T0406647

Global Culture and Sport Series

Series Editors: Stephen Wagg, De Montfort University, UK, and David Andrews, University of Maryland, USA

The Global Culture and Sport series aims to contribute to and advance the debate about sport and globalization by engaging with various aspects of sport culture as a vehicle for critically excavating the tensions between the global and the local, transformation and tradition and sameness and difference. With studies ranging from snowboarding bodies, the globalization of rugby and the Olympics, to sport and migration, issues of racism and gender, and sport in the Arab world, this series showcases the range of exciting, pioneering research being developed in the field of sport sociology.

Damion Sturm • Stephen Wagg
David L. Andrews
Editors

The History and Politics of Motor Racing

Lives in the Fast Lane

Editors
Damion Sturm
Massey University
Auckland, New Zealand

David L. Andrews
Department of Kinesiology
University of Maryland
College Park, MD, USA

Stephen Wagg
International Centre for Sport
History and Culture
De Montfort University
Leicester, UK

ISSN 2662-3404 ISSN 2662-3412 (electronic)
Global Culture and Sport Series
ISBN 978-3-031-22824-7 ISBN 978-3-031-22825-4 (eBook)
https://doi.org/10.1007/978-3-031-22825-4

This Palgrave Macmillan imprint is published by the registered company Springer Nature Switzerland AG.
The registered company address is: Gewerbestrasse 11, 6330 Cham, Switzerland

Acknowledgements

Damion would like to acknowledge his two bundles of joy—Mikaela and Isaac. I love you and am eternally grateful for all the time that we play, grow and develop together. Perhaps you too will grow to enjoy the spectacle and sensations of cars racing at high speeds! This book is dedicated to you both.

He would also like to thank Yi Wei for her love, patience and support along our life journey, as well as my parents, Karen and Bryce, for helping to support our young family.

He especially wants to acknowledge and thank his co-editors for bringing him on board this project and for being so fantastic to work with throughout the process.

Finally, he offers a special acknowledgement to Jacques Villeneuve for providing a pivotal entry point and 'hook' into the world of Formula One that has long since endured.

Stephen would like to acknowledge the invaluable assistance of: Jayne Ashworth at Haynes Publishers, Paul Baxa, Eberhard Reuss, Sandra Esslinger and Aldo Zana.

David would like to acknowledge and thank the diligence, expertise and patience of his co-editors, all of whom were key in bringing this project to fruition.

The editors would also like to extend a heartfelt thank you to all of our contributing authors. Thank you for your willingness to be part of the project and for investing your time and efforts during the challenges and disruptions of a global pandemic. We are delighted with the wide-ranging coverage of motorsport topics across the edited collection, due in no small part to your excellent and timely contributions.

Contents

Notes on Contributors

Derek H. Alderman is Professor of Geography at the University of Tennessee and a past president of the American Association of Geographers. Derek is a cultural and historical geographer interested in race, public memory, tourism, and the politics of place naming and mapping. Much of his work focuses on the rights of African-Americans to move through, claim, and shape places and spaces on their own terms as part of a broader goal of social and spatial justice. He is founder of Tourism RESET, an interdisciplinary and multi-university initiative devoted to analysing and challenging historical and contemporary racialisation of travel, geographic mobility, and transportation.

Mahfoud Amara is Associate Professor in Sport Social Sciences and Management at Physical Education & Sport Science Department, College of Education, Qatar University. Amara has a number of publications, peer-reviewed articles and book chapters, and has been regularly featured in international media outlets. His work focuses on two areas: (1) sport, business, culture, politics and society in the MENA region; (2) sport, cultural diversity and Muslim communities in the West. He has been invited as speaker and expert to a number of working groups, international conferences, symposia, panels and lecture series/ webinars. In 2012 he published a book with Palgrave and Macmillan on "Sport Politics and Society in the Arab World". He co-edited with Alberto Testa "Sport in Islam and in Muslim Communities" (Routledge, 2015), and with John Nauright "Sport in the African World" (Routledge, 2018). He edited "the Olympic Movement and the Middle East and North Africa Region" (Routledge, 2020).

Victor Andrade de Melo is a Full Professor at the Federal University of Rio de Janeiro, where he works in the Program of Graduate Studies in Comparative History and in the Program of Graduate Studies in Education. He is the coordinator of Sport: Laboratory of the History of Sport and Leisure. Author of several books and articles dedicated to the historical studies of sports, he has been a productivity researcher (National Research Council/Brazil) since 2003.

David L. Andrews is Professor of Physical Cultural Studies in the Department of Kinesiology at the University of Maryland, College Park. His research contextualises sport and physical culture in relation to the intersecting cultural, political, economic and technological forces shaping contemporary society. His books include: *Making Sport Great Again?: The Uber-Sport Assemblage, Neoliberalism, and the Trump Conjuncture* (2019, Palgrave): *The Routledge Handbook of Physical Cultural Studies* (edited with Michael Silk and Holly Thorpe, 2017, Routledge); and, *Sport, Physical Culture, and the Moving Body: Materialisms, Technologies, Ecologies* (edited with Josh Newman and Holly Thorpe, 2020, Rutgers University Press).

Tim Angus is Honorary Research Fellow at Coventry University and holds a PhD on the Italian Motorsport Industry in 2001. Tim works in economic development and innovation policy and has a long-standing interest in the global motorsport industry. He has worked with Nick Henry and Mark Jenkins on motorsport industry research for 25 years for clients as varied as the UK Government, trade associations and national and international sporting governing bodies. He co-authored Henry, N., Angus, T., Jenkins, M. and Aylett, C. (2007) *Motorsport Going Global: The Challenges Facing the World's Motorsport Industry* and most recently published Henry, N., Angus, T. and Jenkins, M. (2021) 'Motorsport Valley revisited: Cluster evolution, strategic cluster coupling and resilience', *European Urban and Regional Studies*, 28(4), pp. 466–486. https://doi.org/10.1177/09697764211016039.

Paul Baxa is Professor of History at Ave Maria University, a Catholic Liberal Arts College in Southwest Florida. He is a cultural historian who specializes in Italian Fascism. He has published on the making of Fascist Rome and the relationship between Fascist ideology and motorsport. His recent book is titled *Motorsport and Fascism: Living Dangerously* (Palgrave Macmillan, 2022). Baxa is member of the Society of Automotive Historians and is involved in organizing the annual Michael R. Argetsinger Symposium held at Watkins Glen, NY, the only such event dedicated solely to the history of motorsport.

Youcef Bouandel a graduate of the Universities of Algiers, Algeria and Glasgow, Scotland, Bouandel is Full Professor of International Affairs at Qatar University. He taught at the University of Lincoln England and was visiting professor in Sweden, Bulgaria and the United States. His work has appeared in DOMES—Digest of Middle East Studies, Mediterranean Politics, *The Journal of Modern African Studies*, *The Journal of North African Studies*, *Third World Quarterly* and *Cambridge Review of International Affairs* and has contributed several chapters on Algeria's politics.

Jacob Bustad is an associate professor in the Department of Kinesiology at Towson University, Maryland. His primary research and teaching interests are in the fields of sport management, physical cultural studies, the sociology of sport and urban studies. His research has been published in international journals such as *Cities*, *Qualitative Research in Sport, Exercise and Health*, *International Journal of Sport Communication*, and *The International Journal of the History of Sport*.

Ben Carrington teaches sociology, communication studies and journalism at the Annenberg School for Communication and Journalism at the University of Southern California in Los Angeles. He has written widely on the cultural politics of sports and is the author of *Race, Sport and Politics: The Sporting Black Diaspora* (Sage, 2010).

Bryan C. Clift is Associate Professor (Senior Lecturer) and Director of the Centre for Qualitative Research in the Faculty of Humanities and Social Sciences and Department for Health at the University of Bath, UK. His research is oriented around sport and physical activity in relation to issues of contemporary urbanism, popular cultural practices and representations, and qualitative inquiry. His work has recently been published in: *Sport, Education and Society*; *Body & Society*; *Sociology of Sport Journal*; *Qualitative Inquiry*; and Cultural Studies ↔ Critical Methodologies. Additionally, he recently co-edited with Prof Alan Tomlinson *Populism in Sport, Leisure, and Popular Culture* (Routledge, 2021).

Éamon Ó. Cofaigh lectures in French at NUI Galway. His research interests include twentieth-century French culture, tourism and recreation, the French and Francophone Chanson and French Cinema. He is author of *A Vehicle for Change: Popular Representations of the Automobile in 20th-Century France* (Liverpool University Press, 2022)

Seán Crosson is Associate Professor of Film in the Huston School of Film & Digital Media, and leader of the Sport & Exercise Research Group at the University of Galway, Ireland. His major research interest is the relationship between film, visual media and sport and his publications include the monographs *Sport and Film* (Routledge, 2013) and *Gaelic Games on Film: From silent films to Hollywood hurling, horror and the emergence of Irish cinema* (Cork University Press, 2019). Crosson also co-edited (with Philip Dine) the collection *Sport, Representation and Evolving Identities in Europe* (Peter Lang, 2010) and more recently edited the volume *Sport, Film, and National Culture* (Routledge, 2021).

Timothy Dewhirst is Professor in the Department of Marketing and Consumer Studies and Senior Research Fellow in Marketing and Public Policy at the Gordon S. Lang School of Business and Economics at the University of Guelph in Canada. He is Associate Editor of the journal, *Tobacco Control*, regarding product marketing and promotion, and he serves on the Editorial Review Board for the *Journal of Public Policy & Marketing*. Additionally, he served as an invited expert for the WHO with respect to Article 13 guidelines, concerning cross-border advertising, promotion, and sponsorship of the Framework Convention on Tobacco Control (FCTC). He has provided expert testimony in tobacco litigation in Canada, the United States, and internationally.

Mauricio Drumond holds a doctorate in Comparative History and is a researcher in Sport: Laboratory of the History of Sport and Leisure at the Federal University of Rio de Janeiro. He is the author of books and articles focused on the political history of sports in Brazil, Portugal and Argentina.

Sandra Lotte Esslinger is Professor of Art History in California and holds a PhD from UCLA. Her research focuses on the official art of Nazi Germany, emphasizing the construction of national and cultural identities. She has published and presented on the artwork and museum as Nazi propaganda. Active in disciplinary advocacy endeavours, she has spearheaded the recognition of art history as a discipline in the California Community College System, chaired a College Art Association (CAA) Task Force on Advocacy at CAA, and co-chaired #CAA Advocacy panel (2016) in Washington, DC. In 2011, she and Eberhard Reuss, historian and automotive journalist for ARD/SWR German national public television, began researching Adolf Rosenberger, which in 2019 resulted in the ARD documentary "Der Mann Hinter Porsche–Adolf Rosenberger". She is a cousin of Adolf Rosenberger and founder of the Adolf Rosenberger gGmbH (Adolf-Rosenberger.com), an organization with a mission to support research and projects that promote anti-discrimination policies and support those voices that have been disempowered or marginalized, especially in the automotive industry.

Tom Evens is an associate professor at the Department of Communication Sciences at Ghent University, Belgium, and a senior researcher at the imec research group for Media, Innovation and Communication Technologies. He specializes in the economics and policies of digital media and technology markets, and has widely published on sports and media in international peer-reviewed journals and edited volumes. He is the lead author of *The Political Economy of Television Sports Rights* (Palgrave, 2013) and *Platform Power and Policy in Transforming Television Markets* (Springer, 2018), and the co-editor of *Media Management Matters: Challenges and Opportunities for Bridging Theory and Practice* (Routledge, 2020).

Michael Friedman is a lecturer in the Physical Cultural Studies program in the Department of Kinesiology at the University of Maryland. His research focuses on the relationship between public policy, urban design and professional sports. His first book, *Mallparks: Producing Cathedrals of Baseball Consumption*, is being published by Cornell University Press. He has published several academic articles on sports venues and events, including in the *Journal of Urban Affairs*, *Sociology of Sport Journal*, *International Review for the Sociology of Sport*, *City, Culture and Society*, and the *International Journal of Sport Management and Marketing*.

David Gogishvili is a senior researcher in the Department of Geography and Sustainability at the University of Lausanne, Switzerland. He is interested in the role that large-scale urban development projects, such as mega-events and cultural flagship institutions, play in cities across the globe. His research examines the role of legal exceptions and politics in large-scale urban projects and mostly focuses on the cities of Central Asia and South Caucasus. In his current research, David is building a database of cultural flagships worldwide that will allow drawing conclusions on the prevalence, genealogy, context, rationales and outcomes of these initiatives. He is also conducting qualitative research on the multiple lives and promises of Louvre Abu Dhabi and the Saadiyat Island Cultural District.

Nick Henry is Professor of Economic Geography at Coventry University. Nick undertook his first piece of published research on the UK motorsport industry in 1994 and over the past 25 years has undertaken numerous studies with his long-run colleagues Tim Angus and Mark Jenkins. Nick directed the ground-breaking *MIA (2001) The National Survey of Motorsport Engineering and Services* and Henry, N., Angus, T., Jenkins, M. and Aylett, C. (2007) *Motorsport Going Global: The Challenges Facing the World's Motorsport Industry*. He has provided numerous inputs to studies seeking to understand the regional development possibilities and economic impact of motorsport and performance engineering and its associated events. Most recently he has published Henry, N., Angus, T. and Jenkins, M. (2021) 'Motorsport Valley revisited: Cluster evolution, strategic cluster coupling and resilience', *European Urban and Regional Studies*, 28(4), pp. 466–486. https://doi.org/10.1177/09697764211016039.

Brett Hutchins is Professor of Media and Communications in the School of Media, Film and Journalism at Monash University. His books include *Environmental Conflict and Media* (co-edited), *Sport Beyond Television: The Internet, Digital Media & the Rise of Networked Media Sport* (co-authored), and *Digital Media Sport: Technology, Culture & Power in the Network Society* (co-edited).

Joshua Inwood is Professor of Geography and Ethics at Pennsylvania State University. Inwood is committed to understanding the material conditions of peace and justice and engages with these concerns through a variety of research and teaching projects. At its heart his work seeks to understand the social, political and economic structures that make human lives vulnerable to all manner of exploitations, as well as how oppressed populations use social justice movements to change their material conditions. His research contributes to literatures on urban spaces, political geographies, justice and historical and cultural geographies.

Honorata Jakubowska is a sociologist at Adam Mickiewicz University in Poznań, Poland. She is author of *Skill Transmission, Sport and Tacit Knowledge: A Sociological Perspective* (2017) and co-author of *Female Fans, Gender Relations and Football Fandom: Challenging the Brotherhood Culture* (2021), both based on the research projects funded by the National Science Centre. She has published numerous articles, chapters and two other books related to her main research interests: sociology of sport, gender studies, and sociology of the body. She was the coordinator of European Sociological Association Research Network "Society and Sports" and vice-president of Polish Sociological Association Section "Sociology of Sport" (2017–2019). She is a member of the editorial boards of *Communication and Sport*, *Polish Sociological Review* and *Poznań Journal of Law, Economics and Sociology*.

Mark Jenkins is Emeritus Professor of Strategy at Cranfield School of Management, Cranfield University. Mark's work focuses on competitive strategy, innovation and high-performing teams. He is the author of many journal papers and a number of books on strategic management issues, which include: *Performance at the Limit: Business Lessons from Formula One Motor Racing; Advanced Strategic Management* and *The Customer Centred Strategy.*

Wonkyong Beth Lee is an associate professor at the DAN Department of Management and Organizational Studies, University of Western Ontario, Canada. Her program of research primarily pertains to transformative consumer research (TCR) by focusing on addictive consumption such as smoking, social marketing (especially marketing communications), and the policy environment. She previously served as an adjunct professor at the Department of Advertising and Public Relations, Hanyang University, South Korea and was visiting scholar at the Sydney School of Public Health, University of Sydney, Australia. In addition, she gave a social marketing workshop at the Public Health Summer Camp, University of Otago, Wellington, New Zealand.

Libby Lester is Director of the Institute for Social Change at the University of Tasmania and UNESCO Chair in Communication, Environment and Heritage. She works to understand the place of public debate in local and global decision-making, and her research on environmental communication and political conflict is widely published. Her most recent book is *Global Trade and Mediatised Environmental Protest* (Palgrave Macmillan). Before joining the University, she worked as a journalist for 15 years, reporting for *The Age* and other Australian newspapers and magazines.

Chris Lezotte spent two decades in advertising which included time at McCann-Erickson writing car commercials. After exiting her advertising career she pursued a master's in Women's and Gender Studies at Eastern Michigan University and holds a PhD in American Culture Studies from Bowling Green State University. Now working as an independent scholar, Chris focuses her research on the relationship between women and cars in a variety of contexts. This includes women's participation in various car cultures traditionally associated with masculinity and the male driver, as well as investigations into representations of women and cars in popular culture.

Chris would like to thank archivist Jenny Ambrose of the International Motor Racing Research Center [IMRRC] for her invaluable assistance.

Georgios Paris Loizides Holds a PhD in sociology from Western Michigan University with areas of specialization in social inequality (race, class, gender) and comparative/historical sociology. He published a book and a number of journal articles on the Sociological Department of the Ford Motor Company and is involved in a number of scholarly projects, mainly revolving around social and industrial relations during the Progressive era. He is a professor at the University of Wisconsin—Stout, where he regularly teaches courses in social problems, race and ethnic relations, as well as social theory.

Callie Batts Maddox is an associate professor in the Department of Sport Leadership and Management at Miami University where she teaches classes in the critical socio-cultural study of sport. Her research interests include sport and physical culture in contemporary India, the global governance of sport, and American yoga culture. Her work has appeared in *Sociology of Sport Journal*, *South Asia Research*, *Journal of Sport and Social Issues*, *Annals of Leisure Research*, and *Journal of Sport History,* amongst others.

Andrew Manley is an associate professor in the Faculty of Humanities and Social Sciences at the University of Bath, UK. Manley's research interests centre on the city and issues of urbanism, cultural heritage, and tourism experience. He is also interested in researching human interaction and organizational culture with an emphasis on surveillance and social control. He has published in a broad range of journal articles on these topics including but not limited to the following: *City & Community, Surveillance & Society, International Journal of Cultural Policy, Culture and Organization, and Organization.* His work has been funded by the Jiangsu Provincial Government (PR, China), The Arts and Humanities Research Council (AHRC) and The British Council.

Richard Maxwell is Professor of Media Studies at Queens College, City University of New York. His publications include *The Spectacle of Democracy, Culture Works: The Political Economy of Culture, Herbert Schiller, Global Hollywood* (co-authored), *Greening the Media* (co-authored), *The Routledge Companion to Labor and Media*, *Media and the Ecological Crisis* (co-edited), and *How Green is Your Smartphone?* (co-authored).

Toby Miller is Stuart Hall Profesor de Estudios Culturales, Universidad Autónoma Metropolitana—Cuajimalpa; and research professor of the Graduate Division, University of California, Riverside. His most recent volumes are *A COVID Manifesto, Violence, The Persistence of Violence, How Green is Your Smartphone?* (co-authored), *El trabajo Cultural, Greenwashing Culture*, and *Greenwashing Sport*.

Hans Erik Næss is Professor of Sport Management, Department of Leadership and Organization, Kristiania University College Oslo, Norway. He holds a PhD in sociology from the University of Oslo and is the author of many peer-reviewed articles and books on the relations between business, politics, leadership, and organization of sport, including *A History of Organizational Change: The Case of Fédération Internationale de l'Automobile (FIA) 1946–2020* (Springer, 2020).

Eberhard Reuß began an academic career as a historian but switched direction to become a radio and TV journalist. He developed a specialty for motor racing as a Formula 1 reporter for Germany's Radio ARD, covering many of Michael Schumacher's races. He has produced many TV documentaries on motor racing history and has written a number of books on this topic. His book "Hitler's Rennschlachten", the result of 20 years of research was first published in Germany in 2006. It was named "Motorsport Book of the Year" by the Motor Presse Club, a group of distinguished German motoring journalists. A much-enhanced English translation was published in 2008 by Haynes. In 2019, Eberhard Reuß directed and edited an ARD TV documentary about Adolf Rosenberger. Together with Sandra Esslinger, Reuss researched the case of Adolf Rosenberger and how this Jewish racing driver and co-founder of the Porsche GmbH fell victim to racism, which extended beyond the Third Reich. As a result in 2019, Reuss produced the ARD TV documentary "Der Mann hinter Porsche—Adolf Rosenberger" which reintroduced Rosenberger into the historical record.

Damion Sturm is Senior Lecturer in Sport Management at Massey University, Auckland, New Zealand). With a specialisation in global sport media cultures (inclusive of celebrity, fan and material cultures), he recently co-edited *Sport in Aotearoa New Zealand: Contested Terrain* (with

Roslyn Kerr, 2022), co-authored *Media, Masculinities and the Machine* (with Dan Fleming, 2011), and has published works on mediatisation, technological innovations and sporting events (Formula One, the Indy 500, Formula E, Formula One eSports, cricket, rugby league and the America's Cup).

Samuel Tickell is a postdoctoral researcher with the Institute of Sport and Exercise Sciences at the University Münster in Germany having completed his Doctorate at the Research Group for Media, Communication and Information Technologies at Ghent University in Belgium. His research focuses on media sport and sport management. He has successfully published peer-reviewed articles on the fragmentation of broadcast media delivery and financialisation models with regard to niche sports. Additionally, he has a long professional history in motorsport media in Australia and Europe, having worked mostly in Le Mans style sportscar racing, and various rally championships, including the World Rally Championship.

Daniel S. Traber Is Professor of English at Texas A&M University at Galveston, Texas. He is the author of *Culturcide and Non-Identity across American Culture* (Lexington, 2017) and *Whiteness, Otherness, and the Individualism Paradox from Huck to Punk* (Palgrave, 2007). His work has appeared in journals such as *Cultural Critique*, *The Journal of Popular Culture*, *The Hemingway Review*, *American Studies*, *Popular Music and Society* and *Critical Studies in Men's Fashion*. He is also an invited contributor to the essay collection *The Oxford Handbook of Punk Rock*.

Gustav Venter is an academic with a primary research interest in the historical intersection between sport, politics and race in the South African context. He holds a PhD in History from Stellenbosch University (2016) and his doctoral thesis explored the changing dynamics of professional football as played under apartheid. His career has spanned traditional academic functions as well as the business of sport. He is particularly interested in the application of data science within high-performance sport and previously co-founded a cricket data consultancy which served professional teams in South Africa's domestic structure. He is a National Research Foundation (NRF)-rated researcher in South Africa (Y-rating) and has recently entered the financial sector.

Stephen Wagg retired as a professor in the Carnegie School of Sport at Leeds Beckett University (UK) in 2019 and is now an honorary fellow in the International Centre for Sport History and Culture at De Montfort University in Leicester, UK. He has written widely on the politics and history of sport. His latest books include *Cricket: A Political History of the Global Game 1945-2017* (Routledge, 2018) and *The Palgrave Handbook of Sport, Politics and Harm* (edited with Allyson Pollock, 2022).

Brandon Wallace is a doctoral candidate in the Physical Cultural Studies program in the Department of Kinesiology at the University of Maryland. Broadly, his work examines sport as a vehicle for understanding how hierarchies of race, class, and gender are produced and contested in popular culture, while driven by an optimism that sport can serve as a powerful conduit of social justice. Brandon's past research analysed the cultural politics of athletic apparel, as well as the representations of Black bodies, spaces, and culture in sports media. His current research examines the Know Your Rights Camp led by Colin Kaepernick to explore the transformative possibilities of community-based sporting activism initiatives.

Aldo Zana is a motor historian and journalist. He began writing articles for motor magazines in the mid-1960s as a freelance editor of *Autosprint* and *Rombo* weeklies, developing an inclination towards history and historic cars and races. Since the late 1980s, he has become a regular contributor to Italian and foreign historic car magazines.His recent automotive books deal with the history of the Sports-Prototype FIA World Championship; the Monza 1000 km race (Italian and English editions); the lives and races of Italian drivers Tazio Nuvolari, Achille Varzi, Giovanni Lurani; the motor racing scenario of the 1950s including a biography of Alberto Ascari; the Monza 500-mile races "Monzanapolis—The Race of Two Worlds 1957 and 1958" (Italian and English editions); the story of the forgotten Milano car shows 1901–1947; "Fast on the Sand" (English only) on the LSR triple challenge in Daytona Beach 1928.He also authored the catalogues of the MEF (Museo Enzo Ferrari) in Modena and the exhibit there on Ferrari and Maserati racing cars. He was the key organiser of the 2009 World Forum for Motor Museums in Modena.Outside of the history of motoring, he wrote many articles for science magazines and authored books on an Italian lady CEO, a research on the editors-in-chief of leading Italian newspapers, and the WWII diary of an Italian Red Cross nurse.After a PhD in Theoretical Physics at the Milan University and at the Cern, the European Physics Research Centre in Geneva, he switched to a managerial career in corporate communications while continuing with motor journalism.He is a long-time member of SAH (#2333), Speed Record Club (UK), Aisa (Italian Association of Motor Historians) and the History and Museum Commission of ASI (Italian National Historic Car and Bike Association).

List of Figures

List of Tables

Introduction

Damion Sturm, Stephen Wagg, and David L. Andrews

Through the pairing of people (principally, men) and machines, motorsport has held an enduring fascination for its competitors, interested audiences and invested industries across a history of approximately 125 years. Much of this appeal seemingly percolates around elements of masculine bravado, mastery and risk-taking, often with a yearning for a return to the 'good old days' of 'pure racing and pure racers'. The daring feats of apparently fearless drivers across the ages are regularly lauded and recalled in contemporary motorsport accounts. These accounts repeatedly play on the linkages between men, machinery and risk-taking. Thus,

D. Sturm (✉)
Massey University, Auckland, New Zealand
e-mail: d.sturm@massey.ac.nz

S. Wagg
Leicester, UK
e-mail: stephen.wagg@dmu.ac.uk

D. L. Andrews
Department of Kinesiology, University of Maryland, College Park, MD, USA
e-mail: dla@umd.edu

D. Sturm et al. (eds.), *The History and Politics of Motor Racing*, Global Culture and Sport Series, https://doi.org/10.1007/978-3-031-22825-4_1

traditionally, motorsport has been characterised by dangerous practices and reckless pursuits that were frequently fatal for participants and/or spectators and required, in turn, a series of improvements and refinements in order to safeguard the drivers and preserve their machinery. Furthermore, rather than being staged in some idyllic modernist utopia, motorsport has always been politically contentious, if not highly problematic. For example, the promulgation of motorsport success was variously an assumed symbol of fascism in Italy in the 1930s and of Nazi supremacy under the German Third Reich. This provided a politically contentious boost for national car manufacturers, while the residual privileging of upper-class white masculinities has long presented motorsport as a stereotypical playground for the moneyed 'elite'.

Recently, the status and place of motorsport has been subject to renewed political and scholarly scrutiny. Traditionally wasteful, expensive and somewhat regressive in its operations, critical appraisals have judged motorsport to be out of step with contemporary times, trends and issues. For example, a chequered history of marginalisation, sexualisation and exclusion for women has dogged the development of many forms of motorsport while, regrettably, remaining largely unresolved as an equity and equality issue today (Sturm, 2021). Despite new initiatives, such as Formula One's (2020) 'We Race As One' initiative that focused on diversity, inclusion and sustainability (https://corp.formula1.com/we-race-as-one/ accessed 5 August 2022), the lack of diversification from forms of white, elitist masculinity has also posed challenges for most top tier motorsport categories where the social classifications of gender, race and class seemingly remain impenetrable. Indeed, these initiatives tend to suggest that, rather than meaningfully addressing the identified issues, Formula One has primarily engaged in a public relations campaign of empty corporate social responsibility rhetoric to generate positive publicity rather than instigate real change in a sport that is ostensibly male and 90% white (see chapter "Formula One and the Insanity of Car-Based Transportation"; Sturm, 2023).

In relation to environmental sustainability, long-standing wasteful practices, resource-intensive components and parts, a historical reliance on the extractives industry, and many pollution-inducing elements have legitimated concerns around the deleterious ecological impacts motorsport events can have, both locally and globally. Despite recent attempts to further reduce the environmental impacts of most global motorsport, these renewed sustainability efforts are undermined by the excessively large carbon footprints generated by motorsport series that span the globe annually. For example, despite Formula One's efforts around hybrid technologies and improving event operations, these initiatives only account for approximately 8% of the sport's CO_2 emissions, while global travel and transport together constitute over 70% (see chapters "The Circus Comes to Town: Formula 1, Globalization, and the Uber-Sport Spectacle" and "Formula One and the Insanity of Car-Based Transportation"). It should also come as no surprise that exorbitant costs for the top series, such as Formula One which allegedly operated at approximately $2b per season in the early 2000s (see chapter "Formula One as Television"), further heighten concern with the sport's elitist orientations and escalating costs.

Ironically, although these concerns remain a feature of popular culture, two key aspects have arguably underpinned and remained steadfast for motorsport. First, it remains extremely popular. Motorsport operates in and across a range of levels from local grassroots through to the pinnacle of national or international series such as NASCAR, IndyCar, V8 Supercars, Le Mans/World Endurance, Formula One and the World Rally Championship. Hence on local and global, national and international scales, motorsport is significant and has remained a pre-eminent site and expression of status, tradition and prestige as well as cultural and/or national identity. This significance also translates to live and in-situ audiences—with a regular contemporary annual audience of approximately 450m television viewers for Formula One (subject to positive and negative fluctuations), while the Indianapolis 500 can draw in-situ crowds in excess of 300,000 people on race days (Sturm, 2017). Unsurprisingly, this also generates media and commercial interest. Media conglomerates seek to harness the power, prestige and promotional value of various 'iconic' motorsport events and series across a range of media platforms, technological innovations and cross-promotions. Additionally, transnational corporate sponsors brand and commodify motorsports, often literally turning cars into high-speed billboards, for profit-driven returns.

The second, and more surprising, feature is that, despite its pre-eminence as a significant realm of contemporary sport, for historical sporting traditions and as a form of popular culture (e.g. see chapters ""Men Love Women, But Even More Than That, Men Love Cars": Motor Racing on Film" and "Neoliberal Interpellation in the F1 2018 Video Game" on motorsport films and Formula One video games respectively), motorsport remains under-explored as a valid 'subject' for academic scrutiny, analysis and debate. Indeed, the study of sport from socio-cultural and historical perspectives germinated as an academic field in the 1960s and 1970s, but has overwhelmingly focused on major and mega events, as well as the big sports from predominantly British, North American and Australian contexts and perspectives, often to the detriment and outright exclusion of motorsports. Hence, while remaining popular and globally significant, motorsport itself is largely overlooked or ignored by most scholars despite offering prime sites for explorations of sporting histories, sporting politics and the complex web of globalisation, commercialisation, mediatisation and wide-ranging socio-cultural issues that this book seeks to address.

Of course, there are some notable exceptions. Aside from a range of often one-off accounts that draw on motorsport as a case study to explore aspects such as elite constellation (Nichols & Savage, 2017), event management, sponsorship, tourism and fandom, a select number of authors have offered sustained socio-cultural critiques of motorsport. For example, Mark Lowes and Paul Tranter have explored the politics of motorsport in relation to urban development, the environment and place-making in Canada and Australia predominantly (Lowes, 2004, 2018; Tranter & Lowes, 2005, 2009a, 2009b), while Josh Newman and Michael Giardina have provided critical insights into the cultural politics of southern masculinities, religion and identity in the American NASCAR series (Newman, 2007, 2010; Newman & Beissel, 2009; Newman & Giardina, 2008, 2009, 2010). Furthermore, via the notion of Formula One as a *glamorous and hi-tech global spectacle of speed*, Damion Sturm (2011, 2014, 2017, 2018, 2019, 2021, 2023) has traced how motorsport is constructed as a media spectacle, a sensory experience for audiences, and probed some of its commercial, global and environmental aspects. Finally, Hans Naess (2017, 2019, 2020, 2021) has examined some of the social impacts and political ramifications of various motorsport events, developments and innovations, including explorations of the Formula E series (see also works by Haynes & Robeers, 2020; Robeers, 2019; Robeers & Sharp, 2020; Robeers & Van Den Bulck, 2018, 2021).

While these scholars have also authored or co-authored books which cover aspects of Formula One (Fleming & Sturm, 2011; Naess & Chadwick, 2023), IndyCar (Lowes, 2002), NASCAR (Newman & Giardina, 2011), the World Rally Championship (Naess, 2014) and Formula E (Næss & Tjønndal, 2021), the dearth of edited collections or monographs on motorsport is also surprising, with only a sprinkling of other academic texts available. For example, Beck-Burridge and Walton (2000) focused on leadership and nationalism, while Mourao (2017) probed the economics of motorsport in ways that differ to the specific interest in sporting histories, politics and a critical socio-cultural analysis that inform this edited collection. Alternatively, Baxa (2022) provides a fascinating analysis of fascism in Italian motorsport which is usefully broached via his chapter included in this volume (see chapter "The Fascist Race Par Excellence: Fascism and the Mille Miglia"), while the editors also acknowledge the useful edited work on American motorsport by Howell and Miller (2014), which predominantly focuses on developments for and issues surrounding NASCAR.

In this vein, this edited collection seeks to fill the persistent academic gap surrounding motorsport by bringing together a team of renowned global scholars probing various elements of global motorsport through a critical historical, political and/or socio-cultural lens. In saying this, we acknowledge but seek to go beyond the often valuable journalistic and piecemeal scholarly writing on the sport. In the end, we have found ourselves dealing principally with Formula 1, and this is largely because Formula 1, being, as noted, a sport with a huge global following, has attracted the most attention by academics. We look forward, however, to seeing more historical and/or political scholarship on other motorsport cultures—motorcycle sport, NASCAR, IndyCar, Le Mans and Formula E, to name a few.

The chapters are set out as follows.

Following the Introduction, Part I of the book is concerned with the origins of motor sport. In chapter "The Origins of Motor Sport in France:

Sites of Racing Memory" **Éamon Ó Cofaigh** examines the emergence of motor car racing on the roads of France at the turn of the twentieth century. Chapter "The Long Winding Road: The Politics and Development of the World Rally Championship", by **Sam Tickell**, **Tom Evens** and **Hans Erik Næss**, describes the journey of the World Rally Championship from its amateur roots to a professional championship under the current joint ownership of multi-platform media company Red Bull Media House and KW25.

The four chapters that comprise Part II explore the early political significance of motor racing, looking at its links to Nazism and fascism in Europe, to early twentieth century consumer capitalism in the United States and to right-wing populism in Latin America. Common to these chapters is the notion of motor racing as an important flagship for projects of nationhood and industrial modernity. In chapter "Racing and Racism: German Motorsport and the Third Reich" **Eberhard Reuss** and **Sandra Esslinger** challenge the romanticism that still attends historical accounts of early German motor racing, showing how after the fall of the Third Reich in 1945, the legendary Silver Arrows became strategic in euphemising Nazi Germany and the role of Jewish racers and entrepreneurs was deleted from the official record.

Chapter "Henry Ford and the Rise of US Motorsport", by **Georgios Loizides**, revolves around Henry Ford's involvement in, and influence on, early motor sport in the United States. Its two main parts cover, first, the years of Ford's direct involvement with car racing, 1901–1913, and, second, the years following 1913, when his involvement became more indirect and served the interests of manufacturing and sales. In particular, it covers the 1901 and 1902 races at Grosse Ponte, which proved influential in establishing the Ford Motor Company, as well as other early racing events in which Ford was directly involved.

Chapter "The Fascist Race Par Excellence: Fascism and the Mille Miglia", by **Paul Baxa**, discusses the connection between Italian fascism and the Mille Miglia motor race. His argument is that the Fascist regime used the event to trumpet its road building achievements and its ability to 'discipline' Italians so that fast cars could race on the open roads without impediment. Also, the race itself, given its geographical scope, was designed to bring Fascist and Futurist ideology to the masses of Italy.

Unlike most sporting events, which are held in purpose-built venues, the Mille Miglia was 'brought to the people' and was designed to embody the ideals of the Fascist Revolution and the Fascist New Man. These ideas, Baxa argues, carried over into the post-war revivals of the race.

Chapter "Vargas, Perón and Motor Sport: A Comparative Study on South American Populism", by **Victor Andrade** de Melo and **Mauricio Drumond**, completes this part. Andrade and Drumond analyse the use of motor sport as a political tool during Getulio Vargas's rule in Brazil (1930–1945) and the First Peronism in Argentina (1946–1955). Both Vargas and Juan Perón attempted to mobilise the image of modernity and success related to motor races and their regimes. In Brazil, Vargas supported the staging of international motor races and tried to enhance the national image through a still nationally underdeveloped sport. In Argentina, on the other hand, Perón thrived with the success of star driver Juan Manuel Fangio, closely associating his image to that of the Peronist government itself, in addition to supporting an already well-stablished motor sport field in the country.

Part III consists of two chapters and is about motor racing and the automobile industry. A—perhaps *the*—key historic *raison d'etre* of motor racing has been the promotion of the automobile and the desire to sell cars. As shown in the previous part, several governments in the 1930s gave enthusiastic support to car manufacture and/or to their racing teams. This part offers two case studies—one of Italy where motor manufacturers arguably led the way in the promotion of motor racing, and a contrasting one of the British motor racing scene, which was characterised by a series of comparatively small competing non-works teams with workshops mostly located in 'Motor Sport Valley', north of London. The Italian motor racing mogul Enzo Ferrari once famously disparaged these teams as the 'garagistas', although they dominated motor racing for a time in the 1960s and, in Bernie Ecclestone, produced arguably the most influential entrepreneur in the sport's history.

Chapter "Politics, Motor Sport and the Italian Car Industry, 1893–1947", by **Aldo Zana**, focuses principally on the years from the first appearance of a motor car in the country through to 1940, when Italy entered the Second World War. The years before the Great War were a time of slow-growing mutual understanding amongst politicians, government and the emerging motor car industry, which exploited races for market leverage. The two decades between the Great War and the Second World War saw the apex of motor racing celebrations as the Fascist regime invested it with their key concepts: tight discipline, sheer power, daring and courage, quest for victory and total supremacy. After the Second World War, Italian motor racing, understandably, gained a greater autonomy from the state.

In chapter "British Motor Sport and the Rise of the Garagisti", **Mark Jenkins**, **Nick Henry** and **Tim Angus** present the seven stages of the rise of the British 'garagistas', beginning in the 1920s.

Part IV brings us to the politics of gender. Here the first chapter (chapter "It Was Ironic That He Should Die in Bed: Injury, Death and the Politics of Safety in the History of Motor Racing"), by **Stephen Wagg**, explores the issue of safety in motor racing and begins by describing the masculine codes that dominated the sport in its early decades and which were used to rationalise frequent death on, or at, the track. He then charts the development of a politics of safety in motor racing, attributable, he argues, variously to the emergence of the Grand Prix driver as highly paid celebrity, with an eye to his (likely very comfortable) future; the growth of motor racing as a television event; the (related) acceptance in 1968 of on-car advertising (much of it taken up by tobacco companies) and the corresponding reluctance of these sponsors to have their products associated with death; and the growth of the politics of wellbeing.

Throughout its storied history, motorsport has been unwelcoming to women. Consequently, it has been necessary for female racers to develop unique strategies to enter what has long existed as an exclusive masculine enclave. While entry can be facilitated through a familial relationship with a male driver, women without such connections often get their start through participation in women-only racing events. Although these races have provided women with the opportunity to enter the track, they have not been without controversy. Detractors argue that women will not be considered legitimate racers unless they compete on the same track as men. Proponents view women-only racing not only as a way to attract more women into the sport, but also as an important source of skill development, support and community building. Chapter "From Powder Puff to W Series: The Evolution of Women-Only Racing", by **Chris**

Lezotte, investigates the evolution of women-only racing, from its early introduction as a media stunt, to its current incarnation as a proving ground for serious female open wheel racers.

In chapter "The Awkward Gender Politics of Formula 1 as a Promotional Space: The Issue of 'Grid Girls'", **Honorata Jakubowska** discusses the vexed question of Formula 1 'grid girls', introduced in the 1960s, in the context of the wider socio-cultural changes concerning female status, gender order and feminism that have taken place in the ensuing 60 years. To an extent, Formula 1 has acknowledged these changes, as illustrated by a decision made by Liberty Media in 2018 to drop 'grid girls' from race weekends, but, on the other hand, F1 remains a male-dominated world wherein women are sexualised and 'used' in decorative roles, as evidenced by many of the reactions to this decision. Moreover, the issue of women's agency, which can be expressed, among other ways, by an emphasis on physical attractiveness and the sexuality of a woman's own body, adds a new point of view to this analysis.

Part V is about motor racing and the politics of 'race' and offers three case studies. The first, chapter "A Political and Economic Analysis of South Africa's Historical Relationship with Formula One Motor Racing, 1934–1993" by **Gustav Venter**, is an analysis of the white South African driver Jody Scheckter, Formula One Champion in 1979. Scheckter was a *de facto* poster boy for a pariah state, South Africa's white supremacist apartheid system having caused a range of sanctions to be imposed by international sport bodies. The chapter examines South Africa's historical position within Formula 1 racing. It considers aspects such as the political significance of hosting Formula One races during the apartheid era, and considers how it was possible for this to continue during the turbulent mid- to late 1970s—a period which saw the height of international pressure directed against South African sport. The analysis also seeks to contextualise the role of Scheckter, the 1979 Formula One world champion and to date the only South African to achieve this feat. It looks at how Scheckter was received domestically and internationally, particularly given the vociferous resistance experienced by South African representatives in team sports such as rugby and cricket.

In chapter "On Recovering the Black Geographies of Motorsports: The Counter-mobility Work of NASCAR's Wendell Scott", by **Derek**

H. Alderman and **Joshua Inwood**, the authors explore professional stock car racing, specifically the US-based National Association for Stock Car Auto Racing (NASCAR) and the racialised struggles and resistant 'hard driving' of Wendell Scott (1921–1990) of Danville, Virginia. Scott was the first and only African American driver to win a race in the elite division of NASCAR. He raced throughout the segregated Jim Crow South and in what was otherwise an all-white sport, facing discrimination, humiliation and violence on and off the track. The authors offer a critical (re)reading of Scott's racing career as antiracist counter-mobility work and focus on the bodily, social and technological practices he employed to maintain and even enhance his ability to move around tracks and to and from races. Scott did not represent his efforts in terms of civil rights activism, but it is important to contextualise black resistance outside the confines of formal protest to include the struggle for survival and material reproduction.

Lewis Hamilton is Britain's most successful motor racing driver. In a sport historically associated with the global elite, Hamilton has undoubtedly broken barriers in moving from, as he once put it, 'the slums' of Stevenage (an overspill town, north of London) to the yachts of Monaco. A central part of Hamilton's narrative and his extraordinary career has been his willingness to speak out on racial (and other) issues both within and outside the sport of F1 motor racing. As arguably Britain's highest-profile black celebrity athlete, Hamilton is often seen to embody a new, multi-racial British identity. His very existence is a challenge to contemporary racist discourses that work to produce British identity as exclusively white. Chapter "Can the Formula One Driver Speak? Lewis Hamilton, Race and the Resurrection of the Black Athlete", by **Ben Carrington**, critically examines the role of celebrity athletes as agents of social change, and more specifically focuses on the contradictory ways in which Hamilton has enacted a form of 'celebrity antiracism' and on his representation by the British media.

Part VI is about motor racing, the media and postmodernity, and has six chapters, all concerned both with the historical growth of the relationship between motor racing and the mass media and the cementing of the place of motor racing in postmodern culture. They deal, successively, with motor racing as a television spectacle; the growth and diversification of sponsorship of motor racing; the relationship between motor racing and film; debates about celebrity and driver agency in motor racing; video gaming sanctioned by Formula 1; and, in an apparent consummation of the postmodernisation of motor racing, the purchase in 2017 of Formula 1 by a global media company, Liberty Media.

Chapter "Formula One as Television", by **Damion Sturm**, is about Formula 1 as television. Over the past 30-odd years, Formula One has operated as a television spectacle. In the 1980s, British businessman Bernie Ecclestone repackaged Formula One as a media event, in an effort to streamline what had largely been a haphazard and disjointed series. Today, cameras are placed around the track to provide continuous framing of the race, supplemented by an entertaining and informative emphasis on action, drama and the star drivers. Complementing this highly mobilised fluid framing is the deployment of participatory innovations, particularly the sustained On-Board Camera footage and access to the driver's comments as he races. This coverage is supported by an array of on-screen graphics and information. Yet, although broadcasting rights are still worth an estimated $600 million annually, the television audience has been steadily declining. Nevertheless, new audiences and digital and social media opportunities are also presenting themselves, notably with successful platforms for eSports, live streaming and the *Drive to Survive* series on Netflix.

Next, in chapter "The Shifting Landscape of Sponsorship Within Formula 1" **Timothy Dewhirst** and **Wonkyong Beth Lee** chart changes in the pattern of sponsorship for Formula 1. When Formula 1 was originated in 1950, visible sponsorship was highly limited, with only understated automobile branding apparent on the nose of the race cars. Early examples of Formula 1 sponsorship were typically function-based and largely confined to fuel and tyre suppliers. Prominent Formula 1 team sponsorship liveries emerged during the late 1960s and early 1970s, which marked an important transitional period for sponsorship as tobacco companies began turning towards sponsoring broadcast sports events to compensate for lost broadcast advertising exposure. Cigarette advertising had been banned from the broadcast media in various jurisdictions, including the United Kingdom in 1965 and the United States in 1971. By 2000, tobacco companies collectively were spending an estimated $250 million per year on sponsoring Formula 1 teams. More recently, the technology industry has emerged as prominent sponsors while tobacco sponsorship has diminished in visibility due to regulatory stipulations. Philip Morris International, however, remains a main sponsor of the Ferrari race team, and additional main sponsors currently include Alfa Romeo, Petronas, Red Bull, Renault and sport betting company SportPesa. The magnitude of financial investment from Formula 1 sponsors is huge, yet ethical questions also emerge given many of the sponsors operate in controversial product sectors such as tobacco, gambling, energy drinks and oil.

Chapter ""Men Love Women, But Even More Than That, Men Love Cars": Motor Racing on Film" is an analysis by **Seán Crosson** of the relationship between motor racing and film. Motor racing and film both date from around the mid-1890s. With the development of film into distinctive forms, including fiction and non-fiction, motor racing has continued to feature as a popular subject for film, including both critically acclaimed and commercially successful films across a wide range of genres from drama to comedy, animation and documentary. This chapter examines the historical development of depictions of motor racing on film, identifying some of the salient features of these depictions and their significance with regard to both the development of film and motor racing.

Chapter "'Who D'You Think You Are? Stirling Moss?' British Racing Drivers and the Politics of Celebrity: 1896 to 1992", by **Stephen Wagg**, is about British motor racing celebrity. It explores the nature of the niche that Stirling Moss occupies in the British popular imagination as part of a broader examination of the nature of British racing drivers as celebrities (and otherwise) over a 100-year period. In doing so it pays special attention to the ways in which, in the history of British motor racing, social class and gender have combined with a particular politics of celebrity. British motor racing has its origins largely in the upper reaches of the British class structure and this, along with a specific form of patriotic and predatory masculinity, has for the most part defined the celebrity conferred on the British racing driver. The chapter concludes with four case studies of British racing driver: Moss, Graham Hill, James Hunt and Nigel Mansell. These case studies are aimed to show variations on the theme of British racing driver celebrity and on its construction. Women from wealthy British families have had access to motor cars and have driven them as fast as men and they are also discussed; however, women have invariably been excluded from the elite racing scene, except as adornments, as anxious wives/partners, or as seekers of sexual adventure in the hotels and paddocks of the international racing circuit.

In chapter "The 'Star in the Car': Formula One Stardom, Driver Agency and Celebrity Culture", in what is essentially a sequel to the previous chapter, **Damion Sturm** addresses the matter of contemporary celebrity in Formula 1 (post-1994). He discusses the central question of the extent to which, in a sport dominated by highly sophisticated technology, the car, and not the driver, may be the star. That being the case, how is contemporary racing driver celebrity constructed? Much of his chapter probes how F1 attempts to re-present the 'star in the car' despite these assemblages of technology, machinery and a prevailing corporate culture. Specifically, the case studies of Michael Schumacher, Kimi Raikkonen and Jacques Villeneuve are explored to consider different star-driver responses to these increasing encroachments on F1 stardom.

F1 2018, the only officially licensed Formula 1 Racing video game, is the subject of chapter "Neoliberal Interpellation in the F1 2018 Video Game", by **Daniel S. Traber**. The game is analysed for its ideological properties, and Traber argues that playing the game is, effectively, a tutorial in neoliberalism. Racing in expensive cars with engines built by major manufacturers—some of them categorised as luxury brands—obviously implicates players in the service of naturalising competition and commodity desire. However, to succeed in F1 2018 not only must you win races, but you are required to interact with the technology at a headache-inducing granular level to set up a winning car. Moreover, you must actually manage your own career; for example, choosing the way you answer a reporter's questions about your performance can affect team politics or create rivalries. A game in which your existence and your occupation are so intertwined reads like a digital reproduction of neoliberal rationality. To the normalisation of conducting one's life as a series of 'rational business decisions' is added the worship of technology and science (i.e. privileging closed notions of reason and reality imbedded in both the game's narrative and its very form as a race simulator), as well as embroiling yourself in globalisation, with a seemingly benign cosmopolitan attitude, as you export your product around the world. F1 2018, he suggests, is about much more than pretending to drive fast machines in exotic locales, but so too is the real F1.

Finally in this part, chapter "Ecclestone out, Liberty Media in: A Look into the Shifting Ownership Structure of Formula One", by **Tom Evens** and **Sam Tickell**, examines the consequences, and likely consequences, of the takeover of Formula 1 by the US corporation Liberty Media in 2017. First, the chapter discusses the interplay between sports and the media business and puts corporate integration between sports and media organisations into historical perspective. It claims that any trend towards ownership of sports organisations had been subsiding since the late 1990s, but that vertical takeovers have received renewed interest lately. Second, the chapter describes the shifting ownership structure of F1 and examines the latest acquisition by Liberty Media. With this deal, the former cable company develops into an entertainment conglomerate with multiple activities in the growing leisure business. Finally, the chapter elaborates on the possible commercial future of F1 as a media sport and critically examines Liberty's strategy to grow audiences and fully embrace digital media while protecting its broadcast television revenues.

The final five chapters that make up Part VII cover issues in the globalisation of motor racing.

First we look at the decline of Western—effectively, North Atlantic—hegemony in motor racing and its extension to other previously excluded parts of the world. There follow four case studies—of China, Azerbaijan, the Gulf countries and India—which explore the political motives which have prompted various nations to see, to raise and/or to sanitise their global profile through motor racing. The last chapter—arguably the book's most important—confronts Formula 1 culture as the vehicle for capitalist mythology and environmental destruction.

Chapter "The Circus Comes to Town: Formula 1, Globalization, and the Uber-Sport Spectacle", by **Jacob J. Bustad** and **David L. Andrews**, examines the long-standing, at times haphazard, yet nonetheless processual post-Westernisation of Formula 1, from the North Atlantic origins of its inaugural championship season in 1950 (wherein races were held in Britain, Monaco, the United States, Switzerland, Belgium, France and Italy), to the subsequent spatial distribution of Formula 1 races to

Argentina (originating in 1953); Morocco (1958); South Africa (1962); Mexico (1963); Brazil (1973); Japan (1976); Australia (1985); Malaysia (1999); Bahrain (2004); China (2004); United Arab Emirates (2009); India (2011) and Russia (2014). This discussion examines the complex, and at times contradictory, global (organisational) and local (host) political and economic motivations behind the sport's global expansion, and the existence, or otherwise, of discernible geospatial phases in the post-Western expansion of the sport. In particular, the chapter focuses on the development of Formula 1 as a display of contemporary global sport, characterised by a delivery and experience that emphasises the travelling and comprehensive spectacle of elite motor racing. Yet as the authors argue, this model of global spectacle also has particular implications in regard to sustainability, including in regard to the future development of the sport.

In chapter "Circuits of Capital: The Spatial Development of Formula One Racetracks", **Michael Friedman** and **Brandon Wallace** explore the spatial development of Formula One racetracks, which has followed the pattern of confinement and artifice observed by geographer John Bale (Bale, 2003) as occurring in other sports. The first Grand Prix races were generally held on closed public roads, but as auto racing matured, dedicated tracks began to be built. Since Formula One started in 1950, races have been held on such permanent circuits, street circuits or a combination of the two as cities have sought to profit financially from these high-profile events. Within permanent racetracks, the spectacle of auto racing has been confined to a defined space, often covering a large area as events require several kilometres of road, places for spectators and support facilities. Races on street circuits are held on public roads, often in downtown areas, and local authorities close streets for several days before competitors arrive in order to set up the track, temporary stands and support areas. Civic leaders typically justify this disruption on the grounds that these events are intended to showcase cities to global audiences.

Chapter "Formula 1 as a Vehicle for Urban Transformation in China: State Entrepreneurialism and the Re-Imaging of Shanghai", by **Andrew Manley** and **Bryan Clift**, is a about place-making and the re-imagining of urban space. Taking stock of China's engagement with major sporting spectacles—and with specific emphasis on the Shanghai Chinese Grand

Prix, a round of the Formula One World Championships that began in 2004—the chapter examines the role of sport-mega events in (re)shaping an emergent vision of the nation, one that is reflective of the desire to embrace a persistent drive towards economic modernity whilst simultaneously consolidating the power of the Chinese party-state. In so doing, reflections are raised about this strategy of place-making and place-marketing that point to the problematic of belonging and expose the dominant power relations that work to conceal specific populations and past representations of place deemed inappropriate for the new and preferred portrayal of a city and nation.

In a similar vein, **David Gogishvili**, in chapter "Mega-Event on the Streets: The Formula 1 Grand Prix in Baku, Azerbaijan", analyses the recent inception of the Azerbaijan Grand Prix. Baku, the capital of Azerbaijan, as part of the orchestrated effort for using international sporting events to whitewash the authoritarian political regime there, has been part of the Formula 1 Championship since 2016 and will continue holding the Formula 1 Azerbaijan Grand Prix until at the earliest 2023. Organised on the streets of downtown Baku, the F1 Grand Prix has brought transformations in physical and regulatory terms by imposing temporary regulations and restrictions to host this elite motor sport spectacle. The result was a commercialisation, privatisation and securitisation of parts of the city contained in the race, leading to disruption to the local population's daily practices in the areas directly impacted by the race, including highly popular Baku Waterfront Boulevard, as access to such areas was only made available to F1-related visitors and staff, and for weeks leading up to the event.

Chapter "Motor Sport in the Middle East: Regional Rivalries, Business and Politics in the Arabian Gulf", by **Mahfoud Amara**, is about the Middle East and discusses the growing interest shown by countries in the Gulf Cooperation Council, particularly Bahrain, the UAE and Qatar, in the car and motor racing industries. Bahrain was the first (in 2004) to join the Formula 1 Circuit, followed by Abu Dhabi in 2009 and Qatar and Saudi Arabia in 2021. It is suggested that these countries aim thereby to diversify their revenues and decrease reliance on the oil sector; to satisfy the local growing demand for cars and pickups; and to showcase the mega urban development projects in cities such as Manama, Abu-Dhabi and Doha, organised around the development of airports as hubs for distance travel, as well as tourism, retail and real estate. All these countries also have what is euphemistically described as poor 'human rights records', leaving them open to the same charges of political 'white-' or 'sport washing' as described in the two previous chapters.

On October 30, 2011 Sebastian Vettel won India's first Formula One race in front of 95,000 spectators, Bollywood stars, and the Indian business elite. Framed as the latest sporting iteration of a thriving and cosmopolitan India—joining the Indian Premier League and the Commonwealth Games—the Grand Prix was meant to herald the success of private investment in Formula One, as the race was one of the few on the F1 schedule not subsidised by the local government. There has been no Indian Grand Prix since. In chapter "Stray Dogs and Luxury Taxes: What Happened to the Indian Grand Prix?" **Callie Batts Maddox** outlines the brief and tumultuous history of the Indian Grand Prix and explains why, given in the complex politics of neoliberal India, in this case the promised benefits of privatised sporting development never materialised.

The final chapter (chapter "Formula One and the Insanity of Car-Based Transportation"), by **Toby Miller**, **Brett Hutchins**, **Libby Lester** and **Richard Maxwell**, takes the arguments of the preceding four chapters further, dismissing the notion of 'economic growth' beloved of mainstream economists and 'fan boy' commentators and indicting Formula 1 as a source of waste and environmental damage. As they point out, the costs of participation in Formula 1 are extreme, the companies involved massive, and the host countries engaged in cultural diplomacy shameless. The sport provides these monsters something beyond an Olympics or a World Cup: it occurs annually, year-round and across the world, rather than every four years, for a month and in one region. And it promotes 'the insanity of in-car transportation' with deleterious effects on the environment.

References

Bale, J. (2003). *Sports Geography* (2nd ed.). Routledge.

Baxa, P. (2022). *Motorsport and Fascism: Living Dangerously*. Palgrave Macmillan.

Beck-Burridge, M., & Walton, J. (2000). *Britain's Winning Formula: Achieving World Leadership in Motorsports*. Palgrave Macmillan.

Fleming, D., & Sturm, D. (2011). *Media, Masculinities and the Machine: F1, Transformers and Fantasizing Technology at Its Limits*. Continuum.

Haynes, R., & Robeers, T. (2020). The Need for Speed? A Historical Analysis of the BBC's Post-war Broadcasting of Motorsport. *Historical Journal of Film, Radio and Television, 40*(2), 407–423.

Howell, M., & Miller, J. (Eds.). (2014). *Motorsports and American Culture: From Demolition Derbies to NASCAR*. Rowman & Littlefield.

Lowes, M. (2002). *Indy Dreams and Urban Nightmares: Speed Merchants, Spectacle, and the Struggle Over Urban Public Space*. University of Toronto Press.

Lowes, M. (2004). Neoliberal Power Politics and the Controversial Siting of the Australian Grand Prix Motorsport Event in a Public Park. *Loisir et Socie 'te '/ Society and Leisure, 27*, 69–88.

Lowes, M. (2018). Toward a Conceptual Understanding of Formula One Motorsport and Local Cosmopolitanism Discourse in Urban Placemarketing Strategies. *Communication & Sport, 6*(2), 203–218.

Mourao, P. (2017). *The Economics of Motorsports: The Case of Formula One*. Palgrave Macmillan.

Naess, H. (2014). *A Sociology of the World Rally Championship: History, Identity, Memories and Place*. Palgrave Macmillan.

Næss, H. (2017). Global Sport Governing Bodies and Human Rights: Fédération Internationale de l'Automobile (FIA), the Bahrain Grand Prix and Corporate Social Responsibility. *European Journal for Sport and Society, 14*(3), 226–243.

Næss, H. (2019). Investment Ethics and the Global Economy of Sports: The Norwegian Oil Fund, Formula 1 and the 2014 Russian Grand Prix. *Journal of Business Ethics, 158*, 535–546.

Næss, H. (2020). Sociology and the Ethnography of Human Rights at Mega-sport Events. *Current Sociology, 68*(7), 972–989.

Næss, H. (2021). Is ISO20121 Certification a Detour or Gamechanger for Eco-striving Sport Events? A Conceptual Typology. *Frontiers Sports Active Living, 3*, 659240. https://doi.org/10.3389/fspor.2021.659240

Naess, H., & Chadwick, S. (Eds.). (2023). *The Future of Motorsports: Business, Politics and Society* (pp. 167–182). Routledge.

Næss, H., & Tjønndal, A. (2021). *Innovation, Sustainability and Management in Motorsports: The Case of Formula E*. Palgrave Macmillan.

Newman, J. (2007). A Detour Through "NASCAR Nation": Ethnographic Articulations of a Neoliberal Sporting Spectacle. *International Review for the Sociology of Sport, 42*(3), 289–308.

Newman, J. (2010). Full-throttle Jesus: Toward a Critical Pedagogy of Stockcar Racing in Theocratic America. *Review of Education, Pedagogy, and Cultural Studies, 32*(3), 263–294.

Newman, J., & Beissel, A. (2009). The Limits to "NASCAR Nation": Sport and the "Recovery Movement" in Disjunctural Times. *Sociology of Sport Journal, 26*(4), 517–539.

Newman, J., & Giardina, M. (2008). NASCAR and the "Southernization" of America: Spectatorship, Subjectivity, and the Confederation of Identity. *Cultural Studies ↔ Critical Methodologies, 8*(4), 479–506.

Newman, J., & Giardina, M. (2009). Onward Christian Drivers: Theocratic Nationalism and the Cultural Politics of "NASCAR Nation". In S. Steinberg & J. Kincheloe (Eds.), *Christotainment: Selling Jesus Through Popular Culture* (pp. 51–81). Routledge.

Newman, J., & Giardina, M. (2010). Neoliberalism's Last Lap? NASCAR Nation and the Cultural Politics of Sport. *American Behavioral Scientist, 53*(10), 1511–1529.

Newman, J., & Giardina, M. (2011). *Sport, Spectacle, and NASCAR Nation: Consumption and the Cultural Politics of Neoliberalism*. Palgrave Macmillan.

Nichols, G., & Savage, M. (2017). A Social Analysis of an Elite Constellation: The Case of Formula 1. *Theory, Culture and Society, 34*(5–6), 201–225.

Robeers, T. (2019). "We Go Green in Beijing": Situating Live Television, Urban Motor Sport and Environmental Sustainability by Means of a Framing Analysis of TV Broadcasts of Formula E. *Sport in Society, 22*(12), 2089–2103.

Robeers, T., & Sharp, L. (2020). British and American Media Framing of Online Sim Racing During Covid-19. In P. Pedersen, B. Ruihley, & B. Li (Eds.), *Sport and the Pandemic: Perspectives on Covid-19's Impact on the Sport Industry* (pp. 95–105). Routledge.

Robeers, T., & Van Den Bulck, H. (2018). Towards an Understanding of Side-lining Environmental Sustainability in Formula E: Traditional Values and the Emergence of eSports. *Athens Journal of Sports, 5*(4), 331–350.

Robeers, T., & Van Den Bulck, H. (2021). 'Hypocritical investor' or Hollywood 'Do-gooder'? A Framing Analysis of Media and Audiences Negotiating

Leonardo DiCaprio's 'Green' Persona Through His Involvement in Formula E. *Celebrity Studies, 12*(3), 444–459.

Sturm, D. (2011). Masculinities, Affect and the (Re)place(ment) of Stardom in Formula One Fan Leisure Practices. *Annals of Leisure Research, 14*(2–3), 224–241.

Sturm, D. (2014). A Glamorous and High-tech Global Spectacle of Speed: Formula One Motor Racing as Mediated, Global and Corporate Spectacle. In K. Dashper, T. Fletcher, & N. McCullough (Eds.), *Sports Events, Society and Culture* (pp. 68–82). Routledge.

Sturm, D. (2017). The Monaco Grand Prix and Indianapolis 500: Projecting European Glamour and Global Americana. In L. A. Wenner & A. Billings (Eds.), *Sport, Media and Mega-Events* (pp. 170–184). Routledge.

Sturm, D. (2018). Formula E's 'Green' Challenge to Motorsport Events: The London e-prix as a Case Study. In H. Seraphin & E. Nolan (Eds.), *Green Events and Green Tourism* (pp. 145–153). Routledge.

Sturm, D. (2019). Not Your Average Sunday Driver: The Formula 1 Esports Series World Championship. In R. Rogers (Ed.), *Understanding Esports: An Introduction to the Global Phenomenon* (pp. 153–165). Lexington.

Sturm, D. (2021). The Formula One Paradox: Macho Male Racers and Ornamental Glamour 'Girls'. In K. Dashper (Ed.), *Sport, Gender and Mega Events* (pp. 111–128). Emerald.

Sturm, D. (2023). Processes of Greenwashing, Sportwashing and Virtue Signalling in Contemporary Formula One: Formula Façade? In H. Naess & S. Chadwick (Eds.), *The Future of Motorsports: Business, Politics and Society* (pp. 167–182). Routledge.

Tranter, P., & Lowes, M. (2005). The Place of Motorsport in Public Health: An Australian Perspective. *Health and Place, 11*, 379–391.

Tranter, P., & Lowes, M. (2009a). The Crucial 'Where' of Motorsport Marketing: Is Motorsport Now a 'Race Out of Place'? *International Journal of Sports Marketing and Sponsorship, 11*, 12–31.

Tranter, P., & Lowes, M. (2009b). Life in the Fast Lane: Environmental, Economic, and Public Health Outcomes of Motorsport Spectacles in Australia. *Journal of Sport & Social Issues, 33*, 150–168.

Part I

The Origins of Motor Sport

The Origins of Motor Sport in France: Sites of Racing Memory

Éamon Ó Cofaigh

Introduction

While the motorcar was invented in Germany, it was in France that motor racing was primarily exploited to promote the automobile, whose birth in the late nineteenth century was greeted with a mixture of awe and scepticism. City-to-city races showed the automobile's potential before a series of accidents prompted the establishment of what are now iconic racing circuits in France. The name 'Le Mans' is particularly evocative of the automobile and motor racing. Its circuit, which uses the public roads on the city's outskirts, predates the first twenty-four-hour race held in 1923. Le Mans has maintained strong links with the development of automobile tourism and offers the amateur enthusiast an alternative to the machines that reach incredible speeds on modern-day closed circuits. The town of Deauville, which sports enthusiasts associate more readily

É. Ó. Cofaigh (✉)
School of Languages, Literatures, and Cultures (French), University of Galway, Galway, Ireland
e-mail: eamon.ocofaigh@universityofgalway.ie

D. Sturm et al. (eds.), *The History and Politics of Motor Racing*, Global Culture and Sport Series, https://doi.org/10.1007/978-3-031-22825-4_2

with horseracing, also hosted early Grands Prix and thus occupies an important place in the automobile's history. This chapter examines how French roads became testing grounds for the earliest cars, and how the transition of motor racing from public highways to specially dedicated closed circuits led to the creation of sites of racing memory in France, which remain inextricably linked to the democratization of the car.

Coined by French historian Pierre Nora in his celebrated edited work, the term *lieux de mémoire* refers to places that have been so imbued with commemorative importance that they have become unforgettable, constituent parts of the French collective mentality. Nora's collection of essays by historians and cultural commentators examines such sites of memory to elucidate France's past. These sites may be 'any significant entity, whether material or non-material in nature, which by dint of human will or the work of time has become a symbolic element of the memorial heritage of any community' (Nora, 1997). They vary from war memorials, through the Vichy regime, the *Marseillaise*, and the Cathedral in Reims, to the Tour de France. These *lieux de mémoire* chronicle the history of France from the perspective of its collective memory. It is in this spirit that we now explore sites of racing memory in France.

These sites vary from turn-of-the-century city-to-city races to short dashes in the late nineteenth century aimed initially at breaking the 100 km/h barrier, and later to determine which fuel source was the most sustainable for use in the rapidly democratizing automobile. Paris was the natural starting point for the majority of these endeavours. Indeed, the vast majority of racing sites germinated due to their close links with the French capital. The popular seaside resorts of Dieppe, Deauville and Trouville on the Normandy coast are such well-known tourist attractions because of their proximity to Paris. Moreover, the Parisian upper classes who spent so much of their time on the turn-of-the-century Côte Fleurie were seen as a willing audience to be seduced by the automobile industry. While races from Paris to the Normandy coast and back were consequently gaining popularity, across the country, on the Côte d'Azur, a different form of testing racing cars developed. Called *Courses de côte* (hill climbs), the earliest versions took place from Nice to La Turbie near the Franco-Italian border. As motor sport gradually began to democratize the car, Gordon Bennett Jr., wealthy owner of the *New York Herald*, served as an important catalyst in the growth of the sport when he inaugurated the first international races, precursors to the modern Grand Prix. Le Mans, just 200 km to the west of Paris, also played a significant role in the early development of motoring. In this chapter, the genesis of motor racing in France will be discussed through sites of racing memory, showing how sport helped the automobile establish a foothold.

Paris

Although Gottlieb Daimler invented the internal combustion engine in Germany in the 1880s, the automobile developed more quickly in France for several reasons. Firstly, France's road network allowed the transition from horse-drawn vehicles to the automobile to be made without too much difficulty. Napoleon Bonaparte's creation at the turn of the nineteenth century of a star-shaped road network with Paris as the hub allowed easy access to and from the capital. Paris was itself capable of accommodating the motor car, having been rebuilt in the mid-nineteenth century by Baron Haussmann under Napoleon III's orders. Fashionable houses were built on elegant boulevards with open intersections designed to deter the building of barricades by rebels but which now allowed for the coexistence of horseless and horse-drawn carriages (Pinkney, 1958).

A second major factor was French entrepreneurs' foresight and anxiety to make up ground lost as a result of France's belated and partial industrial revolution. The traditional *famille artisanale* only began to industrialize in the latter half of the nineteenth century. These small businesses typically engaged in metal and woodworking trades and thus had both the necessary flexibility and the existing infrastructure to turn their workshops into automobile manufacturing plants. These family-run workshops rapidly established themselves as the core of what came to be known as the Second Industrial Revolution in France (Levin, 2010). Thus, by the turn of the twentieth century, France had over 600 car manufacturers compared with fewer than 100 in the rest of Western Europe and the United States put together (Laux, 1976).

As regards automobile racing, the French aristocracy was mainly responsible for the first attempts to codify the sport. The nobility actively supported and participated in sports and, indeed, the *Jockey-club de Paris*, a gathering of the elite of nineteenth-century French society, was an example of this close link. Two members of this exclusive club formed two-thirds of the founding members of the *Automobile Club de France* (ACF) in 1895. The Comte de Dion, Baron de Zuylen and Paul Meyan, a journalist with *Le Figaro* and editor of the newsletter *La France Automobile*, met in September 1895 to create the world's first automobile club. De Dion was nominated club president, which he immediately ceded to de Zuylen as he saw his position as a car manufacturer at the time as a conflict of interest. The *Association Internationale des Automobile-Clubs Reconnus*, created in 1904, was the predecessor to the *Fédération Internationale de l'Automobile*, which would come into being in 1947, as the body with which the ACF organized its international races. Its headquarters is located next door to the ACF at 8 Place de la Concorde in Paris.

The growth in automobile racing was also to have its effects on the highly politicized arena of journalism. The Comte de Dion and Pierre Giffard found themselves on opposite sides of one of the most significant political scandals in French history, the Dreyfus Affair, which involved the wrongful conviction (and later exoneration) of a Jewish officer in the French army on charges of treason. Giffard founded sport newspaper *Le Vélo* in 1892 and pursued an active role in promoting both bicycles and automobiles; thus, his paper was widely used for the advertising of these vehicles (Dauncey, 2008). One such manufacturer was the Comte de Dion, a vocal anti-Dreyfusard. De Dion became involved in a highly publicized spat with the French president Émile Loubet at the Auteuil races, for which he was jailed for fifteen days. Having been heavily criticized by Giffard in the newspaper he sponsored extensively, de Dion removed his advertising from *Le Vélo* and with several other industrialists, including the Michelin brothers, created a new newspaper, *L'Auto-Vélo*, in 1900, with Henri Desgranges as editor-in-chief. It became *L'Auto* in January 1903 when Giffard successfully sued the paper for infringement of his own paper's name. Hence, it was *L'Auto* in 1903 that was responsible for the creation and organization of the celebrated *Tour de France* cycle race.

The popular press was experiencing substantial development with growing literacy levels in society, and each newspaper was striving to come up with ideas to increase its readership—a vital link developed between journalism and the expansion of sport. As sport was of growing interest, it was seen by journalists as a means of acquiring and then maintaining a high readership. The coverage of a sporting event that lasted over a number of days or even weeks was used as a tool to promote the regular purchase of newspapers. Giffard, as editor-in-chief of *Le Petit Journal*, the largest-selling newspaper of the 1890s, had organized in 1891 a bicycle race from Bordeaux to Paris; this was followed in the same year by Paris-Brest-Paris. These bicycle races had allowed Giffard to create a daily column relating to the race build-up and the preparations involved, encouraging readers to buy their paper each day for the duration of the race period to learn about each competitor's progress (Dauncey, 2008). This paper-selling technique was the reason for the creation by *L'Auto* of the *Tour de France*. It was only a matter of time before this practice was adapted and used as a model to promote a motoring event.

The first attempts to test automobile efficiency in public were organized as early as 1887 when the French newspaper *Le Vélocipède illustré* announced the holding of a 'reliability' trial (Studeny, 1995). The event involved a short run from Paris to Versailles. Only one competitor showed up, however, and the event had to be abandoned. The following year, the same trial was organized. This time, two automobiles turned up; the trial was carried out and completed, but little importance has been given to it since the two cars involved were both by the same manufacturer, the Comte de Dion. An automobile was allowed to take part in the Paris-Brest-Paris bicycle race of 1891. This race also saw the first instance of pneumatic tyres used in a race. The Michelin brothers convinced the renowned cyclist Charles Terront to use their invention on his entry. While having to stop to repair numerous punctures, the pneumatics' ability to cope with the rough terrain helped Terront to a famous victory (Souvestre, 1907). Terront finished the course some seventeen minutes before the only participating car, which indicates why the first authentic automobile race was not to take place for another number of years.

Having sponsored the Paris-Brest-Paris bike race, Pierre Giffard decided to apply his model to a motoring trial. Having seen the automobile first-hand in 1891, Giffard organized and publicized a trial for *Voitures sans Chevaux* (horseless carriages) to be held on the public roads between Paris and Rouen in 1894 (Studeny, 1995). It was not a race, but a reliability trial intended to assess the potential of the motor car. Unlike previous attempts, this event garnered a considerable level of interest, not least due to front-page promotion by Giffard in *Le Petit Journal.* It began to catch the public's attention, and what has been qualified as a 'significant' crowd turned out at Porte-Maillot for the departure on 11 June 1894 (Varey, 2003). Of the 102 entrants, twenty-one appeared on the start line, and seventeen made it to the finish. As reliability and practicality were the order of the day, the automobile that finished first was not awarded first prize. The Comte de Dion on a steam engine of his invention crossed the line first; his vehicle, as it required a stoker, was deemed impractical. The first prize was jointly awarded to the second- and third-placed vehicles, both petrol-powered. De Dion covered the distance of 127 km in six hours and forty-eight minutes, giving him an average speed of just over 18 km/h with all competitors stopping for lunch during the event.

Giffard was immediately approached to organize an automobile race in 1895 but declined as he was unwilling to run an event on open roads with vehicles capable of reaching what were perceived to be dangerously high speeds. De Dion and Baron de Zuylen duly organized the Paris-Bordeaux-Paris race. The choice of route may have been modelled on the first city-to-city bicycle race, which had successfully run from Bordeaux to Paris in 1891. This route was also chosen to show those still sceptical about the automobile that it could cover a large distance with a minimum of mechanical issues. By linking two of France's largest cities, it demonstrated the functional role of the car.

While car trials were a thing of the past, with people wanting to know which car was the fastest, practicality remained a primary concern. Although French engineer Emile Levassor on a Panhard finished the race first, in a time of forty-eight hours and forty-eight minutes (averaging 24.5 km/h), he was not awarded first prize since his automobile only had two seats and was thus not considered viable (Volti, 2004). However, his achievement is remembered by a statue situated at the start/finish line in Porte-Maillot, Paris. Commissioned by the ACF in 1898, a year after

Levassor's death, the monument was originally to be sculpted by Jules Dalou. However, upon Dalou's death in 1902, one of his students, Camille Lefèvre, completed the Greco-Roman-style triumphal arch in 1907. The arch, which depicts Levassor in his car being watched by onlookers, remains there to this day (Laux, 1976).

The new-born ACF decided to hold city-to-city races on an annual basis. Race organizers chose routes that always incorporated Paris as a starting point but gradually moved further away in their destination. Paris-Bordeaux-Paris covered a total distance of almost 1200 km; the following year, the race distance was extended to more than 1700 km for the Paris-Marseille-Paris race. The year 1898 may have seen a shorter race but with a much more significant destination as it was from Paris to Amsterdam; political borders were crossed as the automobile proved capable of linking countries. Races linking Paris with Berlin, Vienna and Madrid followed; these were interspersed with some national competitions, including the *Tour de France automobile* in 1899, organized by Paul Meyan and *Le Matin*, a full four years before the cycling version (Cadène, 2005).

The largest sporting event in 1903 was not the inaugural *Tour de France* bicycle race but the Paris-Madrid road race organized by the ACF, which left from Versailles on 24 May 1903 in front of a reputed 200,000 spectators (Dauncey & Hare, 2003). A further two million people lined the roads from Paris to Bordeaux. According to newspaper reports, the entire population of Bordeaux (around 200,000) came out to see the arrival at the end of the first stage of this race (Dauncey & Hare, 2003). However, a spate of fatal accidents brought about the cancellation of the Bordeaux-Madrid stage of the race. Among the victims was Marcel Renault, brother of Louis, co-founder of the Renault company. The ill-fated Paris-Madrid race signalled the banning of city-to-city races in France as it was deemed impossible to adequately marshal motor races on open roads (Rousseau, 1985). An early form of circuit racing now came into being. Roads were closed to public use to form a circuit; this became the compromise required by the authorities to allow racing to continue.

While these races tested reliability, many manufacturers remained unconvinced of the feasibility of the internal combustion engine. The late 1890s saw the beginning of a struggle for power between three types of vehicle: internal combustion, steam and electric. Each vehicle had its qualities and its weaknesses. Electric cars were quiet and reliable; however, their battery never lasted more than forty or fifty kilometres, and given the fact that they were challenging to recharge outside urban environs, they were essentially seen as city cars. Steam-powered automobiles worked along the same lines as locomotive engines, albeit in a smaller form; these cars required a *chauffeur*, literally a *heater*, to stoke the engine with fuel to provide the steam to propel the car. Steam cars, therefore, required two people to run and were quite large and cumbersome. They were also slow to start as twenty minutes was generally needed for an automobile to build up a head of steam. Internal combustion engines were noisy, smelly and largely unreliable; however, they could cover large distances, and for those who converted from steam, their *chauffeur* now drove the car.

La France Automobile, essentially the journalistic organ of the ACF, initiated a series of short speed tests in the late 1890s. A straight stretch of road in the Parc Agricole d'Achères near Paris was the venue chosen for these sprints, and in 1898 Gaston de Chasseloup-Laubat set the world's first land speed record when he achieved 63 km/h driving a Jeantaud, an electric vehicle (Chanaron, 1983). In 1899, Belgian driver Camille Jenatzy, nicknamed *The Red Devil*, broke the 100 km/h barrier for the first time, driving another electric car named *La Jamais Contente* (Never Satisfied) (Souvestre, 1907). However, it was becoming apparent that there was no scope for improvement in electric batteries' power or longevity; steam, and particularly internal combustion, remained a more viable option. Engineer Léon Serpollet procured the bragging rights for steam when he broke the land speed record in April 1902, driving his *Oeuf de Pâques* (Easter Egg) along the Promenade des Anglais in Nice, to record a speed of 120 km/h (Chanaron, 1983). Within a matter of months, prominent American William K. Vanderbilt II drove a French Mors at 122 km/h to become the first internal combustion-powered automobile to hold the land speed record. This signalled the beginning of the end for steam power, as petrol, in winning both reliability and speed trials, was proving its ability to answer the needs of drivers.

La Côte Fleurie

Having the closest resorts to Paris, early seaside vacationing in France began in Normandy in the nineteenth century. The upper classes made these resorts their summer destination primarily for their proximity to Paris (Bertho-Lavenir, 1999). It was becoming easier to reach the sea from the capital, and the construction of the rail line to the region in 1848 meant that it was possible to access Normandy's golden beaches within five hours. An iconic poster of the time, which was subsequently commemorated on a stamp, shows members of the upper classes in the sea off the coast of Cabourg trying to catch a bewitching mermaid dressed in white, the caption reading 'Cabourg à 5 heures de Paris'. Hotels and particularly casinos began to spring up in these towns as the wealthy classes made their way there. In the 1850s, the town of Trouville was the preferred holiday retreat of Napoleon III's court, and it was his half-brother, the Duc de Morny, who identified the marshland across from Trouville as the perfect location for a new town to be built specifically to welcome increased tourism to the area (Hébert, 2012). This new town, Deauville, was constructed with upper-class holiday-making in mind.

The growth in popularity of the automobile among the wealthier classes in the early twentieth century gave the so-called Côte Fleurie a new lease of life following the economic downturn which had occurred in the aftermath of the Franco-Prussian war (Smith, 2006). With the advent of the automobile, members of the upper classes enjoyed further autonomy as their latest purchase duly made its way to the nearest seaside resort. In 1911, the Comte Le Marois had the surroundings of the race-course at Deauville-La Touques redeveloped in the image of Longchamp racecourse in Paris (De Villiers, 1921). Coco Chanel opened her second boutique in Deauville in 1913, and the fashion store Printemps also opened its first shop outside of Paris there (Madsen, 2009). The resorts were places in which the gentry wished to be seen, and several artists and writers also made this area their summer home. Marcel Proust was among them, being chauffeur-driven to Cabourg and spending every summer from 1907 to 1914 in the Grand Hotel; he used the town as a model 'Balbec' in his epic novel *À la recherche du temps perdu* (Karlin, 2007).

André Citroën became emblematic of the type of wealthy Parisian who brought his family to stay in a rented villa and strolled along the 'Promenade des Planches' (Aubenas & Demange, 2007). Thus, the perception of the town of Deauville is critical as Bertho-Lavenir refers to the importance of its image in the press and also, crucially, to its role as the standard-bearer for automobile-oriented tourism (Bertho-Lavenir, 1999).

Leisure activities were of particular importance to the upper classes. In consequence, these resorts incorporated the facilities to host events that would amuse their clientele (Huggins, 1994). Horse racing was seen as the principal sport on the social calendar, and with the emergence of Deauville as a resort, horse races began to be held there. The Grand Prix de Deauville (originally called the Coupe de Deauville), a prestigious flat race, first run in 1866, still exists today (Pinçon & Pinçon-Charlot, 1994). The nascent motor industry also invested in this area by running one of the first automobile trials from Paris to Trouville in 1897 (Ribémon & Toombs, 2010). This race was a resounding success as it attempted to exploit the established interest in equine sport and transfer it to the automobile that was gaining currency as a means of transportation. The choice of route for the race was by no means arbitrary, as it showed the possibility to reach the sea outside the constraints of the train timetable. A speed trial was held at Deauville in 1901, and again the following year, the success of which is attested to by the specialist newspaper *La Locomotion* (9 August 1902). Motor racing was to remain popular in the region as Dieppe vied with Le Mans for the hosting of the first-ever motor racing Grand Prix and the inaugural Grand Prix Automobile de France (Bonté et al., 2006). Although unsuccessful in securing this pioneering race, Dieppe went on to host the following four Grands Prix de France in 1906, 1908, and then, after a three-year break, in 1911 and 1912 (Ribémon & Toombs, 2010). Deauville would also go on to welcome the *Grand Prix de France* in 1936 when the race was run in the streets of the town in what was an imitation of Monaco, where the first street race had taken place in 1929 (Jacob, 1973).

Early tourism in Normandy was fuelled by the upper classes as they left Paris to holiday. Initially linked via train and later by car, the Côte Fleurie was the initial seaside destination of choice of the Parisian wealthier classes and remained so until sufficient advances in the road network and the car itself allowed for the possibility of reaching the Côte d'Azur with relative ease. The emergence of the Côte Fleurie as a tourist destination at the turn of the twentieth century was closely linked to that of the car; this was evidenced by the number of automotive events staged in the area. The growth of the resort towns of Dieppe, Cabourg, Trouville and Deauville and their subsequent use as destinations for automobile trials and races are a clear reminder of their place in early motor sport, which was ever-democratizing as new forms of trials were inaugurated to further test and promote the automobile.

Courses de Côte

One of the oldest forms of motor sport, the hill climb, has in more recent times evolved into a spectator-oriented motorcycle event where competitors try to climb an excessively steep grass-covered slope before falling back down again. The original *Courses de Côte* (from the French word for hill) tested not only engines but also brakes and tyres as cars made their way up an undulating route which comprised several hairpin turns while climbing rapidly from sea level up to significant altitudes. A famous example is the *course de côte* du Mont Ventoux, which was inaugurated in 1902. The Mont Ventoux in the Drôme *département* in France is particularly resonant as it is a feature of the Tour de France cycle race and the place where British cyclist Tom Simpson died, near the summit, during the 1967 Tour. The last motoring edition run on Mont Ventoux was in 2002, with the only category being *Véhicule Historique de Compétition.* Perhaps the closest modern example of the *course de côte* is the Pikes Peak International Hill Climb (also known as 'The race to the clouds') in the Rocky Mountains in Colorado, which has been holding an annual event since 1916.

Often integrated into a larger event, the *course de côte* involved a staggered start, much like modern-day rally competitions. The competitors came to the start and left one by one at regular intervals from the bottom of the hill, the goal being to reach the top as quickly as possible. The event generally took place over a weekend, sometimes over a single day if the course's length and the number of competitors allowed it. The drivers were generally entitled to two or three test climbs, which preceded the timed climbs. The final result was determined by the best time, the addition of the times, or the average of the times achieved. Thus, how the winner was determined varied depending on the rules in place.

The town of La Turbie is located on the winding roads that lead from the Mediterranean coast up into the Alps. It is famous for its Trophy of Augustus (*le trophée des Alpes*), a thirty-five-metre-high monument built circa six BC to celebrate Emperor Augustus' military victories over the tribes inhabiting the Alps and which was partially destroyed during the War of the Spanish Succession by order of Louis XIV. The road itself was to become famous later as it was on one of the hairpins that Princess Grace of Monaco suffered a stroke and lost control of her car in the now-famous fatal accident.

The first Nice-La Turbie *course de côte* was the final leg of a larger three-stage race which ran between Marseille-Fréjus-Nice-La Turbie from 29–31 January 1897. The race was the brainchild of journalist Paul Meyan, who had previously been involved in creating the *Automobile Club de France*. Originally from Marseille, Meyan's local roots probably played a role in his decision to launch a race from there. This first hill climb would have tested cars' power and reliability under extreme exertion, notably their brakes and several other technical components. The undulating nature of the climbing route allowed numerous spectators a good vantage point as they crowded into the grassy areas adjacent to the winding road. The race was organized and run by the *Automobile Vélo Club de Nice* created in 1896. This auto club purportedly organized the first *Concours d'élégance automobile* in 1899 (*Le Matin: derniers télégrammes de la nuit*, 1 February 1899). These competitions, which predated the car, initially involved parades of horse-drawn carriages, which were gradually replaced by 'horseless' vehicles. Thus, the early races not only provided the means by which automobiles could be tested, but they also offered platforms for manufacturers to show both the aesthetic and mechanical qualities of their vehicles.

In 1897, the hill climb started from the centre of Nice, went through the Route de Gênes (now the Grande Corniche), then passed in front of the Mont-Gros observatory to end at the entrance to La Turbie, a village located 450 metres above sea level and on the border of the Principality of Monaco. This third stage, the *course de côte*, was to be retained into the early twentieth century. The first edition was won by André Michelin, driving a steam-powered De Dion et Bouton automobile; he covered the 16.6 km in 31 minutes and 50 seconds (an average speed of 31 km/h) (Lottman, 2003). Having previously participated in the Paris-Bordeaux-Paris (1895) and Paris-Trouville (1897) races, the older of the Michelin brothers won two of the three stages in the Marseille-Fréjus-Nice-La Turbie race (*Le Sport universel illustré*, 15 February 1897). As previously explored, the Comte de Dion was instrumental in the growth of the automobile and motor racing at the time, with five of the first ten cars to finish bearing his name.

With the inauguration of the first *course de côte*, this new sporting discipline was to become adopted elsewhere in France, as well as in Belgium and further afield. Also organized by Paul Meyan in 1898, the *course de côte* de Chanteloup on the outskirts of Paris became, arguably, the most famous example of this racing discipline. It was the stage that was retained by the *Automobile Vélo Club de Nice* and continued to be held on an almost annual basis up until 1939.

Gordon Bennett: *Urbi et Orbi*

The aforementioned wealthy American journalist Gordon Bennett played a significant role in the promotion of international motor racing. He sponsored the world's first international race, inviting competitors from different countries to compete for the Gordon Bennett trophy; Bennett was later to sponsor an annual ballooning competition (1906–1938). James Gordon Bennett (1841–1918) was born in New York. He was the son of an Irish-American mother and a Scottish-American father who owned the famous *New York Herald*, the leading American newspaper of the day. When he took over the reins from his father in 1866, he was twenty-five and keen to spread the family firm abroad. Gordon Bennett had a keen sense of the newsworthy and publicized his *Herald* with a series of publicity stunts, such as Arctic and African expedition sponsorships, predecessors to the Citroën 'Raids' (rallies) of the 1920s and 1930s as they used exploration to promote sales. Bennett was also an avid sailor, having won the first transatlantic yacht race in 1866. As a sports fan and, much like Giffard, seeing sports promotion as a means of expanding newspaper readership, he inaugurated competitions in yachting, football and boxing.

Bennett moved to Paris in 1877 where he established the *Paris Herald*; he was, therefore, in France at the birth of the motor car and was ideally placed to observe its progress. Consequently, in announcing the inauguration of his *Coupe Internationale*, his aim was to transform motor sport into an international phenomenon. The first international races followed a set of rules devised by Bennett but enforced by the ACF. Each annual race was open to a maximum of three entries per nation, and they were to be held in the country of the winner of the previous year's race (Besquent, 1985). The cars of each nation were to be painted a national colour irrespective of their manufacturer. French cars were painted blue, American cars red, Belgian cars yellow, Italian cars black and German cars white. As there was no British entry in the inaugural race and since the three traditional colours from the British flag were taken by other countries, the Napier driven by Selwyn Edge in 1901, which won in 1902, was green, and this is reputedly the source of British Racing Green.

While initially quite farcical affairs, with only France filling its quota of three cars, it was not until the French were defeated that manufacturers and the public opened their eyes to the competition's worth. In its third year, a British car, a Napier, won the Paris-Vienna race, albeit in somewhat fortunate circumstances as the three leading cars, all of which were French, each broke down in quick succession. A dramatic rise in the number of entries in the French qualifying competition for the following year is indicative of the importance attached to this result in France. Equally, 1903 saw the largest number of entries in the race, twice the number of the previous year, with full quotas of competitors for the first time from Germany, Britain and the United States.

As a British driver had won the 1902 race, it was now Britain's responsibility to act as hosts, which proved problematic. Britain had been hostile towards the automobile, and the Red Flag Law set a speed limit of twelve miles per hour on British roads and stipulated that all motor cars be preceded by a man on foot waving a red flag (Laux, 1976). Although this law had been repealed by 1903, speed limits were still maintained, so it was decided that the race would be hosted in Ireland, where a relaxation of speed laws was permitted on rural roads but not in towns. The racing track consisted of two circuits forming a figure '8' centred on the town of Athy, County Kildare. On seven points where the track passed through towns, there were non-racing zones where the cars followed a bicycle through the town. This was the first example of an international motor race which took place outside of France; it was also the first time motor sport was attracting global attention. Camille Jenatzy, driving a Mercedes, won the race, thereby taking the Gordon Bennett Trophy to Germany, and with it the privilege of hosting the following race.

The final two Gordon Bennett races in 1904 and 1905 took place in a highly charged political atmosphere. The Franco-Prussian war of 1870 was still a matter of contention in some areas, and this was no more evident than in Alsace, which France had ceded to what was to become Germany in the aftermath of their high-profile military defeat. Léon Théry's 1904 victory on German soil and subsequent triumphant return to France through Alsace, where he and his supporters were ordered to hide their Tricolours, demonstrated the motor car's potential to become a symbol of national pride (Besquent, 1985). The ostentatious welcoming of Théry by the president of France on the Champs-Élysées further augmented the event's political impact (Breyer, 1984). The final Gordon Bennett race consequently took place in France and was the centre of media attention across the globe. Léon Théry's triumph for the second year in a row became front-page news simultaneously in France, Britain and the United States, among other countries; in doing so, it relegated the Russo-Japanese War to page 2 (Besquent, 1985).

The Gordon Bennett Cup (1900–1905) internationalized motor sport when it seemed that France would continue to monopolize the sport for years to come. Bennett harnessed the French method of organizing racing, even going so far as to use the ACF to organize his races. He based his initial race in France, but by stipulating that the winner must host the following year's event, he opened the door for other nations, in time, to establish themselves in motor racing; this also provided a focal point to develop further growth. Bennett's cup acted as a catalyst for motor sport development as it evolved into a phenomenon visible on the world stage. These races, however, left France increasingly frustrated. While other nations often struggled to assemble a team, France held annual qualifiers to choose its representatives. Thus, with only three French cars out of twenty-nine qualifying for the 1904 race, manufacturers like Clément-Bayard, Darracq, De Dietrich, Gobron-Brillié, Hotchkiss, Panhard, Serpollet and Turcat-Méry found themselves absent from the international sporting spotlight. When the Gordon Bennett Cup was born in 1899, the motor industry was still struggling to make their products viable, but by 1905, the United States had overtaken France as the world's largest automobile producer (Laux, 1976).

Turn-of-the-century motor racing was a reliability exercise more than a sporting event; however, the success of the Gordon Bennett Cup meant that the sport was becoming, to an even greater extent, an arena in which constructors marketed their products. Responding to the French inability to cater for all its manufacturers, the ACF decided to boycott the 1906 Gordon Bennett competition. Instead it inaugurated a race in which all car producers could have a chance to compete without limiting entries. Bennett, in turn, withdrew sponsorship from his motor race and created the *Coupe Aéronautique Gordon Bennett* in 1906 for balloons, an event that exists to this day (Dauncey & Hare, 2014). He followed this, in 1909, by sponsoring *The Gordon Bennett* in Reims, an airplane race that continued until World War I. It is particularly apt that the street named in Bennett's honour in Paris is located beside the Stade Roland Garros, the tennis centre that commemorates a renowned World War I pilot who was the first person to fly across the Mediterranean.

Le Mans: Continuities and Changes

When the name Le Mans is mentioned, it is the twenty-four-hour car race that springs to mind for most people. While the *Le Mans 24 heures* is universally recognized, the role of this town in the evolution of motor sport goes back much further than the 1923 start date of the first twenty-four-hour race. As host of the world's first Grand Prix in 1906, Le Mans holds a singular place in motor sporting history, but the automobile tracks stretch back even further in the history of the town and area, which can justifiably claim to be the hub of motor sport in France.

The department of La Sarthe was home to the Bollée family. Originally bell makers, this family took up car construction when steam locomotion was being developed. Amédée-Ernest Bollée invented *L'Obéissante* (the feminine form of the adjective 'obedient'), a twelve-seat estate car that was advertised as the 'first road locomotive' in 1873 (Bonté et al., 2006). This vehicle made national news in 1875 when Bollée drove it the 200 km that separate Le Mans and Paris. In 1878 *La Mancelle*, meaning a female native of Le Mans, became the first automotive vehicle to be presented at the *Exposition Universelle de Paris* (Cadène, 2005). Such was the lack of familiarity with this new mode of transport that, being steam-powered, it was classified in the railroad section. As previously mentioned, the company's *Nouvelle* took part in the first ever automobile race, the 1895 Paris-Bordeaux-Paris. Many vehicles built by Bollée won various small races over this period, including Paris-Dieppe (1897) and Paris-Trouville (1898), and in 1898, Léon Bollée took part in the highly publicized world land speed record attempts averaging 60 km/h. The Bollée family was a prime example of the success that could be had with the automobile. Their success inspired an ethic of innovation in the region of La Sarthe. This spirit infused the ambition of an entire community to mobilize in order to attract what was to become the largest race of the time to Le Mans (Plessix, 1992).

In late 1905 the ACF announced that a new Grand Prix would be held the following year, allowing three entries from each automobile manufacturer. The newspaper *L'Auto* announced 'the Race for the Circuit' on 1 December 1905 (Bonté et al., 2006). Among the seventeen proposals was one from Georges Durand on behalf of the *Circuit du Mans*, received on 15 December, just fourteen days after the original advertisement. Before the end of 1905, Durand had acquired the financial backing of the General Council of the Sarthe and had convinced the board members of the ACF to visit the proposed circuit, a triangular formation joining the towns of Le Mans, St Calais and La Ferté Bernard (Cadène, 2005). After examining the proposal and visiting the proposed circuit between 14 and 16 January, the ACF declared on 17 January 1906 that La Sarthe would host the inaugural *Grand Prix de l'ACF* in 1906. The *Automobile Club de la Sarthe* was created on 24 January 1906 and immediately made the Baron de Zuylen (the then president of the ACF) and Amédée Bollée honorary presidents (Plessix, 1992). Durand was elected general secretary, having turned down the opportunity to become president; it was a role that he was to retain until 1938. An energetic fundraising campaign ensued, the circuit was prepared, and on 26–27 June, the race took place on the 103.16 km circuit, which every car had to complete six times on each of the two days. Twenty-three French cars took part in this race, which, despite a significant attendance, made a loss for the Automobile Club de la Sarthe (ACS), with most of the spectators deciding to watch the race from areas where it was free rather than paying for entry into the main stand (Bonté et al., 2006). This setback notwithstanding, the entire weekend was deemed a success by the ACF, and Le Mans went down in history for having hosted the first Grand Prix.

Le Mans is best known for its twenty-four-hour race, the launch of which came after more than twenty years of groundwork and was to become the world's most famous annual race. The *24 Heures du Mans* was the brainchild of Georges Durand who, becoming worried about the enduring relevance of motor sport in its current form, held a meeting during the *Salon de l'Automobile* of 1922 with Charles Faroux, of the newspapers *L'Auto* and *La Vie Automobile*, and with Émile Coquille of Rudge-Withworth, well-known wheel makers (Bonté et al., 2006). It was decided that motor racing needed to be simplified and made more accessible. It was by now apparent that cars were reasonably reliable and could reach high speeds. However, race cars were moving further and further from the vehicles on the roads, and technical advances were no longer of direct benefit to the everyday driver. Coquille believed that car lights and starters were particularly behind the times and that, in the interests of building a safer car, a high-profile night race was needed (Plessix, 1992). Durand suggested a twenty-four-hour race instead as this would put the lights to the test, while pushing man and machine to the limit. It was agreed that the race of 'tourism cars' would take place during the second half of June, when days are at their longest, and that the race was to run from four o'clock in the afternoon until the same time the following day.

The *Le Mans start* was the initiative introduced to test the cars' starters; this involved the drivers lining up on one side of the road and, once the French flag was dropped at four o'clock sharp, French time, running across the road, jumping into their vehicle, starting it up and driving off.

The advent of racing harnesses did nothing to stop this practice, and it took the actions of a racing driver to show the lunacy of competing at getting into racing harnesses. In 1969, instead of running across to his car, Jacky Ickx, the eventual winner, made a point of strolling across the track and belting up carefully before driving off. The following year would see the race start with the drivers already strapped into their cars. However, the Le Mans start did ensure that Durand and Coquille accomplished the two goals they had set for themselves: testing the starters and lights of the cars.

The *Le Mans 24 heures* has continued to be used as a testing ground for new technologies, and aerodynamics improved immensely over the early years due to the long straights on the circuit. Disc brakes were first used at Le Mans in 1953. Alternative fuel sources have also been tested here, from ethanol, used on a class-winning Porsche in 1980, to a diesel-powered Audi that won three successive races from 2006 to 2008. Audi managed to achieve from diesel a similar speed to that typically obtained from a petrol-powered car. This, allied with the fuel economy of diesel, meant that the Audi pitted fewer times than other cars, giving it the necessary margin to win. More recently, hybrid-engined cars have been successful, with Porsche and Toyota to the fore.

Le Mans is also the site of the single most devastating accident in motor sport, an accident that had severe repercussions not only in France but also throughout the world. In 1955, just seven hours into the race, French driver Pierre Levegh, driving a Mercedes, was forced to swerve wildly by another car, losing control of his car and flying into a packed stand (Ambroise-Rendu, 2007). Levegh died instantly, along with eighty-two spectators. The decision to continue the race was taken to allow emergency services access to the circuit as stopping the race would have flooded the roads with the over 200,000 people in attendance. Later in the race, Mercedes withdrew its two other participating cars and retired entirely from competitive racing until 1987. When the curtain drew on this event, it saw the cancellation of many races throughout the world, including the *Grand Prix de France* for that year. It also brought about a complete ban on circuit racing in Switzerland, which exists to this day (Setright, 2003).

From its beginnings in motor sport, through the early days of Grand Prix racing right up to its current position, Le Mans has remained at the forefront of motor racing in France. Le Mans continues to gather higher and higher viewing and attendance figures, year in, year out, while all forms of motor sport are coming under increasing pressure to survive. Its rich legacy is one of innovation and perseverance, much like the twenty-four-hour race for which it is famous.

Conclusion

The democratization of the automobile and, indeed, motor racing has been enacted at a certain number of privileged sites of racing memory in France. The first races ever run took place with Paris as their focal point, and the first attempts at codification were a result of France's desire to promote this technological innovation. The early growth stimulated the initiative taken by the French nobility, who, along with the vested interests of newspapers, embraced the idea of organizing and taking part in races to build the reliability and reputation of the self-propelled vehicles. Automobile racing spread to the Normandy coast and later to the Côte d'Azur where the upper classes holidayed. The inauguration of the *course de côte* from Nice to La Turbie launched a new trial for these early manufacturers and racers. Gordon Bennett modified the French turn-of-the-century races and successfully internationalized them through French facilities to lay the groundwork until other countries were capable of taking up the baton. Le Mans took up the reins in the further advancement of the product; its name will forever be associated with hosting the first international Grand Prix, but it is for its endurance race that this city is truly famous. These sites of racing memory were the stages upon which the pioneers of motor sport plied their trade as the automobile was gaining a foothold in society. They remain closely linked to the genesis of the sport in popular sporting memory.

References

Ambroise-Rendu, A.-C. (2007). Dangers et tourments du sport. *Le Temps des médias, 9.*

Aubenas, S., & Demange, X. (2007). *Elegance: The Séeberger Brothers and the Birth of Fashion Photography, 1909–1939.* Chronicle.

Bertho-Lavenir, C. (1999). *La roue et le stylo: comment nous sommes devenus touristes.* Odile Jacob.

Besquent, P. (1985). *La coupe Gordon-Bennett 1905.* La Montagne.

Bonté, M., Hurel, F., Ribémon, J.-L., & Bruère, F. (2006). *Le Mans: un siècle de passion.* Le Mans, Automobile club de l'Ouest.

Breyer, V. (1984). *La belle époque à 30 à l'heure.* France-Empire.

Cadène, J. (2005). *L'automobile: de sa naissance à son futur.* Perpignan.

Chanaron, J.-J. (1983). *L'industrie automobile.* La Découverte.

Dauncey, H. (2008). Entre presse et spectacle sportif, l'itinéraire pionnier de Pierre Giffard (1853–1922). *Le Temps des médias*, 35–46.

Dauncey, H., & Hare, G. (2003). *The Tour de France, 1903–2003: A Century of Sporting Structures, Meanings, and Values.* Frank Cass.

Dauncey, H., & Hare, G. (2014). Cosmopolitanism United by Electricity and Sport: James Gordon Bennett Jnr and the Paris *Herald* as Sites of Internationalism and Cultural Mediation in Belle Époque France. *French Cultural Studies, 25*, 38–53.

De Villiers, M. (1921). Comte Le Marois. *Journal de la Société des Américanistes, 13*, 129–130.

Hébert, D. (2012). Deauville: création et développement urbain. *In Situ. Revue des patrimoines*, 1–13.

Huggins, M. (1994). Culture, Class and Respectability: Racing and the English Middle Classes in the Nineteenth Century. *The International Journal of the History of Sport, 11*, 19–41.

Jacob, J.-F. (1973). *Monte-Carlo: 60 ans de rallye.* Laffont.

Karlin, D. (2007). *Proust's English.* Oxford University Press.

Laux, J. M. (1976). *In First Gear: The French Automobile Industry to 1914.* McGill-Queen's University Press.

Levin, M. R. (2010). *Urban Modernity: Cultural Innovation in the Second Industrial Revolution.* MIT.

Lottman, H. (2003). *The Michelin Men: Driving an Empire.* I.B. Tauris.

Madsen, A. (2009). *Coco Chanel: A Biography.* Bloomsbury.

Nora, P. (1997). *Les lieux de mémoire.* Gallimard.

Pinçon, M., & Pinçon-Charlot, M. (1994). L'aristocratie et la bourgeoisie au bord de la mer: La dynamique urbaine de Deauville. *Genèses, 16*, 69–93.
Pinkney, D. H. (1958). *Napoleon III and the Rebuilding of Paris*. Princeton.
Plessix, R. (1992). Au berceau des sports mécaniques: Le Mans. *Jeux et Sports dans l'histoire*, 205–228.
Ribémon, J.-L., & Toombs, R. (2010). *Deauville 1936: un Grand Prix près des planches*. ITF.
Rousseau, J. (1985). *La commémoration de la course Paris-Madrid: 24 mai 1903*. Automobile-Club du Sud-Ouest.
Setright, L. (2003). *Drive on! A Social History of the Motor Car*. Granta.
Smith, M. S. (2006). *The Emergence of Modern Business Enterprise in France, 1800–1930*. Harvard University Press.
Souvestre, P. (1907). *Histoire de l'automobile*. H. Dunod.
Studeny, C. (1995). *L'invention de la vitesse*. Gallimard.
Varey, M. 2003. *1000 Historic Automobile Sites*.
Volti, R. (2004). *Cars and Culture: The Life Story of a Technology*. Westport.

The Long Winding Road: The Politics and Development of the World Rally Championship

Sam Tickell, Tom Evens, and Hans Erik Næss

Introduction

Rallying as a form of motorsport has a rich history, dating back to the 1894 Paris–Rouen Horseless Carriage Competition (*Concours des Voitures sans Chevaux*). In the auto sector's infancy, manufacturers would see rally's unique endurance formats as an ideal place to test their vehicles, and it was accessible for anyone with the necessary equipment and financial means. Rallying took place on all surfaces—in forests, on the streets, on

S. Tickell (✉)
Social Sciences of Sport, University of Münster, Münster, Germany
e-mail: sam.tickell@uni-muenster.de

T. Evens
Department of Communication Sciences, Ghent University, Ghent, Belgium
e-mail: Tom.Evens@UGent.be

H. E. Næss
Kristiania University, Oslo, Norway
e-mail: HansErik.Naess@kristiania.no

D. Sturm et al. (eds.), *The History and Politics of Motor Racing*, Global Culture and Sport Series, https://doi.org/10.1007/978-3-031-22825-4_3

ice and on gravel. Events were run over many days, and throughout the ensuing decades, the sport formed its spirit of adventure and endurance. Slowly, national and regional championships would emerge, bringing on local talent and exporting the sport to different areas of the world. Then in 1973 the World Rally Championship (WRC) was born. Yet its development as a media product was not prioritised until the early 1990s when Bernie Ecclestone and his International Sportsworld Communicators (ISC) group centralised the Championship's promotion. They took control of the sport, putting in place the first steps towards professionalisation and mediatisation (Næss, 2014). At the same time, this led to conflict and controversy in packaging and promoting the WRC in a rapidly changing media landscape. This chapter explores the reasons for the long neglect of rallying, and focuses on the developments from 2000 to 2019 to identify what made the rally promotion of this period fundamentally different from earlier media ventures.

The WRC's journey from 2013 to today will be given particular attention as it has been all but ignored by researchers so far, even though it is one of the most dramatic eras in terms of media innovations. In 2013, after the collapse of the former WRC promoter (TV production company North One Sport), the WRC Promoter GmbH was formed, led by the Red Bull Media Group to navigate a new era in the sport's management and revolutionise media opportunities (Brenner, 2014; Evans, 2012a). The following period saw managerial stability, the reinvention of the television product, and capitalisation on rallying's position as a niche sport, rather than chasing the vast financial rewards that mega-sports like Formula 1 or the English Premier League had achieved. The chapter places this story in a political landscape and applies sport management and media theories to the sport from its inception, through turbulent ownership structures and, finally, the stewardship of the current promoter. The chapter will scrutinise the formation of rallying as a world championship, and its relevance as a global media phenomenon. Then, there will be an emphasis on media-driven financialisation, management and professionalisation, before the chapter reconnects with the history of the WRC at the time when its commercial rights were first centralised. The rest of the chapter discusses the ramifications of 'the promotional turn' in 2000 which has led to the WRC we see today.

The Formation of a World Championship

The WRC formally came into existence in 1973 with a 13-round championship for manufacturers. This followed a three-year trial of a World Cup to provide a global championship in line with sportscar racing and Formula 1. A driver's championship would be introduced in 1977. From the initiation of the Championship through to the late 1980s, there was no central promotion body; rather the governing body would oversee the WRC, create the calendar and set the technical rules, while the manufacturers and promoters of individual events would be responsible for promotion and television (Lovell, 2003; Næss, 2014). The events ran under a variety of different formats, from more flat-out sprint-style events to longer 'raid' (off-road/cross country)-style events providing radically different lengths, with the 1973 East African Safari Rally being over 5000 km, for instance, while the International Österreichische Alpenfahrt was the shortest at 324 km (*1973 WRC Season*, 2021). Furthermore, some events allowed drivers to inspect the roads and create pace notes, while others simply provided maps. Teams would choose drivers according to their local knowledge and speed on the different rallying surfaces of snow/ice, gravel or tarmac.

During this time, the manufacturers and the governing body would wield significant power. In the beginning, rallying mostly featured tuned road cars. However, Italian car makers Lancia created a bespoke car, the Lancia Stratos HF, which would take the 1974, 1975 and 1976 WRC Championships (Davenport & Klein, 2012). This led others to create their bespoke rally cars and pressure the governing body to use the WRC as a testing ground for new technologies and marketing. Due to this pressure, the technical ruleset of Group B was formed. It created powerful and visually spectacular cars, rumoured to rival the pace of a Formula 1 car in certain conditions (McKellar, 2013a). The cultural effects of the rule change would fundamentally change the path of the sport as, in the past, road-derived cars were used with relatively few modifications. With Group B, bespoke cars specifically designed for rallying would be the norm. Never again would a private entrant be able to build a car and successfully compete against a better-funded manufacturer team.

During the Group B era, safety was less of a concern, with the cars proving to be exceedingly dangerous, and hordes of spectators would stand in excessively risky positions. Rallying had never been more popular, but in the end it was a recipe for disaster. It came to a head in Portugal 1986 when four spectators died and two leading drivers, the Finn Henri Toivonen and Italian American Sergio Cresto, were fatally injured on the Corsican Tour de Corse (Davenport & Klein, 2011). This resulted in Group B being banned at the end of the year and Group A regulations coming into force. From 1987 the message was clear: Safety had to be a priority, or the sport could be lost.

From the WRC's inception through to the commencement of the Group A regulations, the power balance, event formats and media had largely remained unchanged. However, this period demonstrated that there could be a significant fanbase for mediated rallying. Therefore, rallying would increasingly be seen by the governing body as a sport to commercialise. It would draw the interest of Bernie Ecclestone and Max Mosley, the latter of whom was working his way from Head of Promotions at the Fédération Internationale du Sport Automobile (FISA) in 1986, to President of FISA five years later and President of the Fédération International de l'Automobile (FIA) in 1993 (Albers-Daly, 2020). The Ecclestone/Mosley duo had achieved success in professionalising and financialising Formula 1 and sought to achieve the same success with other sporting series. Their power had grown to such an extent that Ecclestone saw it as his "God-given right" to control other motorsport entities, and the first steps to recreate the Formula 1 experience in rallying would take place in the late 1980s (Lovell, 2003, p. 235). With Ecclestone entering the fray, the sport would undergo a fundamental shift.

Media-driven Financialisation and Professionalisation

Ecclestone's interest in the WRC (and motorsport in general) coincides with significant developments seen in the global media economy, as the WRC had been as loosely organised as Formula 1 before he took control of the latter in the 1970s (Mosley, 2015). Professionalism and media-driven financialisation of sport is rooted in neo-liberal political ideals wherein privatisation and market forces dominate (Harvey, 2007). That is the case for both mega-sport and niche sport. A niche sport does not receive significant mainstream media attention, does not have much cultural influence and is not the recipient of much financial prosperity (G. Greenhalgh & Greenwell, 2013; Hutchins, 2019; Tickell & Evens, 2021). Due to the lack of cultural and economic clout, niche sports can be more susceptible to political motives, as evidenced in the WRC as their path to professionalisation was highly influenced by political moves in the governing body (G. Greenhalgh & Greenwell, 2013; Næss, 2018). In essence, the WRC stakeholders wanted media-driven prosperity. They hoped that the WRC would become a mega-sport bringing greater cultural kudos; higher revenue; increased interest from government and media; and ease of access for a significant audience base (Boyle & Haynes, 2009; McKay & Miller, 1991; Miller et al., 2001; Rowe, 2011). Some sports, like F1, successfully professionalised, earning billions, and were a source of inspiration for others, like the WRC, to seek the same media-driven financial success (Billings, 2011; Greenhalgh et al., 2011; Rowe, 2011; Thorpe & Wheaton, 2011; Wenner, 1989).

At almost all points, media-driven financialisation through broadcast television was the omnipotent force for mega-sports. Live sport and television were a match made in heaven. Television could present a range of experiences and spectacles that allowed sports to reach their fans week in, week out, with increased accessibility and visibility (Whannel, 1992, p. 96). Financialisation of sports had started in the mid-twentieth century, but throughout the 1980s and 1990s the rise in sports coincided with the proliferation of live television (see Billings, 2011; Rowe, 1999; Wenner, 1989; Whannel, 1992). The relationship between the media and financialisation of sport created what has been called the "sports/media complex" (Jhally, 1984) and the 'sports-media triangle' (Boyle & Haynes, 2009; Rowe, 1999; Whannel, 1992). The sports/media complex makes it possible for cultural and media popularity to draw audiences to consume sport on television, and broadcasters can financialise this audience through avenues like advertising and subscriptions. Two important developments allowed this shift: evolving technology that brought television into most peoples' homes and the neo-liberalisation of the television marketplace (Evens et al., 2013; Evens & Donders, 2018; Milne, 2016). Thus, mediated sport, with its inherent unpredictability, became popular with viewers. Viewing rituals or appointments were made to watch sport, and growing audiences fuelled increases in global sports-rights values (Smith et al., 2016; Whannel, 1992, p. 192).

The primary reason why rallying would find it difficult to make it into the living rooms of fans was 'broadcast scarcity' (Hutchins & Rowe, 2009). With limited media opportunities and broadcast slots only the most popular sports could demand live television, as they brought significant advertising or subscription revenue for the broadcaster, producing a financial win-win (see Rowe, 1999; Wenner, 1989; Whannel, 1992). Culturally significant, live sports would bring in viewers, advertising or subscription packages, resulting in a financialisation cycle. For sports, like rallying, that were not culturally significant or telecast live, it would be difficult to financialise this approach, and the WRC had to seek less financially attractive alternatives. When a sport cannot be shown live, the problem is twofold. Live sport creates tension; once the result has become known or 'spoilt', the viewer interest is significantly reduced. Additionally, a highlights package that is not broadcast at a predictable time fails to create a ritual for the viewer (Rowe, 2011).

However, as technology progressed, and behaviours changed in the internet age, scarcity gave way to 'digital plenitude' (Hutchins & Rowe, 2009). Suddenly, measurable or finite caps on content to be distributed to audiences disappeared. Fast internet and cheap storage enabled streaming video, social media, blogs and more, ensuring almost limitless possibilities to publish content online to reach targeted audiences. Moreover, geographical boundaries became theoretical. The importance of valuable broadcast slots decreased as sports could be broadcast at the mutual convenience of administrators, investors and mediators, and as such the broadcast business models were revolutionised. For mega-sports, the financial pipeline coming from television would still be important and protected, but for niche sports the opportunity to pivot their broadcasting strategy was evident (Evens & Donders, 2018). Sports managers could now stream their events, either through third-party intermediaries (similar to broadcast television) or via owned services (like their own mobile app or portal); directly publish on a variety of social and web channels; and interact directly with their audiences (Hutchins et al., 2019; Næss & Tickell, 2019; Zheng & Mason, 2018). The new model allowed a sports promoter to act like a media company in their own right, and have a direct relationship with their audience (Lefever, 2012). It provided a renewed path to 'branded entertainment', giving more control over the mediated product to convey the sport in a distinct style, integrating commercial aspects into the viewing experience (Kunz et al., 2016, pp. 523–524).

For sports to exploit this changing marketplace, rapid and continuing professionalisation had to occur. Professionalisation of sports resulted in sporting bodies leaving behind volunteer-based structures, with the "transformation leading towards organisational rationalisation, efficiency and business-like management" (Nagel et al., 2015, p. 408). Moreover, the professionalisation of a sporting body can be seen when bureaucratic and formal structures are introduced, and when this structure supports professional employment (Kikulis et al., 1992). Financially, this enables sports promotions to be seen as an investment, rather than a form of charity (Sam, 2009). This change can be seen as 'systematic professionalisation' brought on by external factors like commercialisation or decisions imposed by other companies, and sporting bodies rarely revert to their former status but instead are forced to continue to evolve (Dowling et al., 2014; Sam, 2009; Skinner et al., 1999). While not unique to sports, these managerial shifts help bring standardisation in elements like media, culture or promotion (Washington & Patterson, 2011). Standardisation in Formula 1 resulted in similar tracks, cars, race length and event structure, and this proved to be successful in a global market (Sturm, 2014). Equally, for the WRC, standardisation would occur to assist the creation of a globally popular media product (Næss, 2014). Transformation came for both F1 and the WRC, but with vastly different financial results, and why the WRC's journey is different has seldom been explored.

The Professionalisation of the WRC

Upon Ecclestone's entry to the WRC, motorsport's governing body saw the success of Formula 1 globally and was eager to transform and financialise its other global motorsport properties, and the WRC was part of this plan (Næss, 2014). As Lovell (2003) suggests, this was a time of major political powerplays within the FIA as Mosley and Ecclestone sought to fundamentally shift how global motor racing would be organised and promoted. In total, 19 Championships, including the WRC, would be brought under the control of International Sportsworld Communicators (ISC), the motorsport promotion company headed by Ecclestone (Lovell, 2003). In 1993 this strategy forced the WRC to take steps towards professionalisation. The effects of this decision were quickly felt. A new television distribution model was created which the car manufacturers had to fund, increasing costs and negatively affecting teams' copyright claims on the footage, and television companies could no longer televise the Championship free of charge (Lovell, 2003). From 1994 until its demise in 1999, World Rally Teams Association (WRTA) campaigned against these, and other measures, on behalf of the major teams (Evans, 2020a).

These motorsport-wide decisions were being watched. Within motorsport, there was trepidation after Ecclestone and the FIA took partial control of the World Sportscar Championship in the late 1980s when the series had originally run under the direction of the French automotive group (and originators of the famous 24 Hours of Le Mans race) Automobile Club de l'Ouest. By 1993, costs had risen and interest dwindled to such an extent that the Championship, started in 1953, was discontinued (*FIA Group C Racing (1982–1993)*, 2012; Lovell, 2003; Orlove, 2016). Having seen what happened with sportscars, the manufacturers were wary of the changes in the WRC. While media had been a major factor in the emergence of the WRTA, they were not the only factor. The 1995 Championship featured the fewest rounds since 1974 with eight rounds and the rally rotation scheme (whereby some rallies would be held only every two years), and the "Rally 2000" document was created regarding future car and event regulations (Evans, 2020a). Both initiatives were politically charged as they were designed to find new ways to increase investment in the sport, decrease costs, and standardise more aspects of car specifications and event operation. Within the WRTA and between the WRTA and the ISC, friction was evident. The process to find the balance between tradition and future demands was difficult. Moreover, this was magnified by the fact that Ecclestone personally did not care much for rallying, despite Mosley's efforts to convince him of the commercial value of the WRC, thinking it could become more popular than F1 because of its 'conceivably greater worldwide potential' (Mosley, 2015, p. 232). Despite the backroom disquiet, however, charismatic drivers and popular cars helped to draw an estimated crowd of 2 million to the 1995 RAC Rally, a four-day event (Page, 2019).

This popularity could not be sustained, and even with television coverage that had better production and cost more, the viewing figures in some territories were halved between 1995 and 1997 (Lovell, 2003, p. 262). However, it seemed as though the teams would have to learn to live with the situation as ISC was handed the promoter rights deal for the period 1996–2010 (Goren, 2006). Throughout the following years, political rumblings would continue as Group A gave way to the WRC car regulations and the televisation of the WRC was centralised (O'Connor, 2004, p. 11). The disquiet continued, with some motorsport and WRC stakeholders pressing the European Union to investigate the FIA and Ecclestone for anti-competitive practices, a tactic that would eventually succeed. In 1997, on the back of a possible flotation of Ecclestone's Formula 1 interests, the European Commission launched an investigation into global motorsport (*European Commission*, 1999; Formula One Stalled by EU, 1999; Lovell, 2003; Næss, 2014; O'Connor, 2004). In June 1999, the Commission released a document concluding

> that it considers the FIA to be abusing its dominant position and restricting competition. The Commission has sent the same statement of objections to two companies controlled by Mr Bernie Ecclestone: Formula One Administration Ltd (FOA), which sells the television rights to the Formula One championship, and International Sportsworld Communicators (ISC), which markets the broadcasting rights to a number of major international motor sport events. (*European Commission*, 1999)

This decision from the European Commission would set in motion a series of events that would impact the sport for years. For Ecclestone, the path was clear with the eventual sale of F1 being worth more than a billion dollars, dwarfing the value of the WRC (Lovell, 2003; Mosley, 2015). Ecclestone's decision required a solution for the WRC. Initially, the European Commission courted Patrick Peter, a leading figure in the fight against Ecclestone. Peter was part of a consortium promoting a burgeoning global sportscar series—the BPR Global GT Series—but became a victim of the FIA's draconian approach to motorsport media in the 1990s. The FIA stated that he was operating outside FIA policy by not giving the broadcast rights to Ecclestone, but he would continue in sportscars rather than switching to rally promotion (Grandprix.com, 2000; Lovell, 2003). This opened the door for Welsh motorsport entrepreneur David Richards, who purchased the ISC brand and the WRC promotion rights for a sum that was thought to be around £30 million (Lovell, 2003, p. 313).

A Period of Hope, Instability and Disaster

With multi-million-pound investment and 10 years remaining on the rights contract, Richards' confidence in the future financial success of the WRC was evident. At the time, manufacturer interest was high, with seven manufacturer teams, growing budgets, and an appetite to replicate Formula 1's success as a form of branded entertainment (Davenport, 2000; Næss, 2014; Williams & Klein, 2001). Richards said:

> ...we need to be looking at rallying with some fresh vision. There are two sides to the sport. Looking at the top, it is 100 percent professional. And it is pure entertainment for spectators. It is a medium for the marketing of cars and associated sponsors. (Davenport, 2000, p. 37)

Changes would soon come in an attempt to address the entertainment and marketing aspects of the WRC. Key among these changes was the introduction of a compulsory centralised service park and cloverleaf formats. These two aspects resulted in a standardisation of rallying whereby a central area where all cars would go for repairs, the 'service park', would be used. Stages would surround the service park and be used two or three times in one day before the cars dispersed to different geographical areas the next day for another group of stages, conjuring the image of a cloverleaf (see Image 1). The drivers would drive from the service park to the stages, knows as the liaison, on public roads, driving to a set time but outside of direct competition (Næss, 2014). Previously, cars repairs could occur anywhere and stages could snake across a country.

These changes were primarily for the benefit of the media and spectators. They allowed Richards to take a revolutionary step to control WRC media presentation, creating and delivering consistently branded television products. The number of employees at ISC increased, market research was carried out and, for the first time, broadcasters could expect branded daily highlights delivered at a predetermined time (O'Connor, 2004). Television was the leading asset in trying to make rallying a "much younger and dynamic sport" (O'Connor, 2004, p. 157). Despite the

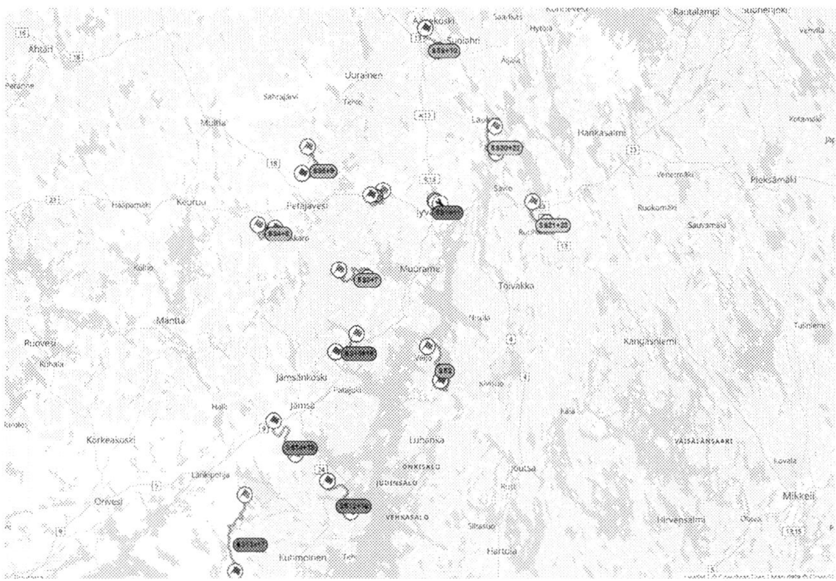

Image 1 A WRC event itinerary: Rally Finland 2019. The flags represent the start and finish of the stages. The wrench denotes the service park, the central area of the rally for car repairs and the media. Via: https://www.rally-maps.com/Rally-Finland-2019

effort and new direction from ISC, however, the FIA were still active in the background, with political discontent becoming more visible in 2004 with efforts to expand the calendar from 14 to 16 rallies, introducing a re-start rule for retired crews (previously teams had to retire from the event if they missed a stage; this rule would allow them to miss stages and incur a time penalty) and consideration of a move away from compulsory centralised servicing (*Season 2004*, 2004; Wilkins, 2003). It was apparent that Richards was becoming increasingly aggravated by the creeping influence from the governing body and, at the time, was quoted as saying:

> The overriding issue for me is the way [the rules are] being imposed on the World Championship. You've got a commission with all the appropriate stakeholders. To take the authority away from that group is wrong. (Wilkins, 2003)

Furthermore, Jost Capito, the boss of Ford's European motorsport arm, outlined the manufacturer discontent:

> Ford budgets are being reduced and if budgets need to be increased—by up to 2 million for Japan and Mexico—the feeling within the company is that might not be right. (Wilkins, 2003)

Other manufacturers were also considering their place in the sport and over time interest declined. By 2007, several manufacturers had withdrawn and Richards was divesting himself of ISC, with the (now defunct) London company, North One Sport (NOS) taking command for that season (Goren, 2006). NOS came in as promoter with apparent sympathy from FIA President Max Mosley, who said:

> The fundamental difficulty is that rallying is wholly unsuitable for television. The public now demand to devour their major sporting events live which simply cannot be delivered in the case of rallies. (Davenport, 2008, p. 105)

At the time, Simon Long, a senior executive at ISC, was looking to the internet with great opportunism. He would say:

> We want to make the possibilities that the Internet has to offer take off and make it a playground for the WRC. The TV coverage is still important but the web enables you to go multi-dimensional. (Davenport, 2008, p. 106)

Having dismissed the possibilities of television, Mosley endorsed the aspirations of the promoter to utilise new media services to improve the reach and financial aspects of the sport:

> In my view, the WRC is made for the Internet with its capability to deliver the action direct to millions of people. North One Television, the new owners of ISC [which retains the WRC rights], recognise this.... (Davenport, 2008, p. 105)

While NOS wanted to exploit the end of 'scarcity' and the start of 'plenitude' on the media side, their management of the WRC would coincide with the global financial crisis of 2008–2009. There was a concerted effort to reduce costs for both competitors and events (Evans, 2009). A secondary tactic was to find new sources of revenue. As a result, rally cars were cheaper, and out went long-held events and in came new rallies and a rotation system—meaning some rallies would be held only every second year. Again NOS and the FIA had differing views here, with the FIA encouraging the rotation system, ignoring the pleas of the promoter (Evans, 2010). The change was designed to bring in additional income while trying to protect the history of the sport. Politically and culturally, this would raise issues in the sport, most notably with the Monte-Carlo Rally, the most prestigious event being subjected to the rally rotation system. Initially, the rally was to skip one season in 2009 (*Monte Carlo Rally to Join the IRC in 2009*, 2008). However, the promoters of the event, the Automobile Club de Monaco (ACM), concluded a deal with the nascent Intercontinental Rally Challenge (ISC) and would remain in that championship for three years. This gave the IRC credibility, and together with Eurosport Events, the then promoter of the ISC, they managed to be the ones to broadcast multiple stages live in 2011, where a star-studded field proved that live rallying could be an entertaining television event (Barry, 2021). While the ACM would move their event back to the WRC, this showed that while the WRC had 'more' rallies, they lacked key aspects of fan interest—innovative television coverage, top-end teams and blue riband events.

Financially, the WRC under NOS continued to struggle. They reported a loss in 2009 and were not confident of making a profit in 2010 (Olson, 2010). However, despite any apparent troubles, NOS retained the promotion rights for the sport for the period 2010–2019, and with the new agreement the ISC name was formally terminated in a rebranding exercise from NOS (Næss, 2014). This ownership structure would be short-lived, with British/Russian firm Convers Sports Initiatives (CSI) purchasing NOS for the 2011 season, though they would keep the same staff (Bennett, 2011). CSI, led by London-based Russian businessman Vladimir Antonov, had been making large acquisitions of "underleveraged sports entertainment businesses and making them a success" (Andronikou & Kubik, 2012). These included sports entities like football teams and racing events. For the WRC, this would push the sport to the edge. CSI would collapse under the strain of investments and alleged criminal transactions including fraud and money laundering by their owners, for which Antonov would later be jailed (Scott, 2011; "Vladimir Antonov", 2019). The fallout left NOS with debts of more than £5.7 million and liquid assets of only £1.1 million (Andronikou & Kubik, 2012; Evans, 2012b). The WRC was trapped in a mess much larger than itself, and while rescue packages were offered, the FIA remained unimpressed. Talks collapsed shortly before the 2012 season, and with less than two weeks before the start of the season, the FIA dictated a stop-gap solution:

> The FIA sought urgent unequivocal assurances from NOS that it could fulfil its contractual obligations and deliver the promotion of the upcoming Rally Monte Carlo and the Championship for 2012 and the future. It is with regret and disappointment that no such assurance has been given to the FIA, and therefore today the FIA has been driven to terminate its contract with NOS. NOS has conspicuously failed to deliver its contractual obligations and is in fundamental breach of contract. (FIA World Rally Championship, 2012)

The 2012 season provided a strange throwback to the early days in that the FIA would take control of the sport's promotion. However, before the season was out, the new WRC Promoter GmbH was created and awarded the promotion rights from 2013 to 2022 with Red Bull Media House and Sportsman Media Group (Evans, 2012a). Through the bankruptcy process for Convers, it became apparent that the WRC had been financially struggling, even during good times. In fact, during the 2000–2011 period, the promoter body only achieved a profitable year three times (Andronikou & Kubik, 2012). It was now evident that the WRC could not achieve its mega-sport ambition and needed to explore a new path.

Red Bull and the WRC Promoter

The New Media Landscape

The aspirations of anyone in control had to be tempered, as it was not realistic to aim for Formula 1's level of financial success and public prominence. After a season with a piecemeal promoter structure, the WRC Promoter GmbH took control of the WRC for the 2013 season. The WRC Promoter GmbH would in turn be led and part-owned by the Red Bull Media Group, a company with a different culture and outlook to previous promoters of the WRC. They had successfully created, promoted and distributed a mega event, the Red Bull Stratos Jump, that broke streaming records, alongside owning a television channel and promoting their own sporting competitions like the Red Bull Air Race (for planes) and Red Bull Crushed Ice, which was composed of extreme winter sports (Rogers, 2014). Their diversified portfolio provided many institutional skills in the operation of sport and sustainable sport mediatisation. Culturally, the organisation had a proven record of agility and risk-taking that could allow them to follow their managerial direction with the WRC. Their strategic legacy would soon become apparent in two primary areas—shifting the relationship with the fans and refining the sporting product.

The changing relationship with the fans would be best demonstrated by the changes to the broadcast television product. Initially, the WRC+ app for mobile devices enabled streaming and enhanced media delivery directly to the consumer. The early formation of the app carried a raft of media including on-board cameras, highlights packages and live radio (WRC App Launched, 2014). Soon live stages would be added, and then in 2018 the AllLive package was introduced, bringing 25 hours or more of coverage per weekend (Nelson, 2018). Through their owned app, they eliminated the need for broadcast partners and, indeed, any external forces for mediated change to the sport, and ensured that they could have a direct relationship with their fans. Effectively, they enacted a 'betting on two horses approach' where the sport would become its own global broadcaster while selling into national and regional markets, often having multiple partners in a single market (Tickell & Evens, 2021). It allowed the sport to progressively increase content to a point where, in 2018, there was a more than 750 per cent increase in broadcast time from the previous year and a world away from the three–four hours of highlights expected in the 2002 season (Carp, 2018; O'Connor, 2004).

Creating the app and showing the leading cars live at each stage of rallies for the first time is a prime example of what was now possible in the digital age. Furthermore, this move changed the way the story of the sport was told. More information was available than ever before, which resulted in teams and media evolving in their storytelling methods, with teams introducing sophisticated trans-media storytelling to further encourage fan interest and engagement (Næss & Tickell, 2019). Additionally, the WRC has been quick to grasp and launch digital products that feature more than the AllLive app, and include products like eSports, podcasting and social media (*WRC Factbook 2020*, 2020). The new direct relationship with the fan, the expanded storylines and the opportunity to create a multifaceted approach to financialising a niche sport showed that broadcast television revenue, once the holy grail of financialisation, was now just one of many opportunities for a niche-sport promoter.

A New Political Outlook

The second key change has been to the sport itself. During the reign of the current promoter, the cars, rallies and sporting regulations have all been changed. The AllLive media coverage affected the running of events, with event length, time between stages and visual aspects all needing tweaks to fit in with the new media technologies (Tickell & Evens, 2021). Changes would also be evident in other areas, as professionalisation and financialisation continued. Alongside the fan experience, the expectations of sponsors and manufacturers had to be met and this was done through development of the service park. Rallying competes for the same sponsorship revenue as other sports, and with motorsports like Formula 1 and sportscar being able to provide high-level corporate entertainment, rallying was almost obliged to follow. Once even the biggest teams just had small tents in the service park. Now large structures that could take days to build and dismantle were demanded to satisfy the needs of corporate guests (McKellar, 2013b). Despite being a niche sport, the changes in the wider sporting landscape could still influence the evolution of rallying.

The manufacturer involvement would continue to change as Red Bull tried to put their stamp on the Championship. New rules for 2017 meant that cars were faster than ever before, and the FIA dictated a rule to disallow amateur drivers to compete in these cars due to safety concerns (Evans, 2020b). Additionally, the FIA would create and standardise the 'ladder' system for drivers and teams aspiring to rally in the WRC, known as 'Group R'. It was a clear statement of intention from Red Bull, the FIA and the manufacturers to create something more spectacular at the front line while creating a coherent structure under the WRC. In effect, however, it ensured that only manufacturer entries could compete at the top level and placed more power in the hands of the richest teams. Away from the cars, standardisation of more event elements was another crucial piece of Red Bull's vision for a spectacular event. Points for an individual stage had been awarded for the first time in 2011, under NOS leadership. However, it would become a key ingredient to create a spectacular ending to any rally and so the sport changed to facilitate an exciting, made-for-TV ending. The final stage would start and finish at a standard time, be part of the AllLive app and be sold to third-party broadcasters. It would come to be known as the 'Powerstage' with the winner receiving five points (second to fifth on stage would receive points) (*WRC Factbook 2020*, 2020). With the rally winner getting 25 points, five points can be considered significant. These stages needed to highlight the WRC's strengths given their importance to sporting and media elements. Consequently, visually spectacular landscapes and action elements like artificial jumps would increasingly be utilised (Hughes, 2018).

Through these changes, and in particular, from the period of 2013–2020, the sport had experienced a period of the sort of political and economic stability it had not enjoyed since the push to professionalisation began. The ownership structure remained relatively stable with Red Bull Media House maintaining its ownership, and in 2015, the Sportsman Media Group was sold to the Swiss multinational corporation Sports Radar and the share of the WRC Promoter GmbH was transferred to KW25 (*KEK, BLM Commission Report*, 2017). Manufacturer engagement remained relatively stable, and while interest at the top level would wane, manufacturers stayed in the sport at other levels, creating cars for national, regional or ladder series. The sport continues to face pressure from consumer motoring and the environmental focus from manufacturers and governments (*FIA Environmental Strategy*, 2020; *Sustainability Report 2020*, 2020; *Strategy 2025*, 2020; *Environmental Report 2020*, 2020). This position was backed by former WRC Managing Director Oliver Ciesla, who referred to the pressure faced as the need to "expand our visibility and that of the manufacturers that have decided to invest and race in the WRC" (Thukral & Rauli, 2020). Furthermore, New Zealand driver turned team owner Hayden Paddon said "[t]he sport of rallying needs to evolve and quickly before it gets left behind. And EVs (electric vehicles) are the solution" (Craig, 2020). This is one aspect of the complex puzzle the sport faces going into the next phase.

The future aside, it is almost impossible to know if the sport has become profitable during this era, as the financial aspects and subscription figures are heavily guarded secrets. However, stability can be viewed as a positive sign. Undoubtedly, the sport's culture has changed over this period, but the use of new technologies and adapting to market pressures helped achieve stability.

Discussion and Conclusion

The path to professionalisation and financialisation for the WRC was far from smooth. The choices presented by the FIA with regard to the promoter were stark. The sport experienced relative stability in its first years and efforts to professionalise were imposed on it, with disastrous results. At the beginning of professionalisation, it was evident that replicating a successful model from another sport was not sympathetic to rallying's culture. Until the Antonov affair at least, the WRC had relied on a fanbase characterised by loyalty to the sport's roots. This meant a fan culture with key ingredients like a working-class atmosphere (due to the widespread 'garage life' of both fans and drivers), spectating outdoors in all kinds of weather, and bantering about the action instead of merely watching it (Næss, 2014). To make things worse in terms of nurturing this culture, efforts to commercialise and professionalise the sport struck a middle ground, leaving everybody dissatisfied—both those who thought the changes were too small to save the sport and those who found the changes to be a mockery of tradition. It was only after the sport almost failed that a new path was forged. Overconfidence in the popularity and financial ability of the media product derived from other motorsport series would hamper the WRC's progress, and a new strategy was needed. When the current promoter arrived, their expertise in niche sport and their culture of sports management enabled quicker reactions to the prevailing media changes regarding rallying.

Lessons can be taken from the WRC's mediatisation, including that the unique cultural aspects of sport need to be maintained and that not all sports can achieve significant financialisation. To achieve this, systematic professionalisation was forced onto rallying, where more modest targets would be more sustainable. Even when viewing the WRC through the lenses of the media-sport complex and media-sport triangle, rapid professionalisation was needed to create a television-friendly product. Undoubtedly, throughout the early stages of the sport, rally media were underutilised. As it turned out, however, the wish to achieve rapid financialisation through media and professionalisation created instability in the sport. This is demonstrated in Fig. 1, which shows that the first 17

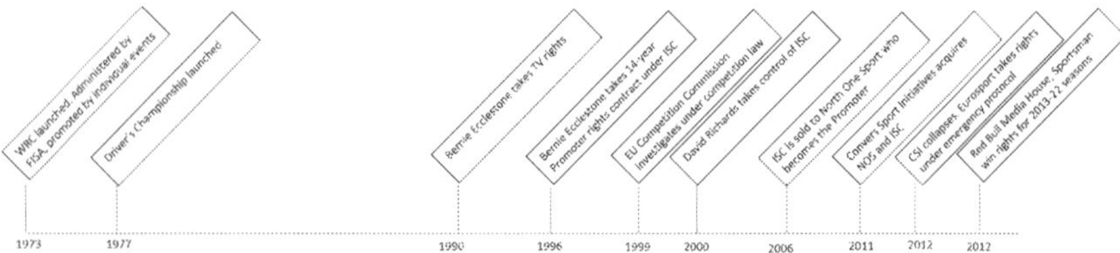

Fig. 1 Timeline of major changes within the WRC management

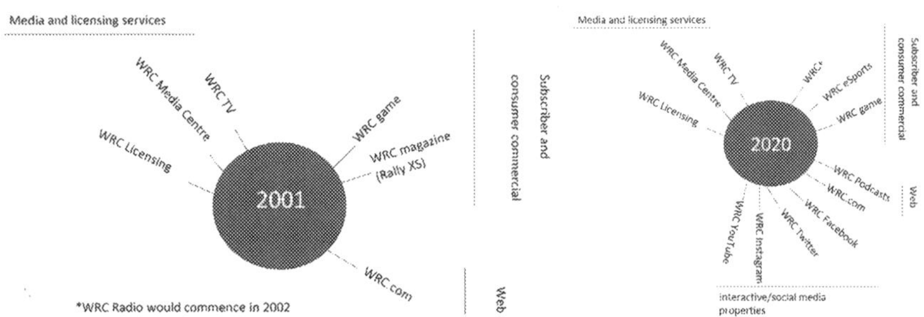

Fig. 2 Owned media properties of the WRC promotion body, 2001 vs 2020

years of the sport had stable ownership and promoter structure, whereas the following 17 years were quite unstable. Once the outlook of the promoter changed again, stability returned to the sport.

Moreover, mediated sport changed drastically over the 25 years of the WRC's professionalisation, as shown in Fig. 2. It has forced changes to the ongoing financial and promotional structures in the WRC. The changes reflect the shift from broadcast scarcity to digital plenitude where there is a necessity to take advantage of technologies and acknowledge where the audience exists. In the WRC Promoter GmbH's situation, creating an owned app with a direct-to-consumer approach was an acceptable step for three reasons. The first was that it proved that increasing the commitment to the previously created branded entertainment base was possible. Secondly, for a niche sport, ensuring television coverage can be difficult, and the owned app eliminated this risk. Thirdly, it opened new paths for media financialisation, where the sport had previously struggled.

Other changes and pressures on the sport like gaming, geopolitics and environmental factors will continue to exert influence. However, niche sport's interaction with professionalisation, financialisation and media-sport is important, as shown by the WRC case. As technologies and skill-sets to reach audiences evolve and effective business models emerge, sports have more options to create a profitable future. In the end, for the WRC, stability was achieved when it stopped trying to adapt the sport according to the successes of other motorsports and started to exploit the sport's inherent culture and strengths.

References

Albers-Daly, T. (2020, May 13). F1 Spotlight—Max Mosley [News/Opinion]. *DriveTribe*. https://drivetribe.com/p/f1-spotlight-max-mosley-I9Y9uMuzTH2NR1u7mq-zcw

Andronikou, A., & Kubik, P. (2012). *Statement of Administrator's Proposals—North One Sport LTD* (Creditor Report No. 1; p. 28). Hacker Young LLP. https://find-and-update.company-information.service.gov.uk/company/01649155/filing-history

Barry, L. (2021, January 19). Monte Carlo Rally 2011 Rewind: The One that Had It All [News, views]. *DirtFish*. https://dirtfish.com/rally/erc/monte-carlo-rally-2011-rewind-the-one-that-had-it-all/

Bennett, J. (2011, March 4). New Dawn for WRC as Series Promoter Changes Hands. *Sports Media Pro*. http://www.sportspromedia.com/news/new_dawn_for_wrc_as_series_promoter_changes_hands

Billings, A. (2011). *Sports Media: Transformation, Integration, Consumption*. Routledge.

Boyle, R., & Haynes, R. (2009). *Power Play: Sport, the Media and Popular Culture: Sport, the Media and Popular Culture*. Edinburgh University Press.

Brenner, M. (2014, August 29). 7 Content Marketing Lessons From Red Bull Media House. *Relevance*. http://blog.newscred.com/article/7-content-marketing-lessons-from-red-bull-media-house/179187d03b9b6144ea92dc27049813c3

Carp, S. (2018, January 24). Leaders in Motorsport: WRC Managing Director Oliver Ciesla Previews the 2018 Season. *Blackbook Motorsport*. https://www.blackbookmotorsport.com/features/leaders-in-motorsport-wrc-managing-director-oliver-ciesla-previews-the-2018

Commission Opens Formal Proceedings into Formula One and Other International Motor Racing Series. (1999). [Text]. European Commission. https://ec.europa.eu/commission/presscorner/detail/en/IP_99_434

Craig, J. (2020, November 4). Paddon: Rallying Risks Being "Left Behind" by Not Embracing Green Technology [News]. *Autosport.Com*. https://www.autosport.com/wrc/news/153276/rallying-risks-being-left-behind-without-green-push

Davenport, J. (2000). From Co-Drive To Prodrive. *Motor Sport Magazine*, May, pp. 23–37.

Davenport, J. (2008). What in the World Is Going on? *Motor Sport Magazine*, April, pp. 102–106.

Davenport, J., & Klein, R. (2011). *Group B—The Rise and Fall of Rallyings Wildest Cars* (1st ed.). McKlein Publsihing. https://www.rallyandracing.com/en/rallywebshop/books/history/group-b-the-rise-and-fall-of-rallyings-wildest-cars

Davenport, J., & Klein, R. (2012). *Group 4—From Stratos to Quattro*. McKlein Publsihing. https://www.rallyandracing.com/en/rallywebshop/books/history/group-4-from-stratos-to-quattro

Dowling, M., Edwards, J., & Washington, M. (2014). Understanding the Concept of Professionalisation in Sport Management Research. *Sport Management Review, 17*(4), 520–529. https://doi.org/10.1016/j.smr.2014.02.003

Evans, D. (2009). WRC Revises 2011 Technical Rules. *Autosport.Com*. https://www.autosport.com/wrc/news/76506/wrc-revises-2011-technical-rules

Evans, D. (2010). FIA Still in Favour of Rally Rotation. *Autosport.Com*. https://www.autosport.com/wrc/news/82182/fia-still-in-favour-of-rally-rotation

Evans, D. (2012a, September 28). Red Bull Becomes World Rally Championship Promoter. *Autosport.Com*. https://www.autosport.com/wrc/news/102926/red-bull-seals-wrc-promoter-deal

Evans, D. (2012b, November 5). How World Rallying Was Almost Saved [News]. *Autosport.Com*. https://www.autosport.com/wrc/feature/4435/how-world-rallying-was-almost-saved

Evans, D. (2020a, April 14). Relive the 1995 WRC Season with DirtFish [News]. *DirtFish*. https://dirtfish.com/rally/wrc/relive-the-1995-wrc-season-with-dirtfish/

Evans, D. (2020b, June 14). Future WRC Cars Will Be Available for National Rallies [News]. *DirtFish*. https://dirtfish.com/rally/wrc/future-wrc-cars-will-be-available-for-national-rallies/

Evens, T., & Donders, K. (2018). Game of Screens. In T. Evens & K. Donders (Eds.), *Platform Power and Policy in Transforming Television Markets* (pp. 47–85). Springer International Publishing. https://doi.org/10.1007/978-3-319-74246-5_3

Evens, T., Iosifidis, P., & Smith, P. (2013). *The Political Economy of Television Sports Rights*. Palgrave Macmillan. https://doi.org/10.1057/9781137360342

FIA Environmental Strategy 2020–2030 (Action for Environment, p. 28). (2020). [Position Paper]. Federation Internationale de l'Automobile. https://www.fia.com/multimedia/publication/fia-environmental-strategy-2020-2030

FIA Group C Racing (1982–1993). (2012, July 6). [Blog]. IMCA SlotRacing. https://web.archive.org/web/20120706034618/http://www.imca-slotracing.com/1982-1993%20GROUP%20C%20RACING%20part%20II.htm

FIA World Rally Championship. (2012, July 2). [Organisational]. Federation Internationale de l'Automobile. https://www.fia.com/fr/node/5092

Ford Sustainability Report 2020 (p. 54). (2020). [CS Report]. Ford Motor Company. https://corporate.ford.com/microsites/sustainability-report-2020/assets/files/sr20.pdf

Formula One Stalled by EU. (1999, June 30). [Financial]. CNN. https://money.cnn.com/1999/06/30/worldbiz/formula_one/

Goren, B. (2006). Richards to Step Down from ISC. *Autosport.Com*. https://www.autosport.com/wrc/news/52239/richards-to-step-down-from-isc

Grandprix.com. (2000, August 9). The FIA and the European Commission [News]. *Grandprix.Com*. http://www.grandprix.com//news/the-fia-and-the-european-commission-2.html

Greenhalgh, G., & Greenwell, T. C. (2013). What's in It for Me? An Investigation of North American Professional Niche Sport Sponsorship Objectives. *Sport Marketing Quarterly, 22*(2), 101–112.

Greenhalgh, G. P., Simmons, J. M., Hambrick, M. E., & Greenwell, T. C. (2011). *Spectator Support: Examining the Attributes that Differentiate Niche from Mainstream Sport, 20*(1), 14.

Harvey, D. (2007). *A Brief History of Neoliberalism* (2nd ed.). Oxford University Press.

Hughes, J. (2018). WRC Should Do Away With "Stupid" Artificial Jumps, Say Drivers. *The Drive*. https://www.thedrive.com/accelerator/21499/rally-drivers-think-wrc-should-do-away-with-stupid-artificial-jumps

Hutchins, B. (2019). Mobile Media Sport: The Case for Building a Mobile Media and Communications Research Agenda. *Communication & Sport, 7*(4), 466–487. https://doi.org/10.1177/2167479518788833

Hutchins, B., Li, B., & Rowe, D. (2019). Over-the-Top Sport: Live Streaming Services, Changing Coverage Rights Markets and the Growth of Media Sport Portals. *Media, Culture and Society, 41*(7), 975–994. https://doi.org/10.1177/0163443719857623

Hutchins, B., & Rowe, D. (2009). From Broadcast Scarcity to Digital Plenitude: The Changing Dynamics of the Media Sport Content Economy. *Television and New Media, 10*(4), 354–370. https://doi.org/10.1177/1527476409334016

Hyundai Motor 'Strategy 2025' (p. 7). (2020). Hyundai Motor Company. https://www.hyundai.news/eu/brand/hyundai-motor-updates-strategy-2025/

Jhally, S. (1984). The Spectacle of Accumulation: Material and Cultural Factors in the Evolution of the Sports/Media Complex. *Insurgent Sociologist, 12*(3), 41–57. https://doi.org/10.1177/089692058401200304

Kikulis, L. M., Slack, T., & Hinings, B. (1992). Institutionally Specific Design Archetypes: A Framework for Understanding Change in National Sport Organizations. *International Review for the Sociology of Sport, 27*(4), 343–368. https://doi.org/10.1177/101269029202700405

Kunz, R., Elsässer, F., & Santomier, J. (2016). Sport-related Branded Entertainment: The Red Bull Phenomenon. *Sport, Business and Management: An International Journal, 6*(5), 520–541. https://doi.org/10.1108/SBM-06-2016-0023

Lefever, K. (2012). Sports/Media Complex in the New Media Landscape. In *New Media and Sport*. ASSER.

Lovell, T. (2003). *Bernie's Game: Inside the Formula One World of Bernie Ecclestone*. Metro. http://archive.org/details/berniesgameinsid0000love

McKay, J., & Miller, T. (1991). From Old Boys to Men and Women of the Corporation: The Americanization and Commodification of Australian Sport. *Sociology of Sport Journal, 8*(1), 86–94. https://doi.org/10.1123/ssj.8.1.86

McKellar, C. (2013a, April 15). Henri Toivonen at Estoril—Exploring the Myth [Corporate]. *Red Bull*. https://www.redbull.com/gb-en/henri-toivonen-at-estoril-exploring-the-myth

McKellar, C. (2013b, July 18). Tech Talk: World Rally Hospitality [Corporate]. *Red Bull*. https://www.redbull.com/int-en/tech-talk-world-rally-hospitality

Miller, T., Lawrence, G., McKay, J., & Rowe, D. (2001). *Globalization and Sport*. Sage Publications Ltd. https://uk.sagepub.com/en-gb/eur/globalization-and-sport/book207268

Milne, M. (2016). *The Transformation of Television Sport*. Palgrave Macmillan. https://doi.org/10.1057/9781137559111_1

Monte Carlo Rally to Join the IRC in 2009. (2008, January 28). [Business]. *SportBusiness*. https://www.sportbusiness.com/news/monte-carlo-rally-to-join-the-irc-in-2009/

Mosley, M. (2015). *Formula One and Beyond: The Autobiography* (UK ed.). Simon & Schuster.

Næss, H. E. (2014). *A Sociology of the World Rally Championship—History, Identity, Memories and Place*. Palgrave Macmillan. https://www.palgrave.com/br/book/9781137405432

Næss, H. E. (2018). Fédération Internationale de l'Automobile (FIA), Power, and Politics: A Socio-Historical Analysis. *Sport History Review, 49*(2), 143–160. https://doi.org/10.1123/shr.2017-0027

Næss, H. E., & Tickell, S. (2019). Fan Engagement in Motorsports: A Case of the FIA World Rally Championship. *The Journal of Media Innovations, 5*(1), 31–44. https://doi.org/10.5617/jomi.6289

Nagel, S., Schlesinger, T., Bayle, E., & Giauque, D. (2015). Professionalisation of Sport Federations—A Multi-level Framework for Analysing Forms, Causes and Consequences. *European Sport Management Quarterly, 15*(4), 407–433. https://doi.org/10.1080/16184742.2015.1062990

Nelson, D. (2018, October 17). How All Live is Changing the Face of Rallying: Foundations. *The F1 Broadcasting Blog*. https://f1broadcasting.co/2018/10/17/how-all-live-is-changing-the-face-of-rallying-foundations/

O'Connor, S. (2004). An Examination for the Marketing Strategy of the World Rally Championship. *Masters*. https://doi.org/10.21427/D7V32R

Olson, P. (2010, February 24). A Shift Up For Rally Racing. *Forbes*. https://www.forbes.com/2010/02/23/world-rally-championship-business-sports-auto-racing.html

Orlove, R. (2016, December 25). How Group C Died [Comment]. *Jalopnik*. https://jalopnik.com/how-group-c-died-1790488527

Page, J. (2019, October 15). Motorsport Memories: When McRae Magic Gripped the Nation [Industry]. *Classic & Sports Car*. https://www.classicandsportscar.com/features/motorsport-memories-when-mcrae-magic-gripped-nation

Rogers, G. (2014). Red Bull—It Gives You Wings! An Examination of the Emotional Experiences that Drive the Brand for the Popular Energy Drink. *Journal of Integrated Studies, 5*(1). http://jis.athabascau.ca/index.php/jis/article/view/133

Rowe, D. (1999). *Sport, Culture & Media: The Unruly Trinity*. McGraw-Hill Education.

Rowe, D. (2011). *Global Media Sport*. Bloomsbury Academic. https://doi.org/10.5040/9781849661577

Sam, M. P. (2009). The Public Management of Sport. *Public Management Review, 11*(4), 499–514. https://doi.org/10.1080/14719030902989565

Scott, M. (2011, November 23). Portsmouth Co-owner Vladimir Antonov is Subject of Arrest Warrant [News]. *The Guardian*. http://www.theguardian.com/football/2011/nov/23/portsmouth-vladimir-antonov-arrest-warrant

Season 1973 Event Statistics. (2021). [Database]. Juwra. https://www.juwra.com/season_1973_event_stats.html

Season 2004. (2004). [Database]. Juwra. https://www.juwra.com/season_2004.html

Skinner, J., Stewart, B., & Edwards, A. (1999). Amateurism to Professionalism: Modelling Organisational Change in Sporting Organisations. *Sport Management Review, 2*(2), 173–192. https://doi.org/10.1016/S1441-3523(99)70095-1

Smith, P., Evens, T., & Iosifidis, P. (2016). The Next Big Match: Convergence, Competition and Sports Media Rights. *European Journal of Communication, 31*(5), 536–550. https://doi.org/10.1177/0267323116666479

Sturm, D. (2014). A Glamorous and High-tech Global Spectacle of Speed. Formula One Motor Racing as Mediated, Global and Corporate Spectacle. In *Sports Events, Society and Culture* (pp. 68–82). Routledge.

Thorpe, H., & Wheaton, B. (2011). 'Generation X Games', Action Sports and the Olympic Movement: Understanding the Cultural Politics of Incorporation. *Sociology, 45*(5), 830–847. https://doi.org/10.1177/0038038511413427

Thukral, R., & Rauli, G. (2020, June 6). WRC Wants to Return to Key Markets United States and China [News]. *Motorsport.Com*. https://www.motorsport.com/wrc/news/united-states-china-return-ciesla/4800018/

Tickell, S., & Evens, T. (2021). Owned Streaming Platforms and Television Broadcast Deals: The Case of the World Rally Championship (WRC). *European Journal of International Management, 15*(2/3), 266–282. https://doi.org/10.1504/EJIM.2021.10032581

Toyota Environmental Report 2020 (p. 42). (2020). [CS Report]. Toyota Motor Corporation. https://global.toyota/pages/global_toyota/sustainability/report/er/er20_en.pdf#page=10

Vladimir Antonov: Former Portsmouth FC Owner Jailed in Russia. (2019, March 18). *BBC News*. https://www.bbc.com/news/uk-england-hampshire-47609147

Washington, M., & Patterson, K. D. W. (2011). Hostile Takeover or Joint Venture: Connections Between Institutional Theory and Sport Management Research. *Sport Management Review, 14*(1), 1–12. https://doi.org/10.1016/j.smr.2010.06.003

Wenner, L. (1989). *Media, Sports, and Society*. Sage Publications Ltd.

Whannel, G. (1992). *Fields in Vision: Television Sport and Cultural Transformation*. Routledge.

Wilkins, R. (2003, September 11). Richards: Dangerous Times for WRC. *Crash*. https://www.crash.net/wrc/news/111273/1/richards-dangerous-times-for-wrc

Williams, D., & Klein, R. (2001). *Rallycourse 2000–01*. Hazleton Publishing.

WRC App Launched. (2014). [Corporate]. WRC—World Rally Championship. https://www.wrc.com/en/news/news-archive/wrc/wrc-app-launched/

WRC Factbook 2020 (p. 84). (2020). WRC Promoter GmbH. https://www.wrc.com/factbook/2022/#40

Zheng, J., & Mason, D. S. (2018). *Brand Platform in the Professional Sport Industry*. Springer International Publishing. https://doi.org/10.1007/978-3-319-90353-8

Zulassungsantrag der WRC Promoter GmbH für das Fernsehspartenprogramm "WRC+" (p. 5). (2017). [Commission Submission]. Kommission zur Ermittlung der Konzentration im Medienbereich (KEK) auf Vorlage der Bayerischen Landeszentrale für neue Medien (BLM). https://www.kek-online.de/fileadmin/user_upload/KEK/Medienkonzentration/Verfahren/kek945WRC_Promoter.pdf

Part II

The Early Political Significance of Motor Racing

Racing and Racism: German Motorsport and the Third Reich

Eberhard Reuss and Sandra Esslinger

Introduction: Revisiting, Revising, and Rewriting Racing History in Germany

> *Today, I believe, nothing that is alive can sidestep politics. Even a refusal of politics is political; it merely abets the politics of evil.*
> —Thomas Mann in a letter to Hermann Hesse, 8 April 1945

The history of automobile racing in Germany is often interpreted through a lens of romanticism, wherein the silver bullets of German automotive racing streak across the track with a simple minimalist aerodynamic elegance and a signature roar—man triumphs over machine and imminent death. No small part of this romanticised myth-making is the

E. Reuss (✉)
Mannheim, Germany
e-mail: Eberhard.Reuss@swr.de

S. Esslinger
Mt. San Antonio College, Walnut, CA, USA
e-mail: sesslinger@mtsac.edu

D. Sturm et al. (eds.), *The History and Politics of Motor Racing*, Global Culture and Sport Series, https://doi.org/10.1007/978-3-031-22825-4_4

ever-present need for marketing—marketing of consumer products as well as of the ideology of the supremacy of Nazi Germany. If one is tied to the well-established automotive corporations or the original equipment manufacturers in Germany, there is a high likelihood that the success of today is strongly supported by their Nazi past. Not to mention that the ties are not just for industrial grants of governmental monies but also slave labour, human suffering, and death.

The romantic racing scene is often tied to the narrative of the heroes behind the wheel, the finish fetish of the cars, the brand or corporation that produces them, and the imminent struggle against death. The post-World War I German racing scene was a perfect setting for political marketing of the relatively new nation state. This was an ideal context for building the myth of a powerful and modern Third Reich beginning in 1933 in the wake of the losses of World War I. Notably, after the fall of the Third Reich in 1945, the legendary Silver Arrows became strategic in the euphemising of Nazi Germany, providing a reason to believe that things had not been *all* bad under this regime. This was another permutation of the romantic myth promoted by the same leading automotive and racing people who profited from the Third Reich and survived World War II.

German Racing History: The Brown Beneath the Silver

> *Germans don't know what they want, but if you tell them they are very efficient at making it happen.*
>
> —Jacques Rivière, *L'Allemand: Souvenirs et reflexions d'un prisonnier de guerre* [*On German nature: memories and reflections of a prisoner-of-war*], 1918/1919

Today's Silver Arrows are once again making motor racing history. When Sir Lewis Hamilton was cruising the line for another Formula One World Championship with Mercedes, the headlines trumpeted the great triumph of the Silver Arrows as though times had never changed. Clearly, in 2013 when he signed with Mercedes-Benz it was most certainly a different historical moment. Unlike his white predecessors, Lewis Hamilton is mixed-race, the son of a black Grenadian father and a white English mother. Facing down discrimination as he rose to fame, he now has a global following and uses his position for environmental and social activism—combating racism and promoting diversity in motor sport. He was knighted in 2021 and was named as one of the most influential people in the world by *Time* magazine.[1] This is a very different world from the days when the Silver Arrows originally hit the tarmac, as mixed-race drivers were absent, and in Nazi Germany, not allowed. There is an aspect Hamilton also addresses that hasn't changed enough since then, which is the persistent exclusivity and racism maintained by institutional barriers in the sport of Formula 1. Lewis Hamilton is fighting Formula 1 history.

Marketing strategists, canny sponsors, and so on were already around in Grand Prix racing in the 1930s in the form of the Nazi regime,[1] its propagandists, and Aryan industrialists. They laid the foundation for the successes of the Silver Arrows that are still celebrated today. They did so with government subsidies, bonuses for winning, and adoration as national heroes. Wheels had to roll for victory, and, especially on important occasions, the seemingly unbeatable national racing cars were even adorned with the trademark of their patrons and exploiters—the swastika. The memory of this form of mutual advertising was suppressed, concealed, and downplayed, for after 1945 the majority of those involved returned to their factories or to the racing circuits. They regarded themselves as profoundly apolitical; doubtless this was why they allowed themselves to be harnessed to the Nazi bandwagon. Even decades after Germany's catastrophic defeat, many people were still citing the victories of the Silver Arrows and the building of autobahns as proof that things were not all bad in 'those' days.

In 1958, former Mercedes-Benz racing manager Alfred Neubauer made the bestseller lists with his memoirs, co-written with journalist and screenwriter Harvey T. Rowe under the title *Men, Women and Engines*,[2] which simultaneously influenced and transformed the image of the racetrack heroes in their Silver Arrows: "Every one of these names has become history today—a part of the history of international motor racing *in its greatest and finest era*".[3] In this way the myths and legends have remained alive and are being cultivated as part of the marketing image. When historicising this comment, the hyperbolic statement romanticises the Nazi past as an idyllic time in car racing.

Today, Mercedes-Benz and Audi are more forthright about the activities of their companies in the days of the Third Reich. Still on the fringes of modern motor sport events, whenever the original cars or even just authentic replicas from the Silver Arrow era are rolled out and make their ear-splitting entrance as in their days of glory, fans are swept up by the spectacle of these engineering wonders of the 1930s. What must it have been like for contemporary observers in the 1930s when cars from Mercedes-Benz and Auto Union raced from victory to victory, proclaiming 'German superiority'? It would have depended entirely on your subject position. The majority would have been inspired and indoctrinated. However, if you were a German race car driver from a marginalized background your perspective was completely different since you were forced off the racetrack as part of the Aryanisation of the sport. Jews, Roma, and black people were *persona non grata* in the performance of national and racial identity in these displays, as this would have bastardised the purpose of the political performance.[4] The propaganda is clear from the vantage point of the marginalised 'other', and it was so successful that one still talks about the legendary superiority of German engineering as part of the national identity.

According to Victor Klemperer in 1946 in *Lingua Tertii Imperii*, his study of the language of the Third Reich:

> Nazism cultivated all forms of sport, and from a purely linguistic point of view it was more influenced by boxing than by all the other sports put together; but the most frequent and most memorable image of heroism is that provided in the mid-1930s by the racing drivers: after his fatal crash, Bernd Rosemeyer was for a while almost on a par with [murdered Berlin stormtrooper] Horst Wessel[3] in the popular imagination.[5]

He continues:

> For a while the victors in international motor racing, behind the wheel of their competition cars, leaning up against them or working underneath them, were the most photographed heroes of the day. If a young man did

> not take his heroic image from the muscle-bound warriors, naked or clad in a stormtrooper's uniform, as seen on posters and commemorative coins, then he certainly did so from racing drivers; what both embodiments of [Aryan] heroism share is the fixed stare, expressing tough, forward-looking determination and the will to conquer.

Beneath the silver that seems to outshine everything there is a dark stain, which can be attributed not to tarnish but to the emergence of the base metal, a suppressed history that is made visible as the silver has been polished thin.

German Motor Sport Before the Great War

In 1870/1871, Germany was united as a nation. The basis had been created by Bismarck with calculated wars, seasoned with bribery and Prussian supremacy represented by the new aristocratic *Kaiserreich*. The aristocratic German leaders, princes, kings, and monarchs were a little late to the stage of nationalism, but nevertheless they soon began their trajectory towards an imperialist and colonial power. This new nationalism was established with great enthusiasm.

In the late nineteenth and early twentieth centuries, Germany exploded with industry and industrialists, who fostered wealth, urban development, and modernism. Villas, department stores, museums, motor cars, aeroplanes, and Zeppelins were introduced into society. The commodities markets brought goods from all over Europe and allowed Germany to export goods, which in turn fostered personal and national wealth and growth. The construction of personal and national identities through cultural/educational experiences and material wealth was the clear next step. The small automotive industry was fuelled by this shift toward industrialisation and the resulting wealth. Motor races were places to see and be seen as part of the great parade of social status and identity. With Jewish emancipation, affirmed at the forming of modern Germany, Jews came to play a significant role in industry and had much at stake to establish themselves as equal citizens and patriots of the new German nation. It is in this adumbrated context that the history of the motor car emerges.

Designer and automotive engineer Carl Benz invented what is considered the first practical motor car in Germany in 1885. However, French engineers and worldly men of great nobility or big money, or both, were the originators of racing with this machinery. The dawn of the twentieth century was accompanied by the sound of cars and airplanes. Men in their racing and flying machines inevitably became the idols of martial and nationalistic times. Land events like the Gordon Bennett Cup (founded in 1900 for competing national automobile clubs) and the Grand Prix de l'ACF (Automobile Club de France) developed the leisure sport of motoring into a professional proving ground for companies, industry, and business tied to the heated patriotism that characterised the life and times of Europe before the Great War, World War I.

Carl Benz was not beguiled by building fast cars, and left his Mannheim company early in 1903 because his financier and commercial CEO Julius Ganss had appointed the French engineer Marius Barbarou and his compatriot crew, who were directed to produce much more powerful cars and push towards racing laurels. In contrast to the German rival of Benz & Cie., the Swabian Daimler company gained great renown by winning the Gordon Bennett Cup also in 1903; by then it was the most important motor race event worldwide. The victorious car was raced by Belgian engineer and professional race car driver Camille Jenatzy, yet the car's name was not Daimler but Mercedes. This was down to Daimler's Austrian client, wealthy Jewish entrepreneur, and patron, Emil Jellinek, who ordered numerous motor cars for his racing pleasures. And these specially ordered Daimlers were named after Jellinek's beloved daughter Mercédès.

The country of the winning car had the honour of organising the following year's Gordon Bennett Cup race. In 1904 Germany presented an event in Roman Imperial style. The headquarters of the circuit, on open roads in the Taunus woods and mountains of central Germany, was centred at the Saalburg, a complete reconstruction and reinvention of an ancient Roman military camp. Hail Caesar (*Kaiser*)! Kaiser Wilhelm II was present at the race weekend and had to witness an ostensibly national defeat to French engineering. Clearly, establishing Germany as a powerful modern nation had been the objective of this event; instead, it had become a theatre for national hubris.

This event was a game changer. Germany had something to prove, which in the end signalled an immense boost for motor racing in Germany. In 1908 racing cars from Mercedes were driven by Germans and cars from Benz were driven by French and Belgian colleagues—the German automakers dominated the Grand Prix de l'ACF. As a result, the French organisers renounced their Grand Prix in 1909 in order to avoid providing another propagandistic platform for their German rivals. Despite this renunciation, Benz in Mannheim built the fastest car in the world. With regard to the European regulations for motor racing, this car was far too large, so they sent their new speed record-breaker to America where US pioneer racer Barney Oldfield presented the so-called Blitzen Benz, *blitzen* meaning 'lightning', and the race car lived up to its nickname. Over the approximately 30 years since Carl Benz had invented the motor car, engine capacities and horsepower had grown increasingly. The Blitzen Benz with its engine size of 21.5 litres producing around 200 hp and enabling top speeds of around 200 km/h executed on open roads without tarmac, was a stunning achievement. In 1911, the Blitzen Benz, designed under the direction of mechanical engineer Dr Hans Nibel with the American driver Bob Burman, achieved the world absolute speed record of 228 kph (141.7 mph).

In those days, wins and records on the racetrack were crucial selling points for a small elite of customers. Victories on road and track provided much more tangible proof of technical competence in production models. And, as in France, the Grand Prix de l'ACF was revived with new technical rules and smaller engine capacities. In 1908 German driver Christian Lautenschlager was victorious. He won a second time in the summer of 1914 in a newly built Mercedes with a 4.5-litre engine only weeks before the Great War erupted. The knowledge and the commitment of German engineers, mechanics, and race drivers ensured the success of German race cars on a racetrack. Now they and their French opponents/antagonists entered into another kind of warfare the likes of which the world never could have imagined, with some of the most nationally and internationally recognised automotive engineers as resources.

Returning to Another Battlefield

The devastation of World War I was palpable in German society. Nearly 1.7 million German men were killed, 4.2 million were wounded, and 1.1 million were prisoners of war. Moreover, the influenza pandemic killed more than 50 million worldwide and impacted families globally. The war-wounded returned home and artists like Otto Dix provided deep-cutting depictions of the ongoing suffering the war had produced. There were many noteworthy features of this war that were fostered by industrialisation. It was the first to feature the large-scale use of aircraft, poison gas, tanks, and submarines. Following the armistice of World War I in Germany, the November Revolution (German Revolution) resulted in the end of the German Empire, which was replaced by a parliamentary republic, known as the Weimar Republic—a fledgling democracy. Out of the war came the burgeoning art, literature, and music culture of the 1920s. A diverse *avant garde* scene including the Bauhaus, Neue Sachlichkeit, the UFA film company, Expressionism, and jazz clubs made Germany a lively intellectual place. Yet, such an 'open' and creative place also carried with it cultural tensions and detractors.

The new German Workers' Party had been founded months after the end of the war, in January of 1919. A year later this party changed its name to the National Socialist German Workers' Party (NSDAP) or Nazi Party. Born out of instability and driven by hate and the promise of change, the NSDAP slowly gained a hold in German society. They were not the only group who harboured these sentiments. The right wing of German society saw these cultural and artistic expressions as degenerate and immoral. The 'degenerate' label absorbed all marginalised identities as well—it included anyone but heterosexual Aryans. The critique of culture brought with it a critique of the Weimar Republic itself. Anti-Semitism was alive and well as Jews were often exemplary of the 'other' in society. Although Jews definitely were not exclusively designated as the 'other', they were seen as the principal outsiders of German society. The Weimar era needed an escape from the devastation and the unsettled tensions left by war. The Versailles Treaty, which extracted heavy reparations from Germany and its allies, was yet another significant source of tension for the Germans as they were not allowed to rebuild or financially recover from the devastating losses of World War I. Post-war instability seems to be the only constant, and provided opportunities for great social and cultural strides, but also advanced the politics of hate and anger. Radical anti-Semitism rose with the turn to populism as a means to build nationhood and national identity, based on a notion of common ancestry, a "nationalist *völkisch* movement". Additionally, the national identity had no place for the Jews, and the anti-Semitic political groups enacted violence against and advocated for the removal of Jews from the citizenry.[6]

Admittedly, in the period of the Weimar Republic motor sport was a highly exclusive pastime. The spectacle might entertain the masses, but this was still far from making motor racing a mass sport. This was in sharp contrast to conditions in other countries, where not only large stadiums and sports halls but also permanent racing circuits were being built. The AVUS circuit was opened in Berlin in 1921. Yet this urban motorway, which was originally intended to generate toll revenue for its private investors, was only temporarily used as a racetrack due to the lack of paying traffic. In those days the AVUS was the modest German variant of an international trend towards shifting dangerous racing away from closed public roads to permanent circuits.[7] Between 1925 and 1927 the Nürburgring was built as a job-creation project in the barren Eifel region near the Belgian border. At the outset the cost was estimated at 4 million reichsmarks (RM), but the racetrack eventually cost 14.5 million. The government was the majority shareholder, so tax revenues continued to flow in to support the racing business. Investing in automotive racing was a mutually beneficial arrangement as this drive towards nationalism and industrialisation served not only the corporations and the economy of Germany, but also the budding modern military nation state.

In the 1920s the motor car was still the luxury toy and means of transport of a well-heeled few. And in Germany, compared with other industrialised nations, there were only very few of these well-placed motorists. In raw statistical terms, the homeland of Herr Benz and Herr Daimler boasted only one car per 100 inhabitants in 1926, while the ratio in France and Britain was 3.2 per 100 and in the USA a striking 21.7 per 100. Defeat in war followed by rampant hyperinflation had put the skids under German car makers. Wins and records on the racetrack were crucial selling points since they provided much more tangible proof of technical competence in series production. Thus, it was only logical that after World War I both leading German companies, Benz and Daimler, would attempt to position themselves in the market by participating in international motor sport again. However, under the Weimar Republic, as elsewhere, success in motor sport was a matter of money. The revolutionary Benz *Tropfenwagen* (a streamlined, teardrop-shaped car) with a mid-mounted engine and floating axles, developed by racing manager Willy Walb and his designers Fritz Nallinger and Hans Nibel and later run and developed by Adolf Rosenberger,[8] made a promising debut in the 1923 Italian Grand Prix at Monza. Driving their non-supercharged Benz racing cars, with only 90 bhp under the bonnet, Fernando Minoia and Fritz Hörner came fourth and fifth respectively. Yet in the wake of the 1923 inflation crisis and an acute shortage of capital, the men from Mannheim, under pressure from the banks, had no choice but to join in an *Interessengemeinschaft* (commercial alliance) with the equally cash-strapped Daimler-Motoren-Gesellschaft. Under the decisive influence of Deutsche Bank, then two hitherto competing companies completed a full merger in the summer of 1926; from 1924 the sole responsibility for motor sport activities had in any case resided with the Daimler branch of the new twin concern. In the Stuttgart suburb of Untertürkheim more emphasis was placed at that time on the design of supercharged engines than on the niceties of bodywork. Since 1923, the man in charge of racing on the Daimler side was Ferdinand Porsche, the 47-year-old Technical Director. He had been appointed to succeed Paul Daimler, because the son of the firm's founder, after violent disagreements in the boardroom, had moved to the Horch car company in the eastern German town of Zwickau.

Many considered Porsche a brilliant 'engine man', while others complained about his penchant for sophisticated but hair-raisingly expensive designs. Since beginning his career with the Austrian firms of Lohner and Austro-Daimler, this self-made engineer had always thought in large-scale terms. He was building giant artillery transporters, with which he made his name in World War I as an armament specialist with a company in Wiener Neustadt. Porsche's move to Daimler came at the right moment, since he was able to combine motor racing and series car production with development contracts for the Army Weapons Office. The latter was all top secret, of course, since the Versailles Treaty banned German companies from involvement in the arms business. However, an imperialist nation state needed a military, and what better way to hide this enterprise than to engineer under the guise of automobile manufacture? In this way, under Porsche's direction, the company developed armoured combat and all-terrain vehicles, tracked vehicles, and a 300 hp aeroplane engine. However, prior to this, Porsche had been allowed to build one more Grand Prix racing car for Daimler in the then prevailing two-litre formula.

On 29 October 1924, at the Gran Premio d'Italia on the Monza circuit, Porsche's new Mercedes eight-cylinder supercharged M218 made its debut. Four cars were entered for the race and their output of about 170 hp at 7000 rpm made them serious contenders for victory. But the complex handling characteristics of these monsters created problems, and 'Count' Louis Zborowski had a fatal accident on the Lesmo bend, whose cause is unknown. Earlier, top Mercedes driver Giulio Masetti had forfeited as a result of a broken fuel pipe, and after Zborowski's accident Max Sailer, the director, withdrew the two remaining cars of Christian Werner and Alfred Neubauer/Otto Merz. The new design would never again be seen in international Grand Prix racing. Any ambitions Porsche had to build another racing car for the newly formed company of Daimler-Benz AG were shattered in 1926/1927, when the Board determined his designs too costly.

The remaining M218 Grand Prix models were converted into sports cars. Two of them showed up in 1926 at the first German Grand Prix on the AVUS track, which, with a view to participation by German works teams, had been opened exclusively to sports cars. The two enclosed Mercedes racing cars were driven by the two most promising young German racing drivers of the time, Adolf Rosenberger and Rudolf Caracciola. Director Sailer, constructor Porsche, and Neubauer, the future Mercedes-Benz racing manager, watched as Caracciola won the race, in pouring rain, maintaining a rock-solid 200 kph (125 mph) in the supercharged eight-cylinder. "It takes a death-defying nerve to drive at such high speed round an old-fashioned circuit like that", wrote the magazine *Das Auto* admiringly. But it was scarcely ten years later that a completely new generation of German racing cars, initiated by Porsche and Nibel, would be tearing round the AVUS at speeds of 340 kph (over 210 mph) with more than 600 hp, and sending virtually an entire nation into a frenzy of enthusiasm.

Yet that spectacle had risks. Even the practice laps for this first German Grand Prix were marred by a death, and on the Sunday of the race itself further serious accidents occurred. Adolf Rosenberger in the lead with the sister works car Mercedes came off the slippery wet track at about 150 kph (90 mph): his car slammed into a timekeepers' cabin and three race stewards were killed instantly. The driver and his mechanic Curt Coquelline, who was also on board, got away with severe injuries. For Rosenberger, this accident was formative. He was anaesthetised by the ether used as an accelerant in the fuel which wafted from the front engine to the cockpit of the car, but he subsequently expressed concerns about the balance of the car as it had lost traction in the rain. Nevertheless, Adolf Rosenberger continued racing for Mercedes-Benz. In 1927 he won the Klausenrennen with the 'Großmutter', the modified Mercedes GP winning car of 1914. In the same year at the inauguration race of the new Nürburgring, he finished in second place behind his teammate Rudolf Caracciola.

The motor racing business had begun to flourish in the 1920s, when France's blue Bugattis and Delages vied for motor sport supremacy with the red Alfa Romeos and Maseratis of Italy and the green Sunbeams of the UK. It was in those years that the single-seater racing car, the Grand Prix *monoposto*, developed into the fastest and most spectacular formula on the continent of Europe. The class of blue-blooded or well-heeled gentlemen, who before the Great War competed with 'running-in' drivers paid by the factory—in other words, racing mechanics still took part in Grand Prix events in the 1920s and 1930s. However, by the early 1930s, and faced with ever more complex racing car technology, they gradually lost out to the driving skills of the specialists. In France, the Monegasque Louis Chiron, and in Mussolini's Italy Tazio Nuvolari and Achille Varzi, ended up being the highest-paid artistes at the wheel, national idols and entrepreneurs on their own account. They were the perfect embodiment of egocentric commercialism, constantly haggling over the best work contracts and the top starting money, and anxious to enhance their own social status. In short, they foreshadowed today's sporting super-rich. The only man thought to achieve this status in German-speaking countries before 1933 was Rudolf Caracciola. The slightly built son of a hotelier from Remagen in the Rhineland, he worked his way up from being a car salesman and weekend racer to signing a work contract with Mercedes. Caracciola's talented friend and colleague Adolf Rosenberger, the young motor racing businessman and Mercedes-Benz works driver from Pforzheim, opted for another plan as his family were involved in commodities, business, and banking. He would take his mentoring ability and automotive knowledge and parlay these to become Ferdinand Porsche's business partner, aiming to get back on the grid of international Grand Prix racing behind the wheel.

Although Porsche was made Technical Director for the merged Daimler-Benz AG, post merger he began to lose a power struggle against Nibel, his counterpart at Benz. After heated disagreements Porsche was forced to leave the group. In 1928, his contract expired and was not renewed; an additional factor was disputes over his sometimes faulty but, in the main, far too costly car and truck models. In the end, Porsche was taken to court over his financial obligations to Daimler-Benz AG. In a bitter frame of mind, the disgraced technician moved to the Austrian Steyr works. But in the wake of the 1929 Wall Street Crash, Steyr's bankers collapsed, and the stricken car maker was bought out by its direct competitor, Austro-Daimler. Porsche was not interested in returning to work for Austro-Daimler as they had refused to renew his employment agreement. He was therefore forced by circumstance to become independent and founded, with Adolf Rosenberger, the firm of Dr Ing. h.c. F. Porsche GmbH, Design and Consultancy in Engine and Vehicle Building. The third man aboard was Anton Piëch, Porsche's son-in-law. The initial share capital in 1930 was 30,000 RM. As founder, Porsche then held 80 per cent of the share capital, his son-in-law Piëch 10 per cent, and the remaining 10 per cent was held by Adolf Rosenberger, who also acted as Managing Director (CEO) of the company. Rosenberger, Porsche, and his handful of Austrian engineers, especially Karl Rabe, were friends and partners, who worked very closely together. They were the 'car guys'. Piëch was the attorney who was seldom involved in automotive building. Thus, the importance of Adolf Rosenberger to Porsche should never be underestimated. He not only made his initial investment in the company, but also gave loans directly and through friends, as well as technical input. He solicited contracts for the fledgling company and brought in venture capital to keep it afloat. The aim of the Porsche GmbH was to develop blueprints for automotive companies, to deliver technical devices, to build prototypes—and to construct a Grand Prix car for the Saxonian Wanderer Company. Furthermore, Adolf Rosenberger planned to race this car on the tracks throughout Europe. At that time, the fact that the former Mercedes-Benz works driver was Jewish did not present an ostensible problem, although anti-Semitism was growing at this time. One did not live in Germany as a Jew without significant challenges.

Meanwhile, the NSDAP had been re-founded in 1925 with a staunch anti-Semitic stance; in 1928 NSDAP members of the Reichstag had asked that Jews be excluded from certain professions and later excluded Jews from rights associated with citizenship, among many others. The years following World War I saw constant political and economic uncertainty. For some, that uncertainty was far greater than for others.

In the wake of the economic slump and mass redundancies even the Daimler-Benz AG closed its works-based motor sport activities for financial reasons in 1932, causing Caracciola to move to Alfa Romeo. That year he won the German Grand Prix in the Italian *monoposto*—an open-wheel car. This was a signal for motoring clubs and the automobile industry to seek subsidies *en bloc* for the construction of a 'German national racing car'. However, the model for financing these very expensive engineering wonders had to be modified as a result of the Great Depression. Initially Daimler-Benz AG benefitted from the consequences of the merger of 1926. The spokesman for the board of Deutsche Bank, Dr Emil Georg von Stauss, who sat on the Supervisory Board of the Daimler-Motoren-Gesellschaft, had, together with Dr Wilhelm Kissel, Finance Director of Benz & Cie, set the foundation for the merging of the two companies. From then on the two managers determined the strategic decisions for the group. From 1926 Kissel acted as *de facto* chief executive of Daimler-Benz AG, even though he was not formally appointed until 1933. The corporation's chief shareholder was Deutsche Bank, which, along with Dresdner Bank and Commerzbank, dominated the Supervisory Board and also provided its chairman in the person of von Stauss.

Together they were active in an apparently 'harmless' movement to 'keep the car industry German'. It was under this banner that Kissel and von Stauss at last planned to commit Mercedes-Benz to motor sport—both in their own business and in national interests. The clientele and the brand image both required and furthered this policy even in difficult times.

The steady reduction in manpower and the high prices of luxury cars had produced sales revenue for Daimler-Benz of 26.85 million RM and 27.76 million RM in 1928 and 1929 respectively. Yet the output figures remained relatively modest: just over 10,000 cars were manufactured annually, and the group's widely scattered production facilities were working at scarcely half their capacity. By the end of 1930 the company's statistics showed a mere 9786 on the payroll, and in March 1932 the all-time low of 4958 was reached. Something *had* to happen.

Porsche, who later created Hitler's *Volkswagen*, or 'People's Car', was not as successful at solving "the problem of an appropriately sized inexpensive car designed for the masses" with the prototypes that his design company later urged Zündapp and NSU to take over. Fortunately, Rosenberger, as General Manager of Porsche's Stuttgart design office, belonged to an exclusive Berlin gentlemen's club where, among others, he got to know Baron Klaus Detlof von Oertzen. The latter was chief executive of the Wanderer car company in Chemnitz and, through Rosenberger, went into business with Porsche. The 30-strong Porsche design team was tasked with upgrading a production model into a sports coupé, and because the car division of a conglomerate better known for its office equipment like typewriters needed a compelling new image, in 1931 Porsche's people were also asked to embark on a racing car project for the new Grand Prix formula. Porsche belonged to the circle of handpicked experts who in late 1931 were commissioned by the International Association of Recognised Automobile Clubs to draw up a set of rules for the new generation of race cars. Starting with the 1934 season, Grand Prix racing cars were not permitted to weigh more than 750 kg. Before each race the weighing of vehicles was to be carried out at the trackside, and the limit to be observed referred to the weight of the empty car (i.e. without fuel, oil, water, and tyres). The Grand Prix monsters of the time were significantly heavier than 750 kg, which is why, given the state of technology, the officials believed that the new designs would need to make use of much smaller and lighter engines to keep within the weight limit.[9] German racing cars were able to harness almost double that power even in the first season of this 750 kg formula thanks to lightweight construction and supercharger technology that was technically beyond their contemporaries and helped establish the success and the myth of the Silver Arrows.

The rough design for his new race car, which Porsche finally submitted in 1932, closely resembled the Benz 'teardrop' car from 1923. This was no surprise, since his business partner Rosenberger had driven that unusual mid-engine racer and even won the 1925 Solitude Mountain climb in it. It was also a solution to the problem he faced in the terrible crash on the AVUS, where the ether and the rear traction had broken loose from the tarmac that caused him to skid out of control into the stands. The engine at the back would maintain the weight over the rear wheels for stable traction. The design was a simple and elegant solution to earlier challenges posed by the older front engine, rear wheel drive race cars, which reduced the weight of a drive shaft. Therefore, it was no coincidence that Porsche now positioned the driver in front of the race car's engine. Rosenberger may not have been primarily a designer, but his technical knowledge and experience as a race car driver were essential to the development of the revolutionary mid-engine race car. It was Rosenberger who funded the project, despite the failure of the Wanderer Corporation and the general struggle the automotive industry was having to stay afloat in Germany during the Depression era. The principal shareholder of the Wanderer Corporation located in Chemnitz was Deutsche Bank, which pleaded for sale or liquidation of Wanderer.

However, the history of the German motor industry now took quite a different turn, because the *Landtag* (parliament) of Saxony leaped into the breach and in mid-February 1932 put up a guarantee of 6 million RM to save over 8000 jobs at the stricken Saxon car makers Audi, DKW, Horch, and Wanderer. On 28 June 1932—with retrospective effect from 1 November 1931—the four companies were merged under a holding company that was given the name Auto Union AG and adopted four interlocking circles as its corporate symbol. With this, the new Auto Union was to become Daimler-Benz's most aggressive competitor within

Germany. The future duels between Mercedes-Benz and Auto Union would be about victories and the resulting subsidies.

With a certain piquancy, the blueprints for the Auto Union racing cars would be provided by the former Technical Director of Daimler-Benz AG, Ferdinand Porsche, and the company's former works driver, Adolf Rosenberger, who was keen to drive this Grand Prix car conceived for Wanderer and now transferred to the newly formed motor group in Saxony. The commitment for Rosenberger to race the Auto Union car was so great that a contract was drafted.[10] But with this promise also came increasing anti-Semitic attacks beginning in 1930. In 1931 and 1932 National Socialists were making demands to remove Jews from public office and even went so far as to suggest that they should be 'removed' in general. On 31 July 1932 the NSDAP secured more seats and influence with the Reichstag elections, resulting in waves of violent attacks and even boycotting of Jewish business and firms.[11] Fiscal and social upheaval were eroding the already weakened Weimar Republic.

Meanwhile, only a few kilometres from Porsche's design office, the executive directors of the Depression-stricken Daimler-Benz AG were also being inspired by the new race car formula. Here too the construction of a German Grand Prix machine was also intended to serve as an advertising medium—and for this purpose government subsidies had to be organised. The German government saw value in the subsidies as German engineering (and implied military prowess) would be put on the global stage. Von Brauchitsch's spectacular victory in the AVUS race of 1932 with the streamlined silver SSK resulted in the radio sports reporter Paul Laven coining the metonym 'Silberpfeil' (Silver Arrow). This race was a perfect pretext for Nibel, the Chief Mercedes Designer, on which to approach the Reich Minister of Transport, Gottfried Treviranus. Three days later the two men had a telephone conversation about governmental sponsorship of the racing car project.

At this stage the intention was simply to make improvements to the ageing SSK sports car for further use in motor sport: "According to information from Mr. Treviranus the sum of 220,000 RM is already guaranteed", wrote Nibel in a file note. "However, he intends to try and get us a total of 110,000 + 180,000". At Mercedes-Benz they may have been sharing the same delusions as the government with its deflation policy

("Only a hundred metres from the goal"). But only five days later, on 30 May 1932, the second Brüning cabinet collapsed, and transport minister Treviranus was among those who lost their jobs. "The system is in free fall", noted Nazi propaganda chief Josef Goebbels with glee. On the very same day Hitler had an audience with Reich President Hindenburg, the ban on the SA was lifted, the Reichstag was dissolved, and new general elections were scheduled for 31 July. The Hitler movement seemed to be close to its goal of taking power in Germany.

These were turbulent times. Mass unemployment was reaching its height, yet, on 20 June 1932 Hans Nibel nevertheless enquired of the new Reich Minister of Transport, Eltz-Rübenach, "whether it might not be possible for us to receive government support for the design and development of our racing cars, since we are unfortunately unable to undertake the exceptionally costly development of racing cars from our own resources. As far as we know, Italian and French factories that build racing cars are supported by their own governments, since international races have a promotional value beyond that for the marque of car in question and give a great boost for the industry of that country".

Four days later Nibel made a personal visit to the ministry and sent two more letters on the subject of financial assistance, before Eltz-Rübenach drafted his final rejection on 30 June. For the moment the political situation following the cabinet change put an end to any hope of government subsidies. To get that kind of money there first had to be a regime that better appreciated the propaganda value of future German racing victories and knew how to exploit them. In this respect, the car-friendly Hitler and the equally keen motor sports enthusiasts among his entourage would come as a blessing for the national racing ambitions of the corporate bosses in Untertürkheim and Zwickau.

In addition to Mercedes-Benz, the newly founded Auto Union, whose plans were famously being forged by none other than Ferdinand Porsche and Adolf Rosenberger, had already lured another senior employee from Untertürkheim for future racing duties—Alfred Neubauer, who was seriously considering joining the opposition. However, Kissel had managed to dissuade him with a generous bonus. Instead, at the beginning of 1933, Auto Union signed up Willy Walb, who until then had been number two in the Mercedes-Benz racing organisation. Another deserter from the executive floor in Untertürkheim was the Chief Press Officer, Dr Richard Voelter, who, as early as 1 October 1932, had joined DKW in Zwickau as Head of Advertising on a salary of 850 RM per month. From then on, Voelter would extract propaganda value from the sporting successes of Auto Union, since their racing division reported directly to the group's advertising department. Voelter, born in 1892, was a qualified lawyer who had served in World War I as a cavalry captain. Even in peacetime this ex-officer regularly turned up for exercises with the military reserve, and, not least, was a member of the Nazi Party from 1925 onwards—as was his wife Else, who liked to be called "the First Nazi Lady of Württemberg". Even before Hitler's men came into power the ambitious couple opened quite a few doors at Daimler-Benz to their Brownshirt party comrades. By 1931 the Voelters had separated, but as we read in an approving assessment by the district military authorities in Chemnitz dated 25 June of 1936, "Dr Voelter has been active for many years on behalf of the National Socialist German Workers' Party". Even in 1931 when Richard Voelter got divorced and launched his new professional as well as marital life in Saxony, the abandoned Else remained under the protection of the Mercedes star in Untertürkheim. After the Nazis seized power, the former Frau Voelter, in collaboration with the Stuttgart management, sold production cars on special terms to upper echelon of the Nazi party. From 1938 onwards Else Voelter was additionally involved in the 'Aryanisation' of Jewish-owned businesses. It was the same Else and Richard Voelter who as early as September 1926 at the trackside of the Solitude race had introduced their party leader, Adolf Hitler, to the Mercedes-Benz team and its then chief designer, Ferdinand Porsche. Hitler was a particularly good customer for the powerful supercharged automobiles of Daimler-Benz AG. They were supplied by another very early member of the Nazi Party, Jakob Werlin, who had been on the Mercedes-Benz payroll since April 1921. As head of the Munich office, he was one of the group's most important and successful car salesmen and at the same time the principal contact for and with the Nazi leadership. Its garages were situated at 39 Schellingstrasse in Munich's fashionably bohemian Schwabing district. The same building housed the printing firm of Adolf Müller. Müller printed for the Nazi Party's publisher, the Franz Eher Verlag, turning out books, pamphlets, and the newspaper

Völkischer Beobachter ("Folkish Observer", which has strong connotations of race). Thus it was inevitable that Werlin would meet the Nazi leader, three years his junior, and the two got on famously. The fact that they both had Austrian roots and shared an enthusiasm for cars was the clincher. As Werlin wrote decades later, Müller introduced Hitler to him with the words: "I've brought a new customer for you". The Nazi leader, who never had a driver's licence, was now famous (or notorious) in Munich, already owned two cars made by the somewhat less renowned Selve company, and wanted to acquire his first big Benz from Werlin.

Forty years later, in a grandiose apologia, Werlin, the former Nazi, tried to present himself as a highly successful yet totally non-political lobbyist on behalf of the motor industry: "I had never made any secret of my acquaintance with Hitler or my role as his advisor, which embraced everything under the heading of motorisation. I was now actually prepared to stick my neck out. It is true, I helped, with all the resources available to me, to do things like promote the construction of autobahns and push through Hitler's plans for the 'People's Car' [*Volkswagen*]. I was the co-founder of the VW factory; and where I could, I promoted motor racing, which in the 1930s brought victory and fame to Germany's Silver Arrows and worldwide sales success for the manufacturers". This is an absolutely accurate statement. Werlin was soon a member of Hitler's closest entourage in Munich, and thenceforth acted as "personal confidant of the Führer" in all matters concerning motor vehicles. In 1932 he joined the SS and in the following year the one-time car salesman made a career leap to join the Management Board of Daimler-Benz AG.

In the critical year of 1932 Daimler-Benz had already activated its contacts with the Nazis. The NSDAP had been gaining more and more votes and supporters, and it seemed likely that Hitler's party would soon be given a position of responsibility from which it would have a modest say in the formulation of national policy. How fortunate for the Untertürkheim company to have a man like Jakob Werlin around. On 14 May Werlin reported to CEO Kissel on a conversation with Hitler: "Naturally, I did not fail to mention that we have always shown the greatest goodwill towards the Party, and I gave some examples". Other companies could probably not make such a claim, "whereas for many years we had cherished and nurtured our links with the NSDAP in recognition of its prospects and always from devotion to the cause". And on 18 May Kissel wrote back to Werlin: "We certainly have no reason to pay any less attention than hitherto to Herr Hitler and his friends; in fact, he will [...] be able to rely on us just as much as he has done in the past".

With German President Hindenburg's appointment of Hitler as Reich Chancellor on 30 January 1933 and the new Reichstag elections immediately set for 5 March, the SA Brownshirts and the Nazi party were masters of the streets. Hitler exploited his position as head of government to consolidate his power.

It was high season for careerists, for the despised *Märzgefallene* (trans: soldiers fallen in the month of March), a bitter nickname for opportunistic followers, sycophants, and profiteers joining the Nazi cause, after Hitler's NSDAP had won the manipulated Reichstagswahl (federal election) on 5 March 1933. The allure of a restoration of national greatness made Nazism palatable to the majority. Furthermore, motor sport in those years became a microcosm of the nation as a whole: the drivers were the pampered idols of a mendacious and criminal system. In return for overblown theatricality and public affirmation of Aryan tropes, Nazi leadership allowed drivers relative freedom of action and gave them undreamed-of benefits.

Thus, the professional racing driver under the Third Reich became the myth of the age, a man ostensibly quite uninterested in politics, who for precisely that reason mutated into a profiteer of Nazi policies. The recovery in both economic and national fortunes—which Hitler had promised the German people—was to occur for a time, and under a policy of massive rearmament gave the German motor industry cause to be grateful, since with the help of government contracts it set new production records. And the works drivers for Mercedes-Benz and Auto Union would, with victories in their Silver Arrows, contribute to the respect and recognition paid to the Nazi regime, lending it an outward glamour. But not all race car drivers would be swept into the 'glamorous' Nazi automotive world of the 'Silver Arrows', nor would they benefit from the social construction of the Aryan hero. Because the automotive industry was a key propaganda tool of Nazi Germany and the drivers key constructors of national Aryan male identity, one had to be the right kind of German. The systemic and ever-increasing pressure of government-sponsored anti-Semitism indicated that Nazi Germany would only make being Jewish exponentially more difficult. On 30 January 1933, when Hitler became chancellor, Adolf Rosenberger resigned the same day as CEO, and he therefore took his first step back from public life as the CEO (Geschäftsführer) of Porsche, while retaining his shares of ownership in Porsche GmbH. Rosenberger understood that the business he had financed, networked, led as CEO, and owned could no longer thrive with a well-known Jew in such a prominent position.[12] The key date in the symbiotic relationship between the Nazi regime and the German motor industry was 11 February 1933, when Hitler opened the International Car and Motorcycle Exhibition in Berlin. He was the first German Chancellor to grace this show with his presence, using it as a platform to announce his programme of 'national motorisation': abolition of the vehicle tax, reduction of corporation tax, and enhanced government support for road-building and motor sport. These proposals were clear signals that in the Third Reich cars and car manufacturers would play a key role. From this, Nazi propaganda would successfully mythologise the Führer as the original 'creator of the autobahns'. Yet, plans for the 'autobahns' had existed since the 1920s and proposed a motorway linking the Hanseatic cities of the north (Hamburg, Bremen, and Lübeck) with Frankfurt in central Germany and Basel just across the southern border with Switzerland. But such connections counted for little; the only thing that mattered was that the new Reich Chancellor was a friend of motorisation, and for that reason the National Federation of the German Motor Industry soon launched a 'Führer Fund' of 300,000 RM. A year after seizing power Hitler would finally start promoting the 'People's Car', the affordable automobile for everyone. Even this had its predecessors, but only Germany's first dictator had the will to put wheels on what had so far been a dream of national mobility. He did so in the face of initial resistance from a less than enthusiastic industry and its umbrella organisation.

The man who would design this *Volkswagen* had already curried favour with Hitler. Immediately after his speech on 11 February 1933, Ferdinand Porsche personally thanked the new Reich Chancellor in a telegram: "As the creator of many notable designs in the sphere of German and Austrian motor transport and aviation and one who has shared your struggle for more than 30 years to achieve today's success, I congratulate Your Excellency on your profound speech at the opening of the German Automobile Exhibition. I hope it will be granted to me and my staff, in future and to an increased extent, to place our skill and determination at the disposal of the German people". Anyone sending such an ingratiating message could be sure of being given an audience: three months later, on 10 May 1933, Porsche and Hitler met in the Reich Chancellery. Together Baron von Oertzen and the newly designated Auto Union works driver, Hans Stuck, not Adolf Rosenberger, were pleading for subsidies for their Grand Prix car project.

Because he was Jewish Rosenberger was now a liability to the Porsche GmbH and to Auto Union. Racing was certainly out of the question, but he hoped to continue his work in a less visible capacity. He kept his 10 per cent of the small company and continued to work out the details of the Grand Prix car contract between Auto Union and the "Porsche Hochleistungs-Fahrzeug-Bau GmbH". The foundation of this private limited liability company in November 1932 had been Rosenberger's idea, in order to secure the financing on all accounts. The Auto Union contract was finally signed in February 1933 in Zwickau by Rosenberger and Porsche. Just a few hours later in Berlin the Reichstag was set on fire, and the hopes of Adolf Rosenberger and so many others would be dashed.

The Money Behind the Myth of the Silver Arrows

Without the incentive of a massive financial boost from the Nazi regime in 1933 neither Daimler-Benz AG nor Auto Union AG would have been able to put their ambitious racing car plans into effect with such speed. True, in the long run the economic recovery of the German motor industry, actively aided by the fiscal benevolence and propaganda of the Nazi regime, would have made it possible to finance the design, construction, and racing of the Silver Arrows from internal resources. Yet, season after season, the National Socialist state generously subsidised the race car industry, which then came to be regarded by these corporations as a rightful State subsidy. The corporations requested these subsidies politely but firmly every year, always accompanied by the routine complaint that expenditure on motor racing had risen massively and that competing for Germany in motor sport was scarcely affordable without the help of the Reich. However, the financial aspect of motor racing activities in Untertürkheim and Zwickau appears to have been perfectly manageable. The expenditure by Auto Union on its racing division accounted for only 0.7 per cent of total sales in 1937/1938, and never exceeded 0.92 per cent (1936/1937). Even at the beginning of participation in Grand Prix racing the corresponding figure for the financial year 1933/1934 was no more than 0.85 per cent. However, since Auto Union's turnover rose strongly year by year until 1938—largely thanks to massive defence contracts and a lucrative business in official cars—the budget for the Zwickau racing division was able to grow in step, along with its expenditure on engineering. In the course of the 1934 Grand Prix season Auto Union had five cars ready to race, and in 1935 no fewer than seven. By 1936 Zwickau had lined up a full dozen of these 16-cylinder monsters. In 1934 Mercedes-Benz could call upon six W25 racing cars and in the following year a total of eight were in Grand Prix trim.

Similarly, the men in Untertürkheim had a budget that fluctuated around 1 per cent of annual sales. However, after 1935 their figure was considerably higher in absolute terms, because business activity was growing significantly faster and was profiting far more from Hitler's massive rearmament than was the case with their competitor in Saxony. In 1933, with a turnover of 100.9 million RM, Daimler-Benz AG was still lagging behind Auto Union AG, which chalked up sales of 116 million RM for the financial year 1933/1934. In 1936 Untertürkheim's sales were 295.1 million RM, against 235 million for Zwickau in the financial year 1936/1937. In 1937 Daimler-Benz pushed its sales up to 399.1 million RM, while those of Auto Union AG were only 276.4 million for the financial year 1937/1938. It was no coincidence that from the 1938 racing season onwards Zwickau had great difficulty in matching the financial and technical outlay of the Mercedes-Benz racing division.

Thanks to the quota system for raw materials imposed by the Nazis as part of their preparations for war, the motor groups only experienced significant growth in production outside their rearmament contracts if there were export opportunities for their own range of vehicles. To that extent German racing victories around the world all too quickly became the proven method of promoting sales of German cars abroad. Yet, every victory for the Silver Arrows simultaneously heralded the success of the new Nazi Germany—a fact that did not make export trade any easier. However, their *political* advertising for National Socialism earned the gentlemen of Daimler-Benz AG and Auto Union good money year after year until well after the war had started.

The direct subsidies were accompanied by additional bonuses based on their racing success. In the case of Auto Union the bottom-line figure from 1933 to the start of the war totalled more than 2.75 million RM. As a proportion of Zwickau's racing budget each year, the generous government contribution ranged from 19.5 per cent to 28.4 per cent. Mercedes-Benz received similar benefits, but in 1933/1934 the percentage contribution was significantly higher. In absolute terms, Untertürkheim pocketed substantially more—up to 1941 a total of over 4 million RM. That was not just on account of greater success on the racing circuit, but also because of preferential treatment. Looking at the absolute financial outlay of the two racing divisions in the period from 1933 to 1941, motor historian Peter Kirchberg calculates that Auto Union spent a total of around 15 million RM, while the Mercedes-Benz figure was about 50 per cent higher. Another historian, Wilfried Feldenkirchen, comes up with a very precise figure for Daimler-Benz's racing costs of 18,246,000 RM, though that only covers the period from 1935 to 1940. It omits not only the racing budget for the year 1933/1934 but also the final 'state assistance for motor sport' of 350,000 RM, dating from February 1941.

We do know, in fact, what it cost Daimler-Benz AG to get into the 750 kg racing formula, from a letter which CEO Kissel wrote on 1 March 1935 to Adolf Hühnlein,[5] the head of the *Nationalsozialistischer Kraftfahrer Korps* (NSKK: National Socialist Motor Corps), asking for support of about 1 million RM for that season. Kissel also mentions the total expenditure for the 1933/1934 period: "Up to the end of last year the costs amounted to some 2.2 million RM. This is made up of the design, construction and trials of racing cars, entering them in races, the application of knowledge gained in races and the adaptation of the racing cars, as well as expenditure on the drivers themselves and auxiliary staff, and any general costs arising from our participation in motor sport". Hence, we can put a figure of more than 20.5 million RM on Daimler-Benz's total expenditure in the cause of motor racing from 1933 to 1941, which is a good five million more than Auto Union spent on its racing endeavours over the same period.

It is no less interesting to note what Kissel has to say, in the same letter to Hühnlein, about the subsidies paid to Daimler-Benz AG for racing in 1933/1934: "As you may be aware, the Reich granted us assistance totalling some 907,000 RM. Remuneration received from private companies, especially those with an interest in racing, and from clubs, amounted to 310,000 RM, so that for the racing season up to the end of 1934 we had a total inflow of about 1,217,000 RM". In other words, almost 60 per cent of the Mercedes-Benz racing budget was externally financed in the early stages of the new 750 kg formula. For the year 1933/1934, the Silver Arrows' debut season, the Nazi regime alone paid more than 40 per cent of the Untertürkheim racing division's total costs of 2.2 million RM. Incidentally, Kissel fails to mention the additional income in the form of starting money and winners' bonuses from the race organisers. These international competitions were particularly lucrative because they brought in foreign currency, money the two companies could use to pay their star foreign drivers and thus circumvent the rigid currency restrictions imposed by the Nazi regime. However, this source of finance began to dry up gradually in the late 1930s, since, faced with the overwhelming superiority of the Silver Arrows, foreign clubs and organisers were increasingly reluctant to stage races under the Grand Prix formula that were essentially a platform for Nazi propaganda and a source of revenue for German motor companies.

As to the level of Nazi subsidies, the two companies were in fact in a position to build an alliance and keep each other informed about their requirements. Both parties could then succeed on the national competitive level, which was strategic in funding, but also played into the Nazi propaganda machine. On 1 March 1935, after reaching agreement by telephone, Kissel sent von Oertzen a copy of his letter to Hühnlein. Three days later von Oertzen sent Kissel a copy of his own letter, beseeching "the same confidential treatment", which he had sent to the NSKK leader the same day, which detailed their expenditures. Von Oertzen told

Hühnlein that the expenditure for the coming 1935 season would be around 1.95 million RM, and Kissel had named a figure of 2.1 million RM. There was an equally similar ring to the doleful justifications by the directors for the assistance that was so urgently needed: "You, my esteemed *Korpsführer*, know what tasks our company has been set, by you and other ministers, which we have to carry out in addition to our normal business and the manufacture of our regular range of models. You also know that Auto Union, as a core German enterprise, is particularly required to resist the pressure exercised by the power of American capital (Opel) and we have to defend our position as the purely German contender in the small-car class". Von Oertzen, as a man with a Jewish wife, writes with an awareness of what was expected at that time. Kissel strikes a similarly plaintive note of a suffering national company committed to motor racing—at a time when Daimler-Benz AG had just rounded off the financial year 1934 with the best results in the company's history: "If it is in fact right in principle that we shoulder some of the burden ourselves, we ask you nevertheless to understand that, in view of our other loss-making assignments, we can only do so to a limited degree. We take the liberty of pointing out that, first and foremost, our branch of industry and our company are rightly being asked to increase our exports extraordinarily steeply, though this causes us considerable and rising losses. The business situation in our industry can be described as reasonably good, thanks to the encouragement received from the Reich government, but in particular from our Führer and Chancellor, Adolf Hitler. However, the fact cannot be ignored that we have to set our prices so keenly that they only permit a very minimal profit, and a series of other considerable cost factors which strongly influence the profit-and-loss account are unavoidable".

The fact that right into the first phase of the war the two groups brazenly asked for and received subsidies and bonuses from the Nazi state was deliberate and was built into their calculations. As the Romans used to say: *Do ut des!* ("I give that you may give!"). Or in more common parlance, you scratch my back and I'll scratch yours. No one hands out subsidies without getting something in return. Both sides profit. From government contracts as much as from government subsidies, from

German racing successes as much as from nationalist propaganda. The deals were mutually beneficial.

Race, Motor Racing, and National Socialist Politics

After 1933, any German who wanted to participate internationally in motor sport had to belong to either the NSKK or another National Socialist organisation. The only exemptions were for those serving in the police or the Wehrmacht. For a personality like Georg 'Schorsch' Meier, the outstanding BMW motorcycle racer and part-time works driver for Auto Union, this requirement was of no small significance at the time: "I was already a successful cross-country rider when I transferred from the police to the Wehrmacht, and then when I started winning road races they all said 'Come and join the Party or the NSKK,' but I always said no and was happy to stay in the Wehrmacht—as a plain ordinary sergeant who was given leave to race with BMW and Auto Union. True, right through the war they never promoted me, so by 1945 I must have been the most senior sergeant in the whole Wehrmacht. But I think I did the right thing".

With the exception of Meier all the top German race car drivers joined a National Socialist organisation. Bernd Rosemeyer, the best and most popular driver of that era, was a member of the SS, as were the successful freelance drivers Bobby Kohlrausch and Huschke von Hanstein. The majority of the other motor sport idols joined the NSKK. In retrospect the National Socialist Corps of Drivers has often been represented as a "fairly non-political association of motor sports enthusiasts". Not a few have claimed ironically that the initials NSKK stood for *Nur Säufer, keine Kämpfer* ("Just Boozers, Not Fighters"), and in doing so try to take the edge off the Nazi ideology of Hühnlein and his henchmen. This rationalisation left its mark, especially after 1945, in the correspondingly lenient sentences of the Denazification Tribunals, to the extent that a senior rank in the NSKK was always taken to be the sign of a fellow-traveller rather than something more sinister; and the later a case was heard—or in some cases the longer it lasted—the more likely NSKK membership was to lead to an acquittal. The Nuremberg war crimes trials had unwittingly reinforced this approach in Denazification hearings by not classing the NSKK—or, incidentally, the SA or the mounted SS—as criminal organisations. This assessment by the International Court may have been made principally for procedural reasons, since the main task of the tribunal was, of course, to investigate and indict the leading war criminals. Nonetheless, it led to the judgement that the NSKK was essentially a playground for harmless car and motorbike buffs. Only in recent years has this viewpoint been substantially corrected.

The NSKK played a prominent part in the crimes committed against the Jewish population in what became notorious as the *Reichskristallnacht* (9 and 10 November 1938).[1] During the war not only was it responsible for the logistics of transport and supply, but also, in conjunction with police battalions, it handled the "pacification of the hinterland in the east". This deceptively mild formulation conceals among other things the operations of NSKK units that, under the guise of 'auxiliary police', took part in the deportation and execution of Jews, first in Poland and later in Russia and Ukraine. Documents held in the Central Office for Administration of Provincial Justice in Ludwigsburg prove that Adolf Hühnlein, in his preface to the NSKK souvenir book *Wir waren mit in Poland* ("We did our bit in Poland"), was anticipating Nazi war crimes as early as the spring of 1940: "It has never been our style in the NSKK to sit on our hands and do nothing until an assignment falls like a ripe fruit into our lap. When we have to get stuck into the fray, the Corps is there with the old fighting spirit. So it was only natural that the NSKK did its bit in Poland like the rest, and in the liberated provinces and the *Generalgouvernement*[2] we showed our mettle in carrying out our assignments".

Followers and Profiteers

After 1945 the racetrack heroes, even if not involved in such crimes, would consistently downplay the role of the NSKK and its leader Hühnlein, to say nothing of their own conduct. Yet almost without exception they had been members of the NSKK—as had been the man who would later become Federal Chancellor, Kurt Georg Kiesinger, the defence minister from Bavaria, Franz-Josef Strauss, the magazine publisher Franz Burda, the classical historian Alfred Heuss, the political theorist Theodor Eschenburg, and many other highly respected Germans. Is this because the NSKK was so 'harmless'? Or was because cars and motorcycles, motor sport, and male bonding attracted the most adventurous sons of the upper and lower middle classes to follow the NSKK banner? Anti-Semites and Nazis, dignitaries and nonentities, young and old were united in their fascination for technology and German motor racing victories. It is even possible that such shared enthusiasms and overlapping interests in Nazi ideology may have undermined the 'moral resistance' which the supposedly 'better circles' swore to uphold, though even that claim was often an empty one.

The heroes of German motor sport thus found themselves in the best of company. Additionally, those who wanted (and were allowed) to compete in races probably did not have many reservations about Nazism. The important thing was to be one of the winners. More than six decades after his races during the Nazi dictatorship, racing driver and journalist Paul Pietsch admitted: "I was just another member of the NSKK. It was only later that I said to myself: You're doing yourself no good, my lad. Then I went off to Italy and did a lot of driving there for Maserati". True, Pietsch was not in the first rank of German Silver Arrow drivers. In the 1935 racing season he was in fact a works driver for Auto Union, but was then—due to his lack of success—forced to drive privately again before making a spectacular appearance for Maserati in the first German Grand Prix at the Nürburgring in 1939, once again attracting the attention of Mercedes-Benz and Auto Union. In this way Pietsch was spared the regular promotions within the NSKK that were linked to success on the circuit.

The Nazi-controlled German press, however, was obliged to take these NSKK ranks very seriously and always mentioned them when reporting on motor sport, so as to indicate clearly for *whose* fame and honour the drivers were racing. Where today a particular sponsor might be mentioned, drivers were identified by military rank: the last pre-war race in the European Championship, the Swiss Grand Prix on 20 August 1939, was, for example, won by NSKK-*Hauptsturmführer* Lang, ahead of

NSKK-*Staffelführer* Caracciola, NSKK-*Sturmführer* von Brauchitsch, and NSKK-*Truppführer* Müller.

One man who at that time adhered to, or was forced to adhere to, this contemporary nomenclature was the influential Berlin journalist Siegfried Doerschlag, who in June 1932 founded his 'DDD' (*Der Doerschlag Dienst*), a news and PR service for transport and motoring that continued to flourish right through the Nazi period. On 27 October 1946, Doerschlag wrote in a letter of mitigation for von Brauchitsch's Denazification tribunal: "If Manfred von Brauchitsch is said to have been a Nazi from 1933 onwards, then by the same token all the great racing drivers, Caracciola, Rosemeyer, Stuck, Lang, Hasse, von Delius, and others were more or less COMPULSORILY forced to join the NSKK, and then after each victory were ceremoniously *promoted* by *Korpsführer* Hühnlein in front of thousands of spectators at the finishing-line. [...] What they were thinking to themselves was a very different matter". In Doerschlag's opinion the politically flexible conduct of the racing drivers could be explained by "the psychosis of the Hühnlein era and the boom in motor racing". By way of straightforward exoneration, he told von Brauchitsch: "Of course there was a dictatorship in sport too, and a top driver like you had to howl with the wolves". However, the propaganda they produced was of unparalleled value in reinforcing and building a national identity of military power and a reputation for German engineering. Yet, these 'virtuous heroes' of the racetrack could maintain a limited culpability.

When Racing and Racism Collide

On 14 November 1946 Dr Anton Piëch, imprisoned with his father-in-law Ferdinand Porsche in a French prison on charges of using French workers as forced labour, wrote a letter to their exiled former partner, Adolf Rosenberger, now living in California. Piëch was requesting 1000 US dollars to assist them in their release. And he praised what Rosenberger had done: "You were right from the beginning; it all started with the race car project...".[13] In the summer of 1935 as part of Aryanising the Porsche GmbH that had begun on 30 January 1933, Adolf Rosenberger had been finally forced to relinquish his 10 per cent ownership to the Porsche family only at face value. However, "they must have been drowning in money", as Rosenberger put it, due to Hitler's *Volkswagen* project the Porsche GmbH was running. But Porsche was at least in part a Jewish business as long as Rosenberger was an owner. As a consequence, in July 1935 Adolf Rosenberger was forced to cede his share of the business, which was transferred to Ferry Porsche. On 5 September 1935, Rosenberger was imprisoned by the Gestapo and on 23 September was sent from a police cell in Pforzheim directly to Kislau concentration camp for alleged *Rassenschande* (racial defilement).[14] He said later that the only person to help him was Hans von Veyder-Malberg, the man who, after the Nazis seized power, took over Rosenberger's position as CEO in the Porsche company. As a Jew in the Nazi Germany of the mid-1930s Rosenberger no longer had any legal leverage with which to protect himself against state-decreed injustices.

Truth and Fiction

After 1945, Germans moved on from the devastation of war. Only a year after the end of the war, motor races resumed in Germany, despite petrol rationing, driving bans, and the suspicions of Allied occupation forces. New racetracks had to be built since racing had become a popular public distraction from the everyday post-war austerity. On 18 May 1947 in Nürnberg, the former Reich Party Arena, known as Norisring, was used for a motorcycle race to advertise the resurgence of that industry in the Franconia region. Many of the great racing heroes of the Nazi era continued their racing careers: Stuck, von Brauchitsch, Meier, Müller, and Hermann Lang were all back on the racing circuit. Lang himself was admittedly still in Denazification proceedings and was later classified as a *Mitläufer*, or, in other words, someone who shared Nazi ideology without directly participating in Nazi crimes. On 26 May 1948, he was sentenced by a tribunal in Stuttgart to pay a fine of 1000 RM[10] as a 'penance'. Lang appealed the judgement stating, "I cannot see why someone should be condemned for driving cars and motorcycles very fast in races—the real reason for my honorary promotions". The sentencing authority at the

Central Denazification Tribunal for Northern Württemberg was slow to respond, but informed Lang in June 1950 that the fine would be reduced to 219.45 deutschmarks, payable in monthly instalments. "In view of the low level of political involvement and the losses suffered by the accused, the court costs represented a hardship. In due consideration of the circumstances, it therefore seemed justifiable to reduce the costs owed and to allow payment by instalments".

In December 1947 Lang's former racing manager, Alfred Neubauer, was also classified as *Mitläufer* by the tribunal for Stuttgart North and fined 100 RM. In February 1948, Neubauer appealed the decision with a detailed rationale. His promotion to NSKK *Oberscharführer* was, he said, "honorary" and "was only due to the fact that the *Werkssturm* (factory unit) of the NSKK in Daimler-Benz AG, to which I was recruited against my will as a supporting member, felt it incumbent upon them to give special recognition to my services as manager of our racing team that had been victorious for so many years". The appeal resulted in the decision being overruled in April that year and ended the proceedings against Neubauer. The former Mercedes-Benz racing manager returned to his traditional place of work—as did all the other leading contenders in Hitler's motor racing battles. At a conference of the Motoring Press Club held in March 1949 in Burscheid under the auspices of the Goetze company, Neubauer asked for permission to show the last Daimler-Benz racing film made in the Nazi period under the title *Victory—Record—Championship*. He wanted to show it "in its international version to this small private gathering", which included, as it had before 1945, Messrs Bretz, Doerschlag, Rosemann, and other old friends. Nothing had changed. "I have in fact found out", Neubauer explained, "that particularly in the British Zone, many sports films with a National Socialist background are shown with no criticism at all, because of course recent events cannot simply be erased".

Former journalist and editor Hans Bretz became the first vice-president of the re-founded Allgemeiner Deutscher Automobil-Club in 1949 and finally served as the unchallenged President of Germany's most powerful motoring organisation from 1964 until his death in 1972. In the post-war period Bretz described the work of the once Nazified ADAC as "without doubt a deliberate demonstration against the high-handed and partisan role of the NSKK in national and international motoring". However, writing during the Third Reich, he had played a very different tune. In 1937, Bretz had written retrospectively about the ten years of the Nürburgring, recounting that "in 1933, through the liberating and revivifying deeds of the Führer, German motor sport received a boost which removed at a stroke all the obstacles with which it had had to battle till then!" He went on to rejoice that "from a multiplicity of clubs [...] a single club has been formed: the Deutsche Automobil-Club (DDAC)". The next year, when writing for Daimler-Benz AG, Bretz had praised National Socialist sports policy, "which has attempted and achieved ever new and greater performances! It is to the credit of the leader of German motor sport, *Korpsführer* Hühnlein, that these internal and external conditions have been created, firstly through the reorganisation of the German club structure, which found expression in the creation of the *Deutsches Automobil-Club*, then most of all in the concentrated power, which the *Nationalsozialistisches Kraftfahrkorps* [NSKK] has won for itself under his leadership. Among the men of the Corps, motor sport is no longer chiefly a striving for personal success but rather an untiring battle for the success and honour of the nation!"

Porsche was a case in point of the failure of post-war de-Aryanisation and denazification. On 30 November 1949 Rosenberger, now known as Alan Arthur Robert, pursued an action before the Stuttgart District Court for the restitution of his shares of Porsche GmbH based on a law made in Germany on 10 November 1947 by the occupying Americans ("Das Rückerstattungsgesets" Law on Restitution—Law Nr. 59). In 1950, Porsche took legal responsibility for having profited from Aryanising Adolf Rosenberger's shares by accepting a settlement in court, which undervalued the true damages faced by Rosenberger. Porsche was motivated to settle, because their company's property was held in Germany by American post-war property control, which could only be released if they settled with Rosenberger. Only four weeks after the settlement in court the property was released.[15]

During the Nazi dictatorship Rosenberger had operated in London, Paris, and elsewhere as the foreign representative of the Porsche company—with no commercial success, or so the lawyers for Ferdinand and Ferry Porsche claimed. Rosenberger riposted that this was due to the great inventor's defective designs and absence of patent rights. Porsche admitted that the Nazi authorities had put pressure on Porsche to part company with their Jewish employees. Was this in fact the case? Or had Porsche fired these staff members to seize the opportunities the Nazi's had to offer, or was this done because they themselves wished to Aryanise their own company because they embraced the Nazi ideology?

This was the claim made by Rosenberger. He declared that it was sheer opportunism to get rid of their Jewish partner. After the war ended, Rosenberger returned to Germany and sought out the Porsches in Stuttgart. Ferry Porsche claims that "…Rosenberger suggested that if we paid him 200,000 DM and he returned half this sum to us 'under the table,' we would not have lost any money. His reasoning was that the 200,000 DM would be tax deductible since it was an indemnification by us. However, this was an unacceptable offer because it would have put the Porsche company in a position of tax evasion. We therefore effected a compromise in which we gave him a new Volkswagen free and several thousand still marks—but no contract".[16] In effect, Ferry Porsche invoked anti-Semitic stereotypes of the "dirty Jewish businessman" in his version of events in a book published in the late 1970s. Porsche provided no evidence to support his allegations, but Rosenberger had already died in Los Angeles on 6 December 1967 at the age of 67 and could not counter the specious claims that assaulted his character. At the time, it seemed as if his contributions to racing history would be buried with him. Rosenberger was almost forgotten as it was the SS officer, Rosemeyer, not Rosenberger, who drove the Auto Union Grand Prix car.

At the same time, the Porsche company became a safe haven for friends and acquaintances closely tied to the upper echelons of Nazi Germany.[17] Albert Prinzing, a highly ranked SS member, became CEO of Porsche, recruited by his friend Ferry Porsche. Prinzing fostered the growth of the small Zuffenhausen sportscar manufacturer into a substantial corporation. Prinzing's friend, SS-Oberführer Franz Alfred Six, was hired as the publicity executive for Porsche. Franz Alfred Six was tried as a war criminal in the *Einsatzgruppen Prozess* at Nuremberg in 1948. The tribunal sentenced Six to 20 years imprisonment, but a clemency court commuted this sentence. Six was released in 1952 and began his work for Porsche. In 1961, he was called as a witness by the defence during the trial of former SS-Obersturmbannführer Adolf Eichmann, a major architect of the Holocaust, in Jerusalem. Six was forced to give his testimony by deposition in West Germany, because he would have been arrested in Israel as a war criminal. Baron Fritz Huschke von Hanstein, former SS-Hauptsturmführer, had a longer tenure in Zuffenhausen. He became Porsche's press officer, racing car driver, and race director, playing an important role within the German racing community. The baron built a reputation for the little VW-based Porsche 365 among the 'better class' of people, making Porsche the 'chic' marque. The charismatic von Hanstein rose to become an internationally respected representative of German motor sport. After serving as Porsche's racing manager, he took up senior positions in the AvD (Automobile Club of Germany) and the World Automobile Federation.

It became public knowledge that Porsche employed Nazi war criminals, when worker protests and international outrage forced former Waffen-SS Oberbannführer Joachim Peiper to leave his job at Porsche. Peiper had been a key member of Himmler's personal staff, was in command of a unit on the Eastern Front, and after the war, in what was known as the Malmédy Trial, was condemned to death for the massacre of Belgian civilians and US POWs in the wake of the Ardennes offensive. He is considered one of the most heinous of the Nazi war criminals. His sentence was commuted to life imprisonment, but Peiper was granted early release in 1956 with the promise of employment by Porsche the following year. Post-war German society maintained a camaraderie fostered by the SS during the Nazi dictatorship. This was particularly true in the 'non-political' world of motor racing. The members of this privileged fraternity benefitted from the specious designation of motor racing as non-political. The juxtaposition of the Rosenberger trial and the immediate population of the company with high-ranking SS points to the fiction of denazification and the mythology of the 'apolitical' status of the automotive industry that is even perpetuated today.

Before the Third Reich, automotive racing had been an elite sport. It became popularised by the Nazi dictatorship and, after 1945, gentrified in a "return to the hands of the 'better classes,' untainted by Nazi ideology". However, the political activities of leaders in the post-war racing world undermine this narrative. Among von Hanstein's closest friends was Prince Paul von Metternich. The prince was also a Spanish grandee, Duca de Portella, Conde de Castillejo, Count von Königswart, a major landowner in the Tyrol, and Grand Prior of the Order of Lazarus in Germany. He had fought for Franco in the Spanish Civil War and had played his part against the 'Communist menace' outside Madrid and at the capture of Toledo and Barcelona. After the war he began his racing, became President of the AvD, and finally ascended to head of the international motor racing federation, the Federation Internationale de l'Automobile (FIA). Years later Max Mosley was President of the FIA in succession to the controversial Jean-Marie Balestre[18] from 1993 to 2009. The contributions and influence of the late barrister and racing driver regarding motor racing, from founding the March Formula One racing team to his work at the FIA, are many and far reaching, not to mention his contributions to road safety. However, Mosley was a son of the former leader of the British Union of Fascists, the late Sir Oswald Mosley. His association with his father's fascist political movement included a job as an election agent running a 1961 by-election campaign featuring racist leaflets warning about immigrants bringing disease and poverty to the UK. Max Mosley appreciated the racing community of the 1960s, where no questions were asked about his father's fascist politics and the extent of his own participation in them. Nonetheless, Mosely's own political views came under scrutiny in 2018 when he told the *Guardian* that he had supported apartheid in South Africa during the 1960s and had felt it "perfectly legitimate to offer immigrants financial inducements to go home".[19]

Up until the late 1980s, there were no discussions within the German racing community about the complicity of the racing business with the Third Reich. Indeed, the end of the war seemed to provide what appeared to be a 'safe haven' for former Nazis. However, the desire to keep the secret of the German racing world's Nazi past and the not so apolitical involvement of its brightest stars came at a price. Keeping one's own secrets demanded keeping the secrets of others. Nonetheless, critiques started to emerge, when the most notable of these figures were deceased and their legends and myths were called into question. These counter-narratives and critiques, like the silenced story of Adolf Rosenberger (Alan Robert), the Jewish entrepreneur, race car driver, and co-founder of the Porsche company, have been established through primary historical documents extant in public and private archives. However, revealing these secrets does not mean that Formula 1 racing has left behind its racist and nationalist past. History is about explaining the present by understanding the past in order to change the future. We have exposed the romanticisation of German automotive racing and its history, which has obscured its discriminatory underpinnings that must be made visible and understood if they are ever to be combatted. Historical and moral questions collide and ought to be confronted in history writing. This disruption of the shining mythological narrative has been long overdue.

Notes

1. Jonathan Noble "Hamilton named among TIME's 100 most influential people". https://www.motorsport.com/f1/news/hamilton-time-100-influential-list/4879940/. Posted 23 September 2020; accessed 10 May 2022.
2. This was followed in 1959 by a second volume, *Master of a Thousand Horsepower*. The memoirs, which Rowe reworked in 1970 and abridged heavily to make a single volume.
3. Alfred Neubauer, Männer, Frauen und Motoren, Hamburg 1958; Alfred Neubauer, Herr über 1000 PS. Erinnerungen des Rennleiters Alfred Neubauer aufgezeichnet von Harvey T. Rowe, Hamburg 1959; cited from: Harvey T. Rowe, Männer, Frauen und Motoren. Die Erinnerungen des Rennleiters Alfred Neubauer, 1. Aufl.[der überarbeiteten, einbändigen Fassung] Stuttgart 1970, p. 10.
4. These were the people named in and targeted by the Nuremburg Laws. However, those outside of the heterosexual 'Aryan' identity were persecuted.
5. Victor Klemperer, LTI. *Notizbuch eines Philologen*. Leipzig: 1996. 10. 14. Aufl. Leipzig 1996, p. 10.
6. Peter Longerich,. *Holocaust: The Nazi Persecution and Murder of the Jews*. Oxford: Oxford University Press, 2010. 10–13.
7. There was a 9 km straight, then a tight bend at the southern end, and another 9 km straight leading to the wide northern bend, and then the whole circuit started again.

8. Adolf Rosenberger has been written out of history, and because there is little to no common knowledge of him, a brief description of who this person was is footnoted here. What has become publicly available regarding Rosenberger has been primarily due to the research and documentaries of Eberhard Reuß, especially *Der Mann hinter Porsche-Adolf Rosenberger* ARD/SWR/NDR aired on 24 June 2019.

   Adolf Rosenberger was born in 1900 in southwestern Germany in the city of Pforzheim. He was Jewish and at the age of 17 volunteered to be a pilot in World War I. He returned from the war as a decorated war hero and began racing motorcycles. He later took up racing Mercedes motor cars, which was a typical path for automotive racing after World War I. He was a record-breaking race car driver and in 1931 became with Ferdinand Porsche and his son-in-law Anton Piëch one of the three founders and CEO of the new Porsche company. When in 1933 Hitler came to power and racing and the industry was Aryanised, the process of forgetting his contributions was actively initiated. He will return to this narrative, as his contributions and his removal from the automotive industry in Germany is illustrative of Aryanising and racist tendencies.

   For more information on some of the wealthiest industrialists who benefitted from Nazi Germany, including Porsche and BMW, please see David de Jong. *Nazi Billionaires: The Dark History of Germany's Wealthiest Dynasties*, New York: Harper Collins. 2022.

   It should be noted here that Porsche AG has shown interest in a discussion with Adolf Rosenberger gGmbH (Adolf-Rosenberger.com) to amend the historical record to include Adolf Rosenberger's contributions to the company and reckon with the Nazi past as it relates to Porsche AG.
9. In theory this meant a smaller cubic capacity and a maximum output of around 250 bhp.
10. Draft Contract, Adolf Rosenberger, gGmbH, Archives of the Adolf Rosenberger gGmbH.
11. Longerich, 18
12. This was the beginning of Aryanisation. 'Aryanisation' is a term that was used by the Nazis that referred to the seizure of property from Jews that removed Jews from economic life, ultimately culminating in the Shoa. Property, jobs, positions, and more were taken from Jewish people and given to Aryans. Initially, Aryanisation was hidden under a cloak of 'nor-

mal' business transactions, until in its later manifestations it was practised as unabashed thievery.

13. Letter from 14 November 1946 from Mendon prison, France, estate of the Adolf Rosenberger gGmbH.
14. It is interesting to note, here, that he was arrested on 5 September for *Rassenschande*, but the Nuremberg Race Laws were not official until 15 September 1935. He was held in Pforzheim until shortly after the Nuremberg Laws were in place and transferred to a concentration camp. Rosenberger's prominence seems to have been why he was targeted. Ferdinand Porsche and his son Ferry later insisted that they had made sure their former colleague was quickly released. Adolf Rosenberger disputes this.
15. Thanks to Dr Christoph Rückel, Attorney, for consulting on the significance of the legal action. Rückel and Collegen, Munich, and Chairman of the Supervisory Board, Adolf Rosenberger gGmbH (Adolf Rosenberger.com), Munich.
16. Ferry Porsche with John Bentley. *We at Porsche: The Autobiography of Dr. Ing h.c. Ferry Porsche with a foreword by Baron Huschke von Hanstein.* New York: Double Day, 1976. 228.
17. As historian Hans Mommsen writes in his standard work on the Volkswagen plant in the Third Reich: "Ferdinand Porsche did not trouble himself with the political implications of putting the task of factory security into the hands of the SS. This measure reflected the strong affinity between the professional technocrats and the SS, who posed as a highly efficient elite". At the same time, Mommsen takes a somewhat benevolent view of this technocrat: "With the sureness of a sleepwalker Porsche succeeded to a great extent in staying aloof from the chronic power struggles between the satraps of National Socialism, and, admittedly backed by the unarguable respect he enjoyed from Adolf Hitler, he was able to maintain a largely independent stance. His unorthodox manner, his relaxed and never subservient way of dealing with the Party notables, and his international renown as a motor car designer, as well as his spectacular successes in racing car construction, gave him an exceptional position within the regime, which in some respects allowed him to break ranks from time to time".

    It could be put another way: Porsche's direct line to Hitler gave him ample opportunity to pursue his own advantage with a ruthless consistency. The central files of the NSDAP record Ferdinand Porsche as member no. 5643287. Having applied for admission on 8 October 1937, he was accepted retroactively from 1 May of that year. And in the final phase of World War II, Porsche, aged nearly 70, was to be found in the ranks of the SS. On 3 April 1944 the central personnel office of the SS in Berlin received a returned and completed 'questionnaire for senior SS officers' in the name of SS-Oberführer Prof. Dr Ing. h.c. Ferdinand Porsche. His son Ferry had already joined the staff of the SS Danube Division as early as 1 August 1941, as no. 346167.

18. Balestre is known to have been a member of the French Nazi division of the SS during the German occupation of France, but later claimed to have been an undercover agent of the French Resistance. See "Jean-Marie Balestre – Obituary", *The Guardian*, 31 March 2008. https://www.theguardian.com/sport/2008/mar/31/motorsports.mainsection. Accessed 16 May 2022.
19. In 1954/1955 there were discussions within the British press about Stirling Moss joining Mercedes-Benz: A Jewish racing driver signing in for a German company ten years after the end of World War II? The late Sir Stirling seemed to have no problem with it; he wanted to race the fastest Grand Prix car and the British could not deliver, so he joined Mercedes-Benz. His compatriot Mike Hawthorn became the first British Formula One World Champion in 1958, thanks to Sir Stirling in the aftermath of the Portuguese Grand Prix. Yet, sometime prior to the 1958 victory, Hawthorn nicknamed Moss 'Moses'.

References

Brünger, S. (2017). *Geschichte und Gewinn. Der Umgang deutscher Konzerne mit ihrer NS-Vergangenheit*. Göttingen.

De Jong, D. (2022). *Nazi Billionaires: The Dark History of Germany's Wealthiest Dynasties*. Harper Collins.

Hochstetter, D. (2005). *Motorisierung und "Volksgemeinschaft": Das Nationalsozialistische Kraftfahrkorps (NSKK) 1931–1945*. München.

Klemperer, V. (1996). LTI. *Notizbuch eines Philologen*. 14. Aufl. Leipzig.

Longerich, P. (2010). *Holocaust: The Nazi Persecution and Murder of the Jews*. Oxford.

Ludvigsen, K. (2021). *Porsche: Excellence was Expected* (4 Vols.). Cambridge.

Mommsen, H., & Grieger, M. (1996). *Das Volkswagenwerk und seine Arbeiter im Dritten Reich*. Düsseldorf.

Neubauer, A., & Rowe, H. T. (1958). *Männer, Frauen und Motoren*. Hamburg.

Neubauer, A., & Rowe, H. T. (1959). *Herr über 1000 PS*. Hamburg.

Neubauer, A., & Rowe, H. T. (1970). *Männer, Frauen und Motoren. Die Erinnerungen des Rennleiters Alfred Neubauer*. 1. Aufl. der überarbeiteten, einbändigen Fassung. Stuttgart.

Nixon, C. (1986). *Racing the Silver Arrows: Mercedes-Benz versus Auto Union 1934–1939*. Oxford.

Nye, D. (2002). *Dick and George: The Seaman Monkhouse Letters 1936–1939*. London.

Porsche, F., & Bentley, J. (1976). *We at Porsche: The Autobiography of Dr. Ing h.c. Ferry Porsche with a Foreword by Baron Huschke von Hanstein*. Double Day.

Porsche, F., & Molter, G. (2002). *Ferry Porsche: Mein Leben*. 5. Aufl.

Pyta, W., Havemann, N., & Braun, J. (2017). *Porsche: Vom Konstruktionsbüro zur Weltmarke*. München.

Reuß, E. (2008). *Hitler's Motor Racing Battles: The Silver Arrows Under the Swastika* (trans. A. McGeoch). Sparkford.

Reuß, E. (2011). *Porsches dritter Mann: Der Fall Rosenberger*. SWR-Documentary.

Reuß, E. (2019). *Der Mann hinter Porsche—Adolf Rosenberger*. ARD-Documentary.

Reuß, E. (2021). Ferdinand Porsche II: Man muss von Arisierung sprechen. Der Fall Adolf Rosenberger. In Hermann G. Abmayr (Hg.), *Stuttgarter NS-Täter. Vom Mitläufer bis zum Massenmörder*. 3. Aufl.

Reuß, E. (2022). Adolf Rosenberger. https://www.leo-bw.de/detail/-/Detail/details/PERSON/kgl_biographien/1012779068/Rosenberger+Adolf. zuletzt aufgerufen am 23.5.2022.

Siems, M. (2022). *Konkurrierende Wahrheiten. Geschichtsbilder in Wolfsburg 1945–1968*. Göttingen.

Viehöver, U. (2021). Ferdinand Porsche I: Hitlers Lieblingskonstrukteur, Wehrwirtschaftsführer und Kriegsgewinner. In Hermann G. Abmayr (Hg.), *Stuttgarter NS-Täter. Vom Mitläufer bis zum Massenmörder*. 3. Aufl.

Walter, M. (2006). Ein vergessener Vater des Volkswagens, der Porsche AG und ein erfolgreicher Rennfahrer. Der Pforzheimer Adolf Rosenberger—ein deutsch-jüdisches Schicksal. Neue Beiträge zur Pforzheimer Stadtgeschichte. Band 1, Ubstadt-Weiher.

Walter, M. (2011). Adolf Rosenberger: Zur Geschichte eines deutschen Juden. Vom erfolgreichen Rennfahrer zum Mitbegründer der Porsche AG. In *Nicht nur Sieg und Niederlage. Sport im deutschen Südwesten im 19. und 20.* Jahrhundert. Oberrheinische Studien, Bd. 28, Ostfildern.

Westemeier, J. (2007). *Joachim Peiper: A Biography of Himmler's SS Commander* (trans. C. Wisowaty). Atglen, Pennsylvania.

Williams, R. (2020). *Race with Love and Death. The Story of Richard Seaman*. London.

ZDF Bilanz. (1966, 11 October). "Wer erfand den Volkswagen?" German TV Broadcast with Adolf Rosenberger Interview Clippings.

Henry Ford and the Rise of US Motorsport

Georgios P. Loizides

Introduction

This chapter revolves around Henry Ford's involvement in and influence on early motorsport in the United States. Although Ford had experimented with automobile manufacture since the mid-1890s, it was not until 1901 that Henry Ford became directly involved in car racing. That year, he created a stir when he defeated accomplished racer Alexander Winton in a race at Grosse Pointe, MI. This event, together with a 1902 race in which Ford's 999 racer (driven by Barney Oldfield) again defeated Winton at Grosse Pointe, skyrocketed Ford's fame and helped him secure funding for establishing the Ford Motor Company. The 1901 race, the only event in which Ford raced himself, marked the start of Ford's 12-year long direct involvement in motorsport, which ended in 1913, the same year that the moving line production was established at the Ford Motor Company's Highland Park plant. This was also the period in which Model

G. P. Loizides (✉)
University of Wisconsin – Stout, Menomonie, WI, USA
e-mail: loizidesg@uwstout.edu

D. Sturm et al. (eds.), *The History and Politics of Motor Racing*, Global Culture and Sport Series, https://doi.org/10.1007/978-3-031-22825-4_5

T sales began to dominate the American automobile market. Following his early flirting with racing, from 1901 to 1913, Henry Ford primarily acted as a major car manufacturer, utilizing racing only to further the interests of developing, manufacturing and selling automobiles.

This chapter will comprise two main parts: the years of Ford's direct involvement with car racing, 1901–1913; and the years following 1913, when his involvement became more indirect and principally served the interests of manufacturing and sales. A short description of the post-1945 period, when Henry Ford retired from the Ford Motor Company and the company leadership was taken over by Henry Ford II is added to this section. The chapter particularly covers the 1901 and 1902 races at Grosse Ponte, which proved influential in establishing the Ford Motor Company, as well as other early racing events in which Ford was directly involved. It also covers Henry Ford's post-1913 indirect involvement, through his Ford Racing team (later renamed Ford Performance), through racing event sponsoring, through the extensive sales of Model T, and through the early Ford Motor Company personnel policies, that arguably facilitated increases in worker leisure time and disposable income (which he directed towards the purchasing of homes and cars). As noted, the main part of this chapter ends with a description of the post-1945 period, when Henry Ford II, grandson of Henry Ford revived the direct involvement of the Ford Motor Company in motorsport. Finally, this chapter concludes with a summary of the main points.

Henry Ford's Direct Involvement in Motorsport: 1901–1913

Although Henry Ford was one of the early players in automobile racing, he certainly did not father the sport in the United States. That title must go to railroad heir and plutocrat William K. Vanderbilt and his friends, who became the first racing enthusiasts in the United States, driving European cars (McCarthy, 2009). Indeed, by 1901, when at the age of 38 Henry Ford ran his first and only race as a driver, motorsport was already beginning to flourish in America. In fact, it was the increasing popularity of motorsport that encouraged Henry Ford to become involved in racing in the first place. Henry Ford's direct involvement in racing lasted, as noted, about 12 years, until 1913. By December 1913, his plant at Highland Park had established the moving assembly line production and was producing an increasing number of Model T. cars. In January 1914, he established his now famous five-dollar-day, and he became fully immersed in automobile production.

Ford's first car, the Quadricycle, took four years to complete and was finished in 1896. It was "essentially a motorized four-wheel bicycle, with chain drive, a tiller for steering, and no brakes or reverse gear" (Goldstone, 2016). The four horsepower Quadricycle could reach a top speed of 20 miles per hour. Ford developed this first car while he was working as a Chief Engineer at the Edison Illumination Company. In 1899, Ford left the Edison company, after a group of investors founded the Detroit Automobile Company, the first Detroit company devoted to the manufacture of automobiles (Goldstone, 2016; Lacey, 1986). This group of investors offered Ford a small amount of company stock and the position of Chief Engineer. Ford remained in the Detroit Automobile Company for only two years, until it was dissolved in January 1901 (see Agreement between Detroit Automobile Company and Henry Ford, 1899).

By the beginning of the twentieth century, the popularity of motorsport in America was increasing rapidly, and so was the average speed in every race. In 1900 for example, William Vanderbilt won a five-mile race at Newport, Rhode Island, with an average speed of 33 mph, while in the same month, Alexander Winton, car manufacturer and famed race driver, won a 50-mile race in Chicago with an average speed of around 38 mph (Lacey, 1986). In 1901 it was announced that on October 10, Winton was going to compete at a newly constructed track in Grosse Pointe, Michigan. History was in the making. In preparation for the Grosse Pointe race, Ford assembled a team, which included an electrician from the Edison plant, Edward "Spider" Huff. Huff and his team developed multiple innovations that became lasting legacies, such as a special spark coil, which was housed in an insulating porcelain case (made of denture ceramic with the help of a dentist)—a predecessor of the modern spark plug (Lacey, 1986). Huff was to be the riding mechanic for Ford in the race.

Ford's racer had modest performance capabilities but was light and of simple construction. It carried a two-cylinder engine that could produce 26 horsepower. By contrast, Ford's registered competitors at the race had more experience and fame and drove racers with much more powerful engines. Henri Fournier for example, the French one-mile speed record holder, drove a car that could produce 60 horsepower, Alexander Winton's racer could produce 40 horsepower, as much as the car belonging to William K. Vanderbilt Jr. In comparison with these famous drivers driving large, heavy and powerful racers, Henry Ford seemed to be less of a competition. When Vanderbilt and Fournier dropped out before the race, there remained but one certain winner, Alexander Winton. Winton was such a big favourite to win the race, that the race organizers allowed Winton's sales manager to essentially collaborate with them in determining the trophy, which was chosen to be a cut-glass punchbowl. Winton even reserved a high visibility spot at his home to exhibit the trophy (Lacey, 1986; Ford, Edsel II, 2015). On the day of the well-publicized race, there were more than 8000 spectators present. At the starting line for the race, there were only three competitors left. One of them developed a mechanical failure and could not start. This left only two competitors, "the new world-record holder and ace motor manufacturer, Alexander Winton, and the Dearborn country boy and failed manufacturer, Henry Ford" (Lacey, 1986, p. 55). Given the few remaining entries and the power differential between drivers and racers, the organizers of the race decided to decrease the number of laps from 25 (25 miles) to just 10, as they felt that there would be little interest in seeing Winton drive 25 laps on his own. This essentially transformed the race from an all-day endurance race to a ten-lap sprint. The race started as expected, with Winton propelling himself to first position and gaining in distance from Ford with every lap. By the end of the third lap, Winton was ahead by more than a fifth of a mile, and the race seemed all but decided, until the sixth lap, that is, when Winton's car developed a problem and began losing power and speed. A cloud began to form behind Winton's racer as it was slowing down. Despite Winton's riding mechanic's frantic efforts at repairing the engine on the fly, the car kept losing speed. By lap six, Ford cut into Winton's lead significantly, and by the seventh lap, they overtook Winton as the crowd went wild. Following the race, clearly intimidated by the dangerous experience, Ford stated that he would "never again" race. He never did!

In November 1901, following his win at the Grosse Pointe race and subsequent fame, Henry Ford secured financial backing once again. Ford and a group of engineers reorganized the company into the Henry Ford Company. Within a few months, Ford left the company (or was fired), following a dispute with his investors in 1902 and went on to establish the Ford Motor Company the following year (see Ford Motor Company Articles of Association). The Henry Ford Company was renamed The Cadillac Automobile Company in 1902. When Ford left the Henry Ford Company, he concentrated on developing Ford 999, with which he won his second major race, with Barney Oldfield as driver this time, at Grosse Pointe, Michigan. Ford's preoccupation with the development of this racing car had been at the core of his disagreement with his backers in 1902. While he was increasingly involved in developing his racing cars, his backers were more interested in developing and constructing a production automobile as soon as possible (Lacey, 1986).

Apart from a short period of fascination with racing beginning in 1901, Henry Ford treated motorsport, like many other automobile manufacturers since the early history of automobile production, as a means to increase the visibility of their brand, thus increasing sales, as a means to develop more efficient automobiles, and as a sort of training and development area for their engineers. In a 2017 editorial titled "Why Do Automakers Spend Big Money on Racing?" *Autotrader*'s Executive Editor Brian Moody argued, similarly, that automobile manufacturers still invest in motorsport to increase product visibility and thus sales, to facilitate product development, and to help train engineers (Moody, 2017). Ford himself, insisted that he did not personally like the idea of racing. Indeed, he played down his own interest in racing, by stating that

> I never thought anything of racing, but the public refused to consider the automobile in any light other than as a fast toy. Therefore, later we had to race. The industry was held back by this initial racing slant, for the attention of the makers was diverted to making fast rather than good cars. It was a business for speculators. (Ford, 1922, p. 86)

However, during the period around the 1901 Grosse Pointe victory, and shortly afterwards, Ford seemed preoccupied with further developing racers. In 1902, while still in the Henry Ford Company, Henry Ford wrote in a letter to his brother-in-law Milton Bryant that "my Company will kick about me following racing but they get the advertising and I expect to make $ where I can't make c [cents] at manufacturing" (Letter from Henry Ford to Milton Bryant Concerning Auto Racing, 1902). Benson Ford Research Center object ID 64.167.1.408. Also see Weiss, 2003, p. 9). Ford's split interests in manufacturing and motorsport was commented on by Watts (2005) thus:

> the marked contrast between Ford the racer and Ford the manufacturer only increased tensions with his financial backers. 'He seemed to be so taken up with the racing car that that is the thing which made the others dissatisfied,' Oliver Barthel observed of Ford's festering relations with his stockholders. 'They merely said that he had the racing fever and they were through with him.' This situation contributed to Ford's dismissal from the Henry Ford Company in March 1902. (also see Pauly, 2012)

When Ford left the company, he took with him the name (as was his legal right) and his drafts for a new racer (Lacey, 1986). It is reported that the disagreement that dissolved the Henry Ford Company was related to his backers being "intent on attracting customers and so opposed to racing." By 1902, Henry Ford was "discontented and pining for a return to racing" (Pauly, 2012, p. 149).

During the 1901 race at Grosse Pointe, Ford met bicycle racer Barney Oldfield (Pauly, 2012). Despite having no prior experience in driving cars, Oldfield was destined to gain fame as a racing driver for the next two decades. In May 1902, a few months after Ford's leaving the Henry Ford Company, he and his team of engineers began building two racers: the 999 and the Arrow. Barney Oldfield drove the 80-plus horsepower 999 to victory in the Manufacturers' Challenge Cup on October 25, 1902, a five-mile race at Grosse Pointe, Michigan. This is often hailed as Ford's second big racing victory. However, it is worth noting that a few weeks before the race, Ford had sold his share of the 999, following a failed test session.

After the 1902 Grosse Pointe race, Ford devoted his attention to establishing the Ford Motor Company and finalizing the development of a general use car. This gave birth to the Model A, a two-cylinder car. Meanwhile, Ford rebuilt his Arrow, which had been involved in a fatal crash, and with his riding mechanic from the 1901 race, "Spider" Huff, set a new land speed record on iced Lake St Clair on January 12, 1904, with a top speed of 91.37 mph (as timed and sanctioned by the American Automobile Association—AAA).

In summer of 1904 Ford partnered with a new race/factory driver, Frank Kulick. Kulick became one of the first Ford Motor Company employees, and stayed with Ford until 1913, when Henry Ford withdrew from racing altogether. Kulick's first races with Ford were with a racer that combined two Model A engines, to make a four-cylinder racer. In June 1907, Kulick drove a six-cylinder production Model K in a 24-hour race for "stock" cars at the Detroit Fairgrounds. He won after driving 1135 miles (using two cars, as allowed by the rules). Following an October 1907 crash, that left Kulick with permanent injuries, Henry Ford stopped developing race cars, until 1910.

The lull in racer development did not prevent Ford from participating in motorsport. In fact, the Ford team participated with two Model T cars in the very first transcontinental car race, the "ocean to ocean" New York-to-Seattle race that was held in June 1909. One of Ford's two participating Model Ts won the race in 22 days (Wells, 2012). It is worth noting that five months after the victory in the New York-to-Seattle race, it was discovered that during the race, while crossing Idaho, the Ford team had replaced the engine of their winning car, and so it was disqualified (Cole, 1991). Meanwhile, after a period of recovery from injuries suffered in the 1907 crash, Kulick continued to win races for Ford. Between 1910 and 1912, he won a number of races around the country driving a specially modified Model T. In 1911, he ran the one-mile oval track at Detroit Fairgrounds in 50 seconds flat, setting a new record and beating a 200 horsepower Blitzen Benz, one of the greatest racers in the world at the time.

As a "stock car," a car designed for public driving as opposed to racing, the Model T proved to be a strong competitor in racing as well. This helped increase public interest in racing (McCarthy, 2007). In 1911, at the inaugural Indianapolis 500, officials barred the Model T team from participating, after drivers refused to carry several hundred pounds of extra weight in order to qualify. Once again, in 1913, Henry Ford's Model T team, with Kulick as driver tried to enter in the Indianapolis 500 race. Race officials demanded that the Model T add 1000 pounds of weight in order to qualify for the race. Indeed, this was a major problem for Ford, as with its smaller engine, the Model T needed to be light to compete with the larger engines and heavier racers of the competition. As the other drivers were driving heavier cars, the Model T was competitive. Add 1000 pounds to it though, and its engine could not compete with the higher horsepower engines of the competition. In response to the demand for more weight, Henry Ford stated "we 're building race cars, not trucks" and withdrew the entry. Following this failed attempt to enter the Indianapolis 500, the Ford Motor Company withdrew from racing altogether, and abstained from major racing programs until the 1950s, after Henry Ford's grandson, Henry Ford II had taken over the company.

Perhaps the greatest reason Henry Ford began to lose interest in racing in 1913 was that by that time, Model T production and sales were increasing dramatically. Indeed, the end of 1913 marks the time of the introduction of the moving line production at the Ford Motor Company plant. By January 1914, the Ford Motor Company had in place a number of innovations that enabled it to mass produce Model Ts. Standardization of production reduced the production time for the Model T to just 93 minutes (Cassia, Fabio and Ferazzi, Matteo, 2018). Ford's ability to mass produce inexpensive cars that won popular races was a recipe for success. Note that 1914 also marked the time when Henry Ford doubled the prevailing minimum wage for automobile workers in Detroit—the now famous five-dollar-day—and established a set of controls to reduce labour turnover and increase the productivity of his workforce (Loizides, 2014). Taken together, these developments absorbed much of Henry Ford's attention. His newfound status as a major automobile manufacturer left little time for racing. For Henry Ford, his engagement with racing had achieved its goal, which was to aid him in increasing car sales. From this point on, racing for him became a side show. His main preoccupation was to maintain and increase production and sales of automobiles. In 1906, Henry Ford stated to a number of visitors to his factory that "it is my whole ambition to build a car that anyone can afford to own, and to build more of them than any other factory in the world" (McCarthy, 2007, p. 31). Ford remained true to his early goal, and this goal seems to have informed much of what he did in his professional life.

Post-1913 Period

The Ford Motor Company remained officially absent from direct participation in racing events for some decades after 1913. However, Ford-made cars continued to take part in racing events and had some notable victories, such as the Romanians Petre Cristea's and Ion Zamfirescu's 1936 victory at Monte Carlo in a modified Ford V8, and Jimmi Florian's NASCAR at Dayton Speedway win in 1950, also with a flathead V8 Ford.

The mid-1950s witnessed a number of highly publicized racing accidents, such as the Le Mans Disaster of 1955, in which more than 75 people were killed and more than 100 injured when two cars collided sending debris into the crowd of spectators. These accidents prompted the Automobile Manufacturers Association to ban participation of its members in racing activities. The Ford Motor Company participated in the ban from 1957 to 1962, when Henry Ford II announced that the company would begin to participate in racing again.

Henry Ford II, grandson of Henry Ford, who was the Ford Motor Company CEO from 1945 to 1979, revived the company's participation in motorsport. In a June 1966 interview in *Sports Illustrated* magazine he stressed the importance of the 1966 Le Mans victory in maintaining the visibility of the company and supporting sales, as well as the importance of motorsport to the development of "better, safer and more efficient automobiles for general use" (*Sports Illustrated*, June 20, 1966, p. 35). The 1960s re-entry of the Ford Motor Company in racing events began a new chapter of the company's participation in motorsport and marked the beginning of the contemporary era of Ford's participation in automobile racing. Since the 1960s, the Ford Performance team has won numerous victories at national and international events, including victories at Daytona 500 and Le Mans. Most famously, in 1966, Ford won a 1-2-3 victory at the 24-hours race of Le Mans, which was depicted in the popular 2019 movie *Ford v Ferrari*. The first three competitors all drove Ford GT 40 mk. II cars. Ford Performance is still a top participant in motorsport.

The publicity and popularity that Henry Ford received from his racing activities during the first decade of the twentieth century proved important in his establishment as a top automobile designer and manufacturer.

Weeks after Henry Ford's historic victory over Winton at Grosse Pointe in 1901, his wife, Clara Ford, wrote to her brother, Milton Bryant, that "Henry has worked very hard to get where he is. That race has advertised him far and wide. And the next thing will be to make some money out of it" (Lacey, 1986, p. 59).

The successful participation of Henry Ford and the Ford Motor Company in racing during the first decade of the twentieth century, culminating to The New York-to-Seattle race of 1909 generated considerable publicity for the Model T. Following the New York-to-Seattle race, which was won by a model T, Ford engaged in "grandiose marketing hype," presenting the Model T as the "Universal Car" (Wells, 2012, p. 50). The marketing campaign that followed the race helped propel Model T sales to newfound heights. The *Ford Times* had a picture of the winning Model T and the two drivers on its cover page (*Ford Times*, No. 19, July 1st, 1909). Another advertisement published in *The Horseless Age*, Ford presented the Model T as "the family car of pleasure, the fast car for the busy businessmen, the reliable car day and night for the doctor, the dependable car on the farm (The Horseless Age, 1910, p. 17). (For a more general discussion on how car racing became very popular and a connection between stock car races and automobile sales see Hall, 2002).

As stated earlier in this chapter, automobile manufacturers typically support motorsport as a means to increase visibility and sales, to increase the efficiency of their automobiles and for training engineers and developing new technologies. To this end, in 2011 the Ford Motor Company (through Ford Racing) published a book titled *Why We Race: Use Ford Racing to Increase Sales*. Clearly intended for distribution to Ford dealers, the book promotes involvement in motorsport as a way of increasing sales. In his foreword, Edsel Ford II stated:

> Back at the turn of the 20th century… my great-grandfather was determined to become an automobile manufacturer… but lacked two things: start-up money, and a reputation of expertise as an automaker. Racing helped him get both… My great-grandfather believed that racing could help him establish himself. If he hadn't believed in the power of racing, the

> Ford Motor Company as we know it probably wouldn't exist today… The fact of the matter is, the basics haven't changed in 110 years. To this day, auto racing remains a highly visible way to generate excitement about an automaker's products, and to demonstrate product superiority and technical expertise. The intense competition has made it a hotbed of innovation in several fields—engineering, fabrication, safety, medicine, and various technologies, to name a few. (Ford Racing, 2011, p. 3)

In his closing remarks, Ford Racing director Jamie Allison argued that:

> Simply put, racing is good for business for Ford Motor Company and Ford dealers… Racing's on-track competition drives us to continually improve our engineering and technology… it also gives us a means of developing and testing a wide-ranging, high-quality line of performance parts… The high visibility of racing allows us to show the millions of fans what we can do and how good our products are… And all this works because the excitement and action of racing draws the fans… It's been 110 years since Henry Ford won his race against Alexander Winton. And today we're still doing it for the same reasons: to help drive innovation and product development; to prove our products in front of a large audience against tough competition; and to market our success. (Ford Racing, 2011, p. 31)

Conclusion—Win on Sunday, Sell on Monday

Ford's direct involvement in auto racing was significant, if somewhat overstated. Ford was a master at public relations and had the ability and financial capability to create successful narratives that maximized his personal benefits. For example, the first racing victory at Grosse Pointe in 1901 was more of a loss to Winton than a victory for Ford. It is not often recalled in the media that it was a series of fortunate events that allowed Ford to claim that victory, such as the dropping out of experienced drivers with much stronger racers and the mechanical failure that Winton's car developed that gave Ford the victory. Similarly, not many remember that the speed record he achieved with his Arrow ("the New 999") at 91.37 mph was broken by William K. Vanderbilt less than a month later, or that the Model T victory in the New York-to-Seattle race of 1909 was taken away five months afterwards. These details did not prevent Ford from utilizing his achievements to increase sales for his cars. Indeed, in a two-page advertisement in the *Saturday Evening Post*, Ford boasted that "Every Model T Ford is an Exact Duplicate of the Car that Won the New York—Seattle Contest" (Saturday Evening Post, 1909, pp. 18–19).

In a fashion similar to the way that Ford utilized his Model T racing victories to increase sales, he also promoted the development of a V-8 racing engine and its incorporation in production vehicles. Ford certainly did not invent the V-8 engine, but he and his team were the first to produce an affordable version of it mounted on a production, mass produced car, once again incorporating racing technology in a production vehicle, the Model B, in order to promote automobile sales. It is indicative of the success of this promotion that upon announcing the car on March 31, 1932, the Ford Motor Company received 100,000 pre-orders, which doubled within a few days (Lacey, 1986).

In all, motor racing enabled Henry Ford to gain the visibility and popularity he needed to secure financial backing for his automobile manufacturing project. Following the great success of his Model T, he did not need racing as much. Other major projects had since come to occupy his time and energy, such as developing his manufacturing endeavours, and securing and maintaining a dependable and efficient labour force (for a discussion of this project, see Loizides, 2007).

The true significance of Henry Ford's direct involvement in motorsport is that it helped establish the Ford Motor Company as a major automobile manufacturer and the Model T as the top general-purpose automobile in America. It should be remembered that at the turn of the twentieth century, the American market for automobiles was small, with only 8000 registered cars in 1900. It was Ford's Model T that propelled the automobile into a mass market (Billington, David P., & Billington, David P. Jr., 2007). By 1917, the Ford Motor Company had up to 40% of the automobile manufacture market (Casey, 1999). The Model T became the most popular car of the era, with 15 million sold between 1908 and 1927. In 1923, the Model T accounted for almost 55% of American Automobile manufacture (Wells, 2007).

Today's involvement of the Ford Motor Company in motorsport is fuelled by the same considerations it did more than 100 years ago. Motorsport is most useful in supporting sales through product exposure, and in development and testing due to the competitive nature of motorsport and the extreme endurance it requires from competitors.

Ford Motor Company and Motorsport Timeline

1895 First automobile race. Paris to Bordeaux, France.
1895 First automobile race in the United States. Chicago to Evanston.
1896 Henry Ford unveils his first car: The Quadricycle.
1901 Henry Ford defeats famed race driver Alexander Winton at Grosse Pointe, Michigan.
1902 Ford 999 (driven by Barney Oldfield) defeats Alexander Winton at Grosse Pointe, Michigan.
1903 The Ford Motor Company is established.
1903 Ford 999 (driven by Barney Oldfield) reaches a record 60 miles per hour.
1904 Model T production begins.
1904 Henry Ford in a rebuilt Ford 999 sets the world one-mile speed record in a frozen Detroit lake.
1907 Ford announced he is abstaining from racing due to safety concerns, following Frank Kulick's injury at the Detroit Fairgrounds track.
1909 Ford resumes involvement in racing following the construction of the Indianapolis Motor Speedway and persistent requests by Frank Kulick.
1912 Frank Kulick drives a modified Model T at 107.8 mph on frozen Lake St Clair, near Detroit.
1913 Moving assembly line production starts at the Ford Motor Company.
1913 The Ford Motor Company ceases its motorsport activities.
1914 The five-dollar-day is established by Ford, essentially doubling minimum wage for automobile employees.
1932 Ford begins production of the Flathead V8 engine; the first affordable eight-cylinder engine available to the public. (Important because it was the first "racing" engine easily accessible.) "Everyman's power for the road, and Everyman's power for racing" (https://performance.ford.com/enthusiasts/newsroom/2018/03/mose-nowland-tells-the-history-of-the-flathead.html, accessed on 3/4/2021).

1936 Petre Cristea and Ionel Zamfirescu win the Monte Carlo race in a specially modified Ford V8.
1945 Henry Ford II takes over the Ford Motor Company as the new CEO.
1947 Henry Ford dies.
1950 Jimmy Florian wins the first NASCAR race at Dayton Speedway with a Ford (flathead V8).
1956 Ford wins its first NASCAR Manufacturer's Championship.
1957 Ford Motor Company participates in the Automobile Manufacturers Association's ban on racing, following serious racing accidents in the mid-1950s.
1962 Ford Motor Company resumes participation in motorsport events.
1963 Tiny Lund wins Ford's first Daytona 500.
1965 Jim Clark (Lotus-Ford) wins Ford's first Indianapolis 500.
Ned Jarrett wins Ford's first NASCAR Grand National title.
1966 1-2-3 victory of Ford GT 40 mk. II (V8) at the 24 Hours of Le Mans.
1968 Graham Hill (Lotus-Ford) wins F1 World Championship.
1978 Mario Andretti (Lotus-Ford) wins F1 World Championship.
1979 Bjorn Waldegard (Ford Escort) wins Ford's first FIA World Rally Championship Manufacturers' Championship
1985 Bill Elliott (Ford Thunderbird) wins Inaugural "Winston Million."
1988 Bill Elliott (Ford Thunderbird) wins NASCAR Winston Cup Championship.
1992 Alan Kulwicki (Ford Thunderbird) wins NASCAR Winston Cup Championship.
1994 Michael Schumacher (Benetton Ford) wins F1 World Championship.
1999 Dale Jarrett (Ford Taurus) wins Winston Cup Championship.
2003 Matt Kenseth (Ford Taurus) wins NASCAR Winston Cup Championship.

2004 Kurt Busch (Ford Taurus) wins NASCAR Nextel Cup Championship.

2011 Trevor Bayne (Ford Fusion) wins Daytona 500. This is Ford's 600th NASCAR Sprint Cup win and the Ford Motor Company's 15th Daytona 500 win.

References

Billington, D. P., & Billington, D. P., Jr. (2007). *Power, Speed, and Form*. Princeton University Press.

Casey, R. (1999). The Vanderbuilt Cup, 1908. *Technology and Culture, 40*(2), 358–362.

Cole, T. M. (1991). Ocean to Ocean by Model T Henry Ford and the 1909 Transcontinental Auto Contest. *Journal of Sport History, 2, Summer, 18*, 224–240.

Ford, H. (1922). *My Life and Work*. Garden City Publishing Co.

Ford Motor Company. (2011). *Why We Race*. Ford Racing.

Goldstone, L. (2016). *Drive!: Henry Ford, George Selden, and the Race to Invent the Auto Age*. Ballantine Books.

Hall, R. L. (2002). Before NASCAR: The Corporate and Civic Promotion of Automobile Racing in the American South, 1903–1927. *The Journal of Southern History, 68*(3), 629–668.

Lacey, R. (1986). *Ford: The Men and the Machine*. Little Brown.

Loizides, G. (2007). "Making Men" at Ford: Ethnicity, Race, and Americanization During the Progressive Period. *Michigan Sociological Review, 21*(Fall), 3–40.

Loizides, G. P. (2014). *Deconstructing Fordism: Legacies of the Ford 'Sociological' Department*. Edwin Mellen Press.

McCarthy, T. (2009). *Auto Mania*. Yale University Press.

Moody, B. (2017). Why Do Automakers Spend Big Money On Racing? Huffington Post. Retrieved February 2, 2021, from https://www.huffpost.com/entry/why-do-automakers-spend-b_b_10863974

Pauly, T. H. (2012). *Game Faces: Five Early American Champions and the Sports They Changed*. University of Nebraska Press.

Saturday Evening Post. (1909). Every Model T Ford Is an Exact Duplicate of the Car that Won the New York – Seattle Contest, August 14, pp. 18–19.

Sports Illustrated. (1966). Here to Show the World (Interview with Henry Ford II). June 20, p. 35.

Watts, S. (2005). *The People's Tycoon: Henry Ford and the American Century*. Alfred A. Knopf.

Weiss, E. H. (2003). *Chrysler, Ford, Durant and Sloan: Founding Giants of the American Automobile Industry*. McFarland & Company.

Wells, C. W. (2007). The Road to the Model T: Culture, Road Conditions, and Innovation at the Dawn of the American Motor Age. *Technology and Culture, 48*(3), 497–523.

Wells, C. W. (2012). *Car Country: An Environmental History*. University of Washington Press.

Benson Ford Research Center Archival Material

Agreement Between Detroit Automobile Company and Henry Ford, 1899. Object ID 64.167.374.1.

Ford Motor Company Articles of Association, June 16, 1903. Object ID 64.167.122.1.

Letter from Henry Ford to Milton Bryant Concerning Auto Racing, 1902. Object ID: 64.167.1.408.

The Horseless Age. (1910). When Ford Speaks the World Listens – For in All the World No Car Like This. November 23; p. 17. Object ID 64.167.19.546.

The Fascist Race Par Excellence: Fascism and the Mille Miglia

Paul Baxa

Called the "beautiful race," the Mille Miglia (MM) continues to fascinate motor sport enthusiasts more than 60 years after it was last staged. Nostalgia for the race continues and a vintage car event is held every year in May. The vintage race is run over three days starting and ending in Brescia and passing through cities like Bologna, Florence, and Rome. The race's participants are mostly wealthy enthusiasts who own cars that once raced in the original MM. In 2007, Philip Selkirk, director of slick documentaries on motor sport, released a film tracing the 2006 Mille Miglia Historic Revival (Mille Miglia: Spirit of a Legend, 2007). The film, like the event it portrays, provides a nostalgic look at the original MM race, run between 1927 and 1957. A travelogue of sorts, Selkirk's film intersperses contemporary images with historic footage from the original race run. In tracing the race's history, Selkirk's film shows an Italy that went from the primitive roads of the 1920s to the Economic Miracle of the

P. Baxa (✉)
Department of History, Ave Maria University, Ave Maria, FL, USA
e-mail: paul.baxa@avemaria.edu

D. Sturm et al. (eds.), *The History and Politics of Motor Racing*, Global Culture and Sport Series, https://doi.org/10.1007/978-3-031-22825-4_6

1950s. Almost entirely missing from the documentary is Fascist Italy, the regime that gave the green light to the first MM in 1927.

In fact, Mussolini's regime is mentioned only once—with reference to the anomalous MM of 1940. That event was notable because it was run on a closed, 100-kilometer circuit around Brescia, not the iconic 1600-kilometre route. Run after the outbreak of the Second World War, the event was festooned with Nazi and Fascist flags in Brescia's Piazza della Vittoria. Won by a German-entered BMW, the winning drivers had swastikas and the SS symbol emblazoned on their driving suits. The impression given by the documentary is that this was the only MM race that was impacted by Fascist ideology. It seems that Selkirk forgot that the previous MM run between 1927 and 1938 were also held under the sign of the *Littorio*. In fact, the MM was a unique product of Fascist Italy, and the race's Fascist DNA was already deeply ingrained in the event. Selkirk's omission of the race's profound roots in Fascism would no doubt take away from the nostalgic haze of the Historic Mille Miglia.

Selkirk's documentary relegates Fascism to the background. According to the film's description, Fascism is not more than a "shadow" (Anon, n.d.). This sums up how the MM is generally viewed today. Like the cycling Giro d'Italia or the Serie A soccer championship, the MM appears to transcend politics and ideology. This view holds that Fascist ideology did not have a great impact on sport despite its attempts to control all sporting activity and use sporting accomplishments as propaganda. Historians like Simon Martin have argued that, despite the successes of Italian sport in the 1930s, sport's ability to promote Fascism's "idealized national identity" was severely limited due to the inconsistencies and contradictions raised by sports like soccer (Martin, 2004). Martin's view has been shared by historians like Daphné Bolz who have pointed out the limits of Fascist ideology in shaping sport (Bolz, 2016). Others like Patrizia Dogliani have recognized that Fascism made sport into a "mass phenomenon" but its goals did not differ from the liberal policies that preceded the regime (Dogliani, 2000). Recent work has suggested that Fascism's restructuring of sport under its authoritarian system did contribute substantially to Italy's successes in sport (Landoni, 2016). Fascism, however, did not significantly change the sports themselves.

A similar argument informs the very few works on motor racing, a sport that has received much less attention compared to soccer and cycling. The only scholarly study of the MM recognizes the importance of the regime in getting the race off the ground but suggests that the race did nothing more than provide Fascism with propaganda in its efforts to modernize Italy (Marchesini, 2001). Enrico Azzini's history of motor racing under Fascism argues that the regime used structures and events that were already in place in the 1920s. Fascism, in other words, did not offer anything innovative to the sport (Azzini, 2011). Motor sport, it is argued, predated and outlived Fascism. Events like the Italian Grand Prix at Monza and the MM outlived Fascism. Both Marchesini and Azzini agree that while Fascism and motor sport were in a mutually beneficial relationship, the latter remained largely independent of politics.

Challenging these viewpoints, the premise of this chapter is that Fascist ideology and motor sport identified with each other on a deeper ideological level, and that the MM in particular was a uniquely Fascist artefact. Of all the sports, motor racing was the best placed to exemplify Fascist values like speed, danger, and the use of avant-garde technology. While all sports made a contribution to the idea of the New Fascist Man, motor sport was the ideal showcase for this Fascist-type since out of all the sports it was the most closely associated to war. Far from being the leisurely tour shown in Selkirk's film, the MM brought high-speed cars to the masses. What they saw was an intensely violent demonstration of speed and noise de-familiarizing an otherwise familiar Italian landscape. Half of Italy became what John Bale has called a "landscape of speed" in a way that cannot be captured by the regulated speeds of the Historic Revival (Bale, 1994). While Selkirk's film shows cars getting caught in modern day Italian traffic, the original race was a flat out exercise in speed in a country that was not yet used to mass automobile ownership.

In order to show how the MM exemplified Fascism, this chapter will focus on the race programmes and writings of motor sport journalists. These purely sporting sources, in fact, contributed to the nexus between Fascist ideology and the MM. The 1935 programme defined the MM as the "Fascist race par excellence" because of its ability to combine "technical with popular" success. The MM brought the world's most advanced racing machines "into the heart of the crowds" via the open roads of Italy, and demonstrated the "warrior spirit of the new Italy" (Anon, 1935b). These words reflected an understanding of Fascism as a revolutionary, "palingenetic"—signifying rebirth—national force (Griffin, 2007). The exaltation of the high-speed racing automobile and its breaking of records and penetration into half of Italy made the MM a part of Fascism's desire to impose a new homogeneity on Italy (Bataille & Lovitt, 1979). Furthermore, the race can be seen as a key element in what Fernando Esposito has called Fascism's "mythical modernity" (Esposito, 2015). Whereas Esposito was referring to the impact of aviation on the Fascist imagination, the same could be said for the high-performance, supercharged racing car in races like the MM.

The following chapter will demonstrate that the MM forged a uniquely Fascist synthesis of elitism and populism through its concept, organization, and route. This event played to both the aristocratic roots of the sport and to the emerging phenomenon of mass sport (Bianda et al., 1983). It also served the Fascist regime's policy of "going toward the people" devised in the early 1930s by Mussolini's regime as a way of bringing the Fascist Revolution to the masses. While the Fascist government did not create the race, its creators, promoters, and participants built up the event as a Fascist exercise, demonstrating that sport and ideology were deeply intertwined. This was evident in the race's genesis in 1927.

The Concept

The MM began as an idea proposed by the Royal Automobile Club of Brescia, a city in the north of Italy. In his 1967 history of the race, journalist Giovanni Canestrini recounts how motoring enthusiasts Franco Mazzotti, Aymo Maggio, and Renzo Castagneto showed up at his home unannounced in Milan in December 1926 to discuss a proposed road race starting and ending in Brescia. The late night discussion was the culmination of a series of discussions that had taken place throughout that year. The plan was to run an "unprecedented and one-off race" between regular production cars using 1600 kilometres of ordinary roads (Canestrini, 1967, pp. 26–27).

These four men, later called the "Four Muskateers," became the organizers of the MM. They were the founding fathers of the event, and their legend has revolved around their sporting achievements—not their politics. The numerous histories of the race have presented them as apolitical sportsmen, motivated primarily by a desire to revive the fortunes of motor sport—at a low ebb in the mid-1920s—and get revenge on the Automobile Club of Milan for stealing the Italian Grand Prix from Brescia. Canestrini, however, did note that non-sporting ambitions also played a role, such as the promotion of road building and automobile ownership. Furthermore, the city of Brescia was ideally suited to host such an event due to the city's reputation for embracing industry and modernization. Canestrini's point suggested that there was more than simply sport involved in the genesis of the MM. In a 1927 article in the *Gazzetta dello Sport*, quoted in his memoirs, Canestrini called Brescia the "city of Italy's rebirth" after the First World War and the race an "homage to the principle of speed" (Canestrini, 1967, p. 33). Clearly, speed as ideology figured prominently in the race's foundation.

For the idea to become reality, the race needed the approval of the regime. This came from the Fascist Party Secretary Augusto Turati. Appointed to his position in 1926, Turati had been a leader of Brescian *squadrismo* in the years leading up the Fascist March on Rome in 1922. One of Turati's *squadristi* was none other than Count Aymo Maggi, one of the Mille Miglia's founders (Chiurco, 1929, p. 407). A veteran of the Great War and scion of the local aristocracy, Maggi became a racecar driver in the 1920s enjoying some modest success. Significantly, Canestrini ignores Maggi's Fascist past, only going so far as to hint at Maggi's "dangerous companions." The downplaying of Maggi's Fascism is also evident in Peter Miller's admiring portrait of the man and his race (Miller, 1988). Maggi's friendship with Turati, however, was decisive in getting the MM approved in the face of opposition from the President of the Automobile Club, Silvio Crespi.

Whatever their degree of Fascist sympathy, these men embodied the idea of the New Fascist Man. Maggi's childhood friend, Franco Mazzotti, became a racecar driver and aviator. Like Maggi, Mazzotti came from a wealthy Brescian family. Although not wealthy, Canestrini also fit the image of the New Fascist Man having served in the Italian air force in the

First World War before racing cars and becoming a motor sport journalist in the mid-1920s. Renzo Castagneto, the oldest of the group, would make his mark as the organizational genius of the event.

In these men and their concept could be found the two key components of Fascist ideology—Futurism and D'Annunzianism. Although they differed in significant ways, these two movements found common cause in exalting speed, technology, and danger. The avant-gardism of Futurism, and the decadent populism of D'Annunzio were present in the MM. To be sure, the Futurists' dynamic, industrial vision for Italy clashed with D'Annunzio's aestheticism and idealized visions of the past; however, both celebrated automobiles and aeroplanes, and both saw dying in the cause of speed as a form of martyrdom. F. T. Marinetti's 1909 Futurist Manifesto famously exclaimed that the "racing car was more beautiful than the Victory at Samothrace"[1] and went on to rejoice in the car crash described in that manifesto (Marinetti, 1972). Marinetti later became one of the founding members of the Fascist Movement in 1919. D'Annunzio had been an aviator and speedboat commander in the First World War. His prewar novels, which exalted heroic deaths, included exciting descriptions of driving and flying. In 1921, after his failed takeover of Fiume, D'Annunzio moved into the Vittoriale on the shores of the Lake of Garda, near Brescia where he became a distant patron of the MM. His chauffeur drove in the first race in 1927 (Canestrini, 1967, p. 33).

The MM was designed to promote speed, technology, and danger. Canestrini noted that the race's founders had rejected the idea of a rally race based on regulated speeds. The race had to be flat out over Italy's public roads. While the first MM was contested by touring cars, the subsequent editions saw increasing participation from high-speed performance cars led by the famous Alfa Romeo 1500 and 1750cc models. By the mid-1930s, the race was dominated by modified Grand Prix cars, like the Alfa Romeo Tipo P3. The legends of Alfa Romeo and the MM were intimately connected and fed off each other. The Alfas pushed the speed limits in the race and made it into an event for high-performance racing cars when it was originally intended to be a race for touring cars which were available to the public. In this way, the MM provided a platform for the truly avant-garde racing car and advanced the development of the sports car and sports car racing (Nicholson, 1969, pp. 5–7).

The idea of running on the open roads also suited the Fascist ethos by bringing these advanced racing machines to the masses. This was not a new idea. Open road races were characteristic of motor racing's pioneer days, but they ended with the tragedies of the 1903 Paris-Madrid Race, after which open road races were banned in many countries (Villard, 1972, pp. 88–111; see Stephen Wagg's chapter in this book). Its revival in Fascist Italy is suggestive of a regime that was willing to risk the hazards in order to promote its call to "live dangerously." Both Renzo Castagneto and Augusto Turati used that slogan after 27 spectators were killed during the 1928 Italian Grand Prix. Responding to condemnations from the Vatican that motor sport exalted a "pagan" obsession with blood sports, Castagneto justified the deaths as the price paid for progress, and as an expression of Fascism's call, once again, to "live dangerously" (Castagneto, 1928). Castagneto's defence of motor racing brought together the two strands of Fascist ideology: the importance of automotive progress and the exaltation of death as a heroic sacrifice, even on the part of spectators.

It is also worth noting that the genesis of the MM came during an important moment in the consolidation of the Fascist dictatorship, and the Fascistization of sport. The meeting of the "four muskateers" in December 1926 came in the same month that the regime centralized all sporting activity under the aegis of the Italian Olympic Committee (CONI). This process included the Automobile Clubs of Italy. With this measure, a rigid hierarchy was imposed on sporting associations that mirrored the establishment of the dictatorship (Landoni, 2016, p. 80). The intersection of the Mille Miglia's founding, and the dismantling of Italy's liberal democracy by the Fascist movement was recalled in the tenth anniversary programme of the race in 1937. Looking back on the race's first edition, Michele Favia del Core, a well-known motor sport journalist who had also served as CONI's Secretary General from 1928 to 1930, noted the particular importance of the year 1927. That year, which served as the "baptismal font of the Mille Miglia," also witnessed the full "charism" of Fascism descend upon Italian sport (Favia del Core, 1937). The MM was thus born in the year that Fascism enjoyed full political power in Italy and the liberal democratic state was dead.

The Event

Fascism's "charism," according to Favia del Core, was evident in the "miracle" of its organization. Foreign observers agreed. In 1928, the famous British motor sport journalist W. F. Bradley praised the Italian government for its ability to run a race like the MM. "The secret of the whole thing was the Fascisti (sic) organization," he wrote in *Autocar* (Bradley, 1928). Inside Italy, commentators like Lando Ferretti, the head of the Italian Olympic Committee from 1925 to 1928, exulted in the military-like organization and martial discipline of the Italians (Ferretti, 1929). Praising the race's organization became a means of emphasizing the race's Fascist identity. The 1933 programme noted how by then, "Italians had grown accustomed to the achievements of the Fascist era" (Anon, 1933). That same year, the *Corriere della Sera* proclaimed that the MM was a "Fascist enterprise that represents a superior will whose most extraordinary prowess has become part of normal life" (De Martino, 1933).

The Fascist "style" permeated the race's organization. Renzo Castagneto, the man in charge of organizing and running the MM, adopted the regime's dictatorial style. In 1930, Castagneto wrote a piece for Lando Ferretti's journal, *Lo Sport Fascista*, outlining the logistics of running the race. Not surprisingly, Castagneto paid homage to the regime arguing that the race was only made possible by the "Fascist and sporting spirit of the Italian people" (Castagneto, 1930). Throughout the article, Castagneto demonstrates how this Fascist spirit was mirrored in the race's organization. Castagneto's method was highly centralized with orders radiating from Brescia to the various "nuclei" in the towns along the route. This required constant communication with "maximum and detailed instructions that are necessary to create a homogeneous work not susceptible to interruptions and sudden changes." Furthermore, with a race like the MM, it was necessary to "know how to command and how to impose oneself" (Castagneto, 1930, p. 29). Emphasizing the militaristic method of the race's organization, the article featured a photograph of a Fascist militiaman blowing a horn to warn spectators of an approaching car.

Castagneto's authoritarian style of stewarding was not only on display while the race was in progress, but also in the months and days leading up to the event. It was demonstrated clearly in his correspondence with officials in the provinces. As the race became more popular, Castagneto and the other organizers became more confident in imposing their will on local party leaders and *podestàs*, especially when route changes were made, requiring the race to pass through new locales. Although the route of the MM did not vary much from its distinctive "figure of eight" shape, there were some significant modifications made in 1934 and 1938. In both cases, Castagneto sent out a form letter to the officials notifying them that the race would pass through their town. After announcing that this "very noble city" had been chosen, Castagneto reminded them of the "ardent passion" Italians have for the event and that the success of the MM was based on the "very rigid application of the rules and the intransigent severity that emanates from the organizers" (Letter from Castagneto to the Officials of S. Pietro in Gu-Lisiera-Ospadoletto-Anconetta, 1934). In the correspondence, Castagneto reminded the officials of the "typically Fascist" character of the race and that this required full cooperation. In order to reinforce this point, Castagneto quoted the Fascist Party Secretary, Achille Starace, who wrote that Fascism, "the generator of energy, glorifier of the tenacity and virtues that assure victory" looked towards the MM with "trust and sympathy." The form letter concludes with an instruction to await circulars from Brescia with Castagneto signing off "Fascisticamente."

In his approach to organizing the race, Castagneto was not above ignoring or dismissing the concerns of party officials. This included overruling Pietro Parisio, the Extraordinary Commissioner of the Royal Automobile Club, appointed by Mussolini in 1932 (Azzini, 2011, p. 55). In a letter from the Venetian Automobile Club, Castagneto was informed that Parisio had visited the Ponte Littorio, the road bridge connecting the islands that constitute the historical centre of the city of Venice to the mainland part of the city where the MM was to pass in 1934, and that he advised that it not be used (Castagneto, 1934). We do not know exactly how Castagneto responded to the letter, but the bridge was used for the race.

The Route

While Castagneto's heavy-handed approach is easily justified by the logistics of running such an event as the MM, it also paralleled the authoritarian nature of the Fascist regime. Castagneto was not afraid to use his Fascist connections and borrow from Fascist terminology to "impose his will" on half the country. In the case of the Ponte Littorio, Castagneto perhaps knew that the inclusion of a recently completed Fascist project trumped any of Parisio's concerns. It also suggested the powerful part played by the route in providing a new reading of the Italian landscape. While some of the modifications to the route were made to enhance the speed of the race—thus exalting an important Fascist value—others were made to emphasize the regime's stamp on the historic landscape.

The route of the MM was arguably its most iconic feature. The Brescia-Rome-Brescia layout was determined in part by the best roads that existed in 1927, but also came to reflect the geographical imagination of the Fascist era. The "figure of eight" layout, immortalized in advertising posters and programme covers, traced the Roman consular roads like the Via Emilia, the Via Flaminia, Via Cassia, and the Via Aurelia. While the route was dictated largely by practical concerns, this nod to *Romanità* suited the Fascist regime's propaganda priorities. Meanwhile, the inclusion of Rome as the hinge point of the route was celebrated as the race's "moral destination" (Anon, 1933). Although Brescia was the home of the MM, the importance of Rome was underlined by the fact that the prize giving was conducted there, at the Headquarters of the Italian Olympic Committee and presided over by the Fascist Party Secretary. Furthermore, Mussolini donated a trophy to the car that completed the Brescia-Rome leg in the fastest time. Arriving first in Rome was thus given a special distinction.

While these proved important markers in "Fascistizing" the MM, the race's layout also provided an opportunity to provide a "Fascist reading" of the Italian landscape via the passage of high-speed racing cars. One of the most prolific examples of Fascism's impact on Italy came through its urban and architectural projects (Jones & Pilat, 2020). The route of the MM offered the regime an opportunity to highlight these projects and the new landmarks, such as highways, bridges, and urban transformations. Since the route remained largely unchanged, these Fascist sites became fixed landmarks of the event thus forging a close identification between the MM and Fascist architecture. This identification was emphasized in the race programmes, especially the "tourist" inserts that started appearing in 1933. Four projects in particular became part of the iconic route of the race: the Piazza della Vittoria in Brescia, the "renewed" Oltretorrente district of Parma, the Ponte Littorio in Venice, and the Firenze-Mare autostrada.

The 1933 programme's extensive "guida turistica" was an opportunity to not only promote Italy but also the public works of Fascism. For example, the city of Parma was singled out as the site of a major urban planning project that transformed the Oltretorrente neighbourhood. The guide noted how the regime had been responsible for eliminating one of the most "folkloristic" quarters of the city replacing it with a newer, and "healthier," urban plan. The guide referred to this process as a "miracle" that was greeted with enthusiasm by the inhabitants of the city (Anon, 1935c). The guide went so far as to point out that Mussolini had been responsible for this "miracle" and even pointed out the date of the telegram that the Fascist leader sent to the prefect of Parma to get the work done. Parroting the language Fascism used to describe its urban planning projects, the guide noted how the changes had brought a breath of fresh air and a modern look to the city. Not lost on the Italian reader was the fact that this neighbourhood had been known for the resistance it put up against Italo Balbo's Blackshirts in the so-called Battle of Parma in 1922 (Franzinelli, 2003, pp. 386–387).

The inclusion of Venice in 1934, as mentioned above, caused some controversy. The addition to the itinerary of the newly opened Ponte Littorio brought automobile traffic to the lagoon city for the first time. Designed by a Brescian architect, Eugenio Miozzi, and inaugurated in 1933, the race offered a prime opportunity to demonstrate how Fascism had injected modernity into the Lagoon City. The route called for the cars to cross the bridge twice as they headed to the check point in the Piazzale Roma where Miozzi had designed what was, at the time, Europe's largest parking garage. The checkpoint was located in front of the garage highlighting its modernist lines. Described by some as an "eye sore," the garage and the bridge gave Venice a distinctly modernist stamp signed by the regime (Plant, 2002, p. 283). The 1935 MM guide celebrated this contribution of Fascism to the Venetian landscape in this way: "The genius of the Duce wanted to connect Venice to *terra ferma*" bringing "new movement to the 'city of dreams'" (Anon, 1935c, p. 24). An illustration is included showing a racecar roaring across the bridge with a counterposing view of a group of gondolas.

The Fascist project that the MM made its own, however, was the Piazza della Vittoria in Brescia. Designed by Marcello Piacentini, Fascism's most prolific and representative architect, the massive square was part of Brescia's urban Master Plan. Inaugurated by Mussolini himself in 1932, the piazza, according to Paolo Nicoloso, became the trademark urban project of Italian Fascism (Nicoloso, 2011, p. 8). The massive complex, built in the heart of the city after extensive demolitions, included Italy's first "skyscraper," a 12-story edifice called the *Torrione*. It did not take long for the tower to become a totem of the MM after it appeared on the cover of the 1935 programme. It also figured prominently in photographs found in the programmes, especially after the Piazza became the site of the race's scrutineering area in 1932. The following year, the Automobile Club moved its headquarters to the square where it became Castagneto's race control. Another part of the square that featured in the iconography of the MM was Arturo Dazzi's 24-foot sculpture of a nude male figure representing the "Fascist Era," a name requested by Mussolini when he saw the statue in 1932 (Robecchi, 1998, pp. 177–178). In this way, the Piazza Vittoria, the "essence of the Fascist spirit," according to architectural historian Richard A. Etlin, and a model of Fascist urban planning, became closely associated with the MM (Etlin, 1991, p. 418). It also became an exemplar of the *Stile Littorio*, a blending of the classical and modern that became Fascism's signature style. The 1935 race programme pointed this out when it described the piazza as being in the "sign of the Littorio" with its classical allusions and "modernist lines" (Anon, 1935, p. 18).

The Mille Miglia's injection of Fascist modernity into the Italian landscape was reinforced by the inclusion of the Firenze-Mare autostrada in 1938. The modifications to the route that year represented the most significant changes since the race began in 1927. The Firenze-Mare autostrada was the latest in the regime's construction of motorways that went back to the early 1920s. It was also, according to Massimo Moraglio, the most useless trunk road and a "more fleeting enthusiasm than a real requirement for the Tuscan region" (Moraglio, 2017, p. 100). What the motorway did offer was a platform to test racing cars. In 1935, Tazio Nuvolari used it to set a new record time in the flying kilometre in the twin-engine Alfa Romeo *bimotore*. In the case of the MM, the entire 50 miles of the motorway was used, allowing the cars to travel flat out between Siena and Florence. The stretch of road did not offer much of a challenge for drivers, nor did it allow the race to exploit the Tuscan scenery. Rather, it was there to increase the overall speed of the race keeping it in line with Fascism's cult of speed and the promotion of the regime's public works.

Higher speeds and the breaking of records informed the MM concept, and with it dramatically new readings of the Italian landscape. The MM turned Italy into what John Bale has called a "landscape of speed" (Bale, 1994). The narrative of the race was shaped by the sectors between the cities. This breakdown made it easier to follow and recount the race but it also emphasized speed. Since the cars were sent off at three-minute intervals, this was the only way to determine the race positions, but it also allowed Italians to re-imagine the distances between the historic towns of Italy. A considerable section of the race programmes broke down the sector times of the previous years' race. A table in the 1935 programme showed how all of the sector times had improved since 1927, emphasizing the Mille Miglia's purpose as a landscape of speed. Not surprisingly, the most important sector of the Mille Miglia was the Brescia to Rome leg. In 1927, it took the leading car seven hours to complete this sector; by 1932, it took less than six hours. The average speed went up from 81 km/h to 114 km/h in 1933 (Anon, 1935c). Far from being a picturesque backdrop for the "world's most beautiful race," Italy was a test bed for the most advanced sports racing cars of the 1930s. The linking of cities also allowed the race to transcend the traditional *campanilismo* (local patriotism) found in other sports, like soccer. The pitting of one city against another in Italy's national game augmented rather than diminish the regionalism that Fascism aimed to suppress (Martin, 2004). The MM promised to unite the cities via speed.

The radical compression of space and time created by the MM transformed how the Italian landscape was experienced. The race programmes attempted to convey this through the accounts of motor sport writers and participants. It was a race where "every kilometer that passes changes the landscape and crowds, and the terrain changes along with the variables faced by the drivers" (Anon, 1933, p. 53). The MM served to shatter the tranquillity of the familiar and seemingly eternal Italian landscape. For an entire day, hundreds of towns and villages were subjected to violent demonstrations of modern speed. Motor sport by its nature is a violent sport, speed, noise, and occasional crashes transformed the otherwise sleepy towns of Italy and their centuries old cityscapes. Federico Fellini perhaps best captured this in his 1974 film, *Amarcord*, which has a scene dedicated to the Mille Miglia's passage through the town of Rimini in the 1930s. Fellini's film was based loosely on his childhood memories of growing up in Fascist Italy, and his MM scene captured what it might have been like for these cars to pass through the towns. The characters in the scene reel off the names of the top drivers, while the main character fantasizes about winning the race.

Fellini's memory of the MM is in line with how the "disruption" of the MM was experienced in the 1930s. Motor sport journalists like Aldo Farinelli often conveyed this in a manner that reinforced Fascist ideology. In the 1938 race programme, Farinelli declared the MM to be a "mythical and legendary" undertaking conducted at high speeds without respite, and that it emanated from "the people" who dreamed of one day conquering the road (Farinelli, 1938). The race's simple formula of "pure speed on the open roads" gave it a heroic nature, continued Farinelli, and this had the "power to form public opinion" and raise national consciousness. The people standing alongside the roadside "feel the voice of the fatherland, the voice of the earth," intoned Farinelli. Furthermore, the course unifies "fifty cities and half of Italy in a fraternal way." The "roar of one hundred automobiles," concluded Farinelli, brings the nation, together.

Implicit in Farinelli's description is the notion that the MM helped form the Fascist nation. This discourse was a common one in the race programme and in the newspapers that covered the race. This included the work of Emilio De Martino, who wrote for Italy's most important national newspaper, *Il Corriere della Sera*, and also wrote sporting novels, one of which centred on the MM (Martin, 2017). In the run-up to the 1933 event, De Martino proclaimed that the MM was a Fascist achievement. The participants did not make this race; rather the race made the participants (De Martino, 1933). That the MM contributed to the legends celebrated by the regime is clear with the rivalry between Nuvolari and Achille Varzi and the rise of Alfa Romeo. While Nuvolari and Varzi competed against each other in numerous races, their battles in the 1930, 1933, and 1934 MM races have contributed most to their legendary status (Marchesini, 2001). Meanwhile, the legend of Alfa Romeo and its preferential status in the Fascist universe was also tied in largely with the MM. While the victories of the P2 Grand Prix car in 1924 and 1925 brought the Alfa name to prominence, the Mille Miglia cemented its mythical status. The race programmes were filled with Alfa Romeo advertising extolling the car's victories in previous editions. While the marque struggled on the Grand Prix circuits in the 1930s in the face of German competition, the MM remained firmly in its hands up until 1938.

Conclusion

The high point of Fascism's identification with the MM came in 1936, when the race was used to promote alternative fuels in the face of the League of Nations' embargo on Italy following Mussolini's invasion of Abyssinia. On the cover of the race programme there is an illustration of a red racing car resembling an Alfa Romeo passing under a large X decorated with two fasces. The subtitle of the programme reads, "140th day of the Economic Siege" (Anon, 1936). Inside the programme, articles by Giovanni Canestrini and Corrado Filippini emphasized the importance of this tenth edition of the race and its response to Italy's current international situation. Filippini described in the detail the alternative fuels that some of the entrants would use and their crucial role in weaning Italy off petroleum-based products (Filippini, 1936). All of this in the cause of Fascism's policy of autarchy. As it turned out, those entrants were hopelessly slow with one of them finishing 28 hours after the race winner (Marchesini, 2001, p. 100).

This failure of the MM to provide for the needs of Fascist propaganda in 1936 should not obscure the very close identification between the values of the regime and the Brescian race. To be sure, there were limits to what the MM could provide for Fascist ideology. Azzini and others have suggested that Mussolini's interest in the race was inconsistent to the point of even expressing frustration at the demands placed upon the regime by the race (Azzini, 2011, p. 43). It is also true that Mussolini never attended the race in person; nor did he preside over the prize giving ceremony. And in 1938, Mussolini was very quick to pull the plug on the race after a car ploughed into a group of spectators killing several spectators including children. Clearly, the call for Italians to "live dangerously" no longer seemed to have the same appeal in 1938 as it had in the late 1920s.

The revival of the MM after the Second World War and its current form as a nostalgic event have blunted the event's Fascist legacy. The original organizers returned minus Mazzotti who had been killed during the war. Gone was the Fascist imagery and language. However, it is notable that the postwar revival had echoes of the Fascist past. Giovanni Canestrini's article in the 1948 programme, for example, borrowed from the Fascist anthem when he praised the "giovinezza"[2] of the MM (Canestrini, 1948). In the same programme, Emilio De Martino recalled the "heroic days" of the 1920s and Nuvolari's record-breaking 100 km/h average on the Brescia to Rome leg in 1928 (De Martino, 1948). Michele Suglia called the MM a "miracle of sport" and a "tonic" for a country that lacks faith in the future. Moreover, the revival of the great race would force Italy to "fix its roads" (Suglia, 1948).

The revival of the race and its repackaging as a sign of Italy's postwar resurrection echoed the original justifications of the race in 1927. Like that race, the new MM would act as a sign for Italy's future greatness and serve to build roads and the automotive industry. The tribute to the late Franco Mazzotti, meanwhile, would not have been out of place in the rhetoric of the 1920s. "From the ardent virility of Count Franco Mazzotti Biancinelli, and overcoming diffidence and obstacles," opened the tribute, "came the MM, which for the next thirteen years provided on the roads of Italy epic and unforgettable battles" (Anon, 1948). Without mentioning Fascism, this description alludes to the values of the Fascist Man and the MM as the event that will bring back the "heroic." The D'Annunzian and Futuristic imagery makes a return in the 1948 programme and this is not a surprise as it draws from the same pool of journalists. By 1951, the iconic "figure of eight" course also returned albeit in a clockwise motion.

By the mid-1950s, the MM had become once again a major sports car event attracting the top teams and drivers. Italy was enjoying its Economic Miracle and the race became a symbol of the new Italy of the First Republic. The race's Fascist DNA, meanwhile, faded into the background. The crashes and deaths continued, however, until a major accident in 1957, which took the life of several spectators, finally ended it. In the meantime, the race became part of Italy's sporting folklore and its historic revival in 1977 a site of nostalgia. Through all of these changes, what remains is the Fascist artefact. Unlike other major sporting events, the MM was a product of Fascist Italy. It demonstrates how Fascist cultural artefacts did not have to germinate within the Fascist state or the party, rather they could come from below, in this case the local automobile club in Brescia. Sport was hardly an innocent or apolitical activity. While historians have recognized that Fascism contributed to sport, such as making it into a mass sport (Dogliani, 2000) or providing the necessary political structures (Landoni, 2016), it is possible to see in events like the MM, a close identification with Fascist values. These values did not disappear with the regime.

Notes

1. A reference to a famous marble sculpture discovered on the Greek island of Samothrace in the nineteenth century and now on display in the Louvre in Paris.
2. Italian for "youth" and the title of the official hymn of the Italian National Fascist Party.

References

Anon. (1933). Mille Miglia: Diana di Progresso e di Giovinezza. In *Settima Coppa Milla Miglia, 8–9 Aprile 1933* (p. 31). R.A.C.I.

Anon. (1935a). I migliori tempi ottenuti sui vari tratti nelle otto dispute. In *IX Coppa Mille Miglia, 14 aprile 1935-XIII* (p. 76). R.A.C.I.

Anon. (1935b). Nona Edizione. In *Nona Mille Miglia.* Reale Automobile Club d'Italia.

Anon. (1935c). Panorama turistico della "Mille Miglia". In *IX Coppa Mille Miglia, 14 aprile 1935-XIII* (p. 18). R.A.C.I.

Anon. (1936). *Xa 1000 Miglia, 5 aprile 1936-XIV.* R.A.C.I.

Anon. (1948). In *XVa Mille Miglia. Coppa Franco Mazzotti.* Automobile Club di Brescia.

Anon. (n.d.). *Selkirk Pictures & Enterprises Ltd.* [Online]. Retrieved Febraury 28, 2021, from https://www.selkirk-movies.com/film-documentary-1/motor-sports/mille-miglia-the-spirit-of-a-legend/

Azzini, E. (2011). *Bolidi Rossi & Camicie Nere: Storia delle Competizioni Automobilistiche durante il Fascismo.* IBN.

Bale, J. (1994). *Landscapes of Modern Sport* (1st ed.). Leicester University Press.

Bataille, G., & Lovitt, C. R. (1979). The Psychological Structure of Fascism. *New German Critique, 16*(Winter), 64–87.

Bianda, R., Leone, G., Rossi, G., & Urso, A. (1983). *Atleti in Camicia Nera.* In *Lo sport nell'Italia di Mussolini.* Giovanni Volpe Editore.

Bolz, D. (2016). Sport and Fascism. In A. Bairner, J. Kelly, & J. Woo Lee (Eds.), *Routledge Handbook of Sport and Politics* (pp. 55–65). Taylor & Francis.

Bradley, W. (1928). Continental Notes and News. *Autocar*, January 6, p. 17.

Canestrini, G. (1948). Giovinezza della Mille Miglia. In *XVa Mille Miglia. Coppa Franco Mazzotti.* Automobile Club di Brescia.

Canestrini, G. (1967). *Mille Miglia.* Autombile Club d'Italia.

Castagneto, L. f. C. B. t. (1934). *Archivio della Mille Miglia.* s.n.

Castagneto, R. (1928). Difendo l'Autodromo. *Lo Sport Fascista*, September, pp. 55–59.

Castagneto, R. (1930). Come si organizza la 'Mille Miglia'. *Lo Sport Fascista, giugno, 3*(6), 28.

Chiurco, G. A. (1929). *Storia della Rivoluzione Fascista, vol. 2: 1920.* Vallecchi Editore.

De Martino, E. (1933). Le vetture piu veloci, i corridori piu forti lanciati sulle strade italiane. *Il Corriere della Sera*, April 8, p. 4.

De Martino, E. (1948). La gara sublime. In *XVa Mille Miglia. La Coppa Franco Mazzotti*. Automobile Club di Brescia.

Dogliani, P. (2000). Sport and Fascism. *Journal of Modern Italian Studies, 5*(3), 326–348.

Esposito, F. (2015). *Fascism, Aviation and Mythical Modernity*. Palgrave Macmillan UK.

Etlin, R. A. (1991). *Modernism in Italian Architecture, 1890–1940*. The MIT Press.

Farinelli, A. (1938). La corsa del popolo: perche? In *XII Mille Miglia, 3 aprile 1938-A. XVI*. R.A.C.I.

Favia del Core, M. (1937). Il Battesimo della Mille Miglia. *XI Mille Miglia*, April, pp. 21–23.

Ferretti, L. (1929). La Gara nei Commenti della Stampa. In *Coppa 1000 Miglia* (p. 28). R.A.C.I.

Filippini, C. (1936). La "1000 Miglia" dell'anno XIV e il suo apporto pratico alla causa dei succedanei nazionali. In *Xa 1000 Mille Miglia, 5 aprile 1936-XIV* (pp. 15–18). R.A.C.I.

Franzinelli, M. (2003). *Squadristi. Protagonisti e tecniche della violenza Fascista 1919–1922*. Mondadori.

Griffin, R. (2007). *Modernism and Fascism: The Sense of a Beginning under Mussolini and Hitler*. Palgrave Macmillan.

Jones, K. B., & Pilat, S. (2020). *The Routledge Companion to Italian Fascist Architecture: Reception and Legacy* (1st ed.). Routledge.

Landoni, E. (2016). *Gli Atleti del Duce: La Politica Sportiva del Fascismo 1919–1939*. Mimesis.

Letter from Castagneto to the Officials of S. Pietro in Gu-Lisiera-Ospadoletto-Anconetta, 1. (1934). *Archivio della Mille Miglia*. s.n.

Marchesini, D. (2001). *Cuori e motori. Storia della Mille Miglia, 1927–1957*. Il Mulino.

Marinetti, F. (1972). The Founding and Manifesto of Futurism. In R. Flint (Ed.), *Marinetti: Selected Writings* (pp. 39–44). Secker & Warburg.

Martin, S. (2004). *Football and Fascism: The National Game under Mussolini*. Berg.

Martin, S. (2017). A "Boys Own" Boy Zone: The Making of Fascist Men in Emilio De Martino's Children's Sporting Novels. *Literature & History, 26*(1), 74–104.

Mille Miglia: Spirit of a Legend. (2007). [Film] Directed by Philip Selkirk. s.l.: s.n.

Miller, P. (1988). *Conte Maggi's Mille Miglia*. St. Martin's Press.

Moraglio, M. (2017). *Driving Modernity: Technology, Experts, Politics, and Fascist Motorways, 1922–1943*. Berghahn.

Nicholson, T. R. (1969). *Sports Cars 1928–1939*. Blandford Press.

Nicoloso, P. (2011). *Mussolini architetto* (2nd ed.). Einaudi.

Plant, M. (2002). *Venice: Fragile City, 1797–1997*. Yale University Press.

Robecchi, F. (1998). *Brescia Littoria. Una citta modello dell'urbanistica fascista*. La Compagnia della Stampa.

Suglia, M. (1948). Miracolo dello Sport. La Mille Miglia e un tonico per molti spiriti e per molte strade. In *XVe Mille Miglia. Coppa Franco Mazzotti*. Automobile Club d'Italia.

Villard, H. S. (1972). *The Great Road Races 1894–1914*. Arthur Barker Limited.

Vargas, Perón and Motor Sport: A Comparative Study on South American Populism

Mauricio Drumond and Victor Melo

On 3 October, 1934, the Brazilian government, under the constitutional rule of Getúlio Vargas, staged its second international Grand Prix in Rio de Janeiro, the country's capital at the time. The date marked the anniversary of the movement that had led Vargas to power in 1930, but the return to democracy with the new constitution in July meant there would be no celebration of the movement that had installed a dictatorship for three years and that had led to a civil war in 1932. Without an official celebration, the Rio de Janeiro Grand Prix, known as the Gavea Circuit, was the next best thing. Accompanied by the Argentine ambassador and other officials, the Brazilian president attended the race and seems to have been deeply impacted by the victory of a Brazilian driver, Irineu Correa, as shown by his personal journal:

> October 3, anniversary of the Revolution, there was no festivity. I watched it bitterly. On this day, we only had the auto race. It was an exciting spectacle: a large crowd, a hard track, a dangerous race, some accidents and

M. Drumond • V. Melo (✉)
Federal University, Rio de Janeiro, Brazil

D. Sturm et al. (eds.), *The History and Politics of Motor Racing*, Global Culture and Sport Series, https://doi.org/10.1007/978-3-031-22825-4_7

> many who stopped before the end. In the end a Brazilian won. How strong is the national feeling! [...] As I struggled to maintain decorum, I was deeply touched, afraid tears would flow if a stranger had won. And I was analysing myself, taken by that strange feeling that I tried to suppress. (Vargas, 1995, p. 331)

Almost two decades later, on 9 March 1952, another populist leader in South America, Juan Domingo Perón, attended a motor race. Accompanied by his wife, Eva Perón, the general inaugurated the Buenos Aires racetrack, named *Autódromo 17 de Octubre*[1]. Just like Vargas, who aspired to celebrate the date that marked the beginning of his rise to power with the motor race, the Argentine president associated the racetrack with the date that symbolized the origin of the Peronist movement. Three races were held on that day, with an estimated attendance of over 100,000 spectators. An opening contest of national car makers started the day, followed by a 500cc motorcycle Grand Prix and a final race with the most prominent drivers, for the Perón Cup. After winning the main race of the day, Juan Manuel Fangio, the Formula 1 world champion, stated that the racetrack was "the best motorway ever built" and that it was "very safe and attractive to racing" (Lupo, 2004, p. 310). In the following year, the circuit was integrated into the Fédération Internationale de l'Automobile's (FIA) Formula One World Championship of Drivers, as the first race of the year.

The staging of international motor races in Brazil and Argentina during the governments of two of their most iconic and notorious presidents is not a mere coincidence. Both Vargas and Perón, to different extents, established close relationships to sports, and motor racing had a special part to play, as seen in the passages above.[2] In order to better understand this connection to motor racing, we must first look at the significance of sports to both populist regimes.

Populism, Sports and Motor Racing

Contiguous in time and space, the first governments of Getúlio Vargas, in Brazil, and Juan Perón, in Argentina, shared many similarities. Empowered at first by a coup d'état known in Brazilian historiography as the "1930 Revolution", Vargas led the country for 15 uninterrupted years. Acting at first as a dictator in the Provisional Government until 1934, he was voted president in indirect elections held by Congress in that same year and staged a self-coup in 1937, beginning a new period of authoritarian rule that ended with a military coup in 1945. Vargas would return for a second administration through popular voting in 1950, and acted as president in a constitutional state until committing suicide in August 1954, on the verge of a new military coup.

Juan Domingo Perón also rose to government after a military coup, in 1943, as a member of the leading military group, called *Grupo de Oficiales Unidos*. Even though he was not officially in charge, his influence over the government was increasingly significant, as was his popularity among the Argentinian people. After a great display of support in a massive labour demonstration held at *Plaza de Mayo* on 17 October 1945, a date that was afterwards called *Día de la Lealtad* (Loyalty Day), Perón emerged as a candidate for the national elections that would be held in February 1946. He was then elected for two consecutive mandates (1946–1952/1953–1955), governing under the rule of law, but maintaining many authoritarian traits.[3] Just like Vargas, his first government ended with a military coup, staged in 1955. He would also return to power though general elections in 1973 to form a second government, remaining in power until his death the following year.

More than military coups leading them into and out of the government, Vargas and Perón coincided in forging a political culture usually referred to as populism. Commonly seen as "paradigmatic examples of populist leaders" (Kaltwasser et al., 2017, p. 20), they brought the urban masses into politics and supported their increased political participation, but restricted political expression if it was not in their favour. Writing about populism in Latin America, Carlos de La Torre offers the following definition of the phenomenon:

> I understand populism as a Manichaean discourse that divides politics and society as the struggle between two irreconcilable and antagonistic camps: the people and the oligarchy or the power block. (...) Populism produces strong popular identities and is a strategy of top-down mobilization that clashes with the autonomous demands of social movement organizations. However, populist glorification of common people and their attacks on

> elites could open spaces for common people to press for their agendas. The tension between top-down mobilization and autonomous mobilization from below is characteristic of populist episodes. (De la Torre, 2017, p. 251-252)

Analysing this definition, it is possible to see the importance of sports in a populist regime and how agents in the sports field embraced politics and put forward their own agenda. Claiming to be the true representatives of the people, populist leaders would seek association with elements with strong popular identification, and sports was undoubtedly an important symbol of national identity, as stated by Vargas in his abovementioned diary entry. Sporting events already promoted the mobilization of crowds and attracted the attention of the urban masses, especially in popular sports such as football.

Motor racing was also an important tool for the mobilization of identities and crowds. Vargas's impressions after Irineu Correia's victory in the Gavea Circuit in 1934 are a clear sign of the symbolic power of the sport. The victory of a national citizen, when competing with qualified outsiders, such as Europeans, was often associated with an alleged natural quality that marked the national type, which resonated with the populist glorification of the common people. The inauguration of the Argentine racetrack in 1952 is also a demonstration of the sport's capacity for mobilizing crowds. Over 100,000 people flocked to the new circuit, celebrating a symbol of Perón's New Argentina.

It is important to stress that this association between populist leaders and sports should not be seen solely as a top-down initiative, but as a two-way street. The sporting community, mainly the ruling elite in each national sport federation, would also seize the opportunity to press for their own agendas. Grand football stadiums were built both in Brazil and Argentina, the governments sponsored many athletes and national delegations, and sports apparel reached regions of the countries where it was previously hard to find. The staging of international races and building of international-class circuits were certainly major parts of the motor racing agenda that was carried out by the government.

If sports were useful for the government, the government was also useful for sports. And when those interests coincided, there were major impacts on the material conditions of sports such as motor racing, for example new cars, renovated tracks, cheaper car parts and racing apparel, and state sponsorship for national events and drivers. This kind of investment was usually met by improvement in performances and national victories. The more important and popular a sport was, the more it could ask and would receive. Far from being just another sport, motor racing played a unique role among other sports.

The ideal of modernity was a strong feature of populist discourse under both Vargas and Perón. These leaders emerged amidst processes of urbanization and industrialization. They fought against electoral fraud and expanded the franchise (De la Torre, 2017, p. 252). They aimed at achieving standards of the so-called modern nations and were portrayed as efficient managers, who knew how to run the country and would lead it to its rightful place in the world order. They were building new countries, the self-proclaimed New State, in Brazil, and New Argentina respectively. Under their rule, a new youthful generation would achieve their full potential. Under the rule of Vargas and Perón, Brazil and Argentina would become modern nations in Latin America.

Due to its relevance of displaying an image of modernity in Brazil and Argentina, motor racing had a distinctive connotation among sports. Fast cars and smooth roads were symbols of modernity, and success in the sport could be portrayed as evidence of being a modern nation.

The Early Days of Motor Racing in Brazil and Argentina

However important Vargas and Perón were for their respective countries' motor racing, there was already a vibrant community dedicated to the sport before their rise to power, a community strong enough to put forward their agenda when negotiating support from the government.

In Brazil, the first official motor race took place in 1908, in the state of São Paulo, a year after the creation of the Brazilian Automobile Club. The sport grew in the following years, restrained by the high costs of imported automobiles and their parts. Nevertheless, races grew in number and diversity, and eventually involved drivers from neighbouring countries, mainly Argentina and Uruguay (Melo, 2011).

The second half of the 1920s saw significant increments in the sport. The first important names in Brazilian motor racing appeared then, such as Irineu Correa and Primo Fioresi, and regional and national political leaders favoured the sport (Melo, 2011). Washington Luís, governor of the state of São Paulo from 1920 to 1924 and President of Brazil from 1926 to 1930, was a strong supporter of the motor industry. His motto was "governing is opening roads" and he had over 1300 kilometres of new roads built in the country during his presidency. In 1928, he built the first paved road in the country, inaugurated the same year, connecting the cities of Rio de Janeiro and Petropolis.

Washington Luís was toppled by the Revolutionaries of 1930, a few weeks before the end of his presidency. His contributions to motor racing, however, endured throughout the new regime. The first important race held during Vargas's government was staged on the very road Luís had inaugurated a few years earlier. In 1932, a hill climb race known as "The Mountain Slope" took place on the Rio-Petropolis road, with the participation of German driver Hans Stuck, one of the most prestigious drivers at the time, who was famous for his hill climbing racing. Stuck had been invited by the Brazilian driver Manuel de Teffé, who had raced in Europe during the 1920s and won the race on two occasions, in 1937 and 1943. The race was also organized in 1933, 1944, 1945 and 1946, with the participation of Brazilian drivers and manufacturers (most assembled their own automobiles and adapted many imported parts from different makers).

In Argentina, motor racing had developed somewhat earlier than in Brazil. The Automobile Club of Argentina was created in 1904 and the first official race was held in December 1906, in Buenos Aires. The *Grand Premio de la Argentina* had its first edition in 1910, from the capital Buenos Aires, on the coast, to Cordoba, in central Argentina, passing through Rosario. According to Eduardo Archetti (2001), the first cars reached Rosario after almost ten hours, and arrived in Cordoba only four days later. Drivers, machines and mechanics were put under extreme conditions.

The cross-country race was staged until 1932 and shows an important difference between motor racing in Brazil and Argentina. If in Brazil the races and drivers were centralized in the cities of Rio de Janeiro and São Paulo (the country's capital and main economic city, respectively), the Argentine races explored the country and were tools for the reinforcement of the connections of the symbolic identities and touristic routes that connected the national territory. From 1933 to 1943, the *Grand Premio* organized by the Automobile Club of Argentina had a different route each year and was seen as a way to "enhance knowledge of the country and foment tourism" (Piglia, 2014).

Meanwhile, a new velocity race was established in 1937, and quickly grew in popularity in Argentina. After a couple of accidents and casualties in 1933 and 1934, the province of Buenos Aires had outlawed street racing in the region. A new set of regulations then established a new form of racing, known as *Turismo Carretera* (touring-car races). Only "touring cars" (regular cars) were allowed in the race, and modifications were severely limited. Their maximum speed was limited to 120 km/h (about 74.5 mph) and they needed to follow the city traffic regulations. *Turismo Carretera* races were organized in many different shapes and sizes, and the most famous Argentine drivers, such as Juan Manuel Fangio, got their start driving the "touring cars" in these races.

In 1935, an international race was established, between Buenos Aires and Santiago. The race, nearly 5000 kilometers long, had a speed limit, and the focus of the race was on endurance, rather than velocity. The route was extended to 6865 kilometres in 1936 (Archetti, 2001, p. 74) and a new international race was staged in 1940, from Buenos Aires to La Paz and Lima, the capitals of Bolivia and Peru respectively, and then back to Buenos Aires. The Pan-American initiative of integration through motor racing even had plans for a Buenos Aires-New York race to take place in 1942, but after 1940, the most significant races were interrupted due to World War II. They would only return in 1947, under the government of Juan Domingo Perón.

Getúlio Vargas, the Gavea Circuit and Motor Racing in Brazil

The process of unifying South America through motor racing, led by Argentina, did not include Brazil. During the 1930s, while the Automobile Club of Argentina was organizing touring-car races that would eventually promote the country at the regional level, Brazilian authorities saw motor racing as an opportunity to present the country on the international stage as a modern nation capable of producing fast cars, daring drivers and exciting races.

The first initiatives were taken at the beginning of the first Vargas administration. The participation of the leading German driver Hans Stuck in the Mountain Slope race was the first attempt at the internationalization of Brazilian motor racing. A bolder initiative was staged in the next year. In 1933, the Brazilian government and the Brazilian Automobile Club promoted the first edition of the Rio de Janeiro Grand Prix, known as the Gavea Circuit, with the recognition of the Association Internationale des Automobile Clubs Reconnus, the future FIA.

The early Grand Prix did not attract much international interest and counted mainly with Brazilians and a few other South American drivers. Attracting some of the most notorious European drivers would take some time. Coming to Brazil with all the equipment and personnel needed to compete in a motor race was difficult, expensive and time consuming.

If in 1933 only a few Argentines and Uruguayans joined Brazilian drivers, in 1934 newspapers reported 15 Argentines and seven Italians out of the 44 competitors (Jornal do Brasil, 3 Oct. 1934, p. 23), but most Italians were in fact Brazilians of Italian ancestry who would represent the European nation in the absence of renowned drivers. In 1935, some Portuguese drivers came to compete in Rio de Janeiro, but the winner was Ricardo Caru, an Argentine. However, the race was marked by the accident that killed Irineu Corrêa, the Brazilian driver who had won in the previous year.

It was only in 1936 that top European drivers crossed the Atlantic in order to compete in Rio de Janeiro: from Italy, Carlo Pintacuda and Atilio Marinoni, driving Alfa Romeos; and from France, the great star was Helle Nice (or Mariette Helene Delangle), who was famous for her public displays of practices that Brazilian society was reluctant to accept. The Frenchwoman was a former dancer and actress who dared to challenge men driving fast and powerful machines. She smoked in public and wore two-piece swimsuits (Melo, 2011). In spite of the presence of famous European racers, however, Vitorio Coppoli, from Argentina, won the race.

The 1937 race also counted with the return of Stuck, driving for Auto Union (the present-day Audi). The dispute between Italians and Germans in European motor racing would be re-enacted in Brazilian lanes. It is important to emphasize that the earlier Italian, and then German, participation in international races in the 1930s was directly related to the Mussolini and Hitler regimes' stances on international propaganda through sport.[4] The Italians took the trophy with the victory of Carlo Pintacuda, who would also win in the following year. With the increasing participation of overseas teams, Brazilian drivers were no longer reaching top positions and so the Brazilian government created a new money prize, for the best national driver in the race under the fourth position (there was already a money prize given to the top four positions).

In 1938, fewer Europeans took part in the race, possibly a sign of the turbulent times Europe was about to face. Pintacuda won for the second time, but he would not have the chance to try it again in the following year. The race did not take place in 1939 and 1940 due to the war in Europe and difficulties in importing fuel and car parts to Brazil. A new version of the race, the "National Gavea Circuit", with Brazilian drivers only, continued the tradition for the following years. The Brazilian government continued to finance the event. Lourival Fontes, the head of propaganda during the Vargas administration, defended the event, stating it was a "sport tradition" in the country and it should be protected during hard times, such as the country was facing.

The Gavea Circuit was the strongest symbol of the relationship between motor racing and the government in Brazil. As Vargas's administration sought new forms of representation and an improved reputation on the international stage, motor racing, among other sports, was a relevant tool used to achieve this goal. At the same time, agents in the motor racing field used this opportunity for their own benefit. The Gavea Circuit brought awareness to the sport, attracted the press and new sponsors, distributed money prizes, and created new opportunities for the establishment of other circuits and races. In 1936, with the arrival of European drivers in Rio de Janeiro, a new race was organized in São Paulo, with an invitation extended to the most notable drivers who had competed in Rio. As they would already be in Brazil, they accepted the invitation and took part in the first São Paulo Grand Prix, which eventually led to the creation of the famous Interlagos Circuit in 1940, once more with financial aid from Vargas's government. This venue, however, would only gain proper attention as the Brazilian leading motor racing arena after the end of the Gavea Circuit, in 1954. Coincidentally or not, this was the same year Vargas took his life on the verge of a coup that would once again remove him from office.

The First Stages of Motor Racing in Peronist Argentina

The same process can be seen in Perón's first administration in Argentina. When he rose to the presidency in 1946, international motor racing initiatives had come to a halt due to World War II. But this scenario would soon change, with the support of the new government. In the following year, international races were resumed with the new version of the International Grand Prix, *Turismo Carretera*, then limited to Argentina and Chile.

The success of the race led to more daring initiatives in 1948, with the creation of the longest and most dangerous version of the *Gran Premio de la América del Sur del Turismo Carretera*, known as the Buenos Aires-Caracas. Spread over 9000 miles divided into two sections and 19 stages, and going through half the countries in South America (Argentina, Bolivia, Peru, Ecuador, Colombia and Venezuela), the race is still remembered for its dangerous roads, especially through the Andes, and its many accidents, such as Fangio's crash in Peru that put him in the hospital and killed his friend and co-pilot Domingo Marimón.

The Argentinian government invested heavily in the prizes in order to motivate drivers to pursue such a dangerous and expensive endeavour. There was a significant cash prize for victory in each section or stage of the race, and the overall winner would receive 10,000 pesos. Moreover, the Eva Perón Foundation, a government-linked foundation heavily associated with sports[5], would award solid gold plaques to the two best Argentines in the race (Donaldson, 2012).

Alongside the return of international racing in *Turismo Carretera*, the Peronist administration also invested in Grand Prix motor racing, held at first in the streets of Buenos Aires. After two Formula Libre initiatives in 1936 and 1941, the Automobile Club of Argentina would seize the moment to gather governmental support for new competitions in the most prominent category in motor racing, with the best drivers in the world. The first two initiatives were composed mainly of Argentinian drivers, with the participation of several Brazilians, including Manuel de Teffé, in 1936, and Chico Landi, in 1941.

In a way, the new initiative was somewhat like the Gavea Circuit in Rio de Janeiro. Public streets were closed in order to receive famous drivers from Europe, invited to promote the image of the new regime in the international arena. Out of the 13 drivers, six were foreigners: four Italians, including the two-time winner in the Gavea Circuit, Carlo Pintacuda, and the famous Achille Varzi, one Frenchman and Chico Landi, representing Brazil. Among the Argentines, Óscar Gálvez and his brother Juan were the most prominent drivers, but neither achieved good results. Two races were held in 1947, and the role of the government is apparent in the very names of the races. On 9 February, the I Buenos Aires Grand Prix was named *I Gran Premio del General Juan Perón*. One week later, the II Buenos Aires Grand Prix was held, entitled *I Gran Premio de Eva Duarte Perón*.

Naming the races after Perón and Evita was a clever, but not unusual, tool in convincing local authorities to support the sporting competitions. However, this does not mean that it was the real motive that led the government to invest in the motor races. Like Vargas before him, in Brazil, Perón's government pursued the creation of a new image for the country on the international stage. Sports played a major role in this process, and motor racing would be a safe bet for government investment. Argentina already had a reputation for having great drivers and dominated most major continental motor racing competitions in *Turismo Carretera*. And as in the Brazilian case, the national motor racing community used this opportunity to push their own agenda. In the process, some flattering moves were common, like naming the Buenos Aires Grands Prix after Perón and Evita, facilitating government support for the motor racing project.

The Buenos Aires Grands Prix were held once again in 1948. This time, the race had more foreigners than Argentinian drivers. Among the six Italians and two Frenchmen who came from Europe, the most notorious were Achille Varzi, who would later inspire the name of the Argentinian racing team; Nino Farina, who would become the first Formula 1 champion two years later; Luigi Villoresi, who won both races in 1947; and Jean-Pierre Wimille, one of the most successful drivers at the time. Six Argentines, a Brazilian and a Uruguayan were the representatives of South America, with Juan Manuel Fangio joining Óscar Gálvez and Chico Landi. Luigi Villoresi won both races once again with his Maserati, and Óscar Gálvez was the runner-up in the *II Gran Premio de Eva Duarte Perón*. The circuit, however, was not the same one as in 1947, as it had moved to the Palermo district of the city. The Palermo street circuit would remain the host of the Buenos Aires Grands Prix in the following years.

The third incarnations of the General Juan Perón and Eva Duarte Perón Grands Prix were held on 30 January and 6 February 1949. The first race of the year had two more countries represented on the lineup: Reg Parnell representing England and B. Bira (Prince Birabongse Bhanudej Bhanubandh, a member of the Thai royal family), representing Thailand. But the race was marked by two fatal accidents. French driver Jean-Pierre Wimille died soon after crashing in his first lap during practice. According to reports, the driver lost control after avoiding a spectator who was crossing the track. The other casualty came during the race itself, when Argentine driver Pablo Pessatti died after crashing his Alfa Romeo. The III Eva Duarte Perón Grand Prix (also known as Premio Jean-Pierre Wimille in honour of the late driver), held one week later, saw the first Argentinian victory. Only ten drivers started the race, and Óscar

Gálvez and Fangio achieved the top positions after all European drivers had left the race due to mechanical problems or minor crashes.

It is important to note that the Argentinian races were part of a growing international motor racing appeal, with several Grands Prix organized throughout the world. Although there was no organized world championship at the time, the races were all recognized by the Fédération Internationale de l'Automobile (FIA). Nevertheless, the Peronist government had already come up with a new strategy for increased success in motor racing: sponsoring an Argentinian team to compete abroad. It was time to display the New Argentina on the European racetracks.

The team was managed by Automovil Club de Argentina (ACA) and had Juan Manuel Fangio and Benedicto Campos as drivers. It was called Equipo Achille Varzi, in honour of the late Italian driver whose family would provide its European headquarters. Amadeo Bignami, an experienced Italian mechanic who had worked with Varzi, would double as team manager and head mechanic. The government had provided each driver with two cars: a Maserati 4CLT for major races and a Simca-Gordini 1430cc for smaller engine races. A few months later, a Ferrari Tipo 166 F2 was also purchased for the team with governmental support (Donaldson, 2012).

The cars were painted blue and yellow, representing the country's colours, and competed in different racing categories in the following months. Starting in minor races, Fangio and the Equipo Achille Varzi had instant success. Fangio achieved six victories in the ten races contested in Italy and France, including his debut race on the famous Monza circuit, driving his Ferrari for the first time. Fangio's success on European tracks was not unnoticed by the Argentine people. When the team returned to Buenos Aires in August, Fangio received the welcoming of a national hero.

A few months later, the fourth and last international General Juan Perón and Eva Duarte Perón Grands Prix were held, in December 1949 and January 1950. With representatives from Italy, France, England, Switzerland, Monaco, Thailand, Argentina and Uruguay, they were the largest versions up to that year. Italians Luigi Villoresi and Alberto Ascari were back to the top, but Fangio continued to show prominence, achieving second place in the first race and the pole position in the second. But victory in the Argentinian main motor sport event would still have to wait.

In sponsoring the Argentine team, Perón's administration took a step further in his relationship with motor racing. Vargas, however, did not go that far, or not openly at least. During his authoritarian rule in the 1930s and 1940s, international motor racing was not as organized as it was after the war. The growing internationalization of the sport would only achieve its height by the time Vargas had been ousted and was already preparing his return by direct elections. In a democratic regime where he was always under suspicion by the Congress, Vargas would not be able to support a Brazilian national team as openly as Perón did. Nevertheless, it is believed that Vargas did support Chico Landi to buy the Ferrari which he drove for several seasons in Europe, an allegation that Landi himself always denied (Melo, 2011). Fangio, on the other hand, was quoted as saying: "When I left for Europe, even if I was happy and pleased with myself, I couldn't forget that the move put me under obligation to the government for backing me, and to the people who supported me" (cited in Donaldson, 2012, p. 81). And that was just the beginning.

Reaching for the Top: Argentina's Move Towards the Motor Racing Elite

In 1950, the international federation decided to create an international championship, the FIA Formula One World Championship of Drivers. It was in this scenario that the Buenos Aires international Grands Prix in the Palermo street circuit were abandoned. A few years later, the Peronist government would build their own world class circuit, which was integrated into the Formula 1 season. Argentina was rapidly moving towards admission to the motor racing elite.

For the first world championship, Fangio was signed by Alfa Romeo and did not race for Equipo Achille Varzi in the new tournament, where he eventually achieved second place in 1950 and won the title in 1951. Fangio would still drive for the ACA team in competitions where the Alfa Romeo squad did not compete, and this was especially true in Argentina.

The Argentinian team would not run in the F1 world championship in 1951. However, the Argentine government had a new approach planned to promote their motor sport prominence—the construction of a national Formula 1 circuit.

There are different versions to the origin of the circuit but these usually revolve around a similar theme. When returning to Argentina from their 1950 Formula 1 tour, the Argentine drivers Froilán Gonzáles, Benedicto Campos, who had run for Equipo Achille Varzi, and Juan Manuel Fangio were invited to meet president Perón, to talk about their experience in the competition and to publicize Perón's image accompanied by the famous drivers. During this meeting, Perón asked the drivers what could be done to improve motor racing even further in the country. Fangio was the one who asked for the construction of a national speedway, to which Perón would have replied positively (Lupo, 2004, p. 308). Mariano Gruschetsky (2019) mentions other possible versions, including an initiative of a wider interest group associated with motor sports, and a meeting with Perón after the deaths of Wimille and Pesatti in the 1949 Buenos Aires Grand Prix.

Despite the different versions, it is important to understand that a project as large as the construction of an international standard circuit is most likely the result of a well-planned initiative, rather than a decision made on a whim. The idea was probably pressed by agents of the motor racing field, perhaps by ACA or by the drivers themselves, hoping to get one more benefit from a willing government. And this was almost certainly followed by thorough studies conducted by government officials. Regardless, the construction was announced by the Buenos Aires municipality in January 1951 (Lupo, 2004, p. 308), with great enthusiasm. The new motor racing arena would be completed about 15 months later and would flatter Perón and his political movement in its name, *17 de Octubre*.

The inauguration of the circuit, on 9 March 1952, was a major political statement. Perón and Evita attended the event, with over 100,000 spectators. Three races made up the opening celebration of the venue. The main race of the day was a Formula Libre race for the *VI Gran Premio del General Juan Perón*, which Fangio won with his Ferrari Tipo 166C. He would then repeat the feat one week later, in the *VI Gran Premio Maria Eva Duarte de Perón*.

The motor race was integrated into the Formula 1 season in the following year. It was the first race of the year, held on 18 January, and was won by reigning world Champion Alberto Ascari, driving for Ferrari. However, the Italian victory was eclipsed by an accident that killed nine and injured over 40 spectators. The race had been heavily advertised by the press and it is estimated that over 400,000 people attended the event. The large crowd, many of whom had entered the venue through holes in or by going over the high wire fences that surrounded the speedway, not only occupied the stands, but were also standing on the sidelines of the racetrack. Donaldson (2012) states that at first the drivers refused to start the race, but after being pressured by the organizers and even by Perón himself, they agreed to do so. On lap 32, Farina lost control of his Ferrari and plunged into the crowd. Danger was still lurking around the Argentinian Grands Prix.

The 1954 season was much better for the Argentinian circuit and drivers. The *Gran Premio de la República Argentina* was once again the opening Grand Prix of the season, and Fangio finally won his home race. He would later achieve his second world title, being second in the tournament to his countryman Froilán González.

Fangio would win the Argentina Grand Prix and the world championship title four years in a row, an impressive feat. However, Perón would not be able to use all these victories for political gain. The president was ousted from power by a military coup d'état on 16 September 1955. Nevertheless, his actions in support of motor racing had led Argentina from being a regional power, organizing *Turismo Carretera* races among its neighbouring countries, to a major country in the motor racing elite. Fangio's success in international speedways and the success of the *17 de Octubre* circuit (called only *Autódromo Municipal*, after the military coup) were long-lasting legacies of his administration's support for motor racing.

Brazil would not have a circuit in the Formula 1 season until the 1970s. The Interlagos circuit, in São Paulo, remained the only major autodrome in Brazil until 1966, when Rio de Janeiro's circuit was inaugurated (Elias et al., 2019). Brazil was once again ruled by an authoritarian regime, under a military government. The dispute between Brazil's two main racing centres, Rio de Janeiro and São Paulo, led the Interlagos circuit to undergo major renovations. A few years later, in 1973, the speedway was inserted in the Formula 1 season. But the government was very different to that of Getúlio Vargas. Nevertheless, the support for major international motor racing competitions continued. The same is true for Argentina, where even after the self-proclaimed Liberating Revolution (*Revolución Libertadora*) that ousted Perón from power in 1955, support for motor racing persisted and the Formula 1 fixture was maintained without interruption until 1960. The populist regimes of Vargas and Perón were not the only ones that invested in the sport and supported motor racing. But they were definitely the ones that most aided the sport in reaching new heights.

Approaching a Finish Line

When comparing Vargas's and Perón's approaches to motor racing, it is imperative to observe and interpret not only the similarities and differences in both cases, but also how they relate to the particularities of each time and place.

When Vargas rose to power in 1930, international elite motor racing was still far from developed in South America. Through the government's support, with the creation and promotion of the Gavea Circuit, Brazil ushered in a new stage in South American motor racing, welcoming some of the most prominent drivers and fastest cars in the sport. Brazilian motor racing enthusiasts, organized around the Brazilian Automobile Club, worked alongside a willing government in order to put Brazil on the international motor racing map.

This movement was only possible due to the international conditions of the period. European drivers crossed the Atlantic to face new challenges and earn more prizes usually with the support of their own governments. They competed on new circuits and profited with the additional fixtures, in a sport that was still growing in popularity on a global scale. The impulse of the fascist Italian regime to use sports for the purposes of international propaganda, associated with the success of Italian constructors in the sport, was also essential at the beginning of the process. Soon, Germany's Silver Arrows joined the Italians in the effort of promoting their flag through motor racing achievements.

The changes to motor racing's international organization that took place in the years following World War II also meant a shift in the way South American populist governments would relate to the sport. The post-war sporting community resumed the staging of international Grands Prix in different parts of the world. In Brazil, Vargas had already been ousted from power, but the government continued supporting the Gavea Grand prix, which was resumed as part of the 1946 season. Argentina, still in the early years of the Perón administration, followed suit in 1947.

It is important then to consider the differences between the two countries and their relations to motor sport to understand the final picture. Given his international success, Fangio achieved the status of national hero, whereas the Brazilian driver Chico Landi, although the most popular driver in Brazilian motor racing, was never quite as popular. This was both a cause and a consequence of the support each driver had received from the national government. Perón invested more heavily than Vargas in sports as a whole as a means of propaganda (Drumond, 2009), and motor racing popularity in Argentina, along with Fangio's success in *Turismo Carretera*, paved the way for governmental investment that eventually helped him become a national icon. Moreover, his unparalleled status in Argentinean sports contributed to further national investment in motor racing as a whole in the country.

Landi was also a renowned sportsman in Brazil. However, he was never quite as popular as Brazilian footballers, the greatest sporting heroes in a country that was less diverse in sports. It was only in the 1970s and 1980s, when the country was going through another period of dictatorial rule, that Brazilian drivers achieved better results and received greater recognition by the population. Emerson Fittipaldi was two-time World Champion in Formula 1, in 1972 and 1974. Furthermore, he was part of the group that constituted a Brazilian team in the category, much like the Argentinean Equipo Achille Varzi, but with poorer results. Nélson Piquet was three-time Formula 1 World Champion, in 1981, 1983 and 1987, when Brazil was undergoing a process of re-democratization. But the Brazilian driver who could be better compared to Fangio in terms of popularity was definitely Ayrton Senna, also three-time champion in Formula 1, in 1988, 1990 and 1991. Senna is the most popular driver in Brazilian motor racing history, and his tragic death, which took place at the 1994 San Marino Grand Prix, caused great national commotion.

In Argentina, Fangio was a star of the first magnitude, recognized as responsible for raising the country's name to the pinnacle of glory. He was represented as an example of the nation's strength and the desired value of its population, demonstrating the country's excellence in international competitions, which served the propaganda purposes and was constantly emphasized by Perón. Vargas, in turn, did not dedicate as much attention to sports in general, much less to motorsport, which was a sport that enjoyed some popularity, though mainly restricted to certain occasions or to the wealthy social strata. As it did not usually attract the attention of the masses, it was often overlooked by government efforts.

This is why the Argentinian government's investment in the sport went even further than the Brazilian government's had. The populist feature of Perón's administration was not matched in the Brazilian regime formed after Vargas. The intense Grands Prix seasons motivated the sponsoring of a national racing team at the first instance, ultimately leading to the construction of the first international standard Formula 1 circuit outside Europe and the USA.

Just like Vargas's administration had done two decades earlier, the Peronist government entered a new stage in the integration of South America into international motor racing. The movement was not the same; it could not possibly be, given the international circumstances of the time. But the ideal was, indeed, very close to that of the earlier populist ruler: that of using motor racing as a tool in the promotion of his country, and of his government, both domestically and abroad. And this movement was not simply a top-down initiative led by a visionary leader who supported the sport. It was initiated and pushed forward by the main agents and organizations of that sporting field, who pressed for their own agendas and worked alongside governmental officials to accomplish their goals.

Notes

1. The circuit was renamed after the end of the Peronist government, in 1955. It was then renamed several more times, and is now called *Autodromo Oscar y Juan Gálvez.*
2. For concise information on the relationship of government and sports during the rules of Vargas and Perón, see Drumond (2014) and Rein (1998). For a comparative approach, see Drumond (2009).
3. There is an extensive debate on the authoritarian features of Perón's first government. For an abridged view, see Wolfenden (2013).
4. For more information on Mussolini's and Hitler's uses of sport as propaganda, see Arnaud and Riordan (1998).
5. For more information on the role of Eva Perón Foundation in Argentinian sports, see Rein (1998) and Rein and Panella (2019).

References

Archetti, E. P. (2001). *El potrero, La Pista y el Ring: las Patrias del Deporte Argenitno [The Paddock, The Racetrack and the Ring: the Homelands of Argentine Sport]*. Fondo de Cultura Econômica.

Arnaud, P., & Riordan, J. (Eds.). (1998). *Sport and International Politics: The Impact of Fascism and Communism on Sport*. Taylor & Francis.

De La Torre, C. (2017). Populism in Latin America. In C. R. Kaltwasser, P. Taggart, P. O. Espejo, & P. Ostiguy (Eds.), *The Oxford Handbook of Populism* (pp. 251–274). Oxford University Press.

Donaldson, G. (2012). *Fangio: The Life Behind the Legend*. Random House.

Drumond, M. (2009). Vargas, Perón e o esporte: propaganda política e a imagem da nação [Vargas, Perón and sport: propaganda and the image of the nation]. *Estudos Históricos, 22*(04), 398–421.

Drumond, M. (2014). Sport and Politics in the Brazilian Estado Novo (1937–1945). *The International Journal of the History of Sport, 31*(10), 1245–1254.

Elias, R., et al. (2019). Automobilismo brasileiro de 1960 a 1966: investimento industrial e interesse governamental [Brazilian motorsport from 1960 to 1966: industrial investment and government interest]. *Revista Brasileira de Educação Física e Esporte, 33*(4), 517–530.

Gruschetsky, M. (2019). Autódromo, corredores y velocidad. Modernismo automotor en la Argentina peronista [Rectrack, Drivers and Speed: Auto Motor Modernism in Peronist Argentina]. In R. Rein & C. Panella (Eds.), *El Deporte en el Primer Peronismo: Estado, Competencias, Deportistas [Sport in the First Peronism: State, Competences, Sportmen]* (pp. 150–176). Universidad Nacional de La Plata.

Kaltwasser, C. R., Taggart, P., Espejo, P. O., & Ostiguy, P. (2017). Populism: An Overview of the Concept and the State of the Art. In C. R. Kaltwasser, P. Taggart, P. O. Espejo, & P. Ostiguy (Eds.), *The Oxford Handbook of Populism* (pp. 16–43). Oxford University Press.

Lupo, V. (2004). *Historia política del deporte argentino (1610-2002) [Political History of Argentine Sport (1610-2002)]*. Corregidor.

Melo, V. A. d. (2011). Before Fittipaldi, Piquet and Senna: The Beginning of Motor Racing in Brazil (1908–1954). *The International Journal of the History of Sport, 28*(02), 253–267.

Piglia, M. (2014). *Autos, rutas y turismo. El Automóvil Club Argentino y el Estado [Cars, Routes and Tourism. The Automobile Club of Argentina and the state]*. Siglo XXI Editores.

Rein, R. (1998). 'El Primer Deportista': The Political Use and Abuse of Sport in Peronist Argentina. *The International Journal of the History of Sport, 15*(02), 54–76.

Rein, R., & Panella, C. (Eds.). (2019). *El Deporte en el Primer Peronismo: Estado, Competencias, Deportistas [Sport in the First Peronism: State, Competences, Sportmen]*. Universidad Nacional de La Plata.

Vargas, G. (1995). *Diário [Diary]*. Fundação Getúlio Vargas.

Wolfenden, Katherine J. (2013). Perón and the People: Democracy and Authoritarianism in Juan Perón's Argentina. *Inquiries Journal/Student Pulse*, 5(02). Retrieved January 3, 2021, from http://www.inquiriesjournal.com/a?id=728.

Part III

Motor Racing and the Automobile Industry

Politics, Motor Sport and the Italian Car Industry, 1893–1947

Aldo Zana

This paper focuses principally on the years from the first appearance of a motor car in the country through to 1940, when Italy entered World War II.

The years before the Great War were a time of slow-growing mutual understanding amongst politicians, government and the emerging motor car industry, which exploited races for market leverage.

The two decades between the Great War and World War II saw the apex of motor racing celebrations as the fascist regime invested it with their key concepts: tight discipline, sheer power, daring courage, quest for victory, total supremacy.

The new Italy that emerged from mid-1945 onwards set a different stage, on which motor sport was still popular yet it became more autonomous without direct connections with politics or government. The focus was on the impact of the car industry on economic and social issues.

A. Zana (✉)
Weston, FL, USA
e-mail: aldo.zana@agenpress.com

D. Sturm et al. (eds.), *The History and Politics of Motor Racing*, Global Culture and Sport Series, https://doi.org/10.1007/978-3-031-22825-4_8

Humble Origins

The story (or, maybe, the tale) goes that the first ever petrol car running in Italy arrived by train on January 2, 1893, in Schio, a small hillside town in the Vicenza county (in the Veneto Region). The unusual destination completed the 1892 order by Mr. Gaetano Rossi, the tycoon founder of one of the premier textile factories in Italy.

The car was a French Peugeot Type-3 animated by a German-designed V2 565 cc engine, with a 2 HP output.

Such a humble entry of the country into the new world of the automobile went unnoticed by the two pioneers striving to produce the first Italian-made petrol car: Michele Lanza in Turin and Enrico Bernardi in Padua.

Once again, the story never determined who was the first Italian to manufacture and drive a roadworthy internal combustion vehicle. The Miari & Giusti company, manufacturers of vehicles based on the Bernardi's invention, produced a handful of motor cars between 1896 and 1901. The former's company factory (rather, workshop) was located in Turin, the town shortly to become the cradle of the Italian automobile industry.

Politics, administration and government didn't care about the nascent industry. Italy was then struggling to find the exit path from decades of widespread illiteracy, high international indebtedness, underdeveloped capital markets, lack of primary energy and raw materials (principally, coal and steel) to feed the new factories of the industrial revolution, which in Italy arrived late.

Social unrest was at its zenith in the years before the new century: in 1898 in Milan, a peaceful march of workers striking to demand better working conditions and decent salaries was attacked by soldiers, who fired on the crowd, killing 82.[1] The revenge came two years later when an anarchist from America shot and killed the king of Italy, Umberto I.

Paradoxically, a superiority complex permeated much of the country, triggered by the government of Francesco Crispi, who wanted to gain a front row place among the leading European countries in military power, colonial acquisition, technology and innovation. This policy won over the industrialists seeking wealth through the new mechanical industries, with the automobile industry leading the way.

Milan was the leading manufacturing centre of the country and the town already numbered 21 marques producing automobiles in 1901: two among them, Bianchi and Isotta Fraschini, were destined for a long life and significant growth. Yet by 1904 it was Turin which was the standard bearer for the Italian car industry thanks to Fiat, established in 1899, Itala (1904) and another seven minor marques located in town. The count had risen to 34 by 1906.

Turin had already been the venue for the first motor car race officially recorded in Italy: on May 18, 1895, five intrepid *automobilistes* left the town aiming for Asti, another town in Piedmont, 29 miles away. It took the winner, a Mr Federman, the whole day, from sunrise to sunset to be back in Turin. He drove a Daimler Victoria Phaeton as he was the Italian representative of the German company.

A total of 917 motor vehicles circulated in Italy in 1901, quite a low figure in comparison to France, US and UK, yet a threefold increase over the previous year. In the same year the overall output of domestic motor car plants amounted to 301, the balance being imports from France and Germany.

Motoring entered the fast lane thanks to the astonishing success of the 1901 Milan and 1902 Turin car shows. The former sold 120,000-plus entry tickets; the latter strengthened the domestic leadership of the local marques as a follow-on of the first ever Italian motor car show in April 1900.[2]

In those early years of the new century neither the government nor the army realized the promise of the automobile despite the increasing attention created by races and their media coverage.

Motor Racing Moves Out of the Cradle

The pioneer of international motor racing in Italy was a rich bourgeois from Palermo, Sicily: Vincenzo Florio (1883–1958) of the Marsala liqueur international fame. Besides the car shows in Turin and Milan as well as some minor local events recorded as racing contests, Florio was the key promoter of the September 1905 Brescia Motor Racing Week. The feature race was the Coppa Florio, 324 miles on a three-sided circuit south of the town. The winner was marquis Giovanni Battista Raggio, a gentleman driver, driving a 100 HP (14.5 litre) Itala, the marque established the previous year in Turin. He won in 4 hours, 46 minutes and 4 seconds, at an average 65.16 mph, and without suffering any trouble with the tyres, while his fiercest competitor, Vincenzo Lancia (1881–1937) driving a Fiat, was forced to finish as a backrunner by too many tyre changes.[3]

Florio decided to launch a new competition in his native Sicily to promote the island as a vacation site for wealthy Europeans. History goes that he conceived the race when he attended the 1905 Gordon Bennet Cup in France. A circuit without railway level crossings was found in the hills and mountains south of Palermo, with start and finish on a straight along the sea, close to the mainline railway to Messina to facilitate the attendance of large crowds. The Grande Circuito (Outer Circuit) delle Madonie was tracked: 92.6 miles a lap, highest elevation at 3413 feet.

For most of the peasants living up the Madonie hills, the vision of a motor car was a devil-like novelty, more exciting than for the inhabitants of the richer north of the peninsula. As customary with Vincenzo Florio, the purse was generous, richer for constructors than drivers. On May 6, 1906, at 6:00 a.m. Vincenzo Lancia, driving a Fiat 24/40 HP, 7.4 litres, was the first of 22 competitors from Italy and France, to be released by the chief timekeeper. At the end of the gruelling three laps, the winner on elapsed time was Alessandro Cagno (1883–1971), in an Itala 35/40 HP, who cashed the 25,000 Lire of the winner purse.[4]

The broad (of course, relative to the times) media coverage and the fascination of motor racing pushed the domestic motor car industry to grow as a significant contributor to the country's economic system. The strongest players in the industry survived the financial crisis of 1907–1908, which forced out of the market the many underfunded and poorly managed small companies producing too few and too expensive vehicles.

The government in those years, known to historians as "Belle Époque," understood, at last, the value of the motor car for the military. Many hundreds of trucks were ordered from Fiat, Itala, Isotta Fraschini and Ceirano for the war against the Ottoman Empire to conquer Libya. The ruggedness of the soil limited the range and scope of the motor trucks: they were the losers against camels and horses. Nevertheless, the connection of the motor car industry with government and politics was finally established.

Such a connection switched the focus from motor racing as the most effective way of promotion to lobbying at the top government levels, while the ever-increasing cost of racing forced the leading marques to establish departments specialized in the design and production of racing cars. The huge investment was only sustainable by the largest concerns, with Fiat virtually alone in Italian motor racing until the mid-1920s.

Since the first decade of the century Fiat had widened the reach of their racing programme to the whole of Europe and America. Vincenzo Lancia and Emanuele Cedrino (1879–1908) became popular in the US due to their achievements in major events like the Vanderbilt Cup and the Beach Races in Ormond Beach, Florida. The American ace-driver David Bruce-Brown (1887–1912) began his meteoric career as riding mechanic on the Fiats driven by Cedrino and met his death in a Fiat in practice for the 1912 American Great Prize in Milwaukee.

A Turning Point: The Great War

The Great War was a turning point for the Italian motor industry. The Italian government, at last, fully understood the need for motor vehicles, ordering 32,000 of them for the army. They were confined to short-range transport behind the lines because the Italian war against the Austro-Hungarian Empire was fought in the mountains and the front was constituted as closely facing trenches. A war of movement supported by motor vehicles was then a concept fully unknown to the Italian Chiefs of Staff. Nevertheless, they were in favour of exploiting the newest warfare weapon: aircraft, even though they were forced to go to French and British manufacturers for them. Nevertheless, Italian motor car companies received fat contracts to produce aero engines under French licence: a more profitable business than delivering trucks to the army. The long delays in outfitting production lines and the overall laggardness of Italian metallurgical and mechanical industries forced the government either to cancel or to pay only a fraction of the price because the products became available too late—at the end of hostilities and, often, even later.

The situation was nearly lethal for Itala, which never fully recovered from the failure to ensure the timely delivery of the 3000 aero engines to be built under licence of Hispano-Suiza.[5]

The severe social and political unrest after the Great War was terminated by the fascist government in 1922. It became a totalitarian regime in 1925, a forerunner of Nazi Germany.

A New Scenario to Exploit

Fiat emerged from the Great War as the dominant motor group in Italy and widened its reach and scope into aircraft and large diesel engines for ships. They also continued with motor racing and developed a series of innovative racing machines: these included the first to show aerodynamic bodies, the first to use reliable and powerful inline-eight engines and the first to win in Europe with a supercharged car in 1923.

Fiat now committed themselves to an unscrupulous political exploitation of motor racing. Fiat victories were rendered as victories of the Italian genius, for its unrivalled superiority, and of course for the will to power in new fascist Italy.

Mussolini himself lowered the blue flag at the start of the Italian and European Grand Prix at Monza Autodromo on September 9, 1923. The media reserved the best of their glorification to the imposing presence of Mussolini, already elevated to the title of "Duce" ("leader," from the Latin "dux") for his, purportedly, bringing back to life the past glories of the Roman Empire.

The *Gazzetta dello Sport*, the largest circulation Milan-based sport daily paper sold across Italy, opened the lead article about the race: "The whole of youthful Italy, the Italy of sports, the Italy always moving ahead, the dynamic Italy of the vital speed that is a multiplier of life, was lined up this morning waiting for the signal from Il Duce, indomitable master of will, his arm was outstretched in the way of the Roman Salute every time the red cars flashed past in front of him." (In truth, Mussolini left the

Autodromo immediately after the start, therefore he couldn't have raised his right arm at every passing of the dominant Fiats.)

Senator Giovanni Agnelli (1866–1945), Fiat's founder, president, CEO and largest shareholder, was in the pits together with the top brass of the company and the designers of the racing department. Of course, they all paid the due respects to Mussolini when he paraded in front of the cars on the grid.

The race, 497 miles, was a long and boring affair. Sunbeam, a brand based in Wolverhampton in the British West Midlands and then the fiercest rival of Fiat, didn't appear and a faint opposition was provided by the single Miller 122 driven by the American star-driver Jimmy Murphy, the unusual and underpowered Benz RH (the first rear-engine Grand Prix car), the French Voisins and Rolland-Pilains.

The Fiats came home with Carlo Salamano (1891–1968) first and Felice Nazzaro (1881–1946) second 24 seconds behind. Only an unbearable pain in the left wrist forced Pietro Bordino (1887–1928) to stop at mid-race and deprive Fiat of a clean 1–2–3 sweep.

When the ageing Nazzaro was called by Fiat to rejoin the team, the *Gazzetta dello Sport* celebrated with the headline: "Felice Nazzaro will race the Italian G.P. for Fiat—Italy's first and foremost." And to further flatter Fiat (one of the largest buyers of advertising in the country) the article added: "We convey our profound appreciation to the men managing Fiat, first of all to the senator Agnelli. He understood that the honour of the company and, even before, the honour of Italy, required Fiat to vindicate the defeat in Tours and to triumph in Monza." The final sentence: "To Fiat, to Alfa, to all our drivers, we address the wish, the appeal, the battle-cry, the order: 'Win for Italy'."

The effect of the Fiat victory found a brilliant recap in the *Gazzetta dello Sport* headline when reporting on the race: "Italy in the forefront again. The red Fiat cars triumphed." And *Corriere della Sera* (the largest circulation daily paper in the Milan and Monza area) wouldn't be outdone. The first lines of the opener on their front page flashed: "Our triumph was and is complete and gigantic. Italian drivers, Italian cars, Italian tyres—Pirelli—won against all competitors."[6]

The media reports confirmed the complete alignment between the fascist regime and the car manufacturers when it came to proclaiming the

Italian superiority in every facet of modernity, automobiles and also aircraft (yet the latter is another long and quite different tale).

Adhering with supine resignation to the orders of the regime, both media and car industry downplayed the incidents and the deaths of drivers: a normal occurrence when driving those unsafe, often unreliable racing cars. Nothing, not even a death, should have disturbed the triumphs of Italian skill and know-how. The news of the death of Ugo Sivocci (1885–1923), works driver of Alfa Romeo, on the eve of the 1923 Italian and European Grand Prix was ignored by the dailies until the day of his funeral in Milano on September 12, four days after the deadly incident.

If racing were for the glory and power of Italy, the dead were "Fallen Heroes" to be glorified and then very quickly forgotten. This was the fate of Enrico Giaccone (1890–1923), Fiat works driver, who was killed on August 28, 1923, during the early trials for the Monza race. Bordino, seated beside him in the car, suffered a fracture of the left wrist which, later in the Grand Prix, forced him out at mid-race.

The censorship by the regime of news about racing accidents found a blatant example in the case of the tragedy in the Italian Grand Prix at Monza on September 9, 1928. Emilio Materassi (1899–1928), then a front row driver, was killed together with 21 persons standing in the front of the grandstand. It would be the worst motor racing incident anywhere until Le Mans in 1955 (see Stephen Wagg's chapter on the politics of safety in motor racing in this book). Nothing was either written or said about it in the news of the day and the whole issue was soon forgotten.

Mussolini, the Number One Testimonial

Such was the aura around motor racing that Mussolini committed himself to mime the role of a racing driver when demonstrating his penchant for Alfa Romeo. He used to drive at such a crazy and unsafe speed that even Enzo Ferrari, then the works racing driver, was scared to death when he had to assist Mussolini in a test run of a new Alfa Romeo RL/SS sports car he had personally delivered in 1924 as a present from the company.

Mussolini also believed in his ability as an aircraft pilot, preferring bombers as background to his photo-ops for which he was clad in flying overalls, goggles and cap. And right arm stretched in the roman salute.

On August 25, 1925, he signed a message to be forwarded to the motor car people, from the bosses to the factory apprentices, from the racing drivers to the (rich, very rich) owners of touring cars. It proclaimed,

> The car is the machine of our time, the typical machine of our period. It is an instrument which multiplies our living opportunities through space. It is a delicate and powerful machine hosting titanic rhythms in its gentle heart. I dream of cars able to easily move through earth, sky, and sea and come back. We will have them, and then we'll adhere to the Corporation of the Integral Speed.[7]

Today, it's too easy a job to mock such an essay of lunatic poetry and foolish foresight. It was then a well-thought move to push the Italian motor manufacturers to adhere to the directives of the fascist government, that is, to focus on the domestic market and avoid costly innovations aiming at keeping up with international competition.

Mussolini's clear and proven affection for motor cars is often generalized to the whole fascist regime as an evolution of "Futurism," the art movement created in Italy in the early years of the century. Filippo Tommaso Marinetti, the magniloquent guru of Futurism, wrote in 1916: "The magnificence of the [all] Creation became richer through the beauty of speed. A racing car sporting a long bonnet adorned with big tubes resembling steel snakes spitting explosive breath is a violent god made of a new steel race."[8]

The theory is an untenable one. When the fascist party was founded by Mussolini in 1919, the battle cry was for violence in order to establish a totalitarian regime in which the State dominated every side and facet of the entire society. Nobody in the party was so educated and acculturated as to be interested in an art movement which promoted war, speed, recklessness as the artistic credo. By sheer chance, those were some of the keywords of the fascists and it became a too easy follow-on to define, many years later, Futurism as the forerunner of Italian fascism.

Protectionism and Victories on the Circuits

The government agreed to Fiat's request to protect the domestic market from foreign competitors seeking to open assembly plants in Italy to avoid the excessive import duties: Ford, for instance, had a plant in Trieste and Citroen had one in Milan. The advances of General Motors to establish a joint venture with Isotta Fraschini in Milan were promptly rejected following governmental pressure triggered by Senator Agnelli. We cannot forget that the 1920s and the 1930s were decades of strong protectionism across the whole of Europe.

The output of motor vehicles in Italy remained low, despite the propaganda generated by every car industry player: in 1923 total production (including trucks and buses) amounted to 37,450 units and this was raised to 63,800 in 1926. Export was the main market: from 12,773 units (56% of total production) in 1923 to 34,191 (54%) in 1926. Fiat alone accounted for 81% of overall 1926 vehicle domestic production. In 1925, 117,500 motor vehicles circulated in Italy, which translated into 1 motor vehicle for every 271 inhabitants. In the same year, the ratio was 1 to 7 in the US, 1 to 52 in UK and 1 to 53 in France.[9]

There was still a long way to go to motorize the country, furthermore because by 1930 exports still amounted to 44% of production. Despite the heavy taxation on imports from other European countries, the foreign market was once again the most profitable for the Italian car manufacturers, due to the focus on medium-high range vehicles preferred by the more affluent foreign customers.

Through the 1920s the victories of Fiat and Alfa Romeo in international races helped to promote the everyday use of the automobile in Italy while supporting the foreign market penetration. By the end of 1926, three prominent and rich gentlemen of Brescia had launched a powerful programme for the effective promotion of the motor car. They were Aymo Maggi (1903–1961), a nobleman fond of Bugatti and other high-performance cars; Renzo Castagneto (1891–1971), a road racing motor cyclist and Franco Mazzotti, count Biancinelli Faglia (1904–1942), whose family was among the largest shareholder of Isotta Fraschini. They were joined by the authoritative journalist Giovanni Canestrini

(1893–1975) of the *Gazzetta dello Sport* daily and won the approval of the Brescia fascist chief, Augusto Turati (1888–1965). On March 27, 1927, the "Coppa delle Mille Miglia" was born of the idea of showcasing everyday automobiles all across the country while racing on the open roads that the government had begun to improve. Yet, neither the most emphatic propaganda nor a people-oriented race could conceal the reality of a modest motor industry, light-years behind the structure, methodology, volumes, commercial and after-sale service organizations of Ford and the other leading US marques. Italian manufacturers offered cars at too a high price because the cost of production was excessive due to the small volumes and the as yet unfinished application of the principles of Fordism and Taylorism.

These principles key managers, technicians and designers of the Fiat concern had observed in their study tours to Detroit and factored into the construction of the new huge plant of the Lingotto, Turin, in 1922. This plant was an industrial complex never seen before across Europe: 1.6 million square feet of covered surface, due to be doubled in a few years, buildings five floors high with a continuous front 1.4 mile long. Raw materials and components entered the ground floor, production moved up through the floors till the finished car (more precisely, the fully finished chassis) was ready to the test run on the track on top of the building, 0.60 mile long with two steeply banked turns.[10]

The interconnection of the motor industry with the government found the institutional go-between in the association of the manufacturers, which became increasingly permeated by the governmental fascist representatives, which reduced, slowly and steadily, its influence as a negotiation platform.

For the manufacturers, motor racing was the most effective way to throw sand in the eyes of the regime and the whole Italian people. The media built up the tale of Tazio Nuvolari (1892–1953) against Achille Varzi (1904–1948), the two greatest Italian racing drivers in the years between the two wars. Their personal behaviour and the driving style were at the opposite: Tazio, vehement, always close to the limit (and, often, even beyond); Achille, cool, rational, straight to the objective. And they always raced one against the other: if Achille drove Alfa Romeo, Tazio chose Maserati, if Achille was due to join Maserati, Tazio joined the

German Auto Union. The perfect recipe to win people's passion even in the difficult times of the 1930s.

And difficult they were. The aftermath of the 1929 Wall Street crash hurt the European racing environment and Italian car manufacturers deeply. Alfa Romeo was saved by the State and diverted to a focus on the production of aero engines under licence of the British Bristol company; Itala went bankrupt, Lancia was too small to feel the troubles, Fiat survived thanks to their size and redirecting production towards entry-level, lower-cost cars.

To maintain positive relations with the fascists was of paramount importance to Fiat: in 1932 their products constituted 74.4% of the total Italian motor vehicle output. In the same year they named "Balilla" the new entry-level sedan, "Balilla" being the nickname of a member of the fascist youth organization (the organization, named Opera Nazionale Balilla, was split in three categories: Figli della Lupa 0–8, Balilla 8–14, Avanguardisti 14–18). To tell the truth, the car wasn't priced low at 10,800 Lire. i.e. three years of the per-capita Italian GDP. Nevertheless, it sold well: in two years 41,000 units entered the market. In the same year 1932 the number of cars owned by Italian families was 188,331.[11]

Fiat terminated their racing presence in 1927 when senator Agnelli ordered the destruction of all the racers still in the department together with drawings, designs and technical documents.

Alfa Romeo had provided the continuation of the winning record of Fiat since 1925. If the GPR-1, the first racer of the marque in 1923, was a failure triggered by its withdrawal from the Italian and European Grand Prix in Monza as a sign of respect for the death of Sivocci, the 1925 Type-P2 was an enduring success. The many similarities with the Grand Prix Fiats came mainly from the design of Vittorio Jano (1891–1965), who was "stolen" by Enzo Ferrari from the Turin racing department and became the chief race car designer at Alfa Romeo.

Alfa Romeo, despite producing a small volume of high-performance and very expensive cars, applied in their racing department the concept, the quality and the organization of a large factory. Furthermore, they could count on a workforce proud to be "Alfisti" with the mission to strive for victories in the name of Italy's glory. Another building block of the marque excellence was the subterranean rivalry with the Turin company, even though the direct one on the tracks lasted less than two years.

On top of this there was the Mussolini's personal penchant for the marque. He was always welcomed by the Alfa Romeo workers while, on the contrary, he understood the hostile feelings of the Fiat workforce and management when in 1932 he paid a visit to the Lingotto plant to celebrate the tenth anniversary of the fascist revolution. The outcome was a permanently negative feeling on the part of Mussolini against Senator Agnelli (named a senator in 1923) while he had to accept that the company was anyway essential to the objectives of the imperial will of power of fascism.

By contrast, Mussolini praised the Alfa Romeos as being: "Fast like my thought."[12] And fast they were, establishing a leadership in Grand Prix racing thanks to their first "Monoposto" Type P3 driven by aces of the like of Varzi, Nuvolari, Louis Chiron (1899–1979), Rudy Caracciola (1901–1959) and René Dreyfus (1905–1993). The surprise victory of Tazio Nuvolari in a P3 Alfa Romeo, in the 1935 German Grand Prix is still inscribed in the myths of motor sport.

The 1934 750 kg Grand Prix formula opened the years of German dominance by Mercedes-Benz and Auto Union. The Italian competition, Alfa Romeo, was annihilated. Politics and propaganda weren't any longer enough to hide the endless string of defeats, made more difficult to accept by the "betrayal" of Varzi in signing for Auto Union to solve the teething troubles of the rear-engine P-Wagen.

The State support to Alfa Romeo got some payback from the October 12, 1936, victory of Nuvolari, driving an Alfa Romeo 12C-36, in the George Vanderbilt Cup on the winding Roosevelt Raceway built in Long Island, a few miles east of New York City. Without the German teams, Nuvolari and the Scuderia Ferrari teammates Antonio Brivio (1905–1995) and Nino Farina (1906–1966) had an easy task. Behind Nuvolari, in second came the Frenchman Jean-Pierre Wimille (1908–1949) in a Bugatti T59/50B. Brivio finished third, 1 minute 4 seconds behind Wimille due to an unscheduled pit-stop in the closing stage of the race. Farina was DNF (Did Not Finish).

It was an event to celebrate well beyond media decency: an Italian victory in the US on Colombus Day (actually a day later). The *Gazzetta dello*

Sport opened with the headline: "Tazio Nuvolari takes a bullying win on the American continent routing all opponents from the Old and New Worlds and proving once again the supremacy of the Italian auto industry." The side article on the front page carried the headline: "Italian triumph on the anniversary of the everlasting glory of Christopher Columbus."

Italian daily newspapers were too eager to glorify the country's motor racing supremacy as the result of the wise and effective politics of the regime to take notice of what Fiorello La Guardia, the mayor of New York City, said at the prize-giving ceremony: "We are all proud of Nuvolari. This is a great day in the history of Italian motor sport. From now on it will be difficult to beat the Italians. The country is on the move and, as long as men like Nuvolari set the pace, Italians will soon be the dominant player in the sport."

La Guardia's statement reflected the now-established custom of presenting motor races as a fight fought by national heroes aiming for the further glory of Italy and fascism. The mid-1930s recorded the climax of the regime, and the largest percentage of Italians felt proud to live in fascist Italy. Enzo Ferrari, the owner and general manager of the Scuderia entering the Alfa Romeos winners in the US, wrote his commentary on the race: "This year in which the Nation wonderfully achieved the supreme mission that history and politics committed to the fascist revolution, the Empire has been at last re-established thanks solely to the power of the rejuvenated Italy."[13]

In 1936 Italy proclaimed the conquest of the Empire of Ethiopia, the independent East African country in the mainland next to Eritrea and Somalia, which were already Italian colonies. It was a war of cold-blooded aggression, tragically late on the colonial conquests of the nineteenth century, which resulted in the death of thousands of civilians by poison gas and mass aerial bombings.

The aggression was condemned by the League of Nations (the pre-war precursor of the United Nations), which imposed embargoes on Italian exports and imports. This embargo lasted roughly a year and was rather easy to circumvent. For instance, the Italian army managed to buy some 3000 Ford medium trucks directly from the company plants in Detroit and Dagenham, UK. Italian-made trucks had proved to be too heavy, large and unreliable to negotiate the tracks on the Ethiopian highlands, the terrain being more suitable for camels, mules and horses.

The Vanderbilt Cup victory was therefore a unique event to revive the links of Italian motor racing with its government. Mussolini went to visit the Milano Alfa Romeo plant on October 27, 1936, to celebrate the American victory and urge everyone to work harder for the glory of Italy.

Once again, it was left to Enzo Ferrari to write the compulsory closing lines of the article reporting on the visit: "The last words of the Duce oration are welcomed with a supreme ovation, never ending."[14]

Sliding Towards a New War

The years 1936 and 1937 saw a new word become widespread across the country: "Autarchy." Italian companies and the populace at large were ordered to buy and use products—food, clothes, motor vehicles and energy—all made 100% in Italy. The order stemmed from the sanctions imposed on Italy by the League of Nations and was exploited by the regime to mitigate the growing international isolation of the country, whose currency was too weak to support imports and whose politics was moving towards the fateful and tragic embrace with Nazi Germany.

The 1937 count of motor vehicles produced by the domestic factories amounted to 26,631 units, pushed +25% up by the success of the new Fiat smallest car, the 500 "Topolino" (Mickey Mouse). Priced at Lire 8900 when the pro-capita GNP amounted to Lire 3200, it didn't comply with the directive of providing every family a car, yet it was affordable enough to stimulate artisans to produce special lightweight bodies and provide the right platform for many racing, "Sports," versions. The engine was usually tuned and bored to 626 cc for a 25 HP output at 4600 rpm (figures of the Siata racing version). The body was shaped as an aluminium light open racer and this car was later widely known as the "Barchetta."

Racing Topolinos soon became the entry-level into motor racing, adhering to the loose government-imposed rules. They became so popular that a new class was established for the domestic races. In 1938, 28 Sports Topolinos started in the Mille Miglia and they also became the backbone of the many local events on dangerous circuits laid across towns and sided by rows of houses. Safety was a forgotten word. The worst accident happened during the Mille Miglia: on April 3, 1938, while racing through Bologna, the driver of a Lancia Aprilia lost control and smashed into a group of bystanders, killing 10, 7 children among them, and wounding 24.

In the late 1930s, the motor car industry deeply modified its relationship with politics, i.e. the fascists: one-way only. Companies scaled down on the government's orders and silently suffered through the restrictions on the availability of imported fuels, the backwardness of the Italian metallurgical industry, the lowered production volumes due to the stagnant and too small domestic market and the shutting down of the export channels.

If Mussolini and the regime had dreamed of a motorized country based on modern roads (the first Italian motorway opened in 1924 and ran from Milan to the north) and state-of-the-art factories producing reliable, elegant, and correctly priced cars, they had tragically failed. The objective of 700,000 units yearly output planned by the fascist government for 1938 was actually not reached until 1961 (759,140) in what was then a completely different world, with regard to GNP and democratic government.

The 1938 output (the final whole year before the war) peaked at less than 54,000.

Anyhow, Italy as a whole had to flatter Mussolini. Senator Agnelli signed a telegram of slavish obedience to Il Duce when the road tax on cars was lowered for 1939 in a last-minute move to improve the circulating fleet: "Fiat technicians and workers join me in acclaiming you, Duce, who opened a new era for empowering the development of the motor car industry and for promoting additional labour. As ever, our products and our personal feelings follow your orders on the autarchy. Yours faithfully."[15]

Gone were the times when the red racers flashed round the European tracks at a winning speed. Alfa Romeo exploited State money to carry the flag against the all-conquering Germans. And they secured positive outcomes only when the German marques Mercedes and Auto Union didn't show up, like in the 1936 George Vanderbillt Cup. Maserati was building a visible presence in the Voiturettes (little cars)[16] races despite being a very small company committed to racing cars only and lacking any significant support from the State, the regime or the media. Nevertheless, racing continued to enjoy the support of the top representatives of the regime, more interested in media publicity when appearing on the circuits than hoping to witness victories like in the past.

Mercedes-Benz made a fool of the Italians at the 1939 Tripoli Grand Prix, the opening event of the season held on the fast Mellaha circuit close to Tripoli in the Italian colony of Libya. It was one of the most modern and better structured racing sites in the world, usually hosting either Formule Libre or Grand Prix races. Knowing that the Germans would have once more been the winners if they had entered their Grand Prix cars, Italians changed the formula only six months in advance: they selected the Voiturette class setting the stage for a triumphal show by the 1.5 litre Maseratis and the new and promising Alfa Romeo 158.

What a surprise when on May 7, 1939, in Tripoli Mercedes-Benz entered two brand new W165 supercharged V8 1.5 litre single-seaters, designed, built, and race-readied in six months. They won hands-down.

Italians, including Marshal Italo Balbo (1896–1940), a top-brass of the fascist regime and governor of Libya, had to swallow from the poison cup once again. It was another blow against additional moves to promote the national motor industry and it terminated the overemphasized government support to racing showcased in the past decades.

Furthermore, World War II was approaching.

The Rise of a New Scenario After World War II

In the final day of April 1945 when the war ended in Northern Italy, which had been occupied by the Wehrmacht and run by a puppet fascist government, 80% of Italian road and rail infrastructure was either destroyed or badly damaged; the hydroelectric plants were still working by 90%; the industrial framework was damaged by bombing yet it was preserved from the complete destruction planned by the retreating German troops thanks to the insurrection driven by the Resistenza (Maquis) fighters and supported by the workforces who protected factories and machinery.[17]

The main Fiat and Alfa Romeo plants in Turin and Milan had been partially destroyed by Allied bombing; yet, the smaller automotive factories and workshops in the countryside were able to start again as soon as raw materials, fuel and tyres became available either on the black or regular markets.

Alfa Romeo saved their precious racing cars, dispersing them in hideouts around Milan. Many racing cars, mostly of the small pre-war classes, had been carefully preserved by a minority of rich privateers and artisans. They all were eager to resume racing.

The first post-war race was held on December 16, 1945, in Naples: it was a short in-town hillclimb won by a Pietro Fordilisi driving a homebuilt Alfa Romeo Special. Many local around-houses races followed in 1946, regardless of the difficult situation in which the national governing bodies of motor sport had found themselves during the fall-out from the fascist past in the aftermath of the war.

The key event was the Turin Grand Prix on September 1, 1946, along the tree-lined alleys of the Valentino Park. It was open to the future F1 single-seaters, i.e. 1.5 litres supercharged and 4.5 litres atmospheric. Thirty-four entrants came from Switzerland, France, UK and Italy driving Maseratis, Delahayes, ERAs and the winners-to-be Alfa Romeo 158s. The winner was Achille Varzi on a 158 in front of teammate Jean-Pierre Wimille, who followed him across the finish line eight tenths of a second in the prearranged order.[18]

Motor racing had restarted despite the Monza Autodromo, the only purpose-built motor racing venue in the country, being still cluttered by thousands of wrecked vehicles scrapped there by the Allied Armies.

The Mille Miglia resumed on June 21–22, 1947, with 153 competitors at the start while the entrants nearly doubled to take advantage of the availability of a set of new tyres (then almost impossible to find on the regular market) and a full tank of fuel. Despite the awful road conditions, 54 made it back to Brescia. The winner was Clemente Biondetti (1898–1955) driving a pre-war 8C 2900B Berlinetta Alfa Romeo owned by Emilio Romano who was seated with him in the car.

The government now ignored motor sport. The priorities were the relaunch of production in the largest plants of the likes of Fiat and Alfa

Romeo as well as the improvement of living conditions of the workforce and the whole country.

Interactions between motor sport and politics were gone for good despite the still strong popular interest theoretically exploitable as an effective source of attraction for political propaganda.

Italian democratic governments stayed alert to the economic and social impact of the car industry. The policies of modernization of the country found a strong platform in motorization, thanks to a network of new state-of-the-art motorways, the improvement of the roads and the availability of affordable cars. Fiat managed only in the mid-1950s to market family cars at a price lower than the yearly average salary of an employee.

The improved social and economic scenario provided the platform for new and existing marques in the car industry. Maserati, no longer under the ownership of the Maserati brothers, continued with the small, yet painstakingly produced, batches of racing and high-performance cars; Cisitalia (derived from Compagnia Industriale Sportiva Italia) was born and had a short yet glorious life in Turin; Abarth, founded in Bologna in 1949, but soon moved to Turin, where their reputation grew, began selling low-cost tuning components which would later evolve into manufacturing winning race cars; Osca (Officine Specializzate Costruzione Automobili—Fratelli Maserati), also begun in Bologna, revamped the skill and the winning tradition of the Maserati brothers; Stanguellini grew out of its pre-war humble origins in Modena in 1900; the many artisans of the "Etcterini" (small jewel-like racing cars) began a long-lasting winning strike; Enzo Ferrari entered the first car manufactured under his own name in the Circuit of Piacenza on May 11, 1947.

Billions of words have been written and told since then about Ferrari and it is beyond the scope of this paper to recap the key steps of the rise of Ferrari among the most praised car marques and to win a prominent worldwide position within the top brands.

Every facet of other Italian post-war marques and cars has been and continues to be scrutinized and added to the knowledge of scholars and enthusiasts.

In post-war democratic Italy, governments showed interest in the motor car industry only when it related to social issues. Racing was no longer a priority symbol of national pride and power.

The State abandoned Alfa Romeo ownership when the firm was already sunk in a black hole of losses. It didn't move a finger when Fiat swallowed every other Italian motor car manufacturer of some significance: Alfa Romeo, Lancia, Maserati and Ferrari. It continued to support Fiat every time their market position or financial performance showed signs of weakness.

In the twenty-first century, Fiat merged with US-based Chrysler company and established the FCA (Fiat Chrysler Automotive) Group in 2014, which was due to become second fiddler in the French PSA Group in 2020.

Ferrari still carries along the mission of representing Italian motor racing at the top, i.e. F 1. And they seek neither interactions with politics nor State support.

Notes

1. This was part of a series of disturbances sometimes known as the Milan Barricade Fights.
2. Based on Bossi, Giovanni; Zana, Aldo: "I Saloni dell'Auto a Milano 1901–1947" (Milan 1901–1947 Car Shows). AISA (Italian Association of Motor Historians), Milano 2021.
3. Published in: "L'Illustrazione Bresciana—Issue 5/1905". Brescia 1905.
4. Published in: Canestrini, Giovanni: "La favolosa Targa Florio". LEA Editrice, Roma 1966.
5. Published in Biffignandi Donatella: "Itala, splendore e declino di una marca prestigiosa" (Itala, splendor and decline of a prestigious marque). AISA Paper No. 64, Milano 2005.
6. Published in Zana, Aldo: "Monzanapolis—The Monza 500 Miles and the endless America-Europe challenge". Società Editrice Il Cammello, Turin 2017.
7. Translated from the original manuscript signed by Benito Mussolini on Ministero degli Esteri (Foreign Affairs Ministry) letterhead, supplied by the Giovanni Bossi Automobile Archive.
8. Published in Castronovo, Valerio: "Fiat 1899–1999—Un secolo di storia Italiana" (Fiat 1899–1999—A century of Italian history). Rizzoli, Milano 1999.

9. Data published in Bossi, Giovanni; Zana, Aldo op. cit.
10. Data published in Castronovo, Valerio op. cit.
11. Data published in Boscarelli, Lorenzo: "Progressi della motorizzazione e società italiana"(Motoring development and Italian society). AISA Paper No. 58. Milano 2003.
12. Published in Bigazzi, Duccio: "Il Portello—Operai, tecnici e imprenditori all'Alfa Romeo 1906–1926" (The Portello—Workers, technicians and managers at Alfa Romeo 1906–1926). Franco Angeli, Milano 1988.
13. The lines about the 1936 George Vanderbilt Cup are taken from Zana, Aldo op. cit.
14. Published in the house organ: "Scuderia Ferrari—Issue 14". Modena, November 5, 1936.
15. Published in Boscarelli, Lorenzo op. cit.
16. This was the official designation of a class of racing cars with engine max. capacity 1.5 litres, less costly and not as fast as the GP racers.
17. Published in Bossi, Giovanni; Zana, Aldo op. cit.
18. Published in Silva, Alessandro: "Back on Track—Grand Prix and Formule Libre racing 1946–1950". Fondazione Negri, Brescia 2019.

British Motor Sport and the Rise of the Garagisti

Mark Jenkins, Nick Henry, and Tim Angus

This chapter charts the evolution of the UK's 'Motorsport Valley' (MSV)[1] from its humble beginnings as a leisure activity for the mechanically minded, to its continued status as 'the jewel in the crown'[2] of British performance engineering, and a globally significant economic cluster. This is an account of the emergence of an industry and economic cluster underpinned by the evolution of specialist technologies and engineering capability. The term 'Garagisti' is used to encapsulate this distinctive engineering culture and production model.

http://www.garagisti.net/ accessed 18 June 2020.

M. Jenkins (✉)
Cranfield School of Management, Cranfield University, Cranfield, UK
e-mail: mark.jenkins@cranfield.ac.uk

N. Henry • T. Angus
Coventry University, Coventry, UK
e-mail: Nick.Henry@coventry.ac.uk; tim.angus@coventry.ac.uk

D. Sturm et al. (eds.), *The History and Politics of Motor Racing*, Global Culture and Sport Series, https://doi.org/10.1007/978-3-031-22825-4_9

Motorsport Valley in the UK is estimated to have a combined turnover of £9 billion, encompassing 4300 firms (mainly small-and medium-sized enterprises, SMEs) and 41,000 employees.[3] We describe six key periods in the evolution of Motorsport Valley ('the Silicon Valley of motorsport') and, critically, the rise of the 'Garagisti'—Enzo Ferrari's disparaging term for the British race car constructors. From early beginnings between the First and Second World Wars we chart the emergence of the first commercial businesses in the nascent motorsport industry of the 1950s and 1960s, through the shift into new technologies and materials of the 1970s and 1980s, to a period of exponential growth and professionalisation in the 1990s and 2000s. This has culminated in the financial, environmental and societal challenges of the period from 2010 to 2020. In the following we outline six key phases and summarise with some conclusions regarding the future of the motorsport industry in the UK.

Beginnings

In which we describe the beginnings of the car clubs and hobbyist engineers who developed light, nimble race cars, using a bricolage of technologies and components, ideal for racing on closed circuits.

The beginnings of the twentieth century saw the establishment of two formal institutions in Europe which became, and remain, central to the sport of motor racing. In 1897 the Automobile Club of Great Britain was formed; this organisation, renamed the Royal Automobile Club (RAC) in 1907, became the official regulatory body for UK motorsport activities. Paris, in 1904, saw the formation of the Association Internationale des Automobile Clubs Reconnus which was to become the Fédération Internationale de l'Automobile (FIA), now the global regulatory body for motorsport worldwide.

As motor racing evolved through the 1920s and 1930s, the UK had started building racing cars with marques, often represented in the traditional British racing green, such as Bentley, Aston Martin and English Racing Automobiles (ERA). These cars were typically large, powerful machines, with the engine located in front of the driver, and which relied on horsepower to deliver performance on public road-based tracks such as Le Mans in France and the Mille Miglia in Italy. During this interwar period grand prix racing was dominated by Germany's white Auto Unions and Mercedes; France's blue Bugattis and Talbots; and the red Italian cars of Fiat, Alfa Romeo and Maserati.

The first purpose-built race circuit in the UK opened in 1907. Brooklands, near Weybridge in Surrey, used a banked oval format, allowing the cars to travel fast round the bends, and was very much the domain of the affluent racing enthusiast. Brooklands became a site not just of the nascent motorsport industry in the UK (both two and four wheeled) but also of the aviation industry. In the early post First World War era it was one of the largest aircraft production facilities in the UK. Brooklands maintained its position as the pre-eminent site of both the sport and industry of motorsport until 1939, when the site was requisitioned for the aviation industry for the war effort in the Second World War, and racing permanently ceased at the venue. In the 1930s, Brooklands monopoly of circuit-based events in the UK was broken by the opening of Donington Park circuit in the East Midlands in 1931. Donington Park became established as the second main UK-based permanent circuit in 1931 until it also was requisitioned for war purposes in 1939. Unlike Brooklands, however, Donington was revived in the 1970s under construction magnate Tom Wheatcroft's patronage. In addition to these two permanent interwar circuits, temporary circuits such as South London's Crystal Palace, a public park which ran events from 1927, bolstered the venues available in this period.

Following the end of the Second World War, two particular motor racing clubs, both located in the south of the UK, provided fertile ground for the germination of the Garagisti. They epitomised the rise of a new form of racing car technology, centred on the UK—and which set in train the global dominance of British-based racing car production for the last 60 years.[4] The first meeting of the Bristol Motor Cycle & Light Car Club had taken place in November 1911,[5] later transforming into the Bristol Aeroplane Company Motor Club, based at Filton near Bristol. This, in turn, became the 500 Club[6] which was established in Bristol in 1946 and continues today. This organisation established regulations for 500cc race cars thereby providing a formal regulatory framework for the small light cars which went on to revolutionise international racing in

Formula 1 (F1) in the late 1950s and early 1960s. Today, as then, regulations remain key to all forms of racing (and the continued power of the regulatory body, the FIA).

One of the more successful initial 500cc designs was created by John Cooper of Cooper Cars in Surbiton, Surrey. Based not far from the old Brooklands circuit, the circuit was where John Cooper had in the pre-war era first discovered his interest in motorsport. First raced at the Prescott hill climb, near Gloucester, in July 1946,[7] the Cooper Mk1 used front suspension assemblies from two scrapped Fiat Topolinos and married these to a J. A. Prestwich (JAP) 500cc speedway motorcycle engine (built in Tottenham, London). There were no engineering drawings, the components were simply laid out using chalk marks on the garage floor. Because the motorcycle engine used a chain drive, the simplest arrangement was to put the engine behind the driver and as close as possible to the driven rear axle, thereby creating a classic 'mid-engine' layout.

The 750 Motor Club was founded in 1939 to exploit the competition potential of the Austin Seven production car. Its simple construction made it ideal for modification and the creation of 'specials' based on the chassis and powertrain. The inaugural meeting of the club was held on 29 March in Willesden, North London.[8] After a number of small events during the summer, including a race at Crystal Palace, it had to make do with a series of occasional meetings at pubs and hotels during wartime, until hostilities ceased in 1945. The club was founded by two journalists, Bill Boddy and Dennis Jenkinson, but its most famous member was Colin Chapman whose successful Lotus specials are probably best exemplified by the front engine Lotus Seven, which is still manufactured in the UK at the time of writing under the Caterham brand.

Initially the most popular form of competition for these clubs was the hill climb, with competitors attempting to set the fastest time to ascend a hill such as those in Prescott in Gloucestershire and Shelsley Walsh in Shropshire. However, after 1945 an abundance of disused military airfields with hard surface perimeter roads made the ideal locations for wheel-to-wheel circuit racing. Both the 500 and 750 Motor Clubs made frequent use of an ex-RAF airbase at Silverstone, north of London, where they could travel, hold an event and return within the day. In 2023 six out of the seven UK based F1 teams (out of a total of 10 F1 teams worldwide) had operations located within a triangle defined by drawing (100 mile) lines between London, Bristol and Silverstone. This demonstrates the locational importance of both the airfield-based circuits, and the technological and engineering influence of the aviation industry to the development of MSV.

The Constructors

Specialist race car constructors, such as Cooper and Lotus, were selling their products to aspiring racers using technologies which created light, nimble and extremely fast racing cars.

Although motor racing was not a new phenomenon post-Second World War, businesses which existed specifically for the purpose of building and selling affordable racing cars and their components were. With Cooper formally creating a race car company in 1947 and Lotus in 1952, the Garagisti were born. Lotus was originally based in London before moving to Hertfordshire and then, finally, Norfolk. However, this didn't translate into British success in grand prix racing for several years. In fact, the first British success in the post-war era came when Vanwall won the inaugural Formula 1 Constructors World Championship in 1958. This was also the first year that a British driver became F1 World Champion, although Mike Hawthorn had done so while driving for Enzo Ferrari. Vanwall founder, Tony Vandervell, had been one of the investors in the British Racing Motors (BRM) project. Frustrated with a lack of progress by BRM, Vandervell purchased a V12 Ferrari—his Thinwall bearing company was already a supplier to Ferrari, Enzo himself having described Vandervell as *the meteoric builder of the Vanwall.*[9] The car was renamed as the 'Thinwall Special'. From using modified Ferrari cars, Vandervell then built his own car at his factory in Acton, West London, using an engine developed by Norton motorcycles and utilising a Rolls Royce military vehicle crankshaft.[10] The tubular spaceframe chassis was designed and built by John Cooper of Cooper Cars and further developed by Colin Chapman of Lotus. Chapman also suggested that they spend time improving the aerodynamic design of the body and enlisted the help of Frank Costin who worked for British aviation manufacturers De

Havilland. Costin had been influential in the aerodynamic development of the early Lotus cars.

During the 1950s Cooper had become the world's biggest manufacturer of racing cars.[11] Having started with the mid-engine 500cc cars, they had also moved into front engine Formula 2, Cooper-Bristol single seaters. The real breakthrough in terms of competitive performance came from a partnership between Cooper and engine builder Coventry Climax. Coventry Climax made fire pump engines from their base in Coventry in the English Midlands, which had become widely used in the UK during the Second World War. The 'feather weight' portable fire pump engine had a capacity of just over 1000cc. Both John Cooper and Colin Chapman recognised that such a light and powerful engine would be ideal for a race car and lobbied Climax to produce a suitable version for automotive use. From these small beginnings Climax went on to produce 1988 automotive engines in 1957.[12] A Cooper Climax car achieved its first grand prix victory at the Argentine Grand Prix of 1958 with Stirling Moss at the wheel. Ironically, this was not a victory for the factory Cooper team, but a private British-based entrant—Rob Walker, heir to the Johnny Walker whiskey fortune, who had decided to use his wealth to go motor racing. This was not only the first win for an engine designed as a fire pump, but the first win for a car with an engine positioned behind the driver ('mid-engine') since the beginning of the Formula 1 World Championship in 1950. In 1959 and 1960 Cooper Climax won the constructors world championship, the first time it had been achieved in consecutive years. The Garagisti had arrived.

Garagisti

Led by Cooper and Lotus the Garagisti develop the dominant designs in Formula 1 motor racing and forced Enzo Ferrari to 'put the ox behind cart'.

The traditional way to design and build a grand prix car was to construct a spaceframe—an arrangement of metal tubes designed to hold the suspension points, the engine, the driver and contain all the major components, including fuel tanks. As the cars became smaller and lower in order to improve handling, fabricating and fitting aluminium fuel tanks inside the spaceframe became increasingly difficult; in addition, the flexing of the chassis often resulted in leaks which could mean retirement from a race. Colin Chapman came up with a typically pragmatic solution[13]—rather than build a frame and fit the tanks into it, why not strengthen the fuel tanks to become a structural part of the car and then bolt the suspension and engine onto them? The Lotus 25 became the first Formula 1 car since the Second World War to use this monocoque chassis.

A major problem for the Garagisti in the early 1960s was a change in engine regulations. In 1963 the FIA had stipulated that from 1 January 1966 F1 engines would have to be either 3000cc normally aspirated or 1500cc turbo-charged. This meant that the hugely successful Coventry Climax power unit was at the end of its time. Faced with the challenge of making significant investment to create a 3000cc engine, Climax decided to step away from racing engines to concentrate on their core business. Colin Chapman made an agreement with two of his former employees, Keith Duckworth and Mike Costin, who had now formed a specialist engine-tuning business—called Cosworth—that they could design and build a 3000cc engine for £100,000. All Chapman had to do was to find the funding. This came from the Ford Motor Company and the result was the Ford Cosworth Double Four Valve (DFV) engine, built at the firm's factory in Northampton, close to the Silverstone circuit and at the heart of what subsequently became Motorsport Valley.[14]

The engine was light and powerful, and most importantly a stressed component allowing the Garagisti to simply bolt the engine onto the rear of the monocoque and then attach the rear suspension and gearbox to the rear of the engine. All of this resulted in a lighter and stiffer race car which had the capacity to win grand prix. Lotus designed their type 49 car specifically for this engine. The car and engine combination emphatically won on its first race—the Dutch Grand Prix at Zandvoort on 4 June 1967. Originally the plan was for the engine to be provided exclusively to Lotus, but Ford's Walter Hayes recognised that this had the potential to totally dominate the sport and, to Chapman's dismay, made the decision to make the engine available to other grand prix teams from 1968.

Cosworth's first customer after Lotus was Surrey-based Tyrrell Racing's Ken Tyrrell: *This meant that anyone with enough money, and in the first year it was only £7500, went to Cosworth and you came away with an engine that was capable of winning the next race and that went on for many years. This is the reason why there are now so many British Formula 1 teams—because that engine was available.*[15]

The Ford DFV changed the balance of power away from the teams who built their own engines such as Ferrari, BRM and Honda, and towards those who concentrated on building the chassis and bought the engines from Cosworth. This included teams such as Lotus, Tyrrell, McLaren (based in Surrey), Brabham (also in Surrey) and Williams (in Oxfordshire). It also moved racing car creation away from the vertically integrated organisations who built all of the car, to horizontally focused specialists who came together to create the racing car. In the UK these were the specialist networks that became the basis of Motorsport Valley and featured other names such as gearbox manufacturers Hewland (based in Berkshire) and fuel cell manufacturers Aero Tec Laboratories (headquartered in Milton Keynes). Race car construction focused on designing car chassis, suspension systems, aerodynamics and other aspects of handling performance, safe in the knowledge that if the constructor had the DFV engine they would be highly competitive. In 1971 and 1973 every grand prix in the World Championship series was won by a car fitted with the Ford DFV engine. The Garagisti didn't just put the ox behind the cart, they revolutionised a production system built on horizontal networks of world-class specialists working together to create race winning cars—networks geographically located in the South and Midlands of the UK (Motorsport Valley).

Aerodynamics had been around the periphery of motor racing for many years. Frank Costin, brother of Cosworth's Mike Costin, worked for aircraft builder De Havilland and had helped influence the design of early Lotus and Vanwall cars. But the idea of aerodynamics as a central, rather than peripheral, technology in race car development only started when full-width 'wings' were first used on grand prix cars at the Belgium Grand Prix of 1968.

The radical shift that really brought aerodynamics to the fore in the late 1970s was led by Lotus, like many innovations during this period. During a period of poor performance Colin Chapman had asked technical director Tony Rudd to take a totally fresh look at racing car design in order to try and find a new breakthrough. This came when aerodynamicist Peter Wright, using the moving-ground wind tunnel at Imperial College London, discovered that by sealing the sides of a wide bodied concept design model a dramatic improvement in downforce could be achieved. This effectively made the underside of the car an inverted wing, with moving skirts along the side of the car used to create a sealed area of low pressure directly under the car. Italian American driver Mario Andretti described the performance of the resulting Lotus 78 as like 'being painted to the road'.[16] Enzo Ferrari initially resisted these innovations from the Garagisti, insisting that his cars would never wear skirts,[17] but eventually he realised that the Scuderia was being left behind and relented. Ferrari was now following the Garagisti.

Growth

Exponential growth in the industry—fuelled by record audience numbers on TV—leads to the constructors growing and branching out into supercars and related businesses.

When Frank Williams founded his Formula 1 team in 1969 there were five people involved, and that included Frank and driver, Piers Courage. By 1980 this had risen to 62 employees, by 1990 to 148 employees and, in the period from 1990 to 2003, the size of the team increased by a factor of over 3 to 475 employees (excluding those involved in creating the engines used by the Williams team). The main reason for this exponential growth during the 1990s was a significant increase in the viewing audiences, primarily for Formula 1, which, in turn, encouraged an influx of sponsors, from a range of sectors including tobacco, drinks, electronics and computing. Motor racing entered a period of globalisation of its sport—and with it the associated global production of racing cars, with its centre in the UK-based MSV, flourished.

With this escalation in revenues the teams found themselves in a race to build up resources to develop their cars more quickly to stay competitive. In the early days of aerodynamics the F1 teams had made use of specialist wind tunnels at research facilities such as the Aircraft Research Association in Bedford and at universities such as Cranfield, Southampton and Imperial College London; but now teams were building their own wind-tunnels in order to test and develop innovations as fast as possible. As these wind-tunnels worked at a reduced scale from the actual car, scale models had also to be built in the early stages at 33 or 40% and then increasing to 50 and 60% to achieve greater accuracy. In addition to using physical wind-tunnels the teams also began to develop their application of computational fluid dynamics (CFD) in order to simulate air flow on a computer, again to speed up and improve the development process. All of these changes meant an increased number of specialists to work in these areas, it also meant that the skills needed to bring together these different technologies in order to design and develop the fastest car were also in short supply and wages and costs therefore increased just as quickly.

During this time the Garagisti were moving ahead not only in Formula 1, but also in terms of developing professional management capabilities and expanding their corporate portfolios. McLaren developed their own 'supercar', the McLaren F1, in a bid to emulate Ferrari both as a brand and in the range of products they offered. Meanwhile Ferrari also established an operation to design and develop their F1 cars in the UK, under the leadership of former McLaren Technical Director, John Barnard. Based in Surrey, this was known as the Guildford Technical Office or GTO for short. Although much of the focus in motor racing is on the development of single-seat racing cars, Motorsport Valley was proving attractive to other formats such as rallying—with the world rally operations of Subaru, Mitsubishi and Hyundai all locating in MSV in this period. Outside single-seat racing cars developed for F1, firms based in MSV also began to dominate other international single-seat racing categories such as the US-based Indycar series. Here, MSV-based firms such as Reynard, Lola and March were market leaders, and the main US-based Indycar manufacturer, Penske, also moved its Indycar chassis design and manufacture to MSV, in a move mirroring that of Ferrari in F1 with GTO.

Global Players

Research into the size, scale and scope of the sector leads to growing evidence of its contribution to the UK economy and, perhaps more importantly, international recognition of the UK's capabilities in high-performance engineering, technology transfer and continuous innovation.

The ban on tobacco advertising instigated by the World Health Organisation was implemented in Formula 1 in 2006 (although some teams still maintained tobacco companies as corporate partners—such as Ferrari with Philip Morris). It paved the way for many new types of sponsor to enter into motorsport: from software to shampoo, telecoms to transportation and banking to beer. But perhaps most importantly in this period was the influx of the global automotive manufacturers and, with it, investment from these OEMs (original equipment manufacturers) into MSV. The relationship between the car makers and the car racers had frequently been close, but rarely enduring. Enzo Ferrari's equipe—Scuderia Ferrari—had started life, not as a builder of race cars, but as the works racing team for Alfa Romeo. The first time the Ferrari prancing horse had appeared on a racing car it was on the side of an Alfa Romeo. It was only in the late 1940s that Ferrari began to construct his own engines and then build cars around them. Ferrari is the only automotive manufacturer that has been competing in Formula 1 since its inception in 1950, Enzo's perspective was always that Ferrari was a racing team; they sold cars to the public in order to fund their racing. In contrast the automotive manufacturers' historical perspective has been that it is a marketing and sales investment to race cars in order to promote them to the public: 'race on Sunday sell on Monday'.

Aside from Fiat who had acquired a stake in Ferrari in 1969, the Ford Motor company had been involved in F1 motor racing for many years mainly through their initial investment in the Cosworth DFV engine, which carried the Ford logo. However, in the early 2000s many manufacturers made the transition from the side-lines to significant investment in F1 teams on the back of the increasing media profile of F1. Ford acquired Milton Keynes-based Stewart Grand Prix at the end of 1999 and created a team around their Jaguar brand. BMW started supplying engines to

Williams in 2000 and then acquired the Swiss-based Sauber team in 2005 to create their own team. In 2000 Renault bought the Benetton team, based in Enstone, near Oxford. In 2005 Honda acquired the British American Racing (BAR) team, located at Brackley, near to Silverstone in Northamptonshire. Toyota made the move from sports car racing to Formula 1 in 2002 when they created their own operation located in Cologne, Germany. Mercedes acquired a majority stake in the UK engine builder Ilmor in 2002, renaming it Mercedes Benz High Performance Engines and eventually moving to becoming a F1 constructor in 2010 when they acquired the Brawn F1 team, which had taken over the Honda operation, and formed Mercedes AMG F1.

In seeking to have a presence in world motorsport, large numbers of OEMs sought out the network of UK SMEs in Motorsport Valley as the suppliers of and/or production centre for motorsport vehicles. In 1995, for example, a supply chain analysis of the world's four most prestigious international motorsport championships noted that all the winning cars were UK-assembled and the UK share of components exceeded 60% in three cases and reached a third in the remaining case.[18] These cars included the seemingly Italian Benetton F1 car and seemingly Japanese Subaru Impreza in World Rally. In 2000 the first ever National Survey of Motorsport Engineering and Services was carried out for the UK-based Motorsport Industry Association (MIA), funded by national government. The survey discovered that total annual turnover for the sector in 2000 was put at £4.6 billion, total employment estimated at 38,500 persons across over 4300 firms engaged in some form of motorsport activity, and exports of £2 billion accounted for 43% of annual motorsport turnover.[19]

Challenges

Bounce-back from two global financial crisis, and responding to the accelerating technological, commercial and societal challenges driven by the low carbon and environmental sustainability agenda.

Over the period 1990–2000, the top 50 UK motorsport engineering firms experienced an (unadjusted) growth in average turnover of some

523% and growth in employment of some 227%.[20] If, however, the 1990s are seen as a period of boom for the UK motorsport industry, then the 2000s are seen as an era when MSV both moved to maturity and saw its competitive advantage challenged on a number of fronts by emergent, or growing, global competitors—and economic recession.

Following a (semi-)global recession, by 2002 many of the sector's leading companies had experienced job losses representing around 5% of total employment (although job loss was not restricted to the UK industry alone), international circuits such as Silverstone and Rockingham were experiencing redundancies and high-profile motorsport engineering companies such as Tom Walkinshaw Racing (TWR) and Reynard had entered into receivership. Furthermore, analysis of the supply chains of winning cars in the leading four global motorsport series (F1, CART, F3000, WRC) over the previous decade showed a worrying trend. By 2002, none of the winning cars were now UK-built and the overall UK average percentage share of the declared supply chain stood at 33%, down from 39% in 2000 and 62% in 1995.[21] Notably, these declining shares were driven by the renewed competitiveness of the traditional competitor industries of Italy, France and Germany rather than those new 'developing economy' entrants who had purchased a global motorsport event in the hopes that performance engineering would follow.

Yet a detailed global mapping of the motorsport industry in 2005 revealed 'bounce back' as the size of the UK industry now stood at £6 billion or 0.5% GDP (a greater share of GDP than in any other national economy), accounted for a 50% share of the key global companies ('constructors') and continued to dominate global supply chains. Nevertheless, the UK industry remained under strong competitive pressure from a resurgent Italy and the acquisitive activities of US global finance.[22]

In 2008–2009, the industry faced a new global financial crisis and its repercussions. Global corporations across the world, including OEMs, retrenched, and one of the investment drivers of motorsport—sponsorship—dried up. Instead, MSV capabilities began to be reimagined as part of the transition to a low-carbon economy and, specifically, as intrinsic to supporting the UK's automotive and transport sectors' low-carbon transition (including light-weighting, energy efficiency and electrification). This move to industry diversification articulated motorsport and its 'performance-engineering' at the centre of 'technology-driven diversification' ranging from new materials such as carbon fibre, composites and nanotechnology through new forms of composite, high temperature, fabrication and digital manufacturing to low-carbon, energy-efficient transport including charging technologies, distributed power systems, (kinetic) energy recovery systems and non-combustion engine powertrains. This initiative reflected how 'low carbon motorsport' became deeply intertwined in a broader 'leveraged' industry offer of prototyping and testing capabilities to accelerate the development of low-carbon, energy-efficient technologies for the global automotive sector and beyond. Motorsport in the UK had truly put 'R&D lab' alongside its historical role as 'marque, brand and billboard'.

Other developments in MSV at the time included: spin-off Flybrid, subsequently acquired by Torotrak, and whose F1 Kinetic Energy Recovery Systems technology was sold to Volvo and put in vehicles such as London buses, trams and JCB diggers; the 2014 global launch of Formula E, an electric-powered single-seat championship, with its global base at Donington Park; a Williams Hybrid Power engine winning the Le Mans 24 Hour Race for Audi; new partnerships in aero/space, defence and special vehicles; energy (Ecofisk); health and well-being (GSK); and, in 2012, 43% of surveyed Motorsport Industry Association members reporting selling into 'other' sectors such as energy, electrical and medical and over half believed that 'energy-efficient, low-carbon technologies will be at the heart of future growth'.[23]

Remarkably, a 'dipstick test' of the largest ten non-F1 MSV motorsport companies showed that by 2012 they had already bounced back (again) with their highest combined turnover ever, and had significantly higher employment than in 2009.[24] Moreover, by 2014, in its core markets, and in the face of global financial crisis and disruptive technological transition, MSV had both retained its historical market dominance and captured significant shares of new technology markets and investment. A supply chain mapping identified a continued global Formula 1 UK share of between 70–75% of supply chain value but, in addition, a 40–60% global supply chain value share of the new Formula E based on electric power and a 40% share of the transitioning Endurance Sports Car market.[25] Thus, a global mapping of all three supply chains showed that whilst Europe, Japan and, to a lesser extent, the East Coast of the USA were strongly represented in these three supply chains, a total of 72 of 151 (48%) firms in these growing high-value global supply chains resided in the UK, most within MSV.

There has been also continued diversification from the motorsport businesses with Red Bull Technologies moving into high performance automotive in collaboration with Aston Martin, as well as event management with their MK7 facility in Milton Keynes. Mercedes AMG have entered into electric racing series Formula E. F1 spin-off Williams Advanced Engineering are providing the battery systems for the third generation of Formula E single-seat electric racing cars due to compete in the 2022–2023 season. They are also supplying the battery systems for a new electric SUV off-road series 'Extreme E' for which cars have been built by specialist French electric car constructor Spark Racing Technologies and which had its inaugural season in 2021. One of the largest non-F1 organisations in the UK motorsport industry, Prodrive, is extending its capabilities in both hybrid and all electric technologies which includes a partnership with Swedish electric truck maker Volta.

Inward investment into MSV continued through this period with a consortium led by Canadian clothing billionaire Lawrence Stroll acquiring Silverstone-based Force India F1 team in August 2018, with further investment in performance car manufacturer Aston Martin leading to a renaming of the team to Aston Martin F1 for 2021. The Williams family stepped down from the motorsport business they started in 1969 with US-based investment organisation Dorilton Capital acquiring the team in August 2020. Further US-based investment was secured by McLaren to support their racing activities with MSP Sports Capital acquiring a minority stake in McLaren Racing in 2020 that will increase to 33% by the end of 2022.

The early decades of the twenty-first century ended as we started with this chapter: namely, British-based performance engineering, and a globally significant economic cluster, based on networks of SMEs, technologists and engineers drawing in global investors and investment to meet the new racing and technology challenges of mobility in the digital age.[26] And, in an initiative to respond to the COVID-19 pandemic, seeing Formula One Management co-ordinate 'Project Pitlane', the development of new ventilator technologies was undertaken by seven UK-based F1 teams to respond to the crisis in March 2020.

Conclusions and Reflections

Sixty years after its emergence, the MSV cluster continues to flourish and hold global economic primacy in its core activity of motorsport production and much further beyond. It remains a cluster comprising a dense and critical mass of numerous interdependent local and globally networked specialists in high value, technologically led testing and development, small-batch production, low-volume manufacturing and aspects of servitisation (such as around agile production systems and big data). The initial Garagisti have become a professional knowledge community of expert individuals and entrepreneurs, while the process of organisational churn so evident in Formula 1 team ownership remains in MSV.[27]

Yet neither is this to say that the cluster's core characteristics have stayed the same—there are signs that aspects of the glue of clustering has changed. One suggestion is indeed that key firms of long-run status such as McLaren (racing cars and automotive), Prodrive (prototyping and racing services), Xtrac (gearbox) or Alcon (brakes) have increasingly become ever more key infrastructural pillars of the cluster. In a system initially renowned for its horizontal SME regional networks, these large pillar companies have become economic anchors in their own right (and even more akin to the highly valued foreign direct investment plants of global manufacturers). A key aspect of this development has been the role of the industry body—The Motorsport Industry Association (MIA)—which has built a series of important networks and channels with both local and national government—and in overseas markets—as this historically anti-state industry (the motorsport industry has traditionally avoided any form of bureaucracy which has included close contact or collaboration with government) has learnt to work with the state (and its support) given hard won recognition of the industry's economic, technological and brand value. With awareness, longevity and brand has come institutional incorporation with cluster members now deeply engrained in local and regional policy-making machinery alongside supporting, for example, skills and education initiatives, global trading and business leadership. With the potential rise of pillar companies of global reach there have been suggestions that supply chains may be inexorably moving offshore and that there is a danger of hollowing out (although even here the cluster is distinctive for the challengers remain Germany, Italy, Japan and the USA rather than the BRICs or global South). Arguably, such fears may mostly be being directed at the mature if globally expanding core of motorsport whereas, in contrast, the cluster's development of high-performance technology within the industrial paradigms of low carbon, big data and Industry 4.0 has seen new forms of collaboration, integration and embeddedness with the broader spatial and regional economic context within which the MSV cluster has historically 'sat'.[28]

So the Garagisti have risen and transformed to become part of one of the most recognised and distinctive industrial clusters in the world, sitting alongside the likes of Silicon Valley, Hollywood and Hong Kong finance. The journey we have described has involved shifts and changes along the way, moving from the artful and pragmatic technologies of Cooper through the modularisation of knowledge with the advent of the Cosworth DFV, through to the branding of UK Motorsport Valley and the institutional engagement of the UK government at local, regional and national level. The cluster continues to evolve and provides a unique capability in technology integration and experimentation which has proved to be both resilient and adaptable. Arguably the Garagisti live on within the cluster's agile networks of people and production today and, although Enzo's epithet 'Garagisti' is often portrayed as contemptuous, one suspects there was also an element of heavily disguised admiration in there as well.

Notes

1. Henry, N., Pinch, S. and Russell, S. (1996) 'In Pole Position? Untraded Interdependencies, New Industrial Spaces and the British Motor Sport Industry *Area* 28, 1, pp. 25–36; Henry, N., Angus, T., Jenkins, M. and Aylett, C. (2007) *Motorsport Going Global: The Challenges Facing the World's Motorsport Industry* Palgrave Macmillan, Basingstoke.

2. Motorsport Industry Association (2013) *Review of Motorsport Valley's Business Cluster*. Motorsport Industry Association, Stoneleigh Park, Warwickshire.
3. Motorsport Industry Association (2013) *Review of Motorsport Valley's Business Cluster*. Motorsport Industry Association, Stoneleigh Park, Warwickshire.
4. Henry, N., Angus, T., Jenkins, M. and Aylett, C. (2007) *Motorsport Going Global: The Challenges Facing the World's Motorsport Industry*. Palgrave Macmillan, Basingstoke.
5. https://bristolmc.org.uk/a-brief-history-of-the-bmclcc/ accessed 16 June 2020.
6. http://500race.org/history/club-history/ accessed 18 June 2020
7. Nye, D. (1983). *Cooper Cars*. Osprey Publishing Limited, Long Acre, London. p. 14.
8. Morgan, D. (2009). *Seven Fifty Motor Club: The birthplace of modern British motorsport*. Haynes Publishing, Yeovil, Somerset.
9. Ferrari, E. (1963). *The Enzo Ferrari Memoirs*. Hamish Hamilton, London.
10. Nye, D. (1993). *Autocourse History of the Grand Prix Car 1945–65*. Hazleton Publishing, Richmond, Surrey.
11. Nye, D. (1993). *Autocourse History of the Grand Prix Car .1945–65*. Hazleton Publishing, Richmond, Surrey.
12. Nye, D. (1993). *Autocourse History of the Grand Prix Car 1945–65*. Hazleton Publishing, Richmond, Surrey.
13. Crombac, G. (2001) *Colin Chapman: The Man and His Cars*. Haynes Publishing, Yeovil, Somerset.
14. Jenkins, M., Henry, N. and Angus, T. (2002) 'Motorsport Valley and the Global Motorsport Industry: The Development and Growth of the British Performance Engineering Cluster'. SAE Motorsport Engineering Conference Proceedings; Henry, N., Jenkins, M., Burridge, M. and Geach, N. (2001) *The National Survey of Motorsport Engineering and Services: 2000*. Motorsport Industry Association, Stoneleigh Park, Warwickshire.
15. Quotation from Case Study: Cosworth Engineering in Jenkins, M. & Ambrosini, V. (2007). *Advanced Strategic Management: A Multi-Perspective Approach*. Basingstoke, Palgrave Macmillan, p. 266.
16. Crombac, G. (2001) *Colin Chapman: The Man and His Cars*. Haynes Publishing, Yeovil, Somerset. p. 284.

17. Interview with Mauro Forghieri, conducted by first author, 18 October 1999.
18. Henry, N., Angus, T and Jenkins, M. (2003) *A Study into the UK Motorsport and Performance Engineering Cluster*. Department for Trade and Industry, London.
19. Henry, N., Jenkins, M., Burridge, M. and Geach, N. (2001) *The National Survey of Motorsport Engineering and Services: 2000*. Motorsport Industry Association, Stoneleigh Park, Warwickshire.
20. Henry, N., Jenkins, M., Burridge, M. and Geach, N. (2001) *The National Survey of Motorsport Engineering and Services: 2000*. Motorsport Industry Association, Stoneleigh Park, Warwickshire.
21. Henry, N., Angus, T and Jenkins, M. (2003) *A Study into the UK Motorsport and Performance Engineering Cluster*. Department for Trade and Industry, London.
22. Henry, N., Angus, T., Jenkins, M. and Aylett, C. (2007) *Motorsport Going Global: The Challenges Facing the World's Motorsport Industry*. Palgrave Macmillan, Basingstoke.
23. Motorsport Industry Association (2013) *Review of Motorsport Valley's Business Cluster*. Motorsport Industry Association, Stoneleigh Park, Warwickshire.
24. Motorsport Industry Association (2013) *Review of Motorsport Valley's Business Cluster*. Motorsport Industry Association, Stoneleigh Park, Warwickshire.
25. Jenkins, M., Henry, N. and Angus, T. (2014) *Developing UK Motorsport: A Supply Chain Analysis*. UK Trade and Investment, London.
26. https://www.sqw.co.uk/insights-and-publications/evolution-of-the-high-performance-technology-and-motorsport-cluster/
27. Henry, N. and Pinch, S. (2000) 'Spatialising knowledge: Placing the Knowledge Community of Motor Sport Valley', *Geoforum*, 31, 2, pp. 191–208.
28. Doel, C. and Green, C. (2016) *The Evolution of the High Performance Technology and Motorsport Cluster at Silverstone*. SQW, Cambridge.

Part IV

Motor Racing and the Politics of Gender

It Was Ironic That He Should Die in Bed: Injury, Death and the Politics of Safety in the History of Motor Racing

Stephen Wagg

Few sports can have taken more human lives, nor inflicted more serious injuries on its participants, than motor racing. Moreover, for much of its history those who came to watch the racing were in as much jeopardy as the drivers themselves and ancillary staff (mechanics and race marshals, for example) have from time to time been added to the sport's substantial death toll. A politics of safety can be discerned in motor racing from the late 1960s, a politics that was not always either uncontested or rooted in altruism. This chapter looks historically and analytically at the development of safety culture in motor racing.

S. Wagg (✉)
International Centre for Sport History and Culture, De Montfort University, Leicester, UK

D. Sturm et al. (eds.), *The History and Politics of Motor Racing*, Global Culture and Sport Series, https://doi.org/10.1007/978-3-031-22825-4_10

Five Minutes After the Second Car Was Built: Danger and Early Motor Racing

Motor car manufacturer Henry Ford is reputed to have said that motor racing began 'five minutes after the second car was built'.[1] This, of course, is hyperbole, but it's true nevertheless that the early decades of the motor car were characterised by the growth of (often lethal) competition. While much pioneering motor technology took place in Germany, most motor racing around the turn of the twentieth century was staged in France or Italy: France, it has been suggested, had many straight roads and Italy was the last country to restrict racing on public highways—it was banned, for example, in Germany and the United Kingdom.[2] These races in the first instance were conducted on public roads and over long distances, usually between cities: the Paris Rouen race of 1894 was among the first. These races were fraught with danger and often resulted in numerous fatalities—the Paris-Madrid race of 1903, for instance, is widely described as the 'Race of Death': eight people (five racers and three spectators) were killed.[3] In Italy the Targa Floria, a race through the mountains of Sicily, was inaugurated in 1906 and the equally prestigious, 1000-mile, Mille Miglia in 1927; it was eleven years later, following the deaths of ten people (including seven children) in the Mille Miglia, that the Italian government called a halt to open road racing.[4] Meanwhile, purpose-built circuits began to appear, the first being Brooklands in Surrey (UK) in 1907.

Drivers of the early motor racing cars were drawn heavily from the higher echelons of western European and American society and related in diverse ways to the prospect of danger and death. Many were European noblemen, such as the Florentine aristocrat Prince Scipione Borghese, an adventurer who won the first Beijing to Paris race in 1907,[5] or Giulio Masetti, who dominated the Targa Floria in the early 1920s and died in the Targa Floria of 1927. Many such men were fascinated by speed and the possibilities of the motor car and had invested commercially in these possibilities: French nobleman Jules-Albert de Dion, for instance, won the first Paris to Rouen race in 1894 and later formed one of the pioneer automobile companies. English racing driver and car importer Charles Jarrott, who raced between 1900 and 1904, expressed the ethos and early dominance of the 'gentleman racer': 'Obviously the competitive element existed between the various manufacturers of cars taking part; they entered a race in the hope that they would [...] beat their rivals; but the general idea underlying the whole event was the desire to prove to the world that motor cars would go, and that they were capable of travelling long distances in a reliable and speedy manner. Dozens of [the drivers] were independent, racing their own cars [and] were so enamoured of the sport as a sport, as to make the mere question of money subservient to the keen desire to drive a racing-car and to race'.[6] This keen desire combined with the fallibility of new, work-in-progress technology to enhance the likelihood of injury or death—to drivers and to curious watchers at the roadside.

In time, however, the industrialisation of car production and the growth of motor racing as a showcase for different brands of vehicle widened the net of recruitment to the driving seats of racing cars. The biographies of the leading racing drivers of the 1920s and 1930s seem to reveal a growing number from working or lower middle-class families. Many—the Americans Barney Oldfield (1878–1946) and Jimmy Murphy (1894–1924), Frenchman Robert Benoist (1895–1944), Swiss driver Christian Lautenschlager (1877–1954), Germany's Christian Werner (1892–1932), August Momberger (1905–69) and Hermann Lang (1909–1987), Italians Ugo Sivocci (1885–1923), Pietro Bordino (1887–1928) and Clemente Biondetti (1898–1955) and others came to motor racing variously from comparatively humble beginnings via jobs as mechanics, engineers, test drivers or racing motor cyclists. They invariably drove what were effectively works cars, thus promoting particular models: in Italy, for instance, motor racing was established in the 1920s, supported notably by the leading car makers Alfa Romeo, Maserati and Bugatti.[7] Such men were racing as a condition of their employment and sheered axles, failing gearboxes, skids and burst petrol tanks were the common coin of their working lives. Death and serious injury thus became occupational hazards for many drivers and they developed strategies for dealing with this. One, it seems, was fatalism. The Italian driver Alberto Ascari, for example, famously withheld affection from his children: 'I prefer to treat them the hard way. I don't want them to love me too much. Because they will suffer less if one of these days I am killed'.[8]

(Both Alberto Ascari and his father Antonio, also a racing driver, died in race crashes—Antonio in the French Grand Prix of 1925, Alberto doing some practice laps at Monza in 1955.) Another acclaimed Italian racer Tazio Nuvolari showed similar sangfroid in, reputedly, never booking return tickets when travelling abroad to race.[9]

Accounts of the career of Nuvolari, who raced cars between 1930 and 1950, provide important insights into the ways in which the prospect of death or serious injury were handled in the culture of motor racing between the world wars. Nuvolari himself was among the first celebrities thrown up by this culture. As such he was marketed as a daredevil. However, New Zealand driver Thomas Cholmondeley-Tapper, who raced against Nuvolari, argued that this sort of publicity belied Nuvolari's professionalism: 'Nuvolari [...] was often called in his own country the 'Son of the Devil'—fearless—but from my acquaintance with him I found this catchphrase inaccurate. He would make no secret of his dislike of a particularly dangerous section of a course and, in spite of what appeared to be extremely abandoned driving, he did in fact know exactly what he was doing and possessed sound judgment and knowledge of his capabilities'.[10] This professionalism, in the cases of Italy and Germany, was often allied to a strident nationalism, blended in the 1930s with fascism. In both countries success at motor racing betokened a thriving automobile industry which in turn heightened international prestige. Of Nuvolari it was said: 'it was only natural and human for Nuvolari to render a machine useless when assailed by a mass of rivals, and when it was a question of defending the national flag and prestige. If he risked his life with inferior means against the German's massive offensive, he did it for these reasons...[...] Again and again he had smashed his car or himself, in one race after another, because of his unflagging determination to overcome the tremendous advantage in power of the German machines'.[11] When professionalism trumped patriotism and Nuvolari accepted an offer of better financial terms from the German team Auto Union, Italian fascist leader Benito Mussolini interceded with Ferrari, Nuvolari's previous Italian employers, to bring him back.[12] Nuvolari incurred many injuries during his racing career and his biographers remark that it was ironic that he should die in his bed;[13] his death, in 1953, seems nevertheless to have been occupationally related—he died of emphysema, brought on by the inhalation of petrol fumes.[14]

In Nazi Germany great political stress was laid upon the notion of death as an honourable outcome while racing for the fatherland. The Third Reich gave much financial support to the principal German car firms—Mercedes Benz, Auto Union and Porsche—and encouraged competition between them.[15] They also saw the German motor racing teams, such as the Silver Arrows (which raced between 1934 and 1939), as important flagships for national regeneration. When leading German racing driver Bernd Rosemeyer, a member of Hitler's paramilitary SS organisation, was killed attempting a land speed record in 1938, Hitler said: 'For all of us it is painful to know that one of the very best and most courageous of those pioneers in the international recognition of German engines and vehicle manufacturing, Bernd Rosenmeyer, had to lose his life so young [he was 29]. But he, and all the men who, in those tough races, sit at the wheel of our cars or ride our motorcycles, are fighting with us to give bread, wages and reward to the German working man'.[16]

It seems fair to say that, while there was disquiet about the deaths caused by motor racing in the 1920s and 1930s, this disquiet was, first, on the whole not expressed by the drivers and, second, it was more likely to follow the deaths of spectators than of competitors. A section of the world's third purpose-built racing circuit at Monza, north of Milan, was abandoned after the death there of driver Emilio Materassi and twenty-eight spectators in 1928 and, as we've seen, deaths of spectators provoked the banning of open road racing by the Italian government in 1938.

Doing What They Enjoyed? Body Count and the Beginnings of a Safety Debate in Motor Racing in the 1950s and 1960s

Formula 1 (F1) was inaugurated in 1950 and, for motor racing, the two decades that followed the Second World War are sometimes recalled as a golden age, a time 'when sex was safe and racing was dangerous'.[17] A picture is often painted of a social milieu in which daring young males defied death at the wheel and, if they survived, mostly spent their non-racing time as 'playboys' in the company of glamorous young females. As the headline of a recent article argued, 'Formula One drivers accepted the risks. This was the life they loved',[18] a rationalisation often heard at race meets in the post-1945 era. In other typical retrospections, David Hobbs, an ex-racing driver who had made his F1 debut in 1969 is reputed to have talked in 2009 of how in his day 'real men'[19] raced at Spa, venue for the Belgian Grand Prix, at which fifteen drivers were killed between 1957 and 1969, and in 2013 Ferrari historian and writer John Lamm reflected thus on the death of Count Wolfgang von Trips at Monza in 1961, in a crash that killed twelve spectators: 'you have to understand that death in motor racing was not uncommon then. At the time, people were still used to people dying around Formula One, even spectators. Sounds weird, doesn't it?'[20]

Accounts, however, suggest that politically the situation as regards death and injury in motor racing during the 1950s and 1960s was far more complex than this. Several factors were in play.

First, while some drivers were live-for-the-day *bon viveurs*, others now embraced the same sober professionalism that had been perceptible before the war. For example, leading tyre technician David 'Dunlop Mac' MacDonald wrote of British driver Dick Seaman, who had died in the Belgian Grand Prix of 1939, 'Seaman had more in common, probably, with our serious young post-war stars who have made Britain pre-eminent in racing than with the devil-may-care fellows of my early days at Brooklands', citing Seaman's 'brilliant ability and close attention to detailed preparation for races'.[21] (Seaman's professionalism derived in part from his admiration for Nazi Germany and it extended to conceding, on his deathbed, that, at the time of his soon-to-be-fatal accident, he had been driving too fast for the conditions.[22]) Tony Brooks, who made his Formula 1 debut in 1956 spoke in similar terms of Stirling Moss: 'Stirling was probably the first really professional driver. Behind the wheel I took it just as seriously as he did, but out of the car I wasn't trying to be commercial, whereas Stirling was'.[23] That would not, of course, mean that Moss and a rising generation of professionally minded racing drivers would lobby for greater safety—indeed Moss himself stated baldly in 1963 that the risks that drivers and spectators took were simply 'their affair' and, as with a number of his contemporaries, he opposed the use of safety belts[24]—but Moss, like other upcoming drivers, would nonetheless now be likely to have a thought-out position on the safety aspects of his work. Now drivers might see it as a test of their professionalism to deal with the prevailing hazards; equally, perhaps, they could see the hazards as an unacceptable barrier to the exercising of this professionalism. In a book of 1961, the Scottish driver Innes Ireland expressed himself broadly opposed to increased safety measures—'I don't go for the business of improving the safety of the track—the circuit—itself. If a circuit is there to be raced on, it's there to be raced on, and, if it includes something a driver doesn't like, such as a brick wall or a house, then he must learn to drive around it. I think one must put up with whatever a circuit presents and drive accordingly. In any case danger is part of the game'. In the next breath however, Ireland admits that the circuits in the French city of Rheims and Cordoba, Argentina, have hazards that must be removed.[25] It would, naturally, be more difficult for drivers concerned about safety to publish their concerns: this could damage their public image and their employability. These concerns were nevertheless expressed privately. The American Phil Hill, who began driving for Ferrari in 1959, was one who developed a more cautious philosophy: years later he recalled his inner conflict, on the one hand wanting 'to race, to excel' and, on the other, 'wishing to stay alive and in one piece'.[26] In the end, he had not, he reflected, been 'gung-ho enough', or prepared to die, for his ruthless employer Enzo Ferrari.[27] Hill's sensitivities were scorned by other drivers, such as the Briton Mike Hawthorn, who called him 'Auntie',[28] masculinity being the predictable subtext to many of these discussions. Nevertheless, feeling about safety sometimes ran high enough for a particular track to be shunned: for example, in 1961, British racing teams boycotted Monza, known in Italy as the 'Death Circuit', because of its notorious high bank, over which cars had often careered, endangering spectators.[29] But, in the late 1960s, drivers who questioned safety at race tracks could still get short shrift. Max Mosley, who began as a Formula 2 driver in 1966, recalled, 'When I suggested to any of the officials I encountered that the racing was unnecessarily dangerous, the response was always: "You don't have to do it if you don't want to, it's entirely voluntary. And, if you think a corner is dangerous, slow down"'.[30]

The second factor which was now promising to change the politics of safety in motor racing was the labour market position of the drivers. This, historically, had been weak. As Moss pointed out, back in 1954, when bravery was thought to be the key ingredient to a successful driving career, Mercedes Benz had received 4000 applications to join their racing team.[31] In these circumstances team bosses such as Alfred Neubauer (Mercedes Benz, 1926–55) and Enzo Ferrari, who had founded the Scuderia team in 1929, had been hard taskmasters, largely because they controlled access to some of the best cars: indeed in 2004 of Ferrari his former mistress recalled, 'He never betrayed his cars. Other things, perhaps'.[32] Increasingly, though, skill and professionalism—scarcer resources—were required. As Mike Hawthorn implied in 1964 an elite corps of drivers had become established on the Grand Prix circuit: there were now 'only about twenty jobs going with the leading continental teams and nobody bothered to advertise them in the Situations Vacant columns'.[33] Hawthorn, who had become Formula One World Champion in 1958, also declared himself to have been 'caught out by the speed with which I had become an international celebrity'.[34] Provenly successful celebrity drivers would, in time, be better able to dictate terms, on safety and other matters, to the racing teams and to the circuit proprietors, as the next few years would show.

A third factor was body count, which was growing. Here there were some fatalities that could not escape the political attention of bodies outside of the sport. The most influential of these incidents was at the Le Mans 24-Hour race in 1955. A collision involving three cars resulted in the death of one driver and, according to recent estimates, around 130 spectators.[35] The race was not stopped; indeed, during this period of races it was not customary to stop races in the event of fatalities. Universally recognised as the worst accident in motor racing history, the carnage at Le Mans in 1955 resulted in the banning of motor racing in several countries; in one—Switzerland—the ban still stands.

The crash that marked the end of the Mille Miglia in 1957 featured a driver who embodied many of the early, devil-may-care myths that had surrounded motor racing. Alfonso de Portago was a Spanish aristocrat, athlete and playboy who had once said that racers lived in 'a world that only a few understand'.[36] In a typically flamboyant gesture, he had stopped his Ferrari during the race to kiss one of his current girlfriends, the Hollywood actress Linda Christian, and had refused a tyre change. When the tyre in question subsequently burst, Portago's vehicle had left the road, killing eleven people—nine onlookers (five of them children), Portago (whose body was cut in two) and his navigator, Edmund Nelson.[37] Besides bringing the Mille Miglia to an end, the incident drew stern criticism from the Vatican[38] and Enzo Ferrari was charged with manslaughter, a charge not dismissed until four years later.[39]

While these incidents did not necessarily lead to many structural changes to motor racing circuits, where safety concerns were still often being rebutted, they did heighten political concerns about the safety of the motor car as a means of transport. After all, a key raison d'être of motor racing was to showcase motor cars for sale to the public and the implications of the catastrophe at Le Mans were clear. With over seventy people already confirmed dead the defiant headline on *Autosport* magazine's principal report of the crash read 'JAGUAR VICTORY AT LE MANS: British Cars Take 13 out of 21 Places'.[40] The following week correspondents wrote to castigate Labour politician Jennie Lee for calling motor racing a 'blood sport'[41] and the week after that a further letter commiserated with Jaguar for 'losing a great deal of publicity from a really great performance'.[42] Mercedes Benz, who had ordered the immediate withdrawal of their drivers, removed their cars from Le Mans and questioned the continuation of the race, pulled out of motor racing and did not return until 1989.

The greatest public concern over the motor car, however, was in the United States, where a political debate over the safety of the automobile itself took place in the mid-1960s. The writer A.J. Baime describes how Ford sales executive Lee Iacocca attended the Indianapolis 500 race of 1964 and grimaced at the sight of two drivers (Eddie Sachs and Dave MacDonald) being killed in cars with 'Powered by Ford' emblazoned on the side: the cars had 'turned in to blazing coffins in front of hundreds of thousands of spectators'.[43] The following year the campaigner Ralph Nader published a book called *Unsafe at Any Speed*,[44] condemning the automobile, and President Johnson declared a crisis on American highways. This brought anxious responses from Ford and Enzo Ferrari, who blamed accidents on careless driving, along with Senate hearings and an

FBI investigation of Nader. With car sales falling in 1966 the US passed the National Traffic and Motor Vehicle Safety Act, compelling safety features in cars.[45] Iacocca argued that such measures were a breach of Americans' civil rights[46] and is reputed to have told President Nixon in 1971 that 'safety has really killed all of our business'.[47]

A fourth factor was technology. Gung-ho masculine codes and philosophies built around the proximity of death notwithstanding, progressive motor engineers were developing safer racing cars and administrators were overseeing the admission of important, if piecemeal, safety innovations into Grand Prix racing. As veteran motor racing commentator Murray Walker reflected, in 1949, the year he began broadcasting, 'drivers were of no consequence. The cars had their engines at the front and the drivers wore thin cotton trousers, short-sleeved T-shirts and linen helmets. They had no safety belts and their cars were flimsy death traps'.[48] Cars in the 1950s were fast but unreliable. Driver reminiscences bear this out. Stirling Moss, for example, remembered driving a Maserati at Monza in 1958 at 160 mph when the steering wheel sheared off.[49] Such mishaps were still common.

Innovations made in the 1950s were few, but significant: crash helmets (affording minimal protection by modern standards) became compulsory in 1952; disc brakes began to replace drum brakes in 1955 and, the same year, Australian driver-engineer Jack Brabham became the first person to enter a Grand Prix (the British) in a mid-engine car; he was also the first person to win in one, in 1959. Rear-engine cars were introduced in 1957 and adopted by all teams by 1961;[50] the last front-engine car to start a Grand Prix was in the British Grand Prix of that year, with occasional driver Jack Fairman at the wheel. Tony Brooks commented years later that this 'makes sense when you're trying to put the power down through the back wheels. Design never looked back after that'.[51] In 1962 the British Lotus team introduced a car with an aluminium monocoque[52] chassis, a major significance of which was that the car was less likely to catch fire; earlier models were made of highly flammable, magnesium-based materials and many drivers had burned to death. The design of this new chassis was credited to engineer Colin Chapman, founder of the Lotus team. Chapman was pro-safety measures and opposed the gung-ho arguments of drivers like Ireland,[53] but he also ran a racing team and innovations such as this were made not solely to improve safety but to enhance the possibility of winning races.

The 1960s saw a number of further important reforms. By the end of the decade F1 cars had roll bars (introduced in 1961), double-braking systems and protected fuel tanks and their drivers were obliged to wear harnesses, fire-resistant clothing and shatterproof visors.[54] Straw bales, long a vestigial protective feature of the motor racing tracks, were finally banned in 1967.

But driver death still stalked the motor racing circuit and the devil-may-care ethic still thrived in parts of the racing fraternity: sometime in the 1960s Piers Courage, a driver from a wealthy brewing family who would die in the Dutch Grand Prix of 1970, was asked by his (disapproving) father why he enjoyed motor racing so much. He replied 'Well, Dad, you had the war'.[55]

In the late 1960s the campaign for greater driver safety had barely begun.

Chicken Noises: Jackie Stewart and the Rise of Driver Militancy

Jackie Stewart, who made his Formula 1 debut in 1965, is often rendered as 'the man who transformed motor racing'[56] and it is certainly the case that no driver campaigned harder for safety measures in motor racing than Stewart. But social change is never the work of one individual alone and it's important to consider the circumstances in which Stewart's initiatives were taken.

A number of things are crucial to note about Stewart's campaign. He rejected the longstanding buccaneer/gladiator notion of the racing driver and embraced instead the growing professionalism—professionalism which, for Stewart, was embodied in the Argentine Juan Manual Fangio who had won twenty-four Grand Prix and been five times World Champion in the 1950s. Fangio had been able to choose the best cars, had avoided serious injury and had provided for his future by setting up a business (a filling station and a Mercedes Benz dealership) in Buenos Aires.[57] Second, as observed earlier, the market position of top drivers was stronger than in the past; they were now heavily in demand and better able to dictate terms. Teams needed them as much as they needed the teams. Stewart, for example, at one point turned down Enzo Ferrari; Ferrari, confident always that any driver would want to drive one of his cars, was not used to such negotiation and is said to have retorted 'What does he want? The factory?'[58] Third, drivers continued to die in large numbers: in his memoirs, Stewart cited an eleven-year window (1963–73) during which he had seen fifty-seven friends and colleagues killed in motor racing, including four established drivers during four months in 1968.[59] Furthermore, Stewart readily recognised both the commercialisation of popular culture of the time and his own business prospects within that: 'There was much to do in the 1960s. Britain was emerging from post-war austerity and bursting out in a colourful blaze of music, fashion and social freedom. Everything seemed so new and, as an F1 driver with a growing profile, I was swept along in all the excitement'.[60] He recalls: 'If there was a corporate function where I knew there would be interesting people to meet, or a business relationship where I thought I could make a worthwhile contribution, I found it [...] almost impossible to say 'no'.[61] Stewart insisted: 'I wanted a life after driving a car'.[62] Such a future orientation was wholly incompatible with the live-for-the-moment ethos to which some drivers still subscribed. (Stewart frequently stressed the importance of family life—by contrast, Stirling Moss, first president of the Grand Prix Drivers Association (GPDA) at its inauguration in 1961, had said that being married to a racing driver was like being married to a soldier. Moss had insisted that the GPDA was not a trade union and talked of modified circuits only in the interests of greater safety for spectators.[63]) Stewart became a client of talent management company IMG (International Management Group) in 1968 and the same year arranged to live in tax exile in Switzerland.

Stewart used a serious accident which he suffered at the Belgian Grand Prix at Spa in 1966 as a catalyst for his initiative. Spa had always been regarded as one of the more hazardous circuits in the motor racing calendar and water on the track had heightened the dangers to drivers on this occasion.[64] The largely inactive GPDA was revived under Stewart's leadership and called for: inspections of Grand Prix circuits; the removal of trees and telegraph poles and the installation of Armco (safety) barriers;

and the compulsory providing to drivers of flameproof apparel, certified helmets and safety belts.[65] Spa was boycotted by drivers in 1969 and the following year the GPDA committee voted 7 to 2 (with two abstentions) to boycott the German track Nurburgring unless certain safety measures were taken.[66] That same year, one of the seven, the Austrian driver Jochen Rindt, who had also gone into tax exile in Switzerland, became Formula 1's first (and only) posthumous champion, having been killed in practice prior to Italian Grand Prix at Monza.

In assessing the Stewart campaign, two things should be added.

First, Stewart's initiatives were resented and resisted in some quarters: track managers were concerned about the expense of upgrading their circuits and there were moves against the GPDA.[67] The authorities had their supporters in the motor racing press: *Motor Sport* writer Denis Jenkinson condemned Stewart for 'his pious whinings [which] have brain-washed and undermined the natural instincts of some young and inexperienced newcomers to Grand Prix racing and removed the Belgian Grand Prix from Spa-Francorchamps'. [...] Can you really ask me in all honesty to admire, or even tolerate, our current reigning World Champion Driver?'[68] Once his campaign was underway Stewart himself recalls Innes Ireland making chicken noises at him at a Grand Prix.

Second, Stewart felt moved to make his own medical provision, hiring medical specialists to be on hand when and where he was racing.[69] This seems to have represented a recognition of the continuing dangers of motor racing and an acknowledgement that thoroughgoing safety policies in motor racing were yet to come. The final section of this chapter explores the reasons for this.

Dead Drivers Are Bad for Business: Sponsorship, Safety and Motor Racing After the Death of Ayrton Senna

Three principal factors—the growth of sponsorship in motor racing, allied to the sports growing global profile; the political struggle during the 1980s and 1990s to control the commercial future of Formula 1; and the concern to make motor racing bodies safe from prosecution—combined to produce a culture of safety in motor racing in the twenty-first century. Although its promotion was contested (and criticisms of it are still heard) this culture has led to minimal loss of life or serious injury in elite motor racing.

As regards safety, the 1970s and 1980s saw a continuation of the pattern of periodic protest and piecemeal reform. There was also some sporadic, safety-related militancy. In 1975 the GPDA threatened a boycott of the Spanish Grand Prix in Barcelona claiming that track safety rails were not bolted properly.[70] The race eventually took place, amid rumours that the cars would otherwise be confiscated by police, and five spectators were killed when the car of German driver Rolf Stommelen went into the crowd. The following year the Dutch driver Niki Lauda suffered severe burns in a crash during the German Grand Prix at Nurburgring, a track of which he had been a vocal critic.[71] Later that year Lauda and other drivers drove only a token lap in the Japanese Grand Prix at Fuji, having deemed the circuit unsafe because of heavy rain.[72] There were dissenters: James Hunt for example, carried on driving when the others withdrew and won the race. Later the same year, prior to the Canadian Grand Prix there, drivers raised doubts about the safety of the venue, the Mosport International Raceway in Ontario and a GPDA meeting was called; James Hunt, although, bizarrely, member of the association's Safety Committee, refused to attend, saying 'To hell with safety. All I want to do is race'.[73]

However, ten Formula 1 drivers died in races during the 1970s and this seems to have triggered an acknowledgement at the level of Formula 1 governance (now in the hands of British entrepreneur Bernie Ecclestone) that something further must be done. In 1978 Ecclestone appointed Prof. Sid Watkins, a neurosurgeon, to be the official F1 doctor, the initial emphasis being placed on measures to treat, rather than to prevent, injury. As Ecclestone recalled in 2012, 'we discussed many aspects of safety and medical issues. We agreed that we needed a proper hospital at the track in the form of a fully equipped medical centre to stabilise injured drivers with immediate treatment, and a helicopter to transport them subsequently to specialist facilities, and that the helicopter pad had to be as close to that trackside hospital as possible'.[74] Helicopter cover, on-site medical centres and designated receiving hospitals were all established over the next few years. If a circuit refused to cooperate, Ecclestone threatened to send the drivers home.[75] Only two drivers—the Italian Riccardo Paletti and Canada's Gilles Villeneuve—died in Grand Prix in the 1980s, although two others (Patrick Depailler of France and Elio de Angelis of Italy) died testing.

This was not all down to altruism. In 1978 Ecclestone had become chief executive of the Formula One Constructors' Association (FOCA) and he drove a hard bargain in his dealings with the race organisers. Patrick Duffeler, executive in charge of sport sponsorship at tobacco corporation Philip Morris (now heavily invested in motor racing) suggested that Ecclestone liked to use safety as a pretext in these negotiations: organisers would have to pay more or risk losing the race because of 'unsatisfactory safety arrangements'.[76] Moreover, FOCA soon came into a long-running dispute with the Fédération Internationale de l'Automobile (FIA), the world governing body for motor sport. FIA was quartered in Paris and held by Ecclestone and FOCA counsel Max Mosley to favour the continental works teams over the British teams quartered in Motor Sport Valley (see the chapter by Jenkins, Henry and Angus in this book), by proposing vehicle specifications that British teams could not afford and/or did not have the time to meet. Here, once again, the vocabulary of motive[77] in the various exchanges was one of safety. For instance, in 1980 the FIA banned skirts—aerodynamic devices adopted by British teams such as Lotus which made cars go faster. The ban was to take immediate effect (instead of after the regulation two-year period) because it was introduced on safety grounds, immediately putting British teams at a disadvantage. Mosley judged that virtually any reform could be given a safety rationale and responded with counter proposals, couched, similarly, in the language of safety—a language likely to prevail if matters came to court in France. This culminated in the so-called Concorde Agreement between FOCA and FIA in 1981.[78]

If Ecclestone himself is any guide to the prevailing attitudes to death and injury in Formula 1 at this time, it appears that the historically masculine and breezy obliviousness to risk was still in play. In 1982, following the two aforementioned driver deaths in quick succession, Ecclestone repeated the rationalisation he would likely first have heard at motor races in the 1950s: 'When a driver dies, he goes out doing what he wants to do. I don't find that depressing at all'.[79] In 1990 he told journalists that driver deaths were 'a form of natural culling'.[80] But whatever the currency of these sentiments in the social world of motor racing, they became unutterable at an official level in 1994, following the deaths of Austrian driver Roland Ratzenberger in practice for the San Marino Grand Prix at Imola and, the following day, of three times World Champion Ayrton Senna in the race itself. Two weeks later another Austrian, Karl Wendlinger, crashed in practice for the Monaco Grand Prix and, although he survived, was in a coma for several weeks.

Reaction to these events showed that motor racing had moved on. It was now a widely televised event with a global audience: each race was seen by around half a billion people in over 180 countries.[81] Senna himself represented the consummation of a process, begun in the 1930s, by which the racing driver had become a national icon: on his death the Brazilian government declared three days of national mourning and Senna was given a state funeral, at which Ecclestone, though he had come to Brazil, was told he would not be welcome. Senna's brother Leonardo told a press conference: 'The motor sport authorities are only interested in money'.[82] More importantly for Ecclestone and Mosley, the latter having just assumed the presidency of the FIA, racing was now heavily dependent on its sponsors, who were understandably very anxious about the torrent of adverse global publicity that followed Senna's death. The roots of this situation went back to 1968 when on-car advertising had been approved. The first companies to have their logos on Formula 1 racing cars were predominantly the tobacco companies and brands, including Gold Leaf, John Player and Marlboro. The last thing that these companies, who were trying to counter widely accepted medical findings that smoking was injurious to health, wanted was to have their products associated with violent death. The writer Russell Hotten put it bluntly: 'Dead drivers are bad for business'.[83] Senna's death crash had taken place at 200 mph, had been witnessed by a huge television audience and his car had borne a huge logo for Rothmans cigarettes. Mosley recalled 'a full-blown crisis. Commentators were asking what was wrong with Formula One; the big car manufacturers and sponsors were talking openly about pulling out; and there were even suggestions from politicians that Formula

One should be banned. I found myself having crisis meetings with senior car industry executives'.[84]

Mosley responded, importantly, with a two-pronged strategy. An FIA Expert Advisory Safety Committee was immediately set up under the chairmanship of Prof. Watkins. Watkins was tasked (a) to investigate ways of making racing safer. This would embrace not only the better response to accidents (more helicopters; safety cars; extrication teams and so on[85]) but ways of mitigating serious injury (head-and-neck protection; collapsible steering columns; and, crucially, the reduction of speed)[86] and (b) to extend his research to cover occupant safety in road, as well as racing, cars.[87] Mosley himself announced restrictions on aerodynamics and engine power; if the teams did not agree to these then the championship for 1995 would be cancelled. As motor sport writer Alan Henry recalled, 'the teams blatantly told Max to his face that he was nuts'.[88] But Mosley had his eye firmly on the broader picture. Motor racing, he argued, would suffer commercially and politically if fatal accidents continued. He had noted that, in theory, FIA was responsible for all motoring. A safety campaign that embraced the ordinary motorist would be seen as an intrinsically good thing, but it would also put motor racing morally in credit in the political sphere—particularly the European Union (EU). Mosley found out that there had been no new legislation in the European parliament to protect car occupants since 1974 and, noting that the EU now had stronger powers under the Maastricht Treaty of 1992 and against motor industry opposition, he led a delegation of experts to the European parliament to discuss sweeping new safety measures. Astutely, he argued to the EU that, as things stood, it was then currently safer to crash in an F1 car than on a typical road. The new measures became effective in 1998 and Mosley claimed subsequently that road deaths across the EU had fallen by 50%.[89] But Mosley made his ulterior motive plain. He had told the FIA Senate 'that if there were ever another major accident like the one at Le Mans in 1955, we would need friends in politics if we were to protect motor sport. It would be too late to start wooing politicians after the event; we would need them onside immediately, already briefed about the lives that were being saved because of what motor sport was doing for the ordinary road user. If we had a big accident without all this in place, we would risk politicians banning motor sport'.[90]

Conclusion

Since 1994, Formula 1 has seen only one driver fatality—that of the Frenchman Jules Bianchi, who died in 2015, nine months after crashing in the Japanese Grand Prix of the previous year. The reforms initiated by Mosley and Watkins appear to have done their work, reducing not crashes, but the fatal consequences of crashes, and thus protecting the Formula One brand. People still die racing motor cars—in 2013 Spanish racing driver María de Villota Comba died as a result of injuries sustained in a crash while she was test-driving at Duxford aerodrome in England the previous year and British driver Sean Edwards perished when his Porsche crashed at the Queensland Raceway in Australia; he was giving a lesson and in the passenger seat. But there is seemingly wide acceptance of the comparative safety of high velocity cars now: indeed, in 2013 British driver Anthony Davidson felt able to tell the motor sport press that motor racing had lost its 'fear factor': 'I feel a driver should be challenged and should be punished for mistakes. It's what makes people follow the sport in quite a gruesome way—it's the danger, racing drivers should be heroes'. He fell short, though, of calling for a return to the hazards and carnage of earlier decades: 'We don't want to see fans get injured or drivers get injured or killed but the drivers should get punished. On some modern circuits it's pathetic when you see drivers going off the track and nothing happens'.[91] And the following year American motoring writer Jordan Golson detailed how Formula 1 cars were now 'so amazingly safe' that drivers could hit a concrete wall nose-first at 150 mph and walk away with only minor injuries.[92] A further endorsement of this view came the same year from retired driver Vic Elford, who had driven in various forms of competition between the 1950s and 1983:

> I think in one respect it has changed for the worse. In virtually all forms of racing, motor racing now has become so safe. I'm not—well, to a certain extent, I am—criticising safety because driving in racing today, it is virtually impossible to get hurt, really badly hurt. It does happen occasionally, but it's almost out of the question getting hurt or getting killed. So, drivers, particularly younger ones coming up, know that they can get away with doing almost anything and they do it, which, to a certain extent, destroys

racing, because you get a whole load of accidents that would have never, ever happened 40 years ago because we wouldn't have dared do the things they do.[93]

If a case is nowadays to be made against motor racing it will be made on environmental grounds and not those of the safety of the participants.[94] One final irony is that, in 2017 with driver safety now virtually assured, membership of the GPDA among Formula 1 drivers stood at an unprecedented 100%, with many drivers feeling that new owners Liberty Media were unclear as to where they 'wanted to take the sport'. Drivers' grievances were now often concerned with motor racing as a spectacle and included 'the rise of pay TV and fewer viewers/followers as a result'; 'negative press spirals due to political fights via the media'; 'badly thought-out television camera angles that do not portray the speed and drama of the cars'.[95]

Notes

1. https://www.pinterest.co.uk/pin/463800461596553855/ Access: 1st October 2019.
2. See Richard Williams *Enzo Ferrari: A Life* London: Yellow Jersey Press 2002 pp. 38–9; Russell Hotten *Formula One: The Business of Winning* London: Orion Publishing 1998 p. 4.
3. https://www.caotica.com/the-race-of-death-paris-madrid-road-race-1903/ Access 2nd October 2019.
4. Williams *Enzo Ferrari* p. 110.
5. See Luigi Barzini *Peking to Paris: Across Two Continents in an Itala* London: Penguin 1986.
6. Charles Jarrott *Ten Years of Motors and Motor Racing* London: E. Grant Richards 1906 p. 97.
7. Williams *Enzo Ferrari…* p. 26.
8. Gerald Donaldson 'Alberto Ascari' https://www.formula1.com/en/drivers/hall-of-fame/Alberto_Ascari.html Access 3rd October 2019.
9. Christopher Hilton *Nuvolari* Derby, UK: Breedon Books 2003 p. 14.
10. Hilton *Nuvolari* p. 219.

11. Count Giovanni Lurani and Luigi Marinatto *Nuvolari* London: Cassell 1959 p. 153.
12. Ivan Rendall *The Chequered Flag* London: Weidenfeld and Nicolson. p. 140. Nuvolari drove once for auto Union in the Swiss Grand Prix of 1938.
13. Lurani and Marinatto *Nuvolari* p. 201.
14. Adriano Cimarosti *The Complete History of Grand Prix Motor Racing* Croydon: Motor Racing Publications 1990 p. 137; Williams *Enzo Ferrari* p. 135.
15. Eberhard Reuss *Hitler's Motor Racing Battles: The Silver Arrows Under the Swastika* Yeovil, UK: Haynes Publishing 2008 p. 67.
16. Reuss *Hitler's Motor Racing…* p. 320.
17. Blake Z. Rong 'The Golden Age of F1 Was Also Its Deadliest' https://www.roadandtrack.com/motorsports/news/a29613/the-golden-age-of-f1-was-also-its-deadliest/ Posted 18th June 2016; access 7th October 2019.
18. Colin Drury "Formula One drivers accepted the risks. This was the life they loved': Italy, 1957' *The Guardian* 3rd November 2017 https://www.theguardian.com/sport/2017/nov/03/1957-mille-miglia-ferrari-louise-king-peter-collins Access 7th October 2019.
19. Quoted in Thomas Macaulay Millar 'When Men Were Men, And Burned to Death' https://yesmeansyesblog.wordpress.com/2009/12/21/when-men-were-men-and-burned-to-death/ Posted 21st December 2009; access 7th October 2019.
20. 'Back in Time: The Tragic Tale of 'Count Crash" (unattributed) https://flagsandwhistles.wordpress.com/2013/11/01/back-in-time-the-tragic-tale-of-count-crash/ Posted 1st November 2013; access 7th October 2019.
21. David MacDonald ('Dunlop Mac') and Adrian Ball *Fifty Years with the Speed Kings* London: Stanley Paul 1961 pp. 49–50.
22. See Jonathan Glancy 'The master race' *Observer Sport Monthly* 1st September 2002 https://www.theguardian.com/observer/osm/story/0,6903,782811,00.html Access 8th October 2019.
23. Bruce Jones *Formula One: The Illustrated History* London: Carlton Books 2015 p. 16.
24. Stirling Moss, face to face with Ken Purdy *All But My Life* London: Pan Books 1965 [First published London: William Kimber 1963] p. 145.
25. Innes Ireland *Motor Racing Today* London: Arthur Barker 1961 pp. 124–6.

26. Michael Cannell *The Limit: Life and Death in Formula One's Most Dangerous Era* London: Atlantic Books 2011 p. 144.
27. Williams *Enzo Ferrari* pp. 225–6.
28. Cannell *The Limit* pp. 143 and 130.
29. Cannell *The Limit* p. xiii.
30. Max Mosley *Formula One and Beyond: The Autobiography* London: Simon and Schuster 2015 p. 36.
31. Moss and Purdy *All My Life* p. 103.
32. Richard Williams 'Mistress of the maestro of Maranello' *The Guardian* 23rd January 2004 https://www.theguardian.com/sport/2004/jan/23/formulaone.comment Access 7th October 2019.
33. Mike Hawthorn *Challenge Me the Race* London: Motoraces Book Club/William Kimber 1964.
34. *Challenge Me…* p. 104.
35. For accounts of the disaster, see Christopher Hilton *Le Mans '55: The Crash That Changed the Face of Motor Racing* Derby: Breedon Books 2004; Mark Kahn *Death Race: Le Mans 1955* London: Barrie and Jenkins 1976; Raphael Orlove 'Just How Horrifying Was The Worst Crash In Motorsports, Le Mans '55?' https://jalopnik.com/just-how-horrifying-was-the-worst-crash-in-motorsports-1589382023 Posted 14th June 2014; access 7th October 2019; David Greenhalgh 'Le Mans 1955, A Lawyer's View' http://www.dailysportscar.com/2013/04/27/le-mans-1955-a-lawyers-view.html Posted 27th April 2013; access 7th October 2019.
36. Cannell *The Limit* p. 203.
37. The best account of the incident is Cannell *The Limit* pp. 152–7.
38. See Hotten *Formula One…* p. 8.
39. See 'One of the toughest moments in Enzo Ferrari's life' https://formula1.ferrari.com/en/happened-today-07-27/ Access 8th October 2019.
40. *Autosport* 17th June 1955 p. 747. Mike Hawthorn, one of the drivers involved in the accident, had won the race in a Jaguar.
41. *Autosport* 24th June 1955 p. 802. The castigation came from Mr and Mrs Holden of Pinner, Middlesex.
42. *Autosport* 8th July 1955 p. 15.
43. A.J. Baime *Go Like Hell: Ford, Ferrari and Their Battle for Speed and Glory at Le Mans* London: Bantam Books 2010 p. 153.
44. Ralph Nader *Unsafe at Any Speed: The Designed-in Dangers of the American Automobile* New York: Grossman Publishers 1965.

45. See Baime *Go Like Hell…* pp. 282–98 for a full account.
46. Lee Iacocca, with William Novak *Iacocca: An Autobiography* New York: Bantam Books 1986 p. 309.
47. Peter Wyden *The Unknown Iacocca* London: Sidgwick and Jackson 1988 p. 189.
48. Murray Walker *Unless I'm Very Much Mistaken: My Autobiography* London: Collins Willow 2002 p. 231.
49. Moss, Purdy *All But My Life* p. 105.
50. Martin Williamson 'A brief history of Formula One' http://en.espn.co.uk/f1/motorsport/story/3831.html Undated; access 8th October 2019.
51. Jones *Formula One…* p. 15.
52. A vehicle structure in which the chassis is integral with the body.
53. Ireland *Motor Racing Today* p.125; for a brief biography of Chapman, see http://www.grandprixhistory.org/chap_bio.htm (undated); access 8th October 2019.
54. See https://www.f1technical.net/articles/24 Access 8th October 2019.
55. Adam Cooper *Piers Courage: Last of the Gentlemen Racers* Yeovil: Haynes Publishing 2010 p. 17.
56. Jackie Stewart: The man who transformed motorsport *The Scotsman* 26th May 2017 https://www.scotsman.com/news/jackie-stewart-man-who-transformed-motorsport-3096630 Access 24th February 2023.
57. Richard Rae 'Heroes' heroes: Sir Jackie Stewart, former Formula One world champion, on Juan Manuel Fangio' *The Sunday Times* 17th October 2004 https://www.thetimes.co.uk/article/heroes-heroes-sir-jackie-stewart-former-formula-one-world-champion-on-juan-manuel-fangio-fq0whrstnbt Access 10th October 2019; see also Gerald Donaldson *Fangio: The Life Behind the Legend* London: Virgin Books 2009 pp. 14, 37.
58. Williams *Enzo Ferrari* p. 272.
59. See Jackie Stewart *Winning Is Not Enough: The Autobiography* London: Headline 2007 pp. 146–51.
60. Stewart *Winning…* p. 209.
61. Stewart *Winning…* p. 207.
62. Jones *Formula One…* p. 112.
63. Moss, Purdy *All But My Life* pp. 129–31.
64. Stewart *Winning…* pp. 134–8.
65. Stewart *Winning…* pp. 154–5.

66. Stewart *Winning...* pp. 162–3.
67. Stewart *Winning...* pp. 172–3.
68. Quoted in Damien Smith 'Stewart vs Jenkinson: safety in motor sport' https://www.motorsportmagazine.com/history/f1/stewart-vs-jenkinson-safety-motor-sport Posted 25th July 2012; access 11th October 2019.
69. Stewart *Winning...* pp. 153–4.
70. James Allen 'Analysis: What happens when F1 drivers become unified' https://www.motorsport.com/f1/news/f1-gpda-drivers-union-association-988401/1383354/ Posted 13th December 2017; access 12th October 2019.
71. See Niki Lauda (with Herbert Volker) *For the Record: My Years with Ferrari* London: William Kimber 1979 p. 47.
72. See Tony Dodgins 'The day Lauda wouldn't risk his life – and there was no stopping Hunt' *The Guardian* 29th September 2007 https://www.theguardian.com/sport/2007/sep/29/motorsports.sport2 Access12th October 2019.
73. Gerald Donaldson *James Hunt: The Biography* London: Virgin Books 2003 p. 211.
74. ESPN Staff 'Ecclestone pays tribute to Watkins' http://en.espn.co.uk/f1/motorsport/story/88903.html Posted 14th September 2012; access 12th October 2019.
75. Professor Sid Watkins *Life at the Limit: Triumph and Tragedy in Formula One* London: Pan Books 1997 pp. 24–6.
76. Tom Bower *No Angel: The Secret Life of Bernie Ecclestone* London: Faber & Faber 2012 p. 84.
77. A concept originated by the American sociologist C. Wright Mills. See C. Wright Mills 'Situated Actions and Vocabularies of Motive'. *American Sociological Review* Vol. 5; No. 6 (December 1940) pp. 904–13.
78. Mosley *Formula One and Beyond...* pp. 139–51.
79. Quoted in Bower *No Angel...* p. 123.
80. Quoted in Bower *No Angel...* p. 164.
81. Susan Watkins *Bernie: The Biography of Bernie Ecclestone* Yeovil: Haynes Publishing 2011 p. 290.
82. See Richard Williams *The Death of Ayrton Senna* London: Bloomsbury 1999 pp. 8 and 16.
83. Hotten *Formula One...* p. 39.
84. Mosley *Formula One and Beyond...* p. 250.

85. See Professor Sid Watkins *Beyond the Limit* London: Macmillan 2001 pp. 30, 41 and 47.
86. Watkins *Beyond…* pp. 6, 31 and 167.
87. Mosley *Formula One and Beyond* p. 254.
88. Alan Henry *The Power Brokers: The Battle for F1's Billions* Minneapolis: Motorbooks International 2003 p. 158.
89. See Mosley *Formula One and Beyond* pp. 357–9 and 363.
90. Mosley *Formula One and Beyond* p. 360.
91. Giles Richards 'Anthony Davidson says motor sport has lost the 'fear factor' to safety' *The Guardian* 20th October 2013 https://www.theguardian.com/sport/blog/2013/oct/20/anthony-davidson-motor-sport-safety Access 13th October 2019.
92. Jordan Golson 'How Today's F1 Cars Are So Amazingly Safe (And Horribly Uncomfortable)' https://www.wired.com/2014/07/formula-one-car-safety-comfort/ Posted 7th July 2014; access 13th October 2019.
93. Terry Shea 'Vic Elford: Versatile racer excelled in every form of motorsport he contested' https://www.hemmings.com/stories/article/vic-elford Access 30th January 2021.
94. See, for example, the editorial 'Motorsport should be banned' in the Scottish newspaper *The Herald* 4th June 2007 https://www.heraldscotland.com/news/12777625.motorsport-should-be-banned/ Access 13th October 2019.
95. Andrew Benson 'Formula 1 drivers' union gets '100%' membership due to concerns over future' https://www.bbc.co.uk/sport/formula1/42314309 Posted 13th December 2017; access 13th October 2019.

From Powder Puff to W Series: The Evolution of Women-Only Racing

Chris Lezotte

Introduction

In October 2018, the W Series—an all-women single-seater racing championship featuring the world's top female racing talent—was introduced with great fanfare to the international motorsports community. The series was heralded as a unique opportunity to promote female drivers into Formula One, universally regarded as the 'absolute pinnacle of global motorsport' (W Series, 2020). Reactions to the announcement fell into two disparate—and vocal—camps. Proponents praised the series as an important platform for women to showcase racing ability, as well as for its potential to carve a pathway for female drivers to higher-level racing. Opponents decried the series as regressive and belittling to women, claiming 'segregated racing' carries the implication that women aren't capable of competing at the same level as men.

C. Lezotte (✉)
Independent Scholar, Ann Arbor, MI, USA
e-mail: clezott@bgsu.edu

D. Sturm et al. (eds.), *The History and Politics of Motor Racing*, Global Culture and Sport Series, https://doi.org/10.1007/978-3-031-22825-4_11

The conflicting responses to the W Series announcement should not be surprising. Whether or not women are best served by separate or equal opportunities has long been a subject of discussion, investigation, and unwavering opinion. Female-only spaces have been praised as locations where women are allowed to test themselves without male criticism or intimidation; conversely, they are also viewed as intrinsically inferior to provinces historically dominated by men.[1] Feminists are also divided on the matter. Liberal feminists view recognition of gender difference as a barrier to equal rights and participation; they promote working within the structure of mainstream society to integrate women into that structure (Gendered Innovations, n.d.). Those who ascribe to difference feminism see value in recognizing male and female differences; they argue that the gender-neutrality promoted by liberal feminists harms women 'whether by impelling them to imitate men, by depriving society of their distinctive contributions, or by letting them participate in a society only on terms that favor men' (Grande Jenson, 1996, p. 3). Motorsports, where women's participation is the exception rather than the rule, has a long and complicated history of women-only racing that affects how the W Series, and all segregated racing activities, is considered by participators and observers alike.

An examination of women-only racing over the past 75 years therefore provides an opportunity to consider how segregated motorsports have both empowered and limited female participation in a historically male-dominated arena. Such an investigation has the ability to uncover the methods by which women have negotiated entry into a venue where men hold the ultimate power, and women are routinely considered as less. The subject of women in racing has not received a great deal of attention in scholarship. Popular literature focuses primarily on exceptional women—individuals who have achieved success and notoriety in the male world of motorsports.[2] In academia, communication and technology studies scholars Sloop (2005) and Pflugfelder (2009) broaden the scope beyond famous female racers through research that explores relationships between gender, women's bodies, and automobility. The association of racing and masculinity is the subject of scholarship produced by Shackleford (1999), Yongue (2014), and Fleming and Sturm (2011). Matthews and Pike (2016) examine the gendered processes that influence attitudes and behaviors toward female racers. While the majority of these investigations bring attention to the woman in racing as an exception, interloper, and curiosity, they rarely consider how a particular motorsports arena can affect how a female racer is perceived, or influence her ability to fail or succeed. Looking at the female racer through participation in women-only events will not definitively determine whether or not women are best served by gender-segregated motorsport opportunities; rather, it will offer insight into how women have constructed alternative avenues into the male-dominated province of auto racing.

Motorsports is an overarching term that encompasses various types of motor-vehicle racing but is most often associated with the automobile. Motorsports takes many forms and is conducted on a variety of courses in event-specific vehicles. The most recognizable racing events are the single-seater, open-wheeled series such as Formula One (F1) and IndyCar, and the multi-seated, closed-wheeled series that include the National Association for Stock Car Auto Racing (NASCAR) and the World Rally Championship. Motorsports is truly international, with drivers hailing from all parts of the globe and events taking place all over the world.

Although motorsports is one of the few activities in which men and women may compete together on a level playing field, women are vastly underrepresented among racing competitors. In the United Kingdom, for example, women comprise only 8% of registered racing license holders (Matthews & Pike, 2016, p. 1534). Due to the small number of female drivers in motorsports in general, this examination does not focus on a specific location, racing category, or vehicle type. Rather, it calls upon a variety of examples from multiple arenas where women have engaged in segregated racing. Extending the inquiry in this manner provides an opportunity to observe how women-only racing has been promoted, performed, and assessed over time.

Early Auto Racing and the Woman Driver

In the early auto age, before mass production brought automobility to 'every man,'[3] the horseless carriage was accessible primarily to those with considerable financial means. In late nineteenth-century America, the automobile was most often regarded as a toy rather than a tool, 'an expensive whirligig produced for the amusement of the effete rich' (Seiler, 2008, p. 62). Although the association of the automobile and masculinity has been accepted as a given throughout automotive history, at the turn of the twentieth century, in both Europe and the United States, it was wealth and status, rather than gender, that determined who could operate a motor vehicle. Thus it was not unusual for well-off women to join men as driving enthusiasts.

The permission awarded to early women drivers allowed them to call upon these 'toys' to expand social, physical, and political horizons. Female motorists of significant means were, in fact, the first to engage in and document cross-country automobile trips. While these tours often served as car company publicity stunts—to demonstrate the ease with which 'even' a woman could operate their vehicles—they also effectively presented women on the national stage as legitimate motorists. As Scharff (1991, p. 77) writes, 'female cross-country drivers, literally revealing themselves to the public eye in their open vehicles, challenged the notion that women ought to remain sequestered at home.'

For some women who engaged in these activities, long-distance tours were not enough. To satisfy a newfound passion for driving, they turned to racing. The world's first organized auto race was held in 1894 in France; a year later, the *Chicago Times Herald* sponsored the first organized American auto race. By the early 1900s, informal and formal racing events were being held in Europe and the United States in a variety of venues. On both sides of the Atlantic, upper-class women gained notoriety, if not success, as female racers. Note Kreszock, Wise, and Freeman (2014, p. 105), 'leisure time and access to resources allowed these women the luxury of stepping outside of socially prescribed conventions for women's behavior.' In 1901, Camille du Gast, a wealthy French widow, became known as the 'first female star of motorsports' due to her performance at the 1901 Paris-Berlin race (Gilboy, 2018b). In Britain, at the

1905 Brighton Speed Trials, Dorothy Levitt won her engine class, the Autocar Challenge Trophy, and 'the right to call herself the fastest woman on earth' (Gilboy, 2018b). US driver Joan Newton Cuneo, who began racing in 1905, broke speed records and defeated some of the top male motorists of the age. She went on to become perhaps the most well-known female motorist in the country until being abruptly shut down in 1909 by the American Automobile Association (AAA) when women were officially and unceremoniously forbidden to participate in AAA events.

Perhaps not coincidentally, the US ban on female racers was implemented shortly after the introduction of the mass-produced, gasoline-powered automobile. The increased performance possibilities of the more powerful engine effectively and irrevocably associated the gas-powered automobile with masculinity. Notes Berger (1986, p. 257), 'everything about the car seemed masculine, from the coordination and strength required to operate it, to the dirt and grease connected with its maintenance.' As cars became more affordable and accessible, framing the gasoline-powered automobile as a masculine technology became a way to limit women's automobility. The association of masculinity and automobility was not only applied to cars, but became part of the motorsports credo. The unfounded belief that women were unable to adequately control automobiles gained increasing traction in the racing world. As Kreszock, Wise, and Freeman (2014, p. 105) assert, 'auto racing, like leisure driving, continued to be portrayed as a male pursuit.' The behavior culturally ascribed to femininity—'natural impulsiveness and timidity, inability to concentrate and single-mindedness, indecisiveness and foolhardiness, weakness, and utter estrangement from things mechanical'—was accentuated to demonstrate the unsuitability of the female body for placement behind the wheel of powerful race cars (Scharff, 1991, p. 26).

After the 1909 AAA ban, female motorists were only welcome at exhibitions, speed trials, and the 'occasional small-town competition that defied the organization's rules' (Macy, 2017, p. 66). The situation differed in Europe, however. Motor racing at Brooklands was beginning to draw large crowds; eyeing a potential for profit, race authorities relented and allowed women onto the track, albeit in special-event, women-only races.

In 1909, seven female competitors entered the Ladies' Bracelet Handicap—Brooklands' first official race for women.

The United States discontinued all racing during World War I; however, this did not stop promoters from organizing 'special' all-ladies racing competitions. In 1918, an event was scheduled for the all-female Speederettes in Stockton, California. Tragically, an accident on the track left two dead; as a consequence, notes McCarthy (2007, p. 75), 'American women's racing faded back into the margins of sporting life for more than three decades.'[4]

While women's racing was suspended in the United States, a change in ownership at Brooklands made female participation possible in the United Kingdom. Taking over the motor racing circuit after her husband's death in 1926, Ethel-Locke King created new opportunities for women. This action—which promoted rather than discouraged female participation—led to what Matthews and Pike (2016, p. 1538) describe as the 'golden age for women in motorsport.' Organizations such as the Ladies' Automobile Club at Brooklands and L'Automobile Club féminin de France became important networks for the development and promotion of women racers. In these European venues, women had the opportunity to demonstrate that they could race as competitively as men.

World War II altered the opportunities for female racers in both Europe and the United States in conflicting ways. In Britain, the postwar period witnessed a change in attitudes regarding female racers; the prevailing mood, writes Bouzanquet (2009, p. 85), was 'no longer conducive to women on the tracks: public-spiritedness required that every woman look after her war veteran and produce children.' Changes at Brooklands, the establishment of new racing venues, the retirement of former female racers, and increased emphasis on the dangers of the sport contributed to the return of traditional opinions 'opposing women drivers' involvement in motor-racing' and the monopolization of motorsports resources in favor of men (Matthews & Pike, 2016, p. 1540).

In postwar America, however, women—nearly invisible on the race track since the AAA ban—were the beneficiaries of new motorsports opportunities. Prior to World War II, less than 25% of women had drivers licenses.[5] Rising prosperity and the move to the suburbs in the decades following World War II, however, led to the necessity of a second car for the woman of the household. Women gained a familiarity with how automobiles worked as well as an appreciation for how cars improved their lives. They also realized how enjoyable driving could be; many sought to experience the car as more than a tool of domestic technology. The 'democratization of American leisure' was quickly taking over post-war America; members of the middle and lower classes sought to experience the same forms of play as the rich (Culver, 2010, p. 9). Notes Kinney (2013, p. 195), 'the use of the automobile as an instrument of play, which ranged from going out for an enjoyable Sunday afternoon drive to serious competitions based on time, speed, and distance reflected that process.'

The Sports Car Club of America (SCCA) began to sanction road racing in 1948. Motorsports, which had long existed as an activity for the rich, soon became accessible to those of lesser means. While sanctioned sports car racing favored the wealthy, other racing venues opened to automobiles and drivers of various persuasions. Stock car racing soon replaced midgets and other forms of open-cockpit racing in popularity throughout the United States. These amateur competitions became fan favorites as anyone with a vehicle and a bit of daring had the opportunity to participate. The majority of competitors in these events 'were in the game for the excitement of it, for the fun, along with the social aspects' (McCarthy, 2007, p. 119). Women who accompanied boyfriends or husbands to the race track were soon offered the opportunity to compete in separate ladies races. These all-female events were referred to by a term forever linked with women's racing: Powder Puff. [6]

Powder Puff

Over the past 70 years, 'powder puff' has served as an umbrella term to describe women-only competitions in sports—US football the most notable example—traditionally associated with male athletes. In motorsports, the phrase most often refers to contests performed in a variety of venues and vehicles in which women compete separately from men. The use of 'powder puff' to describe ladies-only auto races appears to have its origins in the late 1940s and early 1950s. Small town newspapers, reporting results from the local race track, would call upon the term to qualify and single out women's participation.[7] The special ladies races were created to address a number of concerns. Women who accompanied boyfriends or husbands to the track often had little to do once arriving but watch and wait. In the masculine world of motorsports, women served primarily as uniform washers, picnic-lunch makers, and cheerleaders to their male companions. Given that race officials often treated women as 'less important than the cars in attendance,' it is not surprising that female interest in the race experience soon began to wane (Cabatingan, 2013).

Race promotors—fearful that women's lack of enthusiasm would keep boyfriends and husbands from bringing cars to the track—saw an opportunity to keep women occupied and, in the process, increase the gate. Girlfriends and wives were encouraged to 'borrow' cars from male companions and race against each other as a special attraction. On most tracks, the races were often more spectacle than serious competition. Standridge (1988, p. 77) recalls, 'the women also had to participate in a "Gong Show" type agenda. [...] they might have to run so many laps, stop to eat a piece of watermelon, run up into the stands and kiss the man of their choice, then resume the race. Or stop after so many laps to wrestle with a greased pig.'[8] Powder Puff, notes Cabatingan (2013), 'were the type of events in which women were treated as less significant and where the men would kindly lend their race cars to women for just a few laps around the track. Clearly, women competitors were not taken very seriously.'

Powder Puff events also served to appease male egos under a pretense of gender equality. While many women desired to test their skills by competing against male drivers, procedures in place often made it impossible to do so. Of women's SCCA races, contest board representative Ignazio Lozana Jr (qtd in Hull, 1958, p. 104) explained, 'very few of our women drivers have a car to drive during the men's races, since they are usually being driven by a man in those events. Should we discontinue the ladies' races, it would mean we would have at the most two or three women drivers in our program, whereas in the ladies' races we have had as many as 25 starters.' While this explanation suggests that ladies races were implemented to increase female participation, retaining men's interest and involvement in racing was no doubt a greater concern.

Powder Puff participants often had limited driving experience, but were encouraged to take part to show support for a male companion's motorsports hobby.[9] While some men were reluctant to hand over the keys to unschooled wives or girlfriends, most viewed women's participation as a way to gain approval—if not rationalization—for their own racing addiction. Many women participated tentatively, more interested in displaying support than winning trophies. However, there were some women—dissatisfied with roles as tagalongs—who desired to race competitively. But because most tracks prohibited women from racing against men, Powder Puff competitions became the primary way to develop confidence behind the wheel, gain track experience, hone racing skills and strategies, and 'show the guys that they could do it, too' (McCarthy, 2007, p. 210).

Women's passion for racing came from a variety of sources. Some were exposed to cars through male family members.[10] Women connected to men in the sport had a distinct advantage over those who did not. Explains Kreitzer (2017, p. 210), 'female racers relied heavily on male relatives who were already accepted as racing insiders to help jump start their racing careers.' Others, while growing up with a love of cars, did not consider racing until the opportunity presented itself. Vicki Wood—after watching an all-woman's race at the Motor City Speedway—was convinced she could drive better; she subsequently entered a race on her husband's dare. Auto journalist Denise McCluggage, writes Roberts (2015), 'persuaded her editors that she could better report on auto racing from behind the wheel than in the press box.' Yet due to track restrictions, McCluggage began her racing career in Powder Puff derbies, which, as she remarked, 'seemed to me rather like mud wrestling, staged as a spectacle for men to chuckle over rather than serious competition. But it was a chance to drive, so I put up with the hair-pull aspects' (qtd in McCarthy, 2007, p. 147). In the minds of many female racers, ladies races provided the opportunity to 'earn the respect of the men so they could eventually drive in any race' (McCarthy, 2007, p. 210).

Powder Puff women had to navigate significant obstacles. Although racing during this period was an amateur sport, it could be expensive. The price of entry fees, equipment, and upkeep could add up quickly. Women rarely had cars or equipment of their own, so had to beg or borrow cars and racing gear from male relatives or complete strangers. Auto maintenance was an issue, as husbands or significant others wouldn't always be available or willing to help with car repairs or upkeep. Although Powder Puff events varied from state to state and track to track, they were all regulated by men, who, as Forsyth (2016, p. 174) asserts, kept a tight hold and 'steadfastly refused to let the women have more time or more races.'

Yet despite the barriers women encountered, racing often had a positive and powerful effect on their lives. Interviews conducted by Hull (1958) with fellow SCCA members suggest that women raced not only to support male companions, but also to expand social networks, gain confidence, and escape from everyday lives. Powder Puff provided women with the opportunity to develop advanced driving skills, make important contacts, gain a little notoriety, and prove themselves as serious racers. Many who went on to achieve a number of 'firsts' in women's motorsport began racing careers in Powder Puff.[11]

Other than premier events such as the Indianapolis 500 and NASCAR championship, American postwar racing was primarily an amateur pastime. Races were run for trophies; cash prizes were banned, as were donations from sponsors, car makers, owners, or local businesses. It was up to each driver to finance his or her racing habit. While the conditions under which men and women raced were not the same—women received less track time and had fewer and shorter races than male counterparts—all racers were held to the same restrictions in terms of sponsorships and financial remuneration.

As the decade concluded, top drivers from the sports car circuit were being lured by the considerable cash prizes of Formula One and international competition. US racing organizations fought back by creating racing events with comparable financial awards. Smaller venues—losing top drivers and paying crowds—sought sponsors to stay in business. While the move toward the commercialization of motorsports affected all amateur racers regardless of gender, it was ultimately responsible for the decline of all-female racing. Powder Puff events—and the women who participated in them—were not regarded as legitimate and, as such, were unable to attract commercial support. Without amateur ladies races, women lost an important platform from which to gain experience and exposure.[12]

Women's Racing Teams

While ladies races were often the subject of derision and disparagement, they were, without question, instrumental in bringing the racing experience to an increasing population of female motorsport enthusiasts. As the professionalism of racing resulted in reduced possibilities for female drivers, women's racing teams emerged as one of the few opportunities to fill the void. During the 1970s, two racing organizations—in Europe and the United States—developed all-female racing teams. While the primary motivation was the marketing and promotional potential of photogenic female racers, the very existence of these teams allowed for increased women's motorsports participation.

During the early 1970s, Bob Neyret, a French dentist and former rally competitor, convinced Aseptogyl, a brand of toothpaste created by his company, to sponsor a European all-female rally team. The assembled group included individuals with varying degrees of driving skills. *Speedqueens* blogger H.-G. Rachel (2010) writes, 'Neyret always had an eye on the promotional value of his team, and he made little secret of favouring pretty drivers.' Photos of the team—outfitted in matching pink racing ensembles—were part of Aseptogyl's wide-reaching PR campaign. As Bouzanquet (2009, p. 150) asserts, 'The media impact was enormous and magazine *L'Equipe* presented this bright pink stable on its front page (those small saloon cars were painted in red, white, and strawberry pink).'

The team's first outings in 1973 were early-season Alpine rally events in France and provided challenging competition as well as all-important promotional opportunities. Over the next 20 years, Team Aseptogyl had varying degrees of success. The racers claimed a number of Ladies Cups; most noteworthy was the win at the 1975 Morocco Rally. Team Aseptogyl inspired the formation of other all-ladies rally teams in Europe, which included a group of female racers in the Alfa 1500TI selected from the Alfa Romeo network, and Peugeot entering 504s in African rallies. While Team Aseptogyl served primarily as a marketing tool for its owner, sponsors, and race promoters, it also brought attention—both positive and negative—to individual drivers in particular and motorsport women in general. It provided female racers with talent and ambition the opportunity to participate in an activity that had long existed as a masculine enclave. Many who spent a season or two driving for Team Aseptogyl were able to fashion solid careers as rally drivers, no small feat for a female racer. Yet more significantly, Team Aseptogyl and the all-female racing teams it inspired suggested that women in motorsports were not, in fact, exceptions to the rule, but were part of a growing population of serious and competent female racers.

Around the same time in the United States, the Macmillan Ring-Free Oil Racing Team sponsored a group of female racers known as the Motor-Maids. The team was first assembled in 1966 to compete in the Daytona 24 Hours. Yet much like the European racing scene, the focus on the all-female team was more promotional than professional. Publicity focused not on driving skills, but personal appearance. A 1966 press release (Ring-Free, n.d.-b) describes Donna Mae Mins as 'a bubbling, bouncing blonde bombshell of energy. Her famous "Think Pink" wardrobe on the track has become her trademark.' News (Ring-Free, n.d.-a) devoted to Liane Engeman calls attention to her clothing choices: 'Liane's trademarks are her white turtleneck sweaters and a purple racing outfit that emphasizes the fact that this racing driver is all girl.'

Emphasis on physical appearance served two purposes. First, of course, was the utilization of attractive women as a promotional device. As women were a rarity in motorsports, female racers garbed in bright pink racing apparel made them stand out; they were perceived as a novelty, 'eye candy' for male spectators, or an exciting diversion for speed enthusiasts. Secondly, it determinedly and purposefully framed female racers as appropriately feminine. As Kreitzer (2017, p. 206) argues, postwar culture increasingly stereotyped female athletes as 'unfeminine in demeanor, mannish in their appearance, and incapable of maintaining heterosexual relationships with men.' Calling attention to women's sexual attractiveness implied that not only are unfeminine—code for lesbian—women absent in motorsports, but participating in motorsports will not move a woman's sexual orientation in that direction.[13] Selecting heterosexually appealing women and outfitting them in attire to accentuate their 'femininity' assured spectators and participants of both genders that female racecar drivers were 'non-threatening women who continued to adhere to traditional female gender roles as attractive sexual partners [...]' (Kreitzer, 2017, p. 206).

Despite the unwarranted focus on physical appearance, participation as a Motor-Maid did create opportunities for a few of its members. Ring-Free sponsored Suzy Dietrich driving a Lotus 20 in some single-seater races, competing in Formula A and Formula Continental. Janet Guthrie, driving for Ring-Free until 1971, went on to become the first woman to qualify and compete in the 1977 Daytona 500; she was also the first woman and Top Rookie at the Indianapolis 500 the same year. Competing as a Motor-Maid provided its drivers with experience, exposure, and future racing possibilities they were unlikely to have received otherwise.

In September 2020, two all-female crews competed in the 24 Hours of Le Mans, the world's most famous endurance race. The 'Iron Dames' were making their second appearance as members of the all-female Kessel Racing crew. They were joined by newcomers the Richard Mille Racing Team, three talented drivers competing together for the first time. Although faced with shortened training sessions and reduced track time due to COVID, both teams had modestly successful runs. The Iron Dames claimed ninth place from the 22 starters in the LMGTE Am Category, matching their result from the previous year. The Mille team, despite a lack of experience in endurance racing, finished an impressive ninth of the 24 LMP2 crews in their debut outing. The inclusion of these teams resulted in the highest female participation in the 24 Hours since 10 women competed in 1935.

The women recruited for the ELMS (European Le Mans Series) teams were experienced and successful drivers and hailed from all over the globe. While all looked forward to the possibility of driving at Le Mans, some were less than enthusiastic about competing as part of an all-female team. However, as an effort supported and promoted by the Women in Motorsport Commission, the racers came to understand participation as not only beneficial to their own careers, but also as an incentive to get more women involved in motorsport.[14]

Unlike previous all-female racing teams, promotional possibilities took a back seat to talent on the track. When approached to oversee the Mille project, Signatech team boss Philippe Sinault explained, 'whatever the project is, it has to be a real project and not just a marketing tool' (qtd in Brunsdon, 2020). The teams were built around strong, experienced, and serious racers; the marketing focus was on individual and collective ability rather than on femininity or the color of the racing suits. In an informal survey of press surrounding both the 2019 and 2020 events, there is no mention of the women's physical appearance, sexual orientation, marital status, or whether or not they had children. Within the historically masculine motorsport enterprise, there is a perception that female-only teams—and the drivers that inhabit them—are inherently second-rate. Many competitors expressed reluctance to join the teams for that reason. However, the talent and teamwork on display at Le Mans demonstrated that with support, sponsorship, and opportunity, women could achieve success and respect in the motorsport arena.

Women's Racing Series

In the early 2000s, the women's racing series emerged as an alternative all-female racing concept. While the all-female racing team expanded the opportunities for women's participation in high-performance racing events somewhat, women remained a significant minority. The women's racing series was therefore created to address the lack of women in the higher echelons of motorsport by providing more openings for more women to develop the skills and experience necessary to move on to the next level. One of the earliest—and more unconventional—examples of this concept was Formula Woman, an all-female based motor racing championship created and marketed in association with the British media from 2004 to 2007. More than a race series, Formula Woman shared many of its components with the burgeoning reality television and celebrity culture boom taking place throughout the United Kingdom in the early 2000s. Original Formula Woman press officer Alison Hill praised the reality TV structure for its potential to 'put us on the map a lot faster than using a traditional introduction into a race series' (qtd in Falconer, 2004). The series was also promoted as a 'male-free' zone; as the applicant invitation read, 'the charm of Club Formula Woman is that we operate in an entirely female environment, removing the stigma of intimidating, male-dominated driving days' (Men's Stuff, 2005). The promoters did not solicit established racers; rather, a team of 16 finalists was selected from over 10,000 applicants. Prospective drivers were subject to a series of assessments in driving skill, physical fitness, and media and public relations management.

Formula Woman drivers were initially intrigued by the prospect of participating in an all-female motor racing series. As they were relatively new to the racing scene, the women believed the unique experience would mold them for a possible career in the sport, and hoped the television exposure would create lucrative promotional and sponsorship possibilities. However, as Matthews and Pike (2016) reveal, problems with the format, organization, and financial backing led to difficulties on and off the track. The women complained of lack of media coverage—the series was ignored by mainstream motorsport publications—which lessened the opportunity for individual sponsorship and recognition. In the later years of the series, after sponsors withdrew material and financial support, the women were expected to provide their own funding. Thus while Formula Woman was created with the intent to provide increased motorsport opportunities for women as well as to expand female interest in the sport, it ultimately failed to do either well.

That over 10,000 applied to the Formula Woman program certainly suggests a growing female interest in motorsport. And despite its inability to capture a loyal audience in its original incarnation, the Formula Woman series has, in fact, been scheduled to relaunch in post-COVID 2021.[15] The media attention brought to the W Series has unquestionably provided an impetus for various racing organizations—including Formula Woman—to encourage female interest in motorsports.

The W Series was introduced in October 2018 as 'a unique groundbreaking free-to-enter single-seater motor racing series for women drivers only' (W Series, 2020). The all-female Formula 3 championship series was conceived to promote female drivers into Formula One. The W Series objective, notes CEO Catherine Bond Muir, is not only to provide top-notch racing for spectators and viewers on a global scale, but also to 'equip its drivers with the experience and expertise with which they may progress their careers' (W Series, 2020).

In its inaugural season, 18 drivers representing 13 countries—chosen from nearly 100 top female drivers across the globe—participated in six races at some of Europe's premier F1 racing venues. Those selected were required to take part in rigorous training programs centered on driving techniques, simulator exposure, technical engineering approaches, fitness, and media, conducted by instructors with Formula One experience. Efforts were taken to address the inequalities that plague many of the world's premier racing series. Drivers were not expected to attain sponsorships or to shoulder any financial responsibility; all expenses were covered by the series organization. The women competed in identical series-owned Tatuus T-318 Formula 3 cars rotated after each race to remove any hardware advantage from the competition. Not only was the series free to enter for all its drivers, but awarded significant prize money (total of $1,500,000 US) all the way through to 18th place in the final standings.

The 2019 series was a modest success; it experienced an increase in viewer interest and ratings after each race. By the end of the first season, the W Series was broadcast in over 50 countries reaching up to 350 million households. The first W Series champion—Britain's Jamie Chadwick—took home a $500,000 prize and was subsequently named as a development driver for the Williams Formula 1 Team. At the end of the season it was reported that in 2020, the top eight championship drivers would collect points toward an FIA Super License, an important entryway into Formula One.

The COVID pandemic canceled the 2020 W Series. However, as part of a new partnership with Formula One, the W Series will be on the support bill for eight Grands Prix in 2021.[16] The partnership not only lends legitimacy to the all-female series, but further underscores the W Series' role in the preparation and promotion of female racers into the upper tiers of motorsport.

Despite the mostly positive press, W Series entered the racing arena under a cloud of controversy with much to prove. Not everyone—the media, racing organizations, race promoters, and the women themselves—was convinced that a woman-only series was a step forward. Opponents argued that since motorsports is one of the few competitions in which women can compete directly with men, female racers should take every opportunity to do so. Grassroots racer Kiem Tjong exclaimed, 'I absolutely believe women can—and should—race at the same level as men, and I believe a women-only series is insulting and demeaning' (qtd in Gilboy, 2018b). Other objections focused on prize money offered as a 'lure' to female competitors when it could be better spent funding racers in non-segregated events. Veteran racer Pippa Mann asserted, 'I am strongly opposed to segregation as the only option of these female racers to find the funding to continue to compete as a viable pathway forward' (qtd in Hall, 2019). Detractors also claimed that much like the all-female racing competitions that preceded it, W Series is primarily a PR move, as women's success in these venues has little influence within the masculine F1 culture or in providing future opportunities for female racers. As Sturm (2021) explains, accomplished female drivers signed by teams are most often 'relegated to testing or "development roles."'

The debate surrounding the W Series echoes that which has accompanied most configurations of female motorsport since Powder Puffs entered the racing arena. For much of its existence, women's racing has been constructed as a frivolous and inconsequential sideshow, a trivial endeavor, a catwalk of second-rate drivers in pink racing suits. Although women's racing has come into its own in the twenty-first century, it cannot completely escape such long-standing, disparaging associations. It is therefore not surprising that many choose to dismiss all-female racing as a way to distance themselves from these pervasive sexist, stereotypical representations. In addition, throughout automotive history, critics have drawn on gender stereotypes—women as emotionally unstable, physically weak, and intellectually deficient—to frame women as inferior drivers (Scharff, 1991). These assumed biological character deficits have carried over into motorsports, where women are considered less able to perform in a competitive field. Opposition also rests in 'an industry with a long history of conservatism' (Gilboy, 2018b). The focus on female racers as a group rather than individuals with singular objectives and accomplishments is antithetical to the conservative notion of individualism—success based on hard work, perseverance, and personal accountability rather than 'special' assistance—to which many women in motorsports subscribe.[17]

The arguments against the W Series assume an either/or position: only one platform—segregated or non-segregated—best serves female racers.

However, the W Series frames itself as an addition to, rather than replacement for, non-segregated racing. The W Series objective is not to compete with non-segregated events for female support and participation, but rather to increase opportunities for women throughout motorsports. As Bond Muir notes, 'with W Series as a catalyst, we hope to transform the diversity of the sport—and perhaps even encourage more girls into professions they had not previously considered. That will mean as much to us as helping develop a female Formula 1 world champion' (qtd in Gilboy, 2018a). With the completion of its first successful season, and the announcement of the 2021 association with Formula One, many of those originally opposed to the W Series are now its cheerleaders. As 2019 champion Jamie Chadwick exclaimed, 'When you realize it isn't about segregation, we are all trying to achieve the same thing, to get more women involved in motorsport, it's a really positive step' (qtd in Parkes, 2019).

Conclusion

Each side of the gender-segregated vs integrated racing conundrum makes a compelling case for how women in motorsports are best served. Champions of integrated racing argue that women will not be considered equal in motorsport until they compete head-to-head with men. Those on the opposing side contend that, because women have traditionally had fewer avenues into motorsports than their male peers, female racing provides an important and necessary entryway into the higher echelons of competition.

There can be little question that the history of motorsports is a masculine one. Even in its earliest years, when well-connected societal women were conditionally accepted into the racing arena, traditional assumptions and biologically deterministic attitudes toward women framed motoring and motorsports as exclusive male preserves. As Matthews and Pike (2016, 1536) note, 'the monopolization of early motor-racing resources by males, a masculine industry from which the motor car emerged, and pervasive assumptions of driving skill were to become so internalized over time they became commonsensical, with motoring and motorsport constantly identified as a natural masculine quality [...].' One hundred years later, the position of motorsports as a nearly impenetrable male enterprise remains.

Women with an interest in racing have therefore had to devise particular strategies to enter what has long existed as an exclusive masculine fraternity. Without many of the connections available to male racers—rising through the ranks of karting, coming from a family of racing enthusiasts, having an intermediary in the racing community, associating with a social group of other drivers, experience in and an affinity for working on cars, racing mentors—women must often rely on other methods. While some rely on 'intrepidity backed by the simple desire to get out of the bleachers and onto the track' (Gilboy, 2018b), others, as demonstrated here, get their start through participation in women-only racing events.

This examination of female-only racing over the past 75 years does not attempt to answer the question of whether or not women are best served by gender-segregated racing. Rather, it offers insight into how women have constructed alternative avenues into the historically masculine—and often unwelcoming—motorsports arena. Through an inspection of women's engagement in female-racing venues—from Powder Puff to W Series—it provides an opportunity to consider how segregated racing has both limited and empowered women's motorsports participation.

Notes

1. Women-only spaces are often advocated as locations in which women are safe from misogyny in its many forms. See Lewis et al. (2014) and Leathwood (2004).
2. Examples include material devoted to a singular racer—for example, Joan Cuneo (Nystrom, 2013), Guthrie and King (2005), and Patrick and Morton (2007), or 'best of' collections from Bullock (2002) and Bouzanquet (2009).
3. Writes Scharff (1991, p. 55), 'Ford designed the Model T to be literally Everyman's Car: sturdy, thrifty, and powerful.'

4. The Speederettes incident confirmed race organizers' worst fear, that 'an accident involving a woman would bring down the public's wrath upon the sport' (Macy, 2017, p. 65).
5. While there is an absence of statistics on women's automotive participation before 1963, historian Margaret Walsh (2011, p. 59) estimates that in the prewar era, only a quarter of US women of legal driving age held drivers licenses.
6. In 1882, Ellene Alice Bailey was granted a patent for the powder puff, a soft, cosmetic pad used to apply powder to the skin, from which the women's race drew its name.
7. In his collection of stock racing memorabilia from the 1950s, Easton (2014, p. 27) includes a Big Flats Airport Speedway ticket admission stub in which 'Ladies Powder-Puff Race' is listed as a special event alongside the 'rollover of a stock automobile off a ramp!'
8. *The Gong Show* was an amateur talent contest which aired for 13 years on American television. Three celebrities auditioned a series of acts—many of them outrageous—and unceremoniously dismissed the 'losers' by striking a large gong.
9. SCCA racer Hull (1958, p. 11) writes, 'there is no use denying the fact that most women who go in for racing do so because their husbands or someone they are fond of is interested in the sport and, rather than have another woman snap up their men or be a sports-car widow, they go along.'
10. As an example, Ileen Merle Dessie (Forrest) Goodman grew up in a family—three brothers and an uncle—of prominent auto racers. She started competing in Powder Puff races in 1949 at Cejay Stadium in Wichita, Kansas, becoming the women's champion that year (Lawrence, n.d.).
11. Louise Smith, Vicki Wood, Denise McCluggage, Sara Christian, and Ethel Flock Mobley are just a few Powder Puffs who went on to successful racing careers.
12. While Powder Puff events are still held today, the majority are fundraisers for charities such as Races Toward a Cure (breast cancer) and the American Cancer Society.
13. A press release (Ring-Free, n.d.-b) refers to Janet Guthrie as a young lady 'with all her femininity' who spends weekends 'tearing down and rebuilding the engine of her Jaguar.' Guthrie's advanced mechanical knowledge and ability—characteristics most often associated with masculinity—are tempered by referencing her feminine good looks.

14. The Women in Motorsport Commission (FIA, 2019)—presided by Michèle Mouton—was established in 2009 to 'demonstrate that women are recognized by the highest body responsible for the sport,' 'promote the place of women in motorsport through the media [...],' and 'develop social and educational programs to include greater participation of women in motorsport.'
15. For Formula Woman relaunch updates see https://www.formula-woman.co.uk.
16. Britain's Jamie Chadwick successfully defended her W Series title in 2021, and repeated in 2022 after the season was shortened prematurely due to financial reasons. For 2023, Chadwick has joined Andretti Autosport as the first woman in 13 years to compete in Indy NXT—the junior open wheel category just below IndyCar—which, remarks W Series CEO Bond Muir, 'is a sign that the W Series pipeline is working' (qtd in Blackstock, 2022).
17. As noted in my work on women in muscle car culture (Lezotte, 2013), women who subscribe to a conservative ideology do not frame their accomplishments as representative of what women as a group can do; rather, they see themselves as individuals who have attained goals despite gender barriers in a male-controlled automotive culture.

References

Berger, M. (1986). 'Women Drivers!' The Emergence of Folklore and Stereotypic Opinions Concerning Feminine Automotive Behavior. *Women's Studies International Forum, 9*(3), 257–263.

Blackstock, E. (2022, September 2). W Series CEO Catherine Bond Muir is Ready for the Sport to Keep Growing. Jalopnik. Retrieved February 27, 2023, from https://jalopnik.com/w-series-ceo-catherine-bond-muir-is-ready-for-the-sport-1849489545

Bouzanquet, J. (2009). *Fast Ladies: Female Racing Drivers 1888 to 1970*. Veloce.

Brunsdon, S. (2020, September 16). The Renaissance of the All-Female Racing Team. *The Race*. Retrieved December 9, 2020, from https://the-race.com/wec-le-mans/the-renaissance-of-the-all-female-racing-team/

Bullock, J. (2002). *Fast Women: The Drivers Who Changed the Face of Motor Racing*. Robson Books.

Cabatingan, M. (2013, April 23). Race to Equality: History of Women in Racing. *Sports Car Digest*. Retrieved September 9, 2020, from https://sportscardigest.com/race-to-equality-history-of-women-in-racing/

Culver, L. (2010). *The Frontier of Leisure: Southern California and the Shaping of America*. Oxford University Press.

Easton, F. (2014) *Stock Car Racing in the '50s: Pictures and Memories from Western New York and Northwestern Pennsylvania* (Ed. J. Kiernen). Ford Easton.

Falconer, M. (2004, May 19). Formula Woman is the New F1. *GreatReporter*. Retrieved February 10, 2021, from https://www.greatreporter.com/content/formula-woman-new-f1

FIA Women in Motorsport. (2019). Presentation. Retrieved February 7, 2021, from https://www.fia.com/women-motorsport

Fleming, D., & Sturm, D. (2011). *Media, Masculinities, and the Machine F1, Transformers and Fantasizing Technology at its Limits*. Continuum.

Forsyth, D. (2016). *Denver's Lakeside Amusement Park: From the White City Beautiful to a Century of Fun*. University Press of Chicago.

Gendered Innovations. (n.d.). Feminisms. Retrieved August 6, 2020, from https://genderedinnovations.stanford.edu/terms/feminism.html

Gilboy, J. (2018a, October 13). W Series: Everything to Know About the Women-Only Racing Championship. *The Drive*. Retrieved August 7, 2020, from https://www.thedrive.com/accelerator/24146/w-series-everything-to-know-about-the-women-only-racing-championship

Gilboy, J. (2018b, March 8). Women in Motorsports: Their Past, Present, and Future. *The Drive*. Accessed July 4, 2020, from https://www.thedrive.com/accelerator/17072/women-in-motorsport-their-past-present-and-future

Grande Jenson, P. (1996). *Finding a New Feminism: Rethinking the Woman Question for Liberal Democracy*. Rowman & Littlefield.

Guthrie, J., & King, B. J. (2005). *Janet Guthrie: A Life at Full Throttle*. Sport Media Publishing.

Hall, S. (2019, July 3). 3 Reasons We Should Be Paying Attention to the W Series. *Autoweek*. Retrieved January 20, 2021, from https://www.autoweek.com/racing/a21424511/opinion-3-reasons-we-should-be-paying-attention-w-series/

Hull, E. (1958). *Women in Sports Car Competition*. Sports Car Press.

Kinney, J. (2013). Racing on Runways: The Strategic Air Command and Sports Car Racing in the 1950s. *Journal of the International Committee for the History of Technology, 19*, 193–215.

Kreitzer, A. (2017). *Masculinity, Whiteness, and Technological Play in Dirt Track Automobile Racing, 1924–1960*. Dissertation, University of Delaware.

Kreszock, M., Wise, S., & Freeman, M. (2014). 'Just a Good ol' Gal': Pioneer Racer Louise Smith. In M. Howell & D. Miller (Eds.), *Motorsports and American Culture: From Demolition Derbies to NASCAR* (pp. 105–124). Rowman & Littlefield.

Lawrence, B. (n.d.). Women Drivers in Kansas Auto Racing Prior to 1960. *Bob Lawrence's Vintage Auto Racing Web Ring*. Retrieved July 5, 2020, from https://kansasracinghistory.com/Forrest/Women.htm

Leathwood, C. (2004). Doing Difference in Different Times: Theory, Politics, and Women-only Spaces in Education. *Women's Studies International Forum, 27*(5–6), 447–458.

Lewis, R., Sharp, E., Remnant, J., & Redpath, R. (2014). 'Safe Spaces': Experiences of Feminist Women-only Space. *Sociological Research Online, 20*(4). Retrieved February 24, 2021, from https://www.socresonline.org.uk/20/4/9.html

Lezotte, C. (2013). Women with Muscle: Contemporary Women and the Classic Muscle Car. *Frontiers: A Journal of Women's Studies, 34*(2), 83–113.

Macy, S. (2017). *Motor Girls: How Women Took the Wheel and Drove Boldly into the Twentieth Century*. National Geographic.

Matthews, J., & Pike, E. (2016). What on Earth Are They Doing in a Racing Car?: Towards an Understanding of Women in Motorsport. *The International Journal of the History of Sport, 33*(13), 1532–1550.

McCarthy, T. (2007). *Fast Women: The Legendary Ladies of Racing*. Hyperion.

Men's Stuff: The National Men's Resource. (2005). Club Formula Woman. Retrieved February 10, 2021, from http://www.menstuff.org/issues/byissue/formulawoman.html

Nystrom, E. (2013). *Mad for Speed: The Racing Life of Joan Newton Cuneo*. McFarland.

Parkes, I. (2019, September 6). The W Series Silences Its Critics. Next stop: F1. *Nytimes.com*. Retrieved February 2, 2021, from https://www.nytimes.com/2019/09/06/sports/autoracing/w-series-women-f1.html

Patrick, D., & Morton, L. (2007). *Danica—Crossing the Line*. Touchstone.

Pflugfelder, E. (2009). Something Less than a Driver: Toward an Understanding of Gendered Bodies in Motorsport. *Journal of Sport & Social Issues, 33*(4), 411–426.

Rachel, H.-G. (2010, August 26). Team Aseptogyl [blog] *Speedqueens: Women in Motorsport from 1897 to the Present Day*. Retrieved August 20, 2020, from http://speedqueens.blogspot.com/search?q=aseptogyl

Ring-Free Motor Oils. (n.d.-a). Ring-Free Oil Racing Team—Biography Briefs. Retrieved February 12, 2020, from http://www.1966shelbynotchback mustang.com/RingFree/Ring_Free_News_Release_Sebring.pdf

Ring-Free Motor Oils. (n.d.-b). Ring-Free Motor Maids Biographies. Retrieved February 12, 2021, from http://www.1966shelbynotchbackmustang.com/PhotosRingFree.html

Roberts, S. (2015, May 9). Denise McCluggage, Auto Racing Pacesetter, Dies at 88. *Nytimes.com*. Retrieved February 4, 2021, from https://www.nytimes.com/2015/05/10/sports/autoracing/denise-mccluggage-auto-racing-pacesetter-dies-at-88.html

Scharff, V. (1991). *Taking the Wheel: Women and the Coming of the Motor Age*. University of New Mexico Press.

Seiler, C. (2008). *Republic of Drivers: A Cultural History of Automobility in America*. University of Chicago Press.

Shackleford, B. (1999). Masculinity, Hierarchy, and the Auto Racing Fraternity: The Pit Stop as a Celebration of Social Roles. *Men and Masculinities, 2*(2), 180–196.

Sloop, J. (2005). Riding in Cars Between Men. *Communication and Critical/Cultural Studies, 2*(3), 191–213.

Standridge, J. (1988). Childbirth Is Easier than Losing a Ride. *Open Wheel, 8*(10), 77.

Sturm, D. (2021). The Formula One Paradox: Macho Male Racers and Ornamental Glamour 'Girls'. In K. Dashper (Ed.), *Sport, Gender and Mega Events* (pp. 111–128). Emerald.

W Series. (2020, February 6). W Series: A Game Changer. Retrieved January 18, 2021, from https://wseries.com/w-hub/w-series-a-game-changer/

Walsh, M. (2011). Gender and Automobility: Selling Cars to American Women After the Second World War. *Journal of Macromarketing, 31*(1), 57–72.

Yongue, P. (2014). 'Way Tight' or 'Wicked Loose': Reading NASCAR's Masculinities. In M. Howell & D. Miller (Eds.), *Motorsports and American Culture: From Demolition Derbies to NASCAR* (pp. 133–147). Rowman & Littlefield.

The Awkward Gender Politics of Formula 1 as a Promotional Space: The Issue of 'Grid Girls'

Honorata Jakubowska

This chapter aims to discuss the issue of the presence of so-called grid girls during Formula 1 (F1) races. It presents motorsport as a male world within which women play a decorative role. Particular attention is drawn to the decision of Liberty Media, the owner of F1, to drop 'grid girls' from the races in 2018. The discourse on this decision, as the chapter reveals, has been focused on women's objectification and 'modern' values, on the one hand, and women's empowerment and agency, on the other hand. Surprisingly, it has also revealed backlash towards feminism, which the grid girls have accused of having caused them to lose their jobs. As presented in the chapter, despite the F1 authorities' decision, women still play some decorative roles during the races. The concept of 'glamour' is proposed as an analytical tool to understand the permanent presence of models and hostesses during F1 events and the grid girls' attitudes.

H. Jakubowska (✉)
Faculty of Sociology, Adam Mickiewicz University, Poznań, Poland
e-mail: honorata.jakubowska@amu.edu.pl

D. Sturm et al. (eds.), *The History and Politics of Motor Racing*, Global Culture and Sport Series, https://doi.org/10.1007/978-3-031-22825-4_12

Introduction

Although motorsport has been perceived as a gender-equal sport, that is, an activity that "allows men and women to compete against each other" (Matthews & Pike, 2016: 3), from its beginning, it has been dominated by men. Men constitute the vast majority of competitors but also manage motorsport and the development and organization of different types of racing (Charters, 2006; Matthews & Pike, 2016). Additionally, men dominate the motorsport audience and are the main targets of marketing activities. "In short, "It's a guy thing" " (Charters, 2006: 83).

Women as drivers are barely present in professional motorsports, although some of them have been recognized in car racing history (Charters, 2006; Ross et al., 2009). For example, Louise Smith, a NASCAR driver from 1945 to 1956, known as the 'first lady of racing', was the first woman inducted into the International Motorsports Hall of Fame in 1999. Janet Guthrie was the first woman professional driver to compete in both the Indianapolis 500 and the Daytona 500. Finally, Danica Patrick was one of the most successful female drivers, with her historic victory in the 2008 Indy Japan 300 being the only win by a woman in an IndyCar Series race (Arendt, 2021). Regarding Formula 1 (F1), only five female drivers have competed in the races so far. The first of them was Maria Teresa de Filippis, who participated in the races in 1958 and 1959. Maria Grazia "Lella" Lombardi debuted in the F1 in 1974 and is the only woman who has scored points in F1 (1975). The three other female drivers were Divina Galica (1976–1978), Desire Wilson (1979) and Giovanna Amati (1992). In the twenty-first century, women have not participated in F1 races and have been only test drivers (*Women in Formula One – a brief history*, n.d.).

Although women have become more visible in different roles within the teams, such as designers, strategists or even team principals (Sturm, 2021), F1 remains a male-dominated sport. Usually women have played supporting roles, acting as grid girls, models, wives or girlfriends. These 'duties' have not only marginalized their position in motorsport but also maintained the sport's heteronormativity (Matthews & Pike, 2016; Pflugfelder, 2009). The appearance and tasks assigned to grid girls, such as advertising cars, sponsors and locations, as well as posing for pictures and applauding the winning drivers, highlights the sexualization and objectification of their bodies while effectively illustrating the status of women in this male world.

However, F1 has not remained unaffected by socio-cultural changes. On the one hand, women's increasing emancipation and the ongoing battle for gender equality and women's rights, versus, on the other hand, a greater awareness of sexual harassment, women's objectification and increasing resistance towards any form of harassment, as evidenced by the #metoo movement, raised doubts around the continued presence of 'grid girls' during the races. An apt illustration of this was the decision of Liberty Media, the owner of F1, to drop grid girls from its race weekends, beginning with the 2018 season. The decision applied to not only F1 but also Formula 2 (F2) and GP3 series races. As Sean Bratches, F1 Managing Director of Commercial Operations, stated: "While the practice of employing grid girls has been a staple of Formula 1 Grands Prix for decades, we feel this custom does not resonate with our brand values and clearly is at odds with modern-day societal norms" (Formuła 1 już bez grid girls, 2018). Although in the following weeks the F1 authorities agreed to the presence of the grid girls during some events, for example, Sochi Grand Prix (Jakubowska, 2018), the decision constitutes a valuable starting point for analysing the status of the grid girls and the changes in F1 regarding this.

Motorsport as a Male World

The automobile, both in everyday life and professional sports, is perceived as part of a male world; as noted by Balkmar (2012), the relationship between men, masculinity, and cars is perhaps one of the most taken-for-granted gendered relations one can think of. Cars and other motorized vehicles are closely tied to the construction and perception of masculinity (Letherby & Reynolds, 2009; Mellström, 2002, 2004; Uteng & Cresswell, 2008), and they are seen as an "extension of man" (Sloop, 2005: 194).

Motorsport can be described using the term 'homosocial' (Lipman-Blumen, 1976), which refers to the male bonds that reproduce gender order, male dominance and privileges. According to Bird, homosociality is closed related to hegemonic masculinity (Connell, 1987) and, as such, can be defined as "heterosociality" (Bird, 1996: 121), which is characterized by, among other things, competitiveness and the sexual objectification of women. Competition is an intrinsic feature of sport, at least at a professional level, and the objectification of women takes place by excluding them from sporting competition and assigning ornamental roles to them. However, women's objectification and male rivalry can also be referred to the role of sexual activity and sexual storytelling in the creation of male status in a group of men and male bonding (Flood, 2008). Shackleford (1999), analysing the NASCAR racing world, uses the concept of 'fraternity', which is based on, for example, masculine exclusivity, which can be both formal and informal. In the second case, it is often related to the other features of fraternity, such as a proprietary knowledge. Women, through their exclusion, are denied access to knowledge or are perceived as not having enough knowledge. In this sense, the motorsports community resembles football fans, mainly groups of ultras fans that are homosocial and based on the idea of fraternity. Although women have an increased presence among the fans, they still constitute a minority and are excluded from many activities and conversations on football even when they are present in the stadiums (Jakubowska et al., 2020). Similarly, women also constitute a minority amongst motorsport fans (Fleming & Sturm, 2011; Naess, 2014; Sturm, 2014).

Motorsport based on male fraternity and the assumed close relationship between masculinity and cars could be perceived as "a potential retreat from wider social changes in the light of current transformations in gender relations, and what is still loosely termed a crisis of masculinity" (Thurnell-Read, 2012: 250). When other social life fields are feminized (Messner, 1988), fraternity in male sports seems to remain a bastion of hegemonic masculinity (Connell, 1987).

Women in Decorative Roles

The history of grid girls in F1 began in the 1960s in Japan. Rosa Ogawa, the Japanese model and singer, has been recognized as the first 'race queen', advertising an oil company during a motorsports event (Saner, 2018). Over the next two decades, promotional models appeared in other countries, including the United States and the United Kingdom, and tight-fitting outfits became their unofficial uniform (Brennan, 2018). During the races, grid girls held up the grid number and welcomed and cheered for the best three racers on the podium. They were used by the teams for events and promotional purposes. However, they were not only perceived as performing their duties during a particular Grand Prix (GP) event but also, in a wider context, as ambassadors of F1 and the hosting cities and countries. During some races, for example, at the Russian, Austrian or Malaysian Grand Prix, grid girls wore traditional clothes. Although they were often sexualized in this attire, they also represented a cultural connection or symbolic link to the host nation and its traditions. This argument was used to restore grid girls (Now Singapore ignoring F1 'grid girls' ban, 2018) that will be discussed later in the chapter. It should also be noted that for some grid girls, for example, Kelly Brook, Nell McAndrew or Jodie Marsh, their work during F1 races allowed them to become widely recognized and to develop long-term modelling careers (Tippett, 2020).

Matthews and Pike (2016: 10) noted that the gendered roles were well established by the 1970s with "the advent of increased sponsorship and professionalism of motorsport". With the professionalization of car races, women were often excluded from sports competition and its technological aspects while being reduced to a promotional role. As rightly noted by Tippett (2020: 189):

> Although the inclusion of grid girls in F1 served to represent women in some capacity within the world of motorsports, their identity was consistently disconnected from the sport itself and was more readily connected to the sponsors of the event. The grid girls were never involved in the technical, sporting or engineering side of the sport and existed solely as aesthetic—often sexualized—figures.

The sexualization of women in motorsport does not solely concern the grid girls but also the relatively few female drivers. The examination of the advertising images of female racers has led to the conclusion that the pioneer racers were portrayed "with little or no emphasis on traditional femininity", while it is common in the case of more recent racers (Ross et al., 2009: 14). The female drivers who participated in the advertisements in the 1970s, 1980s and 1990s were presented similarly to their male counterparts. Advertising messages drew attention to their competencies and expertise, not gender. In the last twenty years, it has changed, as Danica Patrick's example explicitly illustrates. Although Patrick's sports competencies still have been underlined, much more attention has been drawn to her gender and physical attractiveness. Collectively, a bigger focus on femininity can be seen as an element of heteronormative gender order in motorsports and something imposed by the men who dominate in this world. However, looking at the issue from a neoliberal perspective, as Lippe von der (2013) did in her analysis of beach volleyball's dress codes, one can say that presenting an attractive, feminine and sexualized body is not solely forced on women, but it is a strategy chosen by themselves, a way to attract both media and sponsors' attention (see also Thorpe et al., 2017; Toffoletti & Thorpe, 2018). This approach is similar to how grid girls operate in motorsport, as will be discussed later.

It should be noted that while F1 remains almost inaccessible to female drivers (Sturm, 2021), "in other elite series however, women are competing more regularly" (Matthews & Pike, 2016: 15). Although it requires further analysis, the perception of F1 races as media event could provide a possible explanation. Media coverage depends to a large extent on the assumed tastes of viewers. Men constitute the majority of sports fans and, as the analysis has revealed, are interested in men's events (Jakubowska, 2015). Even though women are formally allowed to participate in F1 races, resistance to their participation may result from the assumption that the (male) audience is interested in male rivalry and prefer to see women in passive and ornamental, rather than active, roles. As the analysis of different sports' media coverage has revealed, in the case of niche or less popular sports, the athletes' gender loses its significance (Jakubowska, 2015: 183). It means media and sponsors perceive female and male athletes in a similar way. It can partially explain why it is particularly difficult for women to compete in F1, the most mediated and popular motorsport, while they are more visible in other motorsports.

This statement can be supported by the example of speedway in Poland, one of the most popular sports in the country. Although women are formally allowed to compete in the races, only a few of them have been given this opportunity, and the dominant image of women in speedway is that of the 'umbrella girls'. Therefore, similar to F1, on the track women mainly have passive roles, contrary to men who play active roles as competitors. However, it should be noted that umbrella girls were removed from participating in some speedway events (e.g., the Grand Prix in Sweden).

The decorative or supporting role of women can also be observed in other sports disciplines (e.g., in boxing, kickboxing and mixed martial arts). Dana White, the chief of the Ultimate Fighting Championship (UFC), when answering the call to drop these girls from the events, stated:

> [...] you can look at any sport you like, nobody treats women better than we do. And I'd suggest these people calling on them to be banned go have a look at what these girls do with the company, the type of money they're making. Do that and you'll realize these girls are as important to our brand as anyone else in the company. And that's exactly the way we treat them. (Stonehouse, 2019)

Hostesses, umbrella girls, ring and octagon girls are all on display during particular sports events and media coverage. Moreover, they have a large, often sexualized, circulation on the Internet. One can easily find many images presenting, for example, the ring girls or rankings of the most beautiful or sexiest umbrella girls. At the same time, they use social media to promote themselves to gain interest and attract attention, which can be converted into financial benefits.

While hostesses are still present during some sports events, the authorities of other sports disciplines have taken a similar position to F1. The Professional Darts Corporation decided to remove walk-on girls, present in the sport since the 1980s, only a few days before F1's announcement. In the case of cycling, criticism was levelled at the podium girls kissing the winner on the cheek and the cyclists' behaviour towards these girls

(Which sports still use, 2018). The decision of the organizer of the UCI Road World Championships in 2017 in Bergen (Norway) to replace hostesses with young female and male cyclists wearing folk costumes can be perceived as one of this critique's consequences. Finally, attention also turned to the presence of cheerleaders during sports events, as evidenced by Tobias Karlson's (a Swedish handball player) statement about cheerleading as an activity that objectifies women during the European Men's Handball Championships in 2016 (Organista & Mazur, 2016). Commenting on the performance of the cheerleaders, the player stated: "I've become somewhat accustomed to it, having played in the Bundesliga, but come on... What year is it now! There are so many other great things you can do during match breaks" (Euro 2016 w piłce ręcznej. Reprezentantom Szwecji przeszkadzają… cheerleaderki, 2016). His statement has been supported by the Swedish television experts, as well as the Swedish handball fans.

Therefore, while some sports disciplines still use women in decorative roles, others, including the majority of motorsport disciplines, have given up this practice. However, somewhat surprisingly, it seems that only the ban on grid girls in F1 has seen a significant backlash emerge. Before presenting the discussion itself, it is worth having a closer look at F1 events and one of their main features—'glamour'.

The 'Glamour' of Formula 1

As noted by Sturm (2014: 68), F1 "is viewed as the pinnacle of motor racing (if not all motorsport), with many of the world's best drivers racing expensive, sophisticated and high-tech machines at circuits around the globe". F1 races attract a significant number of live and TV audiences all around the world. In 2019, a total of 4.16 million spectators attended the 21 Grand Prix F1 races, and the most attended race took place at Silverstone (UK), where approximately 351,000 fans watched the race live over the weekend (Lange, 2020). More than 300,000 spectators also observed the events in Mexico and Australia. The total number of spectators has steadily increased in recent years (e.g., in 2016, it was estimated to be 3.74 million). This growth also concerns the TV audience. In 2019, the cumulative global TV audience stood at 1.9 billion and was 9% higher compared to 2018 (F1 broadcast to 1.9 billion total audience in 2019, 2020).

The numbers show that F1 is not only a live sports event but also an important media event: a "spectacular and seductive" (Kellner, 2010, quoted after Sturm, 2014: 69) global media spectacle. Furthermore, Sturm (2014: 70) states that "representationally, Formula One is constructed as a glamorous and high-tech global spectacle of speed"—a mix of speed, expense, the exotic and glamour. In a similar vein, Noble and Hughes relate F1's glamour to "impossibly fast cars driven by brave and handsome young men of all nationalities in a variety of exotic backdrops throughout the world, with beautiful women looking on adoringly" (Noble & Hughes, 2004: 25, quoted after Sturm, 2014: 70). With reference to glamour, women are overtly emphasized for their significant contribution to making F1 races 'glamorous'. As noted by Kennedy (2000):

> the role of "beautiful women" in providing that glamour is evident (...) like the yachts in the harbor, which are frequently in shot, both in the prelude to the race and when the cars repeatedly drive past them, and the champagne prefigured in the Moet trackside advertisement, they are part of the prize for the victorious hero driver. (p. 65)

Once again, one can see that women do not play an active role in direct competition. They are treated as one of the beautiful objects that create the events' atmosphere and are part of the prize reserved for the men competing on the track. A similar role is played by them during the car shows, where male spectators come to see both luxury cars and beautiful women. In both contexts, women are sexualized, objectified and perceived solely by their attractive bodies.

The glamour of F1 races is based on 'spectacular' sights and cities that can be admired during races, such as the Monaco Grand Prix as well as the money involved, luxurious lifestyles, male drivers and fast cars (Sturm, 2014). Women, playing the role of adornments or trophies, complete this image. From this perspective, as Turner (2004: 205, quoted after Sturm, 2014: 70) states, F1 can be perceived as "the ultimate male fantasist's sport: fast cars, expensive kit, global jet-setting and beautiful women with spray-on smiles".

Tippett (2020), in her analysis of the grid girls' discourse in the British media, also uses the concept of 'glamour'. In doing so, she refers to one of the meanings proposed by the Oxford Dictionary (2018), where 'glamour' is understood as 'denoting or relating to sexually suggestive or mildly pornographic photography or publications'.[1] In this context, as the example of glamour models reveals, using their bodies to earn money and working in the sex/glamour industry can be perceived not only as women's objectification but also as empowering or a form of empowerment (Coy & Garner, 2010; Tippett, 2020). The same can be said about the grid girls in F1.

No More Grid Girls: Between Objectification and Empowerment

Despite its still very masculine nature, motorsport has been influenced by the wider socio-cultural changes concerning women's status, gender relations and the ways of presenting female bodies (also in a sports context). One of the most visible but also questionable manifestations of these changes was a decision to eliminate grid girls from F1. Grid girls were often replaced by grid kids, that is, children selected from the junior drivers who take part in, for example, go-kart competitions. It should be noted that F1 was not the first to decide to eliminate grid girls from its motorsport events. This happened three years earlier, in April 2015, during the Le Mans sportscar race of the World Endurance Championship (Saner, 2018).

The decision of the F1 authorities to drop grid girls from the races provoked a broad discussion that has been analysed by Jakubowska (2018). The data informing the study were taken from a range of news outlets accessed via the Internet between 31 January, that is, the date of Liberty Media's decision, and 20 April 2018. Sixty samples from national newspapers', TV news channels', radio stations' online services, racing websites and sports websites were gathered. In sum, Jakubowska (2018) provided the following findings. The main argument used by F1 management was related to the assumption that the tradition of using grid girls during the races is no longer in line with modern socio-cultural norms. As F1 management stated:

> While the practice of employing grid girls has been a staple of Formula 1 Grands Prix for decades, we feel this custom does not resonate with our brand values and clearly is at odds with modern-day societal norms. (Formuła 1. "Grid kids" zastąpią "grid girls", 2018a)

Specifically, the focus on women's attractive and sexual bodies and their decorative roles has been treated as contradictory to modern norms. This could be read within the frames of 'political correctness'—one of the modern rules; however, there was no single statement in the research sample that presented 'political correctness' as an important principle worth following. On the contrary, it has always been seen in this discussion in a negative way, as 'exaggerated' or 'crazy' and, as a consequence, harmful. This point of view has been presented mainly by the grid girls themselves:

> It is disappointing that Formula 1 has followed the minority's vote to be politically correct. (Charlotte Gash, one of the grid girls for the BBC, quoted after: Prochota, 2018) Wake me up when all this crazy political correctness is over. I love to be a grid girl. (Sophie Wright, quoted after: Prochota, 2018)

In each case, 'political correctness' was viewed as a rule that imposes artificial norms and change on customs and traditions that have existed for many years (Jakubowska, 2018: 122).

The grid girls, who have been active participants in the discourse, have focused mainly on the loss of their jobs, the possibility to earn money and voluntary choice with regard to their jobs:

> Because of these feminists, they have cost us our jobs! I have been a grid girl for 8 years and I have never felt uncomfortable! I love my job, if I didn't I wouldn't do it! No one forces us to do this! This is our choice! (Lauren-Jade Pope, quoted after Kuczera, 2018)
>
> I love my job. I'm respected, paid well & proud to represent the team I'm working for. It's not right for anyone, let alone 'feminists' to judge our job when quite frankly they are putting so many women out of work. Where is the equality & empowerment here? (Lucy Stokes, quoted after: Formuła 1. Grid kids zastąpią grid girls. Środowisko protestuje, 2018b)

The grid girls also emphasized a lack of behaviour that could be perceived as inappropriate (e.g., proclaiming a lack of sexism or sexist practices). They also stressed that their point of view was not taken into account when the decision was made. It should also be noted that their voices were supported by several F1 drivers and by more than 11,000 supporters who had signed a Change.org petition (2018).

Specifically, the grid girls accused 'feminists' of causing the loss of their jobs, although 'feminists' have remained almost inactive in the 'grid girls' discourse. This is even more puzzling as the decision was taken by men—key people in F1 and Liberty Media and those generally dominant in sports, mainly the so-called male sports and organizations (Claringbould & Knoppers, 2012; Hovden, 2000; Pfister & Radtke, 2009). However, in the dominant discourse on women and sport, related to the second wave of feminism, the role of hostesses in sport is considered as one of the prime examples of women's sexualization and objectification. Therefore, it seems that feminism can be considered here as a representative of 'modern' norms and values and as one of the forces that has imposed some decisions on the sports field, although usually not directly. From the grid girls' point of view, as the above quotations reveal, feminism (at least its second, most recognized wave) seems to be perceived as repressive (similarly to political correctness) and/or unprogressive (Tippett, 2020).

The decision to drop grid girls from the races can be read within the frame of different waves of feminism (Jakubowska, 2018). On the one hand, such a ban is in line with the assumptions of the second wave of feminism, where women's sexualization can be seen as imposed by men and used as a tool to attract the attention of male sports fans and sponsors (Davis, 2010; Khomutova & Channon, 2015; McLeod, 2010). Contextually, moving away from such overt and explicit practices is also timely given the increased awareness, discussions and backlash to forms of women's objectification as well as global #metoo movements. On the other hand, as the third wave of feminism or post-feminism suggests, the sexualized body can also be seen as a tool of female empowerment and agency (Gill, 2003, 2008; Heywood, 2008). In this context, a woman is not sexualized by others (men) but decides herself to emphasize her physical attractiveness and sexualized femininity. Taking the example of grid girls, their work will not be perceived here as imposed by heterosexual norms of motorsport worlds, but a free choice of young and attractive women to get attention and make money due to their beauty. In her analysis of the grid girls' discourse in the British media, Tippett (2020: 189) locates the debate with a post-feminism framework:

> The debate over the termination of the F1 grid girls has resulted in a dilemma in British culture over sexual autonomy and choice. Instead of sexualisation being deemed objectifying in this context, there has been a move towards perceiving sexualisation as a form of bodily proprietorship and economic independence for women.

As Tippett (2020) reveals, three main topics dominated the British media discourse on grid girls: (1) [dis]empowerment, (2) choice and (3) disputed feminism. Regarding the first, being a model (hostess) has been perceived as both an empowering and disempowering profession. The grid girls have been perceived as representing either "an emancipated state of modern femininity" or "outdated image that isn't in keeping with modern values" (Tippett, 2020: 193). This dichotomy goes in line with the differences between the feminist movement's waves and their perception of exposing female physical attractiveness and women's agency.

The discussion on choice has concerned the bodily and economic autonomy of grid girls, but also women in general. In the analysed discourse, the grid girls have been seen as celebrating their femininity and using their sexualized images willingly to gain recognition and earn money. However, as noted by Tippett (2020: 194), the chance to obtain empowerment through promotional modelling is only available to a limited category of people, namely those that are young and attractive, usually white, and female, while some social categories, including Black and minority ethnic (BME) groups or older women, are generally deprived of this right. Moreover, men do not usually play decorative roles during sports events; however, some exceptions can be indicated with, for example, the 'grid boys' at Monaco Grand Prix or 'ring boys' during women's fights in mixed martial arts (MMA) (Jakubowska, 2018). Therefore, although grid girls perceive their role as a free choice and women's empowerment, one should be aware that this way of increasing empowerment is limited only to these women who meet the current criteria of physical attractiveness. As Tippett (2020: 192) observes, "Many social groups are excluded from even applying, let alone partaking, in promotional modelling. Due to this, there are inherent contradictions in this form of empowerment".

The third topic that dominated the British discourse on grid girls was feminism and whether it limits or reinforces women's rights. This discussion was related to the grid girls' accusations towards feminism indicated previously in the chapter and dominated by a post-feminism approach. However, some discourse's actors perceived the decision of F1's owner as appropriate in the time of #metoo movement and wider socio-cultural changes (Tippett, 2020).

Conclusion

The decision of F1 has also been criticized by some Grand Prix (GP) race organizers. A few of them have decided to still use hostesses during the events, but in a different, although still promotional, role. For example, during the Monaco Grand Prix in 2018, female models did not hold placards displaying driver numbers but were seen "taking pictures and displaying messages on social media for a luxury watch brand" (Ikonen, 2018). Women also had promotional roles related to airline companies during the Bahrain and China Grands Prix. After negotiations with Liberty Media, grid girls were also present during the Sochi Grand Prix the same year, as well as in Austria and Singapore (Now Singapore ignoring F1 'grid girls' ban, 2018). 'Rebellious' organizers of the GPs have argued that 'beautiful girls' have traditionally been associated with the auto industry (Russia hopes for grid girls return in 2019, 2018). They also emphasized their important role in the events' media coverage (Ikonen, 2018) and in the promotion of the country and local brands, as in the case of Singapore (Now Singapore ignoring F1 'grid girls' ban, 2018). Therefore, although grid girls have been deprived of their previous tasks (so as not to break F1's new regulations), they have not entirely disappeared from F1 races.

Women have managed to break through a glass ceiling in F1 to some extent, and one can see an increasing number of women working for F1 teams in a range of diverse roles previously unavailable to them, including as team principals, engineers, strategists, mechanics and so forth (Sturm, 2021). However, equally, F1 remains a male world as evidenced by a lack of female drivers and the domination of men among the teams' employees (Sturm, 2021). Moreover, women, as mentioned above, still play decorative roles during the F1 events and function to make them, together with fast cars and luxurious lifestyles, 'glamorous'. F1 is not only a sport event, but also run as media, corporate and commodified events that are primarily dominated by men, who also constitute a vast majority of fans. From this perspective, the glamour provided by women can be understood as their objectification. In contradistinction, as the grid girls' discourse has revealed, the role of females in F1 can be perceived within the frame of female agency and empowerment. From this perspective, women's bodies are still on display, but by their choice. A beautiful and sexy body becomes here a source of women's power, and if women are objectified, it is their own choice in accordance with post-feminism (or the third wave of feminism). Therefore, one should speak rather about women's 'subjectification' (Gill, 2003), that is, objectification made by 'subjects' than their objectification. In this context, it should be reminded that the grid girls have emphasized that their work has always been their free choice and that they have liked it very much. Being a model during F1 races can be seen as an example of working in the glamour industry, where money is earned due to the exposition of attractive and sexualized body images. However, one cannot forget that women who do not fit into heteronormative patterns of beauty are deprived of access to such opportunities or industries.

The decision to drop grid girls from the races provides intriguing insights into issues of women's objectification and empowerment, the glamour industry and feminism. One can say that the F1's owner decision has also been in line with the assumptions of second wave of feminism and social movements such as #metoo. At the same time, the grid girls' reaction can be read within the frame of the third wave of feminism (or post-feminism). From both perspectives, the discussion is focused on women's bodies that are sexualized and used to draw attention and, consequently, bring financial profits. Although the decision to ban the grid girls could be seen as favourable to women (against their objectification), the grid girls' opinions have not been taken into account. In this sense, women (grid girls) have been objectified and deprived of the right to decide how they want to use their bodies. A confrontation of different waves of feminism visible in the 'grid girls' discourse reveals that women's agency and empowerment, also expressed by 'subjectification', remains a challenge in male-dominated worlds, such as motorsport.

Note

1. It is worth noting that the dictionary also uses the example of Monte Carlo, where the Monaco GP takes places, defining 'glamour' as 'an attractive or exciting quality that makes certain people or things seem appealing, *the glamour of Monte Carlo*'.

References

Arendt, K. (2021) '10 Best Female Race Car Drivers In Motorsports History (1920s-1990s),' *AutoWise* (online), 22 February. Retrieved March 26, 2021, from https://autowise.com/female-race-car-driver/.

Balkmar, D. (2012). *On Men and Cars. An Ethnographic Study of Gendered, Risky and Dangerous Relations*. University dissertation from Linköping: Linköping University Electronic Press.

Bird, S. R. (1996). Welcome to the Men's Club: Homosociality and the Maintenance of Hegemonic Masculinity. *Gender and Society, 10*(2), 120–132.

Brennan, S. (2018). 'From a '60s Japanese pop star to Katie Price and Love Island's Olivia Atwood: How the grid girl ban spells the end of a long and VERY colourful part of Formula One history,' *Dailymail* (online), 31 January. Retrieved April 20, 2018, from http://www.dailymail.co.uk/femail/article-5336079/Grid-girl-ban-spellsend-colourful-Formula-One.html.

Change.org. (2018). *Formula 1 Keep the Grid Girls*. Retrieved January 8, 2021, from www.change.org/p/liberty-media-formula-1-keep-the-grid-girls

Charters, D. A. (2006). It's a Guy Thing: The Experience of Women in Canadian Sports Car Competition. *Sport History Review, 37*(2), 83–99. https://doi.org/10.1123/shr.37.2.83

Claringbould, I., & Knoppers, A. (2012). Paradoxical Practices of Gender in Sport-related Organizations. *Journal of Sport Management, 26*(5), 404–416. https://doi.org/10.1123/jsm.26.5.404

Connell, R. W. (1987). *Gender and Power: Society, the Person and Sexual Politics*. Stanford University Press.

Coy, M., & Garner, M. (2010). Glamour Modelling and the Marketing of Self Sexualization: Critical Reflections. *International Journal of Cultural Studies, 13*(6), 657–675. https://doi.org/10.1177/1367877910376576

Davis, P. (2010). Sexualization and Sexuality in Sport. In P. Davis & C. Weaving (Eds.), *Philosophical Perspectives on Gender in Sport and Physical Activity* (pp. 57–63). Routledge.

'Euro 2016 w piłce ręcznej. Reprezentantom Szwecji przeszkadzają... cheerleaderki' [Handball Euro 2016. Sweden's national team is bothered by... cheerleaders'] (2016) *Polska The Times,* 18 January 2016. Retrieved March 26, 2021, from http://www.polskatimes.pl/artykul/9302255,euro-2016-w-pilce-recznej-reprezentantomszwecji-przeszkadzaja-cheerleaderki-video-zdjecia,id,t.html.

F1 broadcast to 1.9 billion total audience in 2019. (2020). Retrieved January 8, 2021, from https://www.formula1.com/en/latest/article.f1-broadcast-to-1-9-billion-fans-in-2019.4IeYkWSoexxSIeJyuTrk22.html

Fleming, D., & Sturm, D. (2011). *Media, Masculinities, and the Machine: F1, Transformers, and Fantasizing Technology at Its Limits*. Continuum.

Flood, M. (2008). Men, Sex, and Homosociality: How Bonds between Men Shape Their Sexual Relations with Women. *Men and Masculinities, 10*(3), 339–359. https://doi.org/10.1177/1097184X06287761

Formuła 1. "Grid kids" zastąpią "grid girls" [Formula 1. "Grid kids" will replace "grid girls"] 2018a. Retrieved April 20, 2018, from http://www.sport.pl/F1/7,96296,22987584,formula-1-grid-kids-zastapia-grid-girls.html.

Formuła 1. Grid kids zastąpią grid girls. Środowisko protestuje [Formula 1. Grid kids will replace grid girls. Community protests] (2018b). Retrieved April 20, 2018, from http://www.sport.pl/F1/56,96296,22988041,formula-1-grid-kids-zastapia-grid-girls.html.

Formuła 1 już bez grid girls. Piękne kobiety nie pojawią się podczas wyścigów [Formula 1 without grid girls. Beautiful women will not appear during the races] (2018). Retrieved April 20, 2018, from https://sport.onet.pl/formula-1/formula-1-juz-bez-grid-girls/p5nhz2j

Gill, R. (2003). From Sexual Objectification to Sexual Subjectification: The Resexualisation of Women's Bodies in the Media. *Feminist Media Studies, 3*(1), 99–106. https://doi.org/10.1080/1468077032000080158

Gill, R. (2008). Empowerment/sexism: Figuring Female Sexual Agency in Contemporary Advertising. *Feminism and Psychology, 18*(1), 35–60. https://doi.org/10.1177/0959353507084950

Heywood, L. (2008). Third-wave Feminism, the Global Economy, and Women's Surfing: Sport as Stealth Feminism in Girls' Surf Culture. In A. Harris (Ed.), *Next Wave Cultures: Feminism, Subcultures, Activism* (pp. 63–82). Routledge.

Hovden, J. (2000). "Heavyweight" Men and Younger Women? The Gendering of Selection Processes in Norwegian Sport Organizations. *NORA - Nordic Journal of Feminist and Gender Research, 8*(1), 17–32. https://doi.org/10.1080/080387400408035

Ikonen, Ch. (2018). 'Grid Girls RETURN to Monaco GP – But Have a Different Role: 'It's too much of a fuss", *Daily Star*, 27 May [online]. Retrieved January 8, 2021, from https://www.dailystar.co.uk/news/latest-news/f1-monaco-grand-prix-grid-17141786

Jakubowska, H. (2015). Are Women Still the 'other sex': Gender and Sport in the Polish Mass Media. *Sport in Society, 18*(2), 168–185. https://doi.org/10.1080/17430437.2013.854464

Jakubowska, H. (2018). 'No More Grid Girls at Formula One: The Discourse Analysis on Hostesses' Sexualized Bodies, Objectification, and Female Agency'. *Society Register, 2*(1), 113–130. https://doi.org/10.14746/sr.2018.2.1.07

Jakubowska, H., Antonowicz, D., & Kossakowski, R. (2020). *Female Fans, Gender Relations and Football Fandom Challenging the Brotherhood Culture.* Routledge.

Kellner, D. (2010). Media Spectacle and Media Events: Some Critical Reflections. In N. Couldry, A. Hepp, & F. Krotz (Eds.), *Media Events in a Global Age* (pp. 76–91). Routledge.

Kennedy, E. (2000). Bad Boys and Gentlemen: Gendered Narrative in Televised Sport. *International Review for the Sociology of Sport, 35*(1), 59–73. https://doi.org/10.1177/101269000035001005

Khomutova, A., & Channon, A. (2015). Legends' in 'Lingerie': Sexuality and Athleticism in the 2013 Legends Football League US Season. *Sociology of Sport Journal, 32*(2), 161–182. https://doi.org/10.1123/ssj.2014-0054

Kuczera, Ł. (2018). 'Grid girl uderzają w feministki. Nie pytają nas o zdanie.' *WP Sportowe Fakty*, 2 February. Retrieved April 20, 2018, from https://sportowefakty.wp.pl/formula-1/735612/grid-girls-uderzaja-w-feministki-nie-pytaja-nas-o-zdanie.

Lange, D. (2020). *Formula 1 Grand Prix total attendance worldwide from 2016 to 2019*. Retrieved January 8, 2021, from https://www.statista.com/statistics/1130725/formula-1-total-attendance/.

Letherby, G., & Reynolds, G. (Eds.). (2009). *Gendered Journeys, Mobile Emotions*. Ashgate.

Lipman-Blumen, J. (1976). Toward a Homosocial Theory of Sex Roles: An Explanation of the Sex Segregation of Social Institutions. *Signs, 1*(3), 15–31.

Lippe von der, G. (2013). Discourses on Women's Dress Codes in Beach Volleyball and Boxing: In the Context of the Current Consumer Culture. In G. Pfister & M. K. Sisjord (Eds.), *Gender and Sport: Changes and Challenges* (pp. 140–158). Münster.

Matthews, J., & Pike, E. (2016). What on Earth Are They Doing in a Racing Car?': Towards an Understanding of Women in Motorsport. *The International Journal of the History of Sport, 33*(13), 1532–1550. https://doi.org/10.1080/09523367.2016.1168811

McLeod, C. (2010). Mere and Partial Means: The Full Range of the Objectification of Women. In P. Davis & C. Weaving (Eds.), *Philosophical Perspectives on Gender in Sport and Physical Activity* (pp. 64–82). Routledge.

Mellström, U. (2002). Patriarchal Machines and Masculine Embodiment. *Science, Technology and Human Values, 27*(4), 460–478. https://doi.org/10.1177/016224302236177

Mellström, U. (2004). Machines and Masculine Subjectivity. Technology as an Integral Part of Men's Life Experiences. *Men and Masculinities. Special Issue: Masculinities and Technologies, 6*(4), 368–382. https://doi.org/10.1177/1097184X03260960

Messner, M. (1988). Sports and Male Domination: The Female Athlete as Contested Ideological Terrain. *Sociology of Sport Journal, 5*(3), 197–211. https://doi.org/10.1123/ssj.5.3.197

Naess, H. E. (2014). *A Sociology of the World Rally Championship: History, Identity, Memories and Place*. Palgrave.

Noble, J., & Hughes, M. (2004). *Formula One Racing for Dummies: An Insider's Guide to Formula One*. John Wiley & Sons.

Now Singapore ignoring F1 'grid girls' ban. (2018). Retrieved January 8, 2021, from https://www.f1-fansite.com/f1-news/now-singapore-ignoring-f1-grid-girls-ban/

Organista, N., & Mazur, Z. (2016). '"Piękne kobiety pięknie tańczą" czy „uprzedmiotowienie i upokorzenie"? Analiza dyskursu o cheerleadingu w kontekście mistrzostw Europy w piłce ręcznej mężczyzn w 2016 roku,' ["Beautiful Women Dance Beautifully" versus "Objectification and

Humiliation?" Discourse Analysis of Cheerleading in Respect of European Men's Handball Championships in 2016] *Przegląd Socjologii Jakościowej*, 12(4), pp. 118–143. Retrieved January 18, 2021, from http://www.qualitativesociologyreview.org/PL/Volume36/PSJ_12_4_Organista_Mazur.pdf

Oxford Dictionary. (2018). 'Glamour.' Retrieved January 18, 2021, from https://en.oxforddictionaries.com/definition/glamour.

Pfister, G., & Radtke, S. (2009). Sport, Women and Leadership: Results of a Project on Executives in German Sports Organizations. *European Journal of Sport Science, 9*, 229–243. https://doi.org/10.1080/17461390902818286

Pflugfelder, E. H. (2009). Something Less than a Driver: Toward an Understanding of Gendered Bodies in Motorsport. *Journal of Sport and Social Issues, 33*(4), 411–426. https://doi.org/10.1177/0193723509350611

Prochota, A. (2018). 'Grid girls niezadowolone z decyzji F1. Kochamy naszą pracę.' [Grid girls unhappy with F1's decision. We love our job]. *WP Sportowe Fakty*, 2 February. Retrieved April 20, 2018, from https://sportowefakty.wp.pl/formula-1/735585/grid-girls-niezadowolone-z-decyzji-f1-kochamy-nasza-prace.

Ross, S. R., Ridinger, L. L., & Cuneen, J. (2009). Drivers to Divas: Advertising Images of Women in Motorsport. *International Journal of Sports Marketing and Sponsorship, 10*(3), 7–17. https://doi.org/10.1108/IJSMS-10-03-2009-B003

Russia hopes for grid girls return in 2019. (2018). Retrieved January 8, 2021, from https://www.f1-fansite.com/f1-news/russia-hopes-for-grid-girls-return-in-2019/

Saner, E. (2018). "Grid girls': F1 follows darts by calling time on women in hot pants,' *The Guardian* (online), 2 February. Retrieved January 8, 2021, from https://www.theguardian.com/world/2018/feb/02/grid-girls-f1-follows-darts-by-calling-time-on-women-in-hotpant.

Shackleford, B. A. (1999). Masculinity, Hierarchy, and the Auto Racing Fraternity: The Pit Stop as a Celebration of Social Roles. *Men and Masculinities, 2*(2), 180–196. https://doi.org/10.1177/1097184X99002002004

Sloop, J. M. (2005). Riding in Cars Between Men. *Communication and Critical/Cultural Studies, 2*(3), 191–213. https://doi.org/10.1080/14791420500198522

Stonehouse, G. (2019). 'UFC boss Dana White hits back at UFC 243 Octagon girl criticism,' The Sun, 1 October (online). Retrieved January 8, 2021, from https://www.news.com.au/sport/ufc/ufc-boss-dana-white-hits-back-at-ufc-243-octagon-girl-criticism/news-story/bf79f1391e81b122220a5e326bb74f1b

Sturm, D. (2014). A Glamorous and High-tech Global Spectacle of Speed: Formula One Motor Racing as Mediated, Global and Corporate Spectacle. In K. Dashper, T. Fletcher, & N. McCullough (Eds.), *Sports Events, Society and Culture* (pp. 68–82). Routledge.

Sturm, D. (2021). The Formula One paradox: Macho Male Racers and Ornamental Females. In K. Dashper (Ed.), *Sport, Gender and Mega Events* (pp. 111–128). Emerald.

Thorpe, H., Toffoletti, K., & Bruce, T. (2017). Sportswomen and Social Media: Bringing Third-wave Feminism, Postfeminism, and Neoliberal Feminism into Conversation. *Journal of Sport and Social Issues, 41*(5), 359–383. https://doi.org/10.1177/0193723517730808

Tippett, A. (2020). Debating the F1 Grid Girls: Feminist Tensions in British Popular Culture. *Feminist Media Studies, 20*(2), 185–202. https://doi.org/10.1080/14680777.2019.1574859

Thurnell-Read, T. (2012). What Happens on Tour: The Premarital Stag Tour, Homosocial Bonding, and Male Friendship. *Men and Masculinities, 15*(3), 249–270. https://doi.org/10.1177/1097184X12448465

Toffoletti, K., & Thorpe, H. (2018). Female Athletes' Self-representation on Social Media: A Feminist Analysis of Neoliberal Marketing Strategies in 'Economies of Visibility'. *Feminism and Psychology, 28*(1), 11–31. https://doi.org/10.1177/0959353517726705

Turner, B. (2004). *The Pits: The Real World of Formula One*. Atlantic Books.

'Which sports still use 'walk-on girls?' (2018). *BBC News* (online), 2 February. Retrieved January 8, 2021, from http://www.bbc.com/news/uk-42907570

Uteng, T. P., & Cresswell, T. (Eds.). (2008). *Gendered Mobilities*. Ashgate.

Women in Formula One – a brief history. (n.d.). Retrieved March 26, 2021, from http://www.formula1-dictionary.net/women_in_f1.html.

Part V

Motor Racing and the Politics of Race

A Political and Economic Analysis of South Africa's Historical Relationship with Formula One Motor Racing, 1934–1993

Gustav Venter

Introduction

On 14 March 1993 the Frenchman, Alain Prost, won the opening race of that season's Formula One World Championship held at the Kyalami racing circuit north of Johannesburg in South Africa. To date this represents the last international Formula One race to be held in South Africa, and the intervening 28-year gap belies the fact that the country has had an intimate history with motor racing's ultimate contest, including producing the 1979 World Champion, Jody Scheckter. The 1993 South African Grand Prix was held at a significant political and sporting juncture for the country, falling within a brief but volatile period of transition from the end of structural apartheid in 1990 to the country's first democratic elections—and arrival of black majority rule—in 1994. In sporting terms South Africa was welcomed back into the international fold in 1991 when its national cricket side toured India, followed by

G. Venter (✉)
Stellenbosch University, Stellenbosch, South Africa
e-mail: gbventer@sun.ac.za

D. Sturm et al. (eds.), *The History and Politics of Motor Racing*, Global Culture and Sport Series, https://doi.org/10.1007/978-3-031-22825-4_13

participation in the 1992 Cricket World Cup in Australia and New Zealand and the Olympic Games in Barcelona the same year. Formula One motor racing also returned to South Africa in 1992, having previously visited in 1985.

These important developments within politics and sport during this transitional period were merely an extension of the close historical relationship between these two domains within the South African context. In this regard there is a well-established body of literature probing this relationship, particularly during the apartheid era. Douglas Booth's *The Race Game* (1998) and Robert Archer and Antoine Bouillon's *The South African Game* (1982) stand out as two oft-cited works on this topic. Elsewhere much of the analytical focus has been on the most popular team sports in the country, namely rugby union (Grundlingh et al., 1995), cricket (Murray & Merrett, 2004) and football (Alegi, 2004), as well as the role of anti-apartheid organisations in directing pressure towards the apartheid regime within the realm of sport (Lapchick, 1975). The 1993 South African Grand Prix, however, serves as a useful point of entry for expanding the broader sport-political analysis into motor sport. This paper endeavours to analyse South Africa's historical position within Formula One racing as well as the arc of this relationship—one which is somewhat unique in that South Africa was never formally isolated by the world governing body even at the height of apartheid. This serves as a stark contrast to other major codes which had been isolated since the 1960s. South Africa's Olympic participation also seized in 1960—a full 25 years before the final apartheid-era, South African Grand Prix was held in 1985.

This analysis attempts to probe the particularity of the relationship between Formula One racing and South Africa by focusing on the political, economic and social dimensions during the second half of the twentieth century. Through the use of contemporary writings, media sources and selected private documents it builds on the recent work of Naess (2017, 2020) by adding further depth to South Africa's historical entanglement with Formula One racing. In doing so it makes a novel contribution to the broader literature on the history of South African sport by taking up a hitherto underutilised analytical vantage point.

Origins of Motor Racing in South Africa

The introduction of the automobile in South Africa dates back to 1896 when a local businessman, John Percy Hess, imported a Benz Velo to the Transvaal Republic towards the end of that year. This "horseless carriage" ran under its own power for the first time in January the following year when it was publicly demonstrated in Pretoria (Wheels24, 2016). It did not take long for motor racing to gain a foothold in the country as the Royal Automobile Club (RAC) was established in 1901, followed by the first motor racing event in South Africa held at Cape Town's Green Point cycling track in 1903 (Lupini, 2020a). It took a couple of decades before the arrival of the first motor manufacturing plant in South Africa, when Ford opened what became the company's 16th overseas operation in Port Elizabeth on 19 January 1924. This was soon supplemented by a General Motors plant in the same city two years later (Fourie, 2017, p. 61).

As far as racing was concerned the RAC became the controlling body for motor sport in the country and was affiliated to Association Internationale des Automobile Clubs Reconnus (AIACR)—the forerunner to the Fédération Internationale de l'Automobile (FIA)—in 1931 (Loubser, 2013, 6%). The first motor racing event of any international standing occurred on 27 December 1934, as East London hosted the first ever South African Grand Prix on its 15.2-mile Marine Drive street circuit. This was initiated as a private endeavour by Edward "Brud" Bishop, the motoring editor of the local *Daily Dispatch* newspaper at the time. The thought of creating such an event had come to him in 1933 while taking a morning reconnaissance drive on a completed section of coastal road along the west bank of the Buffalo River which runs through the city. This drive germinated the idea of using the completed road loop as a racing circuit (Bishop, 1965, p. 9). Through his marketing efforts the event—to his surprise—also attracted four international entrants, including British-based American millionaire, Whitney Straight, and English racing driver Richard Seaman. Straight ended up winning the race in front of an estimated crowd of 42,000. According to Bishop (1965, pp. 11–25) this was the first international road racing event held outside of Europe, and the large attendance served as an early indication of the potential interest in high-profile motor racing events in South Africa.

The years leading up to World War II saw the rapid expansion of motor racing events and infrastructure in South Africa. East London hosted four more South African Grands Prix annually in January from 1936 to 1939 on a shortened version of its Prince George Circuit (as it was renamed in 1935). Bishop was also instrumental in the construction of the Earl Howe Circuit north of Johannesburg over a period of four and a half months in 1936—a project that was completed at a cost of £32,000 and just in time to host the first ever Rand Grand Prix on 30 January 1937 with an estimated crowd of 55,000 in attendance (Bishop, 1965, p. 37). Earl Howe, whose full name was Francis Richard Henry Penn Curzon, was a cofounder of the British Racing Drivers' Club and winner of the 1931, 24 hours of Le Mans race. He actively participated in races in South Africa and was a key role player in building up the reputation of these events (Bishop, 1965, p. 45). The Earl Howe circuit would host one more Rand Grand Prix on 16 December 1937 prior to World War II—a race that included a number of international participants—before ultimately becoming the site of a housing estate (Bishop, 1965, p. 50).

During this period leading up to World War II there were similar developments in the Cape as the British property developer, Arthur Edwards—builder of the Grosvenor House Hotel in London—invested a reported £70,000 into the construction of a racing circuit on land which he had acquired in Tokai just south of Cape Town (Bishop, 1965, p. 44). The first Grosvenor Grand Prix was held there on 16 January 1937, followed by two more pre-war events in 1938 and 1939. The success of these races during the 1930s proved that South Africa had the potential to become a significant centre for international motor racing—a process that was ultimately interrupted by World War II. The post-war period saw rapid changes to the country's political and economic landscape which in turn impacted the subsequent trajectory of motor racing.

At this point it is also worth comparing the early development of motor racing in South Africa to competitive sport elsewhere in the country. In this regard the initial formation of organised sports bodies stretched back to the second half of the nineteenth century when British immigrants and soldiers were instrumental in spreading codes such as cricket, football and rugby union, among others. Football, for example, saw the formation of its first national body—the South African Football Association (SAFA)—in 1892 (Bolsmann, 2010, p. 30). This was a whites-only organisation that reflected the colonial relations and practices of the time. Subsequent years saw the formation of similar controlling bodies for other racial groups, with the South African Coloured Rugby Football Board (formed in 1897) constituting the first black national sports body (Alegi, 2004, p. 18). By the early 1950s some codes had up to four separate controlling bodies organised along racial lines (Archer & Bouillon, 1982, p. 153). This was also in line with South Africa's apartheid policy, instituted in 1948, which formally entrenched racial segregation into all aspects of South African life, including sport. For example, the Population Registration Act of 1950 classified citizens into one of four recognised racial groups, namely black (African), coloured, Indian or white. In the South African context the term "coloured" is used to denote people of mixed racial heritage. In addition the Group Areas Act of 1950 designated geographical "group areas" for each population group, and required citizens to carry permits if they wanted to enter different group areas to that of their own racial group.

While organised sport was quick to gain a foothold among South Africa's black, coloured and Indian racial groups during the first half of the twentieth century, motor racing essentially remained a white preserve on account of its high economic barriers to entry. Archer and Bouillon (1982, p. 112), for example, point out that the broad development of organised black sport followed the same trajectory as that of white sport—but with a slight time lag—with "the exception of those minor or technical sports which requires resources black people do not have—such as yachting, motor racing, power-boat racing, skiing and all the aerial sports". This deviation by motor racing from the broader development path of the most popular sport codes in South Africa is worth bearing in mind when analysing subsequent developments during the post-World War II period.

Rapid Change in the Post-War Period

The most significant political development in the years immediately after World War II was the ascent to power of the National Party in 1948 which was accompanied by the implementation of its apartheid policy. This would eventually set South African sport on a collision course with the international community, but during the early years of the policy, sport was able to continue unabated within the international sphere. As far as motor racing was concerned there were some notable developments at international level with the AIACR being renamed as the Fédération Internationale de l'Automobile (FIA) in 1946 (Naess, 2020, p. 31). A key objective at this point was for the FIA to become the sole controlling body for international motor sport. This was soon followed by the creation of the first Drivers' World Championship under the auspices of the FIA in 1950—a seven-race international series won by Guiseppe Farina in an Alfa Romeo that year. This represented the beginning of international Formula One motor racing in the competitive form that we know today (Naess, 2020, pp. 36–37).

On the domestic front East London remained a major racing hub in South Africa after the war, although it would take well over a decade for the South African Grand Prix to make its return to the calendar. By this point both the Earl Howe Circuit north of Johannesburg and the Grosvenor Circuit near Cape Town had been converted to housing estates (Bishop, 2020, p. 59)—perhaps an indication as to the economic challenges in maintaining such facilities sustainably over the long run. The first post-war event of national importance was the Van Riebeeck Trophy race run at Paarden Eiland in Cape Town in 1948 (Loubser, 2011, p. 25). New circuits also sprang up in the Natal Province, and races were held at different locations in the Transvaal including the Germiston Airfield and the Grand Central Circuit between Johannesburg and Pretoria which was inaugurated in 1949 (Loubser, 2011, p. 32). Racing also took place across the border in Lorenço Marques, the capital of Portuguese East Africa at the time, in 1950, while Cape Town began utilising the new Gunners Circle industrial park as a racing venue a year later (Lupini, 2020b).

A significant development took place in 1953 with the establishment of South Africa's own Drivers' Championship consisting of a formalised racing calendar with points on offer at various races around the country (Lupini, 2020b). This competition was conducted on an annual basis until 1986 and formed the backbone of local single-seater racing. The range of racing venues available in South Africa continued to expand during the 1950s, including a new track in the Cape at the Eersterivier airfield as well as the Palmietfontein Circuit near Alberton on the East Rand. Races were also conducted at Salisbury in Rhodesia (Lupini, 2020b). In East London the early 1950s represented a transitional period whereby race organisers were not yet in a position to host events of international standing and instead conducted a series of winter handicap races on a preliminary 1.75-mile Esplanade circuit which proved highly dangerous (Bishop, 1965, p. 57).

By 1958 a local East London hotelier, Cedric Vice, had taken over the chairmanship of the South African Grand Prix Organisers group, and set about establishing the return of this event to the racing calendar. The initial challenge was finding a circuit since the pre-war Prince George Circuit was regarded as being too long for this purpose given the requirement that cars should pass spectators on numerous occasions in order to boost the racing spectacle (Bishop, 1965, p. 58). By June 1959 the organisers had constructed a new 2.5-mile version of the Prince George Circuit which included only a 0.5-mile section of the old layout. The site was still able to capitalise on the Indian Ocean backdrop, and the project was completed at a reported cost of R80,000 to the East London City Council (Bishop, 1965, p. 58). The South African Grand Prix made its return to the national calendar on 1 January 1960—the sixth instalment of this event. Of note was the participation of British racing great, Sterling Moss (who finished second in the race), along with a number of other overseas participants including the likes of Paul Frère (the eventual race winner) and Lucien Bianchi of Belgium, as well as fellow British racers Chris Bristow, Dick Gibson and Bruce Halford (Lupini, 2020c). The seventh South African Grand Prix was held later that same year in December, with Moss again in attendance and this time taking the victory in front of a reported 70,000 spectators. Again a strong foreign contingent was in attendance, with Sweden's Joakim Bonnier taking second place and

Australia's Jack Brabham taking third (Bishop, 1965, p. 60). The following year, in 1961, Jim Clark came away as the South African Grand Prix winner, beating Moss into second and Bonnier into third with 67,000 spectators in attendance (Bishop, 1965, p. 61).

The participation of foreign racers in South African events became commonplace from 1955 onwards (Loubser, 2011, p. 26) and increased into the 1960s, although Bishop (1965, p. 59) pointed to the challenges of attracting high profile names such as Moss, Jim Clark and Graham Hill sustainably over the long term given the high appearance fees they commanded. Another important factor worth considering is the fact that racing events were not exclusively profitable ventures. Bishop (1965, p. 38) himself indicated that they "did not make money" from the prewar Earl Howe Circuit events where he was directly involved. He put this down to the way the hastily constructed track ultimately turned out. Apparently his desire to offer an alternative to East London's fast, picturesque circuit resulted in too many extreme corners being implemented on the Earl Howe Circuit. This, in his view, made for slow racing with little excitement, coupled with other factors such as a lack of sufficient entry roads for spectators. This served as early evidence that purposely built racing circuits were challenging properties to maintain, hence the preponderance of racing events on airfields which were facilities that naturally served a dual purpose.

The gradual expansion up to 1960 of South Africa's racing profile and infrastructure after World War II has to be positioned within the overall economic trajectory of the country at the time. The dawn of the 1960s was to be the start of a period of unprecedented economic growth for the country as a whole, despite the initial political and economic fallout from the events at Sharpeville on 21 March 1960 where 69 black protesters were killed by police (Grundlingh, 2008, p. 143). The event made international headlines and the immediate aftermath saw significant capital flight from foreign investors, but this proved to be a short term trend as the National Party government quickly exerted control by imposing import and exchange controls and clamping down on political unrest. This included the banning of the African National Congress (ANC) and Pan Africanist Congress (PAC) as well as the eventual imprisonment of Nelson Mandela and other leaders within the anti-apartheid opposition

(Grundlingh, 2008, p. 144). These measures ultimately set the table for a period of rapid, extended economic growth as foreign capital began to flow inwards and local investors piled into the stock market. According to Grundlingh (2008, p. 144) South Africa's economic growth for the remainder of the 1960s outpaced "nearly all Western countries by registering an average growth rate of 6%" on an annual basis. South Africa also became a republic and withdrew from the Commonwealth in 1961—a sign that despite the initial political and economic turmoil in the wake of Sharpeville, the country was now confidently striding forward on its own terms under the iron fisted leadership of its prime minister, Hendrik Verwoerd. The aforementioned economic growth during the 1960s is an important factor to foreground when considering the subsequent developments within motor racing during the same period.

South Africa Joins the World Championship Calendar

Having re-established the South African Grand Prix in East London in 1960, the local organisers set their sights on having the race formally included as part of the FIA's World Drivers' Championship series. For this purpose Cedric Vice travelled to Europe in 1961 where he attended the French Grand Prix at Rheims and consulted with the FIA on the process for applying for World Championship status. Upon his return to East London an application was formally lodged and this ultimately proved successful (Bishop, 1965, p. 58). As a result the ninth South African Grand Prix—staged on 29 December 1962—was the first one to be included on the World Championship calendar. It proved to be a championship decider in both the driver and constructor categories of the competition—the latter having been inaugurated during the 1958 season. Graham Hill claimed victory—and his first world title—in front of a record crowd of 90,000 (Loubser, 2011, p. 29), when Jim Clark was forced to retire from the race due to an oil leak while comfortably leading with 20 laps remaining. Hill's British Racing Motors (BRM) team also claimed its first and only constructor's title in the process (Bishop, 1965,

p. 64). South Africa had now established itself as an international racing destination of some repute as the sport continued to grow steadily domestically. From 1960 to 1975 the South African Drivers' Championship was even run under international FIA Formula One regulations, essentially meaning that it was hosting its own national Formula One championship—the only country with such a distinction during that time (Loubser, 2011, p. 28). The next two South African Grands Prix, held in December 1963 and January 1965, retained their World Championship status, but this was not the case for the final South African Grand Prix to be held in East London—the 12th instalment of the race held on New Year's Day in 1966. The FIA had removed the status on account of the introduction of a new three-litre formula that season, maintaining that South Africa would not be a good location to introduce this change on account of its geographical distance from Europe where development was taking place (Loubser, 2011, p. 30).

Another significant milestone during the 1960s was the opening of the Kyalami racing circuit north of Johannesburg in 1961. The Grand Central Circuit had started to age by the late 1950s and the resulting uncertainty surrounding its long-term prospects prompted the tenants, the Sports Car Club of South Africa, to consider an alternative venue (Loubser, 2011, p. 32). Eventually this led to the formation of the South African Motor Racing Club (SAMRAC) in January 1961 consisting of representatives from different Transvaal-based motoring clubs with the intent of financing and planning a new circuit. The group was also able to count on the support of Dave Marais, the mayor of Johannesburg at the time (Loubser, 2011, p. 32). Marais, incidentally, was also the chairman of the recently formed whites-only National Football League (NFL)—the first professional football league in South Africa (Venter, 2016, p. 261)—and was therefore a keen supporter of white sport in his capacity as mayor.

The two central influencers within SAMRAC were Johannesburg natives Francis Tucker—an attorney by trade and the club's chairman—and Alex Blignaut, a racer with some potential who functioned as the club's sporting secretary. Tucker was also a very accomplished rally driver himself, and both would go on to dominate South African motor racing administration in the coming years. In fact Blignaut would in later years be described as "South Africa's Mr Motor Racing" and "South Africa's Bernie Ecclestone" on account of his single-minded and somewhat dictatorial approach to getting things done (Mills, 2013, p. 119). After much consideration and deliberation a site was eventually found for the new circuit that was to become Kyalami—the name being an adaptation of a word from the Sesotho language meaning "my home" (Johannesburg Motor Racing, 1971, p. 23). The site was subsequently purchased from the owner, Mrs Violet Marie Elgey, for a sum of R80,000. Caltex obtained sole advertising rights as an oil company to the venue for three years and the civil engineer and car enthusiast, Basil Read, proceeded with the construction project. Other notable sponsors and advertisers during the early years were the United Tobacco Companies (a Southern African conglomerate formed in 1904), the Coca Cola Export Corporation, South African Breweries and Dunlop South Africa (Johannesburg Motor Racing, 1961, p. 32). The South African arms of the likes of Ford, British Petroleum and Shell also became involved from the mid-1960s onwards (Johannesburg Motor Racing, 1965, p. 25). Another revenue stream came from life membership subscriptions to the newly created Kyalami Grand Prix Club. The total cost of the initial construction of the circuit—including the land purchase—was estimated at R200,000. Kyalami was opened by Dave Marais on 4 November 1961 (Loubser, 2011, pp. 34–36).

The significance of the arrival of Kyalami was captured by the originator of the South African Grand Prix, Edward Bishop, when he wrote in 1965 (p. 59) that he had no doubt that "if the SA Motor Racing Club had not emerged on the Rand in 1961 later to build the Kyalami circuit and share in overseas drivers' starting prices, it would have been impossible for East London to carry on alone". He did also report, however, that according to Tucker SAMRAC had made a loss of about R10,000 on the first four Rand Grands Prix staged at the venue during the early years of the circuit's existence—another indication that generating profits from high-level motor racing was extremely difficult even during an economic upturn. A key factor here was the cost of attracting foreign drivers and teams to participate in these South African events. *The Rand Daily Mail* (1962b, p. 7) reported in 1962 that the British Racing Motors (BRM) team was paid R3600 in starting money to appear in that year's Rand

Grand Prix held at Kyalami on 15 December. Similarly the UDT-Laystall team was reportedly paid R1800 and one can reasonably assume that Jim Clark's Lotus team—the eventual race winners—would also have been well remunerated (no figure is provided in the report). So while the presence of these drivers certainly added to the spectacle of these events—the 1962 race was reported to have had a "big crowd" (Rand Daily Mail, 1962a, p. 6) in attendance—the reality was that attracting them came at a significant expense which made it difficult to generate profits from these races.

The escalating costs of hosting the South African Grand Prix—reported to be more than R70,000—eventually caught up with East London and in 1966 the organisers indicated that the city would no longer be able to host the event. Tucker and Blignaut stepped in on behalf of SAMRAC and offered to host the event at Kyalami (Loubser, 2011, p. 39). By this point the Automobile Association (AA) of South Africa had taken over control of motorsport in the country on 1 January 1966 after the previous controlling body, the Royal Automobile Club (RAC) was disbanded at the end of 1965. The AA therefore became South Africa's representative body on the FIA and subsequently requested that the South African Grand Prix regain its World Championship status (Loubser, 2011, p. 39). According to the South African motor racing enthusiast, Andre Loubser (2011, p. 323), Alex Blignaut went to great lengths to achieve this objective when he attended the 1966 British Grand Prix at Brands Hatch with the intent of stating Kyalami's case directly to prominent FIA officials in attendance. Apparently Blignaut went up to Swedish driver Joakim Bonnier—who was already strapped into a camera car at the back of the grid for the filming of John Frankenheimer's movie, *Grand Prix* (to be released later that year)—and demanded an introduction to the FIA officials. Bonnier replied that he was about to start a race, only for the remark to be ignored with Blignaut "virtually dragging Bonnier from the car's cockpit to effect the introductions". When the FIA met later that year to consider the application the decision was reportedly carried by one vote. Beginning in 1967 Kyalami would go on to host 19 consecutive South African Grands Prix—all but one of which carried World Championship status. The sole exception was the 1981 race which came during the middle of a power struggle between the Fédération Internationale du Sport

Automobile (FISA)—the governing body for Formula One at the time—and the Formula One Constructors' Association (FOCA). Having considered South Africa's post-World War II rise to international prominence within Formula One motor racing the analysis needs to turn to the political dimensions of this trajectory, particularly in contrast to developments within other major sport codes in the country during this period.

Political Forces Enter the Fray

Despite South Africa's surging economic growth during the 1960s the apartheid policy was beginning to prove problematic for sport as far as international relations were concerned. A significant development in this regard was South African football's suspension by the world governing body, FIFA, in 1961. In this regard there had been much effort from within the non-racial sports movement domestically to have the white controlling body expelled from the international football community (Bolsmann, 2010, pp. 37–39). The fundamental characteristic of non-racial sport organisations was that they rejected apartheid's racial classification system. As such they refused to comply with legislation which dictated that sport should be played separately among the different racial groups and instead chose to operate on an integrated basis without government permission. In practice the non-racial sports federations tended to be dominated by members from the coloured and Indian population groups, but they were open to anybody willing to directly challenge the political system of segregation. It also brought them into direct opposition with racially defined sports bodies which cooperated with the white controlling structures within the government system. This represented a significant fissure within black sport more broadly and also bred deep and long lasting resentment between players and officials from either side of this divide. Given this backdrop, political developments within football serve as a useful lens through which to consider South Africa's evolving relationship with international Formula One motor racing. A key consideration here was the existence of alternative controlling structures within South African football that were organised on a non-racial basis and functioned outside formal government-backed structures. This constituted a direct opponent to the white controlling body and it actively campaigned with FIFA to replace the white federation as South Africa's international affiliate. Such a direct opposing structure was absent within domestic motor racing, largely on account of the sport being one largely driven by private wealth and privilege. The absence of such a formal non-racial motor racing federation with its own circuits and events meant that—unlike a sport like football—there was no entity that could function as a domestic pressure point against South Africa's expanding international motor racing connections.

It is also worth reflecting on the activities of arguably the most important body that campaigned against apartheid sport internationally, namely the South African Non-Racial Olympic Committee (SANROC). This entity was originally formed in South Africa in 1962 but had to be reconstituted in exile in 1966. Bruce Murray (2001, p. 668) points out that SANROC's initial focus during the 1960s "was on the Olympic arena", and hence Formula One motor racing represented an activity not immediately within its crosshairs since there were bigger targets to aim for, such as South Africa's potential Olympic expulsion. Here SANROC's efforts proved successful as South Africa's exclusion from both the 1964 and 1968 Summer Olympic Games ultimately led to a full expulsion from the International Olympic Committee (IOC) in 1970. Other notable developments along the sport-political axis during this period included cricket's d'Oliveira affair that resulted in the 1968–69 England tour to South Africa being cancelled in the midst of controversy, thereby focusing the collective gaze of the international sporting community on the political and social situation in South Africa (Venter, 2019, p. 2). During this period the issue of South African representation on the FIA did come up for discussion as the newly formed AA's application for membership was put up for vote. The AA was ultimately admitted and this was a reflection of the FIA's desire to remain non-political in outlook—a common approach adopted by international sports bodies up this point (Naess, 2020, pp. 48–49).

Yet the pressure would continue to mount on South Africa elsewhere, as proposed cricket tours to England (1970) and Australia (1971) were cancelled, while rugby tours to Great Britain (1969–70) and Australia (1971) were accompanied by increasingly strident protests (Venter, 2019,

p. 2). This resulted in the South African government changing tactics and introducing its "multinational" sports policy in April 1971 as a means to deflect some of this international pressure. The policy contained limited reforms to apartheid sport whereby competition between South Africa's four different racial groups was now permitted within certain parameters. This had the bizarre result of allowing different racially defined teams to play against each other, but not allowing individual teams to be racially mixed. It served as an attempt to portray a limited form of racial integration on the sports field to the international community, while still shoehorning this policy into the overall apartheid doctrine of "separate development" for South Africa's different racial groups (Venter, 2019, pp. 2–3). Multinationalism was designed to retain (or regain) South Africa's international status within those codes that had come under pressure from the anti-apartheid movement, but was ultimately unsuccessful as a counterweight to broader political developments within the country. In this regard the Soweto uprising on 16 June 1976 represented a watershed moment for the country politically (Welsh, 2009, p. 101). The uprising saw mass protests by black school children against the imposition of Afrikaans as a language of instruction erupt in Soweto, south of Johannesburg. The protests spread to other areas around the country and elicited a violent response from police who fired on protesters, resulting in 176 official deaths. After this set of events no amount of racial mixing on the sports field would convince the international community to look favourably on the situation in South Africa. This had broad ramifications for sport as South Africa was finally expelled from FIFA at the latter's Montreal Congress that year (Bolsmann, 2010, p. 41), and any hopes of regaining international status in other codes via further reforms to multinationalism were extinguished. Yet Formula One motor racing continued to take place in South Africa annually during this period as Kyalami remained a fixture on the World Championship calendar. In order to understand the circumstances behind this South African sporting anomaly, the analysis needs to consider a number of aspects.

At a very basic level it should be noted that Kyalami was an extremely popular destination for the travelling circus that was the Formula One World Championship. Usually held in March towards the back end of the South African summer, it offered a pleasant contrast to the cold

European winter. A notable ingredient in this mix was the existence of the Kyalami Ranch Hotel in close proximity to the circuit complex. The hotel was founded in 1963 by a South African-born former KLM pilot, Bill Forssman, and his wife, Anneke, with the intent of creating an ideal stopover destination for air crews. The venue subsequently became a key component within the "Kyalami experience" as drivers, team members and the international media were provided with splendid hospitality in luxurious seclusion (Loubser, 2011, p. 292).

More importantly, there were key structural differences between the FIA and an organisation such as FIFA, for example, and it is argued here that this also contributed to South Africa's retention as an international racing destination. While FIFA was significantly impacted by the wave of decolonisation in Africa and Latin America from the 1950s onwards—the issue of South Africa's membership even had a significant impact on the outcome of the contest for 1974 FIFA presidency (Darby, 2008, pp. 259–272)—the same cannot be said for the FIA. An organisational snapshot from 1976 is instructive in this regard. The April issue of *Motor Sport* magazine that year summarises the various structural components within the FIA at that point with a focus on competitive racing. The body which oversaw this domain was the *Commission Sportive Internationale* (CSI)—a branch within the FIA which in turn had eight sub-committees that oversaw different aspects of racing. The most notable members of each committee were listed and the vast majority hailed from Great Britain, France, Italy, Germany, Belgium, Monaco, Switzerland, the Netherlands, Canada and the United States. South Africa's Alex Blignaut even served as a deputy organiser on the Formula One committee (Jenkinson, 1976, p. 368). So despite the fact that FIA membership was increasing and consisted of 81 affiliated countries for sporting purposes by this point, it is clear that decision-making power was mostly concentrated among a group of Western countries with long-standing participation in international motor racing. These countries were far more likely to accept South Africa's continued presence within the Formula One fraternity compared to an influential block of African or Caribbean countries, as was the case in FIFA, for example. It should also be noted that in 1970 the FIA amended its statutes by re-emphasising the fact that it was a motoring organisation and "not engaged in matters of race, politics or of religion" (Naess, 2020, p. 53). This would have provided further justification for ignoring the South African issue.

Finally, any analysis dealing with the institutional dynamics of Formula One from the 1970s onwards would need to consider the role of key individual beginning with the rise to prominence of Bernie Ecclestone. Erik Naess's recent work (2020, pp. 54–59) provides a detailed analysis of this chain of events. By the early 1970s Ecclestone had positioned himself as a power broker between the Formula One teams on the one hand, and race organisers on the other. Teams were happy for him to negotiate on their behalf and he was able to streamline elements of the World Championship by obtaining better terms from freight operators, governments and other stakeholders (Naess, 2020, p. 57). In order to placate the fears of race organisers—who were opposed to his rising influence—he was able to guarantee full starting grids by forcing teams to commit to full race participation as a group. This was a potentially attractive proposition for race organisers since teams were previously able to choose which races they would enter. On the other hand, he was also able to exert greater influence over the racing calendar by maintaining leverage over race organisers—if they were unwilling to accept his package deal offer comprising competition, logistics and hospitality components, he would always be able to turn to an alternative venue (Naess, 2020, pp. 57–58).

From a political perspective this meant that even if there were teams that had reservations about competing in South Africa—highly doubtful at this point—they would not have been in a position to refuse participation on account of the agreement they had in place with Ecclestone. In addition, racing organisers themselves had no incentive to boycott the World Championship on account of racing taking place in South Africa, since their primary concern would have been to generate revenue for their own facility by remaining on the international calendar. Unlike the Olympic Games, the FIA was not in charge of a single global event vulnerable to mass withdrawals such as the African boycott of the 1976 Montreal Olympics (again with South Africa as the central issue). Instead the Formula One World Championship consisted of a relatively small circle of participants, teams and venues that mostly functioned as private enterprises. In this context commercial factors—rather than political ones—were always likely to carry the day. This point was driven home in

1979 when Ecclestone himself purchased the highly indebted Kyalami circuit (and its liabilities) for one Rand from SAMRAC on the day of the South African Grand Prix (Loubser, 2011, p. 43).

Towards the End of the Road

Loubser (2011, p. 42) has highlighted the challenges associated with escalating event hosting costs during the 1970s and that SAMRAC was essentially operating within the volatile entertainment industry which carried a number of risks. The 1973 oil crisis, for example, was an unforeseen international event that had a significant impact on racing in South Africa given the resulting fuel shortage that followed. The precarious financial situation which enveloped SAMRAC during this period can also be gleaned from a cabinet memorandum compiled by Piet Koornhof, the Minister of Sport and Recreation at the time, at some point after the 1975 South African Grand Prix. SAMRAC had made an appeal to Koornhof for financial support, and the memorandum requested the cabinet's approval for an additional R100,000 to be added to the Department of Sport and Recreation's budget for the purposes of hosting the 1976 South African Grand Prix the following year (Koornhof, 1975, p. 3).

According to the memorandum SAMRAC experienced no financial difficulties during their first hosting of the 1967 event, but their financial position had gradually deteriorated beginning in 1968 already, leaving them at a crossroads where they could no longer fulfil the financial obligations required for hosting the 1976 South African Grand Prix. The cost of hosting the 1974 event was listed as R300,000, increasing to R340,000 in 1975, and projected to be R380,000 in1976. This excluded additional administration costs which were R81,854 in 1974 and R114 886 in 1975, leaving SAMRAC with a balance sheet deficit of R70,000 in 1974 and R150,000 in 1975 (Koornhof, 1975, pp. 1–2). It is also revealing that by this point SAMRAC's largest annual administrative expense was listed as interest on existing loans, which was R41,928 for the 1974/75 year—a clear indication of the difficult situation it found itself in.

The reason provided for this state of affairs was the costs associated with ensuring that Kyalami kept up with international standards in order to retain its place on the calendar. This included increased safety measures to prevent deaths, improved media and radio facilities as well as improved facilities for spectators. Up until 1973 Kyalami had been voted as one of the top five racing destinations by the Grand Prix Drivers' Association—a title that it won in 1969. But in 1974 it fell to 12th on the list on account of its media and radio facilities lacking behind (Koornhof, 1975, p. 2). As justification for further financial support Koornhof argued that the South African Grand Prix was by this time the country's only annual world championship event in any major sport, and that it had brought significant media coverage and prestige to the country. Australia and Japan had already tried to usurp its place on the 15-race championship calendar—something that would almost certainly occur in future without additional support (Koornhof, 1975, p. 2).

Koornhof's cabinet request of R100,000 was in fact a watered-down version of SAMRAC's original request of an annual administrative contribution of R125,000 from the department. They also indicated that an alternative option was for the state to purchase Kyalami for R1.3 million with SAMRAC then entering into a long-term lease agreement. Koornhof indicated that his department's budget was itself under pressure and could not make provision for either of these requests as part of normal expenditure. He did, however, make reference to possible use of a general funding scheme comprising financial assistance to "special projects that included projects of national and international scope such as world championship events" (Koornhof, 1975, p. 3).

While it is not exactly clear what the outcome of this specific funding request was, it should be noted that the strategic projects and events later associated with the so-called Information Scandal which erupted in 1978 were unfolding in the background during this period. The crux of the scandal related to a secret slush fund operated by South Africa's Department of Information and deployed across a myriad of strategic projects designed to improve South Africa's image both at home and abroad. One such venture was the establishment of *The Citizen* newspaper in 1976 as an English language counterweight to the existing English media outlets that were often critical of the government and apartheid

(Jones, 1998, pp. 328–329). In order to conceal the government's involvement in the newspaper, the Afrikaner entrepreneur, Louis Luyt, was recruited as a front man. In his autobiography, Luyt (2003, p. 102) states that the government sponsored the South African Grand Prix through *The Citizen*, a fact also confirmed by the Secretary of Information at the time, Eschel Rhoodie, in his own account of the scandal (Rhoodie, 1983, pp. 774–775).

Of note is the fact that in 1976—the very same year for which SAMRAC requested government support for the race from Koornhof—*The Citizen* suddenly arrived as the event's title sponsor. The official race programme contained a note on the sponsorship which was reported to be for an amount of R220,000 "provided by Louis Luyt through his newspaper, *The Citizen*" (Johannesburg Motor Racing, 1976, p. 5). Luyt was being cast as a generous businessman setting an example for others to follow by supporting sport financially. The reality was that the government was channelling the support funding through Luyt with the newspaper as the front mechanism. It was also somewhat unusual that this was being done six months prior to the first copy of *The Citizen* actually seeing the light of day! The race took place on 6 March, while the first edition of *The Citizen* only appeared on 7 September later that year. It is therefore strange that the title sponsor of such a high profile event was a product that consumers could not yet access—although Rhoodie (1983, p. 774) claims that the sponsorship was indeed intended to "generate publicity for *The Citizen*". Ultimately this was probably the confluence of two factors, namely Koornhof's desire to support one of the few high profile international sport events that remained on the South African calendar, coupled with the Department of Information's intention to establish *The Citizen* as a powerful mouthpiece to counteract local and international criticism of apartheid. The sponsorship was continued for two more years in 1977 and 1978, with the reported total spending across the three races totalling more than R700,000. In the 1978 race booklet it was announced that the sponsorship was ending that year (Johannesburg Motor Racing, 1978, p. 5).

In the context of these events and the Information Scandal subsequently becoming public at the end of 1978, it is not surprising that Kyalami was sold to Ecclestone in 1979 given that SAMRAC's financial life support had basically been severed. According to Loubser (2011, p. 43) Ecclestone took on existing liabilities of R460,000 as well as the commitment of carrying the R600,000 cost for hosting the 1979 race—hence a total commitment of more than R1 million. However, a year later in 1980 the circuit was put up for auction—apparently due to accusations of a conflict of interest since Ecclestone was at the time a shareholder in the Brabham Formula One team, the head of FOCA and at the centre of Formula One's commercial rights dealings (Naess, 2017, p. 539). The circuit was purchased for R1.4 million by local developer Bobby Hartslief who formed an events company named Kyalami Entertainment Enterprises (KEE) as a means to generate a return on the investment. According to Loubser (2011, p. 43), Hartslief was supported by an anonymous backer. In later years investigative journalists alleged that Ecclestone might have been this backer and managed to retain his interest in Kyalami by providing guarantees to Hartslief's lender, Rand Merchant Bank, for the same amount (Collins, 1997).

Despite the financial challenges of hosting the South African Grand Prix at Kyalami the event continued uninterrupted until what proved to be the final edition under apartheid in 1985. Some financial relief was obtained through sponsorship legislation that was in place up to 1984, whereby companies sponsoring major events with international profiles qualified for a double deduction of the sponsored amount from their taxable income. This was in line with the government's desire to promote exports, but was ended once entities began to abuse the mechanism (Finansies en Tegniek, 1986). On the political front, Naess (2017, 540) indicates that Ecclestone, along with his close associate Max Mosley, did begin to reconsider South Africa as a venue by 1982. They even engaged in discussions with multiple Zimbabwean ministers over the possibility of moving the Southern African race across the border to the newly independent country, but nothing ultimately came from this.

It was not until the 1985 race that the political question once again took centre stage as the French teams Renault and Ligier were instructed by the French government to withdraw their participation (Naess, 2017, 540). The Australian driver of the Lola-Hart team, Alan Jones, also failed to show up to the circuit on the morning of the race—apparently feeling unwell. However, years later in his autobiography he claimed that this was done after Ecclestone offered him first place prize money to secretly withdraw in order to avoid a backlash against team sponsor, Beatrice Foods Company, in the United States (Jones, 2017). During the build-up to the race the FIA came out strongly by issuing a statement that none of the 64 member nations of FISA (formerly known as the CSI)—including a number of African countries—had raised an objection against the South African Grand Prix during the Plenary Conference held in Paris ten days before the race (Collantine, 2008a, as cited by Naess, 2017, p. 540). Consequently the race did go ahead with Britain's Nigel Mansell taking the victory, but when the provisional calendar for the 1986 season was released a few months later South Africa was demoted to reserve status (Autosport, 1986, p. 4). What was not known at the time was that Kyalami would not return as a Grand Prix venue until 1992.

Sources provide conflicting accounts over the exact reasoning behind Kyalami's eventual disappearance from the Formula One calendar after 1985. According to one of Ecclestone's biographers, Terry Lovell, the announcement by certain television networks that they would no longer broadcast the South African Grand Prix was the final turning point which led to Ecclestone finally scrapping the race (Collantine, 2008b). Journalist Nigel Roebuck, reflecting on the events in 2011, states that once the 1986 motorcycle Grand Prix at Kyalami was officially cancelled "it became clear that neither would F1 be going back to South Africa any time soon"—thereby intimating that political motivations ultimately carried the day. When considering media sources from the time it becomes clear that the door remained open for Kyalami to host a race in 1986. According to local press reports in December 1985 it was in fact South African race organisers themselves who withdrew their application to open the 1986 season on 9 March, citing the weak Rand as the decisive factor (Simpson, 1985, p. 1). Given that the organisers' contract with FOCA was in US Dollars, this created a significant problem once the Rand suddenly nosedived in August 1985 in the wake of President P.W. Botha's infamous Rubicon speech. The historian David Welsh (2009, p. 231) describes it as "an epoch-making speech whose catastrophic impact probably hastened the end of apartheid, as well as provoking more opposition to Botha inside his party". By 28 August 1985 the Rand was trading at 34 US cents—an all-time low (Welsh, 2009,

p. 232). This represented a drastic escalation in costs for hosting the South African Grand Prix, and consequently it was placed on the reserve list in the hope that the situation would improve. Southern Sun Hotels, the main sponsors of the 1985 race, had also indicated that they should not be considered for a race in March the following year given the "current economic climate in South Africa" (The Cape Times, 1985, p. 1). It was reported that the 1985 Grand Prix cost the sponsors 1.7 million US Dollars (Simpson, 1985, p. 1).

In November 1986, Kyalami Entertainment Enterprises (KEE) announced a new development plan for the circuit at a press conference which essentially entailed selling off the top half of the complex to a property developer and remodelling the circuit layout. At that same press conference Laurie Mackintosh, financial director of KEE, blamed the South African government for the loss of the South African Grand Prix by not providing sufficient financial support to the event. He claimed that KEE still had two years remaining on their contract with FOCA and that a Grand Prix could still have taken place if funding could have been sourced. He stated that placing the blame on the political situation was a "convenience" (The Star, 1986, p. 13). In a symbolic end to this historical era even the famous Kyalami Ranch was sold in 1987 due to an extended labour dispute with the Hotel and Restaurant Workers' Union (HARWU) (The Citizen, 1987, p. 11).

Formula One's Return in 1992–93

The abolition of apartheid legislation in 1990, coupled with the freeing of Nelson Mandela, paved the way for South Africa's reintegration into the international community. While the actual political transition was uncertain leading up to the 1994 elections, the sporting transition was much smoother as international federations welcomed South Africa back with open arms. It was in this context that Grand Prix racing was able to return to the remodelled Kyalami in 1992. Motor Racing Enterprises (MRE)—the promoters that owned the operating rights to the circuit at the time—were able to secure a five-year Formula One contract ahead of five other countries, and the event was positioned as a means to showcase the potential of post-apartheid South Africa (Aupiais, 1992, p. 37). *Finance Week* described the race as "the beginning of a mammoth public relations exercise which will turbocharge foreign tourism" to South Africa (Aupiais, 1992, p. 37).

Despite the successful hosting of the race as the 1992 season opener in front of an estimated 100,000 spectators, questions soon emerged regarding the long-term feasibility of the venture. Hosting Formula One races were certainly not getting cheaper, and the South African government began rolling back certain concessions to sponsors of sport events (Coetzee, 1992, p. 11). The exchange rate also continued to hover near three Rands to the Dollar, and consequently many of the historical financial forces were still in play. The situation worsened towards the end of 1992, when it emerged that the holding company that owned the circuit was put into provisional liquidation by a major South African bank. This was part of a rapidly unravelling scandal around a much larger holding company, Tollgate Holdings Group, of which the racing components—including MRE—formed subsidiaries (The Citizen, 1992, p. 1). The 1993 South African Grand Prix went ahead at Kyalami, but on the day after the race the chairman of MRE, Mervyn Key, was arrested on fraud charge ranging between R40 million and R60 million connected to the collapse of Tollgate Holdings (The Star, 1993, p. 1). He was ultimately acquitted, but in the short term this chain of events threw South Africa's Formula One ambitions into turmoil, prompting rumours of an impending sale of Kyalami.

It was also reported that attendance figures for the 1993 South African Grand Prix "were somewhat down" from those of the 1992 race, and that spectators were staying away from other local race meetings at the circuit on account of "the cold, clinical approach of the promotors at Kyalami" which had been widely condemned (Chequered Flag, 1993a, p. 5). Dave McGregor, MRE's other shareholder (along with Key), stated that the 1993 Grand Prix incurred a loss of about R1 million—this despite reported financial support totalling more than R17 million from the government and title sponsor Panasonic (Haler, 1993, p. 14). *Chequered Flag Magazine's* reporting of these events paints a picture of a desperate situation, including a public spat between McGregor and AA Motorsport, a subsidiary of the Automobile Association of South Africa, over unpaid fees by MRE for services provided by AA Motorsport during the 1992 and 1993 South African Grands Prix. AA Motorsport claimed that an amount of R732,000 was still owed by MRE for the 1993 race alone—a figure which McGregor disputed. Subsequent to Key's arrest McGregor was also removed from various AA Motorsport Committees, and he also claimed that his home phone had been bugged during this period (Haler, 1993, p. 14).

Negotiations over the potential purchase of Kyalami by the AA from the circuit's holding company, Kyalami International Circuit, continued into May 1993. Of note were attempts by MRE to attract spectators back to local races by slashing ticket prices for a race meeting held on 1 May and improving the fan experience with measures such as providing public access to the pits. According to McGregor a total of 27,000 spectators attended the event which resulted in the organisers running out of tickets and programmes. He also claimed that he had lined up a consortium of funders to rival the AA's bid for Kyalami, and that they were so confident of acquiring the circuit that they "were already planning their turn of the century party at Kyalami" (Chequered Flag, 1993b, 3). Indeed, a month later it was reported that McGregor's consortium, Catterick Investment Holdings, had been successful in outbidding the AA with a total committed sum of R40 million (Chequered Flag, 1993c, p. 3). However, despite claiming that it had the backing of unnamed Italian property developers, Catterick's funding failed to materialise when it came to concluding the transaction, thereby plunging the future of Kyalami into uncertainty again (Chequered Flag, 1993d, p. 11). To make matters worse, MRE itself was placed into liquidation for failing to come up with R500,000 it still owed to AA Motorsport, resulting in the cancellation of a Kyalami race meeting scheduled for 10 July. MRE was reported to be R17 million in debt at the time of this unravelling (The Citizen, 1993, p. 10).

The saga concluded within a month as the AA finally took ownership of the circuit for a reported purchasing price of R31.2 million. This led to a number of structural changes, including the formation of a new company, AA Racing, with the mandate to run the track and its facilities. However, at the time of this reshuffle the AA was quick to indicate that high profile international events such as the South African Grand Prix would only go ahead if they were going to be financially sustainable

(Chequered Flag, 1993e, p. 2). By August of 1993 the Grand Prix was still provisionally scheduled as the opening round of the 1994 Formula One World Championship, but this was going to require a great deal of external financial backing in order to become a reality. Of particular significance was the political juncture at which South Africa found itself during late 1993. The country's first ever democratic elections were approaching in 1994 and the National Party, having ruled uninterrupted since 1948, was losing its grip on power amidst an atmosphere of instability and uncertainty as the transition to black majority rule approached. In the context of these developments the prospect of securing government backing for the 1994 South African Grand Prix was highly unlikely. In October the FIA issued a calendar for the 1994 Formula One season with South Africa's absence confirmed (Motor Sport, 1993, p. 4). Bernie Ecclestone also indicated earlier that South Africa's challenges with regard to hosting the Grand Prix were down to finances, and that a return to the calendar was going to prove difficult once the race fell away (Chequered Flag, 1993f, 3). That assessment proved to be prophetic as South Africa is yet to host another Formula One race after the 1993 event.

This might seem somewhat incongruous with the country's regular hosting of sport mega-events during the post-apartheid period, including the rugby (1995), cricket (2003) and football (2010) World Cups. Formula One racing lacks some of the crucial aspects present in the other codes, however, most notably South African competitors at the highest level. The sport has also been somewhat detached from the government's unification efforts predicated on sporting prestige and success in the international arena. This is largely a structural issue since racing is a private endeavour which sits outside the purview of the Department of Sport and Recreation. As such racing organisers cannot rely on the same sort of high level government investment available for an event such as the FIFA World Cup, for example. Racing also lacks the widespread appeal of the large team sports since it is a lot less accessible to the poorest members of society. Compare this, for example, to the story of South Africa's 2019 Rugby World Cup-winning captain, Siya Kolisi, who rose from poverty to the pinnacle of his chosen sport.

There are, however, renewed murmurings regarding a possible Formula One return to Kyalami in the future. A bidding group is presently headed up by Warren Scheckter, the nephew of South Africa's 1979 Formula One world champion, Jody, with the intent of getting South Africa back onto the international calendar. Over the years there have been a number of similar attempts without any success, although Formula One did conduct some pre-season testing in South Africa during the early 2000s (Lupini, 2021). It remains to be seen whether this bid will prove to be successful. Naturally an important emotive component to such an attempt is the fact that the Formula One world championship does not contain any races in Africa. Formula One CEO, Stefano Domenicali, and seven-time world champion, Lewis Hamilton, have both expressed a desire to change this state of affairs. However, throughout the history of Formula One commercial considerations have invariably trumped sentiment, and this remains the most significant challenge to a potential South African return.

Conclusion

When considering the historical arc of Formula One motor racing in South Africa a contrasting picture emerges. On the one hand the sport represented a close reflection of the economic development of the country more broadly, particularly in the post-World War II growth period. On the other hand it constituted an outlier as far as its relationship to the political realm was concerned. In this regard it experienced very little disruption from the anti-apartheid movement, and was able to continue uninterrupted throughout the sports boycott until economic forces eventually caught up to organisers in the mid-1980s. The sport's political insulation was partly due to its structure domestically—being a largely white preserve and lacking direct organisational opponents within the non-racial movement. In addition the organisational contours of the world governing body, the FIA, and the role of key individuals such as Bernie Ecclestone, ensured that South Africa faced far less pressure from the international community than was the case with other high-profile sport codes such as rugby, cricket or football. As such the hosting of Grands Prix proved far less precarious from a political perspective, but the situation was significantly different when it came to economics. In this regard Formula One ventures had proven to be a costly exercise from the very beginning, and government support was of critical importance particularly during the rapid commercialisation of the sport during the 1970s. Ironically it was a political event—namely P.W. Botha's Rubicon speech in August 1985—that served as a catalyst for the final economic collapse of the South African Grand Prix under apartheid. Formula One racing made what proved to be a brief two-year return during the post-apartheid period but was ultimately subjected to many of the same challenges faced during the 1980s and was unable to regain a sustainable foothold in the country. The sport's historical relationship with South Africa from 1934 to 1993 does, however, offer a useful vantage point from which to study the country's broader historical, political and economic forces, particularly given its unique trajectory compared to those of other sport codes.

References

Alegi, P. (2004). *Laduma! Soccer, Politics and Society in South Africa*. University of KwaZulu-Natal Press.

Archer, R., & Bouillon, A. (1982). *The South African Game: Sport and Racism*. Zed Press.

Aupiais, L. (1992). Starter's Orders. *Finance Week*, February 12, p. 37.

Autosport. (1986). F1 Calendar Confirmed. *Autosport*, January 9, p. 4.

Bishop, E. (1965). *South African Grand Prix*. Blue Crane Books.

Bolsmann, C. (2010). White Football in South Africa: Empire, Apartheid and Change, 1892–1977. *Soccer & Society, 11*(1–2), 29–45.

Cape Times, The. (1985). SA Withdraws GP Application. *The Cape Times*, December 18, p. 1.

Chequered Flag. (1993a). Kyalami: A Buyer Sought. *Chequered Flag*, March 5–19, p. 5.

Chequered Flag. (1993b). Kyalami Attracts Big Crowd on May 1. *Chequered Flag*, May 1–15, p. 3.

Chequered Flag. (1993c). Kyalami Sale Confirmed. *Chequered Flag*, June 1–15, p. 3.

Chequered Flag. (1993d). Kyalami to the AA? *Chequered Flag*, July 3–19, p. 11.

Chequered Flag. (1993e). AA Confirms Kyalami Purchase. *Chequered Flag*, August 1–15, p. 2.

Chequered Flag. (1993f). No SA GP for 94. *Chequered Flag*, September 16–30, p. 3.

Citizen, The. (1987). Kyalami Ranch Shuts After Staff-Management Rift. *The Citizen*, September 2, p. 11.

Citizen, The. (1992). Kyalami Circuit Goes Bust: GP Goes On. *The Citizen*, December 15, p. 1.

Coetzee, J. (1992). Kyalami stel visier hoër na sukses. *Finansies & Tegniek*, March 6, p. 11.

Collantine, K. (2008a). Mansell Takes Second Win Amid Apartheid Controversy. [Online]. Retrieved March 7, 2021, from https://www.racefans.net/2008/02/05/f1-and-racism-the-1985-south-african-grand-prix/

Collantine, K. (2008b). Did Bernie Ecclestone Really Scrap the South African Grand Prix Over Apartheid? [Online]. Retrieved March 7, 2021, from https://www.racefans.net/2008/11/07/did-bernie-ecclestone-really-pull-the-south-african-grand-prix-over-apartheid/

Collins, G. (1997). Motor Racing's False Start…and a Tollgate titbit. *Noseweek*, September 1997.

Darby, P. (2008). Stanley Rous's 'own goal': Football Politics, South Africa and the Contest for the FIFA Presidency in 1974. *Soccer & Society, 9*(2), 259–272.

Finansies en Tegniek. (1986). Borgskap gunstig vir belasting? *Finansies en Tegniek*, January 24.

Fourie, L. (2017). Made in the RSA. *CAR*, February 1, pp. 60–64.

Grundlingh, A. (2008). "Are We Afrikaners Getting Too Rich?" Cornucopia and Change in Afrikanerdom in the 1960s. *Journal of Historical Sociology, 21*(2–3), 143–165.

Grundlingh, A., Odendaal, A., & Spies, B. (1995). *Beyond the Tryline: Rugby and South African Society*. Ravan Press.

Haler, J. (1993). The Kyalami Saga. *Chequered Flag*, March 25–April 14, p. 14.

Jenkinson, D. (1976). Federation Internationale de l'Automobile (FIA). *Motor Sport*, April, p. 368.

Johannesburg Motor Racing. (1961). IV Rand Grand Prix. [Race programme] Available from: Box 16/1/276 in Library of Franschhoek Motor Museum, Franschhoek, South Africa.

Johannesburg Motor Racing. (1965). Eighth Rand Grand Prix. [Race programme] Available from: Box 16/1/276 in Library of Franschhoek Motor Museum, Franschhoek, South Africa.

Johannesburg Motor Racing. (1971). Fourth Grand Prix of South Africa. [Race Programme] Available from: Box 16/1/276 in Library of Franschhoek Motor Museum, Franschhoek, South Africa.

Johannesburg Motor Racing. (1976). The Citizen Grand Prix of South Africa. [Race Programme] Available from: Box 16/1/278 in Library of Franschhoek Motor Museum, Franschhoek, South Africa.

Johannesburg Motor Racing. (1978). The Citizen and ASSENG Grand Prix of South Africa. [Race Programme] Available from: Box 16/1/278 in Library of Franschhoek Motor Museum, Franschhoek, South Africa.

Jones, A. (1998). From Rightist to "Brightist"? The Strange Tale of South Africa's Citizen. *Journal of Southern African Studies, 24*(2), 325–345.

Jones, A. (2017). *Australian F1 Legend Alan Jones Reveals Untold Story About His Unusual Absence from a Grand Prix*. [Online]. Retrieved March 3, 2021, from https://www.news.com.au/sport/motorsport/formula-one/australian-f1-legend-alan-jones-reveals-untold-story-about-his-unusual-absence-from-a-grand-prix/news-story/8c073066d28aee58b08a27fe394d54d0

Koornhof, P. (1975). Finansiële steun aan die Suid-Afrikaanse Motorwedrenklub vir die aanbieding van die Suid-Afrikaanse Grand Prix. [Memorandum to Cabinet] Available from: File PV 476 1/34/16/1 in Piet Koornhof Private Documents Collection, Archive for Contemporary Affairs, University of the Free State, South Africa.

Lapchick, R. (1975). *The Politics of Race and International Sport: The Case of South Africa*. Greenwood Press.

Loubser, A. (2011). *Kyalami: A Reflection on the History of the Original Circuit, 1961–1987*. Aquarius Publishing CC.

Loubser, A. (2013). *South African Motor Racing: The Early Years*. Kingdomtech.co.za.

Lupini, M. (2020a). *The Beginning*. [Online]. Retrieved November 19, 2020, from https://www.motorsportmedia.co.za/THE_BEGINNING.art14216#:~:text=South%20African%20motor%20racing%20developed,Hoek%20Reliability%20trial%20shortly%20after

Lupini, M. (2020b). *Special Times*. [Online]. Retrieved November 25, 2020, from https://www.motorsportmedia.co.za/article.asp?conID=14218

Lupini, M. (2020c). *The End of the Beginning*. [Online]. Retrieved November 25, 2020, from https://www.motorsportmedia.co.za/THE_END_OF_THE_BEGINNING.art14220

Lupini, M. (2021). *Analysis: The Prospect of a South African Grand Prix Return*. [Online]. Retrieved April 30, 2021, from https://www.grandprix247.com/2021/02/06/analysis-the-prospect-of-a-south-african-grand-prix-return/

Luyt, L. (2003). *Walking Proud: The Louis Luyt Autobiography*. Cape Town.

Mills, G. (2013). *Agriculture, Furniture and Marmalade: Southern African Motorsport Heroes*. Johannesburg.

Motor Sport. (1993). This Month in Motor Sport. *Motor Sport*, December, p. 4.

Murray, B. (2001). Politics and Cricket: The D'Oliveira Affair of 1968. *Journal of Southern African Studies, 27*(4), 667–684.

Murray, B., & Merrett, C. (2004). *Caught Behind: Race and Politics in Springbok Cricket*. Wits University Press and Scottsville, University of KwaZulu-Natal Press.

Naess, H. E. (2017). Sandwiched Between Sport and Politics: Fédération Internationale de l'Automobile, Formula 1, and Non-Democratic Regimes. *The International Journal of the History of Sport, 34*(7–8), 535–553.

Naess, H. E. (2020). *A History of Organizational Change: The Fédération Internationale de l'Automobile (FIA), 1946–2020*. Palgrave Macmillan.

Rand Daily Mail, The. (1962a). Grand Prix. *The Rand Daily Mail*, December 17, p. 6.

Rand Daily Mail, The. (1962b). Grand Prix Visiting Cars Disappoint. *The Rand Daily Mail*, December 17, p. 7.

Rhoodie, E. (1983). *The Real Information Scandal*. Orbis SA Pty (Ltd).

Simpson, H. (1985). No Firm Date for Grand Prix Over Weakness of Rand. *The Citizen*, December 18, p. 1.

Star, The. (1986). Govt Blamed for Grand Prix loss. *The Star*, November 14, p. 13.

Star, The. (1993). Grand Prix Organiser Arrested Over Fraud. *The Star*, March 17, p. 1.

Venter, G. (2016). *Gone and Almost Forgotten? The Dynamics of Professional White Football in South Africa: 1959–1990*. PhD thesis. Stellenbosch University.

Venter, G. (2019). Experimental Tactics on an Uneven Playing Field: Multinational Football and the Apartheid Project during the 1970s. *The International Journal of the History of Sport, 36*(1), 83–103.

Welsh, D. (2009). *The Rise and Fall of Apartheid*. Jonathan Ball Publishers.

Wheels24. (2016). *First Car in SA: Happy 120th Anniversary to the Horseless Carriage!* [Online]. Retrieved November 19, 2020, from https://www.news24.com/wheels/News/Classic_cars/first-car-in-sa-happy-120th-anniversary-to-the-horseless-carriage-20160711

On Recovering the Black Geographies of Motorsports: The Counter-mobility Work of NASCAR's Wendell Scott

Derek H. Alderman and Joshua Inwood

A Reckoning in NASCAR

The summer of 2020 proved to be a consequential moment in confronting the role of racism in American motorsports and specifically NASCAR (National Association for Stock Car Auto Racing). Unlike other major US professional sports, major league stock car racing has remained almost all White. The NASCAR racetrack has a strong tradition of spectators waving Confederate battle flags and other performances of Whiteness, creating for many drivers and fans of colour an unwelcoming place more reminiscent of early- or mid-twentieth-century America than the early

D. H. Alderman (✉)
Department of Geography & Sustainability, University of Tennessee, Knoxville, TN, USA
e-mail: dalderma@utk.edu

J. Inwood
Department of Geography & Rock Ethics Institute, Pennsylvania State University, State College, PA, USA
e-mail: jfi6@psu.edu

D. Sturm et al. (eds.), *The History and Politics of Motor Racing*, Global Culture and Sport Series, https://doi.org/10.1007/978-3-031-22825-4_14

twenty-first century. Yet, in the wake of the murder of George Floyd by Minneapolis police in late May 2020 and Black Lives Matter protests across many American cities, NASCAR decided to prohibit the flying of the Confederate flag at its races and properties. This gesture seemingly signalled an important turn in the sport's recognition of its role in perpetuating racist symbols and thereby racist values. At the very least, NASCAR realized it could not afford to be seen as ignoring the widespread social outcry over the killing of Floyd (Romo, 2020).

As a conservative and entrenched cultural institution, NASCAR was predictably slow in rebuking a racist symbol, even after engaging in significant pro-diversity programming over the past several years. In 2015, rather than issuing an outright ban, racing officials had asked fans to refrain from displaying the Confederate flag at races. While some complied, others were defiant, and waved and defended the flag (Bernstein, 2015; *The Guardian*, 2015). Motivated as much by commercial sponsorship and media market forces as moral responsibility, NASCAR occupied an uneasy relationship with the history and symbols of White Supremacy. NASCAR increasingly recognized the flag was a public relations barrier to the goal of expanding audiences and corporate sponsors, but it also did not wish to alienate or anger its traditional White southern fan base.

Helping to push this long overdue prohibition of the Confederate flag was the demands of Darrell "Bubba" Wallace Jr., the only African American driver currently in NASCAR's top competitive series (Griffith, 2020). Wallace had gone much of his still young career experiencing racism in motorsports, but he had not previously pursued activism. Wallace stated that he was highly affected by the killings of George Floyd, Ahmed Arbery, Breona Taylor, and other African Americans as well as the public protests against these senseless deaths (Cwik, 2020; Macur, 2020b). As a statement of solidarity with these protests for racial equality and calls for unity, Wallace's car for the June 2020 Martinsville, Virginia, race prominently displayed #BlackLivesMatter along with the words "Compassion, Love and Understanding" and the image of interlocking hands—one Black and one White—painted on the front of his car (McCarriston, 2020).

Reaction to Wallace's stand against the Confederate flag and NASCAR's support of him exposed racial fracture lines in the sport, and in America more generally. On the one hand, a large number of drivers, pit crew members, and others stood in support of Wallace, whose activism was also praised by fellow Black athletes in other sports (Long, 2020). One important supporter has been NBA legend and Black entrepreneur Michael Jordan, who in the months after the Confederate flag ban joined forces with champion driver Denny Hamlin to start a new NASCAR racing team that debuted in 2021 with Wallace as the lead team driver. The new team originated partly out of social activism, a desire on the part of Jordan to address systemic racism and increase Black participation in a sport he follows, an interesting shift given Jordan's purported reluctance to speak out against racism in the early phases of his career (McRae, 2017). The involvement of Jordan likely also resulted from his realization of the lucrative brand and sponsorship rewards that await the remaking of NASCAR's racial image (Abrams, 2020).

At the same time, Wallace's denouncement of the Confederate flag also drew sharp criticism (Macur, 2020a; Spear, 2020). Some fans and members of the wider public—including then US President Donald Trump—castigated the Black driver and NASCAR for yielding to what they considered pressure from the left (Quinn, 2020). Around the time of Wallace's opposition to displaying the Confederate flag, his racing team would find a noose hanging in their assigned garage at the Talladega Speedway in Alabama. Although the FBI concluded that the noose had hung in the garage for some time and was not directed at Bubba Wallace specifically, the investigation did nothing to answer the question of how such an insensitive symbol of racialized lynching would ever be found in a NASCAR racing facility to begin with (Martinelli, 2020).

Bubba Wallace's antiracist protests and the still unreconciled place of race within NASCAR culture prompt us to consider the larger history of racism within auto racing. Although receiving limited attention from scholars, motorsports are deeply involved in reinforcing racial inequality while also being a site for resisting that inequality. Racing historian Daniel Pierce (2004) noted some time ago the need to examine the important history of African Americans in auto racing, which he described as largely "hidden" and "untold." As we argue in this chapter, understanding and addressing the racialized aspects of NASCAR requires recovering its "Black geographies" (Bledsoe et al., 2017; Hawthorne, 2019). Black geographies clearly see that racism underpins the organization of motorsports spaces and movements, but it simultaneously recognizes that people of colour have resisted their exclusion from the racing industry by developing antiracist places, practices, and knowledge systems.

In the over 15 years since Pierce's (2004) call, scholarly examinations of African American racers remain limited in number and under-theorized (Poehler, 2020). Racing literature lacks a framework that adequately situates the motorsports experience *as part of* rather than *apart from* the broader operation of White supremacy and attendant Black geographies of resistance. Our chapter offers such a needed historical and theoretical treatment and explores, for illustrative purposes, an African American figure noted for challenging the colour line in NASCAR—Wendell Scott (1921–1990). In 1963, well over 50 years before the rise of Bubba Wallace, Scott became the first of only two Black drivers to win a race in NASCAR's highest competitive division (Wallace would be the second to win at the elite level, in October 2021). In his 13-year NASCAR career Scott had 147 top ten finishes (with one victory) in 495 tries in the Grand National Series (equivalent today to the top NASCAR Cup series). More impressive he competed throughout the segregated South and raced during the tense days of the Civil Rights Movement. He faced discrimination, humiliation, and even violence on and off the track from NASCAR officials, tracks owners, fellow drivers, sponsors, and spectators. Scott did have some assistance from sympathetic Whites, but that help was never a given, and many allies helped quietly or even anonymously without publicly challenging the racism in the industry. Wendell Scott's story reminds us that racism in NASCAR could not be reduced to the stubborn presence of insensitive Confederate symbols, but it also involved a set of wider practices of oppression with major consequences on the self-determination, livelihood, and wellbeing of African Americans within the NASCAR universe. "For Wendell Scott, every race was a struggle and every struggle was about race" (Karpf, 2008, np), and these struggles took major tolls on his health and finances.

Compared to other historic African American racers, Wendell Scott's story is well known. Multiple halls of fame have inducted him to their ranks, including the NASCAR Hall of Fame in 2015. Hollywood loosely based a 1977 feature film (*Greased Lightning*) on Scott's life. Later, documentarians (Holley & Karpf, 2011) and biographers (Donovan, 2008) would treat him and his struggles more deeply. In this same vein, we offer a fresh re-reading of Wendell Scott's career. We situate Scott within a wider understanding of African American antiracist responses to the racialization of motorsports and focus on the Black geographies of mobility he created in stock car racing. Through the course of his career, he actively redefined the conditions under which he and his cars could move freely and competitively within and against a White supremacism in NASCAR. Unlike Bubba Wallace's recent stand against racial inequality, Scott did not easily fit within conventional definitions of protest and activism. Rather, Scott, like many Black drivers before and since, challenged discrimination in auto sports by engaging in "counter-mobility work" (Alderman & Inwood, 2016), such that the very work of driving became part of his political practice. Drawing heavily from Scott's biography (Donovan, 2008), our chapter highlights the bodily, social, and technological practices he employed to maintain if not enhance his mobility around tracks and to and from races—thus ensuring his survivability, material reproduction, right to belong in NASCAR. Before delving into Scott's biography and racing career, we offer some important background discussion on the study of race, mobility, and social justice in and through motorsports from the perspective of racial spatiality and specifically Black geographies.

The Racialization of Racing

Sports cultures, as systems of power relations, are involved in the construction of social identities, both dominant and marginalized, and are thus complicit in the creation of racial inequalities (Shobe, 2008). In exploring how sporting practices become constructed around racial hierarchies, Harrison (2013) introduced the concept of "racial spatiality," a term meant to draw attention to the key roles that place, space, and geographical movement play in racism. Racial spatiality captures how the everyday processes of racism work to secure and legitimize sports-related spaces as White and thus restrict and discourage participation and representation from people of colour and other minoritized communities. Inspired by Harrison's work, Jansson and Koch (2017) argue that sports spaces and spatial practices are imbricated in the uneven processes and politics of exclusion and belonging along a number of different axes of difference and identity, such as nationality, class, gender, and race. They cite the cogent remarks of Coleman (2006, 98), who calls for scholars to "elucidate how sporting arenas and playing fields [and arguably also racetracks] serve as sites where racialized thinking is manifested, performed, and perpetuated – and [most importantly in the context of Black geographies] resisted." The issue of resistance is important here because, as Schein (2006) asserts, the process of racialization is never complete or uncontested. Indeed, despite the long and continuing story of racial discrimination within sports, there are noted historical and growing contemporary examples of African American athletes embracing social justice and challenging racial spatiality in a variety of ways (Cooper et al., 2019).

The scholarly neglect of race and racism in motorsports exists despite the fact that the racetrack, across many different arms of motorsports, is a highly racialized space. As late as June 2020, African American racecar driver and journalist Rob Holland (2020) could identify only a small handful of Black drivers currently competing at highest levels of global motorsports, noting in particular the scarcity of African American competitors. British racer Lewis Hamilton has won multiple championships in Formula One, but he is the first and, to date, only Black driver within that segment of motorsports. Hamilton has been a vocal critic of the weak stand of F1 on fighting racism, and he has established a commission to improve the diversity in grand prix racing (Associated Press, 2020; Smith, 2020). The hegemony of Whiteness and the absence of Black bodies on racetracks are especially evident in NASCAR. Since the founding of the Association in 1948, only eight African Americans have raced a car in its elite series, with only two racing for extended periods of time—Wendell Scott and Bubba Wallace. Aside from Wallace, the only other African American drivers actively competing in NASCAR are Rajah Caruth, Jesse Iwuji, Blake Lothian, and Armani Williams—all driving in lower-tier national racing divisions.

Stock car racing's lack of diversity is not incidental but foundational to its historical development. The sport was "developed primarily by and for White, working-class men" of the southeastern United States and during a time of conservative, if not unreconstructed, views on race and civil rights (Pierce, 2010, 9). NASCAR's founder, Bill France Sr., and other association executives openly believed that competitive Black drivers were bad for business. During NASCAR's first decades of expansion in the 1950s and 1960s, the organization's leaders courted the support of segregationist politicians such as Alabama's George Wallace and South Carolina's Strom Thurmond and their White voting constituencies to build the storied speedways of Talladega and Darlington, respectively (Donovan, 2008; Goodman, 2020). Illustrating the close ties linking NASCAR with right-wing US politics, France would later serve as the Florida campaign manager for George Wallace's failed presidential bid in 1972 (Pierce, 2010). Furthermore, as Kusz (2007) and Newman and Giardina (2008) have discussed, NASCAR became an effective vehicle of White cultural nationalism and a neo-conservative racial politics: a connection amplified during the Presidency of Donald Trump (NASCAR CEO Brain France endorsed Trump for president in 2016). Notwithstanding NASCAR's *Drive for Diversity* programme, created in 2004 to train female and minority drivers, Michael Jordan's ownership of a racing team, and the activism of Bubba Wallace, the racing association continues to resemble what critical sports scholar Kyle Kusz (2007) noted over 15 years ago. He argued that NASCAR projects "a racially exclusive image of America" that reproduces White privilege and power (Kusz, 2007, 81).

Well before the formation of NASCAR in 1948 and throughout much of the first half of the twentieth century, the AAA (American Automobile Association), then the major governing body for much of US motorsports, refused to allow Blacks to compete in its racing events. This pushed early African American drivers such as the noted Dewey Gatson to compete against White drivers in outlaw or unsanctioned races under the pseudonym Rajo Jack DeSoto (Poehler, 2020). Joseph "Joie" Ray Jr., an open-wheel and stock car driver from Louisville, Kentucky, was the first African American licensed by the AAA in 1947, just few days before Jackie Robinson broke the colour barrier in professional baseball. But unlike what we saw in baseball, Ray was not followed by a wave of Black drivers desegregating US motorsports (Anonymous, 2017). Indeed, it would not be until 1991 that the first African American, Willy Ribbs, would qualify for the Indy 500. The only other Black driver to run at the

Indy 500 was George Mack, finishing 17th in 2002. Situated within a Midwest that had become the epicentre of the early twentieth-century rebirth of the KKK, the Indianapolis Motor Speedway's history was rooted in enforcing a Jim Crow racial spatiality that segregated spectators and disallowed people of colour from not just driving but also serving as mechanics or on pit crews at tracks (Gould, 2002). In the wake of Black Lives Matter protests in the summer of 2020, Ribbs lamented the limited progress made in the push for social justice since his historic run and called for the IndyCar series to pursue greater diversity in drivers and fans along with an "African-American presence among mechanics and engineers" (quoted in Brown, 2020, np).

As noted before, our chapter analyses NASCAR and motorsports from a Black geographies approach (Bledsoe et al., 2017; Hawthorne, 2019; McKittrick & Woods, 2007), which centres the situated knowledge, contributions, and struggles of Black communities. Such a perspective names and analyses the harmful effects of racial exclusion, but it does not do so at the sacrifice of acknowledging the dignity, resilience, and resistant agency of people of colour in living with and against White supremacy. Bonds and Inwood (2021) warn against reducing White supremacy simply to racial animus or the actions and worldviews of far-right extremists and hate groups. Rather, it is a more fundamental relation of power and system of racialized privilege embedded in and reproduced through many aspects and spaces of everyday life (including the racetrack) that unjustly structure the life chances and material wellbeing of Black communities. Motorsports are filled with important political moments in which African Americans sought to make a place for themselves within a White-dominated racing industry historically opposed to their right to participate and succeed. In this respect, the careers of Bubba Wallace, Wendell Scott, Willy Ribbs, and others are part of a broader narrative of African Americans challenging racism in motorsports, recognizing that this resistance comes in many forms and cannot be confined to overt protests experienced in 2020.

We encourage readers to appreciate that antiracist activism includes the daily and seemingly common sense practices that African American racers and others carried out in surviving, negotiating, and subverting the racialized spatiality of US auto sports. It is important to pay attention to how Black drivers have historically responded to being excluded from mainstream racing by creating their own Black geographies—those places of competition, promotional strategies, communities of support, knowledge flows, and mechanical innovations that destabilized racist ideas that being a major league racer was a livelihood and cultural identity reserved exclusively for Whites. This history includes, among many chapters, the creation in the 1920s of the Colored Speedway Association, a racing circuit where the best Black drivers and mechanics competed in several Midwestern cities. The Gold & Glory Sweepstakes was its marquee race, held at the Indianapolis State Fairgrounds and drawing tens of thousands of fans of colour along with marches and threats of violence from White supremacists. One of the Association's chief racing stars was four time Gold & Glory winner Charlie Wiggins, known for his great skill under the hood as well as on the track and who was not allowed by the AAA to run in the White-only Indianapolis 500 (Gould, 2002).

Also against the racial spatiality imposed by the AAA, the late 1940s saw the formation of the Atlanta Stock Car Club (ASCC) a league of Black drivers hosting car races on their home track in Lithonia, Georgia, and across the Southeast. ASCC racers included many talented but now largely unknown racers such as George and Ben Muckle, Richard "Red" Kines, Arthur "The Decatur Express" Avery, James "Suicide" Lacey, and Charlie Scott (no relation to Wendell Scott). Charlie later would be the first African American to compete in NASCAR's top division in 1956, although for only one race (Minter, 2014). African American racing pioneer Leonard Miller famously founded a number of racing teams and associations. In 1972, he was the first Black owner to have a car qualify for the Indy 500, and in 2005, Miller and his son would become the first African American owned team to win a NASCAR track championship (at the regional Late Model Stock Car Division). In 1973, Leonard Miller founded the Black American Racers Association. While short-lived (five years), the organization grew to 5000 members and sought to racially diversify spectatorship, develop programmes for developing Black driving talent, reduce sponsorship inequities facing African Americans, and increase the American public's recognition of the forgotten achievements of Blacks in motorsports (Miller & Simon, 2010).

Motorsports as Mobility Politics

As we consider how best to remember and recover the Black Geographies of motorsports, it is not enough simply to record and narrate their histories. Also important is developing a framework for interpreting and casting significance on the practices of African American drivers and how their actions and movements on and off the track constituted a form of antiracism. We suggest that racism within NASCAR is rooted within a racialized mobility politics which restricted the presence and movement of African Americans on racetracks as well as across the wider US landscape. Mobility as we use it here refers to geographic mobility, which is when physical movement becomes invested with social meaning (positive or negative) and embedded within structures of power, including White supremacy (Cresswell, 2006). The extent to which one can move (and where and how one gets there) both inside and outside the context of motorsports is not a socially neutral matter, but historically shaped by one's place within a series of intersecting hierarchies based on race, nationality, gender, and other axes of identity (Itaoui et al., 2021; Kochanek et al., 2021). Importantly, the production of motorsports as a place of and for Whites is made possible, in part, because of the racialization of movement. This racialization of mobility relies upon formal and informal practices enforcing the idea that Whites have some greater right and ability than Blacks to move freely around the sport and its spaces and thus should benefit more from the sport's resources and opportunities. Undergirding our argument is that auto racing demonstrates the high bodily and social stakes of race and mobility. Being allowed to gain access to and move through and around the racetrack is not simply about engaging in a pastime; rather, restricting and controlling of the movements of Black drivers directly impact their material reproduction, safety, and the political negotiation of their lives and futures. In sum, the racetrack is made a racialized place by virtue of the production of Black (im)mobility, recognizing that mobility is a civil right, and the right to move is "fundamentally intertwined with the construction of racial identities" (Hague, 2010, 331).

Motorsports involves multiple mobilities on the part of many parties, from spectators, sponsors, and broadcast crews to pit crews, mechanics, and engineers and participating drivers. For the racecar driver, the focus of our discussion here, their mobilities include the journey to and from different racetracks over a season along with what the competitive movements that occur on the track itself. Moreover, there are the uneven spatial flows of sponsorship money, advanced car technology, labour, and publicity to drivers and their teams, which then shape their competitive mobility and sustainability in the sport. Engaging in these mobilities is daunting for any driver but especially so for drivers of colour who historically were not even allowed to compete against White drivers; and when allowed to race, their movements faced considerable social and economic obstacles, on and off the track, as they challenged racist attitudes, practices, and structures. While the mobilities in NASCAR and other motorsports may seem very different from people's ordinary modes of travel and transportation, and they certainly are in some important ways, they are actually an extension of a wider history and geography of racialized movement and antiracist mobility resistance in America.

The unfettered movement of White America has long relied upon, whether consciously recognized or not, on the immobilization of Black communities and tight control over their right to move. This process began with enslavement and continued through the vagrancy laws and lynching of the Jim Crow era and remains evident today in patterns of mass incarceration. As Lipsitz (2011, 66) aptly says, "The strong desire to move freely across space formed an important part of the Black spatial imaginary, but it has rarely been easy to translate those hopes of moving freely with the ability to actually do so for African Americans." Important to discussions of racial inequality in motorsports is a recognition that the automobile has been a key political technology in the White-controlled mobility regime. This mobility regime included the razing of Black neighbourhoods in the mid-twentieth century because of US federal highway development, cuts in public transit to subsidize car travel and White suburbanization, and the array of hostilities awaiting early Black motorists on the road and those still faced today by drivers racially profiled by police (Alderman et al., 2019; Alderman & Inwood, 2016). NASCAR may seem to some to be a world away from these everyday political struggles over transportation, but stock car racing has been key to valorizing the culture and economy of American automobility. That automobility, while often framed as a democracy open to anyone with a car, actually reproduces if not deepens hierarchies of race, class, and power within the United States (Gilroy, 2001; Seiler, 2008). NASCAR is embedded within rather than immune from these inequalities.

A Black geographies perspective recognizes that African American communities are engaged in complex relationships with oppression and they have a capacity to transform their geographic immobility (or controlled mobility) into movement that subverts the logics and effects of racism. We argue for conceptualizing these resistant movements in motorsports and in the larger arena of social life as "counter-mobility work" (Alderman & Inwood, 2016). "Counter-mobility work captures the bodily, technological, social, and…emotional practices that not only facilitated physical movement [by Black drivers], but which also constituted the racialized labor and resourcefulness of resisting and surviving White supremacy" (Alderman et al., 2019, 8). Seeing Black freedom struggles as counter-mobility work gives direct credit to those performing this labour as well as the broad array of creative and savvy practices required to move in transgressive and resistant ways.

The story of Wendell Scott and so many other Black racecar drivers is part of a broader narrative of African Americans fashioning resistant mobilities as part of their fight for self-determination. There are numerous instances of the Black fight to move and belong on one's own terms—from escaping the bonds of slavery to the Great Migration out of the Southeast, from the freedom rides and stall-ins of the Civil Rights Movement to the development of alternative travel tools, destinations, and networks (Alderman et al., 2019; Dillette, 2021; Inwood, 2014). Within this framework of antiracist mobility making, the automobile and hence auto-racing undergoes an important re-interpretation. At the same time as the automobile sector has participated in perpetuating in various forms racial oppression, Black communities have developed positive identifications with the car, seeing it as a symbol of freedom and uplift, while also engaging in driving as a creative practice of resilience and resistance against inequality. Indeed, African American motorists who were on the road during the same era as Wendell Scott (1940s to

1970s) deployed a range of driving strategies to circumvent and challenge institutionalized discrimination and segregation while travelling by car, including the use segregation era travel guides such as the *Green Book* to locate safe accommodations. Armed with these guides, Black motorists used their cars and driving to find and participate in the major Black urban cultural and political spaces of the day (Harlem, Atlanta's Sweet Auburn Avenue, Chattanooga's 9th Street), and in doing so, challenge and gain some refuge from the control of White supremacy. These same spaces proved to be important incubators for formal political protest during the Civil Rights Movement since they were away from the prying eyes and ears of the White establishment. Because these gathering spaces were at the crossroads of so much car travel, they helped establish critical lines of communication and solidarity across Black communities (Alderman et al., 2019; Bottone, 2020). Turning from the generic Black automobile user, in the remainder of the chapter, we will focus on the specific practices and tactics deployed by Wendell Scott (and conceivably many other semi-professional/professional Black racers) in appropriating and reworking the act of NASAR driving as an antiracist counter-mobility practice.

"The only way I can help…is to just be a… good race driver"

A brief review of Wendell Scott's biography within NASCAR provides insight into the historical construction of a White racial spatiality within motorsports, the kinds of obstacles he faced, and the resistant nature of his presence and movement in racing. Driving first in competitive circuits in his local Danville, Virginia, Scott obtained a NASCAR racing licence and broke the colour barrier in 1953 with no fanfare and with no significant White help. A notable exception was regional official, Mike Poston, who granted him a NASCAR licence—much to the irritation of NASCAR President Bill France, Sr., and other executives. Scott won numerous minor league NASCAR races and two Virginia state championships before joining its elite Grand National Series in 1961. During Scott's racing career, he was never able to secure corporate sponsorship, leaving him to compete using pit crews of family and friends, scavenging for car parts, and mortgaging his home to race. NASCAR officials, including France, had promised help, but did little to assist with badly needed sponsorship or to control racial discrimination at tracks (Donovan, 2008).

Yet, NASCAR's treatment of Wendell Scott was not just a matter of inaction or neglect; it often took the form of active hostility as it enforced stock car racing's White racial spatiality. When the Black driver made his first top series debut in Spartanburg, South Carolina, race officials never mentioned him in pre-race publicity and simply introduced him on race day as W.D. Scott to conceal his identity from potentially angered White stock car fans who would have known a "Wendell Scott." Racing officials unfairly disqualified Scott at pre-race inspections, abused him verbally, denied him compensation and a rookie of the year award, and banned him outright from certain tracks. Bob Colvin, president of the Darlington Raceway and an unapologetic segregationist, blocked Scott from racing on his South Carolina track until 1965, when forced by the passage of the Civil Rights Act. Colvin promoted Darlington's Southern 500 as a "defiant tribute to the Old South," and he used the Confederate flag, instead of a green flag, to start its races. Colvin allegedly said that if a Black man ever won the Southern 500, the driver would "never make it to victory lane" (Donovan, 2008, 100).

If there were one encounter with racism that left the most lasting and bitter impression upon Wendell Scott, it was his lone Grand National Series victory in Jacksonville, Florida, in 1963, just a few months after the March on Washington, which saw 250,000 people gather in front of the Lincoln Memorial to demand economic and political equality for Black America. Scott beat his nearest competitor, Buck Baker, by two laps, but track officials initially declared Baker the winner and he received the trophy and the crowd's adulation. Officials eventually recognized Scott as the winner two hours after the end of the race—long after race fans had left and Baker's departure with the trophy. Scott received the first-place money but a shoddy, wooden trophy with little if any decoration or inscription. While some characterize the sleight as simply the result of a lap counting error (Coble, 2010), others suggest that race promoters delayed the victory because of apprehension about the reaction of spectators to learning of Scott's win and watching him kiss the White beauty queen in the victory circle, a tradition at NASCAR races (Karpf, 2008). It would take 20 years after Scott's death and 47 years after the Jacksonville race before NASCAR would award a suitable trophy to his family.

Even in the face of rampant racism and other obstacles, Wendell Scott proved to be tough competition and regularly finished the racing seasons in the latter half of the 1960s among the top ten in the point standings. Yet, with the 1970s, the African American driver experienced a downturn. His relationship with NASCAR management grew even tenser in the wake of his decision to participate in a boycott of the inaugural race of the new Talladega, Alabama, Speedway because of concerns over unsafe driving conditions. Talladega's construction ushered in a change from the sport's dirt tracks to paved speedways, which often benefited the kind of highly engineered cars that Scott could not afford. In the push to have a more competitive car, Scott went into deep debt to purchase a Mercury with a state-of-the-art engine. He drove that Mercury for the first and last time at a 1973 race at Talladega, completely wrecking the vehicle, causing him serious injuries, and forcing him into retirement that same year (Donovan, 2008).

As we seek to understand the kind of antiracist resistance that Wendell Scott deployed, it is important to note that he would have been the first to admit that he did not identify himself as a civil rights activist. He was reluctant to engage in formal political protest and seldom, if ever, brought up civil rights with other drivers or went public about racism in motorsports—believing that it would lead to his ban from NASCAR. The following comment by Scott to a reporter illustrates the extent to which he distanced himself, at least publicly, from the Movement: "The only way I can help these [civil] rights people and their cause is to just be a…good race driver" (Donovan, 2008, 121, emphasis added). Scott's actions and words might not fall within conventional understandings of activism, but for us they prompt a consideration of the full range of practices that count for resistance, which include the protests of Bubba Wallace but also include Wendell Scott's daily, Black working-class struggle for survivability and material reproduction as much as confrontation. As the lone African American driver operating in a region, time, and sport all of which were hostile to his presence and movements, Scott fashioned a savvy mix of resistance and accommodation, to create a place within a racialized spatiality even as he tried to defy it. According to Litwack (1998), for African Americans in the Jim Crow South, accommodation and survival were political strategies for navigating racism rather than simply the acceptance of oppression, a way of resisting without appearing to do so.

We take to heart Wendell Scott's suggestion that he could help civil rights through his driving. While some critics might dismiss the comment as Scott merely rationalizing his non-involvement in the Civil Rights Movement, we suggest that he, perhaps intuitively, understood the political value of driving a racecar. His very presence and mobility on tracks over several years exposed the racialized dimensions of NASCAR, calling into question the taken-for-granted Whiteness of the sport and representing, in his own way, an articulation of the right of African Americans to bodily occupy, move around, and claim places traditionally devoted to their exclusion and disenfranchisement. But Scott did not exercise this resistance by simply showing up at the track; rather, he did so by "exert[ing] agency over his own geographic mobility and how he used his movement to counter and negotiate the racist ways in which the race track was constructed and realized as a White place" (Alderman & Inwood, 2016, 605). In the following sections, we point to some of the bodily, social, and technological work that Scott deployed to survive and subvert racism and hence carve a Black geography within NASCAR. This work seems to be a matter of mere practicality, but it was always situated within an antiracism politics of survivability and the struggle to make a Black counter-mobility possible and, at times, competitive within a White-controlled motorsports composed of faster, technologically advanced racecars, and well-heeled teams.

Scott's Counter-mobility Work

Bodily Practices

Producing a Black counter-mobility within NASCAR required a range of bodily practices performed by Wendell Scott in navigating the track, controlling his racecar, and negotiating his own body and the bodies of people around him. An important facet of Scott's bodily interaction with the automobile and the track was his power slide technique, which he used effectively on dirt tracks. Throughout much of Scott's career, NASCAR ran races on dirt tracks. In executing the power slide, he would make violent jerks with the steering wheel to make tight, difficult turns on the track, thus allowing him to out manoeuvre and be more agile than the quicker cars driven by White competitors. While other drivers employed a power slide, it played an especially important role in Scott's mobility work since his marginalized position within stock car racing necessitated strategies that would in effect level the playing field between unevenly equipped and financed cars. Scott's driving required reflexes, strength, and endurance—even as he suffered from stress-induced debilitating, stomach ulcers. This along with a tactile understanding of how cars behaved on dirt tracks was important in helping him, as a Black driver, remain resilient and relevant in a sport largely opposed to his existence (Donovan, 2008).

The bodily strategies required for Wendell Scott to keep moving and racing within NASCAR were not restricted to the track. He recognized early in his career that he could not afford to engage in bodily confrontation with angry competitors or fans. Those kinds of confrontations would compromise Scott's credibility in the eyes of the public, and racing officials could use the spectre of White mob violence to justify his exclusion from the sport and legitimize major league stock racing remaining all White. Scott had a uniquely Black knowledge of the social and political realities of White supremacy in the South and how his own bodily actions and Black subjectivity would be interpreted within this racialized hierarchy. When confrontation was necessary, two of Scott's White friends, Buck Drummond and Earl Brooks, would protect him from fights and engage in violence on his behalf. Drummond and Brooks speak to the strategic coalitions Scott established in order to ensure his spatial mobility, which also demonstrated the importance of White allies to civil rights and how White supremacy—even in NASCAR—was never complete or without fractures, which Scott exposed (Chappell, 1996).

On some occasions, Scott exploited the perceived racial ambiguity of his own bodily characteristics—specifically his lighter skin—to navigate and even circumvent the effects of White supremacy, although he never denied that he was an African American to a racing official or track owner.

In doing so, he used the controversial practice of "passing" to gain resources necessary for him to keep moving amid harsh conditions. Biographer Donovan (2008) recounted a situation in which Scott was in desperate need of repairs when travelling home from a race. Like many Black motorists at the time, he found service stations only willing to serve Whites and knew that the longer he remained on the road and not moving, the more vulnerable that he and his family and friends were to harassment or even violence. Covering his curly hair under a cap and posing as the White boss of a Black race crew, he gained access to a garage and made it home safely. To convince the garage owner of his supposed identity, Scott not only looked the part but also sounded like a White supremacist. In what Scott later described as heartbreaking, he referred to his crew, included his own sons, using the n-word, illustrating "how many African Americans in the U.S. South were often placed in a position of having to engage in practices that compromised their racialized position in society" in order to survive White supremacy. Yet, in manipulating how his body and identity were interpreted publicly, Scott "creatively turned Jim Crow's racial politics of the body against itself while also unmasking the illegitimacy of Whiteness as an objective racial identity and thus exposing it as a socially constructed point of superiority and privilege" (Alderman & Inwood, 2016, 606).

Technological Practices

Also important to Scott's creation of a resilient Black counter-mobility in NASCAR was the technological work he performed before and during the race. When hostile pre-race inspection invariably tried to disqualify him, Scott quickly rebuilt engines and made other repairs wherever he could find space, sometimes in alleys and parking lots. The owner of a garage in his hometown of Danville, Scott was known as an innovative, self-taught mechanic, and his contemporaries remember instances in which he would jump out of his car at pit stops during the middle of a race and perform repairs in order to keep the racecar moving (Donovan, 2008). However, these mechanical feats were never just about staying on the track. They were also about how remaining competitive and mobile directly impacted the politics of Scott's own material reproduction in a sport providing little support beyond receiving used parts from sympathetic drivers and crew chiefs or Scott and his sons' foraging for equipment, tyres, and food abandoned by teams after races. When once asked by a reporter why he had worked so hard to mend a car in the middle of a race, Scott responded: "One more position [at the finish line] might be the difference next week in whether I sleep in a motel or in my truck" (quoted in DanvilleVAGov, 2015, np). Importantly, given the inhospitality, police harassment, and possibly even violence awaiting Black motorists on Jim Crow highways during Scott's heyday, finishing races higher in the order (and thus earning money to stay in a hotel) directly affected his safety and wellbeing as he moved from race to race and challenged the White racial spatiality of motorsports.

It is common for any racer to be in tune with their car, and this was especially the case in early stock car racing when so many drivers doubled as mechanics, but Wendell Scott proved to be especially in touch with his racecars and produced an alternative knowledge of his cars without the aid of expensive, sophisticated equipment. Friends recounted to his biographer (Donovan, 2008) that Scott would taste hot motor oil and test spark plugs by hand to detect mechanical problems on a track. Improvisation was key to his antiracist survival and counter-mobility, as illustrated so well in the sole Jacksonville win in 1963. The severe bumps and ruts on the Florida track caused many top racers to bounce, break axles and wheels, and lose traction. In a desperate but fortuitous attempt to improve his car's suspension, Scott removed a shock absorber at each corner of the automobile. The decision allowed him to run faster and outmanoeuvre factory-backed racecars driven by White competitors. In doing so, he was transforming the track from a place that was largely about money and sheer horsepower into a different kind of mobility space in which a Black man with limited means and mechanical prowess and handling skills could belong, matter, and perhaps even win. Squeezing performance and power from inferior cars and making difficult decisions about when and how much to push his car were key to Scott's counter-mobility work and inseparable from the economic inequalities he faced as lone, African American driver refused sponsorship. Because of this racialized necessity, he stressed finishing in the top ten over racing "full out" for a win and hence risking the expense of a blown engine or wrecked car.

Scott's son, Wendell, Jr., captures this resistant survivability and how it informed his father's approach to racing: "Top ten meant the light bill got paid or my third or fourth sister was going to get new shoes. That's the Wendell Scott story" (interviewed in Karpf, 2008). For Scott to be so consistently competitive in so many races in his career is indeed remarkable when one considers that on average sponsored cars ran 10–15 miles per hour faster than his racecars (Donovan, 2008).

Social Practices

While Scott's counter-mobility depended upon certain bodily and technological work, it was also decidedly social in nature, meaning that the driver had to manage the tense social relations that existed on and around the track as a Black driver crossed a highly protected colour line. Scott deployed different strategies in responding to racism in NASCAR and to White opponents; his life experience in the Jim Crow South taught him that certain oppositional actions were possible (and some were not) given the specific racial order of stock car racing. To maintain his counter-mobility and antiracism within NASCAR, Scott deployed a creative mixture of self-defence and tactical avoidance that reminds us that resistance and accommodation are engaged in a dialectical relationship rather than being oppositional binaries.

While Scott recognized the dangers to himself and his position in a White supremacist sport if he engaged in violence, there were instances in which he engaged in self-defence as part of his resistant survivability. As we have noted previously in this chapter, Black motorists on the road during segregation often met with White intimidation and threats of bodily harm. Consequently, Scott never travelled to races alone, and he drove to tracks with a pistol under his seat, not an uncommon practice among African American travellers at the time. Scott tended to avoid overt confrontations with Whites, but he was adamant about defending his family when they faced racialized violence at a track. On two occasions in the 1965 season, Scott confronted groups of White men who threatened his teenage sons: angry spectators at one North Carolina track threatened to castrate them. Scott responded to both tense scenes by promising without hesitation to kill the offenders, which remarkably worked to defuse the situation (Donovan, 2008). The efficacy of Scott's strategy of self-defence was also evident when dealing with fellow driver Jack Smith, who was strongly opposed to Black participation in NASCAR:

> In the 1962 season, Smith repeatedly wrecked, spun out, and crowded Scott on the track. Finally, at raceway in Valdosta, Georgia, Scott pointed a loaded gun at Smith while they were running pace laps on the track. Later, in Hickory, North Carolina, Scott threatened to kill Smith if he ever intentionally hit his car again. No more trouble was had from Smith. (Alderman & Inwood, 2016, 607)

Important to maintaining Scott's mobility around the racetrack was an understanding of how to navigate the wider landscape of American racism. He knew fully well that his ability to drive and compete in NASCAR was deeply embedded in the social practices of racial oppression and anti-racism, and he at times called upon a long tradition of Black self-defence that is sometimes forgotten in popularized narrations of civil rights resistance. Just as the Black driver was calculating about how far he could push his racecar in terms of mechanical performance in order to remain resilient and mobile over the long haul, he also had a keen awareness of how far he could push socially and physically against White supremacy.

Wendell Scott most often approached stressed social relations with fellow drivers by employing a strategy of tactical avoidance. The term "tactical avoidance" is meant to recognize that non-confrontation, or even accommodation, is not necessarily the same as accepting racism. This non-confrontation, while not inherently oppositional, has the potential to become a form of resistance when used strategically. Knowing that NASCAR would relish any chance to ban Scott from the Grand National Series and end his racing career, Scott knew that the self-defence shown against Jack Smith could not be a regular occurrence. He most often focused on striking a delicate balance between driving hard and moving against efforts to sideline him with practising non-aggression on the track. Scott would not hesitate to outdrive and beat White drivers, often to their angry embarrassment, but he would refuse to wreck them and would not retaliate against a White driver who had wrecked him. By making a place on the track for tactical avoidance, Scott would avoid being penalized or disenfranchised by racing officials, while also building sympathy and support among some White fans and drivers witnessing Scott's mistreatment in NASCAR. "In effect, Scott socially fashioned his brand of racing in non-violent ways, which made it possible to create a counter-mobility that exposed the brutality and immorality of racism, the potential fissures in the hegemony of White supremacy, as well as ensuring his own physical and survival on the track" (Alderman & Inwood, 2016, 607).

Unfortunately, although Scott believed that tactical avoidance was necessary for keeping him on the track and moving against White supremacy, the approach may have actually worked against his limited opportunities for sponsorship. Early in Scott's NASCAR career, before reaching the top racing series, he established a relationship with a White trucking executive named Monroe Shook with the hopes it would lead to sponsorship in the top Grand National circuit. But before that investment could happen, Scott needed to show a victory at Virginia's South Boston Speedway. At the South Boston race, Scott was running a close second to White race leader, Gip Gibson. However, when Scott competed, he was not only racing against fellow drivers and teams but also responding to the White public reaction that his movements at the track may evoke—illustrating the added labour of being in and moving through racialized places that are fundamentally opposed to one's existence. Anxious about race fans at the Virginia track getting ugly and turning on him, something he had experienced earlier at other tracks, Scott refused to abandon his established practice of avoiding deliberate contact and nudge Gibson's car out of the way, even though such contact was common among White drivers. Because Scott was not willing to overtake his opponent in this manner, he finished the race in second place (Donovan, 2008).

According to Scott's biographer, "The incident [at South Boston] cost Scott the confidence of Monroe Shook," who angrily removed any possibility that he would sponsor him in Grand National car (Donovan, 2008, 83). This event is indicative of what Du Bois ([1903] 1994) described as the "double consciousness" that Scott and other African Americans live with and socially negotiate as they look at themselves and make life decisions through the eyes of others, namely a White-dominated society. Maurice Shook and arguably other sponsors, although it is unclear how many would have really given Scott a chance in 1950s and 1960s, expected him to follow the same aggressive mobility practices as White drivers. But Scott saw himself in a conundrum, a catch-22: he was not a White competitor and driving as if he were White would most assuredly cause a public backlash and further increase his vulnerability to being wrecked and make him unable to compete for top finishes and financially backing. In this complex racialized world of motorsports, creating an alternative Black geography required Scott to make social manoeuvres that while facilitating his immediate survivability and freedom of movement may have compromised his long-term competitiveness and mobility in the sport. The power of White supremacy is not just in how it directly controls or oppresses people of colour, but also in how it frames or places limits on what may appear as geographically and socially possible within a specific racial order. This was especially the case for someone like Wendell Scott who was trying to use his driving to manage the affect he would have on a track full of White people whose attitudes and actions were frighteningly uncertain to him.

Concluding Remarks

While motorsports in the United States is obviously about racing, it has also always been about race and racism. Recognizing this fundamental fact is critical to understanding and taking on the White racialized spatiality that the sport has long perpetuated and continues to do so today. Important is recovering the often-forgotten Black geographies of competitive driving that have existed in opposition to White supremacy in motorsports and centring these resistant practices, contributions, and movements. Our chapter has sought to begin this process by re-situating the story of Wendell Scott—often heralded as a trailblazer in NASCAR but rarely fully understood—within a broader understanding of a racialized motorsports and an antiracism mobility politics. His countermobility work, in addition to sensitizing us to varied ways that African Americans have resisted and survived marginalization in motorsports, can help us re-evaluate what counts as antiracist political praxis. Scott and other Black drivers actively transformed the meaning and material dimensions of their competitive movements to fashion what contested places they could in motorsports. Their struggles remind us that any serious effort to address racism in motorsports now cannot merely be about paying lip service to diversity or simply challenging White supremacist symbols such as the Confederate flag, although that is important. Rather there must be uncomfortable reparative work of coming to terms with the historical foundations, expressions, and continuing structural legacies of racism in racing.

References

Abrams, J. (2020). Michael Jordan's Big Play in NASCAR Could Help Diversify Its Fan Base. *New York Times*, 25 September. Retrieved January 8, 2021, from https://www.nytimes.com/2020/09/25/sports/autoracing/nascar-jordan-bubba-wallace.html.

Alderman, D. H., & Inwood, J. (2016). Mobility as Antiracism Work: The "hard driving" of NASCAR's Wendell Scott. *Annals of the American Association of Geographers, 106*(3), 597–611.

Alderman, D. H., Williams, K., & Bottone, E. (2022). Jim Crow Journey Stories: African American Driving as Emotional Labor. *Tourism Geographies, 22*(2–3), 198–222.

Anonymous. (2017). Racing without a race: How motorsports never integrated. N/A, 2 February. Retrieved January 16, 2021, from https://medium.com/@NotNamedErik.

Associated Press. (2020). F1 star Hamilton to set up commission to increase diversity. 21 June. Retrieved January 9, 2021, from https://www.bloomberg.com/news/articles/2020-06-21/f1-star-hamilton-to-set-up-commission-to-increase-diversity.

Bernstein, V. (2015). NASCAR asks fans to put away Confederate Flags. *New York Times*, 2 July. Retrieved January 7, 2021, from https://www.nytimes.com/2015/07/03/sports/autoracing/nascar-asks-fans-to-put-away-confederate-flags.html.

Bledsoe, A., Eaves, L. E., & Williams, B. (2017). Introduction: Black Geographies in and of the United States South. *Southeastern Geographer, 57*(1), 6–11.

Bonds, A., & Inwood, J. (2021) Relations of power: The U.S. Capitol insurrection, white supremacy and US democracy. *Society + Space*, 9 August. Retrieved August 10, 2021, from https://www.societyandspace.org/articles/relations-of-power-the-u-s-capitol-insurrection-white-supremacy-and-us-democracy.

Bottone, E. (2020). "Please mention the Green Book:" The Negro Motorist Green Book as Critical GIS. In C. Travis, F. Ludlow, & F. Gyuris (Eds.), *Historical Geography, GIScience and Textual Analysis: Landscapes of Time and Place* (pp. 51–64). Springer.

Brown, N. (2020). As IndyCar Approaches Major Stage, Uncertainty Looms on Its Approach to Social Justice Movement. IndyStar.com, 1 July. Retrieved January 9, 2021, from https://www.indystar.com/story/sports/motor/2020/07/01/willy-t-ribbs-indycar-approach-social-justice-movement-talk-cheap/3277299001/.

Chappell, D. (1996). *Inside Agitators: White Southerners in the Civil Rights Movement*. Johns Hopkins University Press.

Coble, D. (2010). 1963 NASCAR controversy: Racing or race? *The Florida Times Union*, 27 June. Retrieved January 16, 2021, from https://www.jacksonville.com/article/20100627/NEWS/801249575.

Coleman, A. (2006). 'Race' and Sports: How an Historical Construct Continues to Shape Sports, Space and Society. In L. DeChano & F. Shelley (Eds.), *The Geography–Sports Connection: Using Sports to Teach Geography* (pp. 89–101). National Council for Geographic Education.

Cooper, J. N., Macaulay, C., & Rodriguez, S. H. (2019). Race and Resistance: A Typology of African American Sport Activism. *International Review for the Sociology of Sport, 54*(2), 151–181.

Cresswell, T. (2006). *On the Move: Mobility in the Modern Western World*. Routledge.

Cwik, C. (2020). Bubba Wallace's family details racism Wallace faced on his journey to NASCAR. Yahoo Sports, 8 July. Retrieved January 7, 2021, from https://sports.yahoo.com/bubba-wallaces-family-details-racism-wallace-faced-on-his-journey-to-nascar-165908719.html

DanvilleVAGov. (2015). Wendell Scott Hall of Fame induction. Online video clip. YouTube 5 February 2015. Retrieved January 17, 2021, from https://www.youtube.com/watch?v=C01qWU__Zns.

Dillette, A. K. (2021). Black Travel Tribes: An Exploration of Race and Travel in America. In C. Pforr, R. Dowling, & M. Volgger (Eds.), *Consumer Tribes in Tourism* (pp. 39–51). Springer.

Donovan, B. (2008). *Hard Driving: The Wendell Scott Story: the American Odyssey of NASCAR'S First Black Driver*. Steerforth Press.
Du Bois, W. E. B. ([1903] 1994). *The Souls of Black Folk*. Dover.
Gilroy, P. (2001). Driving While Black. In D. Miller (Ed.), *Car Cultures* (pp. 81–104). Oxford Press.
Gould, T. (2002). *For Gold and Glory: Charlie Wiggins and the African-American Racing Car Circuit*. Indiana University Press.
Goodman, J. (2020). NASCAR can't be allowed to whitewash history so easily. *AL.com*, 22 June. Retrieved January 9, 2021, from https://www.al.com/sports/2020/06/nascar-cant-be-allowed-to-Whitewash-history-so-easily.html.
Griffith, J. (2020). Bubba Wallace wants NASCAR to ban the Confederate flag. NBC News, 9 June. Retrieved January 7, 2021, from https://www.nbcnews.com/news/us-news/bubba-wallace-wants-nascar-ban-confederate-flag-n1228546.
Hague, E. (2010). 'The right to enter every other state'–The Supreme Court and African American mobility in the United States. *Mobilities, 5*(3), 331–347.
Harrison, A. K. (2013). Black Skiing, Everyday Racism, and the Racial Spatiality of Whiteness. *Journal of Sport & Social Issues, 37*(4), 315–339.
Hawthorne, C. (2019). Black Matters Are Spatial Matters: Black Geographies for the Twenty-first Century. *Geography Compass, 13*(11), 1–13.
Holland, R. (2020). The World of Cars Has a Diversity Problem. How Are We Going to Fix It? The Drive, 19 June. Retrieved January 8, 2021, from https://www.thedrive.com/news/34228/the-world-of-cars-has-a-diversity-problem-how-are-we-going-to-fix-it.
Holley, K., & Karpf, R. (2011). *Wendell Scott: A Race Story*. ESPN.
Inwood, J. (2014). Great Migration. In C. E. Colten & G. L. Buckley (Eds.), *North American Odyssey: Historical Geographies for the Twenty-first Century* (pp. 103–114). Rowman & Littlefield.
Itaoui, R., Dufty-Jones, R., & Dunn, K. M. (2021). Anti–racism Muslim Mobilities in the San Francisco Bay Area. *Mobilities, 16*(6), 888–904.
Jansson, D., & Koch, N. (2017). Conclusion: Toward a Critical Geography of Sport: Space, Power, and Social Justice. In N. Koch (Ed.), *Critical Geographies of Sport: Space, Power and Sport in Global Perspective* (pp. 235–352). Routledge.
Karpf, R., Director (2008). *NASCAR: Ride of their lives*. NASCAR Media Group, CMT Films.
Kochanek, J., Davis, M., Erickson, K., & Ferguson, D. (2021). More Than "just a driver": A Study of Professional Women Racecar Drivers' Agency in Motorsport. *Psychology of Sport and Exercise, 52*, 101838.

Kusz, K. W. (2007). From NASCAR Nation to Pat Tillman: Notes on Sport and the Politics of White Cultural Nationalism in Post-9/11 America. *Journal of Sport & Social Issues, 31*(1), 77–88.

Litwack, L. F. (1998). *Trouble in Mind: Black Southerners in the Age of Jim Crow*. Knopf.

Long, D. (2020). Athletes from various sports show support for Bubba Wallace. NBC Sports, 22 June. Retrieved January 7, 2021, from https://nascar.nbcsports.com/2020/06/22/bubba-wallace-lebron-james-tyrann-mathieu-max-homa-athletes-across-various-sports-show-support-for-bubba-wallace/.

McCarriston, S. (2020). Bubba Wallace' Black Lives Matter scheme car from Martinsville race can now be ordered online. *CBSSports.com*, 18 June. Retrieved January 15, 2021, from https://www.cbssports.com/nascar/news/nascar-driver-hailie-deegan-apologizes-for-using-slur-during-iracing-event/

Macur, J. (2020a). Bubba Wallace Thankful for Flag Ban, But NASCAR's Fans Might Not Be. *New York Times*, 13 June. Retrieved January 8, 2021, from https://www.nytimes.com/2020/06/13/sports/bubba-wallace-nascar-confederate-flag.html.

Macur, J. (2020b). The Confederate Flag Didn't Bother Bubba Wallace. Until It Did. *New York Times*, 19 June. Retrieved January 7, 2021, from https://www.nytimes.com/2020/06/19/sports/autoracing/bubba-wallace-nascar-Black-lives-matter-confederate-flag.html.

Martinelli, M. (2020). FBI announces noose found in Bubba Wallace's garage had been there since 2019; no federal crime committed. *USA Today*, 23 June. Retrieved January 8, 2021, from https://www.usatoday.com/story/sports/nascar/2020/06/23/nascar-fbi-details-noose-bubba-wallace-garage-talladega/3245722001/.

McKittrick, K., & Woods, C. A. (2007). *Black Geographies and the Politics of Place*. Between the Lines.

McRae, D. (2017). Craig Hodges: 'Jordan didn't speak out because he didn't know what to say'. *The Guardian*, 20 April. Retrieved August 9, 2021, from https://www.theguardian.com/sport/2017/apr/20/craig-hodges-michael-jordan-nba-chicago-bulls.

Miller, L. T., & Simon, A. (2010). *Racing While Black: How an African-American Stock Car Team Made Its Mark on NASCAR*. Seven Stories Press.

Minter, R. (2014). Atlanta racers were racial pioneers. *Atlanta Journal & Constitution*, 16 December. Retrieved January 9, 2021, from https://www.ajc.com/sports/motor-sports/atlanta-racers-were-racial-pioneers/KtbG3GvjQ0CVd7HeBN623M/.

Newman, J. I., & Giardina, M. D. (2008). NASCAR and the 'southernization' of America: Spectatorship, Subjectivity, and the Confederation of Identity. *Cultural Studies, Critical Methodologies, 8*(4), 479–506.

Pierce, D. (2004). A Review of *For Gold and Glory* (2003) by Todd Gould. *Journal of Sport History, 31*(1), 111–113.

Pierce, D. S. (2010). *Real NASCAR: White Lightning, Red Clay, and Big Bill France.* University of North Carolina Press.

Poehler, B. (2020). *The Brown Bullet: Rajo Jack's Drive to Integrate Auto Racing.* Chicago Review Press.

Quinn, M. (2020). Trump targets driver Bubba Wallace while criticizing NASCAR ban on Confederate flag. CBS News, 7 July. Retrieved January 8, 2021, from https://www.cbsnews.com/news/trump-bubba-wallace-tweet-nascar-confederate-flag/.

Romo, V. (2020). NASCAR bans Confederate Flag. npr.org, 10 June. Retrieved January 7, 2021, from https://www.npr.org/sections/live-updates-protests-for-racial-justice/2020/06/10/874393049/nascar-bans-confederate-flag.

Seiler, C. (2008). *Republic of Drivers: A Cultural History of Automobility in America.* University of Chicago Press.

Shobe, H. (2008). Place, Identity and Football: Catalonia, Catalanisme and Football Club Barcelona, 1899–1975. *National Identities, 10*(3), 329–343.

Smith, L. (2020). Lewis Hamilton is demanding change. *New York Times*, 7 August. Retrieved January 8, 2021, from https://www.nytimes.com/2020/08/07/sports/autoracing/lewis-hamilton-formula-1-diversity.html.

Spear, S. (2020). Gov.'s Office condemns speedway owner's racist FB post in wake of Wallace noose incident. Rockingham Now, 25 June. Retrieved January 10, 2021, from https://greensboro.com/rockingham_now/news/gov-s-office-condemns-speedway-owners-racist-fb-post-in-wake-of-wallace-noose-incident/article_059aa668-c85d-5f92-9771-b77bc579e1ac.html.

The Guardian. (2015). Defiant NASCAR fans pledge allegiance to their Confederate flags. 5 July. Retrieved January 7, 2021, from https://www.theguardian.com/sport/2015/jul/05/nascar-fans-wave-confederate-flags-daytona.

Can the Formula One Driver Speak? Lewis Hamilton, Race and the Resurrection of the Black Athlete

Ben Carrington

As the years pass, you realise that success is a wonderful thing. But it feels relatively short-lived. And I don't just want to be remembered as a driver, because I care about so many more different things.
—*Lewis Hamilton*

Introduction

This chapter uses the career and life of Formula One (F1) motor racing driver Lewis Hamilton to assess the recent reemergence of political consciousness among athletes across the globe. In particular I examine the extent to which sport offers a modality for popular forms of anti-racism, and the limits of sports activism. Hamilton's remarkable professional career, that by most metrics has established him as one of the best drivers in the history of F1, has paralleled an astonishing personal

B. Carrington (✉)
University of Southern California, Los Angeles, CA, USA
e-mail: carringb@usc.edu

D. Sturm et al. (eds.), *The History and Politics of Motor Racing*, Global Culture and Sport Series, https://doi.org/10.1007/978-3-031-22825-4_15

transformation, from a once quietly spoken, almost shy, driver, who for the first half of his career cautiously avoided topics beyond the track, into one of the world's most politically conscious and outspoken athletes. Today Hamilton readily and regularly addresses issues ranging from environmental concerns and climate change to women's rights, to showing solidarity for gay and lesbian communities, to explicitly supporting global social movements for racial justice. Hamilton is finally finding his voice, a voice less restricted, limited and policed by the gatekeepers of his sport.

This chapter maps this change and coming to voice by tracing Hamilton's professional career alongside the wider societal shifts that have taken place during this period. I revisit earlier arguments (see Carrington, 2010)[1] wherein I read Hamilton as embodying some of the contradictions of black sporting celebrity engagement with politics. This is a form of cultural politics that has certainly challenged ethno-nationalist accounts of English identity that would otherwise exclude Britain's black and brown communities from the national imaginary, but a politics that, nonetheless, has too often been easily commodified by the dominant cultures of consumer capitalism and the allied industries of public relations, marketing and advertising (see Carrington, 2001). In this context I argue that Hamilton's emergent critical black consciousness is genuine and significant, illustrating the expanded role of athletes within the broader public sphere (Farred, 2022). This moment has resulted in a change within the cultures of not just F1 motor racing but a shift in the wider debates in England too when it comes to discussing race, racism, inequality and identity. The "case study" of Lewis Hamilton demonstrates that sport remains an important and contradictory site of popular hegemonic struggle, a contested terrain of politics.

The Black Athlete (Re)Discovers Their Voice

In the closing pages of *Race, Sport and Politics* (2010), I noted that it was an open question as to whether or not black athletes in the twenty-first century would be able to develop a critical consciousness that would recognize their power as agents of social change and the importance of sports as a modality of cultural contestation. Even if athletes came into such critical consciousness, I argued, it was unclear whether the corporatization and hyper-commercialization of neo-liberal sporting cultures would allow for the types of oppositional voices—voices that in previous historical periods within the sporting black Atlantic world had dared to challenge dominant structures—to be heard (Carrington, 2010, pp. 176–177). I concluded the book with the following sociological observation grounded in a historical reading of future potentialities:

> Black athletes have re-made sports, but not under conditions and rules of their own choosing. The extent to which sport as a racial project can once again, be used for progressive purposes will rest, in large part, on the ability of those invested in sports cultures to hold on to, develop, and articulate a critical consciousness that goes beyond the sports boundary. If that can be done, and if the black athlete can once again find the means to speak, then the 'useless' play of sport may turn out to be an important space for the realization of black dreams of freedom in the long struggle to be accorded the right to occupy the status of the human. (Carrington, 2010, p. 177)

Revisiting those words nearly a decade and a half later, it is striking how the call for black athletes to recognize the political import of sports has been answered. Briefly, a number of factors help to explain the evolving conjuncture of what might be termed a new poetics of sporting politics (Carrington, 2017). These would include the shift towards more public and explicit forms of sports anti-racism driven by various social movements, like Black Lives Matter, alongside the pervasiveness of new social media platforms (sometimes directly controlled by athletes themselves)—and of course a medium that also offers immediate forms of solidarity and support (and criticism) for athletes who do speak out through an expanded public sphere—that has enabled discussion, dissent and dissemination of ideas beyond the restricted spaces of the traditional corporate-controlled legacy sports media, together with a global media culture that elevates sports and amplifies the voices of celebrity athletes when they do decide to speak out. The conservative idea that sports and politics do not mix, and the related charge that athletes should just shut up and play, is increasingly undermined by an emerging consensus that athletes both have the right to speak out on social issues and, even further, that they should do so (Boykoff & Carrington, 2018).

This emerging new centre ground of sporting politics and the coming to voice of athletes in general and black athletes in particular needs to be contextualized. This relatively recent formation requires revisiting the pivotal moments of this shift in collective consciousness among black athletes, against and through which we can better understand both Hamilton's political maturation and his own, singular contributions to this reawakening of the black athlete. Although locating a conjunctural shift is fraught with the danger of overdetermining and misidentifying the socio-political significance of a particular event, and weighing it down with too much agentic and symbolic weight, we can, perhaps, cautiously identify the fatal shooting of the African American teenager Trayvon Martin on February 26, 2012, in Sanford, Florida, by George Zimmerman as being such a moment. Zimmerman was controversially acquitted of murder the following year, which sparked the Black Lives Matter social movement. As Jackson et al. (2020) argue in *#HashtagActivism: Networks of Race and Gender Justice*, it was the 2012 killing of Trayvon Martin, the trial and acquittal of Zimmerman and the broader public reaction to these events that helped to solidify Twitter hashtags as a crucial organizing tool for racial justice activists, directly linking public figures such as politicians and celebrities to the broader public and community activists.

As Jackson et al. (2020) note, Zimmerman was not initially charged with Martin's killing. An online petition at Change.org demanding Zimmerman's indictment, that was supported by celebrities such as director Spike Lee, actress Mia Farrow and the singer Janelle Monáe, as well as the Million Hoodie March organized by activists, helped to raise awareness of the killing, and pressure the Sanford authorities to press criminal charges. During this time "donning a hoodie" became a symbolic marker of solidarity with the Martin family.[2] Significant for this chapter's arguments, on the morning of March 23, 2012, Dwayne Wade of the Miami Heat National Basketball Association (NBA) team posted a photo of himself wearing a hooded sweatshirt ("a hoodie") to his Twitter and Facebook pages. A few hours later LeBron James posted another powerful photo of the entire Heat squad, taken at the team hotel before their game against the Detroit Pistons. The photo showed the players in their NBA gear, wearing their hoodies, heads bowed. James, perhaps the biggest star in the NBA at the time and therefore one of the highest profile black athletes in America, shared the photo on his twitter page along with the hashtags #WeAreTrayvonMartin #Hoodies #Stereotyped #WeWantJustice. ESPN later reported Wade as saying, "This situation hit home for me because last Christmas, all my oldest son wanted as a gift was hoodies … So when I heard about this a week ago, I thought of my sons. I'm speaking up because I feel it's necessary that we get past the stereotype of young, black men and especially with our youth" (ESPN, 2012). ESPN noted that numerous Heat players wrote "RIP Trayvon Martin" and "We want justice" on their sneakers when they played the Pistons later that evening. A few weeks later, on April 11, the Sanford authorities finally charged George Zimmerman with second-degree murder in the shooting death of Trayvon Martin. The following year, on July 13, 2013, and after 16 hours of deliberations over two days, a jury acquitted Zimmerman of all charges.

It would be overclaiming to suggest that the current period of black athletic revolt started with this particular intervention. Such absolute beginnings are rare. Black athletes throughout the diaspora had of course engaged in forms of cultural politics before this moment, even during the "Michael Jordan era," often seen as a period of athlete subservience to the logics of the corporate sports industries and a time of apolitical sports celebrity endorsement of products but not politics (see Andrews, 2001). However, the bold and unequivocal public intervention of high profile players like LeBron James, Dwyane Wade and Chris Bosh, and their NBA teammates, into such a highly charged situation helped to establish a new template for other athletes to speak up and out and began to shift and expand the cultural expectations of athlete engagement with issues beyond the boundary, field and court. Crucially, this project was not just confined to the borders of American sport but took on global dimensions too. In short, this coming to voice of black athletes marked a cultural rupture in the fabric of sports and challenged the dominant white culture that expected and required political silence on the part of (black) athletes up until then, a silence too many had willingly followed.

As the journalist Dave Zirin (2012) noted at the time, highlighting how significantly different the expectations of black athlete were a decade ago, including James's own truncated political consciousness, the connection between Trayvon Martin and the Miami-based NBA players was particularly meaningful. Zirin suggested that "LeBron's actions might surprise fans given that he's never publicly displayed a social conscience," before adding that LeBron had in fact signalled his desire to be the richest athlete in history and to become "a global icon like Muhammad Ali." Zirin pointed out:

> Of all teams in the league, the Heat had the greatest responsibility to step up and be heard. They were Trayvon's favorite and he was killed that late afternoon after leaving his house for a snack during half-time of the NBA All-Star game, which featured the Heat's Big Three of LeBron James, Dwyane Wade and Chris Bosh … The fact that LeBron James has used his exalted platform to speakout for Trayvon and his family even at the risk of his own bottom line, should be in these dark days, a great source of hope. Trayvon's killing has motivated millions to wake up and give a damn about what rots beneath the mini-malls, gated communities and 'security culture' that shades great swaths of our country. We all have a role to play in not only making sure there is justice for Trayvon but also in ensuring no other family or community has to suffer such a loss. If and when there is another killing rooted in fear and ignorance, we now have every right to ask LeBron, 'What are you going to say now?' That's the scary thing about choosing to give a damn. People will expect you to mean it.[3]

And mean it James and others clearly did.

In the years following this moment, an emboldened sports culture emerged in which black athletes and others, across sports, used their "exalted platforms" and engaged in forms of symbolic protest that radically altered the American sporting terrain (Carrington, 2017). To highlight just a few key cultural moments, in November 2014, members of the St Louis Rams National Football League (NFL) team entered the field before the start of the game, and dramatically paused live on national television, raising their hands in the air. This was a "hands up, don't shoot" gesture that had become a symbol for protesters following the fatal shooting of 18-year-old Michael Brown by a police officer in Ferguson, Missouri, earlier in the year. In December 2014, players throughout the NBA wore warm-up T-shirts proclaiming "I Can't Breathe." This was after the killing of Eric Garner by police in Staten Island, New York City, earlier in the summer. Garner died after a chokehold around his neck was used during his arrest. As Garner was taken to the ground, a recording caught his last words, "I can't breathe." The officers continued to restrain him and he died shortly after. In 2016, a number of Women National Basketball Association (WNBA) players from multiple teams in the league, wore "Black Lives Matter" T-shirts before their games and afterwards during their press conferences, using social media and the national press to highlight the need to address racial discrimination and injustice in U.S. society. In the same year, NFL player Colin Kaepernick protested continuing forms of police brutality and anti-black State violence by silently kneeling and raising his fist before the start of games. This powerful gesture, known as "taking a knee," came to symbolize the demand for racial justice in sports.

Significantly, the gesture of taking a knee was taken up by athletes of all ethnicities, in various sports, across the globe. Much like the raised fist and bowed head of Tommie Smith and John Carlos from the 1968 Mexico Olympics, this gesture became the iconic way to protest against social injustice through sport. In subsequent years, and especially from the summer of 2020 onwards following the murder by police officers of George Floyd, the gesture was enacted by cricket players in the Caribbean, by professional footballers, coaches and officials in England before the start of every game, and even, eventually, and, as improbable as it would have seemed in back in 2012, by Formula One racing drivers—an outcome due almost single-handedly to the actions and voice of Lewis Hamilton himself.

Hamilton, Creating the Star: A (Single) Point to Win

Lewis Hamilton entered Formula One in 2007 at the young age of 22. When he joined the McLaren team many motor racing experts doubted whether the young driver would be able to cope with the pressures of competing at the highest level of motor sport. The initial assessment was that Hamilton might achieve the odd podium finish at best, would not win any races and would use his first year gaining experience driving alongside his celebrated teammate, the Spaniard Fernando Alonso, who had just won two back-to-back world championships in 2005 and 2006. As Frank Worrall, sports journalist and author of *Lewis Hamilton: The definitive biography of the greatest racing driver of all time*, notes, he and others thought McLaren had taken a gamble and that the inexperienced Hamilton "would probably get half a season to prove himself." Worrall adds, "I also thought maybe he'd find it all too much and be shunted quietly aside, shell-shocked, perhaps back to GP2 until he was ready for the big-time with a more experienced driver stepping up to bolster Fernando Alonso's assault on a surely inevitable third World Drivers' title" (Worrall, 2021, p. 1). Establishing a narrative that for much of his career he would have to fight against, Hamilton would prove his detractors wrong as they underestimated his abilities and determination, whilst overestimating the strengths of his opponents. Exceeding others' expectations would become a defining motif for Hamilton. In the end, Alonso, the much-admired and talented Spaniard, would not win another F1 World title,[4] whilst his rookie teammate would eventually rewrite the record books of F1 and transform the sport as a result.

Given his early success in his very first season (in the first race, Hamilton finished on the podium in third place at the Australian Grand Prix) and the media attention he generated, Hamilton was immediately compared not just to highly regarded drivers such as John Surtees, Stirling Moss, James Hunt, Nigel Mansell and Damon Hill but, remarkably, to the all-time British F1 greats like Jackie Stewart, Jim Clark and Graham Hill. Profiles and commentators marvelled at Hamilton's steadfast concentration and focus and his willingness not just to learn but to excel. As Damon Hill enthused, "He's come into F1 and dealt with everything that has been thrown at him with no problem at all. He seems to be completely at home. It's as if F1 is simply the next stage in his career, a logical progression—but he's acting like there's another stage beyond F1. I've never seen anything like it" (Hamilton, 2008). British racing driver David Coulthard who retired in 2008, when asked how good Hamilton was and could be said, "Undoubtedly, the guy is very special. I'd say he is a combination of Senna and Prost. We had Senna and Prost, Mansell and Piquet, then

Michael Schumacher. We have now entered the Lewis Hamilton era" (Worrall, 2021, p. 11). The BBC commentator Murray Walker was similarly effusive stating midway through the 2007 season, "It's my considered opinion that Lewis Hamilton will go on to be one of the greatest drivers of all time … There aren't enough superlatives for what Lewis Hamilton is doing, race after race … It is unprecedented in the history of Formula One. I've been watching Formula One since it began and I have never seen anything like this in my life; it is quite incredible. It's more than feasible that he could win the Championship this year, which would be incredible" (Worrall, 2021, p. 12).

Remarkably, Hamilton started the final race in Brazil of the 2007 season leading the driver's championship, just ahead of his teammate Alonso and Ferrari's Kimi Räikkönen. Hamilton qualified in second place, making him favourite to win the title but during the race his car suffered a gearbox problem, dropping him to the back of the field. Hamilton managed to recover a number of positions, eventually finishing seventh but it was not enough. Räikkönen won the Brazil Grand Prix and in so doing amassed enough points to win his first driver's championship. Hamilton lost the tile, in his first year in F1, in the last race, by a single point. Although he had lost the drivers' championship to Räikkönen, Hamilton broke a number of records that year for a debut driver, including achieving the most consecutive podium finishes, he equalled the most wins in a debut season and he scored the most points in a season for a rookie driver. As impressive as those feats were, Hamilton also consistently equalled and occasionally outdrove his McLaren teammate, a double-world champion.[5]

Hamilton's arrival into F1 in 2007 coincided with the retirement, the year before, of Michael Schumacher, widely regarded as one of the greatest drivers to have ever competed in F1, with what seemed, at the time, an unassailable seven world championship wins. Schumacher dominated the sport from the mid-1990s all the way through until his retirement.[6] Some had even suggested that F1 had become boring with Schumacher's red Ferrari winning so often and that the sport lacked few other interesting characters that were known outside the confines of motor racing. With F1's biggest star retiring (the equivalent, perhaps, of Michael Jordan stepping away from basketball), even more attention was focused on

Hamilton. The fear among those associated with the sport was that without a celebrity sports star to compete in the global sports mediascape, F1 would fade from public interest, lose its cultural relevance and with it, the sport would struggle to attract the much needed sponsorship money and lucrative global television rights that funds the F1 travelling circus. Hamilton, then, was given the extra burden of representation that included saving the sport itself. As *The Guardian*'s Richard Williams (2007) put it at the time, "Single-handedly he [Hamilton] has restored public interest in a sport that had sunk up to the axles in its own cynicism." Similarly, Worrall suggests that Hamilton was seen as "the very saviour of a Formula One that had lost its way and no longer had the ingredients to thrill" (Worrall, 2021, p. 4). Writing in *The Times*, journalist Kevin Eason added, "Schumacher was a serial winner, but outside Germany and Italy, home of the retired former champion's Ferrari team, he was a turn-off for millions. Hamilton is pure box office … and the interest is coming from all over the world, with camera crews from places as far afield as Colombia, and Russia queuing for interviews" (Worrall, 2021, p. 8).

Hamilton ended his rookie year as a national sporting figure. He was runner up in the 2007 BBC Sports Personality of the Year (losing to the boxer Joe Calzaghe), awarded *GQ* magazine's Sportsman of the Year, *F1 Racing* magazine's Man of the Year and the British Sports Journalists' Association's Sportsman of the Year and Best International Newcomer, among many other accolades. He had silenced the figures within the sport who claimed he did not deserve to be there, and somehow had managed to keep his composure and optimism despite the devastation of coming so close to winning the drivers' championship in his first year, an achievement that was never guaranteed to occur again.[7] There are many great drivers who came close to but never actually won the drivers' championship, like Sir Sterling Moss.

The following year Hamilton continued his form, improved his racing knowledge and tyre management skills, made less mistakes and honed his craft. He ended the 2008 season with five victories and ten podium finishes. Again, as with the year before, the championship came down to the last race in São Paulo, Brazil, with Hamilton leading the championship but this time just head of Ferrari's Brazilian driver Felipe Massa. Massa needed to win the race to become champion, Hamilton needed to finish fifth or higher to be champion. Massa qualified on pole for the race, Hamilton in fourth. But a rain-affected last few laps produced what was at the time regarded as the most dramatic finish to an F1 season ever. Massa crossed the line first, giving him enough points to overtake Hamilton in the championship, with Hamilton still in sixth place on his final lap (Massa's team and family could be seen celebrating on television, along with the Brazilian fans at the race track). Yet Hamilton somehow managed to catch and pass Toyota's Timo Glock *on the last corner* of *the last lap*, thus beating Massa to the title by *a single point*. Massa would retire from F1 in 2017, without a drivers' championship.

Hamilton thus, in the most dramatic fashion, became the youngest ever Formula One champion. If his profile was rising in 2007, winning in 2008 established Hamilton as Britain's new sports star and set the stage for his emergence as a public figure and a celebrity known beyond the racing circuits.[8] He again finished second in the BBC's Sports Personality of the Year award, this time behind cyclist Chris Hoy. F1 had found its new star, and it was one who did not look like or come from the usual background of most other drivers. Hamilton was not the son of a wealthy billionaire, nor the son of a former driver. Instead, the working class, "mixed race boy from Stevenage" had become the new face of Formula One, and over time, Hamilton would in turn change the face of F1 itself.

Caribbean Roots, British Hero

The very fact that Hamilton was an F1 driver and not, say, a footballer, track athlete or boxer, meant that the earlier coverage of his career struggled to locate him within the predictable and often stereotyped narratives that tend to structure the white sports media complex's depiction of black athletes (Carrington, 2011). Hamilton came from the London satellite town of Stevenage and not the inner cities, the usual originatory birth place for so many tabloid "rags-to-riches," out of the sporting ghetto, narratives. Because of his understated demeanour and his professional respect for his rivals (think Joe Louis more than Jack Johnson), during his early career Hamilton was often described as likeable and humble. Hamilton consciously eschewing the type of "in-your-face" masculine bravado often associated with boxers and track athletes. Hamilton, the first black Formula One driver to consistently compete at the very highest level, could also be read as establishing a new model for what it meant to be black English. Put simply, there were no preexisting scripts when Hamilton first emerged for understanding the symbolic significance of a black English Formula One driver.

Undoubtedly, part of the fascination with "young Lewis" as he was often referred to in overly familial tones, derived from the sheer novelty of a black man in Formula One, one of the most exclusive and wealthy sports in the world. Despite the efforts of McLaren and its team principal Ron Dennis in particular in restricting Hamilton's media exposure and discouraging journalists from directly asking him questions about the racial significance of his achievements, "race" remained a constitutive part of the many narratives about Hamilton. Profiles of the driver often talked in metonymic terms about him being a "breath of fresh air," "irresistibly different" and "new and exciting." "Race" was both ever present and absent in the early media framings of Hamilton. As the journalist Gary Younge (2007) noted, one response underneath a YouTube posting of Hamilton's driving exploits "suggested his driving proficiency came from 'all that practice he's had nicking cars'. At other times the references are more oblique. He has been compared to Tiger Woods, Theo Walcott and Amir Khan—but rarely Nigel Mansell, James Hunt or David Beckham." Frank Worrall's biography of Hamilton includes a section where just such a comparison is made, showing both the problematic tropes of how black public figures are often framed when seen through a white gaze—clean, articulate, grateful etc.—and also Hamilton's early awareness and perhaps even discomfort with how he was being positioned in reference to others, rather than in relation to his own identity. In a chapter titled "The Real Special One," Worrall (2021, p. 8) states, discussing Hamilton:

> His impact on Formula One was both instant and remarkable, drawing comparisons to Tiger Woods and his success in the world of golf. Like Woods, Lewis was articulate, good-looking and possessed a similar talent. He had this to say on the Tiger comparisons: "It's obviously nice to be

compared to somebody like Tiger Woods but you have to remember I'm not Tiger Woods, I'm Lewis Hamilton and this is Formula One—it is not golf. Whether or not it can have a similar impact, I'm not sure. It will be good for the sport if it can. I hope my purpose here serves it place."

Earlier in his career, Hamilton stated that his role models were his father, Nelson Mandela and Martin Luther King, and his musical tastes ranging from Bob Marley and Marvin Gaye to Nas. He appeared on MTV and hung out with black artists like Pharell Williams. Hamilton, from the start, was clearly aware of his race, and the significance of becoming the first black F1 champion. As he noted, "Being black is not a negative. It's a positive, if anything, because I'm different. In the future it can open doors to different cultures and that is what motor sport is trying to do anyway. It will show that not only white people can do it, but also black people, Indians, Japanese and Chinese. It will be good to mean something" (Jacques, 2007). In his first autobiography, quickly published in 2007 to capitalize on his sudden public fame, Hamilton makes great play of the importance of his father's and therefore his own Grenadian roots, even calling it at one point his "real home" (Hamilton, 2008, p. 19). Hamilton says[9]:

I am very close to my roots—to my father's family in Grenada, West Indies, where my real home is, and to the Grenadian people. My grandad lives in Grenada and drives a private minibus … I feel close to all of that. I love Grenada: it is a beautiful country and a place where I have learned a lot … We visited Grenada every year, sometimes twice a year, and during our visits I get a real perspective on things, a better understanding of life altogether—and I realize how blessed I am. My family, my roots and our values are primarily Grenadian although we are British, having been born in the UK. My grandad came to England in the 1950s and then returned to Grenada in the seventies following the death of my grandmother. My dad has always expressed a wish to return and I plan to do the same at some stage in my life but not now. To see the kids in Grenada with smiles on their faces—even if they've got very, very little in comparison with European kids—helps me to understand and manage my way in life. So my principles are always to listen to my dad, cherish my family, compete hard and never give up. Most of all, I try to keep a smile on my face. (Hamilton, 2008, pp. 19–20)

From his entry into public life, Hamilton has clearly been proud of his Caribbean heritage and roots, embracing the values of his black paternal Caribbean lineage that he defines as grounded in values of decency, hard work and positivity. This is a well-worn narrative of migrant communities who seek to show their willingness to work hard and succeed whilst maintaining cultural bonds of attachment to the places they have come from. This is a diasporic reconfiguring and reimagining of "home." Home thus becomes a polyvocal signifier. Sometimes home is a physical place of actual return, as it was for Hamilton's grandfather, or a signifier of cultural connection and identification especially for the children of migrants (second, third etc.) for whom a return to "home" is largely symbolic (though of course still powerful) and projected into some future moment (rarely ever reached) rather than the return to the native lands of the forebears being a literal invocation and actively planned for in the present. In these moments, especially when returns are arranged around vacations, a certain nostalgic and even stereotyped narrative can emerge when depicting the simple, happy-go-lucky, poor-but-positive lives of the people and environments that are visited each year as much in the imagination as they are in actuality. In other words, Hamilton, early in his career, defined his Britishness (and therefore his black Englishness) in very open ways. Hamilton challenges ethno-nationalist ("Tebbit test")[10] conservatism that disallows the right of black and brown migrants to have such flexible, fluid and contingent identifications to their countries of origin alongside their affiliation to Britishness. It is not so much that Hamilton has to choose between being British *or* being Grenadian but that his very black Englishness is produced, in hybrid formation, from that very dialectic or claiming both identities—even as such a positionality can result in outsider-within positionalities. Never being full one thing or the other, but some new identity in formation, a process of becoming that can produce a sense of dislocation, loneliness and uncertainty.

Yet, when it comes to discussing racism (or anything much beyond his sport) the younger Hamilton displays a profound naivety that eschews any consideration of structural factors in shaping social life, and embraces a deeply conservative idea(l) of post-racial harmony reached by ignoring race, working hard and faith in our collective better humanity. For example, in his 2007 autobiography, Hamilton claims that "race" is not an issue for him and that he wishes people would simply behave better and be more polite to one another (Hamilton, 2008, pp. 21–22). He hints at "some very bad, really challenging times" (p. 20) but these experiences he says "have made me stronger" (ibid.). Religious bigotry, prejudice and anti-black racism (my terms, not his) become merely a challenge or hurdle to be learned from and stoically overcome. The sections where he (or more likely his ghost writer) obliquely discusses religion and race (race is used, rarely *racism*) are couched in the language of generalized, almost pious pronouncements: "Some people think race, or skin colour, is an issue; some think religion is. Putting it simply, I do not like to see anyone treated badly. I do not like people who do not behave well, who are not polite or who do not show respect when they should" (p. 22). Hamilton refers to the bullying he received at school and responds by learning karate so that he can defend himself but concludes that ultimately rising above the situation is what is required when confronted with intolerance, violence or racism: "I believe in doing things right and doing them properly" (p. 22). The chapter where these issues are discussed is called "Inspirations."

Lewis Hamilton: My story is instructive as much for what it tells us about the younger Hamilton's world views, views he held in his early to mid-twenties at the start of his career, as it is as a marker for how much Hamilton has grown and matured as a public figure today, into the politically conscious black athlete approaching his forties and his retirement from racing. Hamilton's 2007 uncontroversial autobiography is full of the predictable motor racing incidents and stories from his junior career and (at that moment) his short senior career. The younger Hamilton is remarkably, if unsurprisingly, apolitical. He stresses over and again that his values are rooted in "honesty, loyalty and trust" (p. 25) and contrasts this to the "politics" he and his family found in Formula One. He avoids too many details[11] and simply concludes that "politics sucks" (p. 25). Hamilton relays meeting the then Conservative leader for the first time when both appeared on the Michael Parkinson TV show: "Before I met David Cameron I was not sure what I would make of him. Normally, I don't particularly like politics but he was a really nice guy and I was incredibly impressed. He was a very interesting and genuine person and, as I found out, a great family man" (Hamilton, 2008, p. 272).

Finding His Voice, the Black Athlete Speaks

In some ways the transformation of Hamilton from an athlete who, by his own admission, did not particularly like politics, to the figure we know today is remarkable. The cautious, conservative and largely non-controversial version of the younger Hamilton should not be that surprising. Many athletes come into political consciousness as they mature, gain more control over their lives and management and develop a better understanding of the world beyond their own sporting universe. As the example of LeBron James mentioned earlier in this chapter suggests, certain events can be a catalyst for understanding and introspection on the part of athletes. Similarly, the dedicated focus, hours of practice and single-minded pursuit of success in elite sports requires a personal sacrifice few sports fans are truly aware of. Structurally speaking this tends to result in very conservative sports cultures, wherein the wider pursuit of ideas, political discussions and intellectual interests in non-sporting matters are actively discouraged by managers, coaches and agents. It is not a coincidence that elite athletes tend, for the most part, to become aware of power dynamics when either those structures of dominance force their way into the athlete's sporting lives—thus disrupting their ideological beliefs in the fairness of sports—or when an athlete is coming to the end of their career. This awareness often occurs for the very best athletes who achieve truly historic success, and therefore no longer need to validate their identities purely through the lens of sporting success because they have already achieved and exceeded their sporting goals and become more aware of wanting to shape their legacy beyond the boundary.

In a profile piece in *The Guardian*, Gary Younge observed the political and personal transformation of Hamilton that has taken place in recent years, and especially since 2020. Younge (2021) noted that Hamilton:

> has started to find a voice about his racial identity. He has been taking a knee; raising a clenched fist. Long dormant concerns about racism and discrimination have been rudely awakened following the Black Lives Matter uprisings. In the process, Hamilton has transformed the way he sees himself: from a compliant go-with-the-flow character to a change agent who is determined to make waves. He has shaped the way others see him too, going from an inoffensive, if gaffe-prone, socialite focused only on his sport, to a politically aware role model conscious of his wider cultural significance. Now, he is about to take on the sport that brought him fortune and fame, with a commission demanding racial diversity and meaningful outreach to underrepresented groups—as well as more racial equality in general.

In the interview, Hamilton revealed that part of his reticence in speaking out more, was an insecurity about how his words would be received and a lack of confidence in knowing the issues well enough to speak in an informed way. In 2011, after a series of penalty decisions had gone against him by the race stewards, Hamilton was asked if he was being targeted. He awkwardly joked, "Maybe it's because I'm Black. That's what Ali G says, I don't know" and immediately got pushback for bringing "race" into the sport. Hamilton told Younge, "It often felt that maybe I didn't speak about [race] in the right way, or wasn't great at explaining it, or maybe educated enough to talk about it … Either way, I got a lot of pushback and it seemed like more hassle than it was worth. So I reverted to just doing my talking on the track." Hamilton notes the lack of assistance he was given earlier in his career: "I was never media trained. I was just thrown into a room with people." Hamilton acknowledges the protective but insular world that his father and Ron Dennis created, that shielded him from the worst excesses of discrimination. Rarely directly confronting racism and instead turning the other cheek or using it as motivation to drive better was a strategy that worked, at least in the short term. But it came at a cost, namely a lack of self-awareness and personal growth and an internalization of racial trauma that could not find expression or be dealt with. As with many elite athletes who dedicate their pivotal teenage years to elite sport, there can also be a certain stunted maturation into adulthood, given the enclosed environment of professional sports. Hamilton admits as much when he says, "I'm probably a later bloomer, growing into my adulthood, because I'd been this kid protected by my dad for a long time. And suddenly I'm really in a man's world and I'm being asked all these questions. Everything I say is taken literally, all the mistakes are in plain sight."

That decision to just let his talking take place on the track changed after the murder of George Floyd in 2020. Shortly after Floyd's death under the knee of a Minneapolis police officer, and as Black Lives Matter protests grew across America into the largest social protests in American history, inspiring similar demonstrations across the globe, Hamilton decided to act and to call out the wider F1 community. A week after Floyd's death a clearly frustrated Hamilton wrote on Instagram, "I see those of you who are staying silent, some of you [are] the biggest of stars yet you stay silent in the midst of injustice. Not a sign from anybody in my industry, which of course is a white-dominated sport. I'm one of the only people of colour there yet I stand alone. I would have thought by now you would see why this happens and say something about it but you can't stand alongside us. Just know I know who you are and I see you." The same athlete who years before had said he didn't like politics, and for much of his career had avoided any overtly political stances, wore a Black Lives Matter T-shirt and took a knee before the Austrian Grand Prix in July. The following week he did the same, only this time he raised a fist. In what Younge describes as a heartfelt, genuine and almost confessionary statement, Hamilton revealed the impact Floyd's death and the subsequent global racial reckoning had on him:

> This wrath of emotions came up and I couldn't contain myself. I was in tears. And this stuff came up that I'd suppressed over all these years. And it was so powerful and sad and also releasing. And I thought, "I can't stay quiet. I need to speak out because there are people experiencing what I'm experiencing, or 10 times worse. Or 100 times worse. And they need me right now." And so when I did speak out, that was me letting the Black community know: "I hear you and I stand with you." (Younge, 2021)

Younge adds, correctly in my view, that while "the outrage and activism that followed Floyd's murder gave Hamilton the confidence to speak up, Black Lives Matter did not create his racial consciousness: it emboldened it" (Younge, 2021). In 2019 Hamilton had already initiated research with the Royal Academy of Engineering to better understand the underrepresentation of ethnic minorities and black people in motor sport and to come up with ways to increase representation. The Hamilton Commission as it became known was published in July 2020 with a series of specific recommendations ranging from trying to reduce school exclusions, to anti-racist curriculum design, to promoting science, technology, engineering and mathematics to students of colour. The Commission hopes to increase interest in these science topics in order to expand the pipeline of qualified candidates into the motor racing industry as a whole.

It seems it was in 2019, when Hamilton won his sixth world championship title, that he fully realized that further wins would not suffice as the measure of his personal achievements. With each world title, Hamilton grew more committed to changing F1 as a sport and society more generally. As he put it, "Over time, I've been trying to figure out my purpose. There's got to be a reason that I'm not only the only Black driver but the one at the front. And it's not just about winning. I won the world championship last year and in that year everything became visible—and I felt that my purpose was shown to me and now I'm on that journey" (Younge, 2021).

That journey has, in many ways, been a long time in coming. In 2012, when LeBron James and other African American athletes began to articulate their concerns for social justice and rediscovered the radical voice of the black athlete—a voice that seemed to have disappeared during the 1980s and 1990s—Hamilton was not among them. The significance of 2012 for Hamilton was marked not by his engagement with black politics and his growing political consciousness but by his career aspirations as he left McLaren for Mercedes that year, replacing recently retired Schumacher. The move would prove to be the pivotal one in Hamilton's career. Although his first year with Mercedes in 2013 proved difficult, with only one win in the entire season, and a fourth place finish in the drivers' championship, in the following year Hamilton would win his second world title and then an incredible five championships thereafter.[12] But as Hamilton's global profile grew and his sporting legacy became more assured with each championship, it still took a while for Hamilton to emerge as the cultural icon he is today.

The year 2017 was a transitional year for Hamilton. The year before he had lost the title to his colleague Rosberg. Hamilton clearly refocused to avoid being beaten again by his new colleague, Valtteri Botas, or anyone else for that matter. When F1 arrived in Austin in October 2017 for the U.S. Grand Prix, the world of sports was highly charged. Athletes in the U.S. and elsewhere were "taking the knee" in increasing numbers to protest racial injustice, often at great personal and professional risk. There was widespread support for quarterback Colin Kaepernick who had effectively been denied employment for his political speech by the NFL owners. Just a month before the U.S. Grand Prix, President Trump had attacked black athletes and others who protested as "sons of bitches" who deserved to be fired. Inevitably Hamilton was asked about his views and if he too would show support for Kaepernick and solidarity with the Black Lives Matter social movements. In an article for the BBC, headlined "Hamilton focused on his priority to win race amid protests," which implied an either/or approach to winning versus supporting Black Lives Matter, Hamilton was quoted as saying, "I don't plan on allowing all the BS that's surrounding the topic pull me down in my striving to win the title. While I have opinions and feelings on the situation, I have no plans to do anything" (Benson, 2017). He elaborated further, adding,

> I know a lot of people in America. I get quite a good view of what is happening here in the States and opinions about the movement, which is pretty huge. I have posted about it and I respect it highly; the movement Kaepernick started I think is awesome. I am here to win, that is my priority at the moment, so I am not really focused on anything else at the moment… It is great to see people standing up for their beliefs. Particularly with Kaepernick sacrificing his career for the greater good. Just that alone is admirable and I have huge admiration for him. It kind of puts me on the spot, what do I do? To be continued. (Benson, 2017)

This was a confused and contradictory message of support. Hamilton is clearly wrestling with the desire and urge to "do more," to take a bolder stand and to show solidarity with Kaepernick. Yet Hamilton believes that spending too much time thinking and talking about these issues will detract from his primary goal, which was to win his fourth world title. He frames Kaepernick almost as having willingly sacrificed his own career for racial justice when it had been the actions of the NFL that had taken his job away from him. Hamilton's admiration for Kaepernick's situation does not seem to extend beyond words of support. Hamilton cannot resolve the contradictions of his position. He speaks obliquely about "the situation" avoiding the language of racism and talks as if these matters are external to him, something just happening "here in the States," not, in short, his issues. He ends by noting, in generalized terms, that more is needed to be done and that he will step up, at some future point.

It is worth mentioning of course, that a burden of representation and action was being placed on Hamilton in this period. None of the white drivers were asked similar questions, as though taking anti-racist action was the preserve and responsibility of black athletes alone. We should also remember that in the years between Kaepernick's symbolic political gestures in 2016, up until the summer of 2020, most athletes did *not* feel supported or emboldened enough to take public action beyond a few more prominent athletes like Megan Rapinoe and LeBron James. Athletes that did take a stand by taking a knee were often subject to abuse, retaliation and suspensions (see Zirin, 2021). Yet by the start of the 2018 season, and ahead of the Australian Grand Prix, Hamilton began to find his voice, in part shaped and influenced by the growing, if sporadic support for Black Lives Matter and, no doubt, a continuing frustration on Hamilton's part around the lack of diversity within F1. It was, as he'd say later, a billionaire's boys club that needed to change. An emboldened Hamilton was finally beginning to call out his own sport (and even his own team Mercedes) more publicly and directly than he had done before. In a 15-second video recorded from the Mercedes hospitality suite, Hamilton showed a number of people in the paddock, with a message: "There is barely any diversity in F1, still nothing's changed in 11 years I've been here. Kids, people, there are so many jobs in this sport of which anybody, no matter their ethnicity or background, can make it and fit in. #diversity #ucandoit."

To his earlier response to the reporters in Austin, Texas in 2017, "It kind of puts me on the spot, what do I do? To be continued," Hamilton was now using his platform to put the sport of F1 and the rest of society on the spot instead. And with each victory and each championship Hamilton seemed to gather more confidence to speak more directly and loudly without the cautious and conciliatory tone that he had been told, up until this period, was the only way for him to be accepted and heard. Now Hamilton had found his voice, and was demanding to be heard.

Conclusion: Keep on Movin'

> I've been winning these championships, being so single minded with that, winning them and thinking, 'What does it actually really mean?' We now live in a time when, who would have thought the whole movement with Black Lives Matter would happen? It brought up a lot of emotions for me that I experienced as a kid and even as an adult, the racial abuse I experienced, it brought up a lot of that. (Lewis Hamilton)

The British newspaper coverage on Monday 13, 2021, was near unanimous in its verdict on what had transpired the day before in Abu Dhabi. *The Daily Mail* carried a front page colour photo of Hamilton, looking tired but contemplative as he wiped sweat from his head, next to the headline "Robbery at 200mph," whilst its back page headline read "Grand Theft Auto! Fury as Lewis robbed of eighth world title—now Mercedes set to go to court to overturn result." Inside the *Mail*'s chief sports writer Martin Samuel added "It was a stolen title—by the stewards, by the race director, by the need for drama … in Abu Dhabi, Formula One crossed the divide between competition and the reality shows" (Samuel, 2021, pp. 64–65). The headline of *The Daily Telegraph*'s sports section read: "Hamilton 'robbed'." *The Daily Telegraph's* chief sports writer similarly echoed the same sentiments the next day with an article titled "No escaping injustice of last-lap head-to-head," with Wilson adding, "Good television? Maybe. But fair? Just? Not in the slightest." Owen Slot of *The Times* suggested that whilst Hamilton may have lost on the track, the perceived unfairness of the result by many may turn out to be a victory for Hamilton in the court of public opinion, helping him to be more appreciated than he had been up until that moment: "Whichever corner you are in, though, whether you are Lewis or Max, establishment or revolution, there is one result that cannot be changed by any lawyers or hastily arranged appeals courts, and that is that the Abu Dhabi Grand Prix was a kind of win for Hamilton. For sure, it was not the victory he wanted, but did the court of public opinion ever decide so heavily in his favour?" (Slot, 2021, p. 65).

A range of right wing newspapers, normally critical if not outright dismissive of the types of social justice issues Hamilton has promoted, were reflecting a widely held sentiment that Hamilton had been unfairly denied his record-breaking eighth world title and that he acted with grace and dignity in congratulating Verstappen and his father after the race. *The Sun*, noted that Hamilton had failed to be included in the BBC's shortlist for Sportsperson of the Year. This, they suggested was an outrage. Not only had Hamilton confirmed his status as the best F1 driver of all time, even with this defeat, he was now being talked about as Britain's greatest ever athlete.

In an extraordinary week for Hamilton on Wednesday, 15 December, and as Sunday's controversial race continued to be discussed, Hamilton was made a Knight Bachelor by (then) Prince Charles. All the major English newspapers carried colour photos of Hamilton, kneeling in front of Prince Charles. Hamilton attended the ceremony with his mother.

Sir Lewis Hamilton occupies a unique position in British cultural life. He is, by any reasonable metric of comparison, one of the best F1 drivers in the history of the sport and arguably the greatest British athlete of all time. He has talked with passion about growing up in a working-class family, and the forms of exclusion for those not a part of the "billionaire's boys club." Yet there is also a lingering exclusion from the (white) imagined community of British sports stars that continues to refuse to fully embrace Hamilton, despite his accomplishments. Joseph Harker (2014) has previously argued,

> I suspect the racing great Stirling Moss touched the underlying issue when he was quoted in the *Telegraph* saying of Hamilton: 'He was one of the racing crowd before, and now he's whatever you call those superstars. And that's not really the way we English go. We're more reserved.' Can someone like Hamilton ever be accepted as doing things the way 'we English' do? ...

> For all the huge achievements of black sportsmen and women, it seems the public still struggle to accept them.

Harker adds, "Ultimately, Lewis deserves recognition because his success goes far beyond sport itself. But if he never gains national acceptance through the sports personality vote, it will say more about Britain than about him." That was written in 2014, before Hamilton's coming of age as an athlete-activist but also before the controversial final lap of the 2021 season. Whether the (white) public perception and opinion of Hamilton has changed remains to be seen and a mute point if it implies Hamilton having to accommodate to the views *of* him rather than the other way around. Regardless, Hamilton has changed, and for the better. He is publicly committed to changing motor sports, even if the key actors within the sport try to resist meaningful change beyond issuing tokenistic hashtag campaigns, and sharing short promotional videos on eradicating racism, "racing as one," and embracing diversity and sustainability, that are not connected to meaningful action items.

As I argued earlier in the chapter, black athletes have re-made sports, but not under conditions and rules of their own choosing. Sports can operate as racial projects for social change, affecting and shifting racial formations in progressive directions once athletes are able to articulate a critical consciousness that goes beyond the sports boundary. The "useless" play of sport has proven to be an important space for the realization of black dreams of freedom in the long struggle to be accorded the right to occupy the status of the human. As improbable as it may have sounded a decade or more ago, Hamilton has become a change agent himself, using his platform to raise awareness of various social issues, calling for justice for people killed by anti-black violence, and encouraging his social media followers, as he did in 2020, to read texts by authors and writers such as Afua Hirsch, Malcolm X, Paul Gilroy, Maya Angelou and David Olusoga, among others.

If Hamilton is able to engage with the conversations currently taking place between political activists and black intellectuals, then he will continue to be a figure regarded in the same company of not just the best motor racing drivers of all time, nor even as one of Britain's greatest sportsmen, but as a truly historic figure of the black Atlantic world. "I remember not being able to be myself" Hamilton reflected in his interview with Gary Younge:

> Of not being able to speak the way I want to speak. That's the point of all this inclusivity: including people and not asking them to change in order to fit. I remember feeling that I had to be a different shape. The entry point to my sport was a square and I was like a hexagon, and I thought, 'I'm never going to fit through that bloody thing.' So I had to morph my way in in order to fit into that world, and then try to get back into the shape I was before. (Younge, 2021)

Hamilton is finally reaching a point where he is comfortable with his own shape, his own skin, without having to contort himself to fit into the all-white, class-exclusive worlds where he has developed his professional trade. Having taken these significant steps over the past few years, it will be interesting to see if he is able to keep walking in this forward, progressive direction, to truly find his own voice and develop a more holistic understanding of the issues he has committed to addressing. That last step would require that he is able to make connections between the structuring effects of racism, gender exclusion and discrimination, and environmental degradation, all issues he has spoken powerfully about, with a critique of the global economic system and the related, interconnected, class inequalities that capitalism produces. This would be a move beyond the necessary but limited liberal tropes of inclusion and diversity towards a deeper and more radical understanding of exploitation and transformative justice. A question he may want to return to then is the one he posed to himself back in 2017: "It kind of puts me on the spot, what do I do? To be continued."

Notes

1. This chapter draws upon and updates an earlier argument on Lewis Hamilton, see Carrington (2010, Chapter 4) Sporting Multiculturalism: Nationalism, Belonging and Identity.

2. Trayvon Martin was wearing a hoodie when he was killed, leading a number of conservative and far right commentators to suggest that this item of clothing (the hoodie) was a menacing sign of (black) deviancy. The right claimed that Martin's decision to put his hoodie on had contributed to Zimmerman wrongly but understandably believing that Martin was engaged in potential criminal activity and was thus a threatening body out of place in that particular neighbourhood, despite this being the area in which Martin actually lived.
3. In 2018, in an interview with CNN's Don Lemon, when asked about his political consciousness and desire to use his platform to engage in social issues beyond the court, James himself remarked, "I think it starts with the Trayvon Martin situation and the reason it starts with that, I believe is because having kids of my own—having boys of my own—it hit home for me to see and to learn the story and to think that if my boy left home and he never returned. That kinda hit a switch. From that point on, I knew that my voice and my platform had to be used for more than just sports."
4. At the time of writing (March 2023), Alonso is still driving competitively in F1 having signed a new contract with Aston Martin, likely his last contract, that runs from 2023 until 2025. Despite a promising start to the 2023 season where Alsono outperformed his Mercedes and Ferrari rivals, most F1 commentators believe it is unlikely that Aston Martin will compete for either the drivers' or constructors' championships during this time.
5. Alonso would leave McLaren in 2009 and join Ferrari in 2010, replacing Räikkönen.
6. Three years later in 2010, Schumacher would return to F1, joining Mercedes for two seasons, before finally retiring in 2012, aged 43. His brief comeback was relatively unsuccessful, securing just one podium finish and no victories. He finished his career with 91 race wins, across 19 seasons, another benchmark that few thought would ever be matched and which Hamilton has now surpassed. Interestingly, 2012 was when Hamilton decided to leave McLaren and join Mercedes, effectively replacing Schumacher, a decision many thought was a mistake given how Mercedes, up until then, had struggled to be competitive with the top teams. If Schumacher (albeit an aging Schumacher) had been unable to extract the best from Mercedes, how could Hamilton? At the time Schumacher philosophically reminisced on the end of his career and the

continuation of Hamilton's, when he said, "We did not achieve our goals to develop a world championship-fighting car, but it is also very clear that I can still be very happy about my overall achievements in the whole time of my career … In the past six years, I have learned a lot about myself. For example, that you can open yourself without losing focus, that losing can be both more difficult and more instructive than winning … Sometimes in life your destiny will develop by itself, without any hard feelings and without any regrets. … We all know Lewis is one of the best drivers we have around and I cross fingers that we will have a successful future" (BBC, 2012). A year later, on December 29, 2013, Schumacher suffered a severe head injury following a skiing accident. He was placed in a medically induced coma for 250 days and brought out of the coma in June 2014. Schumacher remains alive but his family have kept his health condition secret. Schumacher has not been seen in public since 2013. His son Mick, who was with his father at the time of the skiing accident, is now an F1 driver too.

7. In his 2007 autobiography *Lewis Hamilton: My story*, Hamilton writes, "To finish second at the end of my first season, as a rookie, in Formula One was certainly no failure, but I could not deny I felt a sense of disappointment to have gone so close to taking the title. I was four points ahead at the start of the day and suffered mechanical problems and bad luck at the wrong time. It was not a sweet moment! But I had to take the positives from it and look ahead to 2008" (pp. 265–266).
8. By chance, Hamilton won the championship on Sunday, November 2, 2008. Thus, on the Monday, many writers in the British press made direct connections to the U.S. Presidential election, taking place in the next day. For example, *The Daily Mirror* wondered if it was a "good omen" that "a young, charismatic black man has shown resilience, skill and determination to win against the odds. Now roll on Barack Obama" (*Daily Mirror*, November 3rd, 2008, p. 10), while Aida Edemariam (2008) in *The Guardian* somewhat hyperbolically mused whether the week would be the greatest ever in black history. Even the right-wing newspaper *The Sun* extolled the significance of the "first black world motor racing champion" in its leader, praising Hamilton, who earlier in the season had to deal with racist Spanish fans, donning black face and mocking his family. Yet, *the Sun* noted, in paternalistic fashion, Hamilton had shown great humility throughout his ordeals and was a true role model and national hero: "It's hard to believe he's done all this at 23. He

has years yet to achieve so much more. Lewis Hamilton is a true superstar on the world stage. We're proud he's ours."

9. As with most autobiographies written by athletes, especially when they are still competing, it is unlikely that Hamilton actually wrote much, if any, of the *Lewis Hamilton: My story*. Nearly all biographies of celebrities are "ghost written," sometimes with the real writer's actual name on the front of the book, normally in much smaller font, or acknowledged inside the text. Hamilton's 2007 "autobiography"—which, as he states, is really "an account of my career to date than an autobiography of my life—I'm too young for that!"—includes the following final sentence in the acknowledgements: "I am grateful to Timothy Collins and his team for assisting me with the writing of *My Story*." That said, for the purposes of this chapter, I will refer to and quote from his text as if he had written the words himself. No doubt Hamilton would have agreed to the wording and perhaps even copyedited the final manuscript before publication.
10. In 1990 the conservative politician Norman Tebbit suggested that a "test" of the loyalty to the nation of Britain's South Asian and Caribbean communities was whether or not they cheered for the England men's cricket team in Test matches against their respective countries of origin. If they supported England they had successfully assimilated, if they supported, say, the West Indies, India or Pakistan, then they were being disloyal British subjects. Tebbit made no such demand of white Australians, New Zealanders or South Africans who had migrated back to the U.K. This requirement of black and brown migrants to prove their loyalty (remembering of course that nearly all of these "migrants" were already British subjects and that Britain is by definition itself a multinational state) subsequently became known as "the Tebbit test."
11. At the time McLaren had been accused of stealing secrets from their main rival Ferrari (so-called spy gate) and McLaren and Ron Dennis were later found guilty of doing so and fined $100 million by the Fédération Internationale de l'Automobile (FIA).
12. Hamilton lost to his teammate Nico Rosberg in 2016. Rosberg retired immediately after. Hamilton controversially lost again to Red Bull's Max Verstappen in 2021, after a contentious decision by the race director, Michael Massi, who altered the rules at the very end of the race to ensure that Verstappen, on fresher tyres, would be directly behind Hamilton at the restart. Hamilton was inevitably overtaken at turn five on the very last lap of the season's final race and lost the championship and with it the chance to surpass Schumacher's seven titles.

References

Andrews, D. (Ed.). (2001). *Michael Jordan, Inc.: Corporate Sport, Media Culture, and Late Modern America*. SUNY Press.

Benson, A. (2017, October 19). *Formula 1: Hamilton focused on his priority to win race amid protests*. BBC. https://www.bbc.co.uk/sport/formula1/41688327

Boykoff, J., & Carrington, B. (2018, January 10). Winter Olympics 2018: The Latest Battleground between Athletes and Trump? *The Guardian*. https://www.theguardian.com/sport/blog/2018/jan/10/2018-winter-olympics-protests-donald-trump-lindsey-vonn

Carrington, B. (2001). Postmodern Blackness and the Celebrity Sports Star: Ian Wright, 'Race', and English Identity. In D. Andrews & S. Jackson (Eds.), *Sport Stars: The Cultural Politics of Sporting Celebrity* (pp. 102–123). Routledge.

Carrington, B. (2010). *Race, Sport and Politics: The Sporting Black Diaspora*. Sage.

Carrington, B. (2011). What I Said Was Racist—But I'm Not a Racist': Anti-Racism and the White Sports/Media Complex. In J. Long & K. Spracklen (Eds.), *Sport and Challenges to Racism* (pp. 83–99). Palgrave Macmillan.

Carrington, B. (2017). Raced Bodies and Black Cultural Politics. In M. Silk, D. Andrews, & H. Thorpe (Eds.), *Routledge Handbook of Physical Cultural Studies* (pp. 132–142). Routledge.

Edemariam, A. (2008, November 4). A Great Week in Black History? *The Guardian*. https://www.theguardian.com/world/2008/nov/04/race-lewis-hamilton-barack-obama

ESPN. (2012, March 23). *Heat don hoodies after teen's death*. https://www.espn.co.uk/nba/truehoop/miamiheat/story/_/id/7728618/miami-heat-don-hoodies-response-death-teentrayvon-martin

Farred, G. (2022). *Only A Black Athlete Can Save Us Now*. University of Minnesota Press.

Hamilton, L. (2008). *Lewis Hamilton: My Story*. Harper Collins.

Harker, J. (2014, November 24). Lewis Hamilton's Lack of Popularity: Is It Cos He Is Black? *The Guardian*. https://www.theguardian.com/commentisfree/2014/nov/24/lewis-hamilton-lack-popularity-black-formula-1-champion

Jackson, S., Bailey, M., & Welles, D. (2020). *#HashtagActivism: Networks of Race and Gender Justice*. MIT Press.

Jacques, M. (2007, October 22). A New Hero for Our Times. *The Guardian*. https://www.theguardian.com/commentisfree/2007/oct/22/comment.race

Samuel, M. (2021, December 12). Max Verstappen's Last Lap Triumph over Lewis Hamilton in Abu Dhabi was a STOLEN Title … By the Stewards, the Race Director Michael Masi and By Formula One's Need for Drama. *The Daily Mail*. https://www.dailymail.co.uk/sport/formulaone/article-10302393/MARTIN-SAMUEL-Max-Verstappens-triumph-Lewis-Hamilton-STOLEN-title.html

Slot, O. (2021, December 14). Arise Sir Lewis Hamilton—A Victor in the Court of Public Opinion. *The Times*. https://www.thetimes.co.uk/article/arise-sir-lewis-hamilton-a-victor-in-the-court-of-public-opinion-5mbpmpthh

Williams, R. (2007, October 22). Novice Pays the Price for Youth but Will be One for the Ages. *The Guardian*. https://www.theguardian.com/sport/2007/oct/22/motorsports.comment

Worrall, F. (2021). *Lewis Hamilton: The Definitive Biography of the Greatest Racing Driver of All Time*. Bonnier Books.

Younge, G. (2007, June 16). Made in Stevenage. *The Guardian*. https://www.theguardian.com/uk/2007/jun/16/formulaone.sport

Younge, G. (2021, July 10). Lewis Hamilton: 'Everything I'd Suppressed Came Up—I Had to Speak Out'. *The Guardian*. https://www.theguardian.com/sport/2021/jul/10/lewis-hamilton-everything-id-suppressed-came-up-i-had-to-speak-out

Zirin, D. (2012, March 25). Trayvon Martin's Death, LeBron James and the Miami Heat. *The Nation*. https://www.thenation.com/article/archive/trayvon-martins-death-lebron-jamesand-miami-heat/

Zirin, D. (2021). *The Kaepernick Effect: Taking a Knee, Changing the World*. The New Press.

Part VI

Motor Racing, the Media, and Postmodernity

Formula One as Television

Damion Sturm

Introduction

Essentially repackaged for the medium, Formula One has had a close and enduring history with television. This chapter explores and unpacks the relationship Formula One forged with television, particularly with regard to the prominence Bernie Ecclestone placed on producing a compelling global media product that could be monetised in the form of lucrative broadcasting rights. A history of ad hoc and sporadic television coverage is traced via developments in the United Kingdom, wherein only occasional races were broadcast live. Our attention then turns to Ecclestone's efforts to both streamline the sport and make Formula One more globally and commercially appealing, particularly through a television broadcast that was consistently high in production values, as well as profitable for the sport. To further interrogate the fundamental role and significance of television for Formula One, key notions of Formula One as a media event

D. Sturm (✉)
School of Management, Massey University, Albany, New Zealand
e-mail: D.Sturm@massey.ac.nz

D. Sturm et al. (eds.), *The History and Politics of Motor Racing*, Global Culture and Sport Series, https://doi.org/10.1007/978-3-031-22825-4_16

and as a media spectacle are then developed. Pertinently, there is an exploration of the specific technologies, techniques and transformations deployed to construct and disseminate Formula One as an engaging contemporary media representation.

Reflective of contemporary developments, consideration is then given to the tensions that have accompanied Formula One's broader shift to forms of pay television during the 2010s. These have occurred both at the expense of free-to-air television and its larger audiences, as well as within a broader context that seems to foreshadow the demise of television and traditional media forms. Finally, a dramatic reorientation towards digital and social media has emerged since Liberty Media acquired Formula One in 2017. This takeover has had significant implications for the future of the sport, with Liberty Media both consolidating the pay television model and diversifying and growing the sport across new media platforms, which include eSports, live streaming, social media and Netflix. First, however, an introduction to Formula One is provided to better understand its global and commercial prominence, as well as to trace its impact and significance as a contemporary media sport.

Introducing Formula One

Formula One is viewed as the pinnacle of auto racing (if not all motorsport), with expensive, sophisticated and hi-tech machines raced at global locations (23 races are planned for 2023). This generates widespread media and audience interest, as well as substantial funding from large transnational corporations who adorn the cars and drivers with their sponsors' logos (Sturm, 2014). Thus, Formula One is clearly a major sporting event while thematically being underpinned by varying elements of commercialisation, corporatisation, innovative mediation, prestige and popular status that, collectively, make it a significant contemporary global sporting competition. Predominantly, the sport makes its money via television (and other media) rights, via hosting rights, as well as track and title sponsors, and through live attendance, while the teams rely on transnational corporate sponsors (Sturm, 2014).

Currently Formula One is disseminated to approximately 500 million television viewers across 185 countries (Sylt, 2020a), with broadcast rights for television (and streaming services) worth approximately $600 million annually (Saward, 2013). Moreover, the sport cost over US$2 billion per season to stage in the 2000s (Sturm, 2014), with more recent budget caps being enforced. For 2022, the budget cap per team is set at $140 million, although Anderson (2022) argues that, due to a range of exclusions, "for a top team you could easily still be talking about an overall budget of $350m+ just to put two cars on the grid on a Sunday afternoon" (para. 4). Additionally, with localities paying over US$400 million annually to obtain host-nation status (Lefebvre & Roult, 2011), the sport has also expanded beyond its European origins to Asia and the Middle East (Bromber & Krawietz, 2013; Silk & Manley, 2012), progressively rising from approximately 16 races in the 1990s to between 19 and 23 races in recent times.

Arguably these orientations are 'grobal' (i.e., imperialistic) rather than global, in that they reflect the ambition of Formula One to realise economic and media interests in non-traditional locales (Andrews & Ritzer, 2007). The localities also harvest the global prestige and reach of Formula One, using the sport's media and marketing platform as symbols of progress and pride and to boost tourism (John & McDonald, 2020; Lowes, 2018; Silk & Manley, 2012). For the 2020 and 2021 seasons, Formula One had to postpone, cancel and/or reschedule a range of races (often without crowds) due to the disruptions caused by the global COVID-19 pandemic. As a result, Baldwin (2021) estimates that Formula One experienced a 43% drop and lost approximately (US)$877 million due to the pandemic.

Nevertheless, new races were staged in the Netherlands (predominantly due to the star power of Dutch driver Max Verstappen) as well as the non-traditional sites of Saudi Arabi and Qatar for the first time in 2021. However, these new events were not without controversy. While clearly financially lucrative for Formula One given the global pandemic (Baldwin, 2021), the money paid to stage the two new Middle Eastern races (both signing ten-year contracts) was criticised, with Saudi Arabia allegedly paying £500 million to be a host nation (McEvoy, 2020). Additionally, both nations were accused of using Formula One as a form of sportswashing in light of perceived issues around human rights and gender equality (McManus & Amara, 2021; 2023). More broadly, a renewed scrutiny surrounding the environmental impact of global motorsport has also been to the fore (Miller, 2017; see chapter "Motor Sport in the Middle East: Regional Rivalries, Business and Politics in the Arabian Gulf"), with notable concerns raised for the Dutch Grand Prix's impact on its surrounding coastal sand-dunes (Crebolder, 2022).

Formula One: Media Origins and Evolution

As Frandsen (2014) reminds us, many sports were developed in unison with modern mass media, particularly as "newspapers would organise sports events in order to both build up interest in the sports and consumption of the papers" (p. 531). With motorsport dating back to France in the 1890s—historians dispute whether the 1894 Paris to Rouen event was a race or mere reliability trial for the 1895 Paris to Bordeaux race (Rendall, 2000)—newspapers were quick to capitalise on the appeal of this new sport. For example, owner of the *New York Herald*, American James Gordon Bennett, sponsored the annual Gordon Bennett Cup for motor-races staged in Europe between 1900 and 1905, a forerunner of the first 'Grand Prix' of 1906 (Rendall, 2000). Additional and irregular races were staged at various venues throughout Europe during the early twentieth century, including the Monaco Grand Prix from 1929 which, by offering a prize money of 100,000 francs for the winning driver, gave the event prestige, glamour and status (Sturm, 2017). Based upon the European Grand Prix series of the 1920s and 1930s, the first fully sanctioned and official Formula One World Championship was established in 1950, commencing in Silverstone, England, with seven 'official' races that also included the Monaco Grand Prix and Indianapolis 500 (Sturm, 2017).

Over time, the history of Formula One would be shaped by media and commercial influences that became more pronounced in later coverage. During Formula One's formative years the grid consisted primarily of individuals, known as privateers and enthusiasts, who raced in their national colours and manufactured their own cars (Rendell, 2000).

However, the complexion of the sport would change in the late 1960s with the advent of tobacco and other sponsor liveries (e.g., corporate colours and logos) adorning the cars, as well as the increased involvement of car manufacturers. Since the 1990s, the sport has become explicitly corporate in its make-up, design and operation (Sturm, 2014; see also chapters “Formula One as Television”: Motor Racing on Film” and “The Shifting Landscape of Sponsorship Within Formula 1”).

In addition, Formula One had been run haphazardly from 1950 until the early 1980s due to the fluctuating numbers of teams and cars per race, as well as the races themselves being independently run (Hotten, 1999). This inconsistency was also reflected in the media coverage at the time with, for example, either the British Broadcasting Corporation (BBC) or Independent Television (ITV) covering only a handful of races in the United Kingdom—notably the British or Monaco Grands Prix. Indeed, despite the BBC broadcasting the 1953 British Grand Prix as the first live race in Britain (Haynes & Robeers, 2020), coverage remained sporadic at best until the mid-1970s.

Additionally, most often broadcasts were highlight packages or provided as delayed or even relayed coverage, with commentators commenting on global trackside coverage from the BBC’s London studios (Walker, 2002). Haynes and Robeers (2020) note that Formula One only gained consistent interest and coverage on the BBC from approximately 1974 due to the star power of James Hunt (the 1976 World Champion and later commentator for the BBC) and commercial sponsorship of the cars, while the BBC secured exclusive broadcasting rights from 1979. Surprisingly, it would not be until 1996 that the BBC first provided live, comprehensive televised coverage of a complete Formula One season for its British and global audiences (Hotten, 1999).

Bernie Ecclestone would become a significant figure in the mediatisation of Formula One, specifically by negotiating the global television rights to the sport. Initially a used car salesman and part-time racer, Bernie Ecclestone turned his interests to Formula One, managing drivers before purchasing the Brabham team in 1971. Ecclestone sensed the commercial possibilities for the sport and, through his position as head of the Formula One Constructors’ Association (FOCA), took on the role of organising and negotiating for all the British teams in order to streamline the sport into a single world championship series. Hotten (1999) suggests "Ecclestone's masterstroke was to promise circuit owners a full grid of teams; teams had to commit themselves to a full season of racing. This pleased the crowds, it pleased the sponsors, and it pleased the television stations" (p. 29). However, infighting still dogged Formula One, with the British teams (FOCA) and the Federation Internationale du Sport Automobile (FISA, the sports arm of the governing body, the Fédération Internationale de l'Automobile [FIA]) squabbling over control of the sport.

Ecclestone's decisive moment was at the 1981 South African Grand Prix when he obtained television coverage and several million viewers for the race in which only FOCA teams competed. This prompted many of the FISA-aligned teams to side with Ecclestone, and he was made vice-president of the FIA that year. Most importantly, however, Ecclestone was made responsible for negotiating worldwide television rights. Years later, in an interview with Henry (1998), Ecclestone commented:

> It was only when I began to get fully involved in the whole scene that I appreciated just how fragmented the television coverage had been. Some people covered a few races, some none at all. My initial motivation was to get the whole business together in an effort to get some decent overall coverage. (p. 16)

By the end of the 1980s, now no longer a team owner, Ecclestone had taken on the role of Formula One's commercial rights holder (leasing these rights for 100 years) through his company Formula One Management (FOM), while his long-time associate, Max Mosley, became FIA president in 1991.

Ecclestone and FOM continued to develop Formula One as a commercial and global brand through a variety of ventures which enticed large companies to finance the sport, such as trackside or title sponsorships for races, or by paying lavish sums to host an event (with many host nations also obtaining government funding to do so). Arguably more significant for the sport's commercial and global success was Ecclestone's handling of broadcasting rights for Formula One, with Ecclestone ensuring a television feed that was strong on production values and highly sought after by an array of global networks. Broadcasting rights were profitable for FOM, as is evident in Ecclestone's transference of the exclusive television rights in Britain from the BBC to ITV in 1997 which, allegedly, increased from £7 million in value to an estimated £60 million (Hotten, 1999; Walker, 2002).

Ecclestone (and FOM) also exerted a major influence across Formula One at all levels, safeguarding the sport through licences and other arrangements to ensure a positive image and global brand (Hotten, 1999). For example, Ecclestone also bought *Formula 1 Magazine* late in 2002, although this would cease publishing in 2004 with Turner (2004) suggesting that the magazine "began to resemble an in-flight brochure in which many articles contained a barely concealed business agenda" (pp. 204-205). Similar criticisms could also be raised for the launch of *formula1.com* in 2003, which was also too focused on self-promotional and sponsor-intensive content (Sturm, 2014). Conversely, early iterations of the 'live timing' function on the website were an invaluable data source for race fans, providing a numeric 'real-time' representation of driver's lap and sector times from all Grand Prix sessions to complement the television broadcast.

Nevertheless, FOM remained blind, if not doggedly resistant, to other digital media possibilities. With a myopic focus solely on television broadcasting rights, FOM rigorously policed and forcibly removed copyrighted Formula One-related clips online (e.g., *YouTube*) while attempting to control other forms of social media during the 2010s (Sturm, 2014). The takeover of Formula One by Liberty Media in 2017 for $4.6 billion would be significant for revamping Formula One's media profile, as well as for future-proofing the sport (Sylt, 2020b; see also chapter "Neoliberal Interpellation in the F1 2018 Video Game" on Formula ownership and Liberty Media). Through Liberty Media, Formula One began to realise and embrace aspects of digital media, as well as to diversify its 'traditional' media offerings—points we will return to in due course.

Formula One as Media Event

As noted above, Formula One was repackaged "as an event *for* the media" (Sturm, 2014, p. 69) in the 1980s to help streamline what had largely been a haphazard and disjointed series with fluctuating numbers of teams and cars per race. The notion of media events was first traced by Dayan and Katz (1992) as a recurrent series of ritual-like events that comprised 'contests, conquests and coronations' (inclusive of sport). The overtly mediatised nature of most contemporary events, inclusive of sport, means that often they are re-conceptualised as a set of mediatised experiences for attendees and for spectators. Therefore, repackaged via collective and individualistic forms of connectivity, co-creation and personalisation, many sport events are potentially reduced to an 'app', digital experience or as shareable media content (Andrews & Ritzer, 2018; Hutchins, 2019; Lawrence & Crawford, 2019; Majumdar & Naha, 2020).

Formula One as Media Spectacle

Kellner (2003) posits that there has been a significant temporal and cultural shift from media events to media spectacles, noting how events, while laden with myths and rituals, are often usurped by and reshaped through the media as spectacles. Kellner (2010) suggests, media spectacles "involve an aesthetic dimension and are often dramatic...They are highly public social events, often taking a ritualistic form to celebrate society's highest values...media spectacles are increasingly commercialized, vulgar, glitz, and...important arenas of political contestation" (p. 76). Collectively, sport events are often drawing upon a rich tradition of history, myth and ritual that are also embedded and infused in this projection of sport as spectacle. Kellner is also cognisant of the convergence of media, technologies, entertainment and commercialisation required to continually reproduce the event as spectacle. Therefore, these media transformations predominantly comprise the spectacular, seductive and sensationalised when representing events, using dazzling representations and excessive displays to amplify the projection and circulation of images (Kellner, 2003).

In this way, many sport and non-sport events construct image-based realities (Baudrillard, 2002) whereby the media are not only influential in terms of re-presenting or re-shaping the sport but, potentially, replace or become the sport. According to Baudrillard (1983), the endless circulation of an abundance of images distorts reality to the point where everything has become simulation or the simulacra: "the generation by models of a real without origin or reality: a hyperreal" (p. 2). Hence, most contemporary sport is re-created and reconfigured via an assemblage of simulated and seductive image-based media representations that are transposed onto hyperreal screens of excess for consumption (Andrews & Ritzer, 2018; Lawrence & Crawford, 2019; Wenner & Billings, 2017).

Relating Baudrillard's and Kellner's arguments to Formula One, Sturm (2014) asserts that its media spectacle comprises a *glamorous and hi-tech global spectacle of speed.* Such a media focus merges and repackages Formula One's global, commercial and mediatised dynamics around technology and 'glamour' through media representations that are dazzling, seductive and alluring. Using the Monaco Grand Prix as a striking exemplar, Sturm (2017) suggests that the race projects "an assemblage of iconic global images that are suggestive of wealth, prestige, elitism and symbols of excess (for example, celebrities, yachts, fashion, jewellery and stereotypically beautiful females)" (177). Such depictions also playfully evoke Formula One's allegedly 'glamorous' elements, albeit, while problematically referencing the largely outdated gender dynamics still underpinning the sport (Sturm, 2021). We will now probe Formula One as both media event and media spectacle by unpacking its televised representation which, via specific techniques and technologies, constructs this *glamorous and hi-tech global spectacle of speed* as a seductive, hyperreal and dazzling display of excess.

Formula One as Televised Media Representation

As media spectacles, Formula One events are carefully crafted to furnish forms of sensory engagement with media representations of speed, risk, drivers and hi-tech machines that are often beyond our real-world experiences or opportunities (such as driving at over 200mph in hybrid rocket cars). For example, Sturm (2017) analyses how the Monaco Grand Prix and Indianapolis 500, both iconic events on the global motor-racing calendar, are transformed through re-presentations of immediacy, liveness and close proximity to the racing action in what, at times, can otherwise become processional or monotonous motorsport events.

Fundamentally, Formula One as media spectacle strives to inform, entertain and retain its large global media audience. Thus, projections of the speed and drama of the racing spectacle are transformed via an entertaining assemblage of television technologies, techniques and production practices. Formula One's speed and danger are re-presented through 20–30 diverse camera placements and perspectives (e.g., trackside, helicopters, cranes, wall mounted), with rapid transitions and frequent intercutting between dramatic angles, long shots and close proximity framing (Sturm, 2017). Since 2007, FOM has controlled race telecasts through a 'world feed' that both maintains its consistently high production values and removes the previous especial focus given to local drivers by local directors (Sturm, 2014). Representationally, the coverage addresses Whannel's (1992) "highly mobile ideal spectator" (p. 98), affording a 'perfect view' for television viewers via continuous trackside transitions and perspectives not available to live attendees. Additionally, the telecast is anchored in 'realism', with the actuality of a race unfolding at a distinct location encoded via the aura of immediacy and liveness to inform the global television audience (Whannel, 1992).

Specifically, a range of techniques and technologies provide mobile, fluid and immersive representations of the racing spectacle. These oscillating techniques render experiential elements of the 'live' first-hand event as witnessed by in-situ spectators (Billings, 2010), furnish all-seeing perspectives of the broader Grand Prix unfolding (including promotional, tourism-inspired and commercially aligned footage) while potentially enticing and enthralling through pseudo-participatory driver perspectives (Sturm, 2014). The use of 'high-fluidity' representational techniques, such as frequent cuts, transitions and the juxtaposition of camera angles and perspectives, contributes to the overall 'infotainment' orientation designed to maintain viewer interest and attention. Moreover, this combination of camera work and editing produces a highly mobilised fluidity to a sport notoriously difficult to frame given the high speeds and geographically diverse terrain, albeit with such techniques often vitiating against rendering the 'real' speed experienced trackside by live event attendees (Whannel, 1992). To combat this, regular transitions from stationary wall-mounted cameras to driver perspectives are used to showcase close proximity racing, how close the cars are running to the barriers and to convey the immense speed at which drivers must operate.

There is often also a video game aesthetic to the televised coverage (Sturm, 2019) with all cars carrying two to three on-board cameras which provide a 'dazzling' array of visual information and pseudo-participatory perspectives. Sturm (2014) asserts that:

> With all cars carrying on-board cameras and footage continually framed and intercut from this point-of-view, viewers are restricted to an illusory shared racer's perspective. Therefore, in a visual, temporal and spatial sense, viewers share the racer's experience and see only what he sees, getting a visceral, spatial and technologically-embodied racing spectacle. (p. 72)

Such perspectives are enhanced by graphic and animated renderings of car dynamics and data (e.g., lap times, tyre wear, fuel usage), overlaid with driver inputs and forces (e.g., application of brakes or throttle, gear changes, g-forces experienced) during the on-board perspectives which potentially further immerse viewers in the televised driving experience.

Additionally, helicopter-, crane- and tower-mounted cameras render the size and scale of various facilities or locations, often foreshortened through the use of telephoto lenses with zoom techniques to easily follow the racing action or to return viewers to close views of the race. Such techniques also reveal, on the one hand, an inherently promotional function linked to placemaking and city-branding, with television cameras locating, transforming and enhancing the host cities and nations through these associated media spectacles (Cairns, 2016; John & McDonald, 2020; Lowes, 2018). Sturm (2017) notes for the Monaco Grand Prix:

> Racing fast cars through affluent city streets provides an idyllic setting; further furnished with the stunning background of historic buildings and an expensive array of yachts in the harbour. Moreover, the rich and celebrated are also shown in attendance, facilitating a mediatised cocktail that mixes celebrities, fashion, corporate sponsors, luxury yachts and beauty in a way that complements and often supersedes screened images of fast cars racing. (p. 178)

On the other hand, a sense of occasion can be heightened by using frequent long shots and dramatic angles from elevated cranes or helicopters. Overall, such techniques afford oscillating 'pleasure points' to attract and retain a wide-ranging viewership (Whannel, 1992).

In summary, Formula One's televisual representation is noteworthy for seeking ways to augment and enhance the traditionally passive role of viewing televised sport, while pushing the envelope of innovations that cater to audience fascination, pseudo-participatory perspectives and all-seeing forms of framing. Hence, a racing action focus allows viewers to take in dramatic moments and provides intimacy with star drivers, while races are often also framed as corporate and promotional spaces, affording marketable televisual commodity-spectacles with attributes attractive to delivering large audiences (Kellner, 2003, 2010). Sturm (2014) asserts:

> By combining sophisticated technologies with innovative camera placements, a continual flow of on-screen textual information, and expert commentary from ex-drivers, the slickly produced Formula One televisual broadcast (often in high definition) transforms the sometimes predictable sport into a glamorous and high-tech global spectacle of speed. (p. 72)

With uncertainty surrounding the future of television, Formula One has retained (pay) television as its prime media outlet while actively diversifying its media platforms and content to attract new markets and demographics to the sport long after television is obsolete.

Formula One and the 'Death of Television'

Despite potentially bleak assumptions surrounding the future of television, the medium remains an experimental site for embedding innovative technologies into sports content. As we have seen, Formula One offers a range of innovative televisual technologies and techniques that aim to appeal to and retain televisual viewers via its close proximity framing and oscillating perspectives. For Formula One, television has also held primacy as a key revenue stream via lucrative broadcasting rights, while ostensibly operating for decades as the prime 'screen of speed' for audiences (Baudrillard, 2002). Additionally, the 'liveness' of televised sport and Formula One's representation as a 'glamorous and hi-tech spectacle of speed' (Sturm, 2014) serves to engage audiences, to shape fan rituals and to forge collective social experiences (Frandsen, 2020; Wenner & Billings, 2017; Whannel, 1992).

Satellite and pay television have been fundamental to Formula One's global strategies, which have steadily moved away from free-to-air content to paid subscriptions, seemingly matched by a long-held ambivalence towards digital media possibilities and transformations. As was noted earlier, in Britain, Formula One had historically operated via free-to-air coverage for nearly 60 years. From inception through until the 1970s, Formula One was available on either the BBC or ITV, albeit largely in an ad hoc fashion as highlight packages or via delayed and relayed coverage. From 1979 to 1996 the BBC held the exclusive broadcasting rights to Formula One, while ITV secured the rights from 1997 until 2008 (Tobin, 2021). Formula One then returned to the BBC in 2009; however, a disruption to free-to-air coverage would occur, with the television rights being 'shared' between satellite provider Sky Sports and the BBC from 2012. Under this arrangement Sky Sports produced live coverage of all sessions while the BBC broadcast only half of the races live (Gallop, 2011).

In many respects, this relationship augured the significant shift to pay television that became the norm in Britain and on a global scale. For example, due to financial pressures, the BBC's rights were transferred to Channel 4 from 2015 to 2018 while, since 2019, Channel 4 has only offered race highlights alongside the British Grand Prix live (Nelson, 2021). Alternatively, operating behind a paywall that is predominantly subscription based, Sky Sports became the exclusive provider of all live Formula One content in an estimated £1 billion deal from 2019 to 2024 (Nelson, 2021). Similar satellite television arrangements are discernible for many other nations. These include France's Canal+ since 2013, as well as Sky Italia and Sky Sports (UK), who both commenced in 2012 but signed exclusive pay-TV-only deals in 2018 (Sylt, 2020a).

For the 2013 season, Mann (2013) noted that Formula One's media coverage was firmly interlocked with, and legally restricted to, FOM's 63 global televisual broadcasts and broadcast partners who were annually spending £30–60 million for the broadcasting rights. Liberty Media has maintained an emphasis on pay television since taking ownership in 2017, including signing new partnerships in Australia in 2019 and Germany in 2021, albeit with the viewing figures dropping by a staggering 70% in Germany as a result (Wilde, 2021).

The reliance on pay television remains a vexed approach. As Noble (2021) observes:

> It is widely accepted that F1's TV audience figures reached their peak in 2008 when there was a tally of 600 million unique viewers that year. A gradual shift to pay TV channels has seen numbers steadily fall away, with it drifting down from 490 million in 2018, to 471 million in 2019 and 433 million in 2020—but last year was impacted by COVID-19 and a shorter calendar. (para. 1-2)

Such points are supported by Sylt (2020a), who reports that in 2019, "Formula One has revealed that it lost 19.2 million viewers worldwide" (para. 1), while also noting that "F1's audience reversed by 3.9% to 471 million last year meaning that it has lost a staggering 129 million viewers since 2008 driven by a move towards Pay TV" (para. 2).

Overall, the Formula One global television audience seems to be in a state of steady decline due to the sport largely being behind a paywall which, Wilde (2021) argues, limits its appeal to motorsport fans rather than having mass circulation via free-to-air coverage. Of course, aside from 2021 and 2022, recent seasons have also, in many respects, been 'non-events' (Sturm, 2014) in terms of the lack of competition and complete dominance of Lewis Hamilton and Mercedes. Conversely, Noble (2021) suggests that while the potential television audience would be bigger on free-to-air television, the pay television partners are perceived to be more beneficial to Formula One due to the infrastructure they put around the sport in terms of media content, marketing, analysis, celebrity coverage and an investment in producing and packaging the sport as spectacle. Moreover, pay television remains lucrative financially for the time being as, accompanying a shift to more pay TV providers, Sylt (2020b) notes that "F1's broadcasting revenue has accelerated by 69.5% to $762.8 million since 2008" (para. 10). Thus, for the short term at least, Formula One seems destined to largely operate behind paywalls globally as Liberty Media looks to grow the broadcasting rights revenue streams.

Nevertheless, we have potentially reached the tipping point for television's relationship with the sport. Many of the Formula One nations offer platforms that can live stream or redistribute the satellite television coverage onto other platforms for paying customers, inclusive of web-based content or digital apps such as Sky Go in the United Kingdom or Kayo in Australia. Unsurprisingly, tight restrictions remain in place around the availability of such online content, with Formula One's national broadcast partners "responsible for ensuring that the action cannot be accessed outside their home territory for fear of impacting viewing figures" (Mann, 2013, para. 2). Moreover, the future of Formula One television broadcasting remains murky given the potential uptake of different paid-streaming options, direct subscriptions or content supplied via media corporations. Indeed, rumours circulated in 2021 that both Netflix and Amazon had an interest in streaming the series (Day, 2021; Tobin, 2021). Finally, various online and televisual paywalls may also threaten the retention of (traditional) Formula One audiences long term, although Liberty Media is seemingly reorientating its focus to a future emphasis on youth and digital media.

Formula One's Digital Future

Formula One, alongside contemporary sport more broadly, has witnessed a shift from traditional broadcast platforms to accelerated digital practices which Hutchins et al. (2019) describes as the 'mobile media sport moment'. Collectively, a myriad of sophisticated digital tools, techniques and devices capture, supplement, shape and disseminate sports content premised on connectivity, networking and mobility (Hutchins, 2019; Hutchins et al., 2019). Reflective of these developments, digital and social media are expanding upon, embellishing and enriching the traditional 'legacy' forms of media (e.g., print and broadcasting), while shifting such content to online and mobile platforms. These permutations, as well as attempts to retain and reinvigorate contemporary Formula One as a televised spectacle via regular technological innovations, afford 'new' interactive capacities for the representation and consumption of sport (Frandsen, 2020; Sturm, 2014).

Focusing on Formula One specifically, Liberty Media has significantly recalibrated the sport and its target market by harnessing the power of digital and social media. Interviewed in 2020 on the 'Beyond the Grid' Formula One podcast (itself an example of the new digital media offerings), Formula One CEO and Executive Chairman Chase Carey noted that part of Liberty Media's strategy was to energise the television broadcast, the live event and the live event experience (Clarkson, 2020). More explicitly, Sylt (2020b) asserts that Liberty Media future-proofed the sport, noting:

> Over the past three years Formula One has transformed the way it interacts with its fans. It has driven up its social media content, introduced an eSports league, developed a Netflix documentary series and launched the F1 TV Pro online streaming platform. These steps have boosted its appeal to a younger audience. (para. 1)

Acutely aware of the generational shift occurring both around traditional versus digital media and the largely untapped under-30s market increasingly tuned out of television, Formula One placed a greater emphasis on non-traditional content that would appeal to and potentially grow a new audience (Clarkson, 2020; Hutchins et al., 2019; Lawrence & Crawford, 2019).

In terms of these developments, the turn to both eSports and digital media is arguably the least surprising. Historically, Formula One video gaming emerged in the 1980s, continuing to evolve towards high levels of photorealism by the late 1990s, with many contemporary drivers also active gamers (Sturm, 2019). Recognising that eSports often has online viewing figures beyond major sports events, as well as the growing phenomenon of (motor)sports turning to forms of eSports to grow their audience and revenue streams, the first official *Formula 1 Esports Series* was launched in 2017 as an annual series (Sturm, 2019). A 'Virtual Grand Prix' eSports series, comprising Formula One drivers, celebrities and other sport stars also ran in 2020 and 2021 due to COVID-related calendar disruptions, allegedly achieving 30 million views across TV and digital platforms, as well as 695 million impressions across social media in 2020 (Dixon, 2020).

Alongside eSports, the F1 TV Pro platform was also made available in 2018, albeit with restrictions that are predominantly geo-blocked within nations that already have existing television broadcasting rights—for example, to ensure that the pay television deals remain 'live' and exclusive. Hence, while live or full replays may be available in different regions with different restrictions, F1 TV Pro (and F1 TV) affords an array of digital content that runs the gamut of live coverage and timings, archival footage, documentaries and historical races through to shows, interviews and podcasts that ideally appeal to a variety of Formula One fans and viewers. Chase Carey suggests that F1 TV Pro is designed to complement the global race feed disseminated by broadcast partners rather than become the sole direct subscription service (Clarkson, 2020), particularly as F1 TV Pro users can switch to pitlane cameras, timing screens as well as the on-board camera on each car to provide a more personalised and user-centric experience alongside the main live race feed.

Intriguingly, alongside the assumption that many contemporary fans demonstrate interactive, consumptive and often (digital) media-savvy orientations and practices, Brown et al. (2018) found that many eSports fans often have little interest in traditional sports and teams. Thus, while potentially appealing to some Formula One fans and gamers, the Formula One eSports series is generally attracting a more youthful and less 'traditional' fanbase, while continuing to grow in popularity, reach and impressions (Sturm, 2019). Arguably, Formula One's digital and social media spaces are creating and underscoring similar trends. For example, F1 TV Pro is envisaged by Chase Carey as offering a rich fan experience through an array of content, data and technology that will appeal to a broad cross section of Formula One fans (Clarkson, 2020), while social media platforms deploy content designed to pique the interest of traditional and non-traditional Formula One fans, audiences and media users.

Arguably, this strategy has been working, with Tobin (2021) reporting that Formula One "recorded 4.9bn video views on its app, website and social media channels in 2020—up by 46% on the previous year, and had 35m followers by the end of last year" (para. 12). For a sport notoriously reluctant to even consider social media prior to the Liberty Media takeover in 2017—notably with Ecclestone in 2014 reportedly dismissing social media as "'short-lived' and not a remedy to falling viewership figures for the sport" (Southwell, 2021a, para. 2), the transformations have been significant. With large growth reported in the 16–25 age bracket, as well as greater reach and impressions across official social media sites, driver social media sites and broader platforms such as Twitch and *YouTube* (Southwell, 2021a), the sport is expanding its content. Most significantly, Formula One is also expanding its fans, audiences, followers and users.

The partnership with Netflix for the Formula One *Drive to Survive* series (2018–present) has arguably also been one of the most groundbreaking and successful transformations introduced by Liberty Media. Specifically, the series has been credited with allowing Formula One to penetrate regions such as the United States and China, as well as increasing the sport's youth audience (Tobin, 2021). For example, Lawrence (2021) notes American audiences are up for both attendance and the televised coverage of races by approximately 40%, while also signposting the growth of female and youth audiences globally, all of which he attributes to the series.

Unsurprisingly, perhaps, there have been critiques centred on some of the editorial decisions and forms of misrepresentation. For example, there have been suggestions that Netflix was seemingly constructing or embellishing rivalries, notably the close friendship between then McLaren team-mates Lando Norris and Carlos Sainz that was, conversely, presented as an intense rivalry (Season 3, Episode 8). As Southwell (2021b) observes:

> For whatever reason, the episode was spliced together with radio messages taken out of context and dialogue hastily chopped with the apparent goal of making it a bitter, jealous rivalry where Sainz was forced from the team by McLaren's favoritism of Norris. It's an outright bizarre narrative to put on a team whose big story last season was going from near-financial-collapse to its best result in years by coming in third in the constructors' title fight. (para. 5)

At times, the contextual specifics that Southwell (2021b) is alluding to remain slippery, if not elusive, in *Drive to Survive*. For example, often each series lacks a connection to broader world championship developments with, remarkably, Season One not even featuring the two title protagonist teams, Mercedes and Ferrari, who refused access for Netflix (Lawrence, 2021). Moreover, the frequent misuse of in-car radio messages has also been critiqued, with Lawrence (2021) noting that "fans have decried the artistic license show creators have taken while stitching in-car radio snippets out of context" (para. 14).

Nevertheless, despite these critiques, the series has been lauded for making the sport more accessible and compelling (Day, 2021; Southwell, 2021a). Thus, rather than replicating the global broadcast of on-track sessions, *Drive to Survive* affords a 'behind the scenes' focus centred on personalities, drama and an explicit blurring of sport and entertainment. For example, Lawrence (2021) sums up the series as "a high-stakes clash of big egos, tense power struggles and stunning betrayals" (para. 8), while noting that "the tension unravels against an ever shifting backdrop of private planes, paddock suits and supercars" (para. 10).

Unlike the live televisual broadcasts, *Drive to Survive* is less concerned with reproducing the results or realities of racing, often focusing on lesser-known drivers and teams through storytelling and dramatic conventions that make them appear more personable and affable for audiences. Thus, *Drive to Survive* not only topped global Netflix viewership in March 2021 but, allegedly, significantly contributed to Formula One gaining 73 million fans in 10 key global locations, most of whom were in the 16–25-year age bracket (Southwell, 2021a).

Concluding Remarks

As we have seen, Formula One has forged a close and significant relationship with television across its history. Although televised coverage existed from its inception, the sport suffered from a disrupted and inconsistent media treatment that, to a large degree, also reflected the disjointed operational practices informing the sport. It would not be until the 1980s where Ecclestone's global vision for Formula One recognised the fundamental role that television could play in encapsulating the elements of speed, glamour and technology as a compelling spectacle. Indeed, by and large, it was Ecclestone's vision and model that underpinned the sport for approximately 35 years, a model premised predominantly on monetising the television broadcasting rights, generally to the exclusion (and, thus, detriment) of other media possibilities. Hence, social media platforms, digital media affordances and streaming options were shunned, if not castigated, within his myopic focus that sought to elevate and retain the pre-eminence of a broadcast model that, over time, became increasingly at odds with other contemporary sports, trends and technologies.

While admittedly Formula One has benefited from the additional (short term) revenue of subscription-based paywalls, as well as the enhanced tie-ins that accompany some of these pay television partners, Formula One's global audience has been significantly impacted upon. Thus, placing the sport behind a paywall in nations that, historically, have resonated with the sport (e.g., the United Kingdom, France, Italy and Germany) bore witness to disruptions, if not a disastrous downturn in viewership, in significant locations such as Germany (Wilde, 2021). Moreover, charging for the telecasts has clearly seen the large viewing audiences that had been accumulated across the decades of free-to-air coverage diminish on a global scale (Sylt, 2020a; Tobin, 2021).

Nevertheless, while pay television may be a short-term (and short-sighted) mechanism for preserving the primacy of television broadcasts for the sport, Ecclestone's emphasis on the televised spectacle, as well as Liberty Media's reorientation to diversifying Formula One's media content, platforms and users, seemingly proffer longer-term benefits and a strategic model of success. Through Ecclestone's vision and endeavours, the sport was transformed via its television coverage, simultaneously operating as a compelling media event and media spectacle. Given the constant innovations, technological refinements and televisual techniques deployed on and across the Formula One telecast, the races afford an alluring assemblage of infotainment, fluidity and sensory engagement with these media representations of speed, risk, drivers and hi-tech machines. Hence, while the future of the sport may not lie in television directly, by having such high production values the shift to live streaming and other modes of delivery that "perpetuate the logics of television coverage and practices" (Hutchins et al., 2019, p. 977) seems potentially less problematic as these telecasts get subsumed by and moved onto new screens and digital devices.

Finally, the acquisition by and subsequent digital media orientation of Liberty Media was a necessary shift to allow Formula One to keep pace with other contemporary sport-media developments. Indeed, for a sport steeped in hi-technology, its resistance to, and repudiation of, digital and social media platforms was surprising given the growth and significance of these across most aspects of socio-cultural life. Sturm (2021) suggests that Formula One may struggle for future relevance if it "cannot find ways to be more economically, environmentally and socially sustainable" (p. 125), which includes addressing its "blinkered vision of progressive gender politics" (p. 125) given that the sport often remains mired in traditional gendered dynamics and practices. Thus, the diversification of its media content and media platforms seems like a necessary transitional component to also diversify its audiences, notably along the more obvious lines of age, gender and race. More broadly, by utilising diverse media content and platforms, the sport is also furnishing different affective access points that percolate around elements of interest, attention and intrigue—whether it be live-streamed races (and/or accessible archival content), viewing or competing in eSports leagues, or following the dramatic insights afforded by series, such as *Drive to Survive* on Netflix, which present the sport in non-traditional ways for non-traditional audiences.

References

Anderson, G. (2022, February 1). Gary Anderson: How the cost cap will really hit teams and F1. *The Race*. https://the-race.com/formula-1/gary-anderson-how-the-cost-cap-will-really-hit-teams-and-f1/

Andrews, D., & Ritzer, G. (2007). The Grobal in the Sporting Glocal. In R. Giulianotti & R. Robertson (Eds.), *Globalization and Sport* (pp. 28–45). Blackwell.

Andrews, D., & Ritzer, G. (2018). Sport and Prosumption. *Journal of Consumer Culture, 18*(2), 356–373.

Baldwin, A. (2021, October 1). Qatar provides a further boost to the balance sheet for F1. *Reuters*. https://www.reuters.com/lifestyle/sports/qatar-provides-further-boost-balance-sheet-f1-2021-09-30/

Baudrillard, J. (1983). *Simulations* (P. Foss, P. Patton & P. Beitchman, Trans.). New York: Semiotext(e).

Baudrillard, J. (2002). *Screened out* (C. Turner, Trans.). Verso. (Original work published 2000).

Billings, A. (2010). *Communicating About Sports Media: Cultures Collide*. Aresta.

Bromber, K., & Krawietz, B. (2013). The United Arab Emirates, Qatar and Bahrain as a Modern Sport Hub. In K. Bromber, B. Krawietz, & J. Maguire (Eds.), *Sport across Asia: Politics, Cultures and Identities* (pp. 189–211). Routledge.

Brown, K., Billings, A., Murphy, B., & Puesan, L. (2018). Intersections of Fandom in the Age of Interactive Media: eSports Fandom as a Predictor of Traditional Sport Fandom. *Communication & Sport, 6*(4), 418–435.

Cairns, G. (2016). The Hybridization of Sight in the Hybrid Architecture of Sport: The Effects of Television on Stadia and Spectatorship. *Sport in Society, 18*(6), 734–749. https://doi.org/10.1080/17430437.2014.985212

Clarkson, T. (Host). (2020, October). Chase Carey on his role in shaping F1's future and guiding the sport through a global pandemic [Audio podcast, Episode 107]. In *F1-Beyond the Grid*.

Crebolder, F. (2022, January 16). Environmental group wants Dutch GP permit revoked. *PlanetF1.com*. https://www.planetf1.com/news/dutch-gp-environmental-wrangle/

Day, L. (2021, September 22). It Sounds Like Netflix Wants to Buy F1 Race Streaming Rights. *The Drive*. https://www.thedrive.com/accelerator/42491/netflix-would-definitely-consider-bidding-for-f1-rights-in-future

Dayan, D., & Katz, E. (1992). *Media Events: The Live Broadcasting of History*. Harvard University Press.

Dixon, E. (2020, June 19). F1 Virtual Grands Prix pull in 30m total viewers. *Sportspromedia.com*. https://www.sportspromedia.com/news/f1-virtual-grands-prix-total-viewers-audience-tv-digital-social-esports/

Frandsen, K. (2014). Mediatization of Sports. In K. Lundby (Ed.), *Mediatization of Communication* (pp. 525–543). Mouton de Gruyter.

Frandsen, K. (2020). *Sport and Mediatization*. Routledge.

Gallop, B. (2011, July 29). New F1 deal explained. *BBC*. https://www.bbc.co.uk/blogs/sporteditors/2011/07/f1_coverage_to_be_shared_betwe.html

Haynes, R., & Robeers, T. (2020). The Need for Speed? A Historical Analysis of the BBC's Post-war Broadcasting of Motorsport. *Historical Journal of Film, Radio and Television, 40*(2), 407–423. https://doi.org/10.1080/01439685.2019.1628418

Henry, A. (1998). *Formula 1: Creating the Spectacle*. Hazleton.

Hotten, R. (1999). *Formula One: The Business of Winning. The People, Money and Profits That Power the World's Richest Sport*. Orion Business.

Hutchins, B. (2019). Mobile Media Sport: The Case for Building a Mobile Media and Communications Research Agenda. *Communication & Sport, 7*(4), 466–487. https://doi.org/10.1177/2167479518788833

Hutchins, B., Li, B., & Rowe, D. (2019). Over-the-top Sport: Live Streaming Services, Changing Coverage Rights Markets, and the Growth of Media Sport Portals. *Media, Culture & Society, 41*(7), 975–994. https://doi.org/10.1177/0163443719857623

John, A., & McDonald, B. (2020). How Elite Sport Helps to Foster and Maintain a Neoliberal Culture: The 'branding' of Melbourne, Australia. *Urban Studies, 57*(6), 1184–1200.

Kellner, D. (2003). *Media Spectacle*. Routledge.

Kellner, D. (2010). Media Spectacle and Media Events: Some Critical Reflections. In N. Couldry, A. Hepp, & F. Krotz (Eds.), *Media Events in a Global Age* (pp. 76–91). Routledge.

Lawrence, A. (2021, December 17). 'Big egos, power struggles, stunning betrayals': How Netflix's Drive to Survive turned Americans into F1 fans. *The Guardian*. https://www.theguardian.com/media/2021/dec/17/netflixs-drive-to-survive-americans-f1-fans

Lawrence, S., & Crawford, G. (2019). *Digital Football Cultures: Fandom, Identities and Resistance*. Routledge.

Lefebvre, S., & Roult, R. (2011). Formula One's New Urban Economies. *Cities, 28*(4), 330–339.

Lowes, M. (2018). Toward a Conceptual Understanding of Formula One Motorsport and Local Cosmopolitanism Discourse in Urban Placemarketing Strategies. *Communication & Sport, 6*(2), 203–218.

Majumdar, B., & Naha, S. (2020). Live Sport During the COVID-19 Crisis: Fans as Creative Broadcasters. *Sport in Society, 23*(7), 1091–1099. https://doi.org/10.1080/17430437.2020.1776972

Mann, C. (2013, May 28). F1 considers online streaming. *Advanced Television*. http://advanced-television.com/2013/05/28/f1-considers-online-streaming/

McEvoy, J. (2020, November 6). F1 announces Saudi Arabia will host its first ever Grand Prix next year. *Daily Mail*. https://www.dailymail.co.uk/sport/formulaone/article-8917853/Formula-One-announces-Saudi-Arabian-Grand-Prix-2021.html

McManus, J., & Amara, M. (2021). Sport at Home, Sport in the World: Evaluating Qatar's Sports Strategy from Above and Below. In M. Zweiri & F. Al Qawasmi (Eds.), *Contemporary Qatar. Gulf Studies, vol 4*. Springer. https://doi-org.ezproxy.massey.ac.nz/10.1007/978-981-16-1391-3_9.

Miller, T. (2017). *Greenwashing Sport*. Routledge.

Nelson, D. (2021, July 29). How the BBC/Sky deal changed F1 broadcasting in the UK. *Motorsport Broadcasting*. https://motorsportbroadcasting.com/2021/07/29/how-the-bbc-sky-deal-has-changed-f1-broadcasting-in-the-uk/

Noble, J. (2021, May 19). The pay TV vs free-to-air conflict at the heart of modern F1. *Motorsport.com*. https://www.motorsport.com/f1/news/the-pay-tv-vs-free-to-air-conflict-at-the-heart-of-modern-f1/6510753/

Rendall, I. (2000). *The Power Game: The History of Formula 1 and the World Championship*. Cassell & Co.

Saward, J. (2013, January 7). Some ruminations on TV rights. *JoeblogsF1*. http://joesaward.wordpress.com/2013/01/07/some-ruminations-on-tv-rights/

Silk, M., & Manley, A. (2012). Globalization, Urbanization and Sporting Spectacle in Pacific Asia: Places, Peoples and Pastness. *Sociology of Sport Journal, 29*, 455–484.

Southwell, H. (2021a, March 25). F1 finally embraces streaming, looks at 1 Billion fans in 2022 thanks to Netflix and Twitch. *The Drive.com*. https://www.thedrive.com/accelerator/39933/f1-finally-embraces-streaming-looks-at-1-billion-fans-in-2022-thanks-to-netflix-and-twitch

Southwell, H. (2021b, March 23). Netflix's Formula 1: Drive to survive season three review: Who is this actually for? *The Drive.com*. https://www.thedrive.com/accelerator/39902/netflixs-formula-1-drive-to-survive-season-three-review-who-is-this-actually-for

Sturm, D. (2014). A Glamorous and High-tech Global Spectacle of Speed: Formula One Motor Racing as Mediated, Global and Corporate Spectacle. In K. Dashper, T. Fletcher, & N. McCullough (Eds.), *Sports Events, Society and Culture* (pp. 68–82). Routledge.

Sturm, D. (2017). The Monaco Grand Prix and Indianapolis 500: Projecting European Glamour and Global Americana. In L. Wenner & A. Billings (Eds.), *Sport, Media and Mega-events* (pp. 170–184). Routledge.

Sturm, D. (2019). Not Your Average Sunday Driver: The Formula 1 Esports Series World Championship. In R. Rogers (Ed.), *Understanding Esports: An Introduction to the Global Phenomenon* (pp. 153–165). Lexington.

Sturm, D. (2021). The Formula One Paradox: Macho Male Racers and Ornamental Glamour 'girls'. In K. Dashper (Ed.), *Sport, Gender and Mega Events* (pp. 111–128). Emerald.

Sturm, D. (2023). Processes of Greenwashing, Sportwashing and Virtue Signalling in Contemporary Formula One: Formula façade? In H. Naess & S. Chadwick (Eds.), *The Future of Motorsports: Business, Politics and Society* (pp. 167–182). Routledge.

Sylt, C. (2020a, January 21). F1's worldwide TV audience crashes by 20 million viewers. *Forbes*. https://www.forbes.com/sites/csylt/2020/01/21/f1s-worldwide-tv-audience-crashes-by-20-million-viewers/?sh=297965d55a66

Sylt, C. (2020b, July 3). How F1 future-proofed its audience. *Forbes*. https://www.forbes.com/sites/csylt/2020/07/03/how-f1-future-proofed-its-audience/?sh=23b7434518b2

Tobin, D. (2021, October 19). F1 looks to cash in on TV bidding war — will it bring better racing? *Motorsport Magazine*. https://www.motorsportmagazine.com/articles/single-seaters/f1/f1-looks-to-cash-in-on-tv-bidding-war-will-it-bring-better-racing

Turner, B. (2004). *The Pits: The Real World of Formula One*. Atlantic.

Walker, M. (2002). *Unless I am Very Much Mistaken*. Collins Willow.

Wenner, L., & Billings, A. (Eds.). (2017). *Sport, Media and Mega-events*. Routledge.

Whannel, G. (1992). *Fields in Vision: Television Sport and Cultural Transformation*. Routledge.

Wilde, J. (2021, October 14). F1 more 'alive than ever' despite pay-TV concerns. *PlanetF1.com*. https://www.planetf1.com/news/f1-ruined-full-switch-pay-tv/

The Shifting Landscape of Sponsorship Within Formula 1

Timothy Dewhirst and Wonkyong Beth Lee

The current sponsorship landscape of Formula 1 is busy and dense. The cars and drivers serve as mobile billboards, being saturated with the branding of multinational sponsors. The overt commercialisation of Formula 1 was established some time ago even though advertisements have not appeared on team uniforms in many professional sports leagues until very recently (see Dewhirst, 2016, 2021a). The race car and uniform of seven-time Formula 1 world champion, Lewis Hamilton, for example, includes branding from Petronas, Mercedes, The Ritz-Carlton, Puma, Tommy Hilfiger, Epson, Pirelli, UBS, Hewlett Packard, Bose, and

T. Dewhirst (✉)
Department of Marketing and Consumer Studies, Gordon S. Lang School of Business and Economics, University of Guelph, Guelph, ON, Canada
e-mail: dewhirst@uoguelph.ca

W. B. Lee
DAN Department of Management and Organizational Studies, University of Western Ontario, London, ON, Canada
e-mail: wlee322@uwo.ca

D. Sturm et al. (eds.), *The History and Politics of Motor Racing*, Global Culture and Sport Series, https://doi.org/10.1007/978-3-031-22825-4_17

Monster. Still, some sponsorships have prompted ethical and moral questions. During the 2021 season, Kingspan—a building materials and envelope company—was named as an additional sponsor. The Kingspan sponsorship, however, proved to be short-lived—visible for one race—after notable backlash, as Kingspan produced insulated panels that featured in the Grenfell Tower building in London, England, that caught fire and resulted in 72 deaths (Booth, 2021). The (brief) naming of Kingspan as a sponsorship partner was coordinated by the Mercedes-AMG Petronas racing team, but Lewis Hamilton—the team's star driver—made it known that he was uncomfortable with the brand association.

In this chapter, we provide an overview of sponsorship-linked marketing in Formula 1 and discuss how it has evolved over time. Formula 1 started in 1950, and initially the visibility of sponsorship was highly limited with understated automobile branding apparent on the nose of the race cars. Originally, a key purpose of Formula 1 was to provide automobile manufacturers—such as Alfa Romeo, Ferrari, and Mercedes—a showcase for their products and technologies. The inaugural season was effectively a European racing series, with seven races held, and six of those races were in Europe (the exception was one race in the USA at the famed Indianapolis speedway). During the 1950s and 1960s, Formula 1 race teams were largely funded by automobile manufacturers or by affluent individuals such as Rob Walker, whose amassed wealth reflected the sales of Johnny Walker whisky (Jenkins et al., 2016). Prominent Formula 1 team sponsorship liveries emerged during the late 1960s and early 1970s, which marked an important transitional period as tobacco companies increasingly turned to sponsorship as a promotional strategy. Outside of tobacco, additional sponsors appeared during this era that were questionable, especially with Formula 1 having appeal as "family viewing" (Jewell, 2016). Condom manufacturer, Durex, for example, was a prominent sponsor of the Surtees race team, prompting the BBC to not broadcast Formula 1 races, including the 1976 British Grand Prix. More recently, the technology industry has emerged as prominent sponsors while tobacco sponsorship diminished in visibility due to regulatory stipulations. Early examples of Formula 1 sponsorship included engine, fuel, and tyre suppliers, which were typically function-based. Over time, however, sponsors have increasingly leveraged symbolic or image-based attributes that are associated with Formula 1. Moreover, as the pervasiveness of sponsorship has increased, there have been further opportunities for co-branding among the sponsorship partners, which focus on compounding the associated image dimensions (Dewhirst & Hunter, 2002).

Sponsorship-Linked Marketing

To clarify the scope of our discussion pertaining to the "sponsorship landscape," we begin this chapter by providing definitions of "sponsorship" and "sponsorship-linked marketing." *Sponsorship* is defined as "an investment, in cash or in kind, in an activity, in return for access to the exploitable commercial potential associated with that activity" (cited in Larson & Park, 1993, p. 97). An important point from this definition is that sponsorship should not be confused with patronage. A patron donates and such generosity is usually based on personal satisfaction and belief in the worthiness of a cause, whereas a sponsor makes an investment wherein motives are commercially based rather than altruistic. Sponsors are involved in a business activity to gain benefits and meet specified and measurable objectives (Townley & Grayson, 1984; Sleight, 1989). Although sponsorship serves a multitude of functions, including hospitality opportunities, primary objectives often encompass the enhancement of brand awareness as well as brand image (Otker, 1988; Irwin & Asimakopoulos, 1992; Irwin & Sutton, 1994).

Corresponding to this definition of sponsorship, Cornwell (1995, p. 15) defines *sponsorship-linked marketing* as "the orchestration and implementation of marketing activities for the purpose of building and communicating an association (link) to a sponsorship." These marketing activities serve to build associations between sports properties and brands in which sponsors strategically identify and promote functional and/or symbolic links. As a sponsor of Formula 1, watch-maker brands such as Tag Heuer can feature on a time clock to demonstrate functional links (i.e., precise timekeeping of the competing race cars). Here, functional properties of the sports become leveraged where the product is visibly used in the operations of the sports property. Additionally, as a sponsor of

Formula 1, Tag Heuer can further build brand image (symbolism) by being associated with the upscale, high quality, and technological attributes of the sports property. Here, symbolic links are highlighted with the aim that the sport property's image associations are credibly transferable towards the sponsoring brand (e.g., see Gwinner, 1997; Gwinner & Eaton, 1999; McDaniel, 1999; Cornwell, 2008; Prendergast et al., 2010). Historically, tobacco brands have been among the more prominent sponsors of Formula 1 wherein congruent image and lifestyle dimensions were strategically highlighted.

Enter the Tobacco Industry as Key Sponsors

Tobacco sponsorship first became apparent in Formula 1 during the late 1960s. In 1968, branding for Imperial Tobacco's Gold Leaf became visible on the championship-winning Lotus race cars (Bartunek, 2007). An important motivating factor behind tobacco companies, such as the UK-based Imperial Tobacco, shifting their promotional spending towards sponsorship was they began to face regulatory restrictions that no longer allowed traditional advertising among media such as television (Philips & Whannel, 2013). Broadcasts of Formula 1 races facilitated *continued* brand exposure among sponsoring tobacco brands, despite the implementation of cigarette advertising bans applicable to the broadcast media in various jurisdictions, including the UK in 1965 and the USA in 1971. An important and yet unintended outcome of prohibitions on cigarette broadcast advertising was tobacco companies notably shifting and redirecting their promotional spending towards broadcasted sports properties (Wichmann & Martin, 1991; Marshall & Cook, 1992). Consequently, sponsoring cigarette brands ably circumvented policy stipulations and effectively compensated for lost broadcast advertising exposure (Warner, 1979; Ledwith, 1984; Stoner, 1992; Cornwell, 1997). Several studies have demonstrated that tobacco companies continued receiving television exposure—with considerable estimated worth—by sponsoring auto racing (Blum, 1991; Siegel, 2001; Morrison et al., 2006). A videotape recording of the Marlboro Grand Prix during 1989, for example, revealed that Marlboro was seen or mentioned 5933 times during the broadcast

(Blum, 1991). While this example pertains to a Championship Auto Racing Teams (CART) race, rather than specific to Formula 1, it points to the tobacco industry quickly understanding that cigarette brand exposure could persist on television if broadcast sports properties such as Formula 1 included cigarette brand sponsorship. Moreover, Formula 1—relative to other auto racing properties—offered broader reach by appealing to a more international audience.

Coinciding with the tobacco industry's entry into sponsorship, Formula 1 would quickly transform into big business during the 1970s with the oversight of its commercial rights by Bernie Ecclestone. Following the lead of the tobacco industry, other companies previously involved with Formula 1, such as engine suppliers, also began to further leverage their sponsorships and add pronounced branding to the liveries of race cars (Bartunek, 2007). The tobacco industry's shifting investment towards sports properties during the 1970s was observed as a prominent contributor towards the general development of sponsorship as a marketing discipline (Meenaghan, 1983; Otker & Hayes, 1987; Meenaghan, 1991; Cornwell, 1995; Sparks, 1997). One notable turning point of Formula 1, becoming a particularly high-profile television event, was during the 1977 season when Ecclestone leveraged the acclaimed interest generated from the previous season between competing race car drivers, Niki Lauda and James Hunt (Philip Morris, 1983). The 1976 season was particularly compelling as the world champion was undetermined going into the season's final race, which was also marked by hazardous weather conditions. The final race showdown between Lauda and Hunt was remarkable because Lauda had suffered horrific burns earlier in the season when his car crashed during the German Grand Prix—he was given last rites at the time—but he returned to the track six weeks later to continue competing (Jewell, 2016). Marlboro was a prominent sponsor of both Lauda and Hunt.

Marketing planning documents from the tobacco industry, made public from litigation, reveal that primary objectives for sponsoring sports properties include increasing brand awareness—through continued brand exposure and visibility—and enhancing or reinforcing brand image (Lavack, 2003; Carlyle et al., 2004; Dewhirst, 2004). This revelation from the tobacco industry is consistent with the common marketing objectives from other product sectors that invest as sport sponsors (Cornwell et al., 2001). According to tobacco industry documentation, "Sponsorship is one of the most effective and durable means of brand communication to consumers because it can significantly enhance brand awareness and brand image among the target consumer group through the media of television" (Brown & Williamson, 1999, pp. 323011268–323011269). While the in-person attendance for a Formula 1 race might be roughly 100,000, the number of television viewers for each race was purportedly 300 million at the turn of the century (Hawaleshka, 2001; "Race report", 2002). For sponsors, Formula 1 is recognised as a leading international sport with considerable reach in terms of media coverage. According to British American Tobacco (BAT) documentation:

> In 1997 Formula One attracted a global audience of 51 billion cumulative television viewers making it by far the world's largest annual media interest activity. Only the Olympics and the World Cup, held only every 4 years, are bigger.
>
> Across 193 countries, satellite and terrestrial networks broadcast 1.1 million minutes of coverage over 53,000 transmissions.
>
> Covering 5 continents with 16 races over 8 months of the year, Formula One provides its sponsors and partners with the greatest marketing opportunities of all leading sporting events. (1997, p. 321463562)

It is acknowledged that some of these audience figures today appear "inflated." Still, regardless of how television audiences are measured, Formula 1 undoubtedly represents a highly attractive property to sponsor due to its considerable and global television audience (see Sturm [2014] for insightful discussion about the various claimed viewing figures that have circulated for Formula 1, with 500 million being the estimated audience in 2012). The 2022 race calendar features a record number of races—23—which serves to enhance the media reach from previous seasons.

Over time, Formula 1 has become ever more international. Initially, Formula 1 races were largely limited to Europe, but races eventually became added to the season calendar in further locations. According to

Philip Morris documentation in 2000, "Formula One racing is considered to be the 'highest' level of racing in the world, and is fast becoming popular in the United States" (AutoWeek, 2000, p. 2084445761). Eventually, races would be held and broadcast from Europe and the USA as well as a broader range of countries, including noted expansion of the racing calendar to Asia and the Middle East (Sturm, 2014). Reflecting the now global reach of Formula 1 and the high sponsorship fees to supplement the exorbitant race team budgets, sponsors tend to be highly established multinational brands.

Formula 1 sponsorship facilitates desirable images associated with the sports property being transferable to the sponsoring brands. For BAT, Formula 1 sponsorship enables being strategically positioned as "a successful innovative World Class company, which is willing to compete at the highest level" (Brown & Williamson, 1999, p. 323011267). According to BAT marketing documentation, "Formula One is perceived as very glamorous and very exclusive" (Cleverly, 2001, p. 325003468). Moreover, Formula 1 is characterised by the company as exciting, lively, vibrant, sexy, and celebrity-laden (BAT, 1999, p. 321449855). Further to being associated with such attributes, Formula 1 sponsorship aims to have the sponsoring brand "stand out from competitive set. To be seen as a leader, innovator," while providing an "opportunity to build consumer emotion" (Brown & Williamson, 1999, p. 323011270).

Philip Morris International (PMI)—a direct competitor to BAT—entered Formula 1 sponsorship in 1972 through its Marlboro cigarette brand (Philip Morris, 1983). Initially, their sponsorship commitment largely consisted of prominent signage alongside the racetracks, which facilitated brand exposure among audiences on-site as well as those viewing on television. At the race team level, PMI's Marlboro was first a sponsor of McLaren before becoming a partner of the Ferrari team. While McLaren has its own illustrious history, Ferrari is regarded as "*the* F1 brand among brands" (Fleming & Sturm, 2011, p. 170). For PMI, one further advantage of Marlboro becoming a sponsor of the Ferrari motor racing team included both brands sharing a common colour—red—which consequently was considered to enhance Marlboro's brand awareness as a sponsor (Philip Morris, 1982). Although McLaren did run red and white imagery with Marlboro for several years, the strength of associating red with McLaren does not match Ferrari's association with the colour (for the 2022 season, the McLaren team is predominantly associated with orange). The findings of PMI's internal market research are supported by scholarly research wherein sponsorship partnerships are regarded as more effective when there is visual congruence among the pairings based on colour (Henderson et al., 2019). Beyond both brands sharing similar red colour schemes, the Marlboro/Ferrari brand alliance is highly complementary for promotional purposes given horses represent key elements of their respective brand identity.

Marlboro is promoted as an expression of masculinity, ruggedness, independence, and power or leadership (Aaker, 1997; Hafez & Ling, 2005). Strategically, Marlboro and motor racing are regarded as congruent symbolically; according to Philip Morris documentation, "overlaps core imagery of confidence, determination, masculinity, independence and control" (1998, p. 2070683679). Ellen Merlo, as Vice-President of Marketing Services at Philip Morris, stated that, "We perceive Formula One and Indy car racing as adding, if you will, a modern-day dimension to the Marlboro Man. The image of Marlboro is very rugged, individualistic, heroic. And so is this style of auto racing. From an image standpoint, the fit is good" (cited in "The Business of Racing", 1989).

As a sponsorship-linked marketing objective, Philip Morris sought to ascribe the positive brand associations of Ferrari, which include sophistication, innovation, premium quality, and speed (power and excitement), to their cigarette brand (Philip Morris, 1991, 1992; Lindstrom, 2005). During the 1980s, in pursuing a possible licensing agreement for the launch of a Ferrari-branded cigarette, interoffice correspondence from Philip Morris identified the prospective target market as young adult males (18 to 34 years of age) who were seeking a brand with macho connotations and high-technology imagery (Dangoor, 1987; Tso, 1987).[1]

By the late 1990s, tobacco companies accounted for more than 70% of sponsorship earnings among race team budgets, which reflected cigarette brands such as Marlboro, Mild Seven, West, Benson & Hedges, Rothmans, Gauloises, and Camel adorning Formula 1 race cars (Brown & Williamson, 1999, p. 323011269). In 2000, tobacco companies collectively spent an estimated $250 million per year towards Formula 1 teams (Grange, 2001). Among American tobacco companies, more than 90% of their sport sponsorship budgets were estimated to be towards motor sports (Turco, 1999). Clearly, sponsorship-linked marketing investments by tobacco companies into Formula 1 and motor sports were significant and noteworthy at the turn of the century. Still, tobacco advertising and sponsorship bans would soon become more commonplace among different jurisdictions hosting Formula 1 races, so race teams initially used alternate and crafty livery that still suggested cigarette brands. For example, the Jordan race car substituted Benson & Hedges with "Buzzin Hornets" while maintaining much of the branding elements, such as the colour scheme, associated with the cigarette brand; similarly, the British American Racing team alternated Lucky Strike with "Look Alike" (e.g., see Carlyle et al., 2004). During the 1999 season, BAT identified three races on the calendar—those held in France, Germany, and the UK—where alternate branding would need to be used (Verlinden, 1999). Accordingly, Formula 1 began shifting the locations of races, which appeared driven in part by seeking sites where tobacco promotion remained permissible. New races were established, for example, in Bahrain, China, and Turkey (Simpson, 2004). Notably, however, legislation became implemented in the UK, where most Formula 1 teams are based, that effectively banned tobacco advertising at sports events in 2005 (Vital Strategies, 2020). Also, in 2005, the World Health Organization's Framework Convention on Tobacco Control (WHO FCTC) took effect. Article 13 of this global public health treaty, which now includes 182 Parties and covers more than 90% of the world's population, calls for a comprehensive ban on tobacco advertising, promotion, and sponsorship (WHO, 2021a). Facing such a reality and public pressure, Formula 1's governing body, Fédération Internationale de l'Automobile, prohibited tobacco sponsorship from the end of 2006 (Vital Strategies, 2020). Still, as we later discuss, this policy measure did not effectively ban tobacco sponsorship, as tobacco companies have persisted in their Formula 1 sponsorship investments and found ways to circumvent policy.

The Sponsorship Landscape in the Twenty-First Century

Crypto.com, DHL, Emirates, Pirelli, and Rolex were identified among Formula 1's global partners for the 2021 season. Many of these global partners can highlight their functional links with Formula 1 while underscoring the high performance and quality of their products and services. For example, Pirelli is the exclusive tyre supplier, while DHL oversees the complex shipping and transport of equipment, including the race cars and replacement parts, from race to race. Emirates is positioned as the preferred airline for Formula 1 participants as well as for passengers seeking to attend races as a part of destination travel. Emirates, as an airline global partner, also speaks to the shifting sites and regions of where Formula 1 races are held. Symbolically, prestige, prosperity, and technology are highlighted attributes of Formula 1 that are transferable to sponsorship partners. Rolex, the watchmaker brand, is recognised as a sponsor of major tennis, golf, equestrian, and yachting events—in addition to motor sports—wherein each of these sports properties are associated with prestige and being upscale. According to its website, Rolex "makes a unique and lasting contribution to global culture, science and exploration." Moreover, Crypto.com, which is a Singapore-based cryptocurrency company, made headlines in replacing Staples as the venue sponsor of the LA Lakers' home arena in a 20-year $700 million naming rights deal (Associated Press, 2021). Crypto.com is seen as representing "an innovative, forward-thinking company" (cited in Dean, 2021). The combination of high-end, luxury items—especially pertaining to cars, clothing, watches, and technology—as sponsorship partners in Formula 1 characterises conspicuous consumption (Sturm, 2014). Cultural anthropologist, Grant McCracken explains that:

> The meaning of a good is best (and sometimes only) communicated when this good is surrounded by a complement of goods that carry the same significance. Within this complement, there is sufficient redundancy to allow the observer to identify the meaning of the good. (1988, p. 121)

When presented as sponsorship partners, particular brands are seen as "going together" wherein complementary cultural identities and statuses are put on display and their meaning compounded. Borrowing from Sahlins (1976), McCracken identifies these meaning systems of goods as "object codes."

High-tech companies have emerged as big players of Formula 1 sponsorship. Among many examples, Oracle is a partner of the Red Bull race team, Cognizant for Aston Martin, and TeamViewer for Mercedes. Since Formula 1's move to turbo hybrid rules in 2014, major technology firms can showcase their ability to combine technology with sustainability as they activate their sponsorship strategies (Noble, 2021a). Red Bull and Oracle's recent partnership also reflects Formula 1's growing appeal among a USA fan base (Baldwin, 2021). Continuing its expansion into the USA market, the Red Bull team struck a one-year sponsorship deal with Walmart in early 2021. The Walmart logo adorned Red Bull's race car during the 2021 season and Red Bull Racing merchandise is available on Walmart's website (Yeomans, 2021). Netflix has apparently played an important role in the recent entry by notable American sponsors and observed audience spikes in the USA (Noble, 2021a). ESPN's Formula 1 ratings are up since *Formula 1: Drive to Survive* debuted on Netflix in 2019 (Abbruzzese, 2021).

The COVID-19 pandemic prompted the cancellation of many sporting events during 2020, including Formula 1 races. While traditional sporting events suffered, the popularity of competitive video gaming, known as esports, has sharply increased. Formula 1, like other sports leagues, has turned their attention to esports (Sturm, 2019; Stubbs, 2020). F1 eSports was launched in 2017 and this initiative proved to be opportune for Formula 1 during the pandemic as sponsors engage with a technologically attuned younger fan base (Indaimo, 2020). For example, the French automotive manufacturer, Renault, which has been involved with Formula 1 since 1977, signed a sponsorship deal in 2018 with Team Vitality, which is France's biggest esports team. This deal showcases Renault's strategic move to interact with new and younger audiences via esports internationally. When the partnership was announced in 2018, the founder of Vitality indicated that, "Our partnership with Renault is a natural match, not only because we share the same values and colours but also because we all want to make it to the very top of the European and international scenes" (cited in Fitch, 2018).

Formula 1's target audiences are becoming younger and thus more tech-savvy. According to a global survey—commissioned by Motorsport Network with Formula 1 and Nielsen—32 was the average age of Formula 1 fans in 2021, which is four years younger than what was observed in 2017 (Bradley, 2021). Coinciding with Liberty Media assuming controlling interest in Formula 1 during 2017, the sports property has become actively involved with social media marketing and reaching out to social media influencers. Tobacco companies, such as BAT and PMI, continue to serve as important partners in Formula 1. BAT sponsors Formula 1 eSports events and the events are streamed live on YouTube. The company sponsored Rudimental—the drum and bass band—for a series of livestreams on their Vuse (an e-cigarette brand produced by BAT) YouTube channel in 2020 (Chapman, 2021). Additionally, McLaren Racing launched a celebrity esports series with BAT's nicotine pouch brand, Velo. The Velo Eseries ran between January and April in 2021, and featured celebrities such as UK musician, Craig David, and social media star, Alex Hirschi, who has more than 34 million Facebook followers and 8.3 million on Instagram racing at McLaren with Velo nicotine pouch title-branding (Dixon, 2021).

Social and Ethical Considerations

The magnitude of financial investment from Formula 1 sponsors is astronomical, yet ethical questions emerge with many of the sponsors operating in controversial product sectors such as tobacco, alcohol, gambling, and oil. Several longstanding and existing Formula 1 sponsorships are controversial based on the contradictory pairing of unhealthy or harmful products with sports and athleticism (Cornwell, 2008). The harmfulness of smoking is especially noteworthy, prompting Wenner (1993, p. 146), for example, to term the association of cigarettes and sports—facilitated by sponsorship—as "patently oxymoronic" when pointing out that, "Athleticism and smoking clearly do not go together." Tobacco use is the leading cause of preventable illness and premature death in the USA, being attributable to nine of ten lung cancer deaths, eight of ten chronic obstructive pulmonary disease deaths, one in three cancer deaths, and countless other preventable conditions (U.S. Department of Health and Human Services [USDHHS], 2014). An approximated 443,000 Americans die prematurely each year from smoking, and one of every five deaths in the USA is attributable to smoking (USDHHS, 2012). Tobacco use is responsible for a greater number of deaths among Americans than the total caused by AIDS, motor-vehicle crashes, suicides, murders, and illicit drug use combined (USDHHS, 2004). Globally, tobacco use is forecasted by the World Health Organization (WHO) to be attributable to more than eight million deaths annually by 2030 (WHO, 2008). An additionally important element in the harm caused by tobacco is the addictiveness of its use (USDHHS, 1988).

Despite cigarette brands such as Marlboro, Camel, and West no longer being depicted on the livery of drivers and racing cars, Formula 1 has notably not entered a post-tobacco sponsorship era. PMI, for example, has sponsored the Ferrari team through an alibi brand known as "Mission Winnow." Additionally, BAT has created an alibi brand, "A Better Tomorrow," for sponsoring the McLaren team. During the 2019 season, the Ferrari and McLaren race teams received an estimated $95 million from PMI and BAT through sponsorship (Vital Strategies, 2020).

The tobacco industry's continued sponsorship of Formula 1 appears motivated by drawing attention to their "next generation" products that are touted as harm reduced. Mission Winnow is registered as a trademark by PMI for "use with respect to tobacco products" (WHO, 2019) with an aim of "developing and testing less harmful alternatives to smoking" (Mission Winnow, 2021). PMI has transitioned such that Mission Winnow is now the branded sponsor (replacing Marlboro). The Mission Winnow brand is about promoting transformation, progress, and innovation—aligning PMI with technology and science—which complement the symbolic qualities associated with Formula 1. Meanwhile, BAT's partnership with McLaren facilitates the promotion of the company's "New Category" products, including branding for Vuse e-cigarettes and Velo nicotine pouches appearing on the drivers' uniforms and the McLaren race cars. During the 2019 Formula 1 season—at 13 races—BAT's taglines "A Better Tomorrow" and "Accelerating Transformation" were also featured (Gratz, 2020). BAT presentations to investors emphasise interrelated strategies for "A Better Tomorrow" and "Accelerating New Category Growth and Profitability" by pointing to products that also include natural remedy cannabidiol (CBD) and others classified as "beyond nicotine" (Dewhirst, in press). Further, for the 2020 season, BAT had "significantly increased branding positions on the Formula 1 car—including highly visible new sidepod branding, inside halo and front wing branding positions," and co-created marketing content to increase awareness about their partnership with McLaren (BAT, 2021, para. 5.). According to BAT's website, "BAT and McLaren share a passion for technology, innovation and design" (BAT, 2021, para. 6.).

Indeed, like other e-cigarette and vaping manufacturers (e.g., JUUL is produced by JUUL Labs), BAT engages in marketing communication that associates their "next generation" products with science as well as innovation and high technology. The corporate website of a BAT subsidiary in Canada, for example, has a dedicated "harm reduction" page where a direct link is provided to "BAT Science" (Imperial Tobacco Canada, 2022). While BAT—and other tobacco companies—have adopted harm reduction in their public relations initiatives, harm reduction is unlikely to be realised because the marketing of "next generation products" such as Vuse is not limited to only those consumers who might genuinely benefit from use (see Dewhirst, 2021b). Instead, reflecting the profit motive of tobacco companies, the marketing of their "next generation products" also attracts new users, dual users (e.g., those continuing to smoke combustible cigarettes while adopting e-cigarettes), and generally discourages outright quit attempts. Given the broad impact of the tobacco industry's marketing on consumer demand (National Cancer Institute, 2008; USDHHS, 2012)—including demand for vaping products (USDHHS, 2016)—the marketing and promotion of "next generation products" is generally inconsistent with the guiding principles of harm reduction. The continued Formula 1 sponsorships by tobacco companies appear motivated by expanding the consumer pool for their nicotine-delivery products.

Alcohol brands also have a prominent sponsorship presence in Formula 1. Heineken—a popular beer brand from the Netherlands—and Ferrari Trento—an Italy-based sparkling wine producer—were identified as

Formula 1 partners for the 2021 season. Heineken became the championship's official global beer in 2016 through a $150 million multi-year sponsorship deal (Reuters, 2016). Champagne still has traditionally featured during the podium ceremonies of Formula 1 races when the winning drivers and teams are recognised and celebrated. Champagne brands such as Moet and Mumm previously had long-time associations with Formula 1 (Noble, 2021b). Additionally, Diageo's Johnnie Walker—a brand of Scottish whisky—began a partnership with the McLaren team in 2005 and became the official whisky of Formula 1 in 2014 (Johnnie Walker, 2021). American brewer, Anheuser-Busch was a notable sponsor of the BMW Williams race team, during the early and mid-2000s, as part of marketing efforts to promote their Budweiser brand globally and broaden the brand's appeal beyond the USA market (Autosport, 2003; BMW Group, 2003). Alcohol companies gain widespread exposure for their respective brands through these partnerships. During the 2017 Formula 1 season, for example, brand exposure was particularly prominent for Heineken and Johnnie Walker, and public health scholars raised concern about the reach of such marketing efforts including a youthful audience (Barker et al., 2018).

Like tobacco, alcohol sponsorship of sports properties has generally undergone scrutiny due to the notable health consequences resulting from alcohol consumption (Sparks et al., 2005; Wenner & Jackson, 2009; Ireland et al., 2019). Alcohol sponsorship of motor racing, in particular, represents a curious combination with impaired driving being a leading cause of death, especially among young adults (MADD, 2021). The sponsorship link between alcohol brands and motor racing events has been identified as problematic with calls for banning alcohol sponsorship (Reuters, 2016). Despite such calls, alcohol sponsorship has persisted, but alcohol sponsors have responded by launching "responsible drinking" media campaigns. Heineken, for example, has created a "If You Drive, Never Drink" campaign to complement its Formula 1 partnership (Reuters, 2016). The brewer's non-alcoholic beer, Heineken 0.0, has also been promoted, which can be interpreted as a pre-emptive attempt to circumvent any future bans of alcohol sponsorship in sport (i.e., brewers would predictably argue that their non-alcoholic products fall outside of the scope of such restrictions and thus should be retained). Meanwhile,

Johnnie Walker has launched a "Join the Pact" campaign—featuring past and current Formula 1 drivers—to demonstrate the brand's commitment to "responsible drinking" (Johnnie Walker, 2021). Consumers are invited to make a pledge online—at Johnnie Walker's website—to never drink and drive. Such "responsible drinking" initiatives suggest it is the *misuse* of alcohol that is problematic, which strategically distinguishes the product category from tobacco when considering the appropriateness of being a sport sponsorship partner (Crompton, 1993).

188BET—a provider of gambling services—was another Formula 1 partner for the 2021 season. Like tobacco and alcohol, gambling has addictive potential, being classified as an addictive disorder according to the Diagnostic and Statistical Manual of Mental Disorders, 5th Edition (DSM-5) (American Psychiatric Association, 2013). Research, including brain imaging and neurochemical tests, shows that the effect of gambling on a consumer's reward system resembles the effect of using substances or drugs like tobacco and alcohol (Reilly & Smith, 2013). Those with gambling disorder are more at-risk for poor general health, suicide, decreased psychosocial and mental health functioning, as well as strained family and employment relationships (Morasco et al., 2006; American Psychiatric Association, 2013). Harm is likely when regular gamblers have instances where they gamble more than initially intended or for those experiencing a loss of control over money or time when they gamble (Blaszczynski et al., 2004). Concerns have been raised that gambling sponsorships, which facilitate brand exposure on television during broadcast sports properties, serve as marketing cues that drive additional sports betting consumption, markedly among those classified as "problem gamblers" (Hing et al., 2013; Hing et al., 2015; Lamont et al., 2016).

Aramco, which is a Saudi Arabia-based (and state-owned) energy and chemicals company that proclaims to produce one in eight barrels of the global oil supply, was an additional Formula 1 partner for the 2021 season. Moreover, Shell is a long-time partner of the Ferrari race team. ExxonMobil—through its Mobil 1 brand of lubricants—was a long-lasting partner of the McLaren team and now serves as a partner for Red Bull Racing (Barretto, 2016). French oil company, Total and BP's Castrol brand have additionally been sponsorship partners for various Formula 1 teams (Reuters Staff, 2017). While the fuel and lubricant brands associated among the racing teams have changed hands regularly over time, the reliance and presence of Big Oil, generally, is long-standing. It is unsurprising that the leading oil companies would serve as prominent sponsors of Formula 1, taking into account the functional links of their products to the sports property as fuel and lubricant suppliers. Still, sponsorship by major oil companies is controversial when consideration is given to the burning of fossil fuels producing carbon dioxide and being a main cause of climate change. Formula 1 faces "greenwashing" accusations by providing sponsorship partners a social licence to operate, and being able to leverage promotional opportunities (e.g., the development of more fuel-efficient engines), despite the events being environmentally destructive (Miller, 2016). The WHO (2021b, para. 1.), has identified climate change as "the single biggest health threat facing humanity"; thus sponsorship by Big Oil serves as a further example of a contradictory pairing of unhealthy or harmful products with sports and athleticism.

The Formula 1 season calendar increasingly includes races in regions known for oil production, such as Qatar and Saudi Arabia, where the hosting of high-profile sports events has also prompted accusations of "sportswashing" (Richards, 2021a). Countries with documented human rights abuses are seen as hosting high-profile sports and entertainment events for the purposes of improving their image and reputation. The inaugural race in Saudi Arabia during the 2021 season generated heightened scrutiny. Canadian musician, Justin Bieber was urged to reconsider and cancel his performance scheduled at the Saudi Arabian Grand Prix. Among those calls for cancelling his concert was a plea from Hatice Cengiz: the fiancée of Jamal Khashoggi—the *Washington Post* journalist—who was murdered by agents with an apparent connection to Crown Prince Mohammed bin Salman (Rachini, 2021).

Seven-time Formula 1 champion, Lewis Hamilton has been outspoken about human rights issues where races are being held. He wore a rainbow-adorned helmet for races in Qatar and Saudi Arabia to show support for the LGBTQ+ community while also directing attention to the repressive laws in these countries that make same-sex relations illegal (Richards, 2021b). Undoubtedly, Formula 1—as a high-profile sports property with global reach—is strategically attractive to companies for fulfilling important marketing objectives and justifying investment as sponsorship partners. Still, companies entering Formula 1 sponsorship must be mindful about which brands—and product sectors—they become aligned with as fellow sponsorship partners from a reputation management standpoint.

Conclusion

Early examples of Formula 1 sponsorship were typically function-based, such as engine, fuel, and tyre suppliers. Sponsorship of Formula 1 served to showcase the performance attributes of brand sponsors or partners. Prominent Formula 1 team sponsorship liveries, however, did not emerge until the late 1960s and early 1970s, when tobacco companies notably turned to sponsoring broadcast sports events to compensate for traditional broadcast advertising exposure no longer allowable. Cigarette advertising became banned from the broadcast media in various jurisdictions—including the UK in 1965 and the USA in 1971—and tobacco companies reallocated significant promotional spending to sponsorship-linked marketing. As tobacco sponsorship became prominent, brand associations leveraged through sponsorship-linked marketing became increasingly symbolic or image-based. Sponsorship spending by tobacco companies in Formula 1 peaked around the turn of the century when they contributed most of the sponsorship revenue among racing team budgets. Since that time, regulations have prompted the removal of cigarette brands from driver and race car liveries, although tobacco companies such as BAT and PMI persist as notable partners in Formula 1.

Today, engine manufacturers such as Ferrari, Honda, Mercedes, and Renault—as well as oil companies being fuel and lubricant suppliers—remain as visible and prominent sponsors. Telecom and technology companies have become known as central Formula 1 partners. Formula 1 is seen as glamorous and exclusive—and linked with elitism and excess in some circles (Nichols & Savage, 2017)—so upscale and high-status brands are drawn to strategically building their associations with the sports property. Despite Formula 1's recent attempts to attract more diverse fan bases, men historically dominate as the actors of Formula 1.

Consequently, some partners have sought to underscore masculine attributes. In their marketing communication, brands such as Marlboro have previously leveraged the rugged and heroic associations of Formula 1. And recently, Red Bull and Monster, which possess mostly masculine attributes in their branding, predictably highlight the adrenaline-filled and exciting associations of motor sports that suitably link with the energy drink sector. Innovation and technology are obviously central attributes of Formula 1 that companies now look to further link with their brands as sponsors.

Over its approximate 70-year history, Formula 1's sponsorship landscape has shifted in several respects. Formula 1 has become increasingly commercialised over time, with the sponsorship landscape visibly denser and more cluttered today. Formula 1 was once largely European in scope, but now represents a global entity. Consequently, brands that serve as sponsors and partners of Formula 1 are notable multinational ones, which are predictably global in ambition and those looking to expand internationally into new and emerging markets. Sponsors may seek links with Formula 1 broadly (e.g., as a global partner) or instead build associations at a racing team level. The global reach of Formula 1 is remarkable with a racing season that typically runs over an eight- or nine-month period. Formula 1 is regarded as an attractive sports property for brands to sponsor as there are opportunities to activate the partnerships nearly year-round. Still, Formula 1 sponsorships have commonly included those from harmful and unhealthy product sectors, which raises several important ethical and social considerations (e.g., the morality of sponsorships that pair products such as tobacco and alcohol with sports and athleticism).

Acknowledgements The authors would like to thank Damion Sturm for his detailed and helpful feedback on an earlier draft of this chapter.

Disclosures Timothy Dewhirst served as an invited consultant for the World Health Organization (WHO), in which he was named as an expert for the elaboration of a template for a protocol on cross-border advertising, promotion, and sponsorship regarding Article 13 guidelines of the

Framework Convention on Tobacco Control (FCTC). He has also served as an expert witness in litigation for governments whose policies regarding the marketing and promotion of tobacco and vaping products were challenged on constitutional grounds.

Note

1. More generally, tobacco companies have commonly associated cigarettes with premium, fast, and powerful motor vehicles in their marketing communication through advertising creative, sponsorship, and licensing agreements. Rothmans—a cigarette brand strategically positioned as representing premium quality, upward status, and internationalism—serves as one example: the brand depicted flashy, extravagant automobiles such as Porsche in earlier advertising (Dewhirst & Sparks, 2011). Additionally, Rothmans served as a predominant sponsor of the Williams racing team from 1994 to 1997. This period of sponsorship included having the legendary Ayrton Senna in the car in 1994, while Damon Hill and Jacques Villeneuve had championship-winning Formula 1 seasons in 1996 and 1997, respectively (Dewhirst & Sparks, 2003). More recently, tobacco producer, Korean Tomorrow and Global (KT & G) launched a Lamborghini-branded cigarette, under licence, for both domestic and international markets (Dewhirst & Lee, 2018).

References

Aaker, J. L. (1997). Dimensions of Brand Personality. *Journal of Marketing Research, 34*(August), 347–356.

Abbruzzese, J. (2021, June 22). Drive to Thrive: Netflix's Docuseries a Boost for Formula 1. *NBC.* Retrieved July 10, 2021, from https://www.nbcnews.com/tech/tech-news/netflix-f1-espn-boost-tv-ratings-espn-rcna1237

American Psychiatric Association. (2013). *Diagnostic and Statistical Manual of Mental Disorders: Fifth Edition.* American Psychiatric Association.

Associated Press. (2021, November 17). LA Lakers' Home to Be Renamed Crypto.com Arena in Reported $700m Deal. *The Guardian.*

Autosport. (2003, July 16). WilliamsF1 Confirms Budweiser Deal. *Autosport*. Retrieved December 1, 2021, from https://www.autosport.com/f1/news/williamsf1-confirms-budweiser-deal-5025182/5025182/

AutoWeek. (2000). Marlboro Brand Formula One Insert: AutoWeek—2001 Racing Fan Guide. AutoWeek by the Numbers, Bates No. 2084445761.

Baldwin, A. (2021, March 25). Motor Racing-Oracle Cloud Partnership Puts the Wind in Red Bull's Sails. *Reuters*. Retrieved July 10, 2021, from https://www.reuters.com/article/motor-f1-redbull-oracle-idUSL4N2LM46N

Barker, A. B., Britton, J., Grant-Braham, B., & Murray, R. L. (2018). Alcohol Audio-Visual Content in Formula 1 Television Broadcasting. *BMC Public Health, 18*, 1155.

Barretto, L. (2016, December 1). F1 Fuel Supplier ExxonMobil Switches from McLaren to Red Bull. *Autosport*.

Bartunek, R.-J. (2007, September 18). Sponsorship, the Big Business Behind F1. *CNN*. Retrieved December 3, 2021, from http://edition.cnn.com/2007/SPORT/09/18/behind.sponsorship/index.html

Blaszczynski, A., Ladouceur, R., & Shaffer, H. J. (2004). A Science-Based Framework for Responsible Gambling: The Reno Model. *Journal of Gambling Studies, 20*(3), 301–317.

Blum, A. (1991). The Marlboro Grand Prix: Circumvention of the Television Ban on Tobacco Advertising. *The New England Journal of Medicine, 324*, 913–917.

BMW Group. (2003, July 17). Budweiser Sponsors BMW Williams F1 Team, Press Release. Retrieved December 1, 2021, from https://www.press.bmwgroup.com/usa/article/detail/T0020636EN_US/budweiser-sponsors-bmw-williamsf1-team?language=en_US

Booth, R. (2021, December 2). Grenfell Survivors Outraged by Lewis Hamilton Car Sponsorship Deal. *The Guardian*.

Bradley, C. (2021, October 21). F1 Fans Becoming Younger and More Diverse, Say Global Survey Results. *Motorsport*. Retrieved February 12, 2022, from https://www.motorsport.com/f1/news/f1-fans-becoming-younger-and-more-diverse-say-global-survey-results-/6696732/

British American Tobacco. (1997). Formula One—A Global Opportunity. Bates No. 321463560–321463592.

British American Tobacco. (1999). Formula One Questions and Answers. Bates No. 321449849–321449864.

British American Tobacco. (2021). Our Global Partnership with McLaren. Retrieved November 25, 2021, from https://www.bat.com/abettertomorrow

Brown & Williamson. (1999). Formula One Sponsorship Proposal. Note to the Chief Executive's Committee, Bates No. 323011267–323011282.

"The Business of Racing". (1989, July 9). Marlboro Advertisement. *The New York Times Magazine.*

Carlyle, J., Collin, J., Muggli, M. E., & Hurt, R. D. (2004). British American Tobacco and Formula One Motor Racing. *British Medical Journal, 329*(7457), 104–106.

Chapman, M. (2021, February 21). New Products, Old Tricks? Concerns Big Tobacco Is Targeting Youngsters. *The Bureaus of Investigative Journalism.* Retrieved May 10, 2021, from https://www.thebureauinvestigates.com/stories/2021-02-21/new-products-old-tricks-concerns-big-tobacco-is-targeting-youngsters

Cleverly, S. (2001). 2001 Formula One Program: Lucky Strike BAR Honda Launch. British American Tobacco documentation, Bates No. 325003466–325003489.

Cornwell, T. B. (1995). Sponsorship-Linked Marketing Development. *Sport Marketing Quarterly, 4*(4), 13–24.

Cornwell, T. B. (1997). The Use of Sponsorship-Linked Marketing by Tobacco Firms: International Public Policy Issues. *Journal of Consumer Affairs, 31*(2), 238–254.

Cornwell, T. B. (2008). State of the Art and Science in Sponsorship-Linked Marketing. *Journal of Advertising, 37*(3), 41–55.

Cornwell, T. B., Roy, D. P., & Steinard, E. A. (2001). Exploring Managers' Perceptions of the Impact of Sponsorship on Brand Equity. *Journal of Advertising, 30*(2), 41–51.

Crompton, J. L. (1993). Sponsorship of Sport by Tobacco and Alcohol Companies: A Review of the Issues. *Journal of Sport and Social Issues, 17*, 148–167.

Dangoor, D. E. R. (1987). Project Red Ferrari Trademark for the U.S. Interoffice Correspondence of Philip Morris USA, Bates No. 2044201818.

Dean, S. (2021, November 16). Goodbye, Staples Center. Hello, Crypto.com Arena. *Los Angeles Times.*

Dewhirst, T. (2004). Smoke and Ashes: Tobacco Sponsorship of Sports and Regulatory Issues in Canada. In L. R. Kahle & C. Riley (Eds.), *Sports Marketing and the Psychology of Marketing Communication* (pp. 327–352). Lawrence Erlbaum Associates, Inc.

Dewhirst, T. (2016, September 17). The NHL Is Eyeing Jersey Ads, But Will Hockey Fans Call Offside? *The Globe and Mail.*

Dewhirst, T. (2021a, March 10). This NHL Game Is Brought to You by (Place Ad Here). *The Toronto Star*.

Dewhirst, T. (2021b). Co-optation of Harm Reduction by Big Tobacco. *Tobacco Control, 30*(November), e1–e3.

Dewhirst, T. (in press). 'Beyond Nicotine' Marketing Strategies: Big Tobacco Diversification into the Vaping and Cannabis Product Sector. *Tobacco Control*.

Dewhirst, T., & Hunter, A. (2002). Tobacco Sponsorship of Formula One and CART Auto Racing: Tobacco Brand Exposure and Enhanced Symbolic Imagery Through Co-sponsors' Third Party Advertising. *Tobacco Control, 11*(2), 146–150.

Dewhirst, T., & Lee, W. B. (2018). Lamborghini Brand Sharing and Cigarette Advertising. *Tobacco Control, 27*(2), 237–239.

Dewhirst, T., & Sparks, R. (2003). Intertextuality, Tobacco Sponsorship of Sports, and Adolescent Male Smoking Culture: A Selective Review of Tobacco Industry Documents. *Journal of Sport and Social Issues, 27*(4), 372–398.

Dewhirst, T., & Sparks, R. (2011). Brand Mismanagement: Rothmans Cigarette Marketing, 1957–2000. *Journal of Historical Research in Marketing, 3*(3), 351–369.

Dixon, E. (2021, January 7). McLaren F1 Esports Series Boosts British American Tobacco Gaming Presence. *SportsPro*. Retrieved July 10, 2021, from https://www.sportspromedia.com/news/mclaren-f1-velo-esports-series-british-american-tobacco-gaming

Fitch, A. (2018, February 13). Renault Announces Partnership with Team Vitality. *Esports Insider*. Retrieved February 12, 2022, from https://esportsinsider.com/2018/02/renault-sport-team-vitality-announced/

Fleming, D., & Sturm, D. (2011). *Media, Masculinities and the Machine: F1, Transformers and Fantasizing Technology at Its Limits*. Continuum.

Grange, M. (2001). Win on Sunday . . . Sell on Monday. *R.O.B. Magazine, 18*, 36-40.

Gratz, M. (2020, December 11). Some Motorsport Teams Remain Addicted to Tobacco Company Sponsorship Deals, Despite Tobacco Causing 8 Million Deaths Each Year. *CNN*. Retrieved July 10, 2021, from https://edition.cnn.com/2020/12/11/motorsport/formula-one-tobacco-sponsorship-deals-spt-itl/index.html

Gwinner, K. (1997). A Model of Image Creation and Image Transfer in Event Sponsorship. *International Marketing Review, 14*(3), 145–158.

Gwinner, K. P., & Eaton, J. (1999). Building Brand Image Through Event Sponsorship: The Role of Image Transfer. *Journal of Advertising, 28*(4), 47–57.

Hafez, N., & Ling, P. M. (2005). How Philip Morris Built Marlboro into a Global Brand for Young Adults: Implications for International Tobacco Control. *Tobacco Control, 14*, 262–271.

Hawaleshka, D. (2001, June 25). Grand Prix Wizardry. *Maclean's, 114*, 40–41.

Henderson, C. M., Mazodier, M., & Sundar, A. (2019). The Color of Support: The Effect of Sponsor-Team Visual Congruence on Sponsorship Performance. *Journal of Marketing, 83*(3), 50–71.

Hing, N., Lamont, M., Vitartas, P., & Fink, E. (2015). Sports Bettors' Responses to Sports-Embedded Gambling Promotions: Implications for Compulsive Consumption. *Journal of Business Research, 68*, 2057–2066.

Hing, N., Vitartas, P., & Lamont, M. (2013). Gambling Sponsorship of Sport: An Exploratory Study of Links with Gambling Attitudes and Intentions. *International Gambling Studies, 13*(3), 281–301.

Imperial Tobacco Canada. (2022). Tobacco Harm Reduction. Retrieved February 13, 2022, from http://www.imperialtobaccocanada.com/group/sites/BAT_AXYKCM.nsf/vwPagesWebLive/DO9T5KLN

Indaimo, A. (2020, September 11). Formula 1 and Esports in the Time of Coronavirus. *Withersworldwide*. Retrieved July 10, 2021, from https://www.withersworldwide.com/en-gb/insight/formula-1-and-esports-in-the-time-of-coronavirus

Ireland, R., Bunn, C., Reith, G., Philpott, M., Capewell, S., Boyland, E., & Chambers, S. (2019). Commercial Determinants of Health: Advertising of Alcohol and Unhealthy Foods During Sporting Events. *Bulletin of the World Health Organization, 97*, 290–295.

Irwin, R., & Asimakopoulos, M. (1992). An Approach to the Evaluation and Selection of Sport Sponsorship Proposals. *Sport Marketing Quarterly, 1*, 43–51.

Irwin, R. L., & Sutton, W. A. (1994). Sport Sponsorship Objectives: An Analysis of Their Relative Importance for Major Corporate Sponsors. *European Journal of Sport Management, 1*, 93–101.

Jenkins, M., Pasternak, K., & West, R. (2016). *Performance at the Limit: Business Lessons from Formula 1 Motor Racing* (3rd ed.). Cambridge University Press.

Jewell, A. (2016, July 8). British Grand Prix 1976: How a Condom Manufacturer Forced F1 Off TV. *BBC Sport*. Retrieved February 11, 2022, from https://www.bbc.com/sport/formula1/35748458

Johnnie Walker. (2021). *Lead the Celebration*. Retrieved July 22, 2021, from https://www.johnniewalker.com/en-sg/whisky-guide/responsible-drinking/

Lamont, M., Hing, N., & Vitartas, P. (2016). Affective Response to Gambling Promotions During Televised Sport: A Qualitative Analysis. *Sport Management Review, 19*(3), 319–331.

Larson, J. F., & Park, H. (1993). *Global Television and the Politics of the Seoul Olympics*. Westview Press.

Lavack, A. M. (2003). An Inside View of Tobacco Sports Sponsorship: An Historical Perspective. *International Journal of Sports Marketing and Sponsorship, 5*, 33–56.

Ledwith, F. (1984). Does Tobacco Sports Sponsorship on Television Act as Advertising to Children? *Health Education Journal, 43*(4), 85–88.

Lindstrom, M. (2005). *Brand Sense: Build Powerful Brands Through Touch, Taste, Smell, Sight, and Sound*. Free Press.

MADD. (2021). *MADD: No Alcohol. No Drugs. No Victims*. Retrieved July 10, 2021, from https://madd.ca/pages/programs/youth-services/statistics-links/

Marshall, D. W., & Cook, G. (1992). The Corporate (Sports) Sponsor. *International Journal of Advertising, 11*, 307–324.

McCracken, G. (1988). *Culture and Consumption*. Indiana University Press.

McDaniel, S. R. (1999). An Investigation of Match-Up Effects in Sport Sponsorship Advertising: The Implications of Consumer Advertising Schemas. *Psychology & Marketing, 16*(2), 163–184.

Meenaghan, T. (1983). Commercial Sponsorship. *European Journal of Marketing, 17*, 5–73.

Meenaghan, T. (1991). The Role of Sponsorship in the Marketing Communications Mix. *International Journal of Advertising, 10*, 35–47.

Miller, T. (2016). Greenwashed Sports and Environmental Activism: Formula 1 and FIFA. *Environmental Communication, 10*(6), 719–733.

Mission Winnow. (2021). *Breaking New Science Ground*. Retrieved May 10, 2021, from https://www.missionwinnow.com/en/pmi/science-and-innovation-at-pmi/

Morasco, B. J., Pietrzak, R. H., Blanco, C., Grant, B. F., Hasin, D., & Petry, N. M. (2006). Health Problems and Medical Utilization Associated with Gambling Disorders: Results from the National Epidemiologic Survey on Alcohol and Related Conditions. *Psychosomatic Medicine, 68*(6), 976–984.

Morrison, M., Haygood, D. M., & Krugman, D. M. (2006). Inhaling and Accelerating: Tobacco Motor Sports Sponsorship in Televised Automobile Races, 2000–2002. *Sport Marketing Quarterly, 15*(1), 7–19.

National Cancer Institute. (2008). *The Role of the Media in Promoting and Reducing Tobacco Use*. Smoking and Tobacco Control Monograph No. 19.

Bethesda, MD: US Department of Health and Human Services, National Institutes of Health, National Cancer Institute.
Nichols, G., & Savage, M. (2017). A Social Analysis of an Elite Constellation: The Case of Formula 1. *Theory, Culture & Society, 34*(5–6), 201–225.
Noble, J. (2021a, April 8). Why 'Fighter Jet' F1 Is Winning a New Wave of Sponsors. *Autosport*. Retrieved June 30, 2021, from https://www.motorsport.com/f1/news/fight-jet-new-wave-sponsors/6129935/
Noble, J. (2021b, March 2). F1 Drivers to Use Sparkling Wine Again in Podium Celebrations. *Autosport*. Retrieved July 22, 2021, from https://www.autosport.com/f1/news/f1-drivers-to-use-sparkling-wine-again-in-podium-celebrations-5557826/5557826/
Otker, T. (1988). Exploitation: The Key to Sponsorship Success. *European Research, 16*, 77–86.
Otker, T., & Hayes, P. (1987). Judging the Efficiency of Sponsorship: Experience from the 1986 Soccer World Cup. *ESOMAR Congress, 15*, 3–8.
Philip Morris. (1982). Pan European Motor Racing Awareness—1982. Bates No. 2044201862–2044201873.
Philip Morris. (1983). Marlboro and Motor Racing. Bates No. 2501060185–2501060186.
Philip Morris. (1991). Proposed Comments on Italy Objectives 1991. Bates No. 2501056407.
Philip Morris. (1992). Adaptation Marketing Plan [Lausanne, Post-Vizzini]. Bates No. 2501060177.
Philip Morris. (1998). Marlboro Racing. Bates No. 2070683673–2070683709.
Philips, D., & Whannel, G. (2013). *The Trojan Horse: The Growth of Commercial Sponsorship*. Bloomsbury.
Prendergast, G. P., Poon, D., & West, D. C. (2010). Match Game: Linking Sponsorship Congruence with Communication Outcomes. *Journal of Advertising Research, 50*(June), 214–226.
Race Report [Report: Canada]. (2002, July). *F1 Racing*.
Rachini, M. (2021, December 1). Saudi Arabia Is Using Justin Bieber, F1 Event to 'Whitewash' Its Human Rights Record: Human Rights Watch. *CBC Radio*.
Reilly, C., & Smith, N. (2013). The Evolving Definition of Pathological Gambling in the DSM-5. *National Center for Responsible Gaming White Paper*. National Center for Responsible Gaming.
Reuters. (2016, June 14). Heineken's F1 Deal Leads to Further Call for Ban on Alcohol Sponsorship. *The Guardian*. Retrieved July 22, 2021, from https://www.theguardian.com/sport/2016/jun/14/heineken-f1-alchohol-sponsorship-eurocare

Reuters Staff. (2017, January 26). BP Replaces Total as Renault F1 Fuel Partner. *Reuters*.

Richards, G. (2021a, December 1). F1 Under Pressure to Speak Out Against Saudi Human Right Abuses. *The Guardian*.

Richards, G. (2021b, December 2). Lewis Hamilton Condemns 'Terrifying' LGBTQ+ Laws before Saudi Arabian GP. *The Guardian*.

Rolex. (2021). World of Rolex. Retrieved December 5, 2021, from https://www.rolex.com/en-us/world-of-rolex.html

Sahlins, M. D. (1976). *Culture and Practical Reason*. University of Chicago Press.

Siegel, M. (2001). Counteracting Tobacco Motor Sports Sponsorship as a Promotional Tool: Is the Tobacco Settlement Enough? *American Journal of Public Health, 91*, 1100–1106.

Simpson, D. (2004). Turkey: F1 Keeps on Coming. *Tobacco Control, 13*, 217–218.

Sleight, S. (1989). *Sponsorship: What It Is and How to Use It*. McGraw-Hill.

Sparks, R., Dewhirst, T., Jette, S., & Schweinbenz, A. (2005). Historical Hangovers or Burning Possibilities: Regulation and Adaptation in Global Tobacco and Alcohol Sponsorship. In J. Amis & T. B. Cornwell (Eds.), *Global Sport Sponsorship: A Multidisciplinary Study* (pp. 19–66). Berg Publishers.

Sparks, R. E. C. (1997). Bill C-71 and Tobacco Sponsorship of Sports. *Policy Options, 18*, 22–25.

Stoner, R. H. (1992). 200 mph Cigarette Ads: A Comparison of International Restrictions on Tobacco Sports Sponsorship. *Hastings International and Comparative Law Review, 15*, 639–670.

Stubbs, M. (2020, August 5). New Report From Fnatic Shows Esports Grew Significantly During The Pandemic. *Forbes*. Retrieved July 10, 2021, from https://www.forbes.com/sites/mikestubbs/2020/08/05/new-report-from-fnatic-shows-esports-grew-significantlyduring-the-pandemic/?sh=4d9f79767de4

Sturm, D. (2014). A Glamorous and High-Tech Global Spectacle of Speed: Formula One Motor Racing as Mediated, Global and Corporate Spectacle. In K. Dashper, T. Fletcher, & N. McCullough (Eds.), *Sports Events, Society and Culture* (pp. 68–82). Routledge.

Sturm, D. (2019). Not Your Average Sunday Driver: The Formula 1 Esports Series World Championship. In R. Rogers (Ed.), *Understanding Esports: An Introduction to the Global Phenomenon* (pp. 153–165). Lexington.

Townley, S., & Grayson, E. (1984). *Sponsorship of Sport, Arts and Leisure*. Sweet & Maxwell.

Tso, D. (1987). Ferrari Project. Interoffice Correspondence of Philip Morris USA, Bates No. 2041510534–2041510544.

Turco, D. M. (1999). The State of Tobacco Sponsorship in Sport. *Sport Marketing Quarterly, 8*, 35–38.

U.S. Department of Health and Human Services. (1988). *The Health Consequences of Smoking: Nicotine Addiction. A Report of the Surgeon General.* U.S. Department of Health and Human Services, Public Health Service, Centers for Disease Control, National Center for Chronic Disease Prevention and Health Promotion, Office on Smoking and Health.

U.S. Department of Health and Human Services. (2004). *The Health Consequences of Smoking: A Report of the Surgeon General.* Atlanta, GA, U.S. Department of Health and Human Services, Centers for Disease Control and Prevention, National Center for Chronic Disease Prevention and Health Promotion, Office on Smoking and Health.

U.S. Department of Health and Human Services. (2012). *Preventing Tobacco Use Among Youth and Young Adults: A Report of the Surgeon General.* Atlanta, GA, U.S. Department of Health and Human Services, Centers for Disease Control and Prevention, National Center for Chronic Disease Prevention and Health Promotion, Office on Smoking and Health.

U.S. Department of Health and Human Services. (2014). *50 Years of Progress: A Report of the Surgeon General.* Atlanta, GA, U.S. Department of Health and Human Services, Centers for Disease Control and Prevention, National Center for Chronic Disease Prevention and Health Promotion, Office on Smoking and Health.

U.S. Department of Health and Human Services. (2016). *E-cigarette Use Among Youth and Young Adults: A Report of the Surgeon General.* U.S. Department of Health and Human Services.

Verlinden, J. (1999). Briefing: Alternative Branding. British American Tobacco Documentation, Bates No. 321613157–321613158.

Vital Strategies. (2020). *Driving Addiction: F1 and Tobacco Advertising.*

Warner, K. E. (1979). Clearing the Airwaves: The Cigarette Ad Ban Revisited. *Policy Analysis, 5*, 435–450.

Wenner, L., & Jackson, S. (Eds.). (2009). *Sport, Beer and Gender: Promotional Culture and Contemporary Social Life*. Peter Lang.

Wenner, L. A. (1993). Tidings for the New Year: On Sport Sponsorship Without the Smoke. *Journal of Sport and Social Issues, 17*, 146–147.

Wichmann, S. A., & Martin, D. R. (1991). Sports and Tobacco: The Smoke Has Yet to Clear. *The Physician and Sportsmedicine, 19*, 125–131.

World Health Organization. (2008). *Mpower: A Policy Package to Reverse the Tobacco Epidemic*. World Health Organization.

World Health Organization. (2019). WHO Urges Governments to Enforce Bans on Tobacco Advertising, Promotion and Sponsorship, Including in Motor Sport. Retrieved June 10, 2021, from https://www.who.int/news/item/14-03-2019-who-urges-governments-to-enforce-bans-on-tobacco-advertising-promotion-and-sponsorship-including-in-motor-sport

World Health Organization. (2021a). Parties to the WHO Framework Convention on Tobacco Control. Retrieved December 5, 2021, from https://www.who.int/fctc/cop/en/

World Health Organization. (2021b). Climate Change—The Biggest Health Threat Facing Humanity. Retrieved December 3, 2021, from https://www.who.int/news-room/fact-sheets/detail/climate-change-and-health

Yeomans, G. (2021, March 15). Red Bull F1 Eyes US Market with Walmart Deal. *SportsPro*. Retrieved June 30, 2021, from https://www.sportspromedia.com/news/red-bull-f1-walmart-america-2021-formula-one

"Men Love Women, But Even More Than That, Men Love Cars": Motor Racing on Film

Seán Crosson

The nomination at the 2019 Academy Awards ceremony of *Ford v Ferrari* (2019) for the Best Film Oscar provided us with a high-profile reminder of the prominence of motor racing in contemporary film. In total the film received four nominations, winning for Best Film Editing and Best Sound Editing; *Ford v Ferrari* also received both critical and commercial acclaim, taking US$225.5 million at the international box-office alone before its release on DVD and via streaming platforms.[1] However the critical response to the film was also revealing with regard to the depiction of motor racing on film, as well as the sports film genre more broadly to which it belongs (Crosson, 2013). Indeed, the sporting context featured was often not the principal concern of reviewers, despite the fact that its lead protagonists are motor racing drivers and its most dynamic sequences feature motor racing. Furthermore, the film's original title de-emphasises its sporting connection—though this was highlighted more clearly in some European territories where the production was retitled *Le*

S. Crosson (✉)
University of Galway, Galway, Ireland
e-mail: sean.crosson@nuigalway.ie

D. Sturm et al. (eds.), *The History and Politics of Motor Racing*, Global Culture and Sport Series, https://doi.org/10.1007/978-3-031-22825-4_18

Mans '66, referring to the French endurance motor race featured prominently within the production. A recurring focus of commentary was on the relationship between the two principal male characters in the film, car designer Carroll Shelby (Mat Damon) and British driver Ken Miles (Christian Bale), described in terms of "bromance" by several reviewers. As noted by Jinal Bhatt, "After Bale and Damon's bromance, my second favourite thing about the film has to be the racing scenes" (Bhatt, 2020). A *New Yorker* review also responded to this aspect, noting that, "the big romance in the movie is bromance, and Mangold conjures it with a touch that's reminiscent of the rowdy friendships found in films by Howard Hawks and John Ford" (Brody, 2019). What both reviewers are responding to are central concerns found throughout the depiction of motor racing on film, particularly when found in fiction. These films may contain drivers and sequences of motor racing; however, what they are more concerned with are the various relationships, challenges and tensions that attend men and masculinity (with women occupying at best supporting roles), in a sport long renowned for its danger. This chapter will map the development of the depiction of motor racing on film with a particular focus (given the limitations of what a single chapter can address) on live-action fiction film emerging from the United States, the country that has by far produced the largest number of relevant depictions. In doing so, major recurring themes evident will be highlighted, as well as the progression of technical advances in the filming of motor racing.[2]

Masculinity and the Sports Film

The focus on men and masculinity within depictions of motor racing reflects a broader theme found across the sport cinema genre where the performance of gender roles has been a defining feature throughout its history (Crosson, 2013, pp. 103–124). Judith Butler has criticised the restriction of "the meaning of gender to received notions of masculinity and femininity" (Butler, 1999, p. viii), viewing it as primarily performative (rather than being an internal essence) and manufactured through a "sustained set of acts, posited through the gendered stylization of the body" (pp. xv–xvi). This is particularly so for masculine identities; as

David Scott has posited, drawing on the work of Elisabeth Badinter and Monique Schneider, "[w]ithin the western tradition from the Greeks onward, masculine identity seems, much more so than feminine identity, something that had to be *constructed*" (Scott, 2010, p. 143). Sport is one of the most revealing sites where this construction is apparent and can be examined. As I have noted previously (Crosson, 2013, pp. 103–104), "sport has historically been concerned above all with the glorification of masculinity and the male body. By masculinity, I refer to qualities such as power, strength, height and wealth which men in the United States and elsewhere in the Western World have been encouraged to aspire to." It is true that women may in more recent years feature more prominently in professional sports and within the sports film genre. However, sport as an institution continues to be a principal site for the "inculcation, expression, and perpetuation of masculine habits, identities, behavior, and ideals, including a belief in patriarchal supremacy over women" (Smith, 2009, p. 160; Dunning, 1986). Indeed, the areas in which sport takes place and is engaged with are spaces that have historically been primarily associated with men from sports fields, to locker rooms, golf clubs, boxing clubs, gambling establishments, bars and motor racing tracks, areas in which women were permitted (at best) restricted access (Smith, 2009, p. 163). Equally, despite the increasing prominence of female athletes, elite sport and its representation is overwhelmingly associated with men who provide the standard for performance. It is not surprising therefore that the sports film is overwhelming focused on male athletes and protagonists, and the broader theme of masculinity, including the sub-genre dedicated to motor racing. Here, women occupy primarily supporting roles as either inspirational muse or femme fatale (Crosson, 2013, pp. 107–110; Mulvey, 1975, pp. 6–18). They can sometimes feature as the focus of conflict, a key requirement in fiction film, between male protagonists (exemplified by the familiar love triangle scenario found repeatedly in mainstream drama) or as foils to highlight salient aspects of male characters, including their vulnerabilities and insecurities. In this respect, female sexuality can be presented as a threatening force in need of both discipline and control. The precarious nature of motor racing itself, where drivers face the real possibility of serious injury or death, has also provided directors with a dramatic arena to focus on masculinity and its vulnerabilities.

The Arrival of Fiction Cinema

As cinema evolved in the 1910s and fiction film increasingly came to the fore, motor racing featured occasionally, particularly as filmmaking technology and the practice of motor racing advanced. The first fiction production featuring motor racing was the eight-minute Keystone Film Company release *The Speed* Kings (1913). Mack Sennet, the founder of Keystone, had developed a personal interest in motor racing to the extent that he purchased his own race car and entered it in the 1913 Santa Monica Road Race. Though he lost the race, the experience gave him the opportunity to film the event (including from a camera mounted on his car) which he subsequently integrated into a fiction film he wrote, hanging a flimsy and unconvincing love triangle scenario on the racing sequences (Kalat, 2015). Despite the weakness of the story and overall narrative, the film has important historical interest as it features major figures in American motor racing at the time. In addition, *The Speed Kings* provides a still fascinating depiction of both the vehicles used and how races were run, including the two-man teams that collaborated in each car, and the huge crowds in attendance. Furthermore, the film anticipated what would continue to be central features of subsequent motor racing productions: the integration of actual race footage into a fictional scenario, and the prominent concern with men and masculinity, and the various challenges they encounter, accentuated by the precarious nature of the sport they participate in. In this context, women occupy primarily supporting roles, often as the love interest or the focus of a love contest, as evident in *The Speed Kings* as the two racers—actual contemporary racers Teddy Tetzlaft and Earl Cooper (her "papa"'s (Ford Sterling) preferred suitor)—compete for Mabel's (Mabel Normand) affections.

The Santa Monica Road Race is also featured in the first feature-length production to depict motor racing prominently,[3] the Famous Players-Lasky release *The Roaring Road* (1919). Described by one online commentator as the film that "started the public's love affair" with motor racing movies (Anonymous, n.d.), the film stars Wallace Reid, who (like Sennet) had a personal interest in the subject. The opening of *The Roaring Road* tells us that the "Grand Prize"[4] road race has never been won three times in a row by a single car manufacturer, though the Darco Motor Company has succeeded twice, and the company's president, J.D. "The Bear" Ward (Theodore Roberts), is determined to ensure a third victory as he awaits the delivery of three new Darco racecars. The depiction of an ambitious automobile manufacturer reflected broader developments in this period where car manufacturing became increasingly important to the US economy and a growing source of employment (Nye, 2015, p. 21).

Motor sales are also a focus of *The Roaring Road* in the profession of the central protagonist "The Bear"'s leading salesman and would-be race driver, Walter Thomas Walden, aka "Toodles" (Reid). Like *The Speed Kings*, a love story is also prominently featured as Toodles seeks to marry J.D.'s "motherless cub," Dorothy (Ann Little). Without J.D.'s knowledge or permission, Toodles enters in the "Grand Prize" driving a car he had built from Darco Motor Company wrecks and duly wins, earning a new more lucrative contract from "the Bear," and eventually (after further twists in the narrative) his permission to marry Dorothy. While *The Roaring Road* made limited technical strides in advancing the filming of motor racing, themes and tropes central to the sub-genre—including the danger of the sport, focus on men and masculinity, and the undermining, marginalisation and infantilisation of women—were already evident.[5]

Motor Racing in Early Sound Cinema

The success of motor racing films featuring Wallace Reid inspired the production of the first English language sound feature to include motor racing, the 1930 pre-code Paramount Pictures production *Burning Up*. According to Fleming (2013), Paramount's Jesse L. Lasky emulated "Wally's films almost exactly," with cinematographer Allen G. Siegler filming "the racing scenes exactly as Wally's had been done" (p. 235). The film received lukewarm reviews, however, on release and was described by the *New York Times* as

> A light and breezy story of the speedways, not calculated to disturb any gray matter … 'Suicide' Larrigan, a racing driver, enters into a conspiracy to defraud citizens of Carfax of their money by being the party to a 'framed' race. But he discovers that the father of the girl he loves has placed $25,000 on the outcome of the race, so instead of losing it, he wins. (Anonymous, 1930)

The review does acknowledge the presence of "excellent 'shots' of racing cars," and there are moments of impressive on-track cinematography, in particular in the final climactic motor race between lead protagonist Lou Larrigan (Richard Arlen) and "Bullet" McGhan (Francis McDonald). While back-projection (the standard for the time) does feature for close-ups, this race includes a sophisticated range of on-track camera angles and positions—including following shots, shots from a car racing ahead of the drivers and from cameras attached to the cars themselves. A further feature evident is the use of the on-track commentator to provide narrative information on the race depicted, a familiar feature of subsequent motor racing films.

The *New York Times* also described Mary Brian (Larrigan's main love interest, Ruth Morgan) as playing "one of those stupid roles in which the girl takes the word of the villain rather than the explanations of the man she loves" (Anonymous, 1930). Some of the dialogue featured in this respect does not date well; when Ruth discovers Lou has been involved with other women in the past, he describes them as "practice … like a fellow goes out and tunes up for a race," a remark that Ruth appears to ultimately accept as they end up together by the end. The world of motor racing, and those who invest or bet on it, is also presented as an essentially male and privileged domain, including shots of well-dressed card players in the "stag club" who discuss bets on the upcoming (fixed) motor race.

Motor Racing on Film in the 1930s

Young and Young (2007) in their discussion of popular culture during the Great Depression describe *Burning Up* as "one of the spate of race-track movies" that emerged as Hollywood "reacted to automobiles and speed" (p. 319). Many of these films were either B movies (including *The Racing Strain*, *High* Speed (1932), *The Big Thrill* (1933), *Speed* (1936), *Speed* Devils (1935) and *Burn 'Em Up O'Connor* (1939)) or low budget independent films (Ten Laps to Go (1936)), or (in the British context) "quota quickies,"[6] as in *Death Drives* Through (1935). This is reflected in a reliance in these films on poorly integrated stock racing footage, unimpressive cinematography or unoriginality in approach. Inevitably, the recurring format of a male protagonist and his romantic difficulties set against the precarity of motor racing feature, with an (equally predictable) final big race encounter providing the climax. However, occasionally a major (often emerging) star of Hollywood did feature, including a young James Stewart (*Speed* (1936)) and Pat O'Brien (*Indianapolis* Speedway (1939)).

Many of Hollywood's 1930s motor racing films were building on the success at the start of the decade of *The Crowd Roars* (1932), which featured one of Hollywood's biggest stars, James Cagney. Directed by seminal director and motor racing enthusiast Howard Hawks, *The Crowd Roars* (remade in 1939 as *Indianapolis Speedway*) is one of the more unsettling depictions of motor racing to emerge—it also engages directly with the sport by including actual motor racing drivers, including Billy Arnold, winner of the 1930 Indianapolis 500, a race featured prominently (McCarthy, 1997). Further authenticity was added with the inclusion of actual crowd and track footage and the collaboration of the Duesenberg brothers, designers of some of the most successful motor racing cars in the period (McBride, 2013). Original releases of the film also included innovative tinted sequences for the final climactic race (Milner, 1932). Despite this, the racing sequences are less impressive than some earlier productions with back projection used liberally. However, as a pre-Code film, *The Crowd Roars* engages more frankly with sexual politics and violence in a manner that would largely disappear from Hollywood films with the enforcement of the Motion Picture Production Code censorship guidelines in 1934.

Moreover, the dangers of motor racing are foregrounded in *The Crowd Roars* with the film beginning with shots of a car race, a car tumbling and crashing in a likely deadly event and the crowd roaring in shock. It is this appeal of motor racing that is both emphasised and critiqued within the film. Cagney plays Joe Greer, a successful motor racing driver who tries to convince his brother Eddie not to enter his profession, describing the crowd as "watching for wrecks and roaring for blood." Despite his protestations, Joe eventually agrees to bring Eddie with him to his races. However, when he finds Eddie drinking with Joe's girlfriend Lee (Ann Dvorak) and her friend Anne (Joan Blondell), he breaks up with Lee leading Anne to seduce Eddie out of anger with the treatment of her friend. The perceived threat of female sexuality is evident in this sequence in the film: "fine couple of tramps you two" Joe remarks to Lee and Anne. Anne is filmed initially with her largely naked legs propped up on the table before her, which Joe knocks angrily to the ground before physically throwing her out of the room. Lee's reaction to the breakup is also revealing as she cries hysterically to her friend Anne: "I can't let him go"; while the woman scorned is depicted as in desperate need of her man, the man feels threatened by her sexuality.

Anne and Eddie fall in love precipitating a fight between the brothers, which leads Joe to rely increasingly on alcohol while bringing his family squabbles onto the race track. When Joe's backup driver "Spud" Connors (Frank McHugh) tries to separate the brothers during a race, he is forced off by Joe, leading to Spud crashing out of the race and his horrific death in his burning car. This is a particularly disturbing scene in the film as we hear Spud's screams and other drivers continue to race around the track despite the smoke, flames and smell of burning flesh which they try to alleviate by covering their faces. Eventually several pull out of the race and Joe crashes out himself. The horrific memory of Spud's crash leads to Joe's rapid decline in racing and dropping out of the sport, before returning at the film's close for a final on-track reconciliation between the brothers. The focus on masculinity, danger and suspicions of female sexuality evident in *The Crowd Roars* would continue in the decades that followed, including in the rare film text that featured a female driver.

The Impact of World War II on Motor Racing on Film: A Female Race Driver?

The advent of World War II contributed to what Mary Ann Abate has described as "a paradigm shift" in American society with regard to the role of women (Abate, 2008, p. 145; see also Chafe, 1991). The impact of women's increasing involvement in positions outside the home during the War also had an influence on depictions of motor racing, though the tensions and fears such changes brought were equally evident in the first English language film to feature a female racing driver, *Blonde Comet* (1941). Directed by William Beaudine, the film stars Virginia Vale as the "Blonde Comet," Beverly Blake who establishes her reputation as a leading driver on the European circuit before returning to the States to race. On her return her main rival is Jim Flynn (Robert Kent) with whom she eventually develops a romantic relationship.

It is noteworthy that this low-budget film (reliant on poorly integrated stock footage) was made by the "Poverty Row,"[7] Hollywood studio Producers Releasing Corporation; no major studio would take on the topic of a norm-breaking female motor racing driver, a role that ostensibly (as the film indicates) breaks the prevailing patriarchal order. As Flynn remarks in an early scene on first hearing of the "Blonde Comet": "what right has she to be in this racket anyway. It's no game for a woman, it's tough enough for a man. If I was her old man I'd spank her good." His subsequent remark "she better not get in my way" also reveals the perceived threat she presents to him (as to all men) as she takes on a role conventionally held by men. However, there is a clear attempt to both assuage such fears and restore the "natural" order, particularly in the climactic race (at the Indianapolis 500) when Blake gives up her opportunity to win (seemingly (as a woman!) exhausted and unable to finish) by asking Flynn to race in her car and ultimately take victory. Following Flynn's victory, we see an intimate moment between the two where he remarks: "I'm not going to let you leave here until you promise that today's race was your last." When Blake protests, Flynn continues "It's a man's job. From now on the man of the family will take care of it." Blake interprets these words as a proposal and the film ends with their kiss, and her seeming acceptance of the return to the "natural order." While there is a real (if incomplete) attempt here to put the genie back in the bottle, returning women to the domestic sphere, the tension regarding the increasing independence and empowerment of women and its threat to prevailing constructions of masculinity and patriarchy is nonetheless clear.

Motor Racing on Film in the Post-War Era

Motor racing appeared increasingly in Hollywood (and world) cinema in the post-war era. This included British (*Mask of Dust* (1954), which included Sterling Moss and further major figures in motor racing in the period, and *Checkpoint* (1956)), East German (*Rivalen am Steuer* (1957)) and French (*Un homme et une femme* (1966)) productions. However, Hollywood continued to dominate the sub-genre with some of its biggest stars appearing behind the wheel including James Caan (*Red Line 7000* (1965)), James Garner (*Grand Prix* (1966)), Paul Newman (*Winning* (1969)), Steve McQueen (*Le Mans* (1971)) and Al Pacino (*Bobby Deerfield* (1977)). Music legend Elvis Presley also played a race car driver in no less than three musicals between 1964 and 1968, including *Viva Las Vegas* (1964), *Spinout* (1966) and the NASCAR[8]-themed *Speedway* (1968). However, as with most Elvis films, the productions contribute little to the depiction of motor racing and are primarily promotional opportunities to foreground Elvis' musical rather than driving (or indeed acting!) abilities.

The first colour Hollywood production to feature motor racing was Henry Hathaway's *The Racers* (1955), starring Kirk Douglas, one of the top box-office draws of the 1950s and 1960s. The film was shot using the still new widescreen Cinemascope process introduced two years previously and this contributes considerably to the cinematic spectacle in which sequences of motor racing, shot by cinematographer Joe MacDonald, dominate proceedings, and are of considerably more interest than the overly familiar, unconvincing and unengaging accompanying narrative. As the *New York Times* reviewer noted on the film's release

> This film about auto road racing is made for those youthful car fans who take pleasure in scorching the highways and wrapping their souped-up jalopies around poles ... For thc constant reiteration in this big CinemaScope color film, which offers Kirk Douglas as a racing driver who is torn between his bright red Ferrari and a dame, is one of fast cars coming at you, sweeping by you, shooting loudly over your head and whizzing with terrifying velocity along crowd-lined streets and roads. (Crowther, 1955)

The danger of the sport featured is also emphasised with serious crashes occurring in most races depicted, and also in the film's retitling in some territories as *Such Men Are Dangerous.* The stress on "men" here is deliberate as yet again it is the physical and emotional trials and achievements of masculinity that are at the centre of the narrative; lead protagonist Italian driver Gino Borgesa (Douglas) almost loses his leg as a result of a serious crash and the second half of the film chronicles his recovery and return to racing.

The "dame" is beautiful ballerina Nicole (Bella Darvi)) and there is some gentle acknowledgement of the changing place of women within Western culture in her depiction. When Gino (playing hard to get) advises Nicole at one point to "stay where you belong and with the people you belong to," Nicole responds that "I belong to myself." This is a rather weak gesture towards independence, however, as Nicole appears largely dependent on male providers throughout the film.

Similar themes and emphases are also evident in the film that is still regarded by many followers of motor racing—and Formula 1 in particular—as providing the most impressive depiction of the sport (See, e.g. Roberts, 2016). American director John Frankenheimer was a motor racing enthusiast and was keen to provide the most detailed and authentic depiction of motor racing to that point. To do so, Frankenheimer and his crew shadowed the 1966 Formula 1 season, following the races and teams participating and compiling the footage that would provide a key component of *Grand Prix* (1966). The film therefore features many of the leading drivers of the era. While American British Racing Motors (BRM) driver Bob Bondurant prepared the lead actors-James Garner, Yves Montand, Brian Bedford and Antonio Sabato Jr.-Bondurant also identified the actor best suited to the lead role (eventually given to Garner), following test laps with each. Garner received additional training as a result and developed into a very competent racing driver (Crowe, 2017). Bondurant had agreed to his role in the production at the request of the film's technical advisor Carroll Shelby, the legendary American car designer and central protagonist in *Ford v Ferrari*. The film's producers also struck a deal with the McLaren racing team who agreed to use an identical livery to that featured on the car driven by Garner's character (American driver Pete Aron), allowing for more convincing integration of actual race footage into the production (Crowe, 2017).

Grand Prix is one of the most successful motor racing films released to date; it was among the top ten films released at the box office in the United States[9] and the film won three Academy awards for Best Sound, Best Film Editing and Best Effects. However, its failure to receive nominations in any of the major categories are suggestive of the film's weaknesses in terms of non-racing narrative, characterisation and plot. It is the visual achievement of Grand Prix that is particularly impressive; cinematographer Lionel Lindon photographed the film in Super Panavision 70, employing a range of innovative camera lenses (with long lenses used for a slow-motion effect), angles and operating techniques to realise the stunning race footage. The final film was also screened in 70 mm Cinerama where possible adding to the overall visual impact on contemporary audiences in 1966.

Linton's work was greatly assisted by a team of innovative camera operators, in particular John M. Stephens. Stephens developed a range of innovations that would transform action cinematography in subsequent decades, including a system to allow the large Panavision cameras to be mounted and balanced on F1 cars and remotely controlled from either helicopter or camera car (Stone, 2014). The film also pioneered the use of in-car cameras to give audiences a more authentic and visceral sense of the driver's perspective; 1961 World Champion Phil Hill drove a modified car in sessions of the Monaco and Belgian Grands Prix to capture these sequences (Roberts, 2016).[10]

As identified with regard to previous motor racing films, masculinity and the various crises that attend it—for which the risks involved in the motor racing is a key metaphor—are central to the non-racing sequences. These consist primarily of each driver dealing with various challenges and traumas with regard to women in their lives highlighting the tensions between developing and maintaining a relationship and trying to sustain a career in the precarious world of motor racing. Though women continue to occupy supporting roles to the central male protagonists, there is evidence of the changing expectations of women. This is particularly evident in the scenes between French driver Jean-Pierre Sarti (Yves Montand) and his (eventual) mistress, journalist Louise Frederickson (Eva Marie Saint). When Sarti asks her, shortly after they first meet, why she is not married, saying it is "very bad for a woman to be too independent," she responds: "very bad for whom?" "I like making my own decisions," she continues, "I like travelling, meeting new people, working, I like to be free." However, ultimately she ends up in a relationship with Sarti (a married man) and appears to accept the limited nature of the commitment he can make with her, particularly as it is clearly indicated he cannot divorce his wife.

The success of *Grand Prix* transformed Hollywood's approach to motor racing on film, in particular the increased focus on the more impressive and authentic visual depiction of races featured. Three years later major Hollywood star Paul Newman played the lead in *Winning*, which was also shot in Panavision, though focused on the American stock-car racing circuit rather than European, or Formula 1, context. The film concerns driver Frank Capua (Newman) and his attempts to reach and win the Indianapolis 500, a race already (as we have seen) the subject of Hollywood motor racing productions. Directed by James Goldstone, the film also featured leading American drivers of the era including Bobby Unser, Bobby Grim, Dan Gurney, Roger McCluskey and Bruce Walkup, as well as the then owner of the Indianapolis Motor Speedway, Tony Hulman. *Winning* also includes actual footage shot at Indianapolis during the 1966 and 1968 races (and at least one actual crash), intercut with further sequences of Newman racing. As with Garner previously, Newman underwent considerable preparation for his role, including training sessions with professional drivers Bob Sharp and Lake Underwood—this experience and his role in the film would lead to a life-long enthusiasm for motor racing, including racing professionally and establishing the very successful IndyCar Newman/Haas Racing team (Mitchell, 2018).

As with previous films featuring motor racing, out of his car, the narrative's principal concern is Frank's love life and the traumas he must come to terms with here as he negotiates between his dedication to motor racing and relationship and (very shortly thereafter) marriage with Elora (Joanne Woodward), a divorcee and mother of a teenage son Charley (Richard Thomas). While Charley develops a close relationship with Frank, working with him to prepare his car for races, his relationship with Elora is greatly damaged when Frank discovers Elora in bed with his main racing rival Luther (Robert Wagner). *Winning* was praised on release for bringing more depth and development to its central characters and their relationship than typically found in motor racing-themed films, largely due to the acting acumen, charisma and chemistry between Newman and Woodward (Thompson, 1969). This focus reflected a movement more broadly in Hollywood towards a grittier and more realistic depiction of relationships and more naturalistic approaches to acting informed by acting schools such as Lee Strasberg's Actors Studio which Newman attended and the growing impact of the New Hollywood movement (King, 2002). However, *Winning* did not depart to any significant extent from the recurring concerns of the sub-genre and added little to the development of the depiction of motor racing as a sport on film.

A further major star for whom motor racing would feature prominently in their non-Hollywood life was Steve McQueen. Though poorly received on its initial release, *Le Mans* (1971), in which McQueen plays race driver Michael Delaney, has garnered increasing respect subsequently as a chronicle of one of the world's most famous endurance motor races. Continuing the concern to depict motor racing as authentically as possible, the film was made on location at the Le Mans circuit in France in the summer of 1970 and featured sequences from the actual race in June that year. McQueen had even planned to participate in the race itself, but the film's insurers forbid it. Nonetheless, a car he had previously driven was entered—McQueen's own Porsche 908/2, #29—equipped with film cameras to capture much of the in-race footage featured.[11]

The most impressive aspect of *Le Mans* is undoubtedly the in-race footage; there is also an almost documentary like quality to the production in certain sequences, particularly in the opening scenes that capture the actual build-up to the race, with crowds gathering outside the race track and drivers preparing to depart. The meticulous chronicling in these scenes of the event continues to have historical importance as a record of the race in the period concerned. Like *Grand Prix*, there is also an almost fetishistic foregrounding of the cars competing and various components of particular vehicles. Indeed, it is 38 minutes into the film before the first dialogue scenes take place. In these non-race sequences the narrative relies on the familiar tropes of a male race car driver dealing with personal crises, the danger of the sport itself and unresolved issues with a member of the opposite sex.

Changing Class and Race Portrayals in the 1970s

The 1970s were an important decade for changing class and race portrayals within American films, including in depictions of motor racing. While characters from working-class backgrounds had featured previously in the sub-genre, films had rarely been interested in engaging with this background in any detail until the release of the Lamont Johnson directed *The Last American Hero* (1973). Based on the true story of NASCAR driver Junior Johnson (played by Jeff Bridges), as Chuck Kleinhans (1974) has observed, this film reflected a larger turn in the 1970s where Hollywood presented "heroes whose working class origins are central to the narrative" (Para. 2). For Kleinhans, these films feature

> working class heroes both in the sense that their class origins are not ignored or hidden, and that they are heroes to the working class. For their intended audience these films are "closer to real life" than films depicting middle class protagonists with middle class problems. (Kleinhans, 1974, para. 2)

In its focus on Johnson's North Carolina working-class origins, developing his driving ability running moonshine for his father, the film continued the more character-driven focus already evident in motor racing films of the early 1970s in a work less concerned regarding the impressiveness of its familiar (if competently realised) racing sequences.

However, the non-racing narrative returned to familiar tropes, including the challenges Johnson encounters in his love life. Here racing groupie Marge (Valerie Perrine) provides both a point of inspiration and trauma for Johnson, as she (as Pauline Kael observed) "floats along with the winners" (Kael, 1973, para. 5).

The Last American Hero was likely influential for the production of *Greased* Lightning (1977); both films focus on the working-class origins of their lead protagonists, including initial driving skills acquired by each through the running of moonshine. However, *Greased Lightning* is distinctive as the first depiction of motor racing to feature an African American driver. As I have previously discussed (Crosson, 2013, pp. 66–85), African Americans and minorities in general have been problematically depicted within the sport cinema genre including regressive stereotypes of African Americans as "infantile, lazy, and subservient" as well as threatening sexual predators, stereotypes Ed Guerrero has identified from the earliest American films (1993, p. 12). This problematic historical legacy partly inspired the establishment of independent production house Third World Cinema Corporation (producer of *Greased Lightning*), founded by African American activist Ossie Davis in 1971 to promote film roles for actors of colour and produce more positive portrayals of African American culture and society (Castillo, 2019).

Directed by African American director Michael Schultz, *Greased Lightning* is based on the true story of Wendell Scott, the first African American to win a race at NASCAR's highest level, the Grand National Series. Comedian Richard Pryor plays the lead role of Scott and while the film follows loosely Scott's life and career in NASCAR, it adopts a largely comedic approach to the subject, perhaps to make the explicit racism evident in the film more palatable to a broader audience. Nonetheless, the liberal use of the "N" word and "boy" when Whites address African Americans, as well as other disturbing scenes of racist language and behaviour makes the film an unsettling watch today.

While *Greased Lightning* undoubtedly provides a more detailed, sympathetic and in-depth depiction of African American society and culture (particularly of the community within which Scott grew up) than previously found in depictions of motor racing, the choice of a comic actor, and comedic approach to the topic arguably unbalances (and at times trivialises) the very serious issues being addressed. There is also a clear attempt to position a White working-class character as a key support and facilitator of Scott's career in the form of fellow driver and friend Hutch (played by Jeff Bridges' brother Beau), a trope I have identified previously as a frequent feature of sport cinema (see, e.g. Crosson, 2013, pp. 78–85). This is most explicitly depicted in a scene in which Hutch brings Scott to a Whites-only restaurant and defends him from attack by a drunken White racist with the aid of a confederate flag. Furthermore, the film recounts the seeming transformation of initially racist and antagonistic White characters into supporters of Scott's, including the local Sheriff (Sheriff Cotton (Vincent Gardenia)). Scott is initially the main target of Sheriff Cotton's attempts to stop the running of moonshine in the Danville area he polices in scenes where his racist attitudes are clearly evident. However, after Scott's success in racing, he visits him in a scene which acknowledges changing race relations and rights in the United States, as Cotton describes Scott as, "the biggest thing that ever hit Danville. I'm proud of you. Everybody's proud of you. Times sure have changed, huh? You folks getting to vote and everything." The final remark here provides insight into the real motivation for Cotton's visit; his attempt to win the Mayorship in the town, which he achieves with Scott's endorsement. The film subsequently includes a scene of Mayor Cotton seeking sponsorship over the phone for Scott's racing team, remarking to those who are hesitant to support an African American driver: "you've got to be colour-blind," a questionable remark given the ongoing challenge of racism in the United States (Smith, 2013).

While innovative in its featuring of an African American lead, and foregrounding of the African American community more broadly, *Greased Lightning* adds little to the depiction of motor racing relying heavily on both back projection and poorly integrated stock footage, both indicators of its low budget origins. The film also features tropes already familiar from the sub-genre, including the romantic life and relationship difficulties of the lead, and the dangers of motor racing, evident in several serious crashes featured, including in a central sequence where we witness Scott almost killed and in hospital with serious injuries.

The 1980s and 1990s and Another (Rare) Female Driver

The changing roles of women continued to impact on the depiction of motor racing in the latter decades of the twentieth century, evident in the 1983 production *Heart like a Wheel*, a biopic of National Hot Rod Association (NHRA) Top Fuel three-time world champion, Shirley Muldowney. The film explicitly addresses in the narrative the challenging proposition for many men of a female driver, evident in the difficulty Muldowney has in getting permission initially to race, and subsequently being accepted by other drivers (and her family) in her profession. The film chronicles the breakup of her marriage due to her husband's (Jack Muldowney (Leo Rossi)) objection to her unconventional profession and Shirley's refusal to adapt to his expectations of a housewife's role, primarily (for him) concerned with child rearing and domestic responsibilities. The film charts changing perceptions of gender as it moves from the 1950s into the 1970s and we witness Muldowney gain recognition and admiration as a leading driver in her chosen sport. While conventional and limited in its approach to the technical filming of motor racing—and in particular drag racing—*Heart like a Wheel* is ultimately less concerned with the sport featured and more with using motor racing as a signifier of changing gender norms. However, the film remains an outlier in depictions of motor racing, notably as the depiction of gender roles (and particularly female representations) would regress in subsequent decades.

The rise of motor racing, and particularly the NASCAR variant thereof, was evident at the beginning of the 1990s when the biggest box office star of the period, Tom Cruise took the lead role of NASCAR driver Cole Trickle in *Days of Thunder* (1990). Directed by Tony Scott, the film did not enjoy the same popular success as Scott's previous collaboration with Cruise (*Top Gun* (1986)), a film that was clearly influential for *Days of Thunder* in the similar choice of music, overall aesthetic and the characterisation of the lead protagonist. This includes Trickle's introduction by arriving to a racetrack on a motorbike, Cruise's signature vehicle (apart from the combat jets he flew) in *Top Gun*.

Days of Thunder has been described as ushering in an era of fiscal restraint in Hollywood due to its production excesses (its budget doubled from $35–70million). The film also went to considerable lengths to bring authenticity to its depiction of the sport, including featuring leading NASCAR drivers, while ESPN reporters also appeared in on-track scenes. The cars featured are also based on actual cars used in NASCAR while the cars driven by the main characters in the film, including Trickle, were entered into actual NASCAR races where additional authentic footage was captured. Indeed, apart from the characters, cars and race tracks, many scenes featured are reputedly based on actual events and this was part of the film's promotional lore (and legacy) (The Associated Press, 2010).

Days of Thunder draws on similar concerns and themes discussed already, including the recurring trope of masculinity in crisis, highlighted by Trickle's involvement with a woman and the danger of the sport concerned. This woman is his doctor, Claire Lewicki (Nicole Kidman), who he subjects to a sexual assault when they first meet, mistaking her for a stripper, after encountering one (disguised as a police officer) earlier in the film. The scene, which is played for humour, is nonetheless unsettling and reflects dated gender politics. However, such problematic depictions of women and gender relations also reflect an attempt to reassert masculinity in a societal context where women's roles and influence have fundamentally changed. There is, nonetheless clearly a tension evident in the film reflected most obviously in the role Kidman plays (as a powerful doctor who will decide ultimately whether Trickle can drive again after a major accident) and also the manner in which she identifies and challenges his own insecurities as a man following a major accident with fellow driver Rowdy Burns (Michael Rooker) accusing him of selfishness in his approach to a sport in which he shares "a racetrack with 40 other infantile egomaniacs." Despite this criticism (which could well be made of the depiction of masculinity throughout the sub-genre), Trickle nonetheless returns to motor racing and Lewicki turns up in support for his final victorious race that closes the film.

Twenty-First-Century Drivers, *Plus Ca Change…*

Motor racing has continued to feature prominently in mainstream cinema in the twenty-first century. It would appear that contemporary directors are very aware (perhaps at times excessively so) of the predominant foci and clichés within the sub-genre, which has contributed to an array of productions of varying quality. Indeed, the recurring themes we have already identified are very evident in contemporary films, including in one of the first major motor racing-themed productions to emerge in the noughties. Sylvester Stallone has been among the most influential figures within the sport cinema genre, particularly as a result of the commercial and critical success of boxing-themed drama *Rocky* (1976). As I have detailed previously (Crosson, 2013, pp. 93–98), *Rocky* was one of the most commercially successful sports films of all time, inspiring a franchise that has produced five subsequent films (and two spin-off-sequels Creed (2015) and Creed II (2018)) to date and chosen at number two on the American Film Institute's (AFI) list of best sports films (AFI, 2008). At the centre of *Rocky*'s narrative is an engagement with various crises that attend White working-class masculinity—as worked through the eponymous central protagonist—while affirming the American Dream trajectory (Crosson, 2013, pp. 93–98), a theme that also chimes with depictions of motor racing on film. It was, nonetheless, surprising when Stallone turned to motor racing as the subject of his 2001 production *Driven*, a work he developed over several years, produced, wrote the screenplay for and acted in as washed up motor racing driver Joe Tanto (a role that again connected with his previous (and subsequent) roles within the *Rocky* franchise). Stallone had initially hoped to focus on Formula 1 in the film, but the challenges of gaining access to Formula 1 teams and developing a production in relation to the sport convinced him ultimately to focus instead on the much lesser known (and no longer existing) CART FedEx Championship Series (Thorn, 2019).

Driven was directed by Finnish director Renny Harlin who makes generous use of both actual race footage recorded during production as well as Computer-generated imagery (CGI) in his depiction of motor racing.

The production was shot over eight months at nine actual races in five countries and employed what was then cutting-edge film technology, including periscope lenses which Harlin described as allowing the camera to "be mounted out of the way, but the lens comes out in front of the driver's eyes so you can get the exact point of view of the driver all the way down the track and all the way up to include his own hands on the steering wheel" (Driven: Production Notes).

Driven was both a critical and commercial failure, generally panned by critics for both its unconvincing characterisations and narrative, and at times preposterous depiction of motor racing. As the *New York Times* critic A.O. Scott remarked at the time of its release

> Though Mr. Harlin blends stunt driving and computer-generated daredevilry with film he shot at actual races, his technique is too jumpy and self-conscious to convey either the meticulous skill the sport demands or the visceral thrill it can produce. (Scott, 2001)

As Scott correctly surmises, *Driven* collapses under the "dead weight of a half-dozen utterly predictable, often indistinguishable plots and sub-plots [and] the horrifying spectacle of actors crashing and burning as they bellow their way through stupefying speeches about faith, will and pure victory" (Scott, 2001).

Particularly unconvincing are the crashes featured. Here Harlin employs CGI to accentuate each major crash, emphasising the extraordinary danger involved and also providing close-ups of the various pieces of wreckage as cars are destroyed. This is particularly apparent in a central sequence—the second to last race featured—when race driver Memo (Cristián de la Fuente) is involved in a horrific crash in which his car is thrown into the air, broken into pieces, with the badly damaged cockpit (with driver attached) landing upside-down in a nearby river. The scene is unintentionally funny, so preposterous it is in its execution and so removed from any actual possible experience in motor racing, including the depiction of the two leading drivers in the race—Jimmy Bly (Kip Pardue) and Beau Brandenburg (Til Schweiger)—leaving their cars and running to rescue Memo from the remains of his car in the river. Ultimately, of course, the purpose of this scene is not primarily about motor racing but rather about emphasising the relationships and masculine bonding between the lead male characters.

While ostensibly concerned with the attempt of rookie racing driver Bly to win the Cart Championship, much of *Driven*'s narrative is taken up with various personal and emotional crises that attend the central male characters, including the familiar love-triangle scenario between Bly and his main race rival, German driver Brandenburg, over Brandenburg's fiancée Sophia (Estella Warren). Tanto (Stallone) is brought back into motor racing by Bly's team manager, paraplegic Carl Henry (Burt Reynolds) to be Bly's support driver, and Tanto's own racing traumas (where he failed to realise his potential) are also recalled by Henry in the film in a speech that explicitly articulates masculinity in crisis:

> I watched you kill yourself! You had everything, and you threw it all away! And I had to sit there and watch! The slowest man in the fastest sport. I wake up every morning, my legs are on fire. I know I'm gonna have to sit in this chair for the rest of the day. But if they gave me one more chance, I'd do it all over again. It ain't gonna happen. We are all damaged.

However, as we have identified elsewhere in the sub-genre, while the central focus is on the male leads, women are portrayed in *Driven* as peripheral, sexualised, if occasionally disruptive figures in men's lives. As the *New York Times* reviewer also noted, "To complete the atmosphere of genial frat-house male bonding, each race day begins with a montage of trackside babes in short-shorts and halter tops" (Scott, 2001), while David Duprey noted that "women here are only window dressing … Treating the whole thing like an MTV beach party, [Harlin] points his camera at every scantily-clad girl (from every angle) whenever he can, giving superficial video game quality attention to the cars themselves" (Duprey, 2018). The poorly developed role of journalist Lucretia (Stacy Edwards) is indicative of the film's engagement with and depiction of gender. Ostensibly following motor racing to write "an expose on male dominance in the sport," no development is given whatsoever to this topic, a further nod to established tropes in the depiction of motor racing though with no interest in interrogating this subject in any depth.

While *Driven* attempted to provide a serious (if melodramatic) depiction of open-wheel racing, *Talladega Nights: The Ballad of Ricky Bobby* (2006) returned to the world of NASCAR to mine the comic potential of the sport, and the culture that surrounds it. Featuring Hollywood comic star Will Ferrell in the lead role of NASCAR driver Ricky Bobby, Ferrell has starred to date in no fewer than four sports films, with *Talladega Nights* the biggest box office draw reaching number one at the US box office.[12] As with *Days of Thunder*, the film also features prominent figures associated with NASCAR, including both drivers and broadcasters. However, the authentic depiction of motor racing is not the principal concern of this production but rather the opportunities these sporting sequences provide for humour.

The recurring themes of masculinity in crisis and the dangers of motor racing also feature in *Talladega Nights*. However, while containing some humorous sequences, the appeal of the film cannot be easily separated from the more problematic race and gender depictions featured. All the drivers featured are White men and the few individuals of colour that appear do so in supporting roles to their White drivers, including Michael Clarke Duncan as Ricky Bobby's crew chief Lucius Washington. Depictions of gender are even more problematic with women in *Talledega Nights* occupying stereotypically marginal roles, there to support and titillate the male characters and viewers. Ricky's eventual wife introduces herself to him after a race victory by lifting her shirt to reveal her breasts remarking: "hey driver, drive these," apparently sufficient basis on which to make a marriage proposal, the following wedding photos suggest. This scene is echoed at the close of the film when Bobby's subsequent partner Susan (Amy Adams) impresses his by then ex-wife (who attempts to win Bobby back) by lifting her shirt to reveal her (apparently equally) impressive breasts, provoking the awestruck remark: "Well, girl, you got some game."

The presence of homosexual driver Jean Girard as Bobby's main rival may appear to challenge conventional conceptions of masculinity, as is evident in the shocked and appalled responses by Bobby and other followers of NASCAR when they first encounter Girard. However, as portrayed in an extraordinarily over-the-top and exaggerated performance by Sasha Baron Cohen, it is hard to take the depiction seriously or view it as more than a further reaffirmation of the peculiarity and inappropriateness of a driver who challenges the prevailing norms of the sport. It is not insignificant that the supposedly ironic inspirational slogan that Bobby adopts from his father—"If you're not first, you're last"—was employed by supporters of Donald Trump during the riots at the Capitol Building on 6 January 2021.[13] This slogan speaks to deep anxieties among Trump supporters (effectively manipulated and exploited by the former president) regarding the increasing empowerment and influence of both people of colour and women in the United States, evident in the backlash on the right to the Black Lives Matter and #MeToo movements (Anderson, 2016; Ross, 2021). *Talladega Nights* provides an ultimately reassuring (and reactionary) depiction of race and gender relations, reasserting masculine values of an earlier era—White, heterosexual and patriarchal—under the guise of ironic comedy.

Masculine values are also at the centre of the 2013 production *Rush* which focused on the rivalry between Formula 1 drivers Niki Lauda and James Hunt, and in particular the events surrounding the 1976 Formula 1 season. However, unlike previous productions discussed above, *Rush* did not include footage of actual races, nor (as with *Grand Prix* and *Bobby Deerfield*) did it shadow a Formula 1 season. The racing scenes were shot in the UK and Germany, with Oscar-winning cinematographer Anthony Dod Mantle ensuring sophisticated cinematography throughout, with heavy emphasis on rapid cutting and dynamic on track and in-car footage, including unusual on-board perspectives, to emphasise the speed, exhilaration and dangers of Formula 1 racing. This footage was combined with judiciously chosen, graded, de-grained and digitally enhanced archive footage (to reduce significant inconsistencies with new material) from relevant races and race tracks. While archive footage has featured before in depictions of motor racing in fiction film, advances in technology allowed for a much more seamless matching with original footage (which was also shot on older lenses for effect, including Baltars and Cooke S2s) in *Rush*, such that these archive sequences provided the skeletal structure around which racing sequences were constructed (Hope-Jones, 2013).

Dod Mantle has spoken of trying to capture the dangers of motor racing effectively (Anthony Dod Mantle, Quoted in Hope-Jones, 2013).

This concern is also evident in the film's dialogue, including remarks by Hunt's eventual wife Suzy (Olivia Wilde) who describes a Formula 1 car as "just a little coffin, really ... a bomb on wheels." However, the secondary position of women like Suzy (eventually divorced by Hunt) to the cars (and men) featured in the sub-genre is also stressed in the words of Lord Hesketh—the British aristocrat who bankrolls Hunt's initial efforts in motor racing—in remarks that underline again the close association between motor racing and masculinity:

> They could never have imagined it, those pioneers who invented the automobile, that it would possess us like this, in our imaginations, in our dreams. Nursie, men love women, but even more than that, men love cars.

Indeed, sex and racing are repeatedly interconnected and related throughout the film. While several scenes of sexual activity and motor racing are intercut, following his victory at the British Grand Prix, Hunt replies to motor racing legend Stirling Moss' question as to how he has achieved "a terrific edge over the rest of the field" with the remark: "Big balls" clearly connecting his performance on the track with his masculine virility. In this context and throughout the film, female characters occupy supporting and highly sexualised roles, with little depth or development provided.

Conclusion

Motor racing has featured from the very earliest decades of film production, with filmmakers attracted to a sport that emphasised and exemplified a defining feature of film: movement. With the emergence of fiction film in the United States (the source of the vast majority of relevant productions), a number of predominant and recurring themes emerged, above all a focus on White men and masculinity, even in the very rare productions that featured women or individuals of colour as drivers. The second half of the twentieth century witnessed a gradual acknowledgement of female independence and agency (reflecting broader social changes), though primarily to accentuate the challenges presented to the leading male protagonists. While the filming of racing sequences has advanced considerably over the past century, assisted by advances in cinematography and digital postproduction technologies and informed by the increasing sophistication of televisual depictions of the sport, the risks associated with motor racing continue to provide an engaging and exhilarating context and metaphor for masculinity and its vulnerabilities. However, in recent decades, there has been a problematic return to sometimes regressive depictions of women, who have at best been marginal figures across the sub-genre, while drivers of colour continue to be largely absent. These traits are evident in the 2019 Oscar winning production *Ford v Ferrari* to which we now return to conclude.

Directed by James Mangold, *Ford v Ferrari* was filmed by cinematographer Phedon Papamichael who received his fourth Oscar nomination for his work on the film. While the majority of the film was shot in the United States, including sequences set in Le Mans, it was possible nonetheless to create a convincing rendering of motor racing in the era concerned (which was heavily influenced by previous productions *Grand Prix* (1966) and *Le Mans* (1971)) due to advances in digital cinematography and post production (Fang Tham, 2019).

The dangers of motor racing are evident from the beginning of *Ford v Ferrari* where we witness both driver and car go on fire during refuelling, followed by the revelation of a serious heart defect for the driver concerned, Carrol Shelby that ends his career behind the wheel. The death of co-lead Ken Mills while testing a race car at the end of the film further underlines the precarity of motor racing. Featuring the combative and competitive relationship between the Ford and Ferrari motor companies in the 1960s, the film focuses on the efforts of a group of American and British engineers, brought together by Shelby (who moved into motorcar design after retirement from racing) in collaboration with British driver Mills and financed by the Ford motor company, to build a car capable of challenging Ferrari in the 24 Hours of Le Mans race.

As evident across most depictions of motor racing on film, the central focus throughout *Ford v Ferrari* is the relationship between the male leads, here Shelby and Mills, which was described repeatedly—as noted in our introduction—in reviews of the production as a "bromance." This relationship is marked by mutual respect but also reveals tensions that erupt as physical violence at one point in the film where both fight outside Mills' house after Shelby arrives to apologise for not taking him with the team to the first attempt to win at Le Mans. With this overriding focus on men and masculinity, women feature little in the diegesis, apart from the occasional (and almost exclusively domestic) scenes with Mill's wife Mollie (Caitriona Balfe). It is here that perhaps the most problematic aspect of motor racing on film continues to be evident: its continuing focus on White masculinity and its challenges to the exclusion of convincing and in-depth portrayals of women and people of colour.

Notes

1. Further information on the box office returns of the film is available here: https://web.archive.org/web/20191118055744/; https://www.boxofficemojo.com/release/rl990348801/
2. While this chapter focuses primarily on American fiction productions, I want to acknowledge a number of significant omissions that deserve further research (beyond the scope of a single chapter); motor racing in non-fiction film (a huge area that comprises a much larger number of productions than found in fiction film), motor racing in animated productions, and motor racing in cinema in films produced outside of the United States. Motor racing-themed films have been made in a wide variety of national contexts and languages, including French, German, Portuguese, Spanish, both Cantonese and Mandarin Chinese, Telugu, Hindi, Italian, Swedish, Russian, Korean, and Malay. Unfortunately most of these films have had limited distribution outside of their national contexts (and are often not available with English-language subtitles) so are difficult to access. To briefly note a number of significant features of non-English speaking motor-racing films: the first (partially) sound film to feature motor racing was the German film *Die Nacht gehört uns* (*The Night Belongs to Us*, 1929), also the first production to feature a female racing driver. Important animated productions have also featured motor racing prominently, including the very popular 2006 Pixar computer-animated comedy *Cars* which launched a multimedia franchise including two sequels and two spin-offs produced by Disneytoon Studios, and the anime and manga inspired *Speed Racer* (2008). Outside of the United

States, the most popular film ever released at the Norwegian box office is the indigenously produced stop motion-animated feature *Flåklypa Grand Prix* (*The Pinchcliffe Grand Prix*, 1975), concerning a motor race and how "local forces win over the international elite" (Iverson, 1998, p. 134). In its successful evocation of the Norwegian landscape and rendering of a range of idiosyncratic characters created by popular Norwegian cartoonist Kjell Aukrust, *Flåklypa Grand Prix* struck a chord with Norwegian people in particular, though it also attracted large audiences across Scandinavia (Crosson, 2021, pp.).

3. While the Charlie Chaplin vehicle *Kid Auto Races at Venice* (1914) doesn't feature motor cars, but rather a children's "baby-cart" race, it is a fascinating depiction of this practice in these years and also notable as the first film exhibited to the public to feature the "Little Tramp" that is most associated with the comic genius of early cinema. Incidentally, the Venice referred to is the Venice neighbourhood of Los Angeles, California, rather than the better known Italian city.
4. This was an actual race started in 1908 (and held on the Santa Monica course in 1914) and originally known as the American Grand Prize, but which is today the United States Grand Prix, part of Formula 1 racing calendar race (Nye, 1978, p. 12)
5. The box-office success of *The Roaring Road* also led not just to a sequel (*Excuse My Dust* (1920)) but to Reid becoming typecast as *the* motor racing star of silent cinema featuring in a string of relevant films, including *Double Speed* (1920), *What's Your Hurry?* (1920), *Too Much Speed* (1921), and *Across the Continent* (1922). Such was Reid's association with race-car-themed film that his son (Wallace Reid Jr.) also featured in several, including *Excuse my Dust* (playing Toodles Walden Jr., the son of the character played by his father) and *The Racing* Strain (1932).
6. "Quota Quickies" were low-cost, and often low-quality film productions commissioned by companies to satisfy the quota requirements (for British cinemas to show a certain percentage of British films) of the Cinematograph Films Act 1927. For further information see Chibnall (2019)).
7. This was a slang term used between the 1920s and1950s to refer to a number of small (and often short-lived) Hollywood B movie studios. For further information see Fernett (1973)).
8. *The National Association for Stock Car Auto Racing*, LLC (NASCAR) is an American auto racing sanctioning and operating company

9. These figures are available at the following link: https://www.the-numbers.com/market/1966/top-grossing-movies
10. The documentary, *Pushing the Limit: The Making of "Grand Prix,"* included in the 2006 40th anniversary Warner Home Video DVD release of the film includes these details also and further information on the innovations the film brought to motor racing.
11. These details are featured and developed in the documentary *McQueen: The Man & Le Mans* (2015) directed by Gabriel Clarke and John McKenna (Content Media).
12. Box office figures for the film are available from Box Office Mojo at https://www.boxofficemojo.com/release/rl2422507009/
13. In recordings of the riots, shortly after the barrier to the capitol was breached a protestor can be heard to exclaim through a loudhailer "If you're not first, you're last." The scene can be watched at approximately 53 minutes 43 seconds at the following link: https://www.youtube.com/watch?reload=9&v=GNQRGohdW9Y&feature=youtu.be

References

Abate, M. A. (2008). *Tomboys: A Literary and Cultural History*. Temple University Press.

AFI (American Film Institute). (2008). America's 10 Greatest Films in 10 Classic Genres. www.afi.com. Retrieved February 10, 2021, from https://web.archive.org/web/20190202004049/; https://www.afi.com/10top10/

Anderson, C. (2016). Donald Trump Is the Result of White Rage, Not Economic Anxiety. *Time*, November 16. Retrieved March 10, 2021, from https://time.com/4573307/donald-trump-white-rage/

Anonymous. (1930). 'BURNING UP' A LIGHT FILM. *New York Times*, 8 February. Retrieved January 10, 2021, from https://www.nytimes.com/1930/02/08/archives/burning-up-a-light-film.html

Anonymous. (n.d.). The Roaring Road. *Silents Are Golden*. Retrieved December 15, 2020, from http://www.silentsaregolden.com/featurefolder7/RRcommentary.html

Associated Press, The. (2010). The Summer That Nascar Received Its Close-Up. *The New York Times*, 26 June. Retrieved 5 December 2020, from https://www.nytimes.com/2010/06/27/sports/autoracing/27nascar.html

Bhatt, J. (2020). *Ford v Ferrari Review: Matt Damon and Christian Bale's Bromance Touches 7000 RPM in This Motorsport Rivalry Mashable India.* Retrieved January 10, 2021, from https://web.archive.org/web/20200324051432/https://in.mashable.com/Entertainment/8421/Ford-V-Ferrari-Review-Matt-Damon-And-Christian-Bales-Bromance-Touches-7000-Rpm-In-This-Motorsport-Ri

Brody, R. (2019). The Airbrushed Racing History of 'Ford v Ferrari'. *The New Yorker*, 19 November. Retrieved January 20, 2021, from https://www.newyorker.com/culture/the-front-row/the-airbrushed-racing-history-of-ford-v-ferrari

Butler, J. (1999). *Gender Trouble: Feminism and the Subversion of Identity*. Routledge.

Castillo, M. (2019). Divided We Fall. *Film Comment*, July–August. Retrieved November 15, 2020, from https://www.filmcomment.com/article/divided-we-fall/

Chafe, W. H. (1991). *The Paradox of Change: American Women in the 20th Century*. Oxford University Press.

Chibnall, S. (2019). *Quota Quickies: The Birth of the British 'B' Film*. British Film Institute.

Crosson, S. (2013). *Sport and Film*. Routledge.

Crosson, S. (2021). European cinema and the football film: 'Play for the people who've accepted you'. In S. R. Millar, M. J. Power, P. Widdop, D. Parnell & J. Carr (Eds.), *Football and Popular Culture: Singing Out from the Stands* (pp. 87–107). London: Routledge.

Crowe, J. (2017). James Garner's Grand Prix. *Auto Action*, January 11. Retrieved January 5, 2021, from https://autoaction.com.au/2017/01/11/james-garners-grand-prix

Crowther, B. (1955). Thrill Show for Hot-Rodders; 'The Racers' Starts Run at Roxy Douglas Drives Car, Chases Dancer. *New York Times*, 5 February. Retrieved February 10, 2021, from https://www.nytimes.com/1955/02/05/archives/screen-thrill-show-for-hotrodders-the-racers-starts-run-at-roxy.html

Driven: Production Notes. (2001). *Cinema.com*. Retrieved February 15, 2021, from https://www.cinema.com/articles/616/driven-production-notes.phtml

Dunning, E. (1986). Sport as a Male Preserve: Notes on the Social Sources of Masculine. Identity and Its Transformations. In N. Elias & E. Dunning (Eds.), *Quest for Excitement: Sport and Leisure in the Civilizing Process*. Basil Blackwell.

Duprey, D. (2018). Why Sylvester Stallone's 2001 'Driven' Does Nothing but Spin Its Wheels. ThatMomentIn.com, 3 May. Retrieved February 20, 2021, from https://www.thatmomentin.com/2001-driven-sylvester-stallone/

Fang Tham, S. (2019). DP Phedon Papamichael on the Vintage Look and Analog Action of 'Ford v. Ferrari'. *Film Independent*, 12 October. Retrieved December 10, 2020, from https://www.filmindependent.org/blog/dp-phedon-papamichael-on-the-vintage-look-and-analog-action-of-ford-v-ferrari/

Fernett, G. (1973). *Hollywood's Poverty Row, 1930–1950*. Coral Reef Publications.

Fleming, E. J. (2013). *Wallace Reid: The Life and Death of a Hollywood Idol*. McFarland & Company.

Guerrero, E. (1993). *Framing Blackness: The African American Image in Film*. Temple University Press.

Hope-Jones, M. (2013). Full Throttle. *American Cinematographer*, October. Retrieved December 10, 2020, from https://theasc.com/ac_magazine/October2013/Rush/page1.html

Iverson, G. (1998). Norway. In T. Soila, A. Söderbergh-Widding, & G. Iverson (Eds.), *Nordic National Cinemas* (pp. 97–134). Routledge.

Kael, P. (1973). The Last American Hero (1973). *The New Yorker*, 1 October. Retrieved November 10, 2020, from https://scrapsfromtheloft.com/2021/01/02/the-last-american-hero-paulinefklein-kael/

Kalat, D. (2015). The Speed Kings—Earl Cooper and Teddy Telzlaft. *Turner Classic Movies*. Retrieved February 10, 2021, from www.tcm.com/tcmdb/title/896317/the-speed-kings/

King, G. (2002). *New Hollywood Cinema: An Introduction*. I.B. Tauris.

Kleinhans, C. (1974). Contemporary Working Class Film Heroes in Evel Knieval and The Last American Hero. *Jump Cut: A Review of Contemporary Media*, 2. Retrieved November 3, 2020, from https://www.ejumpcut.org/archive/onlinessays/JC02folder/lasthero.html

McBride, J. (Ed.). (2013). *Hawks on Hawks*. University Press of Kentucky.

McCarthy, T. (1997). *Howard Hawks: The Grey Fox of Hollywood*. Grove Press.

Milner, V. (1932). Tinted Stock for Better Pictures. *American Cinematographer, 13*(2), 11.

Mitchell, D. (2018). 'Winning' Starred Paul Newman and a Cast of Hoosiers. *IndyStar*, 4 May. Retrieved November 17, 2020, from https://eu.indystar.com/story/news/history/retroindy/2018/05/04/winning-starred-paul-newman-and-cast-hoosiers/580124002/

Mulvey, L. (1975). Visual Pleasure and Narrative Cinema. *Screen, 16*(3), 6–18.

Nye, D. E. (1978). *The United States Grand Prix and Grand Prize Races, 1908–1977*. Doubleday.

Nye, D. E. (2015). *America's Assembly Line*. The MIT Press.

Roberts, A. (2016). Grand Prix: 50 Years since the Greatest Racing Film of All Time. *The Telegraph*, 21 December. Retrieved January 14, 2021, from https://www.telegraph.co.uk/cars/features/grand-prix-50-years-since-greatest-racing-film-time/

Ross, J. (2021). The Trump-Fueled Riot Shocked America. To Some, It Was a Long Time Coming. *NBC News*, January 16. https://www.nbcnews.com/news/nbcblk/trump-fueled-riot-shocked-america-some-it-was-long-time-n1254465

Scott, A. O. (2001). FILM REVIEW; Crashes! Women! But, Hey, What's Under the Hood? *New York Times*, 27 April. Retrieved February 20, 2021, from https://www.nytimes.com/2001/04/27/movies/film-review-crashes-women-but-hey-what-s-under-the-hood.html

Scott, D. (2010). Boxing and Masculine Identity. In P. Dine & S. Crosson (Eds.), *Sport, Representation and Evolving Identities in Europe* (pp. 143–165). Peter Lang.

Smith, E. (2009). *Race, Sport and the American Dream* Carolina Academic Press. 2nd ed. (1st ed., 2007).

Smith, J. (2013). Between Colorblind and Colorconscious: Contemporary Hollywood Films and Struggles Over Racial Representation. *Journal of Black Studies, 44*(8), 779–797.

Stone, M. (2014). *James Garner's Motoring Life: Grand Prix the Movie, Baja, The Rockford Files, and More*. CarTech, Inc.

Thompson, H. (1969). Human Element at Speedway: Paul Newman Starred in 'Winning,' Drama. *The New York Times*, 23 May. Retrieved December 10, 2020, from https://www.nytimes.com/1969/05/23/archives/screen-human-element-at-speedwaypaul-newman-starred-in-winning.html

Thorn, D. (2019). On This Day in F1—Sylvester Stallone Agreed to Make a Movie About F1. *WTF1*, 3 December. https://wtf1.com/post/on-this-day-in-f1-sylvester-stallone-agreed-to-make-a-movie-about-f1/

Young Jr., W. H., & Young, N. K. (2007). *The Great Depression in America: A Cultural Encyclopedia*, Volume 2. Westport, Conn Greenwood Publishing Group.

Filmography

Big Thrill, The. (1933). Directed by Leigh Jason. USA: Goldsmith Productions.
Blonde Comet. (1941). Directed by William Beaudine. USA: Producers Releasing Corporation (PRC).
Bobby Deerfield. (1977). Directed by Sydney Pollack USA: Columbia Pictures.
Burn 'Em Up O'Connor. (1939). Directed by Edward Sedgwick. USA: Metro-Goldwyn-Mayer (MGM).
Burning Up. (1930). Directed by A. Edward Sutherland. USA: Paramount Pictures.
Checkpoint. (1956). Directed by Ralph Thomas. UK: The Rank Organisation.
Crowd Roars, The. (1932). Directed by Howard Hawks. USA: Warner Bros.
Days of Thunder. (1990). Directed by Tony Scott. USA: Paramount Pictures.
Death Drives Through. (1935). Directed by Edward L. Cahn. UK: Associated Talking Pictures (ATP).
Driven. (2001). Directed by Renny Harlin. USA: Franchise Pictures.
Flåklypa Grand Prix (*The Pinchcliffe Grand Prix*). (1975). Directed by I. Caprino. Norway: Caprino Studios.
Ford v Ferrari. (2019). Directed by J. Mangold. USA: 20th Century Studios.
Grand Prix. (1966). Directed by John Frankenheimer USA: Metro-Goldwyn-Mayer (MGM).
Greased Lightning. (1977). Directed by Michael Schultz. USA: Third World Cinema.
Heart Like a Wheel. (1983). Directed by Jonathan Kaplan. USA: Twentieth Century Fox.
High Speed. (1932). Directed by D. Ross Lederman. USA: Columbia Pictures.
Indianapolis Speedway. (1939). Directed by Lloyd Bacon. USA: Warner Bros.
Last American Hero, The. (1973). Directed by Lamont Johnson. USA: Twentieth Century Fox.
Le Mans. (1971). Directed by Lee H. Katzin. USA: Cinema Center Films.
Mask of Dust. (1954). Directed by Terence Fisher. UK: Hammer Films.
Racers, The. (1955). Directed by Henry Hathaway. USA: Twentieth Century Fox.
Racing Strain, The. (1932). Directed by Jerome Storm. USA: Willis Kent Productions.
Red Line 7000. (1965). Directed by Howard Hawks. USA: Paramount Pictures.
Rivalen am Steuer. (1957). Directed by E.W. Fiedler. East Germany: DEFA-Studio für Spielfilme.

Roaring Road, The. (1919). Directed by James Cruze. USA: Famous Players-Lasky release.

Rush. (2013). Directed by R. Howard. USA/UK/Germany: Cross Creek Pictures; Exclusive Media; Working Title Films; Imagine Entertainment; Revolution Films.

Speed. (1936). Directed by Edwin L. Marin. USA: Metro-Goldwyn-Mayer (MGM).

Speed Devils. (1935). Directed by Joseph Henabery. USA: Melbert Productions.

Speed Kings, The. (1913). Directed by Wilfred Lucas. USA: Keystone Film Company.

Speedway. (1968). Directed by Norman Taurog. USA: Metro-Goldwyn-Mayer (MGM).

Spinout. (1966). Directed by Norman Taurog. USA: Metro-Goldwyn-Mayer (MGM).

Ten Laps to Go. (1936). Directed by Elmer Clifton. USA: Fanchon Royer Features.

The Ballad of Ricky Bobby. (2006). Directed by Adam McKay. USA: Columbia Pictures.

Un homme et une femme. (1966). Directed by Claude Lelouche. France: Les Films 13.

Viva Las Vegas. (1964). Directed by George Sidney. USA: Metro-Goldwyn-Mayer (MGM).

Winning. (1969). Directed by James Goldstone. USA: Universal Pictures.

'Who D'You Think You Are? Stirling Moss?' British Racing Drivers and the Politics of Celebrity: 1896 to 1992

Stephen Wagg

Introduction

In 2018, the polling company Yougov conducted a survey to determine 'The most popular all-time sports personalities in the UK'. Eight of the resulting top ten were, arguably, unsurprising: Muhammad Ali, perhaps the most charismatic sportsperson in history, came in at No. 1, followed by widely feted Jamaican champion runner Usain Bolt at 2; recent British Olympic gold medal winners Mo Farah, Jessica Ennis and Kelly Holmes were then joined by Bobby Moore and Bobby Charlton of England's World Cup winning football team of 1966 and Scottish 2013 Wimbledon tennis champion Andy Murray. Perhaps less predictably, German racing driver and seven times Formula 1 World Champion Michael Schumacher, not seen in public since a serious skiing accident in 2013, came fourth and, placed tenth was British driver Stirling Moss, who had retired from elite motor racing as long ago as 1962.[1] Schumacher's high vote seemed

S. Wagg (✉)
International Centre for Sport History and Culture, De Montfort University, Leicester, UK

D. Sturm et al. (eds.), *The History and Politics of Motor Racing*, Global Culture and Sport Series, https://doi.org/10.1007/978-3-031-22825-4_19

to suggest that motor racing had a major significance for sport-minded Britons—in all, ten racing drivers featured in the top one hundred, seven of them Britons. Within that, Moss, who had long since departed the public stage, appeared to have retained a special niche. And the phrase 'Who d'you think you are? Stirling Moss', said often to have been uttered by policemen to motorists caught exceeding the speed limit in the 1950s—and once reputedly uttered to the man himself in such a circumstance—endures: it was the title of a BBC retrospective in 2010, when Moss had turned 80[2] and T shirts bearing the slogan are currently advertised on the internet.[3]

This essay explores the nature of that niche that Moss occupies in the British popular imagination as part of a broader examination of the nature of British racing drivers as celebrities (and otherwise) over a one-hundred-year period. In doing so it pays particular attention to the ways in which, in the history of British motor racing, social class and gender have combined with a particular politics of celebrity. British motor racing has its origins largely in the upper reaches of the British class structure and this, along with a specific form of patriotic and predatory masculinity, has for the most part defined the celebrity conferred on the British racing driver. The chapter concludes with four case studies of British racing driver: Moss, Graham Hill, James Hunt and Nigel Mansell. These case studies are aimed to show variations on the theme of British racing driver celebrity and on its construction. Less is said of another, Sir Jackie Stewart, arguably the most influential of post-Second World War British racing drivers than might otherwise have been the case because his career is discussed at some length in my chapter on the politics of safety in motor racing. And there is scarcely a mention here of Englishman Sir Lewis Hamilton, simply because another chapter in this book (by Ben Carrington) addresses him specifically. Women from wealthy British families have had access to motor cars and have driven them as fast as men and they will also be discussed; however, women have invariably been excluded from the elite racing scene, except as adornments, as anxious wives/partners or as seekers of sexual adventure in the hotels and paddocks of the international racing circuit.

Racing Drivers and the 'Motor Ascot': Speed, Technology and the British Elite

Driving motor cars has been a sanctioned part of British life since the Locomotives on Highways Act, introduced by Lord Salisbury's Conservative government in 1896.[4] This eased restrictions on the use of cars and allowed them to go faster—between 12 and 14 mph (depending on the local authority). The motor car had a growing public—as manifested, for instance, in the founding of *Autocar* magazine the previous year—and this legislation had been lobbied for by the rising numbers of wealthy motor enthusiasts and by leaders of the emergent British car industry—the Daimler Motor Company, for example, formed the same year.[5] The subsequent Motor Car Act (1903), introduced by the administration of Salisbury's successor Arthur Balfour, increased the speed limit to 20 mph.

For those engaged in exploring the technological—and, thus, the commercial—possibilities of the motor car, this limit was unduly constricting. By this time cars had already been produced which were capable of around 70 mph—the German Mercedes-Simplex 60HP, for example[6]—and support grew for a racetrack to be built which would both permit the public enjoyment of automotive speed and provide a testing ground for the nascent British car industry and its drivers.[7] This resulted in Brooklands, near London, the world's first purpose-built motor racing venue, opened in 1907. From the outset, as would be the case for much of its early history, British motor racing drew, for its sponsorship, its drivers and quite often for its engineering expertise, on the upper and upper middle classes.

Brooklands was built on the estate of Hugh Fortescue Locke King in Surrey, drawing on his personal fortune as the owner of swathes of land in the south of England, and was immediately styled by the British press as the 'Motor Ascot', in parallel to Royal Ascot, the elite horseracing event held every June.[8] At Brooklands the link between race drivers and car sales was forged immediately, the first man to drive the circuit being the Australian-born Selwyn Edge, who had worked for the Dunlop tyre company and subsequently promoted Napier cars, largely and simply by writing to the newspapers about them; he averaged 66 mph.[9]

Most of the early British racing drivers were *ascribed* celebrities even before they got behind the wheel, in that they had been born into aristocratic or conspicuously rich families, giving them substantial quantities of what Chris Rojek has called inherited 'attention capital'.[10] In general, they variously combined: great (almost always inherited) wealth; a flair for engineering; a masculine daring; a commercial interest in the car business, or sponsorship from motor-related industries; and a right-wing patriotism, often times manifested in the pursuit of world speed records (in some cases on the sea and in the air, as well as on land) on behalf of the British Empire—a number had been fighter pilots in the Royal Flying Corps (RFC) during the First World War. All these traits were routinely folded into the appellation of 'gentleman racer'[11]—the epitome of the early modern sporting hero. Their trumpeted amateurism and devil-may-care demeanour often belied their integration into the burgeoning nexus of motor car development, sales and promotion.

Leading examples included American-born, naturalised Englishman Sir Henry Segrave (b.1896), educated at Eton and Sandhurst, who was one of the gentleman racer archetypes. A First World War veteran, he drove a British car (a Sunbeam) at Brooklands and in European Grand Prix and was the first racing driver to wear a crash helmet and the first to drive at over 200 mph. He held the world land speed record several times and attempted the world water speed record in craft driven by Rolls Royce engines and financed by Lord Wakefield, whose company marketed Castrol lubricating oil.[12] He died on Lake Windermere, attempting the world water speed record, in 1930. 'With his racing goggles and determined expression', wrote Helen Carter in 2016, 'Sir Henry Segrave epitomised a derring-do British hero from another age'. However, Ben Cussons, a member of the committee awarding the annual Segrave trophy (awarded to a British national who demonstrates 'Outstanding Skill, Courage and Initiative on Land, Water and in the Air' and inaugurated immediately after Segrave's death) emphasised the achieved nature of Segrave's celebrity, stressing his attraction to sponsors and his interest in technological innovation. Segrave, he said, 'did not rely on family money.

[…] He was always looking for the next new technology, which is what inspired him'.[13]

Another driver, John Parry-Thomas (b. 1884), was chief engineer at Leyland Motors and thus centrally involved in the promotion of motor travel—given the costs, to an expectably privileged market. He helped develop the Leyland Eight luxury motor car, which he raced at Brooklands; only 14 were built, each costing £2700 (the equivalent of £194,000 in 2021). He later became a rival to Segrave and his attempts at the world land speed record were sponsored by Shell Mex and Dunlop; his death, in such an attempt in 1927, was reported on the front page of the daily newspapers.[14] Parry-Thomas could claim to be one of the first professional racing drivers.

Similarly, John Cobb (1899–1952), the son of a wealthy fur broker and educated at Eton and Cambridge, was a regular driver at Brooklands in the late 1920s and several times sought the world land speed record. In doing so he enjoyed the support of, and thus promoted, Napier luxury cars and the Mobil oil company. Cobb, too, died in pursuit of a water speed record. He was awarded the Segrave Trophy in 1947 and, like Segrave, although his exploits made him a de facto celebrity, Cobb's main interest appears to have been in technological innovation. According to his widow, 'John was nothing flash, like you might think a racing driver was going to be' and it is said of him that he 'enjoyed speed but he told the Associated Press that his key interest in motor racing and speed testing was in discovering technical improvements such as how tyres and oil react to high speeds that could then be used by the motor industry to finesse cars bought by ordinary motorists'.[15]

The same priorities animated the career of Louis Zborowski (1895–1924). Zborowski was known as 'Count', his father, a New Jersey businessman, having apparently assumed the title after marrying an heiress of the wealthy Astor family. Zborowski was both an inventor and an early works driver. He built a car called Chitty 1 (later the inspiration for Ian Fleming's *Chitty Chitty Bang Bang*) in which he completed a circuit of Brooklands at over 113 mph in 1922. He drove for Aston Martin (founded in London in 1913) and his death prevented him accepting an invitation to drive for the German firm Mercedes. He died at the wheel as his father, also a racing driver, had done in 1903.

Sponsorship of drivers was not confined to the motor trade. Brooklands and RFC veteran Malcolm Campbell, the son of a wealthy Hatton Garden diamond dealer and holder at one time or another of both the world land and water speed records, drove machinery devised by both the Sunbeam and Napier motor companies,[16] but also drew support from the Rolex watch brand. In 1935, *Punch* magazine carried an advertisement by Campbell for the water and dust resistant Rolex Oyster, although it was stressed that he had accepted no payment for this[17]; if he had done so, Campbell, knighted in 1931 and three years later the fourth recipient of the Segrave Trophy, would have undermined his high public profile as a gentleman racer, 'gentlemen' placing themselves above the vulgarity of accepting payment for advertising. Campbell also used his celebrity to promote right wing politics—historically, as several chapters in this book make clear, motor racing and the political right have often converged—standing as a Conservative in the General Election of 1935. Campbell is also known to have been sympathetic to the British Union of Fascists (active 1932–1940), who in turn presented themselves as modernists, supportive of the flight and motor industries.[18]

These men are now often recalled in motoring literature as household names. To the extent that this was so, it would likely have been through the media attention drawn to their feats of speed, on the track and at the venues selected for attempts to break the world record. This media attention came in the form of reports in the national press and on BBC radio, coverage in the motoring journals (*Autocar*, e.g., had begun publishing in 1895 and *The Motor* in 1903[19]) or via newsreels such as Pathe News, shown in British cinemas from 1910: Pathe covered the record attempts of Segrave, Parry-Thomas, Cobb and Campbell, along with events at Brooklands.[20] But these men were only incidentally media celebrities: media publicity was an essential element in their pursuit of speed, technical knowledge, car sales and an enhanced reputation for British engineering. These ingredients were mixed together to form a media spectacle in the form of the 'Bentley Boys' of the 1920s. And to these ingredients was added an upper-class hedonism and a ravening heterosexual masculinity, some version of the latter of which has attended elite motor racing, in Britain and elsewhere, for much of its history.

W.O. Bentley (b.1888) was the son of a wealthy silk and woollens merchant. He and his brother had begun importing French cars to Britain in 1912; they redesigned the cars and raced them at Brooklands.[21] After the First World War, they formed a company to make their own cars, one of which won the Le Mans 24-hour race of 1924. Bentley cars proved a racing success but a commercial failure—Bentley cars then cost around £1000 in 1925, the equivalent of over £60,000 in 2021, and were therefore too expensive for most prospective car buyers. The company's principal financial rescuer, Cambridge-educated racing driver Woolf Barnato, was still another heir to a large fortune, his father having been a key rival of Cecil Rhodes in the South African diamond mining industry.[22] Barnato funded the 'Bentley Boys', a team of men with a similar social profile to the other high-born adventurers currently exploring the possibilities of motorised speed. These included, among others: RFC veteran Sir Henry Birkin (not a natural celebrity, given his shyness and stammer, but notable for his spotted silk neckerchief) whose family had become rich in the Nottingham lace industry[23]; prosperous bacteriologist and *bon viveur* Dudley Benjafield[24]; Jack and Clive Dunfee, whose family were wines and spirits merchants and their father, Colonel Vickers Dunfee Commander of the City of London police[25]; naval veteran and aviator Glen Kidston, heir to metal fortune derived from Clydeside shipbuilding; Bernard Rubin, a wealthy Australian and son of a pearl dealer; and Sydney 'Sammy' Davis, who, as editor of *Autocar* magazine, ensured the Bentley Boys of regular publicity in the automobile world—the magazine hosted a reception for the Bentley team at the Savoy hotel in London, following their (second) victory in the Le Mans 24 hour race of 1927, with Davis himself and Benjafield at the wheel.[26]

The significance of the Bentley men appears to have been manifold. They married the notion of patriotic endeavour cultivated by the seekers of speed records to the matter of motor racing—of Birkin, for example, it has been said that he 'betrayed all the characteristics of a male obsessive spiced by an angry patriotism. He elevated his hobby into a great national cause capable of solving Britain's ills, using his autobiography[27] for a long rant about the lethargy of the British motor industry, the failure to develop British racing cars and to build adequate racing tracks, the ignorance and apathy of the public.'[28] Second, it assimilated racing drivers to the sentimental mythology of the British upper-class amateur sportsman[29] that already surrounded all-round sportsman C.B. Fry, cricketer W.G. Grace and others: they were portrayed as patriotic daredevils despite also being works drivers and, in effect, car salesmen. (The Bentley Boys included one professional driver: Frank Clement, the son of a Hertfordshire watchmaker.) Third, it lent British motor racing some of the same dashing male glamour then currently associated with Hollywood leading men such as Douglas Fairbanks and Ronald Colman—an association strengthened by the Bentley drivers' ostentatiously heterosexual lifestyle. Nick Foulkes, a biographer of the Bentley Boys, suggests, albeit with some hyperbole, that Ardenrun Hall, Barnato's Surrey mansion, operated as 'the de-facto home for the Bentley Boys—the hard-driving, hard-partying playboys who epitomised the cocktail-fuelled, decade-long party that was the Roaring Twenties'. He adds:

> Mothers of 'nice' girls were very careful where he was concerned. Nor, indeed, should any respectable girl accept a lift home with Barnato after an evening out; one particular limousine of his for nocturnal use had just a single seat compartment for the driver, while the rest of the car was converted into a large 'L'-shaped boudoir, equipped with curtains to ensure total privacy. Typical of the women he entertained in the back of this sumptuously appointed luxury vehicle was musical star June Tripp, whose hit songs included the entirely apposite 'Ladies Are Running Wild'. Barnato's life could be followed vicariously through the pages of society magazines such as *Tatler* and *The Sphere*.[30]

Doubtless, too, the Bentley clan's adventures featured in the gossip columns of the upper- and middle-class press (*The Times*, the *Daily Telegraph*) and the lower-middle-class newspapers (the *Daily Mail*, the *Daily Express*). That they were of widespread interest to working-class people seems unlikely, although the *Daily Herald*, the popular working-class newspaper of the time, did have a motoring correspondent. Between the world wars the most pervasive mode of transport for Britons—and certainly, for working-class people—was the chain-driven safety bicycle[31] and working-class people would not come to drive cars in any numbers until after the Second World War. The exploits of fast-driving, hedonistic toffs may therefore have been of marginal interest to them. Besides, the Bentley Boys were hostile to organised labour and formed a 'Brooklands Squad' to assist the police during the General Strike of 1926, earning them the praise of the right-wing *Daily Mail*.[32]

It is important to add that motor racing at this time was not an all-male affair and a number of women raced at Brooklands and elsewhere, although the main organising club at Brooklands did not accept women until 1920. These women invariably gained access to fast cars through their (high) social class and/or their well-placed menfolk in the Brooklands/speed record/luxury car coterie.

An early pioneer and racing celebrity was Dorothy Levitt (1882–1922). Levitt was the daughter of a wealthy Jewish family of jewellers in the London's East End. Her access to cars and thus to speed came via Selwyn Edge at the Napier car company who employed her initially as a typist. Historian of motor racing females Rachel Harris-Gardiner writes:

> Her finest year was 1905, when she won the *Daily Mail Sweepstake* at the Brighton Speed Trials [beachfront speed trials were popular in Edwardian Britain], ahead of several men. At the same event, she set a Land Speed Record for women of 92mph. This was her second speed record, having already set a Water Speed Record of 19.3mph in 1903'.[…] 'She was a real favourite with the press of the time. Reporters lapped up her racing victories and her many adventures' […] Her media fame led to a journalistic career of her own and becoming something of an expert on motoring for women. The high point of this was the publication of her 1909 book, *The Woman and the Car: A Chatty Little Handbook for Women Who Want To Motor*.[33]

It is possible that in a world wherein women were still denied the right to vote, the glamorous Levitt, although courageous and formidably gifted, was exploited for her novelty value. Her Jewishness will likely have made her an outsider in high society—her surname was an anglicised version of her family name 'Levi' and for a while a fictitious upper-class background was concocted for her. She disappeared from public life in 1912.[34]

Another protégé of Edge was Mildred Petre, whose husband the Hon. Victor Austin Bruce worked as a competition driver for AC Cars, which Edge had taken over in 1922. Petre was the daughter of a wealthy Essex landowner and a direct descendant of a leading Tudor politician. In an AC Six car she won the Coupe des Dames at the Monte Carlo rally of 1927, finishing sixth overall. Two years later, she drove a 4.5 litre Bentley at Montlhéry for 24 hours, thus securing the world record for single-handed driving at an average speed of 89 mph, a feat which has never been surpassed by a woman. Like Levitt she also raced speedboats and flew planes.[35]

Other female racers emerged similarly from wealthy, elite families that could afford motor cars and allow their womenfolk time to develop their driving skills. The Renfrewshire family of Margaret Allan owned the Allan Royal Mail Line shipping company, founded in the early nineteenth century. She was educated at Bedales, the progressive private boarding school in Hampshire favoured by more liberal families among the British elite. Allan drove a variety of cars and was one of only four women to hold the Brooklands badge for those lapping the circuit at 120 mph. Importantly, she was taken on as a works driver by MG in 1934. She was married to gentleman racer Christopher Jennings, who became editor of *The Motor* and, latterly, High Sheriff of Carmarthenshire. Allan herself was motoring correspondent of *Vogue* from 1948 until 1957, a post which reflected the growing interest in cars among middle-class women.[36] The less well-known, but equally wealthy, Betty Haig was born (in 1905) into the famous Scottish family of whiskey distillers. Her father was a colonel and she was the grand-niece of Field Marshall Douglas Haig, commander of the British Expeditionary Force on the Western Front during the First World War. She drove principally in rallies and won the Paris-St. Raphael Rally of 1938.[37]

Gwenda Hawkes was the daughter of a major general and the sister of the British imperialist Sir John Bagot Glubb—known as 'Glubb Pasha', commander of the Arab Legion in the 1930s. Another Brooklands regular between the wars, she became the first female to lap the track there at more than 130 mph. Her third husband, Douglas Hawkes, was a car designer, businessman and (gentleman) racing driver and together they ran an engineering company based at Brooklands.[38] Similarly, Jill Scott

Thomas, born in 1902, the daughter of a coal mine owner, and her first husband 'Bummer' Scott were Brooklands enthusiasts and car collectors. They were friends of record-seeker J.G. Parry Thomas, whose Leyland Eight they purchased after his death; John Cobb raced it at Brooklands with Jill as his passenger. She raced intermittently at Brooklands between 1926 and 1939. Her second husband, Ernest Thomas, was also a gentleman racer and, like her, an aviator.[39]

Violette Cordery was the most accomplished of several sisters, all of whom raced cars. Her father worked for a tobacco merchant and her elder half-sister Evelyn was married to Noel Macklin, a racing driver and founder of Invicta cars, based in the Cordery's home town of Cobham in Surrey. She won the first women's race at Brooklands aged 20 in 1920 and, chiefly driving (and thus testing) Invicta cars, she accomplished many feats of speed and endurance. In a column in the *Daily Express* in 1926 (22nd October) she wrote: '[T]here will soon be scarcely an able-bodied woman or girl who cannot drive and generally manage a motor car.' The following year she drove around the world, covering over 10,000 miles, a trip that she described as 'one long, glorious thrill'. In 1929, she won her second Dewar trophy for the Brooklands time trial. The following year, however, she embraced domesticity, largely giving up racing after her marriage to gentleman racer Johnny Hindmarsh, winner at Le Mans five years later.[40]

Elsie (always known as 'Bill') Wisdom, from the South London district of Tooting Graveney, seems to have been comparatively low-born among British female racing drivers of the inter-war period: Her father is described as a 'master watchmaker and shopkeeper'.[41] Wisdom was encouraged to race by her husband Tommy, also a racing driver and the aforementioned motoring correspondent of the *Daily Herald*; he entered her for a race at Brooklands only a week after their marriage.[42]

The history of these women, and their exploits, is now being retrieved and a number of websites feature sepia photographs of them sitting confidently, sometimes in goggles and overalls, sometimes in cloche hats and pearls, behind the wheel of an automobile. In the world of customary male swagger inhabited by Woolf Barnato, who allowed several of them to race his Bentleys, they were partners rather than prey. They reflected the growing aspirations of British middle- and upper-middle-class women in the wake of the Representation of the People Act of 1918, granting the vote to women over 30 and/or meeting a property qualification, and the Sex Disqualification (Removal) Act of the following year, which had removed certain barriers to women joining the professions. Some of the female drivers enjoyed a degree of celebrity and, not only did they win trophies and break records, but they were in several cases (Levitt, Petre, Allan) employed as test drivers. It is at least arguable that, albeit that most of the female drivers were drawn from a charmed social circle, women's star has never been higher in British elite motor racing than it was then.

The Road to Stirling Moss: Class, the Automobile and the (Partial) Democratisation of British Motoring

Before the Second World War, the access of British working-class people—or, indeed, most people outside of the very wealthy—to racing cars was severely restricted: if they had access at all it was most likely as mechanics or as engineers and they got behind the wheel only on test drives. Their relationships with the owners and drivers of these cars generally followed the master-and-servant pattern prevailing at the time, as two examples illustrate. A story told in praise of gentleman racer Earl Howe (Eton and Oxford, Conservative MP and ADC to King George V) has it that, when driving through Europe with his mechanic 'Tommy' Thomas in 1930, Howe would stop at hotels and require Thomas to wait outside; one day, however, he breached protocol and sent a waiter to summon Thomas with the message: '"You are wanted inside, the soup is getting cold". So they ate together, the Earl saying they could "have a good talk about cars"'.[43] And in 1934 Kaye Don, a wealthy Irish racer, who drove at Brooklands and competed regularly for world speed records, ordered his riding mechanic Frank Tayler, to work throughout the day on the brakes of his MG, in preparation for a race on the Isle of Man. Don spent the day playing bridge.[44] That evening, with Tayler on board, Don took the car for a test drive when public roads were no longer closed for race practice. They crashed, killing Tayler, and injuring Don, who served four months for manslaughter. The sympathy of the Brooklands fraternity, however, seemed to reside with Don rather than his deceased servant: in *Autocar*, 'Bentley Boy' Sammy Davis defended Don on the grounds that, as a racing mechanic, Tayler 'knew the risks'.[45]

Davis' remark fed into a wider political debate about cars, in which considerations of class privilege and individual freedom confronted those of public safety. Under the Road Traffic Act of 1930, a 30-mph speed limit had been imposed by the second Labour government of Ramsay Macdonald (the 20-mph limit having been removed in 1930) along with a Highway Code and traffic lights. Under the subsequent National Government, again led by Macdonald, a further Road Traffic Act introduced a driving test in 1934. In that year, 1894 people had been killed the previous year trying to cross roads.[46]

This legislation was bitterly opposed in the House of Commons by Conservative MP Col. John Moore-Brabazon, an aviator and an associate of Charles Rolls, and by *The Motor* magazine, which complained of 'the folly of which pedestrians are capable'. However, *The Times*, historically the mouthpiece of the British Establishment, welcomed the measures, arguing that 'the exclusive or preponderating regard for one class of road users leads nowhere'.[47]

There are clear implications here for the British motor racing. First, driving fast cars was ceasing to be the exclusive and carefree domain of the very rich. Part of the celebrity of public figures like Earl Howe, Dorothy Levitt and Mildred Petre was that they had rejoiced in the frequent fines for exceeding the speed limit.[48] But cars were now an entrenched part of British life and the Brooklands tendency had to be shown some discipline in the public interest.

Second, association with motor vehicles was spreading down the class structure. By 1934, there were over one million private car users in the UK[49] (which would become two million by 1939[50]) and car factories were long established in Birmingham, Coventry, Luton, Oxford and Dagenham. By the mid-1930s cars in the more affordable, non-luxury category—the Austin 7, for example—were widely available at around £165[51] (roughly £12,000 at 2021 prices) and there was a flourishing motor trade, entailing sales, garage maintenance, filling stations and motorists' magazines. Car enthusiasts formed motor clubs: some, as in

Bristol, dated from before the First World War.[52] Tinkering with cars and motorcycles, was, wrote the historian John Stevenson, an introduction to science and technology for many.[53]

This trade had already produced one or two top drivers before the Second World War: for instance, Freddie Dixon (b. Stockton, 1892), a mechanic who was expert on both cars and motorcycles ran a garage business in Middlesbrough and won the British Empire Trophy at Brooklands in 1935; and Reg Parnell (b. 1911), whose garage business was in Derby, drove at Brooklands in the late 1930s and in seven Formula 1 races in the early 1950s. Indeed, the motor trade spawned much of the first generation of post-Second World War British racing drivers. Future World Champion Mike Hawthorn (b.1929) was the son of a Yorkshireman who moved his motor business to Surrey to be close to Brooklands[54]; and the families of Stuart Lewis Evans (b.1930, who raced for Connaught and Vanwall in the 1950s), Peter Collins (b.1931, a Ferrari driver in the 1950s), Cliff Allison (b.1932, who drove for Lotus and Ferrari), John Surtees (b.1934, Ferrari driver and world champion in 1964), Trevor Taylor (b. 1936, also a Lotus driver) and three-times World Campion Jackie Stewart (b.1939) were all variously in the motor trade.

Third, demand was growing for motor racing in the provinces. In 1931, motorcycle racer Fred Craner, another Derby garage owner and member of the Derby and District Motor Club successfully requested that the nearby Donington Hall estate be used for motor racing.[55] Initially this was for motor bikes, but in 1935 and for four consecutive years Donington staged its own unofficial Grand Prix. The winners of these four races together pointed the way ahead for British racing drivers, and racing drivers in general. The first winner, Richard Shuttleworth, was one of the last in the last of archetypal gentleman racers. An Old Etonian and gifted mechanic from a wealthy, old-established engineering family, he owned a range of cars, raced at Brooklands, flew planes and held land speed records.[56] The winner in 1936, Richard Seaman, had a similar profile. Another scion of a wealthy distillers family and a Cambridge graduate, Seaman had defied his wealthy mother (who bought him a plane and a country house) to become a racing driver. He won Donington in a borrowed Maserati and this and other successes brought him to the attention of the German factory team Mercedes Benz, with whom he signed a contract that year. His salary would be '1000 Reichsmarks a month—just under £1000 a year in 1937, or about £65,000 today—plus prize money and bonuses which would quadruple his earnings for the year', although currency restrictions meant that he must remain in Germany.[57] There he openly espoused National Socialism, wherein automotive speed and technology were seen as manifestations of modernism and motor racing funded by the state—in the words of writer Eberhard Reuss 'a car-friendly dictatorship'.[58] Seaman, who gave the Hitler salute on the podium after winning the German Grand Prix of 1938, once wrote to his mother: 'Hitler stands no nonsense. He won't have any slackers about. Everybody has got to work.'[59]

The Donington races of 1938 and 1939 were won by the German Bernd Rosemeyer and the Italian Tazio Nuvolari respectively: two stars of the era, they both drove for Auto Union, the other key automotive company in the Nazi motor racing project. Motor sport was increasingly a matter of national pride on the European continent and the best drivers were in Germany, Italy and France.[60] Seaman could hold his own with them. It was said later that he had 'brilliant ability and [paid] close attention to detail'[61]: the future of British motor racing drivers seemed to call for a greater professionalism and, with it, greater remuneration. The sum £65,000 might not have looked like a lot of money to Dick Seaman but it would certainly appeal to the next generation of British drivers: around the time that Seaman was dying of his injuries in the German Grand Prix of 1939, ten-year-old Stirling Moss was already driving his first car, an old Austin 7, given him by his father.[62]

Stirling Moss, Memorable Moniker

During the Second World, there was significant agitation—much of it conducted via the pages of motor magazines—for a democratisation of motor racing in Britain and the slogan 'motor racing for all' became popular. In July 1941, *Motor Sport* published a letter from freelance motor journalist Joe Lowrey suggesting the development of a new racing car class suited to the special builder and powered by 500 cc motorcycle engines.[63] This idea was taken up by a number of engineers and animateurs who constituted what became known as the '500 cc movement'. A 500 Club was founded in Bristol in 1946, with the Bentley Boy patronage of Earl Howe and Sammy Davis[64] and the firm to respond most successfully to Lowrey's suggestion was the Cooper Car Company of south London. In 1949, nearly half the 40 entrants for the 500 cc race at the British Grand Prix at Silverstone were Coopers.[65] Meanwhile, public enthusiasm (and perhaps the need for motorised speed to be performed in controlled circumstances) was inspiring the creation of new race tracks out of wartime military installations: at Goodwood and Silverstone (1948), Brands Hatch and Thruxton (1950), Oulton Park and Snetterton (1953) and Aintree (1954)—former car dealer Roy Salvadori, who won on many of these tracks, became known as 'King of the Airfields'.[66] Brooklands had closed in 1939.

Affordable cars and new venues brought forth a post-war cadre of variously ambitious young drivers. John Cooper, son of the company's founder, recalled (of Salvadori and others) in 2001: "This was the prototype of today's drivers, if you like. They were more professional, took life and their sport more seriously. They came from the 500 cc movement. Before that, motor racing, in Britain at least, was more of a rich man's pastime. Our cars were so cheap that they introduced a whole new generation of drivers, who took a different approach. Men such as Stirling [Moss] and Roy Salvadori[67] came into it and were quick to realize that there was money to be made. As a result, they were much more professional.'

Formula 1 (F1) began in 1950 and the first F1 British Grand Prix (at Silverstone in Northamptonshire) drew 100,000 people and was attended by the King and Queen. Some of it was also shown on the grainy, black-and-white screens of BBC television. The BBC broadcast its first Grand Prix live in 1953 and F1 remained on the channel until 1996.[68] Motor racing as significantly popular culture in Britain dates from this time and the factors in play provide much of the basis for the mystique that has surrounded Stirling Moss. He is, arguably, British motor racing's first celebrity in the modern idiom: a person of note, whose notability is commodified.

Moss' appeal had several dimensions to it. First, as a public figure he had wide appeal. To a degree he represented a continuation of the

Brooklands tradition: his parents, both racing drivers themselves, had met there. He was a public schoolboy from a prosperous family who were able to support his career financially—his father, for example, met much of the cost of a Maserati 250F in 1954.[69] That said, he was not an aristocrat, had not inherited a vast fortune and was earning his own keep. To the British motor racing—and wider—public of the 1950s, he likely passed for a classless, everyman figure, equally acceptable to the Bentley brigade as to the working-class 'geezer' car enthusiasts, like Bernie Ecclestone, who began to convene at the Brands Hatch circuit in Kent after the war; besides which, for this public, he was the first Briton to excel on the burgeoning post-war international racing scene, constituted after 1950 as Formula 1. He also cultivated a foreign audience: in the absence of much competition in the immediate post-war period in 1950, he accepted an invitation to race abroad and became well known on the European continent[70]; in 1955, he became the only Briton (and one of the few non-Italians) to win the Mille Miglia. At 21, he won the Richard Seaman Trophy for the most points gained overseas. Moreover, he drove for as a wide variety of employers. These included several English racing companies formed after the war—Coopers and HWM (Hersham and Walton Motors) (both begun in 1946), Lotus (1952) and Vanwall, who entered F1 in 1954. But he also drove, on the basis of no more than a handshake, for Rob Walker, privateer and heir to the Johnny Walker whiskey fortune. Walker, a Brooklands veteran, was described simply as 'Gentleman' on his passport.[71] Thus, Moss straddled the old world of the be-goggled upper-class amateur and the new one of the thriving new motor workshops of the post-war era. In his presentation of self, he married this to a plucky individualism: 'I like to feel the odds are against me', he once said. 'That is one of the reasons that I do not drive for a factory. I want to beat the factories in a car that has no right to do so. If I had any sense I would have been driving a Ferrari all these years. Year after year, Ferrari has the best car. But I want to fight against the odds and in a British car'[72] (Moss was actually approached, and then shunned, by Ferrari in 1951[73]).

Second, Moss was a very accomplished and aggressive driver across a range of models and classifications. 'Often', he recalled, 'it would be five different formulae in one day: a race of champions, sports cars, Formula

Two, Formula One and touring cars'. Between winning his first race in 1948 and his enforced retirement in 1962, he registered a world record 212 wins from 529 races in 15 seasons.[74]

Third, Moss never won the World Championship, although between 1955 and 1961 he was runner-up four times and third a further three. This, in an ironic way, further burnished his credentials. If he had won the championship, arguments might have raged over his merits as against other champions; instead that he was 'the greatest driver never to' became a unanimous verdict in the motor racing world and beyond. This reputation was further cemented by an act of sportsmanship which cost him the title. In 1958, a marshal at the Portuguese Grand Prix disqualified Mike Hawthorn for illegally re-joining the track, having spun off it. Moss who had won the race, intervened on Hawthorn's behalf and Hawthorn, who had finished second was reinstated, giving him the title. 'I had no hesitation in doing it', Moss said many years later. 'I can't see how this is open to debate. The fact that he was my only rival in the championship didn't come into my thinking. Absolutely not'.[75] Leading motor journalist Doug Nye has, however, suggested that, in losing the title, Moss had been 'deeply disappointed … perhaps bitter' at the time.[76] It's worth bearing in mind here that Moss is remembered in a way that Hawthorn, Britain's first Formula 1 World Champion, is not.

Fourth, and perhaps most important, Moss desired and understood celebrity. He came, first of all, from a very entrepreneurial family: his father had been a dentist who owned a chain of surgeries. The surgeries, said Moss, were 'mainly in the poorer areas where the patients did not expect the dentists to spend much time generally chatting to them, but rather just do the job. "In quick, yank and out, next please—that's the basis of good business", he might have said'.[77] Moss had a similarly business-like approach, not only to racing, but to being Stirling Moss. This set him apart from other drivers. Tony Brooks, his contemporary, once said 'I wasn't trying to be commercial, whereas Stirling was'.[78] Similarly, in a memoir first published in 1958, the year before his death, Hawthorn declared himself uninterested in celebrity.[79] Hawthorn and leading driver Peter Collins were widely seen as playboys in the pre-war mould.[80] While Moss frequently alluded to the drivers' routine quest for attractive female company, that did not intrude on his business plan.

When he signed for Mercedes in 1954, he sought to capitalise on his growing fame. In 2009, Gordon Cruickshank of *Motor Sport* magazine interviewed Ken Gregory, Moss' manager, about this:

> [Moss said] "I told you I didn't want to drive for them", but I said, "Wait 'til you hear the money. [...]". "By this time", [Gregory] goes on, "Stirling and I had developed complete trust in each other; when he was out of the country I could pass a quote for him, which is why his name was always in the papers. He had marvellous press coverage." By now everyone knew that face—it was gold dust. "I was looking after publicity and the advertising was starting to come in; Stirling Moss as a brand name was developing." More than developing: at the end of '54, when the Mercedes deal was signed, the trio [Gregory, Moss and Alfred Moss, Stirling's father] formed Stirling Moss Ltd., cashing in on what Moss has often said was his biggest asset—his memorable moniker. Gregory is careful to make the point that Moss only endorsed things he approved of—which maximised the power of that memorable visage looking out of a magazine. Sales of *Craven A* cigarettes soared when The Boy lit up.[81]

Moss retired from motor racing after a serious crash at Goodwood in 1962 which left him unconscious for some days. Commercially, though, as Gregory stated, he continued to thrive. While in hospital, Gregory remembered, Moss 'received 400 letters a day, and the press were desperate to get to him. I eventually sold the rights to a bedside interview for £10,000' (the equivalent of £183,000 in 2021).[82] Once recovered, Moss was invited to become the public face of BP, who flew him round the country in a helicopter to open new petrol stations.[83] Moss also understood the transactional nature of celebrity. As Richard Williams said in an obituary for Moss:

> His public image was enhanced by his willingness to invite feature writers and TV cameras into his town house in Shepherd Market, the district of Mayfair in central London where he lived, even when married, in a kind of bachelor-pad splendour amid a panoply of hi-tech gadgets. The aura continued to surround him long after an accident on the track truncated his career at the age of 32, when he was still in his prime. The sight of Moss, in his later decades, entering the paddock at a race meeting [...] never failed

to draw shoals of fans, photographers and journalists keen to hear his opinion on the latest controversy.[84]

Graham Hill: Performing 'Graham Hill'

Graham Hill was Formula 1 World Champion in 1962 and again 1968, while finishing runner-up three years running (1963–1965). He dominated motor racing in the post-Moss period of 'the Sixties', the term being interpreted here as a set of ideas about a less restricted popular culture than as a literal decade.[85] Other leading drivers of this time shunned celebrity. Neither of the two star British drivers of the early to mid-1960s—John Surtees (F1 champion, 1964) and Jim Clark (world champion in 1963 and 1965)—sought to develop a public image. Surtees, whose father Jack had been a dealer in cars and motor bikes and a racer, never strayed from the motor world and on retirement in 1970 opened a Honda dealership in Kent. Jim Clark combined racing with work on the family sheep farm in the Scottish borders (although when he died in 1968 he was living in tax exile in Paris[86]). Graham Hill, by contrast, developed a complex public persona—his son Damon refers to the 'several people that were my father'[87]—which reflected the complex class and less complex gender dynamics of motor racing and wider British popular culture at the time. Whereas Moss simply merchandised his 'memorable moniker', Hill performed 'Graham Hill'.

Born in 1929, the same year as Moss and Hawthorn, Hill's class background can be characterised as lapsed middle class. His father had worked on the London Stock Exchange and had been captain of Mill Hill Golf Club in North London, apparent badges of solid, upper-middle-class respectability but, according to his grandson, Hill Senior had probably been on the wrong end of a deal.[88] This meant that Graham Hill, in contrast to the great majority of British racing drivers hitherto, had begun working life with little money. His wife Bette, an international rower whom he met in 1951, described him then as 'just a chap—and a pretty penniless one'.[89] Hill's route to elite motor racing was via engineering and the burgeoning post-war scene of workshops and Brands Hatch race meetings. He attended Hendon technical college (technical colleges were well down Britain's educational hierarchy, specialising often in teaching craft apprentices) in the late 1940s and did National Service as a Petty Officer in the Royal Navy 1950–1952. He then had a job with engineering firm Smiths Industries which he relinquished to go on the dole and work on cars. When Lotus employed him in 1954 it was, initially, as an engineer; the same year his quest to become a racing driver began when he paid £1 to drive four laps of the Brands hatch circuit. He signed to drive for Lotus in 1957. Meanwhile he earned extra money from a business he set up converting cars to go faster, catering to the growing post-war demand for speed.[90]

His driver's salary, plus retainers from petrol and tyre companies, business dealings and personal appearances made him a wealthy man and he acquired the trappings of achieved celebrity common to top drivers. Like several other drivers he flew his own plane (to races, for business trips, to play golf in Spain with Sean Connery) and in 1971 moved his family into a Hertfordshire mansion in 30 acres. He went shooting with the Queen[91] and his biography, called simply *Graham* and published posthumously in 1977, carried an introduction by the Prince of Wales. He became a member of the London's Clermont Club, opened in 1962 as a meeting place for rich gamblers and, according to one writer, a 'bunker' against egalitarianism.[92] He was invited to address the Institute of Directors' annual convention at the Albert Hall, where he told the assembly how he relished the 'stimulus of competition', and to speak on 'Courage' to an audience in the City of London, temple of British finance capitalism.[93] He was voted After Dinner Speaker of the Year in 1971.[94]

In the course of this ascent, Hill developed a distinct public persona. In an acknowledgement of 'the Sixties' he grew his hair down below his collar and acquired a playfully military bearing and an ersatz upper-class accent. This may have been because Hill, who had turned 21 in 1950, was of a generation wherein upward special mobility still carried with it an obligation to modify one's behaviour accordingly. Alternatively, Damon Hill, speaking of his father's 'ridiculous moustache' says Graham grew it to resemble an 'RAF fighter pilot'. ('Battle of Britain' pilots were, of course, heroes in post-war Britain and drivers often sought to associate themselves with the courage of these airmen.) In Damon's view, however, his father's image recalled actor Terry-Thomas,[95] the 'definitive post-war cad or rotter'[96] in British comedy films of the late 1950s. A more apt comparison might be with Leslie Phillips, who portrayed a string of interchangeably lecherous characters in the *Carry On...* films of the same period, because Hill's *faux* military persona was accompanied by a sexually roving eye. This bordered on caricature, but nevertheless revealed some of the sexual politics of Formula 1 at the time. The Bentley Boys had established the notion of the British racing driver as a suave, predatory male heterosexual. This re-emerged as an element in the performance of the celebrity driver during the 1960s. For example, in 1963 Moss wrote 'I always keep a diary and I do it every night, no matter what. [...] If someone's in bed with me I just say "Excuse me, sweetie, whilst I write a couple of things in m'book"'[97] a mode of writing about women that seemed to borrow from Ian Fleming's (demonstrably sexist) James Bond books. In 1969, Hill, who had been a judge in the Miss World contest the previous year, broke both legs in a crash during the US Grand Prix at Watkins Glen and then embarked on a long recovery. A subsequent BBC sports awards broadcast featured a live link to Hill's hospital bed. Referring to the two nurses attending him, Hill told the camera 'I don't know what you chaps will be doing later, but I will be getting a rub-down from a couple of lovelies. So, if you can beat that, good luck to you'.[98] Hill's wife Bette, in the audience, could almost certainly have seen beyond this moment of *Carry On...* levity and was by then well aware of the attractive young women now converging on the Grand Prix circuit and making themselves sexually available to drivers. 'We disliked the dolly birds', she wrote in her own memoir. 'They were always around and we knew they were going to be there whether we accepted it, tried to ignore it or threw tantrums'.[99] 'The Sixties was not a good time for wives', wrote Damon Hill later, 'The world belonged to the male of the species and macho men like my father had the upper hand'.[100] Indeed, when Bette Hill had given birth to Damon, she had telephoned Graham, then staying in a hotel prior to a race at Snetterton, with the news. Graham's gruff response—'Is that all you woke me up to tell me?'—is recorded in the memoirs of both wife and son; each makes clear that Graham was not joking.[101]

This masculine, heavily heterosexual environment also, needless to say, was difficult for non-heterosexuals to enter. The only known gay British Formula 1 driver was a colonel's son Mike Beuttler, who drove as an amateur in F1 between 1971 and 1973. He was funded by stockbroker friends, some of whom were also gay and whose team was known as Clarke-Mordaunt-Guthrie Racing and his car the 'Stockbroker Special'. He often brought a clutch of 'dolly birds' to races to discourage rumours.[102] He died in 1988 of AIDS.

James Hunt: Consumed by Celebrity

James Hunt (1947–1993) was World F1 Champion in 1976 and, for a time, British motor racing's most lucrative celebrity. Indeed, he is, arguably, a case study of the contradictions of late twentieth-century celebrity. His life has been well documented, and biographies include books by the motoring journalist Gerald Donaldson and a copious 600-plus page tome by Tom Rubython, a writer-publisher specialising in business and motor sport. This section draws on these two accounts.

While British motor racing in the three decades that followed the Second World War threw up comparatively few working-class drivers—a rare example being Roger Williamson (b.1948) whose father Dodge Williamson, a former speedway rider, had, when Roger was four, built him a car powered by a lawn mower engine[103]—growing professionalism had also thinned out the privately educated 'gung ho' tendency. Piers Courage, Old Etonian heir to a brewing fortune and married to Earl Howe's daughter, was a survivor of this tendency, having a fitful F1 career between 1966 and his death in the Dutch Grand Prix of 1970.[104] As an aspirant racing driver, Hunt certainly fit the profile of the unscholarly, privately educated, speed-oriented young man of pre-war years. His father was a stockbroker and his undistinguished schooldays were spent at Wellington College, a minor public (i.e. private) school in England's historic educational hierarchy. In his early employment career he relied heavily on a skilful presentation of self, first in working for a company which rented out telephone systems and, latterly, as a nascent racing driver approaching firms for sponsorship: some upmarket car dealerships responded favourably.[105] He won a prestigious Grovewood award (for promising drivers) in 1969. Between 1973 and 1975 Hunt drove for Lord Hesketh, a wealthy self-styled British eccentric and privateer who maintained the ostentatious Bentley Boy tradition. Hunt, known for his liking for alcohol and recreational drugs, was promoted as a priapic figure with overalls bearing the slogan 'Sex: The Breakfast of Champions'.[106] There's little doubt that the Hesketh team's attempt to revive the 1920s playboy ambience (champagne, caviar, limousines, a liveried butler, parties…[107]) to motor racing was not popular on the circuit. When Hesketh abandoned F1 in 1975 Hunt moved to McLaren, whose manager recalled: '[W]e were a professional racing team and the golden boy-hype business at Hesketh really meant nothing to us. They were just a bunch of wankers'.[108]

The reason that Hesketh withdrew from F1 was the same reason that Hunt continued to thrive: corporate sponsorship, mainly from tobacco companies, now dominated the funding of both teams and drivers. Hunt made a good deal more money out of being James Hunt than he did from racing. The difference between his and the previous generation was that[109] celebrity was now part of the corporate machine that ran in tandem with Formula 1 after on-car advertising had been permitted in 1968. Whereas, for example, the administrative burden arising from Graham Hill's work as a celebrity had been borne by his family,[110] Hunt was signed to the US-based international sport agency IMG, who handled his affairs and had immediately counselled him to live abroad to avoid British tax; under their tutelage he was being paid between $5000 and $10,000 per day for promotional activities. His good looks and growing racing reputation gained him a contract to advertise Marlboro cigarettes, (although he continued to smoke his favourite Rothmans, inserted into Marlboro packets[111]). He also held lucrative contracts with Texaco and Vauxhall. In 1977, his retainer at Philip Morris (owners of the Marlboro brand) alone was worth $250,000 and he rivalled former world champion Jackie Stewart, now four years into retirement and another client of IMG, for earnings. Stewart, readily available to global brands—he worked as ambassador for Rolex (watches), the Ford Motor Company, Moet (winery) and the Royal Bank of Scotland[112]—professed to have earned more money since his retirement than when he had been racing.[113] Hunt was now, it was claimed, the biggest celebrity in Britain.[114]

As a public figure Hunt was notable for doing as he pleased. His prodigious appetite for drink, drugs and casual sex, all widely available on the motor racing circuit, are well documented and he was said to be incapable of embarrassment.[115] He wore what he wanted (his usual attire consisted of jeans, a T shirt and bare feet) and baulked at a 'dress standards' clause in his Marlboro contract.[116] He frequently got into fights and once punched a marshal at a race when he was the reigning world champion.[117] Unsurprisingly, therefore, he featured regularly in the tabloid press: in 1987, for instance, newspapers reported that he had got drunk on a British Airways flight to Adelaide for the Australian Grand Prix and urinated over several passengers.[118]

In the main this troubled neither the sponsors or the public unduly, one strong possibility being that his defiance of convention was appealing, and bringing motor racing, to the rising 'Generation X'—rather in the way the 'bad boys' John McEnroe and Andre Agassi would later do for tennis.[119]

Hunt represented the apotheosis of the racing driver as a symbol of male heterosexual potency. A whole chapter of Rubython's biography of him (and much else of the book) is devoted to Hunt's sexual conquests.[120] His view of women probably differed from that of Moss or Hill only in the degree of discretion with which they conducted their affairs; like Hill, he acted as a judge in the Miss World Contest of 1976 and his reaction to not winning the BBC Sports Personality of the Year award in 1977 is instructive. The winner was figure skater John Curry. Figure skating, of course, was still seen by many as inappropriate for boys (unlike motor racing) and Curry had been outed as gay the year before. Hunt was indignant at not winning and demanded to know what had happened. BBC producer Jonathan Martin told him that 'all the women voted for Curry—they like him'. Hunt's reply—'And they don't like me?'—suggests a mentality rooted in physical attraction and a failure to comprehend the feminine, either in females or in males.[121]

Hunt's celebrity entailed a number of telling ironies. First, his relentlessly off-the-cuff behaviour very possibly meant that, within motor racing, he was more popular as a TV commentator than as a racer. 'I believe that the contribution he made to our sport, through his television commentating and his writing, was enormous', wrote Stirling Moss of (the recently deceased) Hunt—a telling and backhanded tribute to a man who had been a world champion driver in that same sport. 'That was the good side', added Moss. 'For one of my generation, James' behaviour could also be quite appalling'.[122] Hunt had signed to commentate on motor racing for BBC television, following his retirement from driving in 1979. Here he became popular with audiences for balancing the boyish enthusiasm of regular commentator former advertising executive Murray Walker with often scathing professional critique.[123]

Second, in an indulgent adult life littered with apparent *faux pas* and misdemeanour, one of the few rebukes that Hunt received was for a politically liberal statement, which probably said less about him than it did about the social and political circles in which he moved. During commentary on the South African Grand Prix of 1991 Hunt launched into a spontaneous condemnation of the country's racist apartheid system. The BBC held to the notion that such matters constituted 'politics' and should not intrude on sport. The producer immediately passed him a note reading: 'TALK ABOUT *THE RACE*'. Hunt then compounded the felony by adding 'Anyway, thank God we're not there'—the BBC had not disclosed that the commentary was from a live feed and was actually being transmitted from Shepherds Bush in west London.[124]

Third, in 1989 when he sought to divorce his second wife, Hunt, who had already lost a great deal of money as a Lloyds 'name' in the City of London, had to counter claims by his wife's lawyer that he was a bad father. His drinking, drugtaking and, specifically, the British Airways urination incident of 1987 which had taken place when his elder son had only recently been born, were floated as evidence of this. Fearful of losing access to his children, Hunt consented to a very expensive legal settlement.[125] Hunt had always enjoyed the financial benefits of being a public figure while trying to live the life of a private one—he complained that 'the massive invasion of privacy is worse than being at school'.[126] But what might have been relished by Generation X and self-proclaimed opponents of 'political correctness' could scarcely be defended in a legal transaction wherein Hunt's 'good character' was being contested. Celebrity cannot do as it pleases; it is always subject to sanction and punishment, as and when the occasion arises. Hunt was initially known as a racing driver but in time his known-ness came to be based largely upon what Chris Rojek calls 'the charm of notoriety'[127]; his celebrity came to rest in large part on transgression, a gift, depending on time and place, either to the tabloid press, the legal profession, or both.

Nigel Mansell: The Guy You Would Chat to in the Pub

On the face of it, the career of Nigel Mansell, Formula 1 world champion in 1992 whose career at the top included 12 of the 13 years of Margaret Thatcher's premiership, represents the neoliberal dream trajectory, in which (reasonably) humble beginnings, family support, hard work, sacrifice, persistence in adversity and fierce determination lead to success, wealth and fame, followed by business diversification and charity work, as a means of 'giving something back'.[128] Like Clark and Surtees before him, Mansell seems never to have sought celebrity beyond the routine 'ghosted' biography, of which in his case there have been several, although in the most recent of these he readily recognised himself as a 'brand'.[129] The latest one certainly renders his life as a Thatcherite idyll. Other accounts present a more nuanced picture. Given the theme of this chapter, Mansell's career suggests an interesting relationship to the social class history and tradition of British motor racing, to its gender order and, once again, to the transactional nature of celebrity itself. This final section examines the narratives of Mansell's career.

The bare bones of Mansell's early life are set out in his most recent memoir, published by prestigious international publishers Simon and Schuster in 2015; it has no credited co-writer although 'Mart', with whom the book was apparently written, is mentioned in the dedications.[130] As a book, it is a story of dogged struggle but devoid of recrimination.

Mansell was born in 1953 into the technology-based, lower middle class and grew up in Birmingham, the heartland of Britain's motor industry. His father was a senior engineer at Lucas Aerospace and his mother ran a tea shop. The family lived in a modest, semi-detached house. He decided at 8 years old that he would be Formula 1 champion. He came up as a junior on the Midlands karting scene and his father bought him a kart and maintained it for him, his grandparents paying for any necessary parts. He attended the local technical college and, at his father's instigation, joined Lucas as an apprentice, where he became a laboratory technician and then a production manager.[131] At college he had met seemingly his only girlfriend; their first date was at a kart race.[132] They married in 1975.

His route into elite motor racing is marked, first and foremost, by shared sacrifice. His quest to be a top driver was conceived as a family enterprise in which Mansell's wife Rosanne was seen as an equal partner.[133] This enterprise entailed many initial sacrifices. For example, Mansell gave up his Lucas job in 1977 and the couple survived on Rosanne's earnings; they sold their flat in 1978 in order to finance Mansell's move into Formula 3[134] and Mansell worked cleaning windows while writing to 400 companies for sponsorship, without success.[135]

Unsurprisingly, therefore, a hallmark of Mansell's presentation of self is an appreciation of the value of money. For example, fully four pages of his autobiography are expended in telling the reader of an incident in 1975 when a mental patient, who had wandered from a nearby hospital, damaged his car; after a wrangle of several months, he was paid for the repairs. When he was taken on by Lotus, initially to deal with quality control, he slept in his car outside Lotus headquarters in Norfolk, because he couldn't afford bed and breakfast. In 1981, when he made his F1 debut, he stayed in Brazil for six weeks because of the prohibitive expense of going home and then returning for the Argentine Grand Prix. In the Dallas Grand Prix of 1984, his transmission broke so he got out and began to push the car, partly, he explained, because he was on finishing money.[136]

This was allied to considerable physical courage and self-belief. He survived a number of serious injuries, beginning with a crash at Brands Hatch in 1977 which broke several bones in his neck. He was told that he would never race again but records proudly that, backing mind over matter, he was back doing so within six weeks.[137]

Here, surely, was derring-do to match that of the Bentley Boys, the pre-war record seekers and the dashing post-war generations that preceded him. But Mansell seems to have been denied the acclaim accorded to those drivers. James Hunt famously claimed in *The Times* in 1986 that

'Formula 1 insiders' didn't want Mansell to win the world championship, adding 'Above all, they want a worthy winner'[138] (Mansell nevertheless was runner-up and voted BBC Sports Personality for that year.) There was a belief in the motor racing world that the nature of Mansell's ascent had given him a sense of grievance against those drivers who had it less hard. For a time Mansell was No. 2 driver to Elio de Angelis at Lotus. de Angelis' father was the wealthy owner of a construction company in Rome and de Angelis himself had a flat in Monaco, a stark contrast to Mansell's start in life. Peter Warr, team manager at Lotus, said that Mansell 'was still at that time in a frame of mind—and I think it was because of the way he had come up through motor racing—that the world was against him'.[139]

Certainly, Mansell was frequently involved in disputes, with officials and fellow drivers—notably with his Brazilian rival Ayrton Senna, whom he grabbed by the throat following an incident at the Belgian Grand Prix at Spa in 1987. Seemingly by way of explanation, Mansell told a friend later: 'I'm only an ordinary bloke'.[140] Equally, Mansell, who lacked conventional good looks, might have resented the sponsorship that had accrued to drivers on the basis simply of their public image, James Hunt having been the archetype. But resentment of Mansell seemed to run deeper, in at least two ways.

First, Mansell's quiet monogamy seemed to fly in the face of the still-prevailing gender order in Formula 1 motor racing. One of Mansell's biographers, the veteran motoring writer Christopher Hilton, refers pointedly to the fact that de Angelis' girlfriend was a German model; Rosanne Mansell, by contrast, 'would never become like the exotic creatures—and creations—who decorate race meetings and adorn the pit lane'.[141] The Brazilian Nelson Piquet, with whom Mansell had had a fractious relationship as teammates at Williams (1986–7), gave an interview to *Playboy* magazine in 1988 in which he described Rosanne as 'ugly'.[142] At race meetings the Mansell family stuck together: usually they would bring their own motorhome and hang out with relatives, friends and family.[143] Mansell offered no raw material to transgression-hungry tabloid reporters.

Second, and related to this, Mansell as an individual seemed to lack the ingredients from which British motor racing celebrity was customarily confected. Hilton, again, makes this plain and, in doing so, demonstrates the negotiated nature of celebrity.

British sportswriters since before the Second World War have nurtured relationships with performers in their field in the hope of cooperating on a biography or two—this applies to motor racing, as to a number of other sports. Some of the resulting books would be simple celebrations, featuring many photographs and aimed at fans. Others would be more serious interrogations of their subject. In the case of Mansell, an example of the former would be Alan Henry's *Nigel Mansell: World Champion*, in which Mansell is described, among other things, as 'a yeoman racer' and 'like the guy you would chat to in the pub'.[144]

Hilton opted for the latter kind of book, which adopted the same title as Henry's and was published first in 1987, with subsequent editions. In the book Hilton frequently attempts to extol Mansell's perceived ordinariness but instead simply underlines the fish-out-of-water nature of Mansell's relationship to Formula 1 culture. Mansell is depicted variously a 'Brummie, brusque, spade-is-a-spade sort of bloke'; 'moody—perhaps downcast would be more accurate. He always found difficulty concealing that and Birmingham is not noted for its *joie de vivre*'; 'because of that moustache, a subaltern…'; and as possessing a 'firm handshake, those defensive eyes scanning you, that slightly awkward English way of not knowing how to leave'.[145] Mansell, Hilton made clear, simply could not *perform* celebrity. In public, the book argued, he used stilted language, rather in the manner of a police report (Mansell was a special constable for a time when living on the Isle of Man) while rivals provided viable quotes for the reporters' notebooks. Of the leading drivers of the late 1980s, Hilton wrote: 'Senna [is] expressive in Portuguese, Spanish, English and Italian; [Alain] Prost [is] fluent in French, delicious in English, comfy after his fashion in Italian; Mansell [is] sometimes awkward in English'.[146] This, it should be added, is a part of a popular rendering of Mansell as a philistine: a recent article refers to his prosaic culinary tastes—he was a 'burger-chomping' sort of guy, it says, and 'at team dinners, would ask for ketchup to put on his meals'.[147]

Hilton acknowledged Mansell's plain man appeal—of the crowds who flocked to see him drive at Silverstone, he said: 'It was easy to see themselves in Mansell: He had married the sort of girl they might have married, had the sort of family they might have had, spoke the way they spoke.'[148] But, for media purposes, there was little in Mansell from which a celebrity myth to rival that of Moss, Clark, Hill, Stewart or Hunt could be fashioned. 'Mansell had known nothing but the microphones, tape recorders, notebooks', wrote Hilton. 'Moreover, as sport became more democratic—in the sense that anybody could play, not just the born-rich—people came forward with a talent and prospered on that talent while remaining inescapably what they were: ordinary people. Why not? But the extent of their exposure in the media showed, the great talent aside, how ordinary they were'.[149]

This was not mere snobbish pining for the days of the gentleman racers—although it is clearly that. As the leading British F1 contender Mansell had to be the story—he simply didn't help writers like Hilton in the telling of it. Hilton made clear the pragmatic importance of the celebrity-making of Mansell to the motor racing journalists of the time when recalling Mansell's (temporary, as it turned out) retirement in 1990: '[T]hose journalists who didn't have to file immediately started thinking and thinking hard. Where did Mansell's void leave them? Which newspapers would send them round the world at considerable expense to report races without Mansell? This emphasised the stature to which Mansell had grown. He was air tickets to a lot of people'.[150]

In retirement, Mansell maintained a fractious individualism and remained suspicious of those drivers who might not have faced the difficulties that he had faced. In 2010, he was asked what he thought of English driver Lewis Hamilton, who had won his first F1 world championship two years earlier: 'Well, it's fantastic what he has achieved, but he's been manufactured', replied Mansell, 'How many people from seven years of age have been given £2.5 million to go karting?'[151] Mansell also defiantly retained his identification with ordinary people. In 2020, now living in Jersey, with his family he opened a Mitsubishi dealership: Mitsubishi cars, he said (with questionable accuracy), were cars that 'pretty much anybody could afford'.[152]

Conclusion: British Motor Racing and Celebrity—What Ordinary People Lack?

Peevish and maladroit as Mansell may often have been, he seems successfully to have defied the historically entrenched, privately educated, elevated social class ethos of British motor racing and its hyper-masculine gender order. Unlike Moss, whose name, in Hilton's apt phrase, 'became deeply embedded in the national sub-conscious as meaning speed and style with it'[153] Mansell made his way, unashamedly, as a white-bread, ketchup-sloshing everyman, with no glamour to go with his driving expertise. This may not have been forgiven by the copy-hungry motor racing press, who pined for another Moss, another Hunt. And the road is likely to be rockier still for the Nigel Mansells of the future: there is no motor racing now without corporate sponsorship and, as noted, sponsorship seeks celebrity. As the eternally suave Stirling Moss said in one of his last interviews 'Lewis Hamilton races and then straight afterwards he has to go and talk to Vodafone and their guests. When I finished my races, I used to go and chat up the ladies!'[154] Mansell had neither the wit nor the inclination to chat up corporate guests or exotic female pit dwellers, but he communed happily enough with the people, sometimes buying 250 tickets for friends and fans at Silverstone.[155] In his thoughtful autobiography Damon Hill, a Formula 1 world champion and the son of one, suggested that the problem with the 'fame philosophy' was that it presumed a 'normal state of insignificance'; as the singer George Michael once said, famous people aren't famous because they have something that ordinary people lack; it is because they lack something that ordinary people have.[156] While Moss, Graham Hill, Jackie Stewart, James Hunt and many of Mansell's contemporaries might well have rejected such a thought, Mansell himself, his racing expertise notwithstanding, seems to have been its embodiment.

Acknowledgement Thanks to David Andrews and Damion Sturm for helpful comments on the initial version of this chapter and to Kate Linney for kindly lending me her late father's motor racing books.

Notes

1. https://yougov.co.uk/ratings/sport/popularity/all-time-sports-personalities/all. Access 9th February 2021
2. https://www.bbc.co.uk/news/av/entertainment-arts-11706345. Broadcast 7th November 2010; access 2nd April 2021.
3. https://porterpress.co.uk/products/who-do-you-think-you-are-stirling-moss-t-shirt. Access 2nd April 2021.
4. Peter King *The Motor Men* London: Quiller Press 1989 p. 7.
5. https://www.gracesguide.co.uk/1896_Locomotives_on_Highways_Act. Access 18th March 2021.
6. Kyler Patterson 'The Fastest Car of Every Decade Since Cars Were Invented' https://drivetribe.com/p/the-fastest-car-of-every-decade-Ct4c_PlxTqWOQ1OCmlPImg?iid=ORSXpnifRgihRYLWhHZl5Q. Access 18th March 2021.
7. https://www.gracesguide.co.uk/Hugh_Fortescue_Locke_King. Access 24th February 2021.
8. https://www.brooklandsmuseum.com/explore/our-history/birth-brooklands. Access 18th March 2021.
9. Jim Donnelly 'Selwyn F. Edge' https://www.hemmings.com/stories/article/selwyn-f-edge. Posted January 2012; access 24th February 2021.
10. See Chris Rojek *Celebrity* London: Reaktion Books 2001.
11. See, for example, Nick Scott 'A History of Gentleman Racers' https://therake.com/stories/history-of-gentleman-racers/. Access 19th March 2021.
12. https://nationalmotormuseum.org.uk/sir-henry-segrave-the-loss-of-a-hero/. Access 19th March 2021; https://www.britannica.com/biography/Sir-Henry-ONeal-de-Hane-Segrave. Access 19th March 2021; https://www.motorsportmagazine.com/archive/article/february-1941/2/lord-wakefield. Access 2nd February 2021.
13. https://www.bbc.co.uk/news/uk-england-merseyside-35758176. Access 1st February 2021.
14. http://www.parry-thomas.co.uk/. Access 24th February 2021.
15. https://people.elmbridgehundred.org.uk/biographies/john-cobb/. Access 1st February 2021.
16. https://www.gracesguide.co.uk/Malcolm_Campbell. Access 2nd February 2021.

17. https://www.0024watchworld.com/the-first-rolex-oyster-perpetual/. Access 12th February 2021.
18. See Richard Williams 'Return of Bluebird K7 brings memories of golden era speeding back' *The Guardian* 13th August 2018 https://www.theguardian.com/sport/2018/aug/13/donald-campbell-jg-parry-thomas-john-cobb-malcolm-campbell-adventurers. Access 19th March 2012; see also Julie V. Gottlieb 'British Union of Fascists' https://www.oxforddnb.com/view/10.1093/ref:odnb/9780198614128.001.0001/odnb-9780198614128-e-96364;jsessionid=614FE0BB928485A211CC5DBC8514DCA1?backToResults=%2Fsearch%2Frefine%2F%3FdocStart%3D1%26themesTabShow%3Dtrue. Access 2nd February 2021.
19. The magazine had actually been founded a year earlier as *Motorcycling and Motoring*.
20. Clips of all these are easily searched on the Internet.
21. https://www.gracesguide.co.uk/Walter_Owen_Bentley. Access 20th March 2021.
22. https://www.sahistory.org.za/people/barney-barnato. Access 21st March 2021.
23. https://www.bbc.co.uk/news/uk-england-nottinghamshire-23574665. Access 1st February 2021.
24. Bill Boddy 'Dr J.D. Benjafield—Bacteriologist and Bentley Boy' *MotorSport* August 1998 https://www.motorsportmagazine.com/archive/article/august-1998/76/dr-jd-benjafield-bacteriologist-and-bentley-boy. Access 21st March 2021.
25. https://spink.com/lot/20001000650. Access 22nd March 2021.
26. See https://www.bentleymotors.com/en/world-of-bentley/the-bentley-story/history-and-heritage/historic-people/original-bentley-boys.html. Access 22nd March 2021.
27. Sir Henry 'Tim' Birkin *Full Throttle* Edinburgh: T.N. Foulis 1932.
28. https://www.oxforddnb.com/view/10.1093/ref:odnb/9780198614128.001.0001/odnb-Clement9780198614128-e-101179;jsessionid=A7BA55E0A543FDC02861FF4071B4F162?backToResults=&docPos=45. Access 26th February 2021.
29. Tony Collins has referred to the 'sentimental cant of amateurism' and I have borrowed and adapted this apt phrase; see Tony Collins *Sport in Capitalist Society: A Short History* Abingdon: Routledge 2013 p. 64.

30. Nick Foulkes 'The Leader of the Pack: Woolf Barnato' *The Rake* website https://therake.com/stories/icons/the-leader-of-the-pack-woolf-barnato/. Posted June 2016; access 22nd March 2021.
31. John Stevenson *British Society 1914–45* Harmondsworth: Penguin 1984 p. 27.

    Posted 11 December 2020; access 23rd March 2021. Dorothy Levitt *The Woman and the Car: A Chatty Little Handbook for All Women Who Motor Or Who Want to Motor* London: John Lane 1909.
32. Foulkes 'The Leader…' See also Nick Foulkes *The Bentley Era: The Fast and Furious Story of the Fabulous Bentley Boys* London: Quadrille 2006.
33. Rachel Harris-Gardiner 'Dorothy Levitt: A Pioneer for Female Motorists' https://eastendwomensmuseum.org/blog/2020/12/9/dorothy-levitt-a-pioneer-of-motoring.
34. Harris-Gardiner 'Dorothy Levitt…'
35. https://www.gracesguide.co.uk/Mildred_Bruce. Access 23rd March 2021. See also Nancy R. Wilson *Queen of Speed: The Racy Life of Mary Petre Bruce* Bradford on Avon: ELSP 2012: review by Tom Clarke https://speedreaders.info/9623-queen-speed-racy-life-mary-petre-bruce/. Access 23rd March 2021.
36. David Venables 'Obituary: Margaret Jennings' *The Independent* 23rd October 2011 https://www.independent.co.uk/arts-entertainment/obituary-margaret-jennings-1183007.html. Access 24th March 2021.
37. See Roger Farmer *Betty Haig: A Life Behind the Wheel* London: Independent Publishing Network 2018; see also Peter Baker review of Farmer, 2018: https://retro-speed.co.uk/showbooks.asp?art=26543. Access 24th March 2021.
38. See Bill Boddy 'Gwenda Hawkes' *MotorSport* August 1995 https://www.motorsportmagazine.com/archive/article/august-1995/79/gwenda-hawkes. Access 24th March 2021; see also https://www.gracesguide.co.uk/Gwenda_Stewart. Access 24th March 2021.
39. http://speedqueens.blogspot.com/2015/09/jill-scott-thomas.html. Access 23rd March 2021.
40. Quotations taken from Imogen Lyons 'Violette Cordery: 'The Queen of Motoring' http://intriguing-people.com/the-queen-of-motoring/Posted 15th July 2020; access 23rd March 2021; see also Florence Walker 'Legendary Ladies Of Motorsport: Violette Cordery' https://petrolicious.com/articles/legendary-ladies-of-motorsport-violette-cordery. Posted 24th January 2017; access 23rd March 2021.

41. Francesca Wingham 'Brooklands Women: Elsie 'Bill' Wisdom' https://www.brooklandsmuseum.com/explore/museum-from-home/brooklands-women-elsie-bill-wisdom. Posted April 2017; access 23rd March 2021.
42. ibid.
43. Bill Boddy 'Earl Howe: The grand old man of motor racing' *MotorSport* June 1998. https://www.motorsportmagazine.com/archive/article/june-1998/80/earl-howe. Access 2nd February 2021.
44. Archived obituary of Kaye Don in *Daily Telegraph* 1st September 1981 https://www.geni.com/people/Kaye-Don/6000000017231122948. Access 2nd February 2021.
45. Bill Boddy 'Kaye Don's sad mistake' *MotorSport* March 2000. https://www.motorsportmagazine.com/archive/article/march-2000/92/kaye-dons-sad-mistake. Access 26th March 2021.
46. Juliet Gardiner *The Thirties: An Intimate History* London: HarperPress 2010 p. 684.
47. Gardiner *The Thirties…* pp. 680–3.
48. See, for example, Boddy 'Earl Howe…'.
49. Gardiner *The Thirties…* p. 679.
50. Gardiner *The Thirties…* p. 244.
51. Gardiner The Thirties… p. 244
52. Bristol Motor Club was founded in 1911: https://www.bristolmc.org.uk/. Access 26th March 2021.
53. Stevenson *British Society…* p. 431.
54. https://www.mike-hawthorn.org.uk/bio.php. Access 26th March 2021.
55. 'Grand Prix dream comes true for circuit's saviour and thousands of region's race fans' https://web.archive.org/web/20090521161108/http://www.thisisderbyshire.co.uk/news/Grand-Prix-dream-comes-true-circuit-s-saviour-thousands-region-s-race-fans/article-207177-detail/article.html. Posted 5th July 2008; access 26th March 2021.
56. 'Richard Ormonde Shuttleworth 16th July 1909–2nd August 1940'. https://www.shuttleworth.org/richardshuttleworth/. Access 26th March 2021.
57. Richard Williams 'Dick Seaman: England's tainted hero' *MotorSport* April 2020 https://www.motorsportmagazine.com/archive/article/april-2020/112/englands-tainted-hero. Access 26th March 2021.
58. Eberhard Reuss *Hitler's Motor Racing Battles: The Silver Arrpows Under the Swastika* Yeovil: Haynes Publishing 2008 p. 66.

59. Jonathan Glancey 'The master race' *Observer Sport Monthly* 1st September 2002 https://www.theguardian.com/observer/osm/story/0,6903,782811,00.html. Access 26th March 2021; see also Richard Williams *A Race with Love and Death: The Story of Richard Seaman* London: Simon & Schuster 2020.

    David McDonald 'Dunlop Mac' and Adrian Ball *Fifty Years with the Speed Kings* London: Stanley Paul 1961 p. 50.
60. Susan Watkins *Bernie: The Biography of Bernie Ecclestone* Yeovil: Haynes Publishing 2011 p. 41.
61. Stirling Moss and Ken W. Purdy *All But My Life* London: Pan Books 1965 p. 22.

    Mike Lawrence 'A Body is desirable - 500 cc F3' *MotorSport* May 1986. https://www.motorsportmagazine.com/archive/article/may-1986/42/class-1-racing-cars. Access 25th March 2021.

    Moss Purdy *All But …* p. 22.

    Mike Lawrence 'A Body is desirable - 500 cc F3' *MotorSport* May 1986. https://www.motorsportmagazine.com/archive/article/may-1986/42/class-1-racing-cars. Access 25th March 2021.
62. Moss and Purdy *All But…* p. 22.
63. Mike Lawrence 'A Body is desirable - 500 cc F3' *MotorSport* May 1986. https://www.motorsportmagazine.com/archive/article/may-1986/42/class-1-racing-cars. Access 25th March 2021.
64. *Motor Sport* May 1947 p. 119.
65. Watkins *Bernie…* p. 42.
66. See Alan Henry 'Roy Salvadori obituary: Charismatic racing driver who found success at Le Mans' https://www.theguardian.com/sport/2012/jun/06/roy-salvadori. Posted 6th June 2012; access 31st January 2021; Paul Fearnley 'A tribute to Le Mans winner Roy Salvadori' *MotorSport* https://www.motorsportmagazine.com/articles/single-seaters/f1/tribute-le-mans-winner-roy-salvadori. Posted 7th June 2012; access 27th March 2021.
67. The son of Italian immigrants, Salvadori (1922–2012) drove for Ferrari and a variety of British works teams and won Le Mans in 1959. His wife Susan was the daughter of racing drivers Violette Cordery and John Hindmarsh.
68. https://motorsportbroadcasting.com/history/. Access 27th March 2021.

69. Richard Williams 'Sir Stirling Moss obituary' *The Guardian* 12th April 2020 https://www.theguardian.com/sport/2020/apr/12/sir-stirling-moss-obituary. Access 15th February 2021.
70. Moss interviewed by Darren Turner https://magazine.astonmartin.com/people/knights-tale-remembering-racing-legend-sir-stirling-moss. Access 15th February 2021.
71. Paul Fearnley 'The ultimate gentleman racer? Rob Walker and Motor Sport' https://www.goodwood.com/grr/race/historic/2018/8/rob-walker-history/. Access 8th February 2021; See also http://www.grandprixhistory.org/walker_bio.htm. Access 29th January 2021
72. Michael Cannel *The Limit: Life and Death in Formula One's Most Dangerous Era* London: Atlantic Books 2011 p .222
73. Richard Williams 'Sir Stirling…'
74. Press Association 'Sir Stirling Moss: The greatest all-rounder in motor racing's most dangerous era' https://www.cravenherald.co.uk/sport/national/18375185.sir-stirling-moss-greatest-all-rounder-motor-racings-dangerous-era/. Posted 12th April 2020; access 27th.
75. Press Association' 'Sir Stirling Moss…'
76. Doug Nye 'Introduction in Stirling Moss, with Doug Nye *Stirling Moss: My Cars, My Career* London: Guild Publishing 1988 p. 11.
77. Moss and Nye p. 15.
78. Bruce Jones *Formula One: The Illustrated History* London: Carlton Books 2015 p. 15.
79. Mike Hawthorn *Challenge Me the Race* London: Motoraces Book Club/ William Kimber 1964 p. 104.
80. Doug Nye 'Doug Nye—inside the world of the incredible Peter Collins' https://www.goodwood.com/grr/columnists/doug-nye/2016/11/doug-nye-peter-collins/. Posted 9th November 2016; access 28th March 2016.
81. Gordon Cruickshank 'Ken Gregory and Stirling Moss: a winning partnership' *Motor Sport* October 2009 https://www.motorsportmagazine.com/archive/article/october-2009/68/moss-80-gregorys-boy. Access 22nd February 2021.
82. Cruickshank 'Ken Gregory…'.
83. Robert Edwards *Stirling Moss: The Authorised Biography* London Weidenfeld and Nicolson 2014 p. 204.
84. Richard Williams 'Sir Stirling…'.

85. See Julie Stephens *Anti-Disciplinary Protest: Sixties Radicalism and Postmodernism* Cambridge, at the University Press 1998 p. 10.
86. Doug Nye 'Remembering Jimmy Clark—50 years since he passed' https://www.goodwood.com/grr/columnists/doug-nye/2018/4/doug-nye-remembering-jimmy-clark-50-years-since-he-passed/ Posted 6th April 2018; access 30th March 2021.
87. Damon Hill, with Maurice Hamilton *Watching the Wheels: My Autobiography* London: Pan Books 2017.
88. Damon Hill '*Watching*... p. 41.
89. Bette Hill, with Neil Ewart *The Other Side of the Hill: Life with Graham* London: Hutchinson/Stanley Paul 1978.
90. See Graham Hill, with Neil Ewart *Graham* London: Arrow Books 1977 pp. 11–21.
91. Damon Hill *Watching*... p. 19. Sir Jackie Stewart, who followed Hill into the pantheon of British champion drivers, also became close to the British royal family: the Queen attended his 80th birthday party in June 2019; see 'Scots racing legend Sir Jackie Stewart celebrates 80th birthday with the Queen' https://www.scotsman.com/sport/other-sport/scots-racing-legend-sir-jackie-stewart-celebrates-80th-birthday-queen-1415460. Posted 13th June 2019; access 15th October 2021.
92. Laura Thompson *A Different Class of Murder: The Story of Lord Lucan* London: Head of Zeus 2018 p. 105.
93. Bette Hill *The Other*... pp. 109 and 140.
94. Graham Hill *Graham* p. 94.
95. Damon Hill *Watching*... pp. 5 and 9.
96. Andrew Spicer 'Terry-Thomas (1911–1990') http://www.screenonline.org.uk/people/id/461962/ Access 29th March 2021.
97. Moss and Purdy *All But*... p. 59.
98. Damon Hill *Watching*... p. 52.
99. Bette Hill *The Other*... p. 46.
100. Damon Hill *Watching*... p. 30.
101. Bette Hill *The Other*... p. 35; Damon Hill *Watching*...p. 28.
102. Richard Bailey 'Remembering Mike Beuttler' https://web.archive.org/web/20150725065753/http://richardsf1.com/2011/12/29/remembering-mike-beuttler/ Access 29th March 2021.
103. http://www.asag.sk/bio/williamson.htm. Access 11th February 2021.
104. See Adam Cooper *Piers Courage: The Last of the Gentleman Racers* Somerset: Haynes Manuals 2003.

105. Tom Rubython *Shunt: The Story of James Hunt* Northamptonshire: The Myrtle Press 2013 pp. 44–5, 55–6.
106. See, for example, Rod McPhee 'Formula 1 ace James Hunt's son reveals his dad once had marathon sex session with 35 air stewardesses' https://www.mirror.co.uk/sport/formula-1/formula-1-ace-james-hunts-9133348Posted 26th October 2026; access 30th March 2021.
107. Gerald Donaldson *James Hunt: The Autobiography* London: Virgin Books 2003 pp. 91–3.
108. Rubython p. 234.
109. Rubython p. 150.
110. Bette Hill p. 104.
111. Rubython p. 237.
112. Rubython p. 377. See also https://www.celebritynetworth.com/richest-athletes/race-car-drivers/jackie-stewart-net-worth/. Access 15th October 2021; https://www.therichest.com/celebnetworth/athletes/motor-racing/sir-jackie-stewart-net-worth/. Access 15th October 2021.
113. Rubython p. 377. Stewart also had his own F1 racing team, which he sold to Red Bull for £50 million in 1997—see https://www.therichest.com/celebnetworth/athletes/motor-racing/sir-jackie-stewart-net-worth/ Access 15th October 2021.
114. Rubython p. 297.
115. Rubython pp. 63, 128, 240, 342.
116. Rubython p. 236.
117. Rubython pp. 367–8, 419.
118. Rubython p. 66.
119. See Kyle W. Kusz 'Andre Agassi and Generation X' in David L. Andrews and Steven J. Jackson (eds.) *Sport Stars: The Cultural Politics of Sporting Celebrity'* London: Routledge 2001 pp. 51–69.
120. Chapter 29 pp. 379–95.
121. Rubython p. 369.
122. Stirling Moss 'Prologue: A Very Complete Sort of Person' in Rubython p. xxi.
123. Donaldson *James Hunt…* p. 13; Rubython pp. 514–23.
124. Murray Walker *Unless I'm Very Much Mistaken: My Biography* London: CollinsWillow 2002 p. 210.
125. Rubython pp. 561–5.
126. Rubython p. 371.
127. Chris Rojek *Celebrity* p. 174.

128. Mansell is president of UK Youth, a charity in support of which he financed, and rode in, a professional cycling team between 2011 and 2013.
129. Nigel Mansell *Staying on Track: The Autobiography* London: Simon & Schuster 2015 p. 221.
130. Mansell *Staying...* p. v.
131. Mansell *Staying...* pp. 1–15; Christopher Hilton *Nigel Mansell: World Champion* London: Corgi Books 1993 p. 27.
132. Hilton *Nigel...* p. 27.
133. Alan Henry *Nigel Mansell: World Champion* Richmond: Hazleton Publishing 1992 pp. 12–13.
134. Hilton *Nigel...* p. 30.
135. Mansell *Staying...* p. 26.
136. See Mansell *Staying...* pp. 16–19, 57, 61 and 97.
137. Mansell *Staying...* pp. 24–5.
138. Hilton *Nigel...* pp. 148–9.
139. Hilton *Nigel...* p. 52.
140. Hilton *Nigel...* p. 159.
141. Hilton *Nigel...* pp. 52 and 27.
142. See Keith Collantine 'I should have won '86, he should have won '87" – Piquet and Mansell on their rivalry' https://www.racefans.net/2013/01/26/nigel-mansell-nelson-piquet-f1-rivalry/Posted 26th January 2013; access 1st April 2021.
143. Mansell *Staying...* pp. 142–3.
144. Henry *Nigel...* pp. 4 and 10.
145. Hilton *Nigel...* pp. 33, 102 and 155.
146. Hilton *Nigel...* pp. 190–1.
147. Mark Scott 'The good, the bad and the ugly: Nigel Mansell' https://www.planetf1.com/features/the-good-the-bad-and-the-ugly-nigel-mansell/. Posted 30th April 2020; access 1st April 2021.
148. Hilton *Nigel...* p.160.
149. Hilton *Nigel...* p. 201.
150. Hilton *Nigel...* p. 195.
151. Chris Power 'You've had it easy! F1 legend Nigel Mansell slams 'manufactured' Lewis Hamilton' https://www.dailymail.co.uk/sport/formulaone/article-1282561/Youve-easy-F1-legend-Nigel-Mansell-slams-manufactured-Lewis-Hamilton.html?ito=feeds-newsxml. Posted 29th May 2010; access 22nd February 2021

152. Mansell *Staying…* p. 343.
153. Hilton *Nigel…* p. 97.
154. Interview with Darren Turner.
155. Mansell *Staying…* p. 142.
156. Damon Hill *Watching…* p. xxi.

The 'Star in the Car': Formula One Stardom, Driver Agency and Celebrity Culture

Damion Sturm

Introduction

> The Formula One driver has a dual status: he is both an automatic terminal of the most refined technical machinery, a technical operator, and he is the symbolic operator of crowd passions and the risk of death. (Baudrillard, 2002, p. 169)

As Baudrillard (2002) intimates, much of the focus in Formula One is crystalised around the drivers' mastery of their hi-tech machines and their subsequent achievements. Nevertheless, the duality evoked by Baudrillard (2002) operates in a circumscribed fashion, as the agential capacity of the driver is largely *determined by* the machinery of Formula One. In this regard, Formula One confronts traditional notions of sport stardom as the 'car is the star' and is fundamental to any understanding of driver

D. Sturm (✉)
School of Management, Massey University, Albany, New Zealand
e-mail: D.Sturm@massey.ac.nz

D. Sturm et al. (eds.), *The History and Politics of Motor Racing*, Global Culture and Sport Series, https://doi.org/10.1007/978-3-031-22825-4_20

performances and achievements. As such, and to re-project the 'star in the car', Formula One drivers need to become machine-like to be seamlessly integrated with and within the car to maximise their opportunities for success.

Further confronting Formula One sport stardom are the corporate apparatuses that also envelope the sport and impinge on driver agency. Formula One has become increasingly commercialised, commodified and corporatised across the past 25 years due to the acceleration of transnational companies involved in the sport—as either team owners, manufacturers, suppliers or sponsors. In varying ways, these corporations impact on the drivers who need to navigate expectations and obligations surrounding their appearance, marketing and mediated personalities. In concert, this chapter explores the particular conditions for sport stardom in Formula One, asserting that the traditional sport star criteria of meritocracy, authenticity and sporting performances need to be expressed through and in spite of the literal machinery and corporate apparatuses of Formula One.

It should also be noted that, in many respects, this chapter is intended to offer a continuation to Wagg's chapter on early forms of celebrity in Formula One (see chapter "Can the Formula One Driver Speak? Lewis Hamilton, Race and the Resurrection of the Black Athlete"). As such, this chapter takes as its starting point Formula One in 1995, with the sport attempting to recover from the death of Ayrton Senna in 1994. With Senna's death, Formula One instantly lost its star driver and responded by ushering in a greater emphasis on safety, reducing the role of the driver in the car through technology and by becoming ever more corporate in orientation. The chapter probes theories and nuances of Formula One sport stardom before providing individual case studies that examine Michael Schumacher as the robotic corporate man-machine, Kimi Raikkonen's minimalistic hyperconformity and Jacques Villeneuve's brash maverick stardom as three distinct strategies for contemporary Formula One stardom. Each offers a different response to the encroaching deterministic machinery and corporate apparatuses inherent to Formula One, as well as the simulated environments that the drivers navigate to retain a semblance of the 'star in the car'.

Introducing Sport Stardom

Unlike the often-fictional character or creation portrayed and performed within most other mass entertainment realms, there is an alleged sense of realism and an "unrivalled quality of authenticity" (Smart, 2005, p. 194) that surrounds the sport star. In many respects, with star athletes operating as "*real* individuals participating in unpredictable contests" (Andrews & Jackson, 2001, p. 8), sport stardom can also be viewed as meritocratic; earned and measured primarily through sporting achievement, excellence, elite competitions and physical capital (Tulle, 2016; Whannel, 2002). Smart (2005) observes, "it is through the exceptional quality of their sport performances, and media coverage of the same, that individual athletes and players generally become widely known and acquire star status" (p. 194).

Of course, like all sporting codes, Formula One has its own subtleties and nuances that support but also disrupt these generic notions of sport stardom. As such, Formula One stardom is inextricably linked to the performance of the car over the individual driver on the racetrack. Meritocracy is also a contestable assertion given that wealth, whiteness and masculinity have historically underpinned the majority drivers on the grid. Additionally, off track, the drivers need to perform as hyperreal simulations—enacting a mediatised and corporatised version of stardom that appeals to and appeases sponsors. Thus, rather than being idealised 'authentic individuals', drivers are valued for performing narrowly prescribed corporate roles, while meritocracy is further undermined by sponsors influencing the allocation of some race seats.

Sport Stardom and 'On-Field' Performances

Elements of on-field sporting performances remain intrinsic to sport stardom. While not infallible, sport offers a robust site for identifying and articulating the markers upon which sport stardom can be earned and achieved. With performances often rigorously measured and assessed, most sports deploy 'objective' systems of measurement for assessing and rewarding sporting performance (Tulle, 2016; Woodward, 2013). As such and given the ubiquity of sports coverage, both the experts and the public can judge the athletic performance (e.g., time measurements in running, cycling, swimming, motorsport), the level of performance in relation to the sport's internal hierarchical systems (the difference between grades, divisions, and leagues within various sporting codes), and the significance of the performance and/or achievement in relation to the status of various competitions globally (a world championship compared to a national or regional title). Nevertheless, while 'traditional' sports combine achievement, excellence, elite competitions and physical capital to codify sport stardom as authentic and meritocratic (Andrews & Jackson, 2001; Smart, 2005; Tulle, 2016; Whannel, 2002), the 'on-field' performance' is less clear-cut in relation to Formula One stardom.

Performing Formula One Sport Stardom on the Racetrack: Is the Car the Star?

Represented as the pinnacle of motor-racing, there is an assumption that the drivers are also the best in the world. Of course, many of the drivers advance from and usually win junior categories to get into Formula One; for example, various Karting titles (e.g., Fernando Alonso, Max Verstappen), Formula BMW (e.g., Nico Rosberg), British Formula Three (e.g., Rubens Barrichello), Formula 3000 (e.g., Nick Heidfeld), GP3 and Formula 2 (e.g., Charles Leclerc, George Russell) or the rival American IndyCar series (e.g., Jacques Villeneuve, Juan Pablo Montoya). For others, there may be financial avenues to enter Formula One or corporate impositions that affect performance; points we will return to in due course.

Race, gender and class have also been historical barriers, notably with Lewis Hamilton the first black driver to compete in 2007. Aside from twenty-one Japanese drivers, plus Narain Karthikeyan and Karun Chandhok from India, Malaysian Alex Yoong, Alex Albon of Thai descent and Chinese driver Guanyu Zhou (for 2022), historically Formula One drivers have been notable for their 'whiteness' (Spracklen, 2013). Unequivocally, all contemporary Formula One drivers are men, with only five women having ever competed in Formula One; the last in 1992, interspersed with minor female test driver roles (Sturm, 2021).

Additionally, as Wagg's previous chapter highlighted, motor-racing has been grounded in upper-class and elite cultures (see chapter "Can the Formula One Driver Speak? Lewis Hamilton, Race and the Resurrection of the Black Athlete"). Arguably, these 'moneyed' links are not as obvious as they once were, although most drivers tend to come from either affluent and privileged backgrounds (e.g., Nico Rosberg and Jacques Villeneuve being raised in Monaco) or are able to access forms of funding and/or sponsorship to engage in motorsport regularly from a young age (Turner, 2004). Thus, despite growing up with financial hardship, Lewis Hamilton and Michael Schumacher (whose family owned a go-kart track nevertheless), were financially supported from a young age by McLaren and Mercedes, respectively, that allowed them to go racing, ironically in an highly privileged way compared to their peers, in terms of the resources that were made available to them. Hence, race, gender and class (e.g., predominantly affluent or well-resourced white males) have shaped a narrow version of stardom that challenges notions of meritocracy. In addition, technological impositions and commercial imperatives also significantly impact on Formula One sport stardom.

As a technologically dependent sport, the drivers' performance is inextricably tied to the performative capabilities of the cars that they drive. Hilton (2003) suggests that the Formula One driver is "unusual among sports people because for him technology plays such a decisive role. Good drivers do not win in bad cars" (p. 25). Baudrillard (2002) reaches similar conclusions, noting that the "car and driver are merely a living projectile" (p. 167), while observing that "in McLuhan's sense: the car becomes a tactile, tactical extension of the human body" (p. 168). In this vein, technology and the machine determine, to a large extent, the performance of drivers based on the quality of the car.

While ripe for explorations of the implosion of flesh and technology within and through the Formula One car, the body not only melds with the machine, but literally 'disappears' by being cocooned within the cockpit. Indeed, embodiment operates in a contradictory manner in Formula One; providing an 'absent' sporting body which foregrounds technology while viewers rely on inanimate objects (e.g., cars, corporate logos and helmets) as identificatory mechanisms to comprehend the sport and to follow the star drivers. Kennedy (2000) likens the Formula One driver to a knight going into battle, asserting that the "symbolic armour and vehicle for the warrior hero is provided by the helmet, protective clothing and racing car, which so engulfs the driver as to completely obscure him" (p. 65). With the drivers cocooned in their cars and wearing racing garb that conceals their face and body, the car-as-apparatus becomes a primary means for viewer identification that links drivers to the appropriate decals, colour schemes and corporate branding of their cars and helmet designs. An inevitable, indivisible and 'anonymous' man and machine linkage is seemingly also forged.

Nevertheless, this diverges from 'cyborg theory' which argues for a dehumanising condition through the breaching of technology and nature, the increasing symbiosis of humans with machines and a literal reading of the human body as a machine (Haraway, 1991, 1994). Despite the often 'robotic' characteristics of many contemporary drivers (see later discussion of Michael Schumacher), Formula One's man-machine interrelationship does not operate in the same manner as Haraway's (1994) 'machine-organism hybrid' theorised through the cyborg. Rather, the driver remains recognisable as a human agent, albeit with limited degrees of agency, relinquishing much of his performance (and bodily) capabilities to the machine.

Intriguingly, the ever-evolving technological apparatuses are curtailing the driver's role within the machinery, with the need for 'spectacular' driving displays or demonstrable mastery over the machine blunted. Somewhat ironically, despite masculine bravado and risk-taking being entrenched as endemic to Formula One due to wheel-to-wheel racing at speeds in excess of 200mph, alongside the alleged spectre of death that looms over the sport (Baudrillard, 2002), Formula One has become relatively sanitised due to a range of safety features trackside and on the cars. Additionally, Sturm (2021) observes that since 2014, the 'hybrid' technology era "requires drivers to manage, conserve and preserve their cars in a manner that seemingly is at odds with 'racing'" (p. 120). On a primary level, it is fair to assert that driver performance is so intertwined with Formula One's technological apparatuses that drivers acquiesce to the machine, rather than enacting individuated displays.

In the pursuit of Formula One victory, there is an expectation of the seamless integration of the driver (himself also prepared like a machine) within the machine. Formula One teams also employ 'objective' apparatuses to assess driver performances, with banks of team computers providing visual systems of measurement, such as sector and lap times, various simulations and simulators, as well as driver telemetry, which traces exactly *how* the driver *drives* (and should drive) the machine by recording and mapping the application of throttle, brakes, corner entry and exit speeds, etcetera (Sturm, 2014). Often highly regarded, race-winning and indeed former world champions can struggle to adapt to their new teams' cars and systems, with various drivers, including Jacques Villeneuve (2005), Rubens Barrichello (2006), Michael Schumacher (2010) and most recently Daniel Riccardo, Sebastian Vettel and Fernando Alonso (2021) being forced to adapt their own styles to suit the machine.

Teams also measure and map the drivers' bodies and levels of fitness via various tests and biometrics, with some drivers noted for their physical regimes and training exploits, including Michael Schumacher as the 'benchmark' from the 1990s, and later Jenson Button and Mark Webber for participating in competitive endurance events. Collectively, through these systems of measurement a driver's performance (and fitness) is compared to his team-mate first and foremost, as there is an assumption that both drivers are using the same machinery and operating under the same conditions. Hence, the team-mate comparison is fundamental to Formula One stardom as strong performances (e.g., points, podiums, race wins or championships in ascending order) elevate a driver's perceived monetary value, his appeal to other teams and the possibility of a top drive. Simplistically, even if a driver cannot outdrive a poor car, he needs to showcase his ability to outdrive his team-mate. Conversely, reflective of Whannel's (1999, 2002) rise and fall narrative arc, poor performances quickly affect driver reputation, value and are potentially career-ending as drivers slide down the grid to the smaller teams or exit the sport.

Salaries, career earnings and contracts with established top teams are also determinants of Formula One stardom. Most Formula One drivers are well-paid athletes, earning base salaries ranging from US$1 to 10 million a season, while a few have earned closer to (or more than) US$20 million a season—such as Michael Schumacher, Jacques Villeneuve,

Fernando Alonso, Sebastian Vettel, Lewis Hamilton and Max Verstappen. It is assumed that the top drivers will command the highest salaries and be accorded opportunities with the top teams during their careers. Those that can maintain longevity with top teams may be permitted an opportunity to dominate the sport, as the multiple years and championships for Schumacher and Ferrari (1996–2006; 5), Vettel and Red Bull (2009–2014; 4), and Hamilton and Mercedes (2013–present; 6) attest to.

Formula One's star system culminates in the Drivers' Championship as the mark of the man (and implied master of the machine), while projecting and promoting the human dimension to this performance as a crystalised focal point for global audiences (Baudrillard, 2002). In this vein, despite being vitiated by Formula One's technological and machinic assemblages, the concealed and obscure driver furnishes a faint rendering of and appreciation for the 'star in the car'. Rather than an absent or anonymous figure, the agential driver operates as the focal point of attention, of aspiration and as worthy of recognition for his 'human' skills and performances that are, nevertheless, often understood via the car and a series of inanimate identificatory objects. Ranking and evaluating drivers according to championships, race victories, podiums, salaries, career earnings and contracts with established top teams affords useful parameters to potentially demonstrate the attributes of meritocracy and achievement for Formula One stardom, albeit with driver performance very much aligned to and constrained by the technological possibilities of the car. Moreover, the practices of sponsors demonstrate the way that commerce acts as another apparatus within Formula One, literally turning these men into corporate-driving-machines.

Sport Stardom and 'Off-Field' Performances

Outside of a noteworthy and sustained performance on the sport field (or the racetrack for Formula One drivers), an array of off-field performances and expectations also inform contemporary stardom. Hence, how stars can present and perform for and via the media helps to grow local/global audiences and endear sport celebrities to fans (Sturm & Kobayashi, 2022). Specifically, those that have an elevated media profile, presence and the ability to cultivate and perform a charismatic media personality imbued with allegedly admirable and alluring qualities around comportment, appearance and articulation, or at least devoid of banalities, blandness and cliches, are often preferred (Dyer, 1979; Weber, 1968; Whannel, 2002). Unfortunately, due to the corporate nature of the sport, Formula One drivers most often project monolithic media personalities that are bland, sterile and ostensibly operate as corporate shills. Arguably, minus the filters of the traditional mass media, it has only been via the increased use of digital and social media by recent drivers that more engaging insights, access and content has been produced, albeit in often self-promotional and self-branded ways (Andrews & Ritzer, 2018; Fresco, 2020; Sturm, 2019).

Additionally, the potential blurring of on-field stardom and off-field persona may refocus attention towards a range of other constructed components to sport stardom. Hence, an intrigue with celebrity lifestyles and private lives (Turner, 2014) segues to an interest in forms of salaciousness, transgressions and scandals (Wenner, 2013; Whannel, 1999). Sport stars also take on a cultural value and a local/global visibility dependent on the sports that 'matter' in different local and global contexts (Sandvoss, 2012). Sturm and Kobayashi (2022) point to the notable "elevation of select individuals as national 'stars', ambassadors or even evocations as heroic dependent on the scope and scale of achievements" (p. 121) as well as the "national significance of the sport" (p.121). Moreover, Andrews and Jackson (2001) suggest sport stars are often attributed with or as specific cultural identities, sensibilities or representations that tend to run along locally contingent understandings of nation, gender, race, class and so forth. This semiotic and discursive construction and circulation of sport stars in relation to cultural values and norms requires constant affirmation, contestation, negotiation and (re)articulation (Marshall, 2014; Turner, 2014).

By design Formula One is very 'European', with most teams based in Britain or other European localities (e.g., Ferrari and Alpha Tauri in Italy; Mercedes in Britain and Germany), as are the drivers—for example, from Britain, Finland, France, Germany, Italy, Netherlands and Spain. Other nation states have also been represented in recent years, such as Australia, Brazil, Canada, Japan, Mexico and Russia. While Formula One is not a 'national' sport in any specific locale, national sport star status is bestowed on the notable champions including, for example, Michael Schumacher and Sebastian Vettel in Germany, Mika Hakkinen and Kimi Raikkonen in Finland, Lewis Hamilton and Damon Hill in Britain, or the likes of Fernando Alonso in Spain, Jacques Villeneuve in Canada and Max Verstappen in the Netherlands. Status may also be imbued upon those flying the flag for nations not traditionally associated with the sport—for example, for Colombia and the achievements of Juan Pablo Montoya, as well as for drivers that were the first national representative in Formula One despite their relative lack of success, such as Alex Yoong in Malaysia or Narain Karthikeyan and India.

Finally, the marketability, commercial value and commodified performances of sport stars further hints at ascribed or manufactured components to sport stardom (Rojek, 2001; Turner, 2014). For example, Kellner (1996) conceives of a marketable difference shaped around perceived moral, social and cultural values that is often laced with inherent racial connotations. Moreover, while charismatic media performances and personalities can bolster the marketability of stars (Whannel, 2002), there is the innate expectation that sport stars will predominantly operate as compliant and malleable commodities for corporations (Sandvoss, 2012; Wenner, 2013). Manufacturing, projecting and aligning sport stars with select companies and products becomes salient for their global dissemination and potential consumption. This is arguably exacerbated in Formula One as these corporate impositions, commercial expectations and the perceived appeal and marketability of drivers can potentially influence which drivers secure contracts.

Performing Formula One Sport Stardom Off the Racetrack: Corporate Stardom

In relation to the pinnacle and elitist global status of Formula One, Baudrillard (2002) notes, "only in appearance is the circuit the site of the competition. The competition takes place elsewhere—on the world car market, in the drivers' popularity charts, in advertising and the star system" (p. 167). The commercial elements and fundamental role of transnational corporations especially percolate throughout the star system. Formula One increasingly moved to and relied on high-profile corporate sponsors and transnational manufacturers to run many of the teams during the 2000s, including Toyota, BMW and Honda, before each had subsequently withdrawn by 2009 due to the global recession. Additionally, two teams were run as essentially branded corporate entities; first for British American Tobacco (BAT)—as British American Racing (BAR) from 1999–2006—and second as Red Bull Racing since 2005, which also runs a junior Torro Rosso team (recently rebranded as Alpha Tauri). Formula One has continued to attract an array of transnational sponsors, initially heavily reliant on tobacco before shifting to fashion, finance, fragrances, airlines, technologies and alcohol which, collectively, have predominantly funded Formula One for the past twenty-five years (Sturm, 2014). Given the millions corporate sponsors pour into the sport, they often expect to buy some influence within the teams.

In relation to driver selection and expectations, transnational corporations and car manufacturers purchase a degree of influence through sponsorship (Turner, 2004), often favouring or financially supporting a particular driver, pending the team's final approval. Obviously high-profile drivers are preferred yet sponsors also consider other global marketing imperatives; for example, seeking drivers from two different nationalities (and key or untapped markets) to broaden their appeal. Intriguingly, despite the nationalistic team name, Force India (2008–2018) was 'European' in its outlook; being based in Britain, running predominantly European drivers and British technical staff, while comprising few Indian nationals. Some of the major teams also run driver academies, such as Red Bull, Ferrari and Mercedes, which often lock junior drivers into lengthy and restrictive contracts. These junior drivers tend to be strategically placed in developmental roles or unofficial 'second' teams in ways that are often more beneficial to the parent teams rather than the drivers, as Red Bull's recent treatment of Alex Albon and Pierre Gasly suggests (Foster, 2021a).

In addition, the practice of paying for a drive is not uncommon, with some drivers providing either cash or major sponsors to secure a drive with one of the lesser teams in Formula One. The presence of these drivers (commonly referred to as 'pay drivers') dispels the meritocracy myth that all Formula One drivers are the best in the world while demonstrating the corporatised focus of the sport by having sponsors intervening and/or imposing their will (or pay drivers) on the smaller teams. As Turner (2004) cautions, "Don't be fooled into thinking Formula One showcases the twenty best drivers in the world—it doesn't. It offers a stage to those lucky enough to carry the logos of ambitious multinational corporations" (p. 201).

Various 'pay' drivers have provided lavish sums to secure Formula One seats, with such transactions an annual occurrence. In 2006, Honda spent nearly $200 million to create a second team to keep their Japanese driver, Takuma Sato, on the grid (Fleming & Sturm, 2011), while reputedly the Venezuelan Government paid Williams £46 million annually to run Pastor Maldonado between 2011 and 2013 (Sturm, 2014). In 2021, drivers Nikita Mazepin and Lance Stroll received significant financial backing from their father's respective companies—including Canadian billionaire Lawrence Stroll buying the Racing Point team in 2020 (rebadged as Aston Martin in 2021), for whom his son Lance Stroll races.

'Corporate Puppets': The Hyperreal Formula One Star Simulacra

On a larger scale, Formula One itself becomes a site of simulation, of hyperreality and an implosive 'non-event' (Baudrillard, 1983, 1994). Indeed, Baudrillard's (2000) often critiqued assertion that *the Gulf War did not take place* can easily be reworked to a 'Grands Prix do not take place' analogy. Formula One offers an 'implosive' effect, with media coverage converging to reflect Formula One back onto itself through its own 'modelled, precessionary, semiotic production' seemingly devoid of an external reality. Hence television coverage (and a range of contemporary digital technologies) are the 'event' as, according to Baudrillard (2002), "the race takes place on a screen, the screen of speed" (p. 167). Moreover, each 'Grand Prix' is potentially already a non-event given the extensive precessionary modelling and sophisticated simulations that have taken place before teams arrive for a race weekend (Sturm, 2014). Therefore, Baudrillard's (1994) theory of the non-event affords an implosive assemblage of meaning and medium, reality and image, and so forth.

This has a flow-on effect for Formula One stardom. The drivers become a hyperreal projection of a collection of images that are constantly reproduced and recycled—the Formula One star simulacra. Hence driver agency or individuality is pre-coded within Formula One's corporate and technological apparatuses, with the hyperreal celebrity simulacra constantly reproduced via implosive and internal models for what constitutes Formula One stardom in an endless vortex of simulation (Baudrillard, 1983, 1994). These hyperreal driver images are not depthless or lacking in origin or reality but, rather, offer powerful and impenetrable layers of symbol-laden evocations engorged with meaning for global audiences (Baudrillard, 1988) constantly reproduced from a precessionary reality that is modelled upon and embedded within Formula One's systems. Moreover, in the hyperreal, Baudrillard (1990) notes that "the object is always the fetish, the false, the *feiticho*, the factitious, the lure" (p. 184, italics in original) which fascinates but always confounds the subject. In this vein, the Formula One star simulacra affords an alluring or seductive object for subjects—both for overt global commodification—as seen in fan accumulation, practices and displays—and a malleable 'corporate puppet' for the teams and transnational sponsors. By deploying strategies to captivate and corral Formula One subjects, all seductive 'power' resides with the Formula One star simulacra as a 'supreme' media object for, as Baudrillard (1990) asserts, "the object wants only to seduce ... the object always wins" (p. 124).

Applying a Baudrillardian interpretation of the Formula One star simulacra allows us to see that, by being entangled within these corporatised relationships and contractual obligations, the drivers are effectively puppets for transnational corporate appropriation and predominantly operate as bland, blank canvasses via their branded displays and manufactured personas (Fleming & Sturm, 2011). Hence, the Formula One star simulacra furnishes a ready-made or cookie-cutter template for stardom in relation to appearance, grooming and media representation. For example, from approximately 1995 to 2010, the majority of the drivers were generally indistinguishable with short-styled hair, being clean-shaven and resplendent in their team and sponsor intensive attire. Periodically, drivers displayed a degree of 'individuality' to contrast with the otherwise 'uniform' attire and appearances (e.g., Eddie Irvine's dyed blonde hair with Jaguar in 2000 and 2001, Jarno Trulli's long hair with Toyota 2005–2007, or drivers sporting facial hair, such as Barrichello, Button or Alonso). Intriguingly, circa 2010, the Formula One star simulacra seemingly placed a contractual obligation on contemporary drivers brandishing 'designer stubble', with coiffured stubble becoming vogue in Formula One. Hence, what might have been conceived as an 'individuated' display in the 1990s and 2000s became fashionable, marketable and seemingly expected of drivers for the past decade.

Overall, the corporate machinery of Formula One is heavily prescriptive and restrictive for drivers who, through their contractual relationships and obligations, are commodified, constrained and regulated by the corporations, teams and the governing body, the Fédération Internationale de l'Automobile (FIA). In this vein, contractually the drivers are obligated to wear the branded garb, attend to an array of media and/or public relations duties, and to be paraded before various teams' transnational sponsors due to associated expectations for publicity, marketing and appeasing sponsors (Fleming & Sturm, 2011). In this regard, Jacques Villeneuve's (1996–2006) lack of corporate grooming and forthright dissent across his career suggests forms of non-conformity and a repudiation of the Formula One star simulacra, points we will return to later in this chapter.

Commonplace to many contemporary sports, the uniformity of appearance can extend to the uniformity of press releases, with drivers often reluctant to speak openly or directly on topics, while often reproducing and recycling clichéd PR statements. For example, in 2006, Pat Symonds, executive director of engineering for the Renault team, was quoted in *F1 Racing* magazine as bemoaning that "press conferences can be as dull as ditch water—contrived questions, corporate answers, no real thought, no antagonism, no fighting, no one saying what they really mean, no bloody spark. Dreadful" (The future of F1, 2006, p. 94).

Such patterns have persisted in contemporary Formula One although arguably a 'softening' of male driver images and representations has emerged in recent years, such as Lewis Hamilton's ever-changing fashion and style on social media, or Daniel Riccardo's often jocular and self-deprecating interviews (Sturm, 2021). Additionally, the current generation of drivers are more active in cultivating their own profiles and followings on social media to complement traditional media representations. Hence, drivers such as Daniel Riccardo and Lando Norris tend to be less formal or formulaic by responding in more engaging, forthright and comical ways—albeit, with Norris admitting that his PR handlers were responsible for all of his social media accounts and content in 2021 (Scott, 2021). Additionally, forms of activism are also presented by some drivers, such as Lewis Hamilton and Sebastian Vettel (Galily, 2019; see also chapter "On Recovering the Black Geographies of Motorsports: The Counter-mobility Work of NASCAR's Wendell Scott") which can be conceived as both progressive and hypocritical in relation to equality, the environment and human rights given Formula One's problematic operationalisation in these realms (Miller, 2017; Sturm, 2023).

Finally, the Formula One star simulacra affords an assemblage of multiple overlapping structures: the governing body (the FIA); the team that employs the driver; the press and media outlets; the driver's manager and PR agents; the specific corporate sponsors and their requests, and so forth are both woven into the simulacra and operate as impositions to be acquiesced, negotiated and navigated by the driver. For the past 25 years, the Formula One star simulacra has reproduced the driver as a bland corporate-driving-machine susceptible to the whims of Formula One's corporate apparatuses; a human driver who also needs to become robotic in design as a performative and commercial cog within the machine.

Nevertheless, Baudrillard (2002) also reminds us that "the impact of Formula One lies, then, in the exceptional and mythic character of the event of the race and the figure of the driver, and not in the technical or commercial spin-offs" (p. 169). Despite these commercial trappings and machinic emphases, bearing witness to the integration and synthesis between Formula One driver and car retains its appeal to fans. Hence, there is a quest to recognise the primacy of the 'star in the car' which is now probed through three prominent case studies.

The Robotic Winning Machine: Michael Schumacher

In the late 1990s and early 2000s, if one driver personified, if not literally embodied, the corporate racing machine and hyperreal Formula One star simulacra, it was German Michael Schumacher (1991–2006; 2010–2012). Post Senna, he was *the* star driver in Formula One and the generational yardstick for his fellow drivers to be measured against. Schumacher won a record seven world championships (1994 and 1995 with Benetton; 2000–2004 with Ferrari), while establishing new levels of fitness, work ethic and standards of car control. He also set an array of Formula One records, including ninety-one Grand Prix wins, during his 'first' Formula One racing career (Bishop, 2006) before embarking on a second, less successful foray with Mercedes from 2010 to 2012.

Conversely, while Schumacher was revered in this first career for his driving talent and attributes, his near perfect integration within the Formula One machinery and its simulated assemblages seemed too polished, *too seamless*. While perhaps susceptible to national caricaturing, such characterisations tended to reduce Schumacher to an uncharismatic and emotionless figure, with Allen (2000) noting that "Schumacher is often accused of being more like a robot than a human being" (p. 78). Thus, Schumacher adhered to attempts to seamlessly integrate the driver (himself also prepared like a machine) within the machine; with Schumacher operating as a mere performative cog in Formula One's larger simulated, technological and corporate apparatus.

Baudrillard (2002) expounds this point by suggesting that the drivers become instrumentalised and machine-like in their pursuit of victory, with any sense of 'pleasure' consequently eroded for the drivers themselves. Baudrillard (2002) notes,

> There is no passion in this—except the passion for winning, of course, though that is not personal, but an operational passion. It shows up in the driver's brain the way the technical data show on the dashboard. It is inbuilt in the technical object itself, which is made to win, and which incorporates the driver's will as one of the technical elements required for victory.

> This seems inhuman, but to be honest about it, it is the mental logic of the race. (p. 168)

In many respects, the notions of performance, technology, operational passion and the robotic driver mapped thus far are further moulded and redirected by the commercial practices of the sport. Therefore, if we pursue the Schumacher-as-robotic-machine analogy, it comes as no surprise that he has not only won seven world championships (e.g., the performative man-machine) but, also, amassed phenomenal wealth. Schumacher was the highest paid driver on the grid, allegedly paid US$25 million to join Ferrari in 1996 (Freeman, 2021) while being rumoured to earn between approximately US$70 and 80 million annually post-2004, over half of which was derived from endorsements (Fleming & Sturm, 2011). Hence, as both a "streamlined product of sponsors and PR men" (Allen, 2000, p. 84) and a robot in the car, the hyperreal performing man-machine has clear commercial value in this corporate sport.

Returning to the realm of driver performance, Baudrillard (2002) observes that,

> Formula One is a rather good example of the era of performance, in which the heights achieved are the work of man and machine simultaneously, each propelling the other to extremes without it being really clear which is the engine of this meteoric advance and which merely the other's double. (p. 166)

While a robotic man-machine caricature emerged for Schumacher, extraordinary personal skill and physical capital also underpinned his endeavours. Schumacher was revered for his testing and set-up work, his driving ability (notably in wet weather) and his adaptability in altering race tactics during Grands Prix. During his Ferrari team years (1996–2006), Schumacher took his own personal fitness regimes and driving abilities to exceptional levels while expecting both team and car to be moulded around him (the one organisationally, the other physically). Thus, Schumacher immersed himself in relentless hours of testing to perfect his set-up, often at the expense of his teammates in terms of their own car development, access to data, and via preferential strategies come race weekend.

Indeed, despite repeated denials of the existence of complicit 'number 2' drivers, there was no mistaking that all components within Ferrari were reorientated towards, completely focused on and crystalised around a version of 'team Schumacher' (Freeman, 2021). Collectively, contractually subservient (but financially renumerated) second drivers and an influx of his hand-picked personnel were deployed to continually adapt Michael to the car and vice versa, all in order to perfect the performative dominance of the Schumacher/Ferrari 'machine'. In this vein, Baudrillard (2002) notes that,

> If man is haunted by the evil genius of technology, which pushes him to the limits—and even beyond his capabilities—then technology is haunted by man, who identifies with it and projects all his passions into it. The alliance between the two, the pact between them, can be brought about only through an excessive expenditure, a spectacular sacrifice. (p. 166)

Thus, despite the often 'seamless' accounts, an uneasy symbiosis between man and machine also underscores Schumacher's complete devotion and projection of passion towards the machine. Indeed, teammates and relationships are potentially sacrificed and expendable in his relentless quest, while Schumacher is seemingly also pushed to his limits in terms of what he is willing to do to achieve Formula One glory.

Schumacher's dominance, coupled with his 'ruthless ambition' to win at all costs, seems to reflect the robotic, human-machine fulfilling an 'operational passion' for winning devoid of 'human' emotion and unmoved by accusations of unsportsmanlike conduct across his career (Bishop, 2006; Vergeer, 2004). For example, while cleared of any wrongdoing by the FIA in 1994, Schumacher appeared to deliberately run into Damon Hill at Adelaide to claim the title, while there were rumours that his car may have also been running illegal software that season (Allen, 2000). Furthermore, at the title deciding race at Jerez in 1997, Schumacher appeared to ram rival Jacques Villeneuve despite initially not being charged for the incident. The 1997 decision caused a public backlash, with the off-season dominated by reactions to Schumacher's tactics, discussions of a suitable punishment for his move and Schumacher's attempts to repair his tarnished reputation (Allen, 2000).

Ultimately, Schumacher would be stripped of his second-place ranking in the Drivers' Championship for 1997 which, as Vergeer (2004) suggests, "the penalty is a joke, of course, but how else can you treat your main attraction?" (p. 204). Collectively, Schumacher's successful yet controversial career is punctuated by accusations of deliberately ramming title rivals (e.g., 1994 and 1997) or ex-teammates (e.g., Rubens Barrichello in 2012) off the track, alongside punishments for intentionally impeding other cars, including deliberately blocking the other drivers during qualifying at the 2006 Monaco Grand Prix (Bishop, 2006).

There was also increasing frustration at the nature of the Ferrari-Schumacher machine dominance between 2000 and 2004, which came close to being alienating for many Formula One fans given that Schumacher had little external competition, while teammate Barrichello was contractually obliged to let Schumacher win (Freeman, 2021). The 2002 season exemplified this dominance. Schumacher finished on the podium in every race (11 x 1st; 5 x 2nd; 1 x 3rd), scoring 144 total points and remarkably winning the Drivers' Championship by Round 11. Somewhat ironically given this level of Ferrari dominance, Fleming and Sturm (2011) observe that "the 2002 season was infamous for Ferrari stage-managing the Austrian Grand Prix result by having Barrichello, who led for the entire race, pulling over meters from the finish line to gift Schumacher the race victory" (p. 194). The resounding booing by fans and within the press gallery post-race hinted at the displeasure felt towards the inhuman and passionless driver displays evoked by Baudrillard (2002) and now manifest in Schumacher's and Ferrari's actions, which Schumacher tried to deflect as a team decision.

Throughout this five-year period of dominance and success with Ferrari, Schumacher would enact and perform the hyperreal elements of his robotic corporate stardom, 'revealing' during press conferences how difficult his victories were, feigning ignorance to concerns that the races were becoming 'boring' for spectators and, especially, remaining nonplussed at any criticism of manipulative team tactics. In many ways, an exposition of Formula One's technological, simulated and corporatised machinery were afforded to fans at this time, with Schumacher's sport stardom operating as the 'perfect embodiment' of a corporate driving machine that, necessarily, is subordinated to the team, sponsors and technology.

Fleming and Sturm (2011) suggest that to effectively embrace, succeed and performatively deliver upon this robotic corporate role requires for Schumacher the "total absorption of the human into the machinic dimension, into a corporately sponsored object world dominated by an impersonal logic" (p. 198) in which Schumacher must "perform as a corporate and technological marionette" (p. 197). Nevertheless, despite the publicly displayed man–machine interactions, Schumacher still tries to retain and reveal traces of the human, however fleeting, problematic or strained such representations may be. In this regard, the 2021 Netflix *Schumacher* documentary (Kammertöns et al., 2021) is noteworthy for its purposely humanising treatment of Schumacher that eschews a complete career trajectory or detailed interrogation of his driving misdeeds. Instead, the documentary revels in the warmth of a person, a personality and an intensely private family man that perhaps, in some ways, demythologises his hyperreal projection as a robotic corporate driver avatar.

Hyperconformity and Minimalism: Kimi Raikkonen

At first glance, Finnish driver Kimi Raikkonen (2001–2009; 2012–2021) also seemingly fits the robotic Formula One corporate-driver template seamlessly. Arguably, by adopting such an approach, Raikkonen achieved longevity in Formula One, driving for a record 349 race starts until the age of 42 and predominantly for top teams across his career—notably McLaren (2002–2006) and Ferrari (2007–2009; 2014–2018). Of course, financially he was well renumerated, including doubling his salary at Lotus (2012 and 2013) by exceeding expectations based on performance bonuses per point scored (Clarkson, 2019). His driving performances were also noteworthy as the 2007 World Champion and having finished second (twice) and third (three times) in the Championship. However, much is also made of Formula One only seeing glimpses of the 'real' Raikkonen—an allegedly more effervescent, humorous, socially engaged and hard-partying individual away from the track (Clarkson, 2019; Hotakainen, 2018). Thus, the archetypical corporate 'cookie cutter' persona inherent to the Formula One star simulacra that Raikkonen projected seemingly belies and conceals a more enigmatic individual that remained highly popular with Formula One fans.

Arguably, Raikkonen's 'blandness' is itself intentional and a carefully cultivated star persona—with Raikkonen's minimalistic and apathetic attitude towards the corporately scripted, driver-as-commodity hyperreal performance strategically deployed to reduce further demands on his non-driving Formula One commitments. Specifically, it could be argued that Raikkonen deployed Baudrillard's (1988, 1990) notion of a 'fatal strategy' for its agential capacity; toying with the media and fans that sought to know 'him', and the corporations and teams that sought to control him by, rather, simulating his hyperconformity to the corporate ethos, expectations and projection of the 'Kimi Raikkonen' Formula One star simulacra. This fatal strategy was a ruse and mere artifice as it fulfilled yet also minimalised his Formula One commitments, obligations and engagements by simulating his blind obedience to the system. Moreover, such a fatal strategy freed up a private and agential space for an unfettered 'Raikkonen' to flourish away from Formula One stardom, celebrity culture and its simulated, commodified and mediated constraints.

Collectively, with Raikkonen there is an ambivalence, an indifference and a minimalistic approach outside of the car whereby his monosyllabic answers, his phlegmatic projection and his seeming absence of a charismatic persona arguably were being strategically deployed to frustrate those that seek a deeper, more engaging 'real' star image. In fact, the lack of emotion was one of his character traits, where Raikkonen seemed recalcitrant and indifferent to describing the Formula One driving experience, to exuding enthusiasm in press statements (with a monotone response remaining whether he won or retired from a race), and in providing short, deadpan and closed responses.

Additionally, he frequently seemed nonplussed at inane questions, requests or obligations—for example, offering only one-word responses (or no responses) to interviewers, failing to match the excitement of interviewers or fans at PR events, refusing to 'perform' as expected by those in attendance (e.g., often refusing to take off his sunglasses) and only providing brief or fleeting forms of engagement with waiting fans. These non-Formula One driving duties are contractual obligations but, by default, Raikkonen provided the impression that he did not want to attend to such duties and, indeed, frequently confirmed this perspective during interviews (Clarkson, 2019; Hotakainen, 2018).

Nevertheless, seemingly off-script moments during races endeared him to fans. In 2006, after his car broke down mid-race at the Monaco Grand Prix, cameras tracked Raikkonen heading to his private yacht rather than back to the pits for a team debrief. Later footage from the race still in progress has Raikkonen soaking shirtless in a hot tub while his mates continue their weekend of partying. In 2009, with heavy rain suspending the Malaysian Grand Prix mid-race, cameras catch Raikkonen out of his racing overalls eating an ice cream while the other drivers still prepare to race. Finally, his at times terse and abrupt radio exchanges with the team were broadcast. Arguably most famous was his 2012 response to team instructions when leading the Abu Dhabi Grand Prix, retorting "just leave me alone, I know what to do", which became an instant catchphrase and branded slogan when referencing Raikkonen, as did other playful 'ice cream' motifs. Collectively, such moments hint at an apathy, an ambivalence and a disdain for the expected performative roles within Formula One.

In many ways Raikkonen evokes York's (2018) notion of reluctant celebrity, whereby famous individuals navigate and negotiate the structural impositions surrounding their global fame and media attention, while finding strategies to deflect and defer their 'celebrity' roles. Poignantly, York (2018) suggests "reluctance marks an ambivalence rather than a rejection: a condition of simultaneously positive and negative reactions while acting in a way that suggests compliance" (p. 4). Hence, through her case studies, the celebrities don't explicitly reject celebrity or become reclusive per se but, operating primarily from privileged positions, they brandish strategies that negotiate and evoke their seeming reluctance. Specifically, York (2018) discusses Robert De Niro's notoriety for his silence and taciturnity in effectively 'saying nothing' in most non-filmic appearances that often frustrates interviewers or those trying to gain 'deeper' insights into or understandings of the method actor (see also Smith, 2002). York (2018) also explores Daniel Craig's reluctance at being a promotional vehicle for his films, despite the fact companies frequently use his star capital (and often eroticised body) in ways that position him as the 'poster boy' for such films.

These two case studies elicit remarkable similarities to Raikkonen. For example, Hotakainen (2018) suggests that Raikkonen is "famous for his reticence" (p. 34), before noting that elements such as taciturnity, three-word sentences and particularly silence were commonly deployed by the Finn to navigate inane questions and his press-related duties. Raikkonen's disinterest and unenthusiastic approach to promotional work has also been hinted at above—seemingly fulfilling his contractual obligations but shunning any overt displays of interest, enthusiasm or excesses. As such, it could be countered that his minimalistic and seemingly disinterested approach was a strategic ruse and lure by Raikkonen; simulating his own hyperconformity (Baudrillard, 1988, 1990) to the hyperreal Formula One star simulacra to retain an agential space away from Formula One. Additionally, this could also be interpreted as an individual politics of indifference and apathy (and perhaps was at first glance), albeit with his hyperconformity subsumed by and absorbed into Formula One's corporate apparatus as its own simulacra.

Not surprisingly, an overt manufactured image—a 'personalised' Formula One star simulacra—was constructed for Raikkonen whereby he was projected as the 'Iceman', an assumed emotionless image/persona that was given to him by McLaren team boss Ron Dennis in 2002. As Hotakainen (2018) recounts:

> *Iceman.* Ron Dennis gave this name to Kimi. It…defines his professional identity accurately: he comes from a cold climate, drives fast and talks little, he doesn't explain anything, does his job to the best of his ability, and then moves on to the next race. A little later, the role will entail wearing dark glasses everywhere. (p. 131)

Interrelated and perhaps unsurprisingly (see later section), Jacques Villeneuve reportedly rebuked Raikkonen for being a manufactured driver image, allegedly noting that, "It's sad that you don't see drivers being real people. Kimi's image is so obviously fabricated because he's not the Ice Man. It goes back to the corporations. You end up fabricating this image because that's what they want" (Villeneuve in McRae, 2005, para. 5).

Although clearly corporately complicit, arguably this constructed persona was also beneficial for Raikkonen as it seemingly furnished a stable and readily identifiable Formula One character for him to perform. The Iceman provided Raikkonen with the corporate driver avatar, the hyperreal simulacra that permitted his playful politics of apathy and indifference—all permissible as Raikkonen performed the expected role with aplomb. Indeed, perhaps through his ambivalent adherence, his seemingly blind obedience to the role and his apparent subsummation by the corporately imposed apparatuses, Raikkonen undermined the entire hyperreal Formula One circus. Because Raikkonen's hyperconformity was so overt, so explicitly manufactured and so easily discerned by both insiders and outsiders, there was no veneer, no pretence nor explanatory framework offered or needed. Rather, there is a revelling in his hyperconformist approach as the ultimate form of resistance. He has been absorbed, consumed and co-opted by the teams, corporations, media and fans alike who seemingly 'have him' as the Formula One star simulacra (Baudrillard, 1990). Nevertheless, this remains a lure and ruse, as his individual politics of indifference, minimalisation and apathy suggest otherwise, while Raikkonen remains the supreme seductive 'object' with all interested parties in on the game.

Hotakainen (2018) seems cognisant of some of the possibilities that embracing the Iceman persona afforded Raikkonen, observing that "it's an alias, a shield, a tool. You can drive a car under it; it's a good name for that purpose. But it melts outside of the car and evaporates once he reaches his own doorstep" (p. 34). Unfortunately, Hotakainen (2018) then opines contradictory claims that the persona was 'organic' and rooted in Raikkonen's place of origin, despite having previously acknowledged its overt construction and activation as a brand. Nevertheless, what is intriguing is the performative shield and function this allowed for Raikkonen. In many respects, he did not need to cultivate a charismatic persona for—as the Iceman—ambivalence, indifference and a disdain for press and PR duties were understood, subsumed by and complementary to, if not expected of, this hyperreal corporate image. Hence, Raikkonen seemingly only needed to publicly enact this performance to showcase his apparent reluctance and hint at a recalcitrant individual uneasy with the corporate expectations of Formula One. All the while, of course, he was adhering to and conforming to such expectations in a manner that appeased the teams and sponsors while appealing to the fans. As such, Raikkonen could simply don this corporately complicit hyperreal Iceman mask and/or shield, perform its marionette-esque functions (which included an implicit reliance on fearless and fast driving, buttressed by performances on the track), and then remove many of its vestiges in his private, non-Formula One life.

Indeed, so much of the fascination with Raikkonen was the awareness that away from Formula One there was a wilder private life, hedonistic lifestyle and risk-taking thrill seeker who was at odds with the bland personality performed and projected to Formula One audiences. Hence, his dangerous pastimes, hijinks, one-time excessive lifestyle and earlier Finnish celebrity circulation through marriage to former Miss Scandinavia Jenni Dahlman (2004–2012) garnered large media interest and attention, although would barely be acknowledged or commented upon by Raikkonen. Moreover, his hard partying and binge-drinking were seemingly well-known albeit rarely reported, aside from his antics at a London strip club making the tabloids in 2005 (Henry, 2005). Intriguingly, Raikkonen recently revealed having a 16-day 'bender' between two races in 2012, while confirming a broader trend of regular binge-drinking earlier in his career (Clarkson, 2019; Hotakainen, 2018).

Conversely, Raikkonen seemed acutely aware of the intense media scrutiny and corporate expectations that accompanied Formula One stardom. Therefore, strategically, he intentionally offered no perceptible individuated personality outside of the corporately projected Iceman simulacra that he performed for teams, sponsors and the press. As such, Raikkonen demonstrated aspects of York's (2018) reluctant celebrity through his ambivalence, taciturnity and minimalisation via a contractually imposed celebrityhood. Raikkonen also seemingly recognised the agential value and capacity of a 'fatal strategy' (Baudrillard, 1988, 1990) that simulated his hyperconformity to the corporate ethos and projection as the Iceman—adhering to and appeasing team/sponsor expectations replete with the apathetic and indifferent traces that endeared him to fans. Thus, while Raikkonen allegedly remarked to Hotakainen (2018) that "it would be brilliant to drive in Formula One incognito" (p. 36) arguably, Raikkonen already had a ready-made solution and strategy that allowed him to compartmentalise his performances both as a Formula One star driver and as a promotional 'vehicle' for corporate appropriation as the hyperreal Iceman persona.

A Joker in the Pack? Jacques Villeneuve as Formula One Maverick

With a famous racing father (Gilles Villeneuve) and the accomplishment of being a Formula One World Champion (1997), IndyCar Champion (1995) and Indy 500 race winner in the same year, French-Canadian Jacques Villeneuve demonstrates ascribed and achieved celebrity (Rojek, 2001). However, outside of these lofty achievements, Villeneuve's Formula One career (1996–2006) is one of steady decline, arguably best understood as a rise-and-fall sporting narrative (Whannel, 1999, 2002) of instant success confounded by failure and disappointing results. Failing to win a race again post-1997, Villeneuve's stardom seems in sharp contrast to the polished corporate robotic winning machine that Michael Schumacher embodied. Rather, Villeneuve's perceived maverick personality becomes more poignant, wherein his risk-taking, scruffy appearance, dissent and reluctant commodification seemingly operated in contradistinction to the hyperconformist Iceman persona of Kimi Raikkonen and corporately oiled world of Formula One.

Fleming and Sturm (2011) observe that Formula One websites, books and magazines tend to discuss Villeneuve in two ways:

> The first, taking a career 'profile' format, focuses on an early career rich with successes (often tying in connections to his famous racing father and Jacques' own Indy accomplishments in the United States), then attainment of the F1 championship before relative mid-field obscurity in performance terms. The second, however, quite clearly embellishes Villeneuve's 'personality', depicting him as free-spirited, his own man, standing apart, a rebel, eccentric, an individual, opinionated, and so on. (p. 196)

Primarily focused on the second trend, it is posited that Villeneuve provided individuated traces of 'grit' within the smooth and seamless Formula One machine. Permeating all aspects of Villeneuve's engagement with and within Formula One are evocations of the scruffy 'rebel', the reluctant commodity, the anti-corporate dissenter and the macho risk-taker who apparently operated in a distinctive manner from the expected Formula One star simulacra.

This notion of the maverick can usefully be explored as a response to York's (2013) challenge to reintroduce and to reconceptualise agency in studies of celebrity. Avoiding the dialectics of production and consumption, York (2013) advocates situating agency "as one of the many forces operating in celebrity when it is considered as an industry" (p. 1332) wherein authors understand "celebrity as various sets of industrial relations, rather than as a purely individual phenomenon" (1340). Thus, deploying and recasting the notion of the 'maverick' furnishes the unpacking and interrogation of York's (2013) situated agency in terms of Villeneuve's integration and determined subject position within the structures of the sport, counter-posed by his ability to reflexively navigate this corporately complex terrain. Hence, it is acknowledged from the outset that Villeneuve is co-opted into a series of practices, processes and relationships as a hyperreal Formula One star simulacra.

Alternatively, Villeneuve's own attempts to retain an agential space and mobilise a sense of individualism within these simulated assemblages also afford visible sites for contestation. Seemingly an exemplar of Dyer's (1979) "Rebel Hero", such a label problematically implies a binary relationship of the celebrity rejecting the field or industry which then, in fact, is revealed to be mere corporate chicanery. Specifically, despite elements of resistance, most 'rebel' sports stars are *always already* complicit and co-opted, being repackaged for and resold via corporate cultures that subsume their posturing and projections of 'anti-corporate' sentiments (Andrews & Jackson, 2001; Fleming & Sturm, 2011).

Whannel's notion of the maverick seems most appropriate for explaining Villeneuve's Formula One stardom. In defining the maverick, Whannel (2002) notes that,

> Maverick masculine individualism is something that coaches, and governing bodies are concerned to root out. In a world that is constrained, maverick sport stars appear to offer the power to live a life of masculine individualism—defying constraints, rebelling against regulation, whilst still performing. (p. 262)

As a pointed example, Villeneuve's appearance was literally and visibly bereft of the expected corporate grooming practices commonly adopted by his peers. With messy hair often bleached an assortment of blonde, pink, red and even blue at different times, baggy rather than tight-fitting apparel, spectacles and regularly sporting a beard or excessive stubble Villeneuve, symbolically at least, resisted the expectation of a clean, cookie-cutter image inherent to the Formula One star simulacra.

For example, during his three years at Williams, Vergeer (2004) suggests that key sponsors had become infuriated by the "eccentric, variable colour of his hair" (198), while in Brazil in 1998, Donaldson (2001) notes that FIA officials had told Villeneuve,

> Wearing his habitual 'high grunge' clothing, sporting a scraggly beard and with his hair dyed a bizarre shade of blonde, that he should clean up his act and pay more attention to his appearance because he was bringing the sport into disrepute. (p. 56)

Villeneuve continued to sport various hair colours and seldom was without stubble across his career, even on occasion growing a full beard. His scruffy appearance with BAR (1999–2003) led two *F1 Racing* magazine writers to proclaim that "JV is motor-racing's answer to rock'n'roll" (Clarkson, 1999, p. 84) and that "Jacques Villeneuve remains a rebel, remains his own man, and F1 is better for it" (Bishop, 2000, p. 46). Fleming and Sturm (2011) note, "of course, Villeneuve's non-conformist image was also being encouraged and capitalised upon by BAR, BAT and key sponsors as a marketing ploy to promote their 'rebel' star, whose image might be even more saleable off-track than on" (p. 52).

Pertinently, Whannel (2002) also acknowledges the emergence of corporate influences for sport stardom, arguing that, "maverick masculine individualism also increasingly conflicts with the new corporate paternalism, whereby institutions become the moral guardians of their employees, supervising the way they live" (p. 262). Villeneuve's 'traces of grit' further manifest via his assumed reluctant commodification and due to his forthright dissent. Allegedly protective of his image, Villeneuve's relationship with sponsors and corporations was widely represented as abrasive. For example, despite being a contractual obligation, Villeneuve refused to perform extensive public relations duties. After leaving Williams in 1998, Villeneuve redefined his contractual stipulations and demands with BAR by, in effect, limiting his press commitments and promotional work while only being obligated to four PR days annually. Such an approach was exceptional and lauded by Formula One journalists at the time, particularly as most drivers provided thirty (or McLaren drivers over eighty) PR days in 2000 for example (Clarkson, 1999; Bishop, 2000). Windsor (2006) surmised that, during Villeneuve's BAR years, "never had an F1 driver been paid so much to do so little out of the car … for the sponsors" (p. 59).

Villeneuve's reputation as a forthright, brash and, at times, controversial speaker was also valued by some within the press, whereby he was lauded for being "so fabulously quotable" (Bishop, 2005, p. 85) and for providing "a welcome bite to the bubbles of cliché which clog the paddock" (McRae, 2005, para. 2). Specifically, Villeneuve was represented as a regular dissenter on Formula One's corporate ethos, orientation and structure. For example, Villeneuve was quoted in *Formula 1 Magazine* as stating, "F1 has become a corporate sport and corporations don't want human beings driving, they want robots. Nobody sees the difference" (Other comments, 2003, p. 146). Villeneuve's dissent was also directed at the broader complicity of his peers, while deploring the voracious demand for young and compliantly groomed drivers from many teams. Notably scathing of the manufacturing of driver images, Villeneuve allegedly asserted in 2005 that, "all these corporations don't want their drivers to ruin their image so you can't say what you think. You're basically not allowed to have a personality. How can you have any heroes if you don't allow personalities?" (Villeneuve in McRae, 2005, para. 1). Hence, Villeneuve affords the materialisation of a more individuated driver persona, one that agitates against the dominant Formula One star simulacra, despite fluidly circulating within its simulated parameters and assemblages.

Additionally, despite an early-career official FIA reprimand in 1997, Villeneuve derided various attempts by the governing body to regulate safety or to 'improve' the spectacle. For example, in 1996 Villeneuve was quoted as saying, "I also need the danger. I need to be in that situation where I know one mistake could kill me" (Villeneuve in Shirley, 2000, p. 130), while also observing in 1997 that "the risks drivers take now are 10 times less than they were a few years back and we make 10 times more money" (Donaldson, 2001, p. 55). In this respect, Villeneuve seems to encapsulate Baudrillard's (2002) notion of the driver as a "symbolic operator of crowd passions and the risk of death" (p. 169), potentially exciting crowds with his aggressive style and penchant for risk-taking. Through a combination of his reported bravado, big crashes and later struggles to adapt to the evolving technological machinery of Formula One (replacing individuality with electronic driver aids), Villeneuve seemed to be a driver still clinging to his own pursuit of some form of 'personal pleasure' in driving, despite Baudrillard (2002) noting that such pleasure, as well as the personal risk of death, was disappearing from the contemporary circuits.

Arguably, permitting such endeavours was Villeneuve's later mid-field machinery and obscurity that contrast with Raikkonen and Schumacher often driving front-running cars in championship campaigns. Both drivers are also vocal in their 'passion' for driving, although for Raikkonen this consists of a minimalistic, 'no fuss' plug in and drive fast logic (Hotakainen, 2018), ideally uncomplicated by Formula One assemblages. Conversely, Schumacher seems to embody a neoliberal logic of masculine technological mastery: revelling in the minutiae and technical details forever perfecting the car, while privileging a strict operational logic that balances risk, 'operational pleasure', skilful execution and mastery of man, machine and performative perfection.

In summary, Villeneuve seemingly operated in contradistinction to Schumacher and the established pathways to stardom in Formula One despite both being the title protagonists in 1997. Villeneuve's reluctance to acquiesce to Formula One's simulated assemblages saw his rise, fall and eventual departure across the same years as Schumacher went on to dominate as *the star* driver in Formula One. Nevertheless, despite not being the performative man-machine in terms of race results—scoring only two podiums and a mere 55 points post-1998 compared to the 843 points and five championships Schumacher accumulated at the same time—there remained traces of the 'star in the car'.

Whannel (2002) notes that, "the persistent fascination with the errant, the maverick and the erratic suggests at some broader unwillingness simply to embrace the routinised professionalism of work-ethic-driven sport stars" (p. 142). Coupled with his championship and the large salary that reified his star status, Villeneuve's seemingly reluctant commodification, dissenting viewpoints and risk-taking exploits provide the traces of an enigmatic figure for fans, in varying degrees, to 'engage' with. Moreover, despite being embedded within the very corporate apparatuses that he was critiquing, Villeneuve's apparent resistance to the corporate puppetry of Formula One's hyperreal stardom became financially lucrative. Indeed, Fleming and Sturm (2011) note that "there was some irony in Villeneuve's projection of that particular personality at a time when BAR exemplified a high-cost corporate organization focused around him" (p. 52), while also suggesting that "his supposedly unfettered time with the BAR team could be seen as a matter of marketing convenience, allowing BAR to promote their 'rebel' star driver in order to position their team's 'personality'" (p. 197). As such, Villeneuve seemingly offers a vestige of maverick individualism agitating against while operating within Formula One's simulated assemblages.

Concluding Remarks

In conclusion, the three case studies bear witness to the structures, machinery and apparatuses that impinge upon an array of 'performances' relating to Formula One stardom. In this vein, drivers need to acquiesce to hi-tech machines that largely govern their on-track performances, while most strive to enhance their 'star power' potential via race wins, championships, lavish salaries and/or career earnings by driving for a top team. However, top drives come at a price, with the corporate orientation of Formula One requiring drivers to seemingly operate as blank canvasses and 'corporate puppets' via the hyperreal projection of endlessly reproduced images derived from implosive and precessionary models of and for the Formula One star simulacra. Hence, as contractual obligations, such practices curb the agential possibilities for drivers to exhibit degrees of individuality although, of course, an established star, such as seven times World Champion Lewis Hamilton, clearly has more agential potential to project a personality than a 'pay driver' or a corporately groomed junior development driver seeking to secure his future. Conversely, current drivers have access to and are, for the most part, expected to self-promote across an array of media spaces—notably via social media, online gaming and other digital platforms—which potentially affords a more playful space than the strict corporate orientation and impositions of the 1990s and 2000s.

As witnessed through Michael Schumacher, his complete acquisition to all of these components harnessed a dominant winning man-machine. Schumacher's seamless integration into the Formula One 'machine' catered to record-setting performances that arguably became the template for most aspiring drivers to follow and emulate. Schumacher became an influential figure for the next generation of successful drivers—notably Jenson Button, Sebastian Vettel and Mark Webber (by contrast Hamilton cited Senna as his idol)—while a production line of technically proficient, physically fit and corporately groomed young drivers would also emerge to reproduce and reify the hyperreal Formula One star simulacra, particularly via the junior driver academies of established top teams. However, despite all the plaudits and accolades for an exceptional career of achievements, wealth and success, there were accompanying perceptions that Schumacher was always *too seamless, too polished, too corporately aligned.* His tendency to also transgress and exhibit unsporting indiscretions due to his 'win at all costs' mentality further polarised his critical reception. Nevertheless, as the 'star' driver post Senna, his influence was profound, if not problematic, for those navigating their way into Formula One.

Conversely, a 'Kimi Raikkonen' offers another iteration of the seemingly corporately complicit and puppet-like figure that, alternatively, may well be a more nuanced public performance than it first appears. Precisely how agential, reflexive or strategic Raikkonen's approach to the Formula One star simulacra was remains debatable but, by deploying an ambivalent adherence to the hyperreal and hyperconformist Iceman persona,

Raikkonen's reluctance and minimalism was allowed to manifest. Such performances also intrigued and endeared him to many fans and Formula One insiders. Perhaps most telling was the parallel career trajectory for Fernando Alonso (2001–2018; 2021–present) who seemingly shared many of Raikkonen's attributes. Alonso also debuted in 2001, achieving two world championships (2005 and 2006) and is widely regarded as one of the best all-time Formula One drivers. Like Raikkonen, Alonso drove for many of the top teams—Renault (2003–2006; 2008–2009), McLaren (2007; 2015–2018) and Ferrari (2010–2014)—but, arguably, Alonso's temperament, 'ego' and public criticism of teams limited his opportunities for sustained roles or further success (Foster, 2021b). Alternatively, Raikkonen's ability to acquiesce to the corporate ethos by simulating his own hyperconformity meant he retained his place on the grid with top teams for most of his career.

Finally, the reluctance of top teams to embrace a mercurially quick but volatile driver like Alonso has links to our other case study. Jacques Villeneuve was disinterested in simulating the robotic man-machine that Schumacher embodied nor, seemingly, could stomach performing Raikkonen's hyperconformist role, with his maverick individualism arguably proffering 'traces of grit' within Formula One's machinic structure. Nevertheless, Villeneuve's approach was always precarious as it also relied on teams acquiescing to accommodate him, particularly within a context wherein most sponsors wanted the corporately complicit Formula One star simulacra. Villeneuve was fortunate to advance his prior American successes with an early World Championship to safeguard a notable history and legacy of achievement but, ultimately, failed to maintain performative longevity despite spending ten full seasons in Formula One. Thus, while being financially rewarded to drive poor cars with BAR and potentially being encouraged to agitate as their 'rebel' star for five years—whether conceived as a promotional strategy by BAR or as Villeneuve's inherent maverick individualist attributes—these developments quashed any redemption phase for his rise and fall star narrative (Whannel, 1999).

Despite the numerous apparatuses that percolate around (Formula One) sport stardom, demonstrable and quantifiable sporting performances remain paramount. Hence, Raikkonen's ambivalence and Alonso's petulance are accepted or at least tolerated as they have consistently evidenced strong performances for their teams and cars (notably Alonso who seemingly outperforms the limitations of his machinery annually). Similar points could also be made for Hamilton who is still always performing amidst a backdrop of high-profile socialising and global jet-setting, through to his newfound outspoken political activism (Sturm, 2023). Unlike Schumacher's near decade of dominance, Villeneuve progressively slid down the grid to irrelevance and obscurity, often failing to outperform poor cars in his later years as he had in 1999 and 2000. Additionally, Villeneuve opted not to pursue other contractual offers—albeit most likely for less pay and a stricter corporate ethos in return for potentially 'better' cars—to remain as the integral 'rebel' star driver for BAR.

Hence, while Villeneuve's forms of maverick individualism could still reverberate around the Formula One mid-field, his approach showcases and underscores the relevance of sport star performances. Intriguingly, Formula One both challenges and reinforces traditional theories of sport stardom grounded in meritocracy, authenticity and sporting performances. While the top drivers are there on merit, the sport has predominantly comprised white, affluent men of privilege. Equally, despite any agential intent, talent or ability on behalf of the individual driver, it is fundamentally the machinery and technologies that largely define, furnish and circumscribe the driver's performance, creating a sense that the 'car is the star' within Formula One. Finally, notions of 'authenticity' are also dubious given the associated commercial apparatuses and simulated assemblages that manufacture drivers as hyperreal star personas. And yet, at its very essence, there is an intrigue in locating the performative man in the machine, and the man behind the corporate mask—in recognising the 'star in the car' that engenders much of the global passion for Formula One.

References

Allen, J. (2000). *Michael Schumacher. Driven to Extremes*. Bantam.

Andrews, D., & Jackson, S. (Eds.). (2001). *Sport Stars: The Cultural Politics of Sporting Celebrity*. Routledge.

Andrews, D., & Ritzer, G. (2018). Sport and Prosumption. *Journal of Consumer Culture, 18*(2), 356–373. https://doi.org/10.1177/1469540517747093

Baudrillard, J. (1983). *Simulations* (P. Foss, P. Patton & P. Beitchman, Trans.). Semiotext(e).

Baudrillard, J. (1988). *The Ecstasy of Communication* (B. Schütze & C. Schütze, Trans.). Semiotext(e).

Baudrillard, J. (1990). *Fatal Strategies*. Semiotext(e)/Pluto.

Baudrillard, J. (1994). *Simulacra and Simulation* (S. Faria Glaser, Trans.). University of Michigan Press. (Original work published 1981).

Baudrillard, J. (2000). *The Gulf War Did Not Take Place* (P. Patton, Trans.). Power. (Original work published 1991).

Baudrillard, J. (2002). *Screened Out* (C. Turner, Trans.). Verso. (Original work published 2000).

Bishop, M. (2000, September). Hot Property. *F1 Racing*, Australian Edition. pp. 42–47.

Bishop, M. (2005, October). The Long Interview: Jacques Villeneuve. *F1 Racing*, Australian Edition, pp. 80–89.

Bishop, M. (Ed.), (2006, December). *F1 Racing* (Schumacher Tribute), Australian Edition.

Clarkson, T. (1999, September). Easy Rider. *F1 Racing*, Australian Edition, pp. 76–84.

Clarkson, T. (Host). (2019, March). Kimi Raikkonen: 'Racing and Partying—For Me It Was Normal' [Audio Podcast, Season 4, Episode 29]. In *F1-Beyond the Grid*. Formula1.

Donaldson, G. (2001). The Daredevil Inside Jacques Villeneuve. *Formula 1 Magazine, 1*(2), 54–61.

Dyer, R. (1979). *Stars*. BFI.

Fleming, D., & Sturm, D. (2011). *Media, Masculinities and the Machine: F1, Transformers and Fantasizing Technology at Its Limits*. Continuum.

Foster, M. (2021a, October 14). Gasly Has Been 'f****d' by Red Bull and 'Uncle Marko'. *PlanetF1.com*. https://www.planetf1.com/news/christijan-albers-pierre-gasly-uncle-marko/

Foster, M. (2021b, November 5). Wolff on Alonso Having Only Two Titles: You're Not the Sun. *PlanetF1.com*. https://www.planetf1.com/news/toto-wolff-fernando-alonso-two-titles/

Freeman, G. (Host). (2021, July 15). How Schumacher's Ferrari Move Shocked F1 [Audio Podcast, Season 4, Episode 2]. In *Bring Back V10s—Classic F1 Stories*. The Race.

Fresco, E. (2020). In LeBron James' Promotional Skin: Self-Branded Athletes and Fans' Immaterial Labour. *Journal of Consumer Culture, 20*(4), 440–456. https://doi.org/10.1177/1469540517745705

Galily, Y. (2019). 'Shut Up and Dribble!'? Athletes Activism in the Age of Twittersphere: The Case of LeBron James. *Technology in Society, 58*(101109), 1–4. https://doi.org/10.1016/j.techsoc.2019.01.002

Haraway, D. (1991). *Simians, Cyborgs, Women: The Reinvention of Nature.* Routledge.

Haraway, D. (1994). A Manifesto for Cyborgs: Science, Technology, and Socialist Feminism in the 1980s. In S. Seidman (Ed.), *The Postmodern Turn: New Perspectives on Social Theory* (pp. 82–116). Cambridge University Press.

Henry, A. (2005, January 25). Raikkonen 'Strip' Mars Car Launch. *The Guardian.* https://www.theguardian.com/sport/2005/jan/25/formulaone.alanhenry.

Hilton, C. (2003). *Inside the Mind of the Grand Prix Driver. The Psychology of the Fastest Men on Earth: Sex, Danger and Everything Else* (2nd ed.). Haynes.

Hotakainen, K. (2018). *The Unknown Kimi Raikkonen.* Simon & Schuster.

Kammertöns, H. B., Nöcker, V., & Wech, M. (Directors). (2021). *Schumacher* [Film]. Netflix.

Kellner, D. (1996). Sports, Media Culture, and Race—Some Reflections on Michael Jordan. *Sociology of Sport Journal, 13*(4), 458–467. https://doi.org/10.1123/ssj.13.4.458

Kennedy, E. (2000). Bad Boys and Gentlemen: Gendered Narrative in Televised Sport. *International Review for the Sociology of Sport, 35*(1), 59–73.

Marshall, P. (2014). *Celebrity and Power: Fame in Contemporary Culture* (2nd ed.). University of Minnesota Press.

McRae, D. (2005, March 2). Interview: Jacques Villeneuve. *The Guardian.* http://www.sport.guardian.co.uk/formulaone/story/0,,1426962,00.html.

Miller, T. (2017). *Greenwashing Sport.* Routledge.

Other Comments (2003, February). *Formula 1 Magazine*, 2, 12, p. 146.

Rojek, C. (2001). *Celebrity.* Reaktion.

Sandvoss, C. (2012). From National Hero to Liquid Star: Identity and Discourse in Transnational Sports Consumption. In C. Sandvoss, M. Real, & A. Bernstein (Eds.), *Bodies of Discourse: Sports Stars, Media, and the Global Public* (pp. 171–192). Peter Lang.

Scott, M. (2021, May 27). Norris Has 'Got Rid' of Social Media: 'It Sucks'. *PlanetF1.com.* https://www.planetf1.com/news/lando-norris-rid-of-social-media/

Shirley, P. (2000). *Deadly Obsessions. Life and Death in Formula One.* HarperCollins.

Smart, B. (2005). *The Sport Star: Modern Sport and the Cultural Economy of Sporting Celebrity.* Sage.

Smith, G. (2002). Choosing Silence: Robert DeNiro and the Celebrity Interview. In A. Ndalianis & C. Henry (Eds.), *Stars in Our Eyes: The Star Phenomenon in the Contemporary Era* (pp. 45–58). Praeger.

Spracklen, K. (2013). *Whiteness and Leisure*. Palgrave Macmillan.

Sturm, D. (2014). A Glamorous and High-Tech Global Spectacle of Speed: Formula One Motor Racing as Mediated, Global and Corporate Spectacle. In K. Dashper, T. Fletcher, & N. McCullough (Eds.), *Sports Events, Society and Culture* (pp. 68–82). Routledge.

Sturm, D. (2019). 'I Dream of Genie': Eugenie Bouchard's 'Body' of Work on Facebook. *Celebrity Studies, 10*(4), 583–587. https://doi.org/10.1080/19392397.2019.1601808

Sturm, D. (2021). The Formula One Paradox: Macho Male Racers and Ornamental Glamour 'Girls'. In K. Dashper (Ed.), *Sport, Gender and Mega Events* (pp. 111–128). Emerald.

Sturm, D. (2023). Processes of Greenwashing, Sportwashing and Virtue Signalling in Contemporary Formula One: Formula Façade? In H. Naess & S. Chadwick (Eds.), *The Future of Motorsports: Business, Politics and Society* (pp. 167–182). Routledge.

Sturm, D., & Kobayashi, K. (2022). Global/Local Celebrity and National Sport Stardom: Examining Sonny Bill Williams, Brendon McCullum and Lydia Ko. In D. Sturm & R. Kerr (Eds.), *Sport in Aotearoa/New Zealand: Contested Terrain* (pp. 119–132). Routledge.

The Future of F1: Discuss. (2006, December). *F1 Racing*, Australian Edition, pp. 90–96.

Tulle, E. (2016). Living by Numbers: Media Representations of Sports Stars' Careers. *International Review for the Sociology of Sport, 51*(3), 251–264. https://doi.org/10.1177/1012690214525157

Turner, B. (2004). *The Pits: The Real World of Formula One*. Atlantic.

Turner, G. (2014). *Understanding Celebrity* (2nd ed.). Sage.

Vergeer, K. (2004). *Formula One Fanatic*. Bloomsbury.

Weber, M. (1968). *Max Weber on Charisma and Institution Building; Selected Papers* (S. N. Eisenstadt, Ed.). University of Chicago.

Wenner, L. (Ed.). (2013). *Fallen Sports Heroes: Media, and Celebrity Culture*. Peter Lang.

Whannel, G. (1999). Sport Stars, Narrativization and Masculinities. *Leisure Studies, 18*(3), 249–265. https://doi.org/10.1080/026143699374952

Whannel, G. (2002). *Media Sport Stars: Masculinities and Moralities*. Routledge.

Windsor, P. (2006, April). Old Dogs Bark Louder. *F1 Racing*, Australian Edition, pp. 54–59.

Woodward, K. (2013). *Sporting Times*. Palgrave.

York, L. (2013). Star Turn: The Challenges of Theorizing Celebrity Agency. *Journal of Popular Culture, 46*, 1330–1347. https://doi.org/10.1111/jpcu.12091

York, L. (2018). *Reluctant Celebrity: Affect and Privilege in Contemporary Stardom*. Palgrave Macmillan.

Neoliberal Interpellation in the *F1 2018* Video Game

Daniel S. Traber

This chapter explores the topic of ideological interpellation via Codemaster's *F1 2018*, the sole officially licensed Formula One Racing video game. It appears that racing-game fans have tended to sidestep the online culture war skirmishes of recent years in which some self-identifying gamers participated (e.g., Gamergate in 2014), reveling in misogyny and reactionary politics ranging from anarcho-capitalism to outright fascism. In this light, I will analyse elements unique to *F1 2018* (both the narratological and the ludic) which reveal imbued beliefs and values that "hail" a player as a neoliberal subject. Driving expensive cars with engines built by major manufacturers—some of them categorized as luxury brands—obviously implicates players in the service of naturalizing competition and commodity desire. *F1 2018* has another layer of meaning underneath pretending to drive fast machines in exotic locales. That's why it is worth getting our hands dirty by removing the engine cover to

D. S. Traber (✉)
Texas A&M University at Galveston, Galveston, TX, USA
e-mail: traberd@tamu.edu

D. Sturm et al. (eds.), *The History and Politics of Motor Racing*, Global Culture and Sport Series, https://doi.org/10.1007/978-3-031-22825-4_21

inspect the ideological machinery controlling these devices of metal and flesh.

F1 2018's specialty is offering players the experience of participating in a full race weekend, including three practice sessions to set up the car for each different track, qualifying to determine your starting position in the line-up of twenty cars, and finally the race itself. But the game is about much more than winning races by mastering how to pilot the car around different tracks, each with its own unique demands and effects upon the physics of the vehicle. *F1 2018* takes it to another level, adds a further demand in order to become a successful player, an "authentic" participant, a "good" employee hired to drive a race car. You are expected to acquire the necessary "human capital" (a neoliberal notion) that makes you a more desirable occupational commodity. Philip Mirowski assesses this concept as "reduc[ing] the human being to an arbitrary bundle of 'investments,' skill sets, temporary alliances (family, sex, race), and fungible body parts" (59). In the game this includes interacting with the car's mechanical technology by making adjustments at a migraine-inducing granular level—be it tyre pressure, transmission gearing or brake bias—in order to set up a winning ride, which is not actually part of real racer's job requirements, albeit the better drivers do have advanced knowledge about car handling so they can effectively communicate with a team's technical squad. However, to succeed in *F1 2018*—if you choose to fully enter the game designers' universe of the professional racing experience as a job—not only do you have to win races, you must actually manage your own career; for example, the way you answer a reporter's questions about your track performance can agitate intra-team politics or create rivalries, and both have a potential effect upon your future career and earning potential.

None of this may seem to be motivated by neoliberal ideology on the surface, other than being rooted in the value of competition that informs sport in all its forms. In a sense, it works like an accidental exposé of the real-world professional racer's experience on a team and the demands of the sport outside actual competition. However, the process becomes more evident if we incorporate Louis Althusser's theory of interpellation, of how ideology creates like-minded Subjects through a "hailing"—likened to calling out, "Hey, you!"—because ideology cannot survive, let alone succeed, without people who identify themselves as being in accord with a particular set of beliefs. So, to achieve this identification through hailing requires the person recognizing himself or herself as the one addressed, which is to say correctly addressed: "Yes, that is me, I am like you, one of you, part of you"; thus, an individual is made into a Subject, which Althusser says he or she always already was due to ideology.

Paradoxically, for all the structuralist lack of individual choice this concept implies, one actually finds a modicum of agency in this model in that the subject is not simply saying, "Who, me? Well, sure I'll join you, since you hailed me." The Subjectified still has to consider himself or herself to be "someone like this" to recognize himself or herself in the parameters of the ideology. In other words, even if you are being conned you choose to be the kind of someone swayed by such lies, because you want the illusion to be true, want it to define your belief system—your very desires, fears, assumptions—as undeniable Truths. It is more comforting when what I *want* to believe is also what I am required to believe. You are labeled as free through the system that imprisons you in the required Subjectivity you comprise. With the caveat, however, that you are not thinking or acting like a "bad subject," meaning one whose behaviour, or lack of the approved kind more specifically, "provoke the intervention" of the institutional arms of the ruling class (Althusser, 1971, p. 181). The bad subject possibility answers the criticism of interpellation theory that it dissolves agency, asking how is one capable of disagreeing with the ruling ideas, of thinking differently, of adopting an identity that doesn't just blindly follow the rules of the ruling class or dominant culture? That critique mistakenly reads Althusser as saying all hailing is always successful.

Driving fast on race courses in pricey virtual automobiles may raise moral questions; it certainly addresses players through the experience of a specific kind of pleasure. The act of hailing is an essential function of video games. Alfie Bown makes it political in a 2018 *Guardian* article:

> Games are ideological constructions which push a set of values on the user. Like television and film, they often support the ideologies of their context … [They] put the user to work on an instinctual level, making the gamer feel impulsive agreement with these ideologies. Playing *Resident Evil* is not equivalent to watching the movie, because the controller-wielding

> gamer experiences the desires of the game as their own desires–not as the desires of another … [so] the rationale of gaming is to unite pleasurable impulse with political ideology, a process which renders gamers susceptible to discourses that urge people to follow their instincts while also prescribing what those instincts ought to be. (para?)

Interpellation rather than interactivity constitutes the *real* connection between game and gamer, the one that continues even after the console has been turned off and the unreal world of algorithmic play has been set aside for a world *made* real by ideology. Bown (2017) expands on his theory in *The Playstation Dreamworld*:

> [T]he subject is forced to respond to a prompt in a way that constitutes their subjectivity as the responder in the process. If gaming interpellates fragmented subjects, giving them a sense of purpose, then it does so in the service of dominant ideologies. … Of course, games reflect unconscious dreams, wishes, and desires, but they also play a role in constructing these unconscious assumptions [by] naturalizing the dreams, desires, and wishes of a political moment by making us experience those dreams, desires, and wishes as our own. … The patters of enjoyment found in the video game dreamworld tend toward the enforcement of traditionalist and conservative values which support the core values of contemporary capitalism or move them further to the political right. This is less because the structure of video games is inherently conservative or reactionary per se and more because the dreamworld is a reflection and even anticipation of coming political and social trends. (22, 38, 38)

The ludic aspect conceals how video games offer no escape from real life, just the opportunity to act it out in a digitized, code-controlled costume. But what is being offered players on a socio-political level is not so easily discerned in a racing game like *F1 2018*, unlike the militarism of war games or the stereotyping of ethnicity and gender found in the *Grand Theft Auto* series. The first tactic of ideology for any text is to convince the audience it is not ideological, that it instead holds a naturalized, dehistoricized Truth to be accepted as common sense. Likewise, the neoliberal message of *F1 2018* is more indirect.

The scholarly marketplace shelves are filled with work on "neoliberalism," yet David Harvey's (2005) well-quoted summary of the concept is still a good starting point:

> [A] theory of political economic practices that proposes that human well-being can best be advanced by liberating individual entrepreneurial freedoms and skills within an institutional framework characterized by strong private property rights, free markets, and free trade. The role of the state is to create and preserve an institutional framework appropriate to such practices. (2)

The social sphere is viewed through economic principles—"like a business"—and all decisions are made to accord with that perspective. In essence, to challenge what it views as the perennial threat of collectivism (be it socialist, fascist, or just an excessively regulatory liberal state), neoliberalism strikes a bitter compromise between the *laissez-faire* model of capitalism (classical liberalism) and John M. Keynes's general theory allowing for state intervention in the economy (embedded liberalism), thereby creating a hybrid approach founded upon the "recognition that the maintenance of a competitive market system required certain state powers" (Peck, 2010, p. 52). The neoliberal scheme for protecting the market limits government influence to ensuring capitalism's survival through deregulation, deunionization, widespread privatization of public services, disabling social-welfare programs, reducing or removing the labor protections that helped spread profits across post-war American society, and reinforcing the power of an elite class with the goal of disintegrating the threat of democracy negatively affecting the economy.

Milton Friedman, economist and famed cheerleader of neoliberalism, insisted free markets will inevitably lead to free people. Wendy Brown, political theorist and famed critic of neoliberalism, addresses how this notion's theory of "[economic] rationality, while foregrounding the market, is not only or even primarily focused on the economy; rather it involves *extending and disseminating market values to all institutions and social action*." (2005, pp. 39–40). Thus, in neoliberalism, human freedom can only be understood, indeed only thought of, through the logic of a market. As Brown further argues, "Neo-liberalism does not simply assume that all aspects of social, cultural and political life can be reduced to such a calculus, rather it develops institutional practices and rewards for enacting this vision" (2005, p. 40). Which means the state is called upon to instigate a new subjectivity and code of behaviour across society that benefits this system. This is part of what Michel Foucault calls "governmentality," or the process of "leading" the population by "conducting the conduct" of subjects to have them adopt, and therefore live out, some normative regime of truth by coercing their consensus via techniques of "management" (1994, p. 341). This is the process of normalization Foucault calls biopolitics.

The driving game genre is subdivided into simulation and arcade. Arcade racing is less realistic than a simulator which "emphasizes high accuracy and realism—a devotion to verisimilitude—in the car's appearance, sound, and, most especially, handling. The simulator's dedication to a code of honesty, even purity, marks it as a genre for the more serious gamer due to its steeper learning curve" (Traber, 2018, p. 479). Gameplay is split into two styles in most simulator-style driving games. There is typically some form of "Free Play" that allows the player to choose a track to drive solo or with AI racers; one engages in this activity just for fun or to improve one's skills. But the nucleus of any driving game is its "Career Mode" in which the player enters competitions to earn cash so as to buy more cars and upgraded parts, as well as gain some form of skill points in order to progress by entering higher level races and access to better cars. A truly innovative career mode, one that depicts neoliberal rationality deeper than just an act of athletic rivalry, is found in *F1 2018*. The player competing in a full Formula One season must not only drive the car and manage engine components to make the allocated number of "power units" adhere to the official rules of the race series, also help tune the car with the same micro-level of adjustability as found in *Project CARS 2* and *Forza 7*, but now you must also think about managing your career off the track via the panopticon of self-surveillance.

The most obvious form this takes in *F1 2018* is the game's quite unique element of having a player be confronted with a reporter's post-race questions about their performance and to then choose from the provided answers. Your answer is then evaluated on how it affects your levels of "reputation" (with your own team and the competition) and "respect" (on a spectrum bookended by "sportsmanship" and "showmanship"), with both represented as increasing or decreasing along bars. For example, there are four choices to the question, "Well, looks like your luck has changed. Things went a lot better than last weekend didn't they?" I chose to answer, "They did! We've been working on the engine and it's paying off." My choice was marked as being noticed by the "Power Unit department." In affecting the reputation and respect levels, there is then an effect on team morale (hence their dedication to helping you win), and the potential to create rivalries with other teams.

A rivalry adds another degree of pressure upon your performance as you are "watched" and evaluated by the team, sponsors, reporters and fans, such that not only do you have to win or have the best lap time but must also beat your rivals, including your teammate since F1 teams race two cars. In fact, intra-team competition can be more heated and brutal than the inter-team battles. If your performance lags behind your teammate you want to blame the engineering team assigned to you, then you can blame the car's set-up, your squad's dedication to you, the team's limited finances for testing or better parts, anything but your own deficiencies as a professional racer to account for your inability to stand on the podium and get sprayed with champagne. These tensions are relevant to the real world of Formula One racing as intra-team rivalries are a very real and serious part of the sport as evidenced in the first season of the Netflix series *Formula 1: Drive to Survive*. In episode 6, Sergio Pérez and Esteban Ocon battle—literally crashing into each other on track—to keep a seat at Force India after the team is bought by Lawrence Stroll, who will put his son Lance in one car. Eventually Pérez got the ride, some speculating it was a decision based on having sponsorship money more than his talent. So, after tabulating the numbers through a neoliberal calculator, it appears Ocon's human capital was just not as developed.

There are some less realistic benefits of these reputation points in that they provide more options for improving the car by allocating resources to research and design or upgrading the mechanical parts—choices the player must make in addition to driving the car. However, the most significant impact of the player's reputation score, and relevance to imbuing neoliberal rationality, is the way it affects the player's ability to negotiate his contract with the team. Along a bar showing your "Contract Value" is a marker designating "Your Value." You are only valuable as long as you are meeting the team's goals, or if other teams show an interest in hiring you. Then you become a "good" employee, a valuable commodity. Thus, *F1 2018* is a game in which your existence and occupation are so intertwined it plays like a digital reproduction of neoliberal rationality: the normalization of approaching every element of one's life, every choice one makes, through the cost–benefit filter of an entrepreneur. Career mode requires the successful player to think like both a scientist and a savvy brand manager. As Mirowski states, the neoliberal subject "is all at once the business, the raw material, the product, the clientele, and the customer of her own life" (108). If you do not have that capability, then your loss is your own fault with no regard for systemic explanations.

A less common issue in racing games is that of the actual race of the drivers, not to mention the other categories of identity, but this topic has its neoliberal edge as well. Neoliberalism presents and defends itself by arguing it is interested in making a meritocratic, colour-blind society yet still engages in activities like gentrified non-white neighborhoods which create an economic infrastructure that prices out the original residents, predominantly through higher rental rates—all because it's just business, the numbers say it is a good financial decision.

> The major neoliberal theorists Friedrich Hayek and Milton Friedman each willfully co-opted liberalism's political vocabulary of freedom and individuality to justify their economic visions. Jodi Melamed (2006) provides a later example of this phenomenon in her study of "neoliberal multiculturalism." She traces how an idea originally used to celebrate diversity outside the dominant culture was appropriated to yoke anti-racism and capitalism in the name of expanding global markets "while obscuring the racial antagonisms and inequalities on which the neoliberal project depends" (2006, p. 1). This shows that class and the economy are not so easily cleaved from other kinds of identity, as well as how a shared vocabulary does not automatically reveal complicity since ideas can be manipulated to suit an unrelated purpose:
>
> Concepts previously associated with 1980s and 1990s liberal multiculturalism—"openness," "diversity," and "freedom"—are recycled such that "open societies" and "economic freedoms" (shibboleths for neoliberal mea-

> sures) come to signify human rights that the United States has a duty to secure for the world [by using government military action to secure private financial expansion]. (2006, p. 16)

Gamers themselves, who may not be consciously neoliberal, have exhibited their own difficult relationship with a growing multicultural society. Its roots are typically traced back to the 2014 Gamergate controversy—in which a female critic who analysed the prevalent misogyny of video games was pilloried—and the gamers' subsequent parroting of the growing alt-right political ideology. Their declarations of misogyny bled over into rejection of social justice positions, blaming feminism and pluralism as sources for their felt loss of social status because the objects of their fandom, through which they understood their identity, came under critique. Megan Condis (2018) notes how a pluralist notion of identity became an explosive issue in gaming culture: "Gamers are self-identified members of a subcultural group organized around video game fandom. They do not dabble with video games: they live video games. They think of gaming as constituting an important part of their identity." (2). This is why the gamers took offense to no longer being the primary demographic catered to by the industry when a wave of others, those who are not white middle-class straight males, invaded their insular universe as players and game creators and started voicing demands for more diverse representation in games, as well as wanting online players to reduce the offensive banter during matches—in which players insult each other to upset their opponent's focus on the game. In effect, these outsiders were depicted as disrupting an established, protected culture and the attendant sense of self that feels organically attached to it. Moreover, Condis (2018) historicizes the politics undergirding this growing belligerent attitude among the gamers:

> [The] early 1990s was a time of when the rise of neoliberal politics and postfeminist discourse had a chilling effect on discussions of social justice around issues of race and gender. As with other neoliberal systems, the veil of hoped-for meritocracy promised by … [the] Internet actually resulted in the privilege of white male middle-class subjects over all others. The sup-

> posedly bodiless dwellers of the utopian Internet came to be read as straight white men by default. (8)

Can you experience the Other via your avatar in *F1 2018*? Are they treated differently, get different questions from the reporter? If they don't then one might read the game as not using essentialism, however, then the game not only fails at realism because it would definitely be a topic of discussion, but is also actually racist by pretending that race and sexuality do not make a difference in people's life options. In effect, a utopian colour-blindness enacts a policy of colour-disappearance, fueled by indifference to the real social effects of difference, its historical lineage and systemic inheritance. (To be fair, who wants to be the designer who has to take on the minefield burden of crafting identity-based personas for a high-level racing game which then necessitates specific interview questions and answers based on race and/or sexuality?) The game allows for creating your driver avatar along quite diverse sexual and racial lines. As an experiment, I decided to race as a black female driver for the Ferrari team with the name Danielle, even choosing a game-provided nickname for the announcers to use: "The Professor." The game presented absolutely no recognition of my race or gender other than the face and body during cut scenes on the podium. Even then, when sitting at a computer workstation to make racing decisions, if I made the avatar look down it showed the hands of a white male, so the designers didn't put much extra effort into creating a multicultural playing field. This hardly means the game is poised to back voices promoting misogyny and racism, very much unlike the libertarian leaning pro-capitalism reactionary pundit types found all over YouTube and the podcasting media-sphere who tend to drift into that area eventually, seeing the Other of multiculturalism as a force poised against traditionalism (which all too often amounts to an unrecognized defense of white, cis, straight privilege feeling duress, finding the growth of equality in Western societies as an unwelcome historical fact and social process.)

These mixed ludic facets of the game nod to Foucault's (1994) notion of governmentality—that process of conducting the conduct of people—which leads to an important aspect of ideological hegemony which prevents the agency of the individual from being completely shut down.

There is always the possibility of resistance as society is comprised of multiple, varied sites for struggle and compromise in an ongoing "war of position." A counter-hegemony can conceivably arise, voicing a different consciousness and set of values to address the needs and problems of the subordinated. So there are still spaces open for expressing oppositional values and beliefs. Foucault (2007) creates his own term for this in what he calls *counter-conduct*, a conscious resistance to a prevailing governmentality, like that instigated by neoliberalism, by choosing to "struggle against the processes implemented for conducting others" (201). Furthermore, it is the impetus "to refuse what we are," by which Foucault (1994) means what we have been made into, so we can "promote new forms of subjectivity through the refusal" (336). Relevant to the gaming context, Judith Halberstam (2011) writes of the transgressive power of *failure* in a culture that emphasizes winning. We should, she claims, reconceptualize

> failure as a way of refusing to acquiesce to dominant logics of power and discipline and as a form of critique. As a practice, failure recognizes that alternatives are embedded already in the dominant and that power is never total or consistent; indeed failure can exploit the unpredictability of ideology and its indeterminate qualities. … [Making instead a positive] association of failure with nonconformity, anticapitalist practices, nonreproductive life styles, negativity, and critique. (88, 89)

Ultimately, in *F1 2018*, like all racing games, one must decide the kind of citizen you are going to be. Will you risk penalties and car damage by bashing your way to the front by knocking the artificial intelligence (AI) cars out your way, which you have to do much of the time because they will not give up their spot freely, regardless of whether or not they are maintaining the correct racing line through the corners—besides, the programmed bastards would do the same to you without a nanosecond of hesitation in the kill or be killed world of professional racing (and so many video games), or so you convince yourself if you get too close to their wheels or rear end. Megan Condis (2018) defines a game's mechanics as "types of moves available to the player that are discovered over the course of play" (9), while an "emergent dynamics" are the "accidental, unpredicted behaviors that a game allows in addition or even in spite of the intentions of the designer" (9). This may present a field on which a bad subject can operate to enact a Foucauldian counter-conduct. With regard to *F1 2018* gameplay, a form of negotiation would be a mode of play that switches between using the game's prescribed driving line and finding your own way through corners, creating an individualized driving style. That is because:

> These games' science becomes representative of an ideology that informs gameplay by demanding hegemonic consensus from the players. The physics programmed into the game create a textbook racing line covering the proper braking point, corner entry, apex, and exit point to initiate reacceleration. … Since the AI seemingly do not know how to realistically react to the human gamer's presence, they stay on the line, obey it, because of their programming. In other words, it is all they know how to do. What the games do not promote is the fact that a strict adherence to that line is not always the best option in racing, in part because real drivers must constantly respond to the mayhem of chance. … [C]oincidence and accident are absolutely fundamental elements of motor racing; nonetheless, it must still be built into the game, chaos must be made ever more mathematically organized and predictable. (Traber, 2018, p. 480)

In this manner, the game *does* allow players a degree of choice, but it remains restricted, boxed within its own clearly demarcated algorithmic boundaries. Additionally, and perhaps more subversively, you could deliberately choose to crash your reputation and respect scores by choosing answers to the reporter's questions that will turn the team and the competition against you, so that even though you win races—the sole purpose of being a professional racer—you openly challenge the contract value system to lower "your value" according to their system. You will become a champion, perhaps even rise to still be a desired commodity in the economy of Formula One racing, yet a "bad" employee; or, to use Althusser's terminology, a "bad" subject in this ideological market.

Sometimes when you lose, you actually win.

References

Althusser, L. (1971). Ideology and Ideological State Apparatuses. In B. Brewster (Trans.), *Lenin and Philosophy and Other Essays* (pp. 127–186). New York: Monthly Review Press.

Bown, A. (2017). *The Play Station Dreamworld. Polity.*

Bown, A. (2018, March). How Video Games Are Fueling the Rise of the Far Right. *The Guardian*. Retrieved February 28, 2021, from https://www.theguardian.com/commentisfree/2018/mar/12/video-games-fuel-rise-far-right-violent-misogynist

Brown, W. (2005). *Edgework: Critical Essays on Knowledge and Politics*. Princeton University Press.

Condis, M. (2018). *Gaming Masculinity: Trolls, Fake Geeks and the Gendered Battle for Online Culture*. University of Iowa Press.

Foucault, M. (1994). The Subject and Power. In P. Rabinow (Ed.), *Power: Essential Works of Foucault 1954–1984* (Vol. 3, pp. 326–348). The New Press.

Foucault, M. (2007). *Security, Territory, Population: Lectures at the Collège de France 1977–1978* (G. Burchell, Trans.). Palgrave Macmillan.

Halberstam, J. (2011). *The Queer Art of Failure*. Duke University Press.

Harvey, D. (2005). *A Brief History of Neoliberalism*. Oxford University Press.

Melamed, J. (2006). The Spirit of Neoliberalism: From Racial Liberalism to Neoliberal Multiculturalism. *Social Text, 24*(4), 1–24.

Mirowski, P. (2013). *Never Let a Serious Crisis Go to Waste: How Neoliberalism Survived the Financial Meltdown*. Verso.

Peck, J. (2010). *Constructions of Neoliberal Reason*. Oxford University Press.

Traber, D. (2018). Motorsports as Popular Culture as Politics: *Le Mans*, F1, and Video Games. *The Journal of Popular Culture, 51*(2), 466–486.

Ecclestone out, Liberty Media in: A Look into the Shifting Ownership Structure of Formula One

Tom Evens, Sam Tickell, and Hans Erik Næss

Introduction

After years of speculation about the future of Formula One (F1), the iconic global motorsport series changed ownership in 2016. In a US$4.4 billion-worth deal, US media conglomerate Liberty Media Corporation, hereafter Liberty Media, agreed to buy the controlling interest of private equity firm CVC Capital Partners (Liberty Media Corporation, 2016). The deal not only signalled one of the most important moments in the

T. Evens (✉)
imec-mict, Ghent University, Ghent, Belgium
e-mail: Tom.Evens@UGent.be

S. Tickell
University Münster, Münster, Germany
e-mail: Samuel.Tickell@UGent.be

H. E. Næss
Kristiana University College, Oslo, Norway
e-mail: HansErik.Naess@kristiania.no

D. Sturm et al. (eds.), *The History and Politics of Motor Racing*, Global Culture and Sport Series, https://doi.org/10.1007/978-3-031-22825-4_22

commercial history of Formula One, but the landmark deal was also the beginning of the end of the remarkable reign of Bernie Ecclestone. The eccentric British business magnate, who was credited with overseeing Formula One's transformation and professionalisation, and had run the sport for nearly forty years, would step down first as chairman and later as chief executive. Ecclestone was replaced by Chase Carey, a media businessman who had previously worked for News Corporation, DirecTV, 21st Century Fox and Sky. Obviously, this takeover by Liberty Media represents the most significant shift in Formula One Group's management since Ecclestone took over in the late 1970s, and is illustrative of the expanding sport-media relationship that brings new opportunities around marketing, promotion, digital rights and social media.

Whereas Bernie Ecclestone has, arguably, been globally renowned as sport business owner, Liberty Media is anything but a household name, especially not outside the United States. Although it has grown into a major media conglomerate building significant stakes in the sports (Formula One, Atlanta Braves), media (Sirius XM, Pandora, Soundcloud) and entertainment (Live Nation, Ticketmaster) businesses and therefore acts as a perfect example of how these different businesses interact with each other, Liberty Media has remarkably received limited attention in sports and media industries literature (e.g. Evens & Donders, 2018). Birkinbine et al. (2016) provide a detailed profile of twenty-eight global media giants including the 'usual suspects', such as Disney, Time Warner and Facebook, discussing their global activities and the extent of political and cultural power they exert, but did not include Liberty in their overview. As such they failed to acknowledge the significant economic and cultural influence Liberty Media has through many of its subsidiaries in sports and entertainment. After all, Liberty Media is the number one and most valuable sports brand in the world, with an enterprise value of US$ 13 billion according to business magazine *Forbes* (Ozanion & Badenhausen, 2021).

The lack of critical attention for or analysis of Liberty Media is surprising and regrettable given its corporate footprint. Whereas the transformative impact *broadcasting* media conglomerates Fox, ESPN or Disney have had on the sports industry—commercialisation processes regularly referred to as 'Foxification' and 'Disneysation'—is widely acknowledged (e.g. Andrews, 2004; Vogan, 2015) and a rapidly growing number of studies have considered the impact of video streaming platforms on the exploitation of sports rights and fan experience (Hutchins et al., 2019; Tickell & Evens, 2021), the involvement of media *distribution infrastructure* companies in the sports industry, through rights acquisition or team/league ownership, has remained largely underexplored. Nevertheless, cable and telecommunications operators have been fueling the market for sports rights since mid-2000s, mainly with the intention to spur the launch of digital television and connectivity services, and to enhance their competitive position (Smith et al., 2016); although only a few of them are in the business of sports franchising (see Comcast's ownership of the Philadelphia Flyers and Philadelphia Wings). The latter also applies to Liberty Media, which has its roots in cable television and gradually managed to converge into a sports and entertainment group. Through its founder and chairman John Malone (cf. infra), Liberty Media continues to hold significant interests in the media distribution infrastructure market (e.g. Charter Communications and Liberty Global).

The goal of this chapter is twofold. First, this chapter focuses on the shifting ownership structure of Formula One since Ecclestone's entry and highlights its purchase by Liberty Media, potentially affording new insights into motorsport. By providing an exhaustive account of how control of the commercial and television rights enabled Ecclestone to build the Formula One empire, it puts the corporate integration between sports and media activities into a historical perspective. Second, the chapter examines the acquisition of Formula One by Liberty Media enabling the former cable television company to further develop into a sports and entertainment conglomerate. By unfolding the untold story of the diversified business activities of Liberty Media, it adds to the literature of media giants and expands the growing understanding of how sports and media businesses embrace digital media while protecting broadcast television revenues.

Ownership and Control in Media Sports

The symbiotic relationship between sport and the media has already been described and illustrated extensively. In economic terms, sport has been transformed from a spectator-based model relying on ticket income into a global business mainly driven by the exploitation of media rights, sponsorship and merchandising (Milne, 2016). Corporate interests began transforming the structure and nature of sports competitions, and format changes were imposed to maximise audience ratings and commercial revenues. Hence, the mediatisation of motorsport deeply affected the organisation of sport activity by repackaging the product as a mass-mediated 'spectacle' that serves the commercial interests of the many stakeholders involved: race promotors, racing teams, marketing agencies, sponsors and advertisers, clothing manufacturers, travel agencies and so on (Sturm, 2014). Because of the strategic importance of media rights, and the enormous economic benefits arising from the control of these rights, sport organisations and media businesses have developed a mutual beneficiary alliance. Even more, digital technology allows sport organisations to upgrade their position in the sport-media value chain and to explore digital services, such as F1 TV streaming platforms, as an untapped source of revenue. These developments lead to the blurring of boundaries between sport and media businesses.

The sport-media relationship is most visible through the corporate integration between sport and media conglomerates like Qatar Sports Investment controlling the Ligue 1 football club Paris Saint-Germain (PSG) and the global beIN Media network, News Corp Australia's ownership of NRL teams Brisbane Broncos and Melbourne Storm, or US cable operator Comcast owning the NHL's Philadelphia Flyers. Another prime example is Amaury Sport Organisation (ASO) that built a business empire in the organisation of grand sport events such as cycling race Tour de France and the Dakar rally, and that also owns the influential sport newspaper L'Equipe. In Europe, cases of media groups owning sport teams have always been fairly limited, not least in part because teams are significantly less profitable than in the United States. The acquisition of AC Milan by Berlusconi's Mediaset (in 1987) and Paris Saint-Germain by Canal+ (in 1991) have been the most successful examples of this trend towards ownership of sport organisations. In the early 2000s, a number of broadcasters, including BSkyB (Chelsea, Leeds United, Manchester City, Manchester United, Sunderland); NTL (Aston Villa, Newcastle, Leicester City); Granada/ITV (Arsenal, Liverpool) and Canal + (Paris Saint-Germain) sold their stakes in various football teams. For the most part, these were decisions driven by the commercial reality that owing a sport organisation was not particularly, if at all, profitable (cf. Hoehn & Lancefield, 2003).

In the case of some UK broadcasters, however, the decision was also prompted by regulatory intervention in arguably the most significant attempted takeover of a sports team by a broadcaster. In September 1998, pay-television broadcaster BSkyB began negotiations to buy Manchester United, which was, and still is, by some distance the Premier League's most commercially successful club (see Parkinson, 2018). BSkyB's bid was motivated by a desire to reduce the uncertainty surrounding the future collective selling of Premier League rights (Smith, 2007). The competition authority blocked the proposed merger on the grounds that, if not through the 'toehold effect', then from more privileged access to information about the rights auction through its ownership of the club, it would unfairly enhance the pay-television's operator's ability to secure Premier League rights, which would lead to reduced competition in the UK market for pay-television services (Harbord & Binmore, 2000). Had BSkyB acquired Manchester United, it would have benefited from an information asymmetry, or a 'toehold', in the bidding process for sports rights. Whilst the competition authority's report did not set a formal legal precedent, it made clear that the public interest would be best served by keeping the ownership of football teams and broadcasters separate. It was this decision, as much as the blocking of the merger itself, that led UK broadcasters to abandon any plans they may have had to own Premier League football teams (see also Evens et al., 2013).

The aggressive takeover move by BSkyB, at that time part of Murdoch's News Corporation empire, is illustrative for a business strategy Cashmore (2000, pp. 292-293) calls 'Murdochisation'. This refers to a 'process by which corporations primarily involved in mass media of communications appropriate and integrate into their own organisations sports clubs. In doing so, the media groups gain access to and control of the competitive activities of the clubs, which they can distribute through their networks'. According to Horne (2006), media mogul Rupert Murdoch has used sport as part of a global corporate expansion strategy more than any other media corporation. News Corporation has used exclusive sports rights as a strategic resource—or 'battering ram'—for developing television markets in the United States (Fox), the United Kingdom (BSkyB), Australia (Foxtel), Japan (JSkYB), New Zealand (Sky Television) and Southeast Asia (Star TV); a successful strategy that was widely imitated by almost all pay-television networks in the world, including ESPN (USA), Globo/SporTV (Brazil) and MultiChoice/SuperSport (South Africa). This, in turn, led to a spectacular increase in the commercial value of television sport rights. Aside from securing exclusive access to sports rights, News Corporation also purchased the iconic Los Angeles Dodgers baseball franchise (for a record payment of US$311 million), which was highly complementary with its ownership of regional sports networks in the Southeast area of the United States.

Whereas there previously was a clear distinction between the *sport* organisation and the *media* corporation, blurring boundaries between media and sport holdings have produced tensions 'between organisations that *hold* the sport product' and 'those organisations that *need* it in its transformation as media product' (cf. Wenner, 1998, p. 9; our emphasis). In their ongoing quest for new ways to commodify sports products, sports teams are benefitting from the opportunities that new media technology gives them to be transformed into media organisations themselves. Many of the world's largest franchises including FC Barcelona and the NBA started their branded television networks, mobile applications and/or streaming platforms to mostly paying fans, extracting additional commercial value and claiming their own voice in the globally expanding sports media market. This hybrid multimedia strategy not only allows franchises to generate more revenue, but also enables sport organisations to increase negotiation power for future rights discussions (Tickell & Evens, 2021). In an attempt to bring in the needed expertise in the production and marketing of their content, sport organisations are partnering with media corporations. This, in part, explains the involvement of

Red Bull Media House in the World Rally Championship (WRC) as well as Liberty Media's purchase of Formula One.

Formula One Group Ownership Structure

Shifting our focus to Formula One, since its inaugural season in 1950, the World Drivers' Championship, which became the FIA Formula One World Championship in 1981, was anything but a tightly structured organisation. It was only until Ecclestone took leadership and the notorious FISA-FOCA war was settled with signing the First Concorde Agreement that Formula One started on its path of becoming a multi-billion-dollar enterprise.

Ecclestone Takes Control

In the late 1960s Formula One was far from the streamlined show it is today. After the FIA's had approved direct sponsorship most teams waited for the Formula 1 Constructors Association (F1CA) to organise a joint effort to capitalise on the commercial turn. As such a response failed to materialise, Ecclestone, as owner of the Brabham team, together with part team owner of March, Max Mosley, suggested a different solution in 1972: they would take care of the commercial deals and logistics, in return for a fee from the remaining teams. Renamed the Formula One Constructors Association (FOCA) in 1974, it soon served the interests of the teams without factory backing (all teams except Ferrari, Renault and Alfa Romeo) and of which Ecclestone would become chief executive in 1978. The goal of this association was to professionalise the organisation of Formula One and to seize control of the sport's commercial rights. Unsurprisingly, FOCA clashed with the motorsport governing body FISA (Fédération Internationale du Sport Automobile, part of the FIA) and threatened to start a rivalling championship. The dispute was settled in 1981 when FOCA managed to secure the right to negotiate television contracts for the races and teams were able to secure a greater slice of the commercial revenues (television, prize money etc.). This First Concorde

Agreement ensured that all of the teams guaranteed to participate in all of the races and provided the necessary stability to the championship (Bose, 2012).

Collectively, the Concorde Agreement boosted the commercial development of Formula One. For example, it enabled Ecclestone to convince major European broadcasters to show all the races of the championship instead of negotiating the rights on an ad hoc basis. Whereas previously most races were being given highlights or not being broadcast at all, broadcasters started consistent live coverage with commentary after a three-year deal was signed with the European Broadcasting Union (EBU)—an alliance of ninety-two mainly public service broadcasters—in 1982. With guaranteed television exposure and increasing sponsorship rates, in addition to the fact that the EBU agreement was extended by five years in 1985, Ecclestone's influence was on the rise. He not only became vice-president of promotional affairs for the FISA, but was also appointed as administrator for the Second Concorde Agreement in 1987. Under this new contract with the FIA, 47% of the revenues were given to the teams, 30% to the FIA and 23% to Formula One Promotions and Administration (FOPA), a company established in 1987, owned and run by Ecclestone, who also ceased to be team owner that year.

The Third Concorde Agreement commenced in 1992 and was even more favourable to Ecclestone. In total, FOPA's revenues rose from US$12.5 million (in 1990) to US$127.6 million (in 1995). Sources suggest that in reality Ecclestone earned around 73% of the television revenues with the teams dividing the remaining 27%—it was believed that FIA lost US$65 million as a result of the deal (Bose, 2012). As such, FOPA's television income of US$341 million stood in sharp contrast with the US$37 million the FIA made between 1992 and 1995. Ecclestone justified his lion's share of commercial revenues by arguing that he, not the teams, was taking the financial risk (Bower, 2012). By the end of 1995, Ecclestone was granted by the FIA—with Max Mosley now as president—a controversial fifteen-year lease on the commercial rights. In effect, this allowed Ecclestone to be the sole broker of these rights, through his own company Formula One Administration Ltd (FOA) and not FOCA, the organisation representing the teams (Stuart, 2018). Not only was the new agreement criticised by the teams, who wanted a higher share of the revenues, the fifteen-year contract also came under the scrutiny of European competition law. Commissioner KarelVan Miert announced he would investigate whether the contract was a serious infringement of EU competition rules and to what extent FIA, FOA and International Sportsworld Communicators (ISC), another company controlled by Ecclestone that held the television rights to all FIA-governed motorsports, had abused their dominant position and restricted competition (for a detailed discussion, see Næss, 2020).

In anticipation of a possible flotation, Ecclestone transferred ownership of his companies to Petara Ltd, a Jersey company owned by his wife Slavica (Bower, 2012). In March 1997, Petara was renamed Formula One Management (FOM) and was transferred by Slavica to SLEC Holdings (presumably **Sl**avica **Ec**clestone), another jersey company. Then Slavica transferred the same SLEC shares to Bambino Holdings, a third Jersey company, that ultimately became the legal owner of Formula One. Bambino itself was owned by the Bambino Trust, of which Slavica and her two daughters (but not Bernie) were financial beneficiaries, and which was based in Liechtenstein (Næss, 2020). Ecclestone had now completely divested himself of any legal ownership of Formula One, resulting in the complex ownership structure depicted in Fig. 1.

Ecclestone Sells Shares

In October 1999, Morgan Greenfell Private Equity (MGPE) acquired 12.5% of SLEC for US$275 million. Only a few months later, in February 2000, Ecclestone reduced his stake in SLEC to 25% after Hellman and Friedman purchased a 37.5% stake in SLEC for US$725.5 million. Both transactions led to the formation of Speed Investments, which was sold to German media company EM.TV & Merchandising for US$1.65 billion in March 2000 (in exchange for shares). EM.TV also obtained an option to buy another 25% (BBC, 2000). However, EM.TV's role in Formula One was only short-lived as its corporate development was driven by the excessive optimism typical in the months and years before the dot.com bubble busted—by the time the company took over Formula One its share price had grown 3000% in three years' time. A

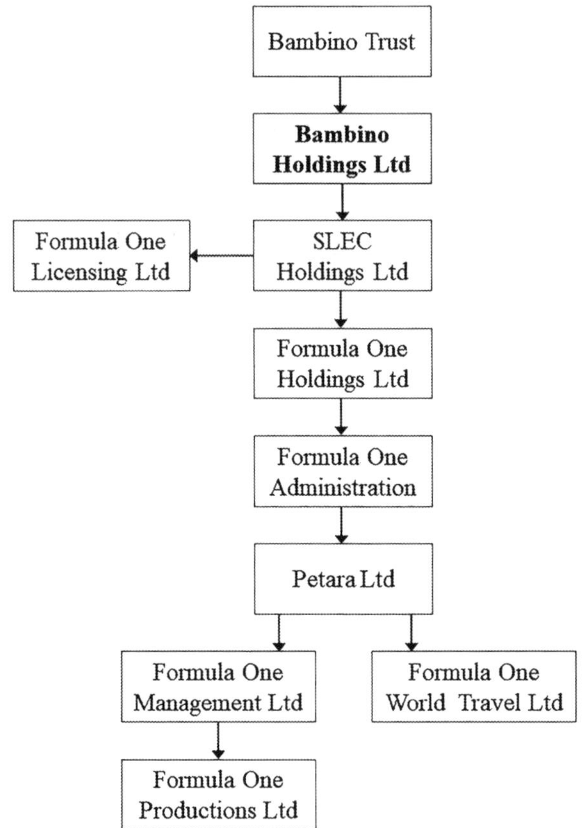

Fig. 1 Formula One ownership structure in 1997

rapidly declining share price (down from €120 to €1.49) and financial fraud committed by its controversial founder and chairman Thomas Haffa called for a divestiture in order to lower the company's huge debts and save it from bankruptcy.

In the end, German media magnate Leo Kirch paid out US$586 million to acquire a minority share of EM.TV and 50% control of Formula One (through SLEC). In February 2001, Kirch Gruppe also took up the option to obtain another 25% of Ecclestone's stakes for US$987.5 million—despite his minority share of 25% Ecclestone retained strategic control of Formula One through Bambino Holdings. To finance the transactions, Kirch Gruppe borrowed €1 billion from Bayerische Landesbank and €600 million both from JP Morgan and from Lehman Brothers. The teams were sceptical of the Kirch-Ecclestone deal as they feared that the German media company would broadcast the races via its pay-television service Premiere, which would lead to a decline in viewing audiences. Meanwhile, Ecclestone had closed a deal—referred to as the Umbrella Agreement—with the FIA for the rights to host the FIA Formula One World Championship for one hundred years after the current contract expired in 2011. In return for US$313.6 million, the 'Hundred Year-deal' enabled Ecclestone to become the exclusive owner of the commercial rights enabling him to collect lucrative hosting fees from circuits and sell television rights to broadcasters (Stuart, 2018).

However, by December 2001, it became clear that Kirch Gruppe was no longer solvent. Not only did Premiere have difficulties in adding subscribers, the company had been buying expensive FIFA World Cup rights as a result of which its debts had grown to US$5.5 billion. With Kirch going into administration, the banks took full control of the 75% share of SLEC: Bayerische Landesbank held 62.2% and JP Morgan and Lehman Brothers each 18.9%. Following Kirch's meltdown, the teams now had the chance to buy Kirch's 75% stake in Formula One. Despite their desire to control Formula One and transfer the revenues to the teams, they did not want to take the financial risk that came with it (Bower, 2012). Ecclestone, for his part, saw this as an opportunity to buy his share back for a bargain price and offered US$600 million. The banks waived away the bid and set a price tag of US$1.8 billion for SLEC's 75% share. Although the banks and Ecclestone became involved in a series of legal fights, the latter was protected by a complex company structure and relied on his usual conquer and divide strategy to retain control of Formula One (Næss, 2020). As it became clear that the banks were ready to sell, Ecclestone introduced private equity firm CVC Capital Partners as a possible buyer for Formula One that would also allow him to stay on as chief executive.

At the end of 2005, CVC Capital Partners announced that it had acquired a majority share (63.3%) in Delta Topco, a newly formed and Jersey based company that would be known as Formula One Group (FOG). While the banks' 75% stake was valued at $1.2 billion, CVC also purchased Ecclestone's remaining stake for US$450 million and spent some US$300 million on buying Formula One's corporate hospitality and trackside advertising divisions. The move brought all money-making divisions under one roof while the teams were offered a 50% share of the company's operating profit. In addition to CVC's majority share, Lehman Brothers (15.3%), Bambino Holdings (8.5%), Ecclestone himself (5.3%), JP Morgan (3%) and Churchill Capital (0.7%) stepped into the capital (see Fig. 2). In 2012, CVC lowered its stake when they sold 21.3% to financial groups BlackRock, Waddell & Reed and Norges Bank Investment Management for US$1.23 billion and a further 7.6% to Waddell & Reed for around US$500 million. With these deals, CVC managed to repay its initial investment in a company that in the meantime was valued at around $9.1 billion.

The anticipated exit of CVC Capital Partners came in September 2016, when Liberty Media agreed to acquire Formula One's parent company Delta Topco from a consortium of sellers led by CVC. In the first

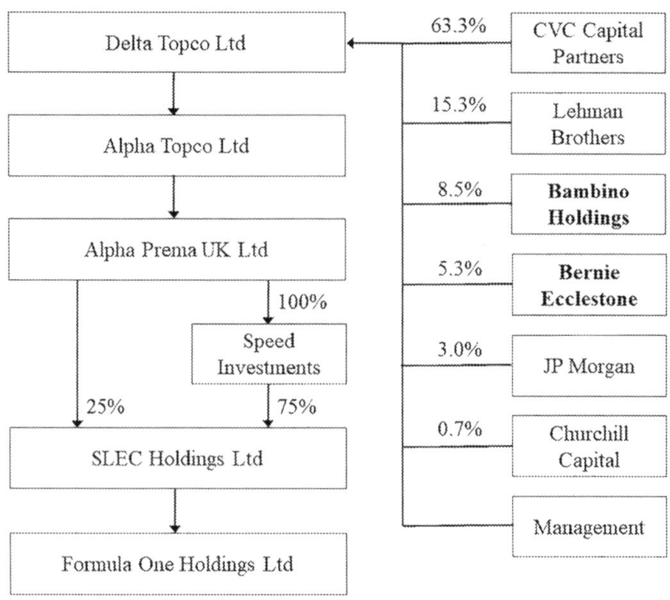

Fig. 2 Formula One ownership structure in 2005

instance, Liberty Media completed the acquisition of a 19.1% minority stake for US$746 million. After regulatory clearance, ownership was increased to 100%. The transaction price valued the company at US$8 billion and represented an equity value of US$4.4 billion. With the acquisition, Formula One was attributed to corporate division Liberty Media Group, which were to be renamed the Formula One Group. In this new Liberty Media division, the consortium of sellers led by CVC continues to own 64.7% of the Formula One Group's equity (with board representation) (Liberty Media Corporation, 2016). Although it was rumoured that Ecclestone, who remained on board as a shareholder through Bambino (5.4%) and himself (2.1%), would stay on as chief executive for three more years, he was replaced by Chase Carey in early 2017. Since January 2021, Stefano Domenicali has taken over as president and CEO of Formula One.

The fact that CVC has stayed on board as a controlling shareholder for about eleven years—the typical investment horizon of private equity firms is usually three to seven years—is illustrative of the money-making machine Ecclestone has turned Formula One into. CVC managed the sport through another round of Concorde Agreement negotiations, avoiding another threatened breakaway from FOTA and made an above-average return on their initial US$2 billion investment, and has, according to critics, pursued that ruthlessly in Formula One. It has been accused of 'raping the sport' with the intention 'to extract as much money from the sport as possible and put in as little as possible' (Richards, 2018). Under CVC's ownership, hosting fees for race promotors rose exponentially, with state-backed circuits in Abu Dhabi and Baku willing to pay a fortune (up to $60 million compared to the average of $30 million), and classic European tracks such as Monza and Silverstone being left with financial issues (Baldwin, 2018). Furthermore, live coverage moved from free-to-air broadcasters to pay-television channels in most countries during this time. Although this secured higher income from selling television rights, the worldwide audience fell from about 600 million to 352 million between 2008 and 2017, which had a negative effect on the sport's popularity, ticket sales and sponsorship income. Finally, limited use of and promotion on digital and social media led to difficulties to engage with younger audiences, while losing opportunities to monetise digital content.

Liberty Media Corporation

Whereas Formula One remains one of the most popular and spectacular sports franchises in the world, its major shareholder Liberty Media is arguably less well recognised. The conglomerate is owned and controlled by John Malone, an American businessman who unlike other media moguls, such as Rupert Murdoch or Michael Bloomberg, tends to shun the limelight. Together with HBO founder Charles Dolan, Malone is known as one of the pioneers of cable television. In the early 1970s, the 'cable cowboy' saw his chance to strengthen his grip over the US cable industry, build media distribution infrastructure and establish his name as a media mogul (Robichaux, 2005). From 1973 to 1996, Malone served as president and chief executive of cable television provider Tele-Communications (TCI), which had grown out of Western Microwave. Under the leadership of Malone, TCI had grown into the largest cable company by 1981. In 1987, TCI acquired a 12% stake in the highly indebted Turner Broadcasting System (TBS), which would be the beginning of a diversified portfolio of cable networks. Perfectly timed acquisitions would become one of the keystones of Malone's successful strategy. In 1991, TCI spun off what it considered to be its 'least valuable' assets into a new company called Liberty Media Group. However, Liberty Media was integrated again a few years later. In 1998, both companies announced the merger of premium network Encore and STARZ! into a new company owned by Liberty Media. The growth of digital cable television was beneficial to both cable network Encore Media and cable provider TCI.

Despite its commercial success, TCI continued to carry a high level of debt. In 1999, AT & T, the largest telephone service provider, bought TCI, the second largest cable operator, for US$48 billion (US$32 in stock and US$16 billion in debt). This marked the first major merger between phone and cable businesses since the 1996 Telecommunications Act had lifted cross-ownership between broadcasters, phone companies and cable television providers. A new subsidiary—AT & T Consumer Services—was created to combine AT & T's wireless and internet services with TCI's cable and high-speed internet activities; Liberty Media remained a separate stock. However, it did not take long before conflicts of interest between AT & T and Malone appeared, which eventually led to a split in 2001. Whereas AT & T seemed mainly interested in TCI's cable infrastructure, Malone believed that the utility of the infrastructure depended upon the quality of the content it carries (and not the other way around). Liberated from AT & T, Malone was seeking to advance Liberty's interests in other content providers. He sold his shares in FOX, but was able to purchase, among others, 18% of News Corporation, which made him the second largest owner within News Corporation (Davis, 1998).

In the following years, Liberty Media was in a continuous state of merging and divesting businesses. In 2005, for example, it spun off its international businesses into a separately traded company, Liberty Media International, that merged with UnitedGlobalCom to form Liberty Global. Through an expansionist acquisition strategy, Liberty Global has grown into the leading cable operator in the world, owning and operating cable networks in numerous European countries (such as Virgin Media, UPC and Ziggo) and having a large footprint in Latin America and the Caribbean. Whereas Liberty Global's strategy was mainly focused on fixed infrastructure, it has pursued deals with mobile operators including Vodafone, Base and Sunrise to be able to launch multi-play offerings (bundling pay-television with fixed and mobile services). Moreover, Liberty Global has invested heavily in content production and television broadcasting in recent years. It owns, among others, production independent All3Media (together with Discovery Communications) and has stakes in a portfolio of television broadcasters such as ITV (UK), UTV Ireland and SBS Belgium (Evens & Donders, 2018). Although Liberty Media has no direct stakes in Liberty Global, it is indirectly linked through its main shareholder and chairman Malone. Through a complex maze of ownership and affiliation, Malone is the spider in the web who has control of Liberty Media and its subsidiaries, but also holds shares in, among others, Discovery Communications (Discovery Channel, Animal Planet and Eurosport), Liberty Global and Lionsgate Entertainment. He, therefore, continues to occupy an influential position in the international media production and distribution landscape.

As it stands today (January 2021), Liberty Media owns interests in a broad range of sports, media and entertainment businesses structured around three divisions. The Sirius XM Group consists of Liberty Media's interests in radio satellite service Sirius XM, music services Pandora and Soundcloud, and concert promotor Live Nation Entertainment. Through the Braves Group, Liberty Media wholly owns the Atlanta Braves Major Baseball club, the Atlanta Braves' stadium and its associated real estate projects (between 1997 and 2000 Liberty Media also owned NBA team Denver Nuggets and NHL team Colorado Avalanche).The Formula One Group includes the abovementioned Formula One activities and a few minority investments. Furthermore, Liberty Media has interests in Liberty Broadband (Charter Communications, the world's third-largest pay-television), Qurate (a leading mobile ecommerce platform) and TripAdvisor. To conclude this overview, Table 1 shows the relative importance of each division to Liberty Media's total revenue and contribution to profit, while suggesting that Formula One accounts for about one fifth of the corporation's total revenue (with a declining share, however). COVID-19's dramatic impact on (motor)sport is further reflected in Formula One's decreased revenue and operational loss for 2020. Although renewed pay-television deals brought in extra revenue, income from race promotion fees, sponsorship and hospitality went down. In addition, costs went up as team payments increased partially due to one-time fees paid to teams upon signing the new Concorde Agreement.

Table 1 Liberty Media Financials (in US$ Million) (Liberty Media Corporation, 2020)

	2017	2018	2019
Revenue			
Sirius XM Group	71.4%	71.8%	75.7%
Braves Group	5.1%	5.5%	4.6%
Formula One Group	23.5%	22.7%	19.6%
Liberty Media Corporation (in US$ million)	7594	8040	10,292
Profit			
Sirius XM Group	111%	107%	105%
Braves Group	-8.2%	0.01%	-2.6%
Formula One Group	-2.8%	-7%	-2.4%
Liberty Media Corporation (in US$ million)	1394	1511	1470

Conclusions

This chapter provided a historical account of the ownership structure of Formula One from the entrance of Bernie Ecclestone in the early 1970s until its most recent acquisition by US media conglomerate Liberty Media in 2017. It presented Formula One as an illustration of the 'unholy alliance' between sport and the media, while sketching how the ownership of the commercial (and television) rights became a decisive factor for Ecclestone to establish his reign over the sport and to turn Formula One into a global success, both in cultural and in economic terms. For its part, Liberty Media is a prime example of a media distribution infrastructure company that became involved in the control of sports franchises. Although media activities, predominantly situated in the music industry, are still at the heart of the company and account for the lion share of revenues and profits, the acquisition of Formula One shows how boundaries between sport organisations and media businesses are fading. Many of the world's largest sports franchises started their branded television networks, mobile applications and/or streaming platforms to mostly paying fans, extracting additional commercial value and claiming their own voice in the globally expanding sports media market.

When Liberty Media bought Formula One in 2017, it made its strategy overtly clear: the goal was, first, to revitalise and grow the popularity of the championship and, second, to rejuvenate the declining and ageing fan basis of motorsports. Under Ecclestone's reign, Formula One had developed into a global media spectacle but was largely steeped in the traditional broadcasting model. Despite its commercial success, Formula One gradually lost connection with the rapidly digitalising media landscape and the transforming (sports) media consumption that came with it. In that respect, Liberty Media has been able to overturn declining audience figures and managed to improve viewership. In 2019, the global cumulative television audience went up to 1.9 billion, the highest since 2012, and the number of unique viewers grew to 471 million (from 352 million in 2017). In addition, digital platforms saw significant growth (+32.9% followers compared to 2018), particularly on Instagram and Twitter, which confirmed Formula One's status as the fastest growing of all major sports competitions in the world. Video views and impressions on Formula One's core digital platforms—the F1.com website and official F1 App—almost doubled (Carp, 2020). The live streaming platform F1 TV, however, remains problematic as its potential for full coverage is restricted by a series of existing, more lucrative deals with broadcasters and pay-television operators (Sylt, 2020).

The strategy of providing more digital content to grow the global fan basis and engage with younger audiences seems to have paid off. In 2017, Liberty Media launched the *eSports Series* to create more touchpoints for younger fans to engage with motorsports (Sturm, 2019). The 2019 edition drew an online audience of 5.8 million viewers; 79% of these were below the age of 35. In response to the COVID-19 pandemic, that caused the cancellation or postponement of several races, Formula One held a *Virtual Grand Prix Series* with the participation of current and former drivers, eSports Series drivers and celebrity guests (including top soccer players Sergio Aguero, Ciro Immobile and Thibaut Courtois). The eight races achieved more than 30 million views across television and digital platforms. 21.8 million views were reached on digital platforms alone including the official Formula One YouTube, Twitch and Facebook channels as well as Chinese platforms Weibo and Huya. In total, the virtual racing series achieved 695 million impressions on social media (Dixon, 2020). The documentary series *Formula 1: Drive to Survive* is another example of Formula One's efforts to expand the fan basis. This collaboration with Netflix provides an exclusive behind-the-scenes look at the championships and received critical acclaim. Whereas these initiatives may hardly be profitable in itself, especially not in the short term, they should be seen as long-term 'investments' to attract a new demographic to Formula One. Liberty Media is reaping the fruits of this digital strategy: 62% of the new fans in the last two years are under the age of 35 (Carp, 2020). The next, and more difficult, challenge is now to extract any financial value from these digital activities. Eventually, this greater fan engagement will need to be monetised by new revenue streams including media subscriptions. For Liberty Media, the strength of Formula One as a global brand may help to expand into new markets outside the United States and develop its position in the worldwide media and entertainment industry. In turn, Liberty Media's footprint and media expertise may help grow Formula One in the United States, where the sport is hardly popular.

Despite Formula One's history as a money-making machine, the championship has not been able to make any profit for Liberty Media since its purchase in 2017. Rumours of a possible sale—either in the form of a full exit or in the introduction of a new equity partner—have never been far away, but the looming financial impact of COVID-19 has certainly removed any short-term deal off the table: continued losses make any takeover very unattractive to prospective buyers. In the following years, when the COVID-19 dust has fallen and the financial damage is done, Liberty Media will need to continue Formula One's tradition of exploring new, potentially lucrative markets, in terms of both territories and services, without giving in to the rich tradition of the sports. The conglomerate will need to rely on its longstanding expertise with media and sports assets to respond to dramatic changes in the media landscape and create value-added services that enhance (and monetise) the fan experience. Possibly more importantly, however, will be its balancing act between chasing innovation and preserving traditions. Liberty Media was already criticised for its 'American approach' when it expressed its intention to increase exposure in the United States and to make more race meetings like Super Bowl weekends (see Richards, 2019). According to former Formula One CEO Carey, however, 'you have to be careful that you don't gimmick-up the sport, that you're recognising the importance of history and the importance of what has made this sport special, but not let that become a straightjacket that doesn't enable you to consider changes that may truly enhance the sport for fans' (Issatt, 2020). It would be naïve to believe that Liberty Media is not in the business to get a return on its investment, but it should, and probably will, not borrow from CVC's example, who merely considered Formula One a cash cow to be milked for profit. The main priority for Liberty Media is now to turn the sport into an attractive and competitive championship while expanding this story along digital platforms to create a compelling fan experience that transforms Formula One into a future-oriented and profitable event in the long term.

References

Andrews, D. (2004). Speaking the Universal 'language of entertainment': News Corporation, Culture and the Global Sport Media Economy. In D. Rowe (Ed.), *Critical Readings: Sport, Culture and the Media* (pp. 99–128). Open University Press.

Baldwin, A. (2018, 25 May). Baku wants a June race date and revised F1 contract, *Reuters*. Retrieved online from https://www.reuters.com/article/us-motor-f1-monaco-azerbaijan-idUSKCN1IQ1MH [15 April 2021].

BBC. (2000, 22 March). *Muppet owners buy Formula One*. Retrieved online from http://news.bbc.co.uk/2/hi/business/686941.stm [14 November 2020].

Birkinbine, B., Gómez, R., & Wasko, J. (Eds.). (2016). *Global Media Giants*. Routledge.

Bose, M. (2012). *The Spirit of the Game: How Sport Made the Modern World*. Constable.

Bower, T. (2012). *No Angel: The Secret Life of Bernie Ecclestone*. Faber & Faber.

Carp, S. (2020, 22 January). F1 global TV audience reaches 1.9bn but unique viewership falls 3.9%, *SportsPro Media*. Retrieved January 11, 2021, from https://www.sportspromedia.com/news/f1-tv-ratings-2019-digital-social-media-figures.

Cashmore, E. (2000). *Sports Culture: An A-Z Guide*. Routledge.

Davis, L. J. (1998). *Billionaire Shell Game: How Cable Baron John Malone and Assorted Corporate Titans Invented a Future Nobody Wanted*. Doubleday.

Dixon, E. (2020, 19 June). F1 Virtual Grands Prix pull in 30m total viewers, *SportsPro Media*. Retrieved January 11, 2021, from https://www.sportspromedia.com/news/f1-virtual-grands-prix-total-viewers-audience-tv-digital-social-esports.

Evens, T., & Donders, K. (2018). *Platform Power and Policy in Transforming Television Markets*. Palgrave Macmillan.

Evens, T., Iosifidis, P., & Smith, P. (2013). *The Political Economy of Television Sports Rights*. Palgrave Macmillan.

Harbord, D., & Binmore, K. (2000). Toeholds, Takeovers and Football. *European Competition Law Review, 21*(1), 1.

Hoehn, T., & Lancefield, D. (2003). Broadcasting and Sport. *Oxford Review of Economic Policy, 19*(4), 552–568.

Horne, J. (2006). *Sport in Consumer Culture*. Palgrave Macmillan.

Hutchins, B., Li, B., & Rowe, D. (2019). Over-the-top Sport: Live Streaming Services, Changing Coverage Rights Markets and the Growth of Media Sport Portals. *Media, Culture & Society, 41*(7), 975–994.

Issatt, B. (2020, 17 October). Carey tells F1 fans: History can't 'become a straightjacket' to change, *Insider Racing*. Retrieved January 31, 2021, from https://insideracing.com/formula-1/13235-carey-tells-f1-fans-history-can-t-become-a-straightjacket-to-change.

Liberty Media Corporation (2016). *Liberty Media Corporation Agrees to Acquire Formula One*. Retrieved online from https://ir.libertymedia.com/news-releases/news-release-details/liberty-media-corporation-agrees-acquire-formula-one [13 April 2021].

Liberty Media Corporation (2020). *2019 Annual Report*. Retrieved online from https://ir.libertymedia.com/static-files/f619ef5d-d7fb-4cdc-ba1c-5b2082cbb780 [11 November 2020].

Milne, M. (2016). *The Transformation of Television Sport. New Methods, New Rules*. Springer.

Næss, H. E. (2020). *A History of Organizational Change. The Case of Fédération Internationale de l'Automobile (FIA), 1946-2020*. Palgrave Macmillan.

Ozanion, M., & Badenhausen, K. (2021, 8 January). The World's Most Valuable Sports Empires 2021, *Forbes*. Retrieved online from https://www.forbes.com/sites/mikeozanian/2021/01/08/the-worlds-most-valuable-sports-empires-2021/ [13 April 2021].

Parkinson, G. (2018, 9 September). Rupert Murdoch's Manchester United? How BSkyB nearly bought the Red Devils, *FourFourTwo*. Retrieved online from https://www.fourfourtwo.com/features/rupert-murdochs-manchester-united-how-bskyb-nearly-bought-red-devils [14 April 2021].

Richards, G. (2018, 10 September). CVC ownership of F1 should serve as a warning to Premiership Rugby, *The Guardian*. Retrieved online from https://www.theguardian.com/sport/blog/2018/sep/10/cvc-ownership-f1-warning-premiership-rugby-union [10 November 2020].

Richards, G. (2019, 6 February). Liberty Media underestimated what it took on in F1, says Christian Horner, *The Guardian*. Retrieved online from https://www.theguardian.com/sport/2019/feb/06/christian-horner-liberty-media-underestimated-f1-red-bull [11 January 2021].

Robichaux, M. (2005). *Cable Cowboy: John Malone and the Rise of the Modern Cable Business*. John Wiley & Sons.

Smith, P. (2007). *The Politics of Television Policy: The Introduction of Digital Television in the UK*. Edwin Mellen.

Smith, P., Evens, T., & Iosifidis, P. (2016). The Next Big Match: Convergence, Competition and Sports Media Rights. *European Journal of Communication, 31*(5), 536–550.

Stuart, S. A. (2018). Bernie Ecclestone: Formula One's Entrepreneurial Ringmaster. In E. Bayle & P. Clastres (Eds.), *Global Sport Leaders: A Biographical Analysis of International Sport Management* (pp. 363–394). Palgrave Macmillan.

Sturm, D. (2014). A Glamorous and High-tech Global Spectacle of Speed: Formula One Motor Racing as Mediated, Global and Corporate Spectacle. In K. Dashper, T. Fletcher, & N. McCullough (Eds.), *Sports Events, Society and Culture* (pp. 68–82). Routledge.

Sturm, D. (2019). Not Your Average Sunday Driver: The Formula 1 Esports Series World Championship. In R. Rogers (Ed.), *Understanding Esports: An Introduction to the Global Phenomenon* (pp. 153–165). Lexington.

Sylt, C. (2020, 6 March). F1 live stream audience plummets to just 70,000 viewers per race after switch to Sky Sports, *The Independent*. Retrieved January 11, 2021, from https://www.independent.co.uk/sport/motor-racing/formula1/f1-live-stream-viewing-numbers-tv-sky-sports-formula-one-lewis-hamilton-a9380406.html.

Tickell, S., & Evens, T. (2021). Owned Streaming Platforms and Television Broadcast Deals: The Case of the World Rally Championship (WRC). *European Journal of International Management*. https://doi.org/10.1504/ejim.2021.10032581

Vogan, T. (2015). *ESPN: The Making of a Sports Media Empire*. University of Illinois Press.

Wenner, L. A. (1998). Playing the Media Sport Game. In L. A. Wenner (Ed.), *Media Sport* (pp. 3–13). Routledge.

Part VII

The Globalisation of Motor Racing

The Circus Comes to Town: Formula 1, Globalization, and the Uber-Sport Spectacle

Jacob J. Bustad and David L. Andrews

Introduction

Involving high-profile drivers, teams, and sponsors, and often times taking place at heavily mythologized racing circuits, from its inception in 1950 Formula One (F1) has advanced itself—if not always incontrovertibly—as the pinnacle of motorsport. While the origins of F1 are distinctly British and European (with regard to the preponderance of teams and tracks located in the UK and Western Europe), from its earliest stages of development the sport has nonetheless consistently incorporated, and developed, interconnections with other parts of the world. F1's longstanding international orientation includes the sport's first dominant driver—Juan Manuel Fangio, an Argentine who won five World Driver's

J. J. Bustad (✉)
Department of Kinesiology, Towson University, Towson, MD, USA
e-mail: jbustad@towson.edu

D. L. Andrews
Department of Kinesiology, University of Maryland, College Park, MD, USA
e-mail: dla@umd.edu

D. Sturm et al. (eds.), *The History and Politics of Motor Racing*, Global Culture and Sport Series, https://doi.org/10.1007/978-3-031-22825-4_23

Championships in the 1950s—as well as the early involvement of non-European host nations and cities, for example the South American Grand Prix (first held in Argentina in 1953), and the Moroccan Grand Prix (held in 1958). However, the global expansion of F1 over the past 60 years has been anything but a linear process: The globalization of the sport has encompassed different stages of extensity, intensity, and velocity, and arguably reached its apotheosis following the reformation of the sport in the 1970s and 1980s under the guidance of Bernie Ecclestone. In collectively restructuring team's commercial and media rights, Ecclestone provided a 'package' deal to host circuits, which furthered the development of F1 as a coherent, and indeed highly lucrative, corporate and media entity. As a result of such generative commercial reworkings, and whether accurate or otherwise, Ecclestone became widely perceived as an autocratic figure within the sport: he was 'Mr. Formula One' (*Economist*, 1997).

Ecclestone's commercially driven restructuring of F1 was concomitant with—indeed, it facilitated—the broadening global reach of the sport, principally through a concerted expansion in the number and location of host circuits, including the debut of the Brazilian Grand Prix in 1973, the Japanese Grand Prix in 1976, and the Australian Grand Prix in 1985. Latterly, this global expansion focused primarily on the addition of races in Asia (Malaysian Grand Prix in 1999, Chinese Grand Prix in 2004, Singapore Grand Prix in 2008, Korean Grand Prix in 2010, Indian Grand Prix in 2011, and Russian Grand Prix in 2014), as well as the Middle East (Bahrain Grand Prix in 2004, and Abu Dhabi Grand Prix in 2009). The sport's global status would be transformed again in January 2017, when Formula One announced the completion of an acquisition of F1 as an "iconic global motorsports business" by US-based Liberty Media Corporation, with a "transaction price" of $8.0 billion including debt of the previous owning group (Formula1.com, 2017). With Ecclestone moved to the largely symbolic position of Chairman Emeritus, this corporate takeover signaled a new phase of F1's corporate and sporting strategy under the leadership of American media executive Chris Carey as CEO, former ESPN executive Sean Bratches as managing director for commercial operations, and former Ferrari and Mercedes director Ross Brawn as managing director for motorsports (Baldwin, 2017).

From the outset, the Liberty's revamped F1 management team has pursued the goal of growing the popular and commercial appeal of the sport, through: a focus on the sport as a form of entertainment; finalizing media rights deals with various global partners for coverage of race weekends; and, developing F1 content for streaming providers. In particular, the streaming docuseries *Drive to Survive*—featuring "a mix of personal backstories, inter- and intra-team feuds and 300 km per hour racing"—has been cited as evidence of the ongoing 'Netflix-ization' of the competition, as F1 seeks out new audiences and markets across the globe (Pender, 2021). However, while social and streaming media have provided an opportunity for enhanced publicity and popularity, the mediatization of motorsport in regard to F1 is simultaneously reliant on a specific strategy regarding the geographic distribution of the races comprising the annual calendar of F1 championship. Thus, along with further developing the relationship between F1 and the media, the goals of the Liberty group at the time of the 2017 takeover also included aspirations to expand the geographical reach of F1, through staging additional races at previous or new venues and locations, thereby increasing the internationalization of the *circuit of circuits* that collectively make up the competition calendar. This strategy has been evident in the development of various races that are now part of the annual calendar, including the Qatar Grand Prix and Saudi Arabian Grand Prix both of which debuted in 2021, the inaugural Miami Grand Prix in 2022, and plans for potential future events in Las Vegas, United States and Panama City, Panama, as well as the return of the South African Grand Prix (last held in 1993).

In this chapter, we contribute to the study of the sociological significance of F1 as a global form of motorsport, through a discussion of the implications of the competition's growing international compendium of circuits, and corresponding host cities and nations. Importantly, rather than focus on a single circuit and event, we provide an analysis of the increasingly global reach of the championship's host venues. This speaks to Formula 1's positioning as an exemplar of the *uber-sport* (Andrews, 2019) model of elite global sport structure, delivery, and experience, the ubiquity of which should not negate the fact that each stop on the championship circus is, to some degree, rooted in the spaces, cultures, and populations of the hosting local. Our analysis therefore engages with the cumulative global experience that constitutes the peripatetic 'circus' of an F1 season, in examining the dimensions of *spectacle* and *sustainability* within contemporary elite motorsport. In particular, our analysis suggests that these themes are inextricably linked to the present and future of F1: The sport is predicated on a cosmopolitan variety of settings and international locations for its events, yet simultaneously (and increasingly) constrained by the unsustainability of F1's expansive carbon footprint (derived largely from the international travel/transportation demands that make the *circuit of circuits* possible).

F1, Globalization, and Uber-Sport

When analysing the impacts of globalization on sport and the sport industry, many studies have emphasized the relationship between the 'global' and 'local' as fundamental to how sport has developed within specific contexts. This focus on sport as part of a dynamic 'global–local nexus' (Morley & Robins, 1995) enabled scholars to examine how global actors and forces engaged with local societies and cultures, and to demonstrate how particular forms of sport were transformed through this global–local articulation. However, other scholars noted the limitations of this framework, in that such approaches are "too often structured by an assumed opposition between the local and the global, where the local is offered as the intellectual and political corrective of the global" (Grossberg, 1997, p. 8). In order to address these limitations, research on globalization and sport incorporated a conceptualization of 'glocalization' (Giulianotti & Robertson, 2004) that was premised on the interactions between the global and local, with these aspects situated on a continuum rather than placed as polar opposites. Subsequent studies then sought to further explicate the mutual constitution of the global and local in specific sporting contexts, providing empirical detail to particular types of sporting glocalization (see Andrews & Granger, 2007).

Within these discussions of globalization and/as glocalization, there was also a concern for the broader historical development of sport at the global level, and how international relations have contributed to the modern sport system. Following Van Bottenburg (2001), this history includes several distinct yet interrelated phases, in which pre-modern forms of sport were in turn consolidated by economic, social, and military elites into a relatively concise economy of rationalized and standardized team and individual sport forms. More importantly for this analysis, while Van Bottenburg (2001) theorized that Britain (in the nineteenth century) and the United States (in the twentieth century) had been the dominant forces of cultural influence on the previous development of sport around the world, other scholars noted that the twenty-first century prefigured a more open and undecided era in which other nations might gain and wield influence within the global sport industry. As Maguire (2000) explains, the more recent phases of the development of global sport have therefore been "characterized by the rise of non-Western nations to sporting prominence, and, sometimes, to pre-eminence" (p. 366). In analysing this reorientation of sporting importance and influence away from the previous dominance of Western nations, Rumford (2007) describes this transformation as the 'post-Westernization' of sport, and specifically the impact of this process on the structure and governance of cricket. In this analysis, the contemporary form of cricket can be characterized as post-Western in regard to three developments: (1) the relocation of the International Cricket Council, as the sport's governing body, from London to Dubai; (2) the restructuring of gameplay to allow for both traditional test match cricket, as well as shortened one-day (ODI and T20) forms of the game; and (3) cricket's relationship to the growing Indian middle-class population, placing cricket's economic centre of gravity firmly within the subcontinent (Horne, 2010). Gupta (2009) contributes to the study of contemporary cricket, while also broadening the framework of global sport's post-Westernization by drawing attention to the role of non-Western nations in hosting sport mega-events, including the 2008 Beijing Olympics (see also Dowse & Fletcher, 2018), and in regard to foreign ownership, including the 2008 purchase of Manchester City by the Abu Dhabi sovereign wealth fund (Gupta, 2009, p. 1787). Taken collectively, these developments might signal a larger shift in the locus of control and popularity for major global sports, as "non-Western nations have gone from being the recipients of sporting dictates to actual shapers of decision making in various games" (Gupta, 2009, p. 1788).

When assessing the more recent evolution of Formula 1, it may be possible to connect to some aspects of the broader post-Westernization of sport, in particular through the inclusion of an increasing number of host cities and tracks from Asia and the Middle East (and as discussed in other chapters of this volume). However, within this chapter we offer an alternative framework for understanding the present and future development of F1, in regard to a revised approach for examining the relationship between globalization, sport, and spectacles via the concept of 'uber-sport'.

In our framework, uber-sport encompasses the reformation of elite sport and physical culture through the late capitalist processes of corporatization (institutional and management reorganization designed to realize profit-driven structures and logics); commercialization (sport brand diversification and non-sport brand promotion across multiple sectors); spectacularization (entertainment-focused delivery of popular sport spectacles, realized through a combination of structural reformation and cross-platform mass mediation); celebritization (sporting contests constructed around, and a site for the embellishment of, specific public persona); and, digitalization (digital technologies and content increasingly integrated into sport delivery and experience). Uber-sport therefore describes a highly rationalized, diversified, yet culturally integrated popular sport phenomenon that is primarily designed to generate mass audiences and consumer markets, and thereby popularity and profit, across an array of culturally and economically multiplying streams (products, bodies, services, and spaces). As Andrews (2021) explains, uber-sport entails that:

> The shape of the ball, the nature of the physical contest, cast of characters on display, or litany of corporate sponsors differ even if the mode, means, and relations of uber-sport production remain unerringly similar. … Although not a word used in common parlance, uber-sport thus represents a condition of formulated ubiety: a state of being or existence derived from location in a given time or space, a whereness. (p. 76)

In this analysis, uber-sport affords the possibility of a different approach to studying the relationship between sport and globalization, and in particular the type of elite, ultra-commercialized, media-driven sport of which Formula 1 serves as an example *par excellence*. This is in part due to the 'rhizomatic' nature of uber-sport as a "chaosmosis, a chaotic osmosis of varied and variable connections rather than an ordered cosmos" (Conley, 2009, p. 33), instead of macro-to-micro, top-down hierarchies of power and influence. As rhizome, uber-sport is a flattened multiplicity of connections between heterogenous component elements, including athletes, coaches, animals, teams/franchises, performances events (games/matches/contests), media broadcasts and content, products, services, spectators, viewers, consumers, sponsors, retail spaces, natural and/or built environments, leagues, competitions, tournaments, multi-sport events organizations, and governing bodies. The rhizomatic relations that characterize uber-sport formations (such as Formula 1) mean each of these elements has the possibility of being connected in affecting ways, yet no connection is guaranteed, nor does any element possess some pre-ordained affecting ascendancy or descendancy within a hierarchal structure. Moreover, the rhizomatic approach of uber-sport means that the 'spectacle' of the performance event and its hypermediated representation—in the context of Formula 1, a specific Grand Prix weekend—is not considered the integrative core of uber-sport, from which ancillary elements are derived. Instead, the spectacle of a singular Grand Prix might be analysed as part of the larger assemblage of the sport's seasonal structure and experience, in which the collective races, event, and corresponding host cities are all considered as interrelated aspects of a broader sociological object: the *circuit of circuits* that comprises the global scale and scope of contemporary F1.

F1 as Uber-Sport Spectacle

More recent sociological and cultural studies of Formula 1 have often engaged with the individuated 'spectacle' events of the sport, in the form of Grand Prix races hosted by specific cities and nations. This approach includes research on the impact of hosting a Formula 1 Grand Prix in regard to tourism and event management (see Dávid et al., 2018; Choe et al., 2017; Kim et al., 2017; Liu & Gratton, 2010; Watanabe et al., 2018), as well as studies focused on the relationship between F1 Grand

Prix events, urbanization, and the particular social, political, and economic forces involved in the development and hosting of a race weekend (see Fairley et al., 2011; Gezici & Er, 2014; Gogishvili, 2018; Lefebvre & Roult, 2011; Yu et al., 2018).

In contrast, other scholars have sought to examine the social meanings and effects that are involved in the development and distribution of Formula 1 as a more comprehensive mediated, global consumer experience. Silk and Manley (2012) include the Singapore Grand Prix in their discussion of the linkages between urban spaces and sport events, asserting that "the event offered unique signifiers for global consumption—highly visible (or perhaps hyperreal) images of the material landscape" (p. 465). For Sturm (2014), analysing the sport across the various races that make up an annual season allows for a recognition of how F1 "projects a glamorous and high-tech global spectacle of speed that evokes elitism, the exotic and an aura of expensive sophistication, often directly associated with its technologies, localities or assumed luxurious jet- set lifestyle" (p. 80). In this analysis, the representation and experience of F1 as an "overarching spectacle" is premised on three elements, including (1) the dissemination of the sport as an "accessible and engaging" spectacle via global media, (2) the relationship between the mediated spectacle and specific locations and their corresponding cultural signs and symbols, in order to emphasize the localized "scale and grandeur" of each Grand Prix and (3) the development and deployment of transnational sponsorships, which "through their prominently displayed logos, brand and commodify Formula 1 cars, drivers and fans as a consumptive corporate spectacle" (p. 80).

Lowes (2018) then connects this focus on the more general and collective spectacle of F1 with the 'place-marketing' strategies of host cities and nations, in regard to a "merging of image, spectacle, sport, and capitalism" (p. 215). In discussing the interactions between imagery and urban experience, Lowes' analysis asserts that the collective spectacle of F1 includes "distinctly promotional performances of local cosmopolitanism intended for both domestic and global audiences. … F1's glamorous global spectacle revolves around corporations, branding, and leveraging F1's symbolic cultural capital" (p. 204). In doing so, the representation and experience of the F1 season draws on the cultural signs and symbols of specific host cities and circuits, while always reinterpreting these meanings within the larger framework of the spectacle. As Sturm (2017) explains in regard to the Monaco Grand Prix, this event provides an opportunity to communicate "elitist, aspirational motifs of Formula 1 to its already global audience":

> through an assemblage of iconic images and associated symbols that reiterate its status, privilege, luxury and conspicuous consumption … Monaco's illusions of European glamour dovetail seamlessly with Formula One's prestigious global image and maintain its 'megamediasport' event status. (p. 183)

In the uber-sport framework, this analysis of F1's annual calendar as global, mediated, consumer-oriented, and involving forms of urban cosmopolitanism signal how the individual spectacle of a specific Grand Prix might be decentered, in order to better understand the more comprehensive experience of the sport and its aggregated cultural meaning and significance. More specifically, conceptualizing F1 as the *circuit of circuits* can help emphasize how uber-sport exists as 'deterritorialized' (Andrews, 2019), in that the broader F1 spectacle is no longer dependent on specific and local cultural contexts from which it derives significance: F1 has come to represent a spatial differentiated spectacle in general terms, but not one anchored or reliant upon specific, unchangeable, sources of spatial difference. The transnational scale and scope of F1 entails an uber-sport spectacle that can be produced and presented both effectively and affectively nearly anywhere around the world. Thus, as Andrews (2021) explains, such uber-sport formations are "able to exist and operate within disparate societal setting, be they authoritarian, state socialist, or neoliberal capitalist"—this characteristic is definitively evident within the sport's annual calendar, as it features Grand Prix races in all of these various socio-political contexts. As such, the deterritorialized nature of the F1 uber-sport spectacle lends itself to the logic and strategy of global expansion that has served as a primary goal for the sport in its most recent era, in particular following the Liberty takeover in 2017. While the seasonal number of races had steadily increased during the sport's development into the 2000s, this figure had remained between 18–20 races per year during the beginning of the hybrid turbo era of the 2010s. When Liberty assumed control of the sport, the organization proclaimed the goal of expanding the schedule to 25 races, with the prospect of locating new host cities and nations as well as possibly returning to previous race sites (Sloan, 2021).

Liberty's expansion strategy has included the aforementioned debut of the Qatar Grand Prix and Saudi Arabian Grand Prix, as well as the return to venues in France (Circuit Paul Ricard) in 2018, the Netherlands (Circuit Zandvoort) for the 2021 season, and the debut of the Miami Grand Prix in 2022. Additionally, race cancellations due to COVID restrictions resulted in the championship returning to Portgual (Alagarve International Circuit) from 2020, Turkey (Intercity Istanbul Park Circuit) in 2020 and 2021, and Imola, Italy (Emilia-Romagna Grand Prix) 2021 through 2025. In announcing the ten-year deal for the Miami race, F1's chief executive Stefano Domenicali emphasized the agreement as indicative of the sport's mission to continue and increase fans and sponsors in areas that serve as a "key growth market", as demonstrated by the addition of a second race in the USA (Matar, 2021). More broadly, Liberty's future planning envisions approximately a third of races in Europe, with 'heritage' races (including the Monaco, Silverstone, Spa-Francorchamps, and Monza circuits) essentially protected within the schedule—the remainder of the schedule would provide flexibility allowing for potential expansion to various other cities and nations with FIA Grade 1 approved circuits, with the very real and potentially lucrative possibility of 'bidding wars' between interested sites (Sloan, 2021).

Beyond the possible expansion to new locations, however, the deterritorialized uber-sport spectacle of F1 also entails a particular relationship between the global vision and strategy of Liberty and the local intermediaries associated with the various race locations. In the uber-sport era, this relationship is increasingly characterized through an incorporation of the local host culture, including national and urban signs, symbols, and other cultural expressions such as music, food, and festivities that correspond with the host nation and/or city. However, while these aspects of the local culture may be central to the production of urban cosmopolitanism (Lowes, 2018) as a defining feature of the contemporary F1 spectacle experience, the actual interaction or engagement with the local is nonetheless limited. Following Dirlik (1996, p. 34), within F1 "[t]he recognition of the local ... does not mean any serious recognition of the local, but is intended to recognize the features of the local so as to incorporate localities into the imperatives of the global". Within the context of the contemporary F1 *circuit of circuits*, the local is a discernible yet largely superficial and formulaic allusion to the metropolitan, regional, and/or national context in which the race is taking place (see Sturm, 2014). The extent of this conjoined spatial and symbolic localization is, to some degree, determined by the longevity, and thus accumulated F1 provenance, of the circuit within the sport. The heritage circuits (Monaco, Silverstone, Spa-Francorchamps, and Monza etc.) have—over the course of their storied histories within the sport—developed a spatial familiarity associated, and in many cases resonant of their place and culture of location. Equally, urban or downtown-located street circuits provide the spatial and symbolic parameters for races, imbuing them with a tangible sense of the local (see Friedman & Wallace, this volume).

However, our specific interests lie in the proliferation of relatively recent circuits built as part of F1's expansion in the 2000s. These facilities were often built for the express purpose of attracting and hosting F1 races as the pinnacle of their motorsport offerings, and included: the Bahrain International Circuit (Bahrain GP, Sakhir GP); Buddh International Circuit (Indian GP); Circuit of the Americas (United States GP); Jeddah Corniche Circuit (Saudi Arabia GP); Korea International Circuit (Korean GP); Intercity Istanbul Park (Turkish GP); Sepang International Circuit (Malaysian GP); Shanghai International Circuit (Chinese GP), and Circuit de la Comunitat Valenciana Ricardo Tormo (European GP). Hermann Tilke, a German racing driver turned engineer, was the lead architect responsible for the design many of these circuits (and the redevelopment of numerous established circuits), and is widely acknowledged to have initiated a new era of motor racing with his designs. However, Tilke is not without his critiques, with some accusing him of "penning boring tracks and, even worse, of butchering legendary ones" (Briggs, 2009). Despite the homogenizing constraints imposed by the voluminous FIA track regulations and guidelines, criticisms targeted at Tilke's circuits tend to focus on their spatial/design similarity, much of which derives from his recurrent use of extended run-off areas. Intended primarily to improve driver safety purposes, for some these run-off areas provide drivers more room to mitigate their mistakes, thus leading to less jeopardy and excitement in races. In broader spatial terms, Tilke's formulaic and widely replicated circuit designs could also be considered boring, in that he has effectively and efficiently reduced F1 circuits to being, in Augé's (2009) terms, spectacular "non-places". According to Augé (2009), "non-places" are the spatial expressions of supermodernity—such as hotel rooms, shopping malls, airports, and motorways—whose generic aesthetic and highly replicated constituent elements render them largely disassociated from their local surroundings, and little more than transient points of engagement for largely anonymous populations. Despite Tilke's assertion that much of his design effort goes "into conceiving dramatic architecture that reflects the host country, like Sepang's lotus-leaf grandstands in Malaysia" (Briggs, 2009), recent F1 circuits can be considered "non-places" (Augé's, 2009): They possess key constituent elements that spectators (even if they are not party to them) have come to expect of the F1 spectacle, such as architecturally striking main grandstands, luxury spaces and amenities, entertainment zones, and phantasmagorically branded commercial environments. For instance, each of various tracks is adorned with hoardings and banners from the same corporate sponsors (in recent years, including Heineken, Rolex, Liqui-Moly, Aramco, and DHL), such that while curves, straights, and/or chicanes may be given unique names, spatially (Tilke's design orthodoxies) and symbolically (corporate sponsors' brand prevalence) the circuits appear to be conforming ever-more closely to some F1 prescribed norm (see Sturm, 2014). This is equally apparent in the multiple-branded pop-up team garages, whose component elements are transported from race to race, such that the "paddock" becomes yet another consistent (if temporary) element of the F1 race circuit. As such, recently constructed and renovated circuits tend to exude a somewhat discomforting sameness and familiarity, as if they occupy some transnational F1-scape linking them more to the organizational structure and sensibilities of the sport, than to any meaningful specificities of the local host culture (see Sturm, 2014). In this manner, F1 circuits are the spatial expressions, and perhaps the epitome, of ubersport's condition of being ubiquitous and ubietous. The global *circuit of circuits* ensures F1 exists spatially and symbolically "in multiple settings around the globe", yet their ubiety, or state of "existence derived from location in a given time or space", is conclusively formulated and indeed formulaic (Andrews, 2019, p. 12).

Within contemporary F1 circuits, any allusion to the local—as in Sepang's lotus leaf grandstands—is little more than an aesthetic flourish: They are superficial constructed expressions of what is a caricatured localness. Devoid of any distinctive localness, or what Ritzer would call somethingness, these F1 circuits provide a spatial example of a sporting nothingness in that they are "centrally conceived and controlled and relatively devoid of distinctive content" (Ritzer & Ryan, 2003, p. 51). Furthermore, if F1 circuits could be considered a form of spectacular, locally indistinct nothingness for race attendees, this is even more the case for global viewing audiences tuning in to the F1 spectacle. Since 2007, races have been broadcast via a standardized world feed, providing generic coverage for the global television and internet audience, for whom any allusion to the local is offered by national marketed-oriented "client" broadcasters who are likely to frame any reference to the host race location and/or culture according to the perceived values and expectations of the "client" viewing market (Silk, 2001). In this manner, and from the vantage point of the external viewing audience (as opposed to that of the host city organizers), F1 offers a televised "space of global cosmopolitan imagery" (Lowes, 2018, p. 204), which distinguishes it from more narrowly place-bound uber-sport expressions, such as the National Basketball Association, Indian Premier League, or Australian Football League, each of which derives a sense of its brand identity from its specific (as opposed to compound) ubiety (sense of whereness). Nonetheless, rather than any meaningful material or symbolic articulations of specific locals, the F1 brand's distinguishing transnational cosmopolitanism derives from the accumulation of superficial representations of its socio-spatially distinct component parts (or races).

F1, Spectacle, and Sustainability

Conceptualizing F1 as an example of uber-sport—a corporatized, commercialized, spectacularized, celebritized, and digitalized phenomenon—enables an analysis of the social, and cultural implications of the sport's *circuit of circuits*. Additionally, the uber-sport model's economic imperatives—particularly its overriding rationally driven efficiencies and expansionist logics—explain how the global cosmopolitanism of the F1 circus justifies the weighty cumulative ecological footprint of the sport's annual race calendar. In this mode, the 'itinerant circus' (GPblog.com, 2022) of F1 can be examined in relation to environmental sustainability and the current and future development of the competition. In particular, we focus on the tension between the combined travel and transport involved in producing multiple events around the globe, and ongoing discussions and policies aimed toward making the sport more sustainable. Our analysis emphasizes that this tension is the underlying fault line for the prospects of elite motorsport (Dingle, 2009), in that the capacity to provide a global, deterritorialized spectacle is both a primary factor in the popularity and influence of F1, while also serving as the most probable threat to the future existence of the sport in its current form.

This does not mean that Liberty and F1 have not sought to address environmental issues within their governance—on the contrary, the sport has moved over the last decade to develop and promote different policies and practices related to the ecological impact of its operations. Indeed, the recognition of sustainability as a key aspect of motorsport development was evident in the 2009 FIA report stating the competition's intention to support and promote research including:

> information on the best environmental procedures, practices, and technologies that can be applied to motorsport. … This will cover areas such as vehicle design and technology, infrastructure management, emissions monitoring and control, offsetting procedures, energy optimization and storage, and preservation of the natural environment … [as well as] training of officials, circuit and race personnel in environmental procedures and practices … [and] encouraging environmental education and awareness of

participants, officials and members of the public at international motor sport events. (as cited in Dingle, 2009)

In the more recent planning for the 2021 season, F1 went further in announcing specific sustainability goals, including: (1) the development of future engine power via sustainable fuels, including the aim of a 100% sustainably fueled hybrid engine by 2025; (2) the implementation of policies and practices toward becoming zero net carbon as an organization by 2030; (3) governance of operations and events toward zero waste on and off the track, and a reduction of the carbon footprint of all operations; and (4) efforts to position sport to "leave a lasting positive impact" (F1, 2021). As part of the zero net carbon goal, F1 has stated particular 'On the Move' sustainability initiatives related to the travel and transport necessary to enable a global tour of speed. The proposed measures include:

- Maximize logistics and travel efficiency through process and volume optimization, using the least CO2 intensive transport available.
- Accelerated plans to introduce a more sustainable way of broadcasting our races, known as remote production. This has resulted in a 34% reduction in technical cargo and a 36% reduction in travelling staff sent to every race.
- Adopting an innovative honeycomb structure for the walls of our travelling broadcast centre has reduced the total weight and related GHG emissions for filming our races globally.
- Designing innovative 'flexible' ULD shipping containers—allowing F1 to adopt more fuel-efficient means of transport such as rail and sea freight. This will also enable a move away from 747 to newer 777 cargo planes (F1, 2021).

As with other commercially impelled manifestations of uber-sport—and as Miller (2016) explains—the commitment to sustainability with elite motorsport can be a "complex field" given the competing priorities involved in the development and performance of F1 cars, as "the sport's advanced engineering seeks ever-greater fuel efficiency, which is in turn passed on to everyday business and domestic motoring, supposedly diminishing the latter's carbon footprints" (p. 720). Yet while the proposed forms of sustainability that are being incorporated into F1 have the potential to address the ecological impact of the cars, teams, and individual Grand Prix events, there remains an imbalance in regard to the sport's larger environmental effects via international travel by administrators, sponsors, media, drivers, and fans. A sustainability report released by F1 following the 2018 season indicated that 27.7% of the CO2 emissions from that season came from business travel, while another approximately 45% of the season's CO2 emissions came from transportation of teams and equipment, with the resulting 256,551 tons of CO2 emissions equating 55,795 passenger vehicles being driven for one year (Harding, 2021). In comparison, emissions from the sources that are most directly addressed by existing F1 sustainability policies—cars and individual events—are marginal. For example, the same 2018 report indicated that 'power unit emissions', including the operation of cars from all ten teams during testing, practices, and races, totaled just 0.7% of the annual emissions; meanwhile 'event operations', including circuit energy use, broadcasting, and hospitality, totaled 7.3% (O'Shea et al., 2020).

These figures underscore the imbalance between the sport's proposed sustainability initiatives and travel and transport as the primary causes of un-sustainability, leading to questions about how—or whether—F1 will continue to exist. In this analysis, the transnational scale and scope of the sport's *circuit of circuits* therefore entails a potentially unavoidable conflict between the logic and strategy of growth and expansion, specifically in regard to additional races at an ever-growing collection of host cities and nations, and the stated priorities of making F1 sustainable and possible in the future. Following Miller (2016), this problem is compounded through the most direct form of support for teams and drivers, as "sponsors like the fact that [F1] events are global and its season eternal…Formula 1 is akin to an Olympics or a World Cup where the key events occur annually, year round, and across the world, rather than every four years, for a month, in one region" (p. 721). Moreover, the planned increases to the race calendar—including a record 23 races scheduled for 2022—often demonstrate the tensions between corporate and consumer growth and environmental sustainability in particular cities and markets. As Harding (2021) notes, climate change has been identified as a primary factor in the future development of multiple existing host cities, while the inclusion of Miami as the most recent addition to the annual calendar means that the sport has committed to a ten-year deal for a circuit that will stand just 10 feet above sea level, in a city in which sea levels are expected to continue to rise over the same period. Within the context of F1 as uber-sport spectacle, such concerns might lead us to also question the "somewhat perverse" nature of F1 in effectively contributing to climate change by traveling to and hosting events in parts of the world that are at the forefront of those changes (Harding, 2021).

Conclusion

This chapter has analysed Formula 1 as not only a pre-eminent form of elite motorsport, but also as a mediated and commercialized uber-sport spectacle centred less on any individual race or event, and more on the presentation of a truly global/transnational sporting experience constituted by a season of races spread across the globe. Moreover, this version of the F1 spectacle is underpinned by a strategy and logic of growth, specifically regarding the expectation of perpetual increases in particular metrics (revenues, sponsorships, viewers, etc.): a market growth logic that necessitates hosting races at the most commercially expeditious host locations at any given moment. The most recent figures announced by F1 demonstrate the (commercially) positive outcomes of this strategy over recent seasons, as an announcement in February 2022 stated that "Our fans reacted to the [2021] season, new formats, and new venues, very positively and Formula 1 has seen growth in our TV audiences and on our digital platforms", (F1.com, 2022) including:

- Followers (across Facebook, Twitter, Instagram, YouTube, Tiktok, Snapchat, Twitch and Chinese social platforms) were up 40% to 49.1m, video views increased 50% to 7bn and total engagement up 74% to 1.5bn.
- Total video views across F1.com, the F1 app and social media were up 44% vs 2020 to 7.04bn, unique users were up +63% to 113m and page views were up +23% to 1.6bn.

- Digital share of total minutes consumed (across broadcast and digital) has grown from 10% in 2020 to 16% in 2021.

Digital viewership and social media engagement provide measures of the relative success of Liberty's directives for transforming elite motorsport, described in the organization's corporate strategy as the "repositioning of F1 into an Entertainment and Media company with our first ever Marketing, Digital, Strategy and Research divisions, [and] expanded teams managing our key revenue streams" (F1, 2020). However, our analysis emphasizes that these forms of growth all depend on the global scale and scope of the sport's annual season, and the continued potential for expansion in terms of host cities and nations, as well as the number of total races. Again, this is included in the corporate strategy outlined by Liberty, specifically through the goal of developing a "geographically diverse race calendar, maintaining heritage circuits and adding new races in iconic locations and destinations" (F1, 2020).

This approach to global expansion means that while particular host cities can be discussed as part of the media and social media content surrounding the sport, the more important factor is the constant possibility of additional races that could accommodate a larger number of host locations. Indeed, the existence of other potential circuits has also provided valuable flexibility in regard to the race calendar during periods of disruption, including during the COVID pandemic (races were rescheduled or changed to different or new locations), and in response to Russia's invasion of Ukraine in February 2022 (Russian Grand Prix cancelled and changed to a different location). The ability to effectively pivot to a different global destination reflects the broader global strategy of the sport, as F1 CEO Stefano Domenicali explained in January 2022:

> It's true that there is a big interest for new places—or old places!—to be part of our calendar…I think that with no doubt, without any kind of limitation that is correct to keep, there could be easily over 30 venues that we could do [a deal with] tomorrow, but we cannot go in this direction. (Mitchell, 2022)

These comments underscore the global scale and scope of the F1 season as an uber-sport spectacle, while also highlighting sustainability as the key issue involved in the current and future development of the sport. As Sturm (2018) notes, "motorsport rarely offers a model of sustainability":

> Economically it is expensive, socially it is often exclusive and privileges the elite, while politically it is most often used as symbolic tool for ambitious nations and corporations to self-brand and self-promote. Motorsport's environmental reputation is also problematic: burning fossil fuels, leaving large global carbon footprints and the wanton waste of resources including its impacts on green spaces and locations. (Sturm, 2018, p. 145)

As discussed in this chapter, F1 has been actively seeking to develop and implement initiatives aimed at addressing issues of sustainability across the sport, including the operations of teams, events, and the regulation of hybrid technologies in the cars themselves. Yet these measures do less in engaging with the overwhelming source of the majority of carbon emissions—and therefore ecological impact—of an annual season of racing across countries and continents. F1 as a contemporary sporting spectacle therefore faces a crossroads involving the future direction of elite motorsport, in that it can continue to emphasize and potentially expand the geographic reach and temporal duration of the season, but it cannot do so while actively acknowledging and addressing the most unsustainable aspect of the sport in terms of travel and transport to a variety of locations around the world. Our analysis therefore demonstrates that conceptualizing F1 as uber-sport provides a means for engaging with the cultural meanings and environmental effects of the seasonal structure and experience of the sport, and the inescapable tensions between these elements within motorsport more generally. As a traveling circus strategically roaming the globe, F1 as a *circuit of circuits* draws attention to the shifting compendium of races and host cities as individual components of what is, ultimately, an unsustainable global uber-sport assemblage.

References

Andrews, D. L. (2019). *Making Sport Great Again: The Uber-Sport Assemblage, Neoliberalism, and the Trump Conjuncture*. Springer.

Andrews, D. L. (2021). Getting to the Uber-Sport Assemblage. In *The Palgrave Handbook of Globalization and Sport* (pp. 59–81). Palgrave Macmillan.

Andrews, D. L., & Granger, A. D. (2007). Sport and Globalization. In G. Ritzer (Ed.), *The Blackwell Companion to Globalization* (pp. 478–497). Blackwell.

Augé, M. (2009). *Non-Places: An Introduction to Supermodernity*. Verso.

Baldwin, A. (2017). Liberty Completes F1 Takeover, Ecclestone Replaced. *Reuters*. https://www.reuters.com/article/us-motor-f1-ecclestone/liberty-completes-f1-takeover-ecclestone-replaced

Briggs, G. (2009, March 21). Tilke, Tailor, Circuit Maker. *The Guardian*. https://www.theguardian.com/sport/2009/mar/21/hermann-tilka-formula-one-designer

Choe, Y., Park, H. Y., & Kim, D. K. (2017). Holding or Not Holding a Mega-Event: Case of the F1 Korea Grand Prix. *Asia Pacific Journal of Tourism Research, 22*(1), 88–98.

Conley, V. A. (2009). Of Rhizomes, Smooth Space, War Machines and New Media. In M. Poster & D. Savat (Eds.), *Deleuze and New Technology* (pp. 32–44). Edinburgh University Press.

Dávid, L. D., Remenyik, B., Molnár, C., Baiburiev, R., & Csobán, K. (2018). The Impact of the Hungaroring Grand Prix on the Hungarian Tourism Industry. *Event Management, 22*(4), 671–674.

Dingle, G. (2009). Sustaining the Race: A Review of Literature Pertaining to the Environmental Sustainability of Motorsport. *International Journal of Sports Marketing and Sponsorship, 11*(1), 75–91.

Dirlik, A. (1996). The Global in the Local. In R. Wilson & W. Dissanayake (Eds.), *Global Local: Cultural Production and the Transnational Imaginary* (pp. 21–45). Duke University Press.

Dowse, S., & Fletcher, T. (2018). Sports Mega-Events, the Non-West and the Ethics of Event Hosting. *Sport in Society, 21*(5), 745–761.

The Economist. (1997, March 13). Mr Formula One. *The Economist*. https://www.economist.com/business/1997/03/13/mr-formula-one

F1. (2017, January 23). Liberty Completes F1 Acquisition. *Formula1.com*. https://www.formula1.com/en/latest/article.liberty-completes-f1-acquisition.html

F1. (2020, January). Corporate Strategy—Formula One World Championship Limited. *Formula1.com*. https://corp.formula1.com/corporate-strategy/

F1. (2021, January). *Formula1.com*. https://corp.formula1.com/sustainability/

F1. (2022, February 17). Formula 1 Announces Audience and Fan Attendance Figures for 2021. *Formula1.com*. https://corp.formula1.com/formula-1-announces-audience-and-fan-attendance-figures-for-2021/

Fairley, S., Tyler, B. D., Kellett, P., & D'Elia, K. (2011). The Formula One Australian Grand Prix: Exploring the Triple Bottom Line. *Sport Management Review, 14*(2), 141–152.

Gezici, F., & Er, S. (2014). What has been Left after Hosting the Formula 1 Grand Prix in Istanbul? *Cities, 41*, 44–53.

Giulianotti, R., & Robertson, R. (2004). The Globalization of Football: A Study in the Glocalization of the "Serious Life". *The British Journal of Sociology, 55*(4), 545–568.

Gogishvili, D. (2018). Baku Formula 1 City Circuit: Exploring the Temporary Spaces of Exception. *Cities, 74*, 169–178.

GPblog.com. (2022, January 20). How does Liberty Media Reconcile Hunger for More F1 with Sustainability? *GPBlog.com*. https://www.gpblog.com/en/news/103262/how-does-liberty-media-reconcile-hunger-for-more-f1-with-sustainability.html

Grossberg, L. (1997). Cultural Studies, Modern Logics, and Theories of Globalisation. In A. McRobbie (Ed.), *Back to Reality? Social Experience and Cultural Studies* (pp. 7–35). Manchester University Press.

Gupta, A. (2009). The Globalization of Sports, the Rise of Non-Western Nations, and the Impact on International Sporting Events. *The International Journal of the History of Sport, 26*(12), 1779–1790.

Harding, J. (2021, May 11). How Much Longer Can Formula 1 Drive to Survive? *DW*. https://www.dw.com/en/how-much-longer-can-formula-1-drive-to-survive/a-59722750

Horne, J. D. (2010). Cricket in Consumer Culture: Notes on the 2007 Cricket World Cup. *American Behavioral Scientist, 53*(10), 154.

Kim, M. K., Kim, S. K., Park, J. A., Carroll, M., Yu, J. G., & Na, K. (2017). Measuring the Economic Impacts of Major Sports Events: The Case of Formula One Grand Prix (F1). *Asia Pacific Journal of Tourism Research, 22*(1), 64–73.

Lefebvre, S., & Roult, R. (2011). Formula One's New Urban Economies. *Cities, 28*(4), 330–339.

Liu, D., & Gratton, C. (2010). The Impact of Mega Sporting Events on Live Spectators' Images of a Host City: A Case Study of the Shanghai F1 Grand Prix. *Tourism Economics, 16*(3), 629–645.

Lowes, M. (2018). Toward a Conceptual Understanding of Formula One Motorsport and Local Cosmopolitanism Discourse in Urban Placemarketing Strategies. *Communication & Sport, 6*(2), 203–218.

Maguire, J. A. (2000). Sport and Globalization. In J. Coakley & E. Dunning (Eds.), *Handbook of Sports Studies* (pp. 356–369). Sage.

Matar, D. (2021, April 18). *Miami GP to Join F1 Calendar from 2022 in 10-year Deal.* Associated Press. https://apnews.com/article/miami-sports-europe-florida-austin-texas-be0f12ccd0497ef91f518f6d5b952f32

Miller, T. (2016). Greenwashed Sports and Environmental Activism: Formula 1 and FIFA. *Environmental Communication, 10*(6), 719–733.

Mitchell, S. (2022, January 5). F1 has So Much Interest It Could 'Easily' have 30-Race Calendar. *The-Race.com.* https://the-race.com/formula-1/f1-has-so-much-interest-it-could-easily-have-30-race-calendar/

Morley, D., & Robins, K. (1995). *Spaces of Identity: Global Media, Electronic Landscapes and Cultural Boundaries*. Routledge.

O'Shea, M., Perry, N., & Duffy, S. (2020, January 14). Formula 1 Says It's Going Carbon Neutral but Fans Must Demand Greater Detail on How. *The Conversation.* https://theconversation.com/formula-1-says-its-going-carbon-neutral-but-fans-must-demand-greater-detail-on-how-127328

Pender, K. (2021, September 24). Daniel Ricciardo the Star in the Netflix-isation of Sport. *The Guardian.* https://www.theguardian.com/sport/2021/sep/25/daniel-ricciardo-the-star-in-the-netflix-isation-of-sport

Ritzer, G., & Ryan, M. (2003). The Globalization of Nothing. *Social Thought & Research, 25*, 51–81.

Rumford, C. (2007). More than a Game: Globalization and the Post-Westernization of World Cricket. *Global Networks, 7*(2), 202–214.

Silk, M. (2001). Together We're One? The "Place" of the Nation in Media Representations of the 1998 Kuala Lumpur Commonwealth Games. *Sociology of Sport Journal, 18*(3), 277–301.

Silk, M., & Manley, A. (2012). Globalization, Urbanization and Sporting Spectacle in Pacific Asia: Places, Peoples and Pastness. *Sociology of Sport Journal, 29*(4), 455–484.

Sloan, G. (2021, August 10). Liberty Media Spoilt for Choice for New Races. *F1 Chronicle.* https://f1chronicle.com/liberty-media-spoilt-for-choice-for-new-races/

Sturm, D. (2014). A Glamorous and High-tech Global Spectacle of Speed: Formula One Motor Racing as Mediated, Global and Corporate Spectacle. In K. Dashper, T. Fletcher, & N. McCullough (Eds.), *Sports Events, Society and Culture* (pp. 68–82). Routledge.

Sturm, D. (2017). The Monaco Grand Prix and Indianapolis 500: Projecting European Glamour and Global Americana. In L. A. Wenner & A. Billings (Eds.), *Sport, Media and Mega-Events* (pp. 170–184). Routledge.

Sturm, D. (2018). Formula E's 'Green' Challenge to Motorsport Events, Spaces and Technologies. In H. Seraphin & E. Nolan (Eds.), *Green Events and Green Tourism: An International Guide to Good Practice* (pp. 145–153). Routledge.

Van Bottenburg, M. (2001). *Global Games* (B. Jackson, Trans.). Urbana, IL: University of Illinois Press.

Watanabe, Y., Gilbert, C., Aman, M. S., & Zhang, J. J. (2018). Attracting International Spectators to a Sport Event Held in Asia: The Case of Formula One Petronas Malaysia Grand Prix. *International Journal of Sports Marketing and Sponsorship, 19*(2), 194–216.

Yu, L., Xue, H., & Newman, J. I. (2018). Sporting Shanghai: Haipai Cosmopolitanism, Glocal Cityness, and Urban Policy as Mega-Event. *Sociology of Sport Journal, 35*(4), 301–313.

Circuits of Capital: The Spatial Development of Formula One Racetracks

Michael Friedman and Brandon Wallace

This chapter explores the spatial development of Formula One racetracks, which follows the pattern of confinement and artifice observed by Bale (2003) in other sports. The first Grand Prix (GP) races were generally held on closed public roads, but tracks dedicated solely to racing began being built as auto racing matured. Since Formula One started in 1950, races have been held on such permanent circuits, on street circuits, or a combination of the two as cities seek to profit from these high-profile events. Within permanent racetracks, the spectacle of auto racing has been confined to defined spaces as events require several kilometres of road, places for spectators, and support facilities. Races on street circuits are held on public roads, often in downtown areas, and close streets for

M. Friedman (✉)
Department of Kinesiology, University of Maryland, College Park, MD, USA
e-mail: mtfried@umd.edu

B. Wallace
Department of Kinesiology, University of Maryland, College Park, MD, USA
e-mail: bwallac3@terpmail.umd.edu

D. Sturm et al. (eds.), *The History and Politics of Motor Racing*, Global Culture and Sport Series, https://doi.org/10.1007/978-3-031-22825-4_24

several days before competitors arrive in order to set up the track, temporary stands, and support areas. Civic leaders justify this disruption as events are intended to showcase cities to global audiences. Such large investments of capital and space reflect on the increasing prominence of Formula One racing within the processes of globalization.

Few sporting events garner as much international attention as Formula One (F1) Grand Prix races. In 2019, the F1 circuit included 21 events, each in a different country, on five continents. Races had a total attendance of 4,164,948 people and were viewed by global media audiences exceeding 1.9 billion people (Formula One, 2019; Formula One, 2020). While much of the research on F1 focuses on the drivers and their machines, the spatial elements of Grand Prix racing in terms of the circuits, their development, and position within urban environments have been subject to much less attention. This chapter seeks to be a starting point for such examinations.

In becoming the premier global motor sports competition since its founding in 1950, F1 built upon a legacy of Grand Prix races and other auto racing events starting in the late nineteenth century (Guzzardi & Rizzo, 2001). As automakers and car enthusiasts sought to popularize and promote the new technology of automobiles, the first races were held on public roads between cities. Following numerous accidents causing the deaths of drivers, spectators, and bystanders from cars becoming faster and more dangerous, public outcry led to the enclosure of events into temporarily closed circuits of public roads and permanent motor sports venues early in the twentieth century. This mixture of temporary circuits and permanent venues continues to define the spaces of F1 racing as event promoters, track operators, and cities balance the spatial requirements of motor sports with issues of public safety and the general commodification of sport.

To truly appreciate the spatial development of F1 racetracks, it is necessary to understand the relationship between speed and the spatial requirements of motor sports. In track and field, the fastest athletes can sprint 100 metres (m) in just under 10 seconds. At top speeds nearing 360 kilometres per hour (about 224 miles per hour), a race car will travel a full kilometre during those same 10 seconds. This ten-fold increase in speed requires tracks that are exponentially larger than tracks dedicated to running. A standard 400-m running track and the 4-km Indianapolis Motor Speedway (Indy) may be comparable in the time it takes the fastest competitors to complete one lap (approximately 40–45 seconds). However, the running track fits into a 1.6-hectare space, while Indy encircles an area that is more than 60 times larger—exceeding 100 hectares. Once spectator, consumption, and performance support spaces are included, Indy is the world's largest sports venue at 226 hectares (O'Kane, 2011).

Although their massive scale differentiates motor sports venues, their evolution as sporting landscapes follows a pattern similar to venues for other sports. Sport geographer John Bale (2003) identified a process of confinement and commodification evident within the modernization of sport and the development of sporting spaces over the past 150 years. Along with the codification of rules and practices, informal activities became sports as they were enclosed within distinct spaces that defined areas for competition and separated performers from spectators. This process enabled the commodification of sport as gates and fences limited spectator access and as internal partitioning enabled sports venues to become ever more sophisticated generators of revenue.

To aid understanding of the spatial dimensions of F1, this chapter will first discuss the evolution of sports venues generally. This is followed by a survey of the early years of Grand Prix racing as events moved from public roads into dedicated motor sports venues. With this context in place, we then examine the development of F1 since the 1950s as circuits have been increasingly commodified, as F1 has become a globalized sport, and as cities have competed for global media attention and for tourists.

Confinement and Commercialization of Sporting Landscapes

Karl Raitz (1995, p. ix) describes sporting venues "as a kind of theater," explaining that "sporting events, just as for plays, purposeful, directed and structured activity is enhanced with props and performed with the end of providing a gratifying experience for participants and spectators alike." Sporting landscapes have evolved into integral parts of the sporting experience as they have shaped events for performers and provided a context for spectators to consume the event.

This evolution began with the modernization of sport in the late nineteenth century. Bale (2003) outlines a four-stage process for the development of sports stadiums, beginning with folk games in which games lacked standardized rules or defined spaces. Permeable boundaries allowed participants and spectators to mix, and games were played in spaces that were used for other purposes (Bale, 2003). As rules were established and formalized, sports were enclosed into defined spaces to separate participants from spectators. Although spectators could no longer enter the playing field, they faced no other limitations on their movement (Bale, 2003). The third stage of partitioning enabled the commodification of sport. Dedicated venues were separated from surrounding neighbourhoods with gates and walls that limited spectatorship to ticket holders and through internal segregation enabling sport promoters to offer enhanced experiences to people who were willing to spend more money (Bale, 2003).

Bale's (2003) fourth stage—which he termed "surveillance"—suggests increasing control of spectators through facility design and technology. In post–World War II stadiums, spectators came to be confined to individual seats and subjected to panoptic observation from video cameras, wealthy spectators receive upgraded experiences within luxury boxes, and videoboards structure and direct spectator actions. As Bale produced his typology following the 1989 Hillsborough tragedy and subsequent Taylor Report that resulted in many football stadiums around the world being redesigned to increase spectator safety through surveillance and control, we suggest hypercommodification over the past three decades as a fifth stage of development. In this most recent stage, sports venues and surrounding spaces have been spectacularized and transformed into highly sophisticated consumption environments (Friedman, 2023).

This process can be seen in the evolution of baseball spaces from Hoboken's Elysian Fields, where the first baseball game occurred in 1845 to the most recent stadiums where teams control development within ever-growing portions of their surrounding neighbourhoods. Within the first stage, bat and ball games were played in colonial America as settlers continued playing English folk games such as stoolball, one cat, town ball and rounders. Games were played within various community spaces and followed traditional customs that neither limited the number of players nor delineated a dedicated field of play (Seymour, 1989). As the Knickerbocker Base Ball Club of New York created a standard set of rules during the 1840s, one was to enclose the field of play within a 90-degree arc. Such enclosure not only defined whether batted balls were in or out of play but separated players from spectators (Goldstein, 1989). The popularization of baseball through the 1850s and 1860s led to the partitioning of baseball spectator spaces. In 1862, William Cammeyer developed the first commodified baseball venue, the Union Grounds, with a business model seeking to profit from renting a first-class field to the leading clubs and by selling tickets to spectators for admission (Friedman, 2023).

While movement from undefined sport spaces to enclosure and partition moved fairly rapidly, the process of commodification has continued for 150 years; Raitz (1995, p. xi) recognized that "as sporting events have become more popularized and accepted as entertainment, the sports landscape has been increasingly subject to economic influences." Following Cammeyer's lead, entrepreneurs built baseball grounds throughout the late nineteenth century to host games for their professional teams (Riess, 1989). Built from wood, grounds could be constructed quickly and economically as team owners purchased or rented inexpensive land, often in places where they had financial interests in trolley lines, real estate, or other commercial ventures (Friedman, 2023). However, these were impermanent structures with severe safety problems and subject to replacement once landowners found more lucrative uses for their real estate (Ross, 2016). Baseball's maturation into a stable business at the start of the twentieth century led to the construction of brick-and-steel ballparks that were built to last.

Ballparks represented a significant upgrade from baseball grounds (Goldberger, 2019). Still built with private investment in places like Boston's Fens, where Red Sox owners had significant real estate interests, ballparks were increasingly sophisticated consumption environments with the development of permanent food and merchandise concessions (Friedman, 2023). As facilities aged and suburbanization changed the racial composition of cities, stadium development became a public activity as governments built sports venues to be spaces of mass recreation and large public gatherings (Friedman & Beissel, 2020). These new super stadiums were highly technologically advanced, designed to maximize public use and accommodate multiple sports with circular designs, artificial surfaces, and occasional domes, and they offered large parking lots with convenient access to highways (Bale, 2003). Super stadiums enhanced consumption environments with expanded food and merchandise concession stands on concourses broader than those in ballparks, improved restrooms, and a few luxury amenities within luxury suites and loge levels, albeit spectators still generally had similar experiences (Lisle, 2017).

Illustrating the principles of hypercommodification that have contributed to the spatial development of F1 circuits, design trends since the late 1980s have prioritized consumption with "mallparks" following the principles of shopping mall and theme park design (hence the portmanteau "mallparks"). Contemporary stadiums provide a diversity of consumption experiences on gamedays and anchor downtown entertainment districts by showcasing cities and drawing millions of potential consumers (Friedman, 2016). Mallparks offer retail, restaurants, tours, and private event spaces towards ensuring year-round use and impact. However, by relying upon private investment to develop surrounding areas, mallparks have been unreliable producers of economic development (Friedman, 2023; Rosentraub, 2010).

Towards addressing this shortcoming, the most recent Major League Baseball venues to open, Atlanta's Truist Park and Globe Life Field in Arlington, Texas, have been built as part of Integrated Stadium Development (ISD) projects (Friedman & Beissel, 2020). In general, ISDs ensure economic development occurs around sports venues by requiring teams to be lead investors in broader projects incorporating office, retail, residential, and recreational elements. ISDs are intended to produce vibrant neighbourhoods that are active and generate economic activity throughout the year rather than just on event days. Other examples of ISDs include District Detroit around Little Caesars Arena in Detroit, LA Live surrounding Staples Center in Los Angeles, and Green Bay, Wisconsin's Titletown development outside Lambeau Field (Rosentraub, 2010).

A similar process of spatial development has occurred within auto racing, which quickly moved from public roads onto increasingly commodified circuits. Yet, the structure of the auto racing spectacle is very different from the seasonal nature of baseball and other major sport leagues as races are week-long events visiting multiple cities within national and international circuits. As a result of this schedule and the extensive spatial needs of racetracks, there are relatively few permanent motor sports venues, and most are located far from downtown areas. However, given the global competition for media attention and visitor spending, F1 circuits are significant elements in many urban and national economic development and placemaking efforts.

The Enclosure and Partitioning of Auto Racing

Historians of auto racing generally locate the sport's beginnings in late nineteenth-century France due to its relatively high-quality roads and limited legislation regulating travel speeds (Twitchen, 2004). Twitchen (2004) identifies the first recorded automobile competition as a reliability trial held between Paris and Rouen in July 1894, in which 5000 francs were awarded to the vehicle that best combined safety, handling, and economy. The first race was held the following year as the *Auto Club de France* and newspaper sponsors offered a prize money pool of 75,000 francs to the fastest finishers in a race from Paris to Bordeaux and back (Adair, 1998). Such events were then organized in different countries, with the first American auto race occurring in fall 1895 and interest growing in Great Britain, Germany, and Italy before the end of the nineteenth century (Guzzardi & Rizzo, 2001; Pillsbury, 1995).

Early auto races were intended to popularize and advertise this emerging technology by proving "vehicles [to be] strong, fast and reliable" (Pillsbury, 1995, p. 273), to enable manufacturers to demonstrate the relative capabilities of their machines (Twitchen, 2004), and for elite groups to display their social position (Adair, 1998). Moreover, auto races were implicated within nationalistic discourses with victories exemplifying a nation's technological and manufacturing prowess. James Gordon Bennett Jr, publisher of the *New York Herald* and *International Herald*

Tribune newspapers, sought to capitalize on this connection by sponsoring the Gordon Bennett Cup, a series of international competitions between 1900 and 1905 which invited three cars to represent each competing nation (Dick, 2013).

Major early races were between large cities and utilized public roads. However, as automobiles became faster, races created increasing dangers for drivers, spectators, and bystanders, and were a nuisance for communities situated along the routes. Drivers damaged roads and broke rules of the road, and their races disturbed the peace of countryside towns as cars skidded and stirred up dust, produced loud noises and noxious odours, killed animals, and endangered people (Dick, 2013; Twitchen, 2004). During a 1901 race between Paris and Berlin, a small boy was killed by a competitor, while eight deaths occurred during the 1901 Paris-Bordeaux rally. With growing opposition to motor racing events, these tragedies led the French Prime Minister to announce that no more racing permits would be granted in the country (Twitchen, 2004).

Pressure from the emerging automobile industry and driving enthusiasts led a permit being issued for a Paris-Madrid race in 1903. Starting with great fanfare, a crowd of 100,000 gathered to watch the beginning of the race and an estimated 3,000,000 spectators lined the road to Bordeaux (Adair, 1998). However, as Adair (1998, p. 125) notes, spectators were "largely ignorant about the difficulties faced by drivers trying to control speeding motor vehicles," and there were not enough police to maintain public safety, which resulted in the race "ending in disaster." After several accidents led to eight deaths, including five among spectators and soldiers, the French government cancelled the race at Bordeaux and required the cars be returned to Paris by train (Twitchen, 2004). The failure of the Paris-Madrid race led many newspapers to report the end of auto racing (Dick, 2013).

As Hamilton (2017, p. 187) explained, "the inherent danger to spectators brought an awareness of the need for more control in the shape of a circuit that could be more easily managed and provide some form of crowd constraint." With public confidence in the safety of open road racing waning, Great Britain hosted the Gordon Bennett Cup race of 1903 on a 200-km circuit of closed roads starting at Athy in County Kildare in Ireland (Guzzardi & Rizzo, 2001). This race was not the first to be held on a circuit,[1] but it may have been the most important for the development of auto racing in Europe. To protect the public, race organizers employed 7000 police officers who enforced orders requiring residents to remain in their homes. Although the race was viewed by few spectators, it produced no fatalities or serious injuries. According to Twitchen (2004, p. 134), the race's success "did much to allay the criticisms of motor racing and helped to rebuild the confidence among the public towards motor racing as an acceptably safe sport."

Such enclosure of races into closed circuits helped fuel the sport's growth through Europe during the first half of the twentieth century. In 1906, Le Mans, France, hosted the first Grand Prix race in which competitors completed 12 laps around a 105-km circuit over two days. The first French Grand Prix (GP)[2] had several safety advances (Adair, 1998). Rather than racing through the town of St Calais, traffic was diverted away across a specially built wooden bridge. Forty miles of wooden barricades helped protect and control spectators, while a tunnel was dug beneath the track to allow spectators to safely cross (Adair, 1998). The race also had an important economic advancement with a grandstand built for thousands of paying spectators (Adair, 1998). Other circuit races were soon held in Sicily and Germany, but only France and the United States (U.S.) hosted Grand Prix races before World War I.

While many early circuits ran for 75–150 kilometres, their size became shorter between the wars. For example, the first Italian GP in 1921 was held on a 17.2-km circuit at the northern town of Montichiari, the first 24 Hours at Le Mans was held on a 17.26-km circuit in 1923, and the first Monaco GP in 1929 was held on a 3.145-km circuit through the city's narrow streets (Guzzardi & Rizzo, 2001; O'Kane, 2011). Such races were safer for drivers, who developed familiarity with the course, and were much more accessible for spectators, who were assured of seeing frequent action.

Several of the Grand Prix races that would later become some of the most prestigious F1 events developed between the wars. Generally held on closed road circuits that were shaped by surrounding landscapes, each course offered unique challenges for drivers. Spa-Francorchamps, where the first Belgian GP was held in 1925, offers 15 km of "undulating" roads through the Ardennes Forest (Hamilton, 2017). The narrow streets of the

Monaco GP emphasize skill, precision, and concentration as they leave drivers with no margin for error (O'kane, 2011). In France, the Circuit de Reims-Gueux (Reims) connected the historic city with two small villages along a 7.8-triangular course distinguished by two long straightaways (straight sections of a roads or racetracks) that placed a premium on speed (Hamilton, 2017). The 7.3-km Bremgarten circuit, described by Hamilton (2017, p. 187) as a "relentless sequence of curves and high-speed corners," hosted the first Swiss GP in 1934.

Although Hamilton (2017, p. 187) observed that "public highways and byways continued to provide the easiest, if not the most socially convenient form of racetrack" for Grand Prix races, the first half of the twentieth century saw the development of several permanent venues that "soon became popular and offered more potential for profit." Although Brooklands in Surrey, England, opened as the first purposefully built, paved motor sports venue in 1907, racetracks were more common in the U.S. than Europe as Americans "demonstrated a clear preference for races on the fast and compact Indianapolis-style ovals that were equipped with comfortable grandstands at all points" (Guzzardi & Rizzo, 2001, p. 35). Several early races were held in horse racetracks due to their long straightaways and existing grandstands. In 1903, the Wisconsin State Fairgrounds built a one-mile circular dirt track in Milwaukee, which was paved in 1954 and remains the oldest operating motor sports venue in the world (Guzzardi & Rizzo, 2001). Opened in 1909, the Indianapolis Motor Speedway is the first paved motor sports venue in the U.S.

As American tracks tended towards speed-maximizing ovals surrounded by grandstands, European tracks sought to reproduce the challenges of open road racing within controlled settings (Sturm, 2017). Brooklands, despite its status as the first paved motor sports venue, had limited utility for the development of racing due to its "more exclusive code of participation" that was similar to elite British horse racing spaces and events (Adair, 1998, p. 129). After hosting the first two British GP in 1926 and 1927, Brooklands was surpassed by the opening of Leicestershire's Donington Park raceway in 1933 (Adair, 1998). In 1922, the Milan Automobile Club built Monza in an enclosed park, whose original circuit covered 10 km over a 340-hectare area. Monza remains the oldest Grand

Prix circuit in use as it has hosted 86 of 91 Italian GP. Germany built three major racing circuits: Berlin's AVUS in 1922, Nürburgring in 1927, and Hockenheimring in 1932 (Hamilton, 2017). AVUS consisted of two 9-km straights that were connected by banked hairpin corners, which placed a premium on speed and power (Setright, 1973). Nürburgring's original 28-km course, once described by Scottish world champion Jackie Stewart as "the Green Hell," snakes through the Eifel Mountains and includes more than 170 curves, a maximum grade of 17%, and nearly 1000 feet of elevation changes (Gold, 2020; Hamilton, 2017). Though Hockenheimring lacks the history and reputation of Nürburgring, it has hosted all but four German GP since 1976. Beyond Europe, developers in São Paulo, Brazil, built the 7.96-km Interlagos[3] circuit in 1940, which has hosted 40 of the 50 Brazilian GP held since 1972.

For the most part, early Grand Prix circuits were designed to reproduce open road conditions to challenge drivers and their automobiles with relatively little focus on spectators or other concerns. The Monaco GP stands apart as a notable deviation to this pattern, as the race has been synonymous with European glamour since its founding in 1929 (O'Kane, 2011). Located on the French Riviera, Monaco's status as a tax haven and its world-famous casino in Monte Carlo has given the principality a reputation as a playground for the elite (O'kane, 2011). As described by Sturm (2017), much of the race's status comes from the way it symbolically links the event with Monaco's reputation as the GP provides patrons with opportunities for ostentatious displays of wealth and status and the pursuit of business opportunities.

The Development of Formula One Racetracks

As Grand Prix racing resumed after World War II, it became increasingly organized and commodified through the creation of F1 in 1950. Lefebvre and Roult (2011) identify four phases of expansion (1950–1961, 1962–1980, 1981–1998, 1999–the present) that follow particular economic, urban, and spatial logics. During the first phase, F1 was primarily held within European cities as they incorporated many pre-war Grand

Prix races at historic circuits such as Monza, Monaco, Bremgarten, Spa-Francorchamps, Nürburgring, and Reims, and the newly built Silverstone in Great Britain. While counting towards the World Drivers' Championship between 1950 and 1960, the Indianapolis 500 was generally ignored by F1 teams as primarily an American race (O'kane, 2011). Comprising 20% of F1 events during this period, only 11 races were held outside Europe: the Argentinean GP (seven times), the United States GP (three), and the 1958 Moroccan GP (Lefebvre & Roult, 2011).

The Silverstone circuit typifies post–World War II race circuit development. Built in 1948 in the midland county of Northamptonshire, Silverstone had operated as a Royal Air Force bomber station during the war (Guzzardi & Rizzo, 2001). Decommissioned during peacetime, its three runways, taxiways, and perimeter roads offered foundational elements for a racing circuit. Although Silverstone flourished as a race circuit and test track for Great Britain's automobile manufacturers, it only provided a limited experience to spectators (Sheard, 2001).

Silverstone's focus on track quality reflected the priorities of F1 executives in determining race locations. According to Lefebvre and Roult (2011, p. 334), "the only organisational necessities were the presence of a well-designed circuit and an existing culture of the sport in the local population." In their considerations, economic and media concerns were secondary to the quality of circuit, paddocks, and supporting race infrastructure (Lefebvre & Roult, 2011). As a result, F1 race circuits tended not to be highly commodified and were built away from downtown areas.

European locations continued to be dominant during Lefebvre and Roult's (2011) second era, 1962–1980, by hosting 70% of F1 races. Yet, F1 began seeking international expansion in this period with new events in South America (Mexico and Brazil) and Commonwealth countries (Canada and South Africa) as permanent circuits were built in each country (Lefebvre & Roult, 2011). F1 continued to demonstrate its emphasis on track qualities over economic concerns and showed a clear preference for race circuits as, not including Monaco, only 30 Grands Prix were run on public roads during F1's first 31 years (Lefebvre & Roult, 2011).

Transforming the F1 Spectacle (1981–1998)

By the mid-1970s, F1 racing was beginning a significant transformation. This is partly due to the deaths of drivers and spectators that led to the recognition that races needed to protect driver safety to the maximum possible extent (Guzzardi & Rizzo, 2001). Also, F1's expanding global popularity led to the increasing commodification of races and the annual competition, especially as British entrepreneur Bernie Ecclestone established control over the competition through acquiring its international television rights. As F1 moved into Lefebvre and Roult's (2011) third period of development between 1981 and 1998, changes resulted in the renovation or closure of many older circuits, races being established in new locations, and the construction of new circuits that emphasized revenue production and the telegenic presentation of races to global media audiences. As noted earlier in this chapter, these changes were part of broader trends of commodification and spectacularization that were reshaping the sports industry and urban spaces more generally.

By the 1970s, safety concerns forced the relocation of Grands Prix away from Spa-Francorchamps and Nürburgring, which resulted in both being significantly shortened and renovated during the early 1980s (Hamilton, 2017). As classic circuits were renovated, several new European venues opened that offered increased safety for drivers and new revenues for F1 and race operators. Lefebvre and Roult (2011, p. 335) described new circuits at Barcelona, Imola, and Budapest as the "first to get important and touristic amenities in and around circuits," specifically identifying luxurious corporate suites, bars and restaurants, and other commercial and festival activities. Such development was similar to the trends Bale (2003) described within mid-twentieth-century stadiums and the changes within American racing venues as superspeedways offering higher levels of spectacle and services to spectators replaced older tracks during the 1980s and 1990s (Pillsbury, 1995).

While Silverstone did not have the same safety concerns as Spa-Francorchamps and Nürburgring, economic considerations underpinned its renovation during the early 1990s. Rob Sheard, now a Senior Principal at global sports architectural firm Populous, was hired by track operators in 1988 to produce a masterplan guiding its redevelopment. Sheard (2001, p. 110) wrote, "it quickly became clear to the design team that the Silverstone site was not planned efficiently, was underused, and could be made considerably more efficient and therefore profitable." Sheard's (2001) masterplan created five categories of price-differentiated spectator areas, each of which would be supported with food and beverage concessions, toilets, and areas for retail sales. To enhance the site's year-round profitability, the masterplan included a hotel, office space marketed to companies related to the motor sports industry, improvements to a business park, and potential to create an exhibition space or museum (Sheard, 2001).

As races were moving into new and renovated permanent circuits in Europe, F1 began aggressively working to expand its global reach, often with spectacular street circuits. Towards gaining greater acceptance in the U.S., five different American cities hosted street races before the United States GP was run on a circuit constructed within the infield of the Indianapolis Motor Speedway between 2000 and 2007 (Lefebvre & Roult, 2011). After being held on a race circuit more than 100 km from Toronto, the Canadian GP was moved to a street circuit in Montreal in 1978. While not downtown, Circuit Gilles Villeneuve was built on Notre-Dame Island, an important space within Montreal's tourist economy which hosted EXPO 1967 and aquatic events during the 1976 Olympics and is the site of the Montreal Casino (Lefebvre & Roult, 2013). Towards becoming established in Australia, F1 held 11 races on a street circuit in Adelaide before moving to Melbourne in 1996 (as described below). Beyond these English-speaking nations, in 1973, F1 established the Brazilian GP in Sao Paulo's historic Interlagos circuit, though the race was held for most of the 1980s at the Jacarepagua circuit in Rio de Janeiro. In Japan, F1 racing began at the Mitsubishi-owned Fuji Speedway in 1976, but the Japanese GP has been largely run at the Suzuka Circuit, which was originally built in 1962 as a Honda test track (Guzzardi & Rizzo, 2001).

Globalizing the F1 Spectacle in the Twenty-first Century

Lefebvre and Roult (2011) fourth stage of F1 spatial development begins in 1999 with the intensive globalization and mediatization of the sport. In this era, F1 has moved away from several traditional European locations in favour of "dominant-emerging" cities in Asia and the Middle East, such as Singapore, Kuala Lumpur, and Dubai, which could be more interesting to viewers as novel events in exotic locations. As a result, "the infrastructure itself (circuit and paddocks) is no longer sufficient to draw the hosting of a F1 race; the urban surroundings have become a variable just as important as the financial details of the race" (Lefebvre & Roult, 2011, p. 335).

While many cities have built arenas and stadiums in downtown areas in hopes of realizing economic development benefits, the spatial requirements of motor sports have resulted in the construction of permanent venues far from urban cores. Although their locations are not ideal in terms of image promotion, F1 races are mega events that attract global television audiences and tourists (Gezici & Er, 2014; Lowes, 2018; Silk & Manley, 2012). This combination has incentivized national and local governments of dominant-emerging cities to subsidize circuit construction of facilities that are fitted out with upscale amenities to satisfy F1 executives and sponsors and to pay large rights fees to F1 (Ishak, 2005; Lefebvre & Roult, 2011). However, as F1 maintains sponsorship and broadcast revenue and events last for less than one week per year, circuit operators have difficulty being profitable (Gezici & Er, 2014).

Often the construction of new permanent circuits is central to efforts to attract F1 to establish races in new countries (Lefebvre & Roult, 2011). In Turkey, race organizers built a $130 million venue with a capacity of 125,000 in a forested area 45 kilometres outside of Istanbul. Supported by the Turkish government—which sought to use the race within international marketing efforts—the Turkish GP was held between 2005 and 2011 (Gezici & Er, 2014). In Malaysia, the Sepang International Circuit opened in 1999 with an ambitious architectural design to "correspond to the marketing image of Malaysia as a modern developed state"

(Stürzebecher & Ulrich, 2002, p. 119). Located nearly 45 km outside of Kuala Lumpur, Stürzebecher and Ulrich (2002, p. 116) describe the Malaysian GP, held between 1999 and 2017, as "afford[ing] unbridled image promotion for the South-East Asian state." In Shanghai, organizers of the Chinese GP built a $240 million facility that could hold 200,000 spectators along its 5.45-km circuit. While the race is estimated to lose $30 million annually, civic leaders admitted that "economic impact is not the only criterion" as global broadcasts render the Chinese GP as an important opportunity for promoting Shanghai's image (Liu & Gratton, 2010, p. 631). Even the U.S. has a new permanent F1 venue, as the United States GP is now held in Austin, Texas' $300 million Circuit of the Americas, which is located outside the city centre in the southeastern part of Travis County around 15km from the Austin International Airport (Lefebvre & Roult, 2011).

However, the cost and size of venues, along with the structure of F1 competition, creates substantial challenges for race operators. Because F1 is an international competition in which no country hosts more than a single race, venues can hope for only one event per year. Moreover, given significant national and international competition for events, race organizers, governments, and tourism promoters offer F1 large rights payments and control over sponsorships (Gezici & Er, 2014). With race organizers receiving revenue from just ticket and concession sales, new motor sports venues open with diverse consumption amenities and operators must attempt to attract other motor sports and non-motor sports events for circuits to be economically viable.

Faced by these economic challenges, motor sport venues are beginning to engage in integrated forms of development similar to other sports venues. As described by Lefebvre and Roult (2011, p. 335), "in some cases, these new circuits become true team (theme?) parks, mixing sportive, cultural and touristic structures and activities into commercial, business residential, or even university spaces." This can be seen in Abu Dhabi's Yas Marina Circuit, which is part of a $5 billion development project embedding the race circuit, capable of hosting 50,000 spectators, alongside a 500-room luxury hotel, a marina for yachts, and areas for commercial development, residential units, and public recreation (Lefebvre & Roult, 2011).

Given the cost, scope, and limited use of motor sports venues, several F1 races are held on temporary circuits that can combine public and private spaces and roads for a limited duration. Despite their temporary nature, street circuits often provide spectacles of consumption similar to those staged in permanent circuits as cities host races within their most attractive spaces; unlike the permanent circuits that are distant from downtown areas, global audiences see waterfronts, public parks, government areas, and iconic downtown buildings as dramatic backdrops for F1 cars speeding through city streets (Lowes, 2002; Lowes, 2018).

The Australian GP, which began in 1985, exemplifies this type of temporary circuit. Originally held on a street circuit in downtown Adelaide, the race moved in 1996 to Melbourne's Albert Park, a 225-hectare public park surrounded by inner-city residential neighbourhoods. Backdropped by downtown just two kilometres away, the race circles Albert Park Lake; runs alongside the Albert Park Golf Course; winds between football ovals, cricket grounds, and bowling greens; and passes the Melbourne Sports & Aquatic Centre (Lowes, 2004). The Singapore GP provides a spectacular night-time view of the city's landmarks, as Singapore's leaders installed 1500 pylons and aluminium trusses for lights above the course to reproduce daylight conditions for drivers (Hamilton, 2017; Henderson et al., 2010). Since 2016, the Azerbaijan GP has been run through the streets of Baku, where the race passes along the Caspian Sea Waterfront and near the city's UNESCO World Heritage old town and Azerbaijan's Government House in Freedom Square (Gogishvili, 2018).

However, providing such attractive views of cities through F1 Grand Prix races creates several problems. First, preparing city streets to host a high-speed race requires substantial infrastructure investments that provide little public benefit beyond the event (Henderson et al., 2010; Lowes, 2002). Second, events can be highly disruptive to urban life due to the time it takes to complete infrastructure improvements and the closing of public areas for weeks around events as cities set up and disassemble race-related structures (Lowes, 2004). Third, beyond losing access to important public spaces, F1 often requires cities to give up control of these spaces during events and allow F1 to profit from their use for sponsorship and corporate hospitality (Tranter & Lowes, 2005).

In terms of infrastructure, city streets need significant upgrades to accommodate the speeds of F1 cars. In Singapore and Baku, roads were resurfaced, widened, and had curbs removed for the safety of drivers and to facilitate competition (Gogishvili, 2018; Henderson et al., 2010). Pit roads and race-related buildings were built at public expense in Melbourne and Singapore (Henderson et al., 2010; Lowes, 2004). Races also required substantial temporary infrastructure of track barriers, 4-m fencing, entry gates, buildings for food and beverages, toilets, and grandstands (Henderson et al., 2010).

F1 events also are highly disruptive to urban life. The road improvements required for the Grand Prix circuit impacted traffic in Baku for more than one year (Gogishvili, 2018). In Melbourne, the Australian GP can limit for up to four months the use of fields and other recreational infrastructure in Albert Park, one of the city's most popular spaces for physical activity (Lowes, 2004). As F1 demands control over race spaces during the week of the event, the public loses access to many urban spaces (Tranter & Lowes, 2005). In Baku, the luxurious corporate hospitality of F1's "Paddock Club" occupied Freedom Square and limited the ability of Azerbaijan's residents to interact with public officials in Government House. Additionally, two layers of concrete and steel fences covered with advertising curtains designed to prevent unticketed viewing also prevented Baku's residents from visiting or even seeing much of the city's core and waterfront (Gogishvili, 2018). The public even loses control over the messages seen in public spaces as advertising from F1 sponsors privilege hypermasculine messages promoting fast cars, smoking, and drinking (Tranter & Lowes, 2005).

Conclusion: Spaces of F1 Racing

While the spatial development of auto racing spaces is subject to local contexts and conditions, each instance shares common themes. Following the general enclosure and partitioning of auto racing beginning in the early twentieth century, development of F1 racing demonstrates patterns of surveillance and spectacularization identified by Bale (2003), as venues themselves have become profitable commodities designed to promote spectatorship, consumption, and destination images to global audiences. What differentiates the spatial politics of auto racing from other sports is the sheer size and scale of venues capable of meeting the physical requirements demanded by speeding cars and their broader scope following F1's intensifying globalization. Such a combination has spurred the evolution of auto racing spaces into profitable global commodities that serve as spectacularized platforms for the transmission of images and messages about urban spaces to global audiences. Whether within dedicated motor sports venues or temporary circuits located in public spaces, the spatial development of F1 racing tracks exemplifies the ways in which auto racing—as well as sport in general—is influenced by the dictates of (hyper) commodification and globalization.

Notes

1. There remains debate around the first closed circuit race. Dick (2013) identified the first circuit race as being held in Pau, France in 1901, while Guzzardi and Rizzo (2001) identify the Circuit des Ardennes in Belgium.
2. Specific names of races will be identified as "[national] GP" going forward.
3. The Interlagos circuit has been renamed the Autodromo Jose Carlos Pace but is commonly known by its original name.

References

Adair, D. (1998). Spectacles Of Speed And Endurance: The Formative Years Of Motor Racing In Europe. In D. Thoms, L. Holden, & T. Claydon (Eds.), *The Motor Car And Popular Culture In The 20th Century*. Ashgate.

Bale, J. (2003). *Sports Geography*. Routledge.

Dick, R. (2013). *Auto Racing Comes Of Age : A Transatlantic View Of The Cars, Drivers And Speedways, 1900-1925*. Mcfarland & Company, Inc., Publishers.

Formula One. (2019). *Grand Prix Attendance Surpasses 4 Million In 2019* [Online]. Retrieved December 2, 2021, from https://www.Formula1.com/en/Latest/Article.Grand-Prix-Attendance-Surpasses-4-Million-In-2019.61fehe3wb7wl8thfp8cbtd.Html.

Formula One. (2020). *F1 Broadcast To 1.9 Billion Total Audience In 2019* [Online]. Retrieved December 2, 2021, from https://www.Formula1.Com/En/Latest/Article.F1-Broadcast-To-1-9-Billion-Fans-In-2019.4ieykwsoexxsiejyutrk22.Html.

Friedman, M. T. (2016). Mallparks and the Symbolic Reconstruction of Urban Space. In N. Koch (Ed.), *Critical Geographies of Sport: Space, Power and Sport In Global Perspective*. Routledge.

Friedman, M. T. (2023). *Mallparks: Baseball Stadiums and the Culture of Consumption*. Cornell.

Friedman, M. T., & Beissel, A. S. (2020). Beyond "Who Pays?": Stadium Development And Urban Governance. *International Journal of Sports Marketing and Sponsorship, 22*, 107–125.

Gezici, F., & Er, S. (2014). What Has Been Left After Hosting The Formula 1 Grand Prix In Istanbul? *Cities: Part A, 41*, 44–53.

Gogishvili, D. (2018). Baku Formula 1 City Circuit: Exploring The Temporary Spaces Of Exception. *Cities, 74*, 169–178.

Gold, A. (2020). Must Read: A Concise History Of The Nürburgring: Learn The Story Behind What Is Arguably The World's Most Famous, Fearsome Racetrack. *Motortrend.*

Goldberger, P. (2019). *Ballpark: Baseball In The American City*. Alfred A. Knopf.

Goldstein, W. J. (1989). *Playing For Keeps: A History Of Early Baseball.* Cornell University Press.

Guzzardi, G., & Rizzo, E. (2001). *Motor Racing: A Century of Competition and Human Challenges*. Chartwell Books.

Hamilton, M. (2017). *Formula 1: The Pursuit of Speed.* Aurum.

Henderson, J. C., Foo, K., Lim, H., & Yip, S. (2010). Sports Events And Tourism: The Singapore Formula One Grand Prix. *International Journal Of Event And Festival Management, 1*, 60–73.

Ishak, M. M. (2005). *The Sports, Politics and Economics of The Hosting of Mega Sports Events In Malaysia: Exploring the Commonwealth Games of 1998 and the F1 Grand Prix.* Penerbit Universiti Utara Malaysia.

Lefebvre, S., & Roult, R. (2011). Formula One's New Urban Economies. *Cities, 28*, 330–339.

Lefebvre, S., & Roult, R. (2013). Territorial And Touristic Branding: Urban History And The Festive And Economic Perspectives Of Montreal's Formula One Grand Prix. *Loisir Et Société / Society And Leisure, 36*, 43–59.

Lisle, B. D. (2017). *Modern Coliseum: Stadiums And American Culture*. University Of Pennsylvania Press.

Liu, D., & Gratton, C. (2010). The Impact of Mega Sporting Events on Live Spectators' Images of a Host City: A Case Study of the Shanghai F1 Grand Prix. *Tourism Economics, 16*, 629–645.

Lowes, M. D. (2002). *Indy Dreams and Urban Nightmares : Speed Merchants, Spectacle, and the Struggle Over Public Space in the World-Class City*. University Of Toronto Press.

Lowes, M. D. (2004). Neoliberal Power Politics and the Controversial Siting of the Australian Grand Prix Motorsport Event in an Urban Park. *Loisir Et Société / Society And Leisure, 27*, 69–88.

Lowes, M. D. (2018). Toward a Conceptual Understanding of Formula One Motorsport and Local Cosmopolitanism Discourse in Urban Placemarketing Strategies. *Communication & Sport, 6*, 203–218.

O'kane, P. (2011). A History of the 'Triple Crown' of Motor Racing: The Indianapolis 500, The Le Mans 24 Hours and the Monaco Grand Prix. *The International Journal of the History of Sport, 28*, 281–299.

Pillsbury, R. (1995). Stock Car Racing. In K. B. Raitz (Ed.), *The Theater Of Sport*. Johns Hopkins University Press.

Raitz, K. B. (1995). The Theater of Sport: A Landscape Perspective. In K. B. Raitz (Ed.), *The Theater of Sport*. Johns Hopkins University Press.

Riess, S. A. (1989). *City Games: The Evolution of American Urban Society and the Rise of Sports*. University Of Illinois Press.

Rosentraub, M. S. (2010). *Major League Winners: Using Sports And Cultural Centers as Tools for Economic Development*. CRC Press.

Ross, R. B. (2016). *The Great Baseball Revolt: The Rise and Fall of the 1890 Players League*. Lincoln.

Setright, L. J. K. (1973). *The Grand Prix: 1906 to 1972*. W. W. Norton & Company.

Seymour, H. (1989). *Baseball: The Early Years*. Oxford University Press.

Sheard, R. (2001). *Sports Architecture*. Spon Press.

Silk, M., & Manley, A. (2012). Globalization, Urbanization & Sporting Spectacle In Pacific Asia: Places, Peoples & Pastness. *Sociology of Sport Journal, 29*, 455–484.

Sturm, D. (2017). The Monaco Grand Prix and Indianapolis 500: Projecting European Glamour and Global Americana. In L. Wenner & A. Billings (Eds.), *Sport, Media and Mega-Events* (pp. 170–184). Routledge.

Stürzebecher, P., & Ulrich, S. (2002). *Architecture For Sport: New Concepts And International Projects For Sport And Leisure*. Uk, Wiley-Academy.

Tranter, P. J., & Lowes, M. D. (2005). The Place of Motorsport in Public Health: An Australian Perspective. *Health And Place, 11*, 379–391.

Twitchen, A. (2004). The Influence of State Formation Processes on the Early Development of Motor Racing. In E. Dunning, D. Malcolm, & I. Waddington (Eds.), *Sport Histories : Figurational Studies In The Development Of Modern Sports*. Routledge.

Formula 1 as a Vehicle for Urban Transformation in China: State Entrepreneurialism and the Re-Imaging of Shanghai

Andrew Manley and Bryan C. Clift

The spectacle manifests itself as an enormous positivity, out of reach and beyond dispute. All it says is: "Everything that appears is good; whatever is good will appear."
—Guy Debord (1995, p. 15)

Introduction

As monuments to both temporary and long-term urban transformation, sporting mega-events and the staging of sporting spectacles are often imbued with a promise of heightened global visibility for hosting cities. Predominantly adopted by dominant groups—be they the political and/or economic elites—sporting mega-events perpetuate a discourse promoting the positive financial, social, environmental, and political legacy that is said to transform host communities and their surrounding

A. Manley (✉) • B. C. Clift
Department for Health, University of Bath, Bath, UK
e-mail: A.T.Manley@bath.ac.uk; B.C.Clift@bath.ac.uk

D. Sturm et al. (eds.), *The History and Politics of Motor Racing*, Global Culture and Sport Series, https://doi.org/10.1007/978-3-031-22825-4_25

landscape (see Andrews, 2017; Hall, 2006; Horne, 2007; Horne & Manzenreiter, 2006; Roche, 2000). Thus, nations and cities—and indeed their respective local governments—have come to portray sporting mega-events as vehicles for economic investment, infrastructure development, cultural expression and exchange, the re-imaging of place and the re-positioning of local destinations on a transnational scale (Silk, 2002). Historically, this strategy of place-making has encouraged nations and cities to engage with the wider logics of late capitalism and neoliberal economic rationalities (see Andrews, 2009; 2017, 2019; Newman & Giardina, 2011). Often incorporating an assemblage of public institutions and private corporate interests, aspirational cities navigate the operational mechanisms of the free market, deregulation policies, and private enterprise in a bid to enhance economic conditions and attain—or perhaps even revive—a competitive position in the world economy (Hall, 1992; Waitt, 2008).

Advocates of these pro-growth strategies endorse the symbolic, built, and economic restructuring of cities to support such place-making with the understanding that longer-term economic development and job creation will ensue (Hiller, 2000). However, critics have consistently pointed toward the dubiousness of such boosterish urban change on several grounds, including for example: challenges to assumed economic benefit; fiscal requirements to do so and risk of significant public debt; tensions between temporary and post-event infrastructure usage; misplaced sense of public priorities; distance between urban transformation and the lived realities, problems, and challenges of inhabitants; disruption of social networks and cohesion; magnification of human rights issues; and environmental and ecological concerns (see Broudehoux, 2007; Roche, 2000; Shin, 2012). Still, despite lack of certainty around positive domestic and international outcomes, mass-mediated sporting events continue to be leveraged by pro-growth advocates as key facilitators in realizing the global growth aspirations of many major city regions, operating as irresistible drivers for economic expansion through accelerated urban transition. Thus, and with reference to Ong (2011a), sporting mega-events are considered experimentations in the "art of being global", "urban initiatives that compete for world recognition in the midst of inter-city rivalry and globalized contingency" (p. 3).

Contemporary examples of this strategy of urban growth and place-making have become prevalent throughout Asia's cities and Mega-Urban Regions (MUR). Over the past 40 years, China has demonstrated the desire to position the city as an engine for economic development (Douglass, 2000). Since the introduction of Deng Xiaoping's 'open door policy' in 1978, China has experienced a rapid rate of economic growth and pursued a strategy of urban development that has invested heavily in infrastructure and urban renewal projects, re-making cities through an intensified engagement with transnational flows of capital, information, and expertise (Logan & Fainstein, 2008; Wu, 2002; Ren, 2013). The hosting of past mega-events—such as the Beijing 2008 Summer Olympic Games, Shanghai 2010 World Expo and the Guangzhou 2010 Summer Asian Games—has formed a prominent aspect of this strategy, functioning as tools to construct a positive self-image of place (see Silk & Manley, 2012; Zhang & Silk, 2006; Zhang & Zhao, 2009). While still contingent upon the mutually reinforcing processes of globalization and urbanization—and firmly connected to globalizing circuits of capital—the hosting of mega-events and China's approach to territorially based entrepreneurialism is, however, still largely governed by the state (Wu, 2003). Deviating from neoliberal sensibilities common in Western nations—where the state gives way to market-based forces—China's entrepreneurial activities associated with urban growth are predominantly organized at the local state level, utilizing financial instruments to tap the market and implement development projects through state-controlled land resources under the principles of 'state entrepreneurialism' (see Wei, 2012; Wu, 2020). Similar to large-scale events such as the Summer or Winter Olympic Games, Asian Games, and the World Expo, the Chinese Formula One Grand Prix encapsulated this approach towards urban governance and the re-imaging of place. Primarily planned and endorsed by state agencies, state-owned enterprise, and local public actors—yet operating in conjunction with global enterprise and foreign direct investment—these global-local forces coalesced to endorse the ephemeral and exclusive aspects of mega-events that enable cities to climb the global urban hierarchy (Lefebvre & Roult, 2011; Lowes, 2004, 2018).

Strategies aligned to the re-imaging of 'place' that operate around principles of urban governance in this form, however, unevenly impact an urban populace. As several have observed, effects of these strategies include: spatial segregation of inner-city neighbourhoods into exclusive colonies for transnational elites; encouragement of enclave urbanism with the rise of gated, privatized and packaged suburban districts; and displacement of poorer urban populations—in some instances forcibly and with little compensation—through the planned processes of gentrification (see Gogishvili, 2018; Silk & Manley, 2012; Ren, 2013; Shin, 2009). Whilst sporting mega-events provide cities with the opportunity to engage in the processes of place marketing, nation branding, and extensive urban transformation, the economic and political prosperity derived from and affiliated with urban sporting spectacles typically resides with those invested in public–private partnerships (e.g. public officials, agencies, state-owned and international private business leaders) (see Armstrong et al., 2011; Clift & Andrews, 2012; Friedman & Andrews, 2010; Manley & Silk, 2014a; Silk, 2004). Within this chapter, we draw upon the Chinese Grand Prix in Shanghai as an illustrative example of strategic place-making, a political economic project allied to China's broader policy agenda of urban and regional development. Expressive of China's state entrepreneurialism, the place-making project seeks to recast Shanghai's image—and ultimately the nation's identity—primarily for the purpose of driving capital accumulation and promoting the symbolic values attached to a consumptive, modern, and entrepreneurial urban spirit under the guise of "being global". In doing so, we critically demonstrate how the delivery of this sporting project has led to the exclusion and removal of specific urban inhabitants both in terms of spatial relocation and representational identity. A process of sport-based urban place-making that sought to propagate a preferred and carefully managed civic identity, whilst concealing a past representation of place deemed undesirable in light of China's contemporary approach towards urban modernization and distinctive strategies of political-economic expansion.

State Entrepreneurialism and Sport-based Urban Place-Making in China

Entrepreneurial cities are often portrayed as implementing strategies of spatial reconfiguration on the basis of maintaining or enhancing economic competitiveness, a process of urban transformation centred on the logics of "capital space" (Harvey, 2001). In doing so, such strategies work to accelerate the establishment of public–private partnerships in an attempt to attract new direct financial investment, and focus upon the political economy of place to promote local economic growth and the upgrading of a city's image (see Harvey, 1989; Hall & Hubbard, 1996; Jessop & Sum, 2000; Wu & Zhang, 2007). Whilst the promoters of entrepreneurial cities are commonly guided by neoliberal sensibilities—endorsing market conditions that call for a retrenchment of state intervention—a variability exists between differing geographic contexts concerning the state's relationship with encroaching free market forces (see Brenner & Theodore, 2002; Ong, 2006, 2011a). China provides one such example where the development of its cities is still largely guided by centralized authoritarian control, mediating international economic relationships through state agencies and demonstrating an amalgamated market-oriented economy; highlighting the complex interplay between an inherited institutional infrastructure and the dominant logics of the global marketplace (see He & Wu, 2009; Liew, 2005; Wu, 2008). Thus, China's contemporary approach towards urban development and place-making has become shaped by the historic legacy of its socialist centrally planned economy and the resultant economic and political transition towards a socialist market economy.

Under the leadership of Mao Zedong (1949–1976) and China's socialist ideology, urban governance was dominated by a strong presence of the state that exacted control over the ownership of production materials, urban planning and the organization of a collective consumption (Wu, 2002). Emphasis upon an administrative hierarchy and central planning policy restricted the size and growth of China's cities, delineating urban space as a site of active governance through which the state created, sponsored, and managed organizations (see Derleth & Koldyk, 2004; Heberer,

2009; Read, 2003). Since the introduction of Deng Xiaoping's economic reforms in 1978, policies were imposed to open trade, partially decentralize decision-making capabilities away from the state, and engage with market-led urban development initiatives (Ren, 2013; Yeh & Wu, 1999). The relaxation of state control over the private sector through economic reform shifted China towards a city bias and away from rural areas and the agricultural sector, restoring private control over land use and establishing housing as a free-market commodity (Wu, 2006). With the introduction of an 'open door policy' in the Post-Mao era, and a clear engagement with wider global economic forces, prior practices of urban planning were challenged by a growing number of actors and interests infiltrating China's land development process (Yeh & Wu, 1999). The departure from a political ideology steeped in socialist 'egalitarianism', and the introduction of foreign investment into China's local economies, encouraged the municipality to pursue a more growth-oriented planning philosophy (Bian & Logan, 1996; Yeh & Wu, 1996). As such, the combination of local, state, and private enterprise sought to promote rapid urban redevelopment as a key component for spatialized capital accumulation, the promotion of place, and the economic development of China's cities (He & Wu, 2005, 2009).

Despite China's accelerated adoption of strategies for growth that reflect the values and tactics of urban entrepreneurialism—such as city branding, marketing, and promotion—the state still maintains a prominent and proactive role in supporting such entrepreneurial activities. The state deploys market instruments to generate economic growth and to legitimize its power. In doing so, local government officials are presented with the capability to cultivate economic development activities, allowing the state to operate as an agent acting through the market under the guise of principles commonly aligned with 'state entrepreneurialism' (Wu, 2017, 2020). Unlike the pro-growth strategies for urban development evidenced by many Western nations—largely driven by private sector interests and a reorientation towards a consumer-driven focus (Lees et al., 2016)—China's cities draw upon the influence of local governments to instigate policy initiatives and orchestrate entrepreneurial activities that are invested with significant national economic development objectives (Wu & Phelps, 2011). Proposed land development projects—often associated with the tourism industry, the development of high-tech zones or educational districts—are thus utilized by the local state as a tool to expand urban administrative areas in a bid to generate growth (Wei, 2012). Here, the interventionist role of the Chinese state—at both the central and local level—in controlling the land development process has been of key importance to this particular model of urban governance, shaping China's contemporary pathway of urban (re)development, strategies of place promotion and the economic growth of municipalities and cities (Wu, 2003; Wu & Phelps, 2011; Wei, 2012).

Evidence of China's engagement with state entrepreneurialism has become increasingly prominent in relation to sport-based urban place-making initiatives. Instigated by the introduction of fiscal revenue-sharing contracts, which provided revenue incentives for local authorities to engage in land development activities during the early 1990s (see Ran et al., 2010), China began to construct large-scale sports venues throughout major cities (Xue & Mason, 2012). These measures have been strategically implemented by local governments to acquire and trade land for the purpose of realizing economic growth, mobilizing resources and capital for continued public investment, to evidence a strong adherence to the central state's new urbanization plan, and competitively position cities through planned projects of urban renewal that coalesce around the advent of sporting mega-events (Xue & Mason, 2011, 2019). As such, the staging of mega-events and the development of sport stadia fold into China's existing urbanization processes and the global growth aspirations of cities, strategically deployed by local governments to construct and subsequently promote new images of place amidst intercity competition (Silk & Manley, 2012; Yu et al., 2018; Xue & Mason, 2019). Whilst many of China's cities have utilized the development of large-scale sport venues to enhance their image on a global scale, the planning and spatial reconfiguration of place is strongly embedded in local and territorial politics. The arrival of the Chinese Formula One Grand Prix in Shanghai provides a salient example of this approach towards sport-based urban place-making, and the relevance of state entrepreneurialism as a guiding hand for urban governance. Although not a nation traditionally associated with motorsport, the Shanghai International Circuit, and stage for the Chinese Formula One Grand Prix, formed a prominent part of a much wider large-scale process of suburbanization and new town development in the city's surrounding metropolitan area. This strategic shift in city construction away from central districts to the suburbs was largely driven by the municipal government's entrepreneurial ambitions to remold Shanghai as a global city, an aspect of urban governance that drew upon market imperatives introduced, developed, and deployed by the local state apparatus (Wu, 2003, 2020).

Regenerating Metropolitan Shanghai, New Town Development, and the Arrival of the Chinese Grand Prix

Since the post-reform era, China has adopted strategies of urban and sporting reform as part and parcel of its national efforts towards international political and economic competition. Sport's role and presence in the nation's urban agenda has been deployed strategically to leverage urban development projects with a focus on economic, political, social, and cultural enhancement at local, national, and international levels (Broudehoux, 2007; Cook, 2007). The arrival of the Chinese Grand Prix to Shanghai was no different in this regard.

In 2001, under the Shanghai municipal government's "One-City-Nine-Towns" (一城九镇) urban policy plan, a new development of suburban satellite-town construction was initiated as an entrepreneurial endeavour to attract residents away from the city centre, stimulate the local economy, and continue to elevate Shanghai's global profile (Shen & Wu, 2012). This new decree would aim to promote urbanization through the development of nine experimental towns built as authentic Western townscapes in the city's suburbs (Wang et al., 2010). As part of this development, the Shanghai International Automobile City (SIAC: 上海国际汽车城)—and subsequent construction of the Shanghai International Circuit—reflected this aggressive adoption of place-promotion strategies and land development projects to stimulate local economic growth. Situated in Shanghai's Jiading District—approximately 30 kilometers northwest of the city centre—the SIAC was designated as one project of the "One-City-Nine-Towns" plan instigated by the municipal government (Shen & Wu, 2012). Following this approach to urban planning, the Jiading District government merged two townships—Anting and Fangtai—under the administration of the SIAC and redeveloped the area based upon the existing automobile manufacturing industry (Chen et al., 2009). Incorporating the Shanghai Volkswagen Industrial Park—developed to encompass manufacturing plants for the production of automobile parts and accessories—the SIAC became host to educational institutions (Tongji College of Automotive Engineering), trade and exhibition centres, a new 5.4 square kilometer real estate development entitled 'Anting New Town' (安亭新镇) as well as the Shanghai Formula One International Circuit (Chen et al., 2009; Li & Wu, 2012).

In the promotion of a modern identity, the SIAC's Anting New Town was designed by the German architectural firm Albert Speer & Partner, with the first phase of this major residential development completed by 2004 and in conjunction with the opening of the Shanghai International Grand Prix Circuit. Seemingly disconnected from China's traditional cultures, Anting New Town is a modern housing development incorporating 5334 residential units for 50,000 residents that mimic the Bauhaus architecture and landscape of Weimar, Germany (Chen et al., 2009; Gutzmer, 2011). Through adopting this particular trend of 'duplitecutre' (see Bosker, 2013), Anting New Town's Euro-style Weimar Villas were marketed towards emerging consumers seeking Western comfort and style, architectural replicas that would traditionally appeal to Shanghai's wealthy households looking to invest in property, China's burgeoning middle class and middle-to-senior-level employees at the Shanghai Volkswagen joint venture company based within Jiading District (Wang et al., 2010). Thus, with the arrival of the Chinese Grand Prix, the redevelopment of Jiading District sought to further position Shanghai as a modernized socialist cosmopolitan city, a project of urban renewal that worked to accelerate the urbanization of suburban and rural communities, incite consumption and competitiveness across the city, promote economic growth and continue to raise Shanghai's global image (Yu et al., 2018; Xue & Mason, 2019). Alongside large-scale real estate development, Jiading District accelerated the improvement of green space and transportation infrastructure—constructing metro railways for a connection to Shanghai's city centre—in a bid to attract sports enthusiasts and an increased number of tourists to better serve the Formula One Chinese Grand Prix (Xue & Mason, 2011).

As part of a mechanism for initiating a wider planned project of suburbanization, the development of Anting New Town and the Shanghai International Circuit followed specific features of urban design, planning processes, and development outcomes that came to reaffirm China's approach towards state entrepreneurialism. Heavily guided by the central government and its influence over Shanghai as a province-level municipality, Jiading's urban redevelopment incorporated local government stakeholders—primarily the Jiading District Government; state-owned corporations, such as the Shanghai Juss Event Management Co., Ltd; foreign direct investment; and foreign design firms invested in urban renewal (Xue & Mason, 2012). The Jiading District Government were responsible for facilitating the development projects surrounding the FI circuit, whereas the State-owned Shanghai Juss Event Management Co., Ltd was created to operate, manage, and finance the F1 Chinese Grand Prix (Xue & Mason, 2012). Foreign direct investment was generated through business groups seeking official sponsorship contracts and an opportunity to enter the Chinese market. This amalgamation of actors and interests illustrated the influence of China's central government, and the relative power of both the municipal and district government, in guiding projects of place-making that are contingent upon national interests and partnerships that operate with/through the influence of global capital. Thus, new processes of cooperation between elite Party cadres and local, or indeed global, entrepreneurs created avenues to acquire new sources of capital for investment in infrastructure and property development projects, replacing the traditional state-directed central planning and financed forms of China's urban development (Walcott & Pannell, 2006).

Although Jiading District reported to experience growth that corresponded with the arrival of the Formula One Grand Prix—increasing the district's Gross Domestic Product (GDP) by more than 20% and annual revenues by 36% (see Xue & Mason, 2011)—such transformation is not without concern. Reliant on the disparate connections that held together this project of spatial reconfiguration, the outcomes of such regeneration—as with many urban redevelopment projects based around sporting mega-events (see Silk, 2002, 2011; Silk & Manley, 2012, 2017; Shin, 2009, 2012; Yu et al., 2018)—altered the original landscape and fractured the social balance and dimensions of the region (Wang et al., 2010). The transformation of rural land into an internationally oriented race track and the arrival of Anting New Town symbolized the Chinese state's broader shift from agrarian to post-industrial uses of urban space, serving as a platform for racing's capacity to exploit diverse and varied forms of entrepreneurial activity. In doing so, the voices of the (former) local residents were seemingly unheard or disregarded as this project came to redefine the suburban population to align with newly engineered and pre-planned spaces of consumption (Chen et al., 2009). As such, the motives for sport-based urban place-making become increasingly clear amidst the context of inter-locality competition and a political agenda that is seeking to provide districts, regions and indeed cities with new avenues for capital accumulation. Therefore, it is imperative to pay heed to the social impacts of urban mega-events as they become an increasingly important strategy for city branding and the re-imaging of place, addressing the particular consequences for citizenry as they speak to notions of belonging, inequality and social polarization amidst the wider framework of China's urban policy (Shin & Li, 2013).

Suburbanization and the Socio-spatial Consequences of the Chinese Grand Prix

The regenerative investment surrounding Shanghai's Chinese Grand Prix presented an opportunity to transform the city's Jiading District by engaging in a large-scale project of urban reconfiguration that empowered local states in the pursuit of growth. Yet, this process of (trans) national urban redevelopment calls into question the socio-spatial consequences of such grand projects of renewal and regeneration (see Zhang & Silk, 2006).

Since securing a contract with the Formula One Constructors' Association (FOCA) in 2002 that permitted Shanghai to officially host the Chinese Grand Prix, both land prices and housing prices within Jiading District increased at an exponential rate (Wang & Wang, 2011). Whilst real estate developments surrounding the Shanghai International Circuit were marketed on the principles of "new urbanism" in China—espousing qualities of diversity, community, accessibility, and improved living conditions—the rise of new town construction and residential housing was primarily predicated on the speculative aspirations of developers, the local government's desire to generate city competitiveness and the ambition of transnational design companies to enter into the Chinese market (Shen & Wu, 2012). Anting New Town's embodiment of urban duplitecutre worked towards exacerbating social segregation in the form of exclusive gated communities, and generated further inequity between spatial users of this new development and the surrounding residents (Wang et al., 2010). Excluding the urban poor from the decision-making processes of planning and construction, new town facilities and conveniences, the real estate developments bordering Shanghai's Grand Prix Circuit displaced former residents to the surrounding area of poorer locations within the new towns (Wang et al., 2010). This (re)shaping of Shanghai's socio-spatial structure pursued a more segregated and unequal pattern of urban development, one that benefitted the local government from the sale of state-owned land and real estate developers invested in promoting image-building projects. Consequently, growing social inequality has become synonymous with the bifurcation of China's urban landscapes, marginalizing lower-income families that are constrained to a life on the urban periphery and denied access to the modern amenities, lifestyle preferences and aspirations that are associated with new suburban growth (Shen & Wu, 2013).

In line with market-led approaches to urban development, the construction of high-end gated communities built to replicate Western suburbia raise questions that are not only aligned to the wider logics of transnational gentrification and the reproduction of class-based identities, but also speak to the loss of place attachment, sense of community and way of life associated with collectivist cultural traditions and practices (see Breitung, 2012; King & Kusno, 2000; Manley & Silk, 2019). While sport-based urban place-making initiatives throughout Asia have come to reflect the complex interdependencies of the global and the local (see Cho et al., 2012; Giulianotti & Robertson, 2012; Silk & Manley, 2012; Waldman et al., 2017; Yu et al., 2018), projects of urban transformation established in the pursuit of capital have, as with Ong (2011b, p. 206), subjected "'local' spaces to the overarching logic of a capitalist system with translocal or placeless determinations". As is often the case throughout urban China—and in many cities subject to rapid transformation—the commodification of urban developments has become exploited by developers and place marketers seeking to (re)create a particular sense of place, or spatial identity, that is representative of the exclusivist housing aspirations of the upper- and middle-classes (Pow & Kong, 2007). The suburban regeneration surrounding Shanghai's International Circuit within Jiading District was reflective of China's trend towards Western urban mimicry (see Bosker, 2013; Manley & Silk, 2014b), and the construction of a social environment characterized by social homogeneity (Pow & Kong, 2007). As such, these vast urban projects foster a particular sense of place that becomes devoid of ties to the historic characteristics of locality, generic spaces or *non*places that are defined by their homogeneity and imposition—as opposed to inclusion or integration—on the urban landscape (see Ritzer, 2007).

Shanghai's suburban dynamics surrounding the arrival of the Chinese Grand Prix, couched within the wider logics of a rapidly globalizing megacity, faced additional challenges from the further development of new towns in the surrounding area. With multiple real estate and urban development projects being undertaken within the locale, Anting New Town and the surrounding small-town urban planning had lost its territorial and formal cohesion (Henriot, 2017; Li & Wu, 2012). As original residents were displaced to surrounding areas, and white-collar workers preferring to commute from Shanghai proper, the residential development has become somewhat of a ghost town with few commercial, hotel, recreation, and public amenities constructed (see Gutzmer, 2011; Lang, 2017; Wang et al., 2010). Despite the proposed plan of serving Anting New Town's population locally, the housing developments encompassing Shanghai's International Circuit have been viewed as a failure in providing commercial, medical, and educational facilities that meet the needs of residents (Wang et al., 2010). With the majority of property purchased for investment and subsequently remaining empty (Gutzmer, 2011), this process of urban redevelopment emulated a pattern of marginalization, polarization, and detached social networks that often arises as a by-product of hosting sporting mega-events, acting as a catalyst to exacerbate inequalities endemic among poorer urban inhabitants (Shin, 2009; Shin & Li, 2013).

The repetition of dispossessing and displacing economically disadvantaged urban inhabitants in the name of sporting mega-events has become all too common (Gold & Gold, 2008; Lenskyj, 2020). Over the course of the twentieth century, mega-events have emerged as *the* new urban spectacle that, on the one hand, promises positive benefits, revenue, infrastructure legacies, and global recognition. Yet, on the other hand, propagates the demolition of local housing, the forced displacement of people, and repressive enforcement tactics. Such features of sport-based urban place-making have thus come to create disparate consequences for communities, seemingly effacing the traditions, histories, and heritage of populations tied to former representations of place and a shared sense of civic identity (Silk & Manley, 2012).

Conclusion

The hosting of sport mega-events across cities and many MURs have sought to secure their legitimacy through the premise of positive legacy outcomes manufactured upon ideological constructs (Gibbons & Wolff, 2012). Firmly embedded within the machinations of the global market and in the pursuit of transnational capitalism, Formula One motorsport is no exception. The spectacle of the event itself offers an influential tool to cultivate an image of political value, a symbolism for contemporary urban cosmopolitanism that supports a nation-building agenda by reinforcing images of a powerful, modern, and progressive state (Gogishvili, 2018; Lowes, 2018). Additionally, host cities profess to provide socio-economic benefits to local communities through investment in infrastructure and projects of urban renewal. With respect to the Shanghai Chinese Grand Prix, the event operated effectively as an instrument for place marketing, working to positively project the image of a modern, open, and metropolitan city towards live spectators (Liu & Gratton,

2010). In forging connotations of progress, vitality, and a sophisticated self-image through the lens of a high-tech global media event (see Sturm, 2014), the perception and awareness of Shanghai could be enhanced to elevate the affective qualities—such as local and national pride—associated with these spectacular spaces of cultural consumption (Huang et al., 2014; Liu & Gratton, 2010).

Although Shanghai's Grand Prix has been regarded as a key identity card for positioning the city on a global scale (Liu & Gratton, 2010), the benefits associated with hosting a Formula One Grand Prix are often never fully realized—contributing towards the mythification of legacy attached to the staging of sport mega-events (Gibbons & Wolff, 2012)—and, in certain instances, have come to impact negatively upon local residents (see Gezici & Er, 2014; Lefebvre & Roult, 2011; Lowes, 2004, 2018). As projects that emanate from political decision-making and rarely through public discourse, local assets and resources conducive to the tourist gaze are exploited in a bid to showcase a preferred image of a city, one that is often detached from the local culture and marketed with the intent of generating economic growth to benefit local state officials, media entrepreneurs, real estate developers and the tourism economy. The suburban development of Anting New Town that neighbours the Shanghai Formula One International Circuit is indicative of this strategic approach towards place marketing, and the manipulation of place itself, to attract investment and boost economic growth (Shen & Wu, 2012). Such urban 'duplitecture' (Bosker, 2013) offers an image that coalesces around, and seeks to reinforce, the consumptive lifestyle, urban identity, and local cosmopolitanism attached to the performative aspects of Formula One motorsport (Lowes, 2018). However, this process of image building and place marketing holds real connotations for poorer urban populations. Low-paid domestic workers who serve these new exclusive communities (e.g. gardeners, maids, and security guards) are relocated to rural areas, exemplifying the growing trend of social and spatial polarization between the rich and poor as new circuits of capital come to revalorize suburban districts and the urban fringe (Chen et al., 2009). Through this course of displacement and development, a new urban narrative is created that functions to serve a particular and selected global city imagery, an image of place that acts to suppress, and indeed efface, local identities attached to cultures and communities subjected to relocation.

By drawing upon the Shanghai Chinese Grand Prix as an example of urban place-making, we sought to demonstrate the conflicts that arise from an enthusiasm to renew and (re)position the city based on state entrepreneurial tactics, reflecting the local and territorial politics that govern China's urban development in the post-reform era (Li & Wu, 2012). The large-scale project of suburbanization surrounding Shanghai's International Circuit is representative of China's contemporary approach towards urban policy and development, emphasizing a model of state entrepreneurialism that operates through the market via an assemblage of quasi-government agencies (e.g. urban development and investment corporations), state-owned enterprises and under the control of the local state (Wei, 2012; Wu, 2020). While global financial instruments, capital flow, and revenue are key considerations for such large-scale land development projects, this process of suburbanization is not guided by consumer choice nor overwhelmed by a market logic, but planned, driven, and primarily controlled by state-owned enterprise (Wu, 2017). In this instance, state entrepreneurialism within urban China is 'deeply political' (Wu, 2020), and calls for a contextual understanding of the particular assemblages that govern urban development and the manner through which contemporary China is seeking to (re)make its cities and select parcels of transnational space (King & Kusno, 2000).

To conclude, the potential negative impacts of a mega-event can be widespread, influencing host communities in a multitude of ways that contribute towards social inequality, damage to the environment, economic burden, and issues of surveillance and securitization (Coaffee & Wood, 2006; Gezici & Er, 2014; Geeraert & Gauthier, 2018; Klauser, 2012; Manley & Silk, 2014a). As such, preparation to assuage these negative realities may indeed provide an opportunity to maximize the intangible benefits of mega-events—often associated with national pride, knowledge development, and governance reform (see Huang et al., 2014)—as they become integral components of the legacy planning for host cities. In the specific context of China, the alleviation of detrimental outcomes arising from the hosting of mega-events and the reconfiguration of urban space increasingly becomes a matter for the Chinese state apparatus. State-owned enterprise is considered the 'primary builder'—both in terms of scale and defining role—in the development and commodification of urban space under globalization (Shen & Wu, 2012). Thus, whether such future land development projects that seek to build on the exposure of sporting mega-events will contribute towards any form of spatial democratization is perhaps reliant upon a dramatic shift in political agenda, and a desire to recognize the exclusionary model of spatial, social, and economic stratification that is so often found within China's contemporary strategies for urban place-making, development, and expansion.

References

Andrews, D. L. (2009). Sport, Culture, and Late Capitalism. In B. Carrington & I. McDonald (Eds.), *Marxism Cultural Studies and Sport* (pp. 213–231). Routledge.

Andrews, D. L. (2017). Sport, Spectacle and the Politics of Late Capitalism. In A. Bairner, J. Kelly, & J. W. Lee (Eds.), *Routledge Handbook of Sport and Politics* (pp. 225–237). Routledge.

Andrews, D. L. (2019). *Making Sport Great Again: The Uber-Sport Assemblage, Neoliberalism, and the Trump Conjuncture*. Palgrave Pivot.

Armstrong, G., Hobbs, D., & Lindsay, I. (2011). Calling the Shots: The Pre-2012 London Olympic Contest. *Urban Studies, 48*(15), 3169–3184.

Bosker, B. (2013). *Original Copies Architectural Mimicry in Contemporary China*, University of Hawai'i Press.

Bian, Y., & Logan, J. R. (1996). Market Transition and the Persistence of Power: The Changing Stratification System in Urban China. *American Sociological Review, 61*, 739–758.

Breitung, W. (2012). Enclave Urbanism in China: Attitudes towards Gated Communities in Guangzhou. *Urban Geography, 33*(2), 278–294.

Brenner, N., & Theodore, N. (2002). Cities and the Geographies of "Actually Existing Neoliberalism". *Antipode, 34*, 349–379.

Broudehoux, A.-M. (2007). Spectacular Beijing: The Conspicuous Construction of an Olympic Metropolis. *Journal of Urban Affairs, 29*(4), 383–399.

Chen, X., Wang, L., & Kundu, R. (2009). Localizing the Production of Global Cities: A Comparison of New Town Developments around Shanghai and Kolkata. *City & Community, 8*(4), 433–465.

Cho, Y., Leary, C., & Jackson, S. J. (2012). Glocalization and Sports in Asia. *Sociology of Sport Journal, 29*, 421–432.

Clift, B. C., & Andrews, D. L. (2012). Living Lula's Passion: The Politics of Rio 2016. In H. J. Lenskyi & S. Wagg (Eds.), *The Palgrave Handbook of Olympic Studies* (pp. 210–232). Palgrave Macmillan.

Coaffee, J., & Wood, D. M. (2006). Security is Coming Home: Rethinking Scale and Constructing Resilience in the Global Urban Response to Terrorist Risk. *International Relations, 20*(4), 503–517.

Cook, I. G. (2007). Beijing 2008. In J. R. Gold & M. M. Gold (Eds.), *Olympic Cities: City Agendas, Planning, and the World's Games, 1896–2012* (Studies in History, Planning and the Environment Series) (pp. 183–196). Routledge.

Debord, G. (1995). *The Society of the Spectacle*. Zone Books.

Derleth, J., & Koldyk, D. R. (2004). The *shequ* Experiment: Grassroots Political Reform in Urban China. *Journal of Contemporary China, 13*(41), 747–777.

Douglass, M. (2000). Mega-Urban Regions and World City Formation: Globalisation, the Economic Crisis and Urban Policy Issues in Pacific Asia. *Urban Studies, 37*(12), 2315–2335.

Friedman, M. T., & Andrews, D. L. (2010). The Built Sport Spectacle and the Opacity of Democracy. *International Review for the Sociology of Sport, 46*(2), 181–204.

Geeraert, A., & Gauthier, R. (2018). Out-of-Control Olympics: Why the IOC is Unable to Ensure an Environmentally Sustainable Olympic Games. *Journal of Environmental Policy & Planning, 20*(1), 16–30.

Gezici, F., & Er, S. (2014). What has been Left after Hosting the Formula 1 Grand Prix in Istanbul? *Cities, 41*, 44–53.

Gibbons, A. and Wolff, N. (2012). Games monitor. *City: Analysisof Urban Trends, Culture, Theory, Policy, Action 16*(4), 468–473.

Giulianotti, R., & Robertson, R. (2012). Glocalization and Sport in Asia: Diverse Perspectives and Future Possibilities. *Sociology of Sport Journal, 29*, 433–454.

Gogishvili, D. (2018). Baku Formula 1 City Circuit: Exploring the Temporary Spaces of Exception. *Cities, 74*, 169–178.

Gold, J. R., & Gold, M. M. (2008). Olympic Cities: Regeneration, City Rebranding and Changing Urban Agendas. *Geography Compass, 2*(1), 300–318.

Gutzmer, A. (2011). *New Media How Brand-Driven City Building is Virtualizing the Actual of Space*. Thesis (PhD). Goldsmiths College, University of London, London.

Hall, C. M. (1992). *Hallmark Tourist Events*. Belhaven Press.

Hall, C. M. (2006). Urban Entrepreneurship, Corporate Interests and Sports Mega-Events: The Thin Policies of Competitiveness within the Hard Outcomes of Neoliberalism. *The Sociological Review, 54*(s2), 59–70.

Hall, T., & Hubbard, P. (1996). The Entrepreneurial City: New Urban Politics, New Urban Geographies? *Progress in Human Geography, 20*, 153–174.

Harvey, D. (1989). From Managerialism to Entrepreneurialism: The Transformation in Urban Governance in Late Capitalism. *Geograflska Annaler, Series B, Human Geography, 71*, 3–17.

Harvey, D. (2001). *Spaces of Capital: Towards a Critical Geography*. Routledge.

He, S., & Wu, F. L. (2005). Property-led Redevelopment in Post-reform China: A Case Study of Xintiandi Redevelopment Project in Shanghai. *Journal of Urban Affairs, 27*(1), 1–23.

He, S., & Wu, F. L. (2009). China's Emerging Neoliberal Urbanism: Perspectives from Urban Redevelopment. *Antipode, 41*(2), 282–304.

Heberer, T. (2009). Evolvement of Citizenship in Urban China or Authoritarian Communitarianism? Neighborhood Development, Community Participation, and Autonomy. *Journal of Contemporary China, 18*(61), 491–515.

Henriot, C. (2017). In the Shadow of Shanghai: A New Small Town, Relay of Urbanization and Metropolitan Urbanity. *L'Espace géographique, 46*(4), 329–345.

Hiller, H. H. (2000). Mega-events, Urban Boosterism and Growth Strategies: An Analysis of the Objectives and Legitimations of the Cape Town 2004 Olympic Bid. *International Journal of Urban and Regional Reearch 24*(2), 439–458.

Horne, J. (2007). The Four 'Knowns' of Sports Mega-Events. *Leisure Studies, 26*(1), 81–96.

Horne, J., & Manzenreiter, W. (2006). Sports Mega-Events: Social Scientific Analyses of a Global Phenomenon. *Sociological Review, 54*(Suppl. 2), 1–24.

Huang, H., Mao, L. L., Kim, S.-K., & Zhang, J. J. (2014). Assessing the Economic Impact of Three Major Sport Events in China: The Perspective of Attendees. *Tourism Economics, 20*(6), 1277–1296.

Jessop, B., & Sum, N.-L. (2000). An Entrepreneurial City in Action: Hong Kong's Emerging Strategies in and for (Inter) Urban Competition. *Urban Studies, 37*, 2287–2313.

King, A., & Kusno, A. (2000). On Be(ij)ing in the World: Postmodernism, "Globalization," and the Making of Transnational Space in China. In A. Dirlik & X. Zhang (Eds.), *Postmodernism and China* (pp. 41–67). Duke University Press.

Klauser, F. (2012). Spatialities of Security and Surveillance: Managing Spaces, Separations and Circulations at Sport Mega Events. *Geoforum, 49*, 289–298.

Lang, J. (2017). *Urban Design a Typology of Procedures and Products Second Edition*. Routledge.

Lees, L., Shin, H. B., & López-Morales, E. (2016). *Planetary Gentrification*. Polity Press.

Lefebvre, S., & Roult, R. (2011). Formula One's New Urban Economies. *Cities, 28*, 330–339.

Lenskyj, H. J. (2020). *The Olympic Games: A Critical Approach*. Emerald Group Publishing.

Li, Y., & Wu, F. (2012). Towards New Regionalism? Case Study of Changing Regional Governance in the Yangtze River Delta. *Asia Pacific Viewpoint, 53*(2), 178–195.

Liew, L. H. (2005). China's Engagement with Neo-liberalism: Path Dependency, Geography and Party Self-reinvention. *Journal of Development Studies, 41*(2), 331–352.

Liu, D., & Gratton, C. (2010). The Impact of Mega Sporting Events on Live Spectators' Images of a Host City: A Case Study of the Shanghai F1 Grand Prix. *Tourism Economics, 16*(3), 629–645.

Logan, J. R., & Fainstein, S. S. (2008). Introduction: Urban China in Comparative Perspective. In J. R. Logan (Ed.), *Urban China in Transition* (pp. 1–25). Blackwell Publishing Ltd.

Lowes, M. (2004). Neoliberal Power Politics and the Controversial Siting of the Australian Grand Prix Motorsport Event in an Urban Park. *Loisir et Société/Society and Leisure, 27*(1), 69–88.

Lowes, M. (2018). Toward a Conceptual Understanding of Formula One Motorsport and Local Cosmopolitanism Discourse in Urban Placemarketing Strategies. *Communication & Sport, 6*(2), 203–218.

Manley, A., & Silk, M. (2014a). Liquid London: Sporting Spectacle, Britishness and Ban-Optic Surveillance. *Surveillance & Society, 11*(4), 360–376.

Manley, A., & Silk, M. (2014b, August 18). *The Rise of the Replica: China's Urban Imitation and a Push to Protect the Nation's Heritage*. Jersey City: Forbes.

Manley, A., & Silk, M. (2019). Remembering the City: Changing Conceptions of Community in Urban China. *City & Community, 18*(4), 1240–1266.

Newman, J. L., & Giardina, M. (2011). *Sport, Spectacle, and NASCAR Nation: Consumption and the Cultural Politics of Neoliberalism*. Palgrave Macmillan.

Ong, A. (2006). *Neoliberalism as Exception: Mutations in Sovereignty and Citizenship*. Duke University Press.

Ong, A. (2011a). Worlding Cities, or the Art of Being Global. In A. Roy & A. Ong (Eds.), *Worlding Cities Asian Experiments and the Art of Being Global* (pp. 1–26). Wiley-Blackwell.

Ong, A. (2011b). Hyperbuilding: Spectacle, Speculation, and the Hyperspace of Sovereignty. In A. Roy & A. Ong (Eds.), *Worlding Cities Asian Experiments and the Art of Being Global* (pp. 205–226). Wiley-Blackwell.

Pow, C.-P., & Kong, L. (2007). Marketing the Chinese Dream Home: Gated Communities and Representations of the Good Life in (Post-)structuralist Shanghai. *Urban Geography, 28*(2), 129–159.

Ran, T., Su, F., Liu, M., & Cao, G. (2010). Land Leasing and Local Public Finance in China's Regional Development: Evidence from Prefecture-Level Cities. *Urban Studies, 47*(10), 2217–2236.

Read, B. L. (2003). Democratizing the Neighbourhood? New Private Housing and Home-Owner Self-organization in Urban China. *The China Journal, 49*, 31–59.

Ren, X. (2013). *Urban China*. Polity Press.

Ritzer, G. (2007). *The Globalization of Nothing 2*. Pine Forger Press.

Roche, M. (2000). *Megaevents and Modernity: Olympics and Expos in the Growth of Global Culture*. Routledge.

Shen, J., & Wu, F. (2012). The Development of Master-Planned Communities in Chinese Suburbs: A Case Study of Shanghai's Thames Town. *Urban Geography, 33*(2), 183–203.

Shen, J., & Wu, F. (2013). Moving to the Suburbs: Demand-Side Driving Forces of Suburban Growth in China. *Environment and Panning A, 45*, 1823–1844.

Shin, H. B. (2009). Life in the Shadow of Mega-Events: Beijing Summer Olympiad and Its Impact on Housing. *Journal of Asian Public Policy, 2*(2), 122–141.

Shin, H. B. (2012). Unequal Cities of Spectacle and Mega-Events in China. *City, 16*(6), 728–744.

Shin, H. B., & Li, B. (2013). Whose Games? The Costs of Being "Olympic Citizens" in Beijing. *Environment & Urbanization, 25*(2), 559–576.

Silk, M. (2002). Bangsa Malaysia: Global Sport, the City and the Refurbishment of Local Identities. *Media, Culture and Society, 24*(6), 253–277.

Silk, M. (2004). A Tale of Two Cities: Spaces of Consumption and the Façade of Cultural Development. *Journal of Sport and Social Issues, 28*(4), 349–378.

Silk, M. (2011). Towards a Sociological Understanding of London 2012. *Sociology, 45*(4), 733–748.

Silk, M., & Manley, A. (2012). Globalization, Urbanization & Sporting Spectacle in Pacific Asia: Places, Peoples & Pastness. *Sociology of Sport Journal, 29*, 455–484.

Silk, M. L., & Manley, A. (2017). Urban and Securitized Spaces. In M. L. Silk, D. L. Andrews, & H. Thorpe (Eds.), *Routledge Handbook of Physical Cultural Studies* (pp. 344–355). Routledge.

Sturm, D. (2014). A Glamorous and High-tech Global Spectacle of Speed: Formula One Motor Racing as Mediated, Global and Corporate Spectacle. In K. Dashper, T. Fletcher, & N. McCullough (Eds.), *Sports Events, Society and Culture* (pp. 68–82). Routledge.

Waitt, G. (2008). Urban Festivals: Geographies of Hype, Helplessness and Hope. *Geography Compass, 2*(2), 513–537.

Walcott, S. M., & Pannell, C. W. (2006). Metropolitan Spatial Dynamics: Shanghai. *Habitat International, 30*(2), 199–212.

Waldman, D., Silk, M., & Andrews, D. L. (2017). Cloning Colonialism: Residential Development, Transnational Aspiration, and the Complexities of Postcolonial India. *Geoforum, 82*, 180–188.

Wang, L., Kundu, R., & Chen, X. (2010). Building for What and Whom? New Town Development as Planned Suburbanization in China and India. *Research in Urban Sociology, 10*, 319–345.

Wang, L., & Wang, F. (2011). Sustainable Land Use under the Influence of Mega-Events. *2011 International Conference on Multimedia Technology*, Hangzhou, pp. 1265–1272. https://doi.org/10.1109/ICMT.2011.6002954

Wei, Y. H. D. (2012). Restructuring for Growth in Urban China: Transitional Institutions, Urban Development, and Spatial Transformation. *Habitat International, 36*, 396–405.

Wu, F. (2002). China's Changing Urban Governance in Transition towards a More Market-Orientated Economy. *Urban Studies, 39*(7), 1071–1093.

Wu, F. (2003). The (Post-)socialist Entrepreneurial City as a State Project: Shanghai's Reglobalisation in Question. *Urban Studies, 40*(9), 1673–1698.

Wu, F. (2006). Globalization and China's New Urbanism. In F, Wu (Ed.). *Globalization and the Chinese City*, (pp. 1–18).

Wu, F. (2008). China's Great Transformation: Neoliberalization as Establishing a Market Society. *Geoforum, 39*, 1093–1096.

Wu, F., & Phelps, N. A. (2011). (Post)suburban development and state entrepreneurialism in Beijing's outer suburbs *Environment and Planning A 43*, 410–430.

Wu, F. (2017). State Entrepreneurialism in Urban China. In G. Pinson & C. M. Journel (Eds.), *Debating the Neoliberal City* (pp. 153–173). Routledge.

Wu, F. (2020). The State Acts Through the Market: 'State Entrepreneurialism' beyond Varieties of Urban Entrepreneurialism. *Dialogues in Human Geography*, 1–4. https://doi.org/10.1177/2043820620921034

Wu, F., & Zhang, J. (2007). Planning the Competitive City-Region: The Emergence of Strategic Development Plan in China. *Urban Affairs Review, 42*(5), 714–740.

Xue, H., & Mason, D. S. (2011). The Changing Stakeholder Map of Formula One Grand Prix in Shanghai. *European Sport Management Quarterly, 11*(4), 371–395.

Xue, H., & Mason, D. S. (2012). Mapping the Major Sport Events Strategy Environment in Shanghai. In M. J. Williams & J. J. Anderson (Eds.), *Urban Development: Strategies, Management and Impact* (pp. 31–60). Nova Science Publishers.

Xue, H., & Mason, D. S. (2019). Stadium Games in Entrepreneurial Cities in China: A State Project. *Journal of Global Sport Management, 4*(2), 185–209.

Yeh, A. G. O., & Wu, F. (1996). The New Land Development Process and Urban Development in Chinese Cities. *International Journal of Urban and Regional Research, 20*(2), 330–353.

Yeh, A. G. O., & Wu, F. (1999). The Transformation of the Urban Planning System in China from a Centrally-Planned to Transitional Economy. *Progress in Planning, 51*, 167–252.

Yu, L., Xue, H., & Newman, J. I. (2018). Sporting Shanghai: Haipai Cosmopolitanism, Glocal Cityness, and Urban Policy as Mega-Event. *Sociology of Sport Journal, 35*, 301–313.

Zhang, L., & Zhao, S. X. (2009). City Branding and the Olympic Effect: A Case Study of Beijing. *Cities, 26*, 245–254.

Zhang, T., & Silk, M. (2006). Recentering Beijing: Sport, Space, Subjectivities. *Sociology of Sport Journal, 23*(4), 438–459.

Mega-Event on the Streets: The Formula 1 Grand Prix in Baku, Azerbaijan

David Gogishvili

Introduction

Mega-events, as agents of temporary and long-term urban transformation and policy change, are increasingly globalizing and diversifying. Their staging is often justified by the increased global visibility for event host cities and countries (Hall, 2006), together with promises of influxes of tourists and foreign capital (Gruneau & Horne, 2015; Sánchez & Broudehoux, 2013). Whether these promises are realized or not, it is becoming a common practice for event organizers to use public funds and public areas (parks, squares or street networks) as 'event infrastructure' to hold spectacular but strictly regulated and commercially ticketed, frequently private, events (Smith, 2015; Smith & McGillivray, 2020).

Though mega-events are temporary happenings, they often provide an example for permanent practices of spatial regulation and private-sector appropriation of daily civilian life, producing long-term impacts on their

D. Gogishvili (✉)
Department of Geography and Sustainability, University of Lausanne, Lausanne, Switzerland

D. Sturm et al. (eds.), *The History and Politics of Motor Racing*, Global Culture and Sport Series, https://doi.org/10.1007/978-3-031-22825-4_26

host communities and built environment (Hall, 2006; Smith, 2015). These lasting actions are often facilitated by temporary regulations or executive decisions that permit practices typically forbidden in the host cities, but accepted on account of their alleged short-term nature (Gogishvili, 2021; Gray & Porter, 2015) The Formula One World Drivers Championship, or just Formula 1, attended essentially by the global wealthy elite (Lefebvre & Roult, 2011) has become a significant part of this mega-event business, and their urban impacts such as public space commodification gentrification, securitization have also been increasing over the last decades. Still, there is little academic research examining the evolving relationship between the F1 and its host cities (on F1 and host cities see Gezici & Er, 2014; Lefebvre & Roult, 2011; Roult et al., 2020; Tranter & Lowes, 2005, 2009).

Baku, the biggest city in the Caucasus and the capital of the resource-rich Azerbaijan, is also one of the newest additions to the Formula 1 Championship hosts where the impact of event is particularly interesting to trace due to race being hosted right on the central public street network. After regaining its independence from the USSR in 1991, Azerbaijan's capital went through a dramatic process of urban changes supported primarily by state revenues derived from hydrocarbon resource export (Marriott & Minio-Paluello, 2012; Valiyev, 2013). This major economic growth of Azerbaijan, entirely dependent on the extractive industries, also strengthened the existing authoritarian regime. The political and economic elite, spearheaded by the authoritarian political regime of the President Ilham Aliyev, put effort into attracting global attention to Azerbaijan, both as a tourist destination and as a regional economic centre (Valiyev, 2014). Major international events, such as the 2012 Eurovision Song Contest or the 2015 European Games, in Baku were considered as important state-funded occasions for putting the country on the map (Gogishvili & Harris-Brandts, 2022). In 2016, Baku hosted its first F1 race, later known as the Azerbaijan Grand Prix, on its newly created Baku City Circuit (henceforth, BCC). The city even inaugurated a special statue dedicated to the Formula 1 and dressed central iconic buildings in event colours and banners creating a spectacular urban environment (Gogishvili, 2018) (Fig. 1).

Fig. 1 BCC map laid on a public street network of Baku. (Source: BCC, Compiled by the author in 2016)

Through on-site observations, media analysis, and in-depth interviews in Baku, this chapter explores the role mega-events such as the F1 race play in transforming cities and examines its temporary legacies. The main sources for this chapter are the field observations conducted in Baku before, during and after the event (June 13–21 and October–December 2016). News from local and international media and reports from the BCC and the Formula One Group (FOG) published between 2015 and 2020 were used to construct the event profile. Further information was gathered from ten semi-structured interviews with representatives of the BCC, journalists, academics and prominent activists all having knowledge or experience with large international events, or with the process of urban development in Baku.

Using the work of Giorgio Agamben on the state of exception as a theoretical framework, this chapter examines the impact of event-related temporary exceptional practices and restrictions upon the use of public space in Baku during the 2016 Formula 1 race, and also in the later editions of the race. Agamben's state of exception concept theorizes the abandonment of the rule of law by the sovereign during a supposed crisis in the name of the greater public good. In Baku, a similar development can be traced, as exceptional practices are applied to stage the costly private event in public space within a limited time frame justified by the promise of overarching global promotion and socio-economic progress.

The chapter begins with the outline of the theoretical framework underpinning this work by presenting the concept of (state of) exception and its uses in urban environment and mega-events. An introduction to the mega-event phenomenon and the developing relationship between the F1 and its host cities follows. This leads to a discussion of the case of Baku that conceptualizes the Baku City Circuit as a (wealthy) temporary space of exception relying on state support financially, legally and politically while excluding the needs of Baku residents.

Mega-Events as Private Spaces of Exception

Italian philosopher Giorgio Agamben in his seminal work *State of Exception* (Agamben, 2005), Italian philosopher Giorgio Agamben, explores the suspension of the rule of law by the sovereign to preserve public good which is realized by the provisional abolition of the distinction between legislative, executive and judicial powers fundamentally altering the structure and meaning of legal and political form. Agamben discussed the state of exception that occurs via the suspension of the constitution and the extension of military authority into the public realm. However, the same concept can also be applied to the different governance level when rules and regulations are sidelined to streamline particular activities or projects. Urban life is no stranger to the practices of exception "both within and beyond the confines of existing legal frameworks" (Baptista, 2013, p. 40). Scholars have demonstrated the use of exceptional practices on the urban level. For example: the controversial practices of privatization in Hong Kong in the aftermath of the Asian financial crisis of 1997 (Chu, 2010); urban policies in Rotterdam based upon securitization and gentrification of deprived areas (Schinkel & van den Berg, 2011); the urban regeneration project, The Polis Programme, in Portugal (Baptista, 2013); the Greenwich Park transformation for the

London 2012 Olympics (Smith, 2012); and others. Advancing the concept, anthropologist Aihwa Ong (2006) claims that the creation of a particular space of exception can be characterized as simultaneously positive and negative: Exceptions can be used both for "negative" exclusion but also "positive" application to create a new entity or an opportunity. However, an indicating Ong's (2006) dualistic understanding of spaces of exception, this positive inclusion disregards the non-exceptional populations and practices associated with the same space.

This argument can be extended to the F1 race in Baku, or many other mega or major events, realized through the formation of spaces of exception in the city. Müller (2015b) describes mega-events as: ambulatory occasions of a fixed duration that attract a large number of visitors, have largely mediated reach, come with large costs and have large impacts on the built environment and the population (p. 3). The preparation for mega-events within a strict time frame and rules often creates the necessity to modify the existing legal structure of the host. This means changes in laws and regulations covering urban planning, taxation, immigration, environmental protection, use of public infrastructure (Sánchez & Broudehoux, 2013). This is possible through the unofficial imposition of a state of exception that is justified by the political class and the events-rights holders by the temporary character of the event as well its alleged longer-term positive impacts. However, often such actions leave behind a legacy of permanent changes to the host city built environment or legal framework (Smith, 2014, p. 250). These changes require massive use of public funds and are rarely based on public consensus.

Increasingly, governments use mega-events to impose a temporary state of exception on host cities during the event period. Moreover, cities are often developed through exceptional and often exclusionary pre-event legal actions. Marrero-Guillamón (2012), outlines that the colossal transformation of the legal and spatial landscape brought by mega-events relies on the unofficial declaration of a state of exception—the suspension of the ordinary legal order. Brazilian scholar Carlos Vainer, studying the 2016 Summer Olympic preparations in Rio de Janiero argued that the mega-events are realized in its intense and full form is the city of exception where "everything goes beyond the formal institutional mechanisms. … The city of mega-events is the city of ad hoc decisions, exemptions, special permits" (Vainer, 2016, p. 99). Mega-events act as an instrument for imposing the state of exception. Not only are they used to create a state of exception, but they are also realized through exceptional, often exclusionary, practices.

Up to now, only limited number of studies have discussed the exceptional practices introduced for hosting Formula 1 events in various cities. Lowes (2004) examined how in Australia the Victoria State Government relocated the race from Adelaide to Melbourne's Albert Park as the organizers were attracted by the proposed race location. Staging the event in a vast green space, protected by environmental and planning laws, in downtown Melbourne became the exclusive condition for the relocation. Thus, the state government used its executive authority to impose a state of exception, and to evade potential legal limits, and converted a significant portion of the public park into a private playground for the spectacular event. The decision was officially justified by the tourism benefits and potential inward investments. An analogous development with a different outcome took place with the Turkish Grand Prix held since 2005, and marketed as a prestige project for Istanbul. Here, the location was an issue again. However, the proposed race site was situated close to a protected forest within the Istanbul Master Plan and placed within the boundaries of a drinking water basin where construction was prohibited. To create territories of the exceptional rule, the central government of Turkey intervened and modified the implementation plan of the basin (Eryilmaz & Cengiz, 2015, p. 245). The authorities mobilized vast public funds for this project. Yet, the race did not succeed in attracting the desired visitor attention. Finally, due to disagreement over the franchising costs, in 2011 the race was removed from the Formula 1 calendar. The Turkish Grand Prix was reintroduced in 2020 after several host cities could not host the event due to the COVID-19 pandemic.

Formula 1 as Urban Mega-Event

Similar to many other mega-events, Formula 1 grew from a small-scale competition limited to Western Europe and the United States to a global phenomenon hosted by large cities or metropolises all over the world.

Thus, it has transformed into a mega-event, increasing globally, and starting to affect the urban built environment at the significant scale. An urban impact of the F1 race differs according to how and where it is staged. Most of the races are held on specially constructed permanent circuits that require a large and static facility. Thus, the host cities do not have to dismantle their structures after the race. Still, to add extra thrill and sell the event destination, some races are held on street circuits laid out on public roads, and are marketed by FOG as more exciting for the locals as "it is right in the heart of the city" (Hamilton, 2016). In 2021, Monaco, Singapore, Baku and Jeddah host F1 on their public street network. Despite its temporality, F1 races on street circuits requires significant disruptions to public life in the area the event is hosted and its adjacency to prepare the event infrastructure, host the event, and then to dismantle it. This extra thrill and entertainment that is highly valued by the FOG imposes additional problems on the host cities and their residents.

The transformation of F1, which initially was a sport with low media and public interest, is linked to its commercialization, mediatization and to the concerted diffusion of sports globally (Lefebvre & Roult, 2011; Sturm, 2014). Initially, the technical quality of circuits was prioritized over the urban scenery of event hosts. However, the influence of the British business magnate, Bernard Ecclestone, as the head of FOG, changed the paradigm and amplified the commercial value of F1. Everything changed in 1974 with the precedent-setting introduction of sponsorship. Today, the event is heavily branded according to guidelines set by FOG. Private companies and governments invest heavily to get an association with this motorsport in general, or to a racing team more particularly. FOG began capturing broadcasting rights since the 1970s, which reached almost USD 770 million in the general profit of USD 2.02 billion earned in 2019 (Dixon, 2020). Sponsorship deals and franchising also make a significant contribution (Sylt, 2015). Yet, the direct gains for host city from the event are limited to the income from ticket sales accompanied with spending from the visitors on hotels, food, etc. However, this often might often come at the expense of reduced number of general visitors during the event as it is commonly known to happen during mega-events (REF-mega-event encyclopaedia on economic impacts).

The extreme mediatization of F1—as well as growing competition to host the race among cities—has increased the role of the urban built environment or scenery in attracting the event to the new host cities. Since the 2000s, Ecclestone led a worldwide expansion effort for F1 as European events were replaced on the calendar with cities including Abu Dhabi, Bahrain, Istanbul, Jeddah, Kuala Lumpur (removed in 2017) or Shanghai, Sochi. Emerging countries, often lacking democratic rule and public oversight, were prepared to invest millions in hosting the race. As of 2021, the F1 is still increasing globally with the newest editions in Baku, Azerbaijan (since 2016), Bahrain, Bahrain (since 2004), Doha, Qatar (since 2022), Jeddah, Saudi Arabia (since 2021), Singapore, Singapore (since 2008) and Sochi, Russia (since 2014). The F1 championship races have been also hosted in Shanghai, China from 2004 to 2019 and Greater Noida, India from 2011 to 2013.

Baku's Eventful Turn

Baku, the capital of Azerbaijan, is home to more than 2.2 million people. This is also where almost 80% of the nation's GDP is generated, which mostly relies on hydrocarbon resources export (Valiyev, 2014). Regaining independence in 1991, the country's transition to a market economy brought dramatic changes to Baku's built environment. Oil and gas revenues, and population increase due to in-migration, have triggered a construction boom in Baku frequently realized by evading existing planning regulations (Buchanan, 2012, p. 26; Valiyev, 2016, p. 133). The major economic growth of Azerbaijan also strengthened the existing authoritarian regime, together with the political and economic elite in close ties to the regime, which controlled the oil profits (Hughes & Marriott, 2015).

Azerbaijan is a semi-presidential republic, with the president of Azerbaijan as the head of state, and the prime minister of Azerbaijan as head of government. Baku is governed by a mayor and twelve district heads appointed and accountable to the president of Azerbaijan (Valiyev, 2013). Thus, the decision-making power is predominantly in the hands of the latter. Judiciary also depends heavily upon the executive and fails to provide recourse against violations of human rights (Buchanan, 2012).

Since independence, Azerbaijani political regime (which has been largely in the hands of the Aliyev family and New Azerbaijan Party from 1993) has continually been criticized for its poor human rights record, authoritarian-style government, high levels of corruption and restricted media (Freedom House, 2020; Transparency International, 2019). New Azerbaijan Party is in power on all political levels starting from the local to the national. This confluence of political factors greatly impacts the urban development of Baku as decisions made on the national level are realized in Baku without transparent discussion. Frequently, decisions made on the national level are implemented in the city without transparent discussion or scrutiny by the lower-level government. Baku's approach to hosting mega-events further underlines the authoritarian nature of this regime, which is often even preferred by various mega-event rights holder organizations (Fett, 2019). For example, hosting the F1 race has been presented as the initiative of President Ilham Aliyev and as the Minister of Sports concluded: "[A]ll the brightest ideas are born in his (president's) head".

Since 2010, Azerbaijan put forward a plan to transform itself into the main tourist node of the South Caucasus region and its economic heart (Valiyev, 2014, p. 630). A range of major events were staged in Baku such as the Eurovision Song Contest, the inaugural edition of European Games, the Islamic Solidarity Games and the UEFA EURO Men's Championship in 2020. Iconic architectural projects by prominent international architects such as GMP Architects and Zaha Hadid Architects, and numerous luxury hotels, were realized to reflect the novel glamorous image of the capital, and to host potential visitors attracted by the aforementioned mega-events. In preparation, the government also devoted billions from public funds into urban infrastructure projects and event venues. These efforts also included the beautification campaign (Valiyev & Wallwork, 2019), causing forced relocation from central Baku to the peripheries of around 80,000 people living within areas slated for redevelopment (Burger, 2010; Grant, 2014). Displaced families—sometimes violently evicted—received compensation well below market value and were left with few options for legal recourse (Human Rights Watch, 2012, p. 3). City beautification also took the forms of view protection—high walls along prominent roadways were installed to seclude informal or deteriorated housing from the sightlines of visitors. Similar cases directed towards excluding unwanted groups and sites from urban environment have been reported from the Seoul 1988 (Davis, 2011) and the Rio 2016 Summer Olympics (Broudehoux, 2017).

After the Eurovision Song Contest in 2012 (the first major event hosted in Baku), many attempts to equally high-profile events followed: Such state efforts were mainly directed to improve the urban portfolio of the city for its (unsuccessful) Olympic bids. In 2015, Baku hosted the inaugural edition of the European Games, brought more than 6000 athletes to the city at the expense of the Azerbaijani state and with a public budget of over USD 10 billion (Waal, 2015). Baku also gained the hosting rights of the F1, the Islamic Solidarity Games 2017, the European Youth Olympic Festival 2019 and UEFA 2020. According to the Azerbaijani officials, their event hosting strategy is built to support nation-building, boost civic pride and promote Azerbaijan worldwide (Militz, 2016).

The Azerbaijan Grand Prix's Temporary Spaces of Exception

A ten-year contract was signed between FOG and the Azerbaijani Government in 2016, binding the latter to host the F1 race for at least five successive years and was further extended to 2023 (Formula 1, 2019; Trend AZ, 2016). The Baku City Circuit Operations Company, established by the son of Azad Rahimov (the Minister of Youth and Sport since 2006) Arif Rahimov in 2015, is responsible for organizing the AGP. Preparations for the event started in 2014 with the creation of Baku City Circuit. Running through the downtown core, the waterfront boulevard, the twelfth-century UNESCO world heritage site old town showing "the beauty of the historical and modern sights of Baku" (Tilke, 2016). Media reported that costs for the inaugural event in 2016 reached a remarkable USD 230 million and were fully covered by the national budget (Recknagel & Geybulla, 2016). The licence fee paid to FOG alone accounted for USD 40–60 million and will increase annually by

10% (Khristich, 2016). The yearly organizing costs decreased later as major equipment required for the event was purchased in 2016 but organizing costs still reached at least USD 60 million (Clayton, 2019). No official figures exist regarding the cost or the economic impact.

Together with the general planning, national government made other attempts to facilitate a flawless event. Aliyev published a special decree simplifying country's complicated visa system for F1-related visitors (Carrion, 2016, p. 23). This overall had a positive impact as issuing tourist visas were simplified after the experience with event-hosting. Furthermore, the universities in the capital were requested to postpone their final exams, happening during to the race, to reduce the flow of students in the downtown. This measure was repeated for the later editions of the F1 race.

Between 17th and 19th June 2016, Baku was transformed into a large-scale playground for the global elite and media to host the F1 race (Williams, 2016). The event was hailed by FOG for being well-organized and visually fascinating (Azertag, 2016; Walker, 2015). The AGP is overall considered as one of the most challenging and visually fascinating due to its scenic background and the complexity of the track (Maher, 2021; Walthert, 2016). This praise, however, overlooks the facts that the organizers were unable to sell a substantial number of tickets (ranging from USD 90 to 665) during the inaugural edition. While the number of attendants increased for the later years, one can still see substantial number of empty seats along the race. The detailed statistics on the number of tickets are not made readily available. The comments from various government officials prior to the race indicated that despite a huge expenditure a high attendance was not expected, justified by the fact that Baku was an inaugural event.

Assembling the Event Infrastructure

The residents of Baku experience heavy disruptions to their daily practices every year as the event date nears. This happens not only during the event but also within the lengthy preparation and dismantling periods (1news.az, 2021; BCC, 2017). Building works to arrange the circuit for the inaugural race lasted for about a year. For the later years, this happened faster but on some cobble-stoned areas asphalt is laid every other year which takes about 2–3 weeks at least (BCC, 2017). Temporary event structures, such as grandstands, garages, barriers were built occupying roads, sidewalks, and squares. The Paddock Club, the exclusive VIP hospitality trackside viewing area above the team garages with gourmet cuisine and open bars, was also cited in one of the city's most prominent areas—Freedom Square situated in front of the Government House.

Baku's medieval UNESCO World Heritage old town was one of the key factors initially appealing to FOG. However, the cobblestone streets had to be resurfaced with special asphalt to meet the race requirements. The sidewalks on narrow parts of the circuit were also removed to accommodate the width of two racing cars. Race organizers claimed that these changes would be reversed within one month after the 1st race However, these promises did not materialize.

The Baku City Circuit was realized in the city by erecting two layers of concrete and steel walls along its street network delimiting the circuit from the urban environment. The walls are covered by F1-branded curtains installed to market the event but also avoid unauthorized viewing. The extensive network of barriers gives physical shape to the event but also adds a level of inconvenience to city dwellers. This results in the shutting of a substantial amount of the city's public spaces (including one of the largest public areas in Baku, its boulevard) and partly closed sidewalks often leaving only a meter-wide passage there for pedestrians (Fig. 2).

While the planning and construction of the event-related facilities in Baku caused disruptions and distress to the everyday lives of the residents it has benefited the Baku City Circuit Operations company founded by Mr. Arif Rahimov, the son of Mr. Azad Rahimov who served as the head of the Ministry of Youth And Sport from 2006 to 2021. The company has been granted exclusive rights to organize the F1 event in Baku since 2016 while the latter also contracted DDLAR Group, a construction company that has been managed by Mr. Rahimov for six years before committing to the F1 race organization. The same company has been involved in the delivery of the many of the projects related to hosting other mega-events in Baku (DDLAR Group, 2016).

Fig. 2 Barriers and fences erected in Baku downtown. (Source: Author, 2016)

Securitization and the Militarization of Public Space

Tightened and ubiquitous security measures are increasingly common features of the F1 race in Baku, which are intensified during the race weekend for what seems the largest security operation in peacetime Azerbaijan. In 2016, the military and the police were mobilized to ensure "public order" for patrolling the streets, ensuring the security of individual officials and overseeing the city from rooftops (kaspi.az, 2016). The security extended to all strategic urban areas, including the waterfront ports, transport hubs, malls along with that of the hotels accommodating guests and athletes. The coastline of the Caspian Sea was patrolled by military ships, which normally are not present in this area (Armiya.AZ, 2018).

Security is also extreme inside the event territory. The ticket holders, staff, and media have to pass through airport-style security checks to enter the circuit zone and F1 Village. This job is done by the events private security forces screened and provided by the state.

Since the first edition of the F1 race, additional security measures are also implemented in the parks and public areas adjacent to the race to produce a buffer space where at times access is fully restricted, or certain activities (such as loitering, photography, and video recording) are banned. Metro stations at the lines leading to the city circuit and at the stops close to the circuit are under tight control. Users of public transport are screened by security while entering or exiting the station.

Restriction on Movement

Due to the central location of Baku's racetrack, different parts of the city are closed to pedestrians and traffic (including parking) for at least two weeks during the event. Closure starts with the preparation of the road surface but the geography of restrictions extends in the city as the event approaches. In 2016, the limitations were imposed around the track marked on the traffic restrictions map including the Old City and Azadliq (Freedom) Square. The restrictions are most severe for three weeks around the race period and cover the race area itself combining residential, administrative, and commercial buildings. The government worried about possible traffic jams and the visual appearance of the individual vehicles bans the cars registered outside Baku.

During the first F1 race in Baku, pedestrians were limited to streets adjacent to the racetrack. Crossing streets was only possible via a limited number of distantly located underpasses or temporary overpasses. Lifts for those with limited mobility were not present. Importantly, similar to the other events hosted in Baku, it became accepted to reroute public transport passing through the event area, causing problems to its users and traffic jams elsewhere within the city (Figs. 3 and 4).

Since the 2016 race in Baku, the event organizers held lengthy promotional activities mostly in the downtown using portion of the Caspian Sea Boulevard already a few months before the event. The area later transformed and expanded into the 2-kilometre-long F1 Village—an entertainment space established exclusively for ticket holders. The boulevard space was heavily commercialized and configured in a manner desired by the commercial interests of the event's sponsors.

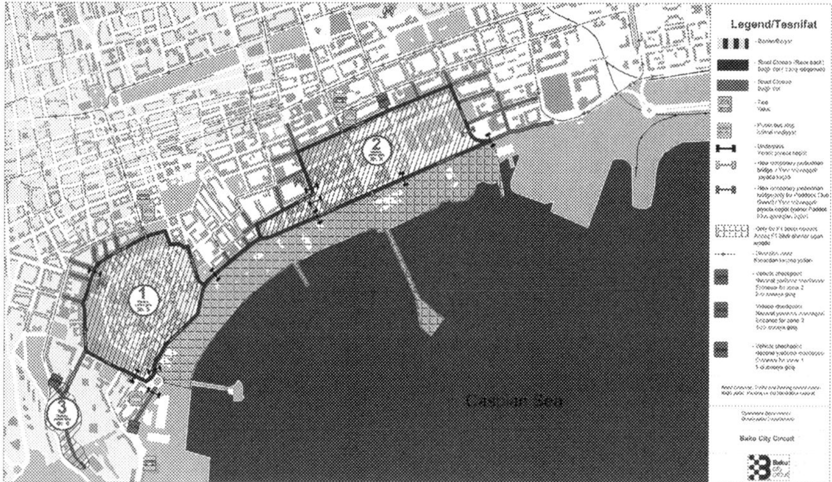

Fig. 3 Map of the Baku City Circuit and traffic restrictions. (Source: BBC, 2016)

Fig. 4 Blocked entrance of the Old Town and the spectators stand (back). (Source: Author, 2016)

Post-Event Baku

After the event, most of the related infrastructure is removed and the closed areas of the city resume normal operation. However, physical interventions and the reconfiguration of the city's landscape for the event was not fully temporary. For example, from the first edition of the AGP in Baku, objects of varying size and significance—concrete traffic medians to abandoned advertising—remained throughout the city pointing towards the grandiose presence of the F1 (Fig. 5).

The street circuit in Baku is hailed for its exceptional fragments such as a dual carriageway, a part of the circuit where cars drive in opposite directions from one another. This was realized by erecting a 600-meter-long concrete barrier to split one of the main arteries of Baku, the Neftchilar Avenue, into two. As security criteria required a solid structure, it was built in situ and left as is during the non-event period. Moreover, a decision was made to leave the Paddock Club structure until the city ceases to be on the F1 calendar.

The adaptation of Baku streetscape to the race needs sacrificed pedestrian spaces, and experiences, and continues to do. The street passing in

Fig. 5 October 2016, the Baku City Circuit paddock club and the Hilton Baku Hotel on the left. (Source: Author, 2016)

the old town has now permanently been widened to provide more space and the sidewalk was removed. Similarly, the remaining physical structures of the racetrack caused the abandonment of former street crossings, road signs or changes in traffic regulations.

Discussion

The F1 Azerbaijan Grand Prix in Baku takes place as a result of a collection of state-funded lengthy and disruptive practices. The residents have to tolerate weeks and months of disturbing construction, blocked traffic, and ongoing modifications to their public transit routes for ten days minimum and normally for much longer to organize the event largely oriented towards the out-of-town visitor class. Considering the fly-in and fly-out nature of event tourism, these problems are hardly experienced by visitors coming to the race especially as the city is adapted to their needs. This resembles the cases from the cities in the United States discussed by Eisinger (2000) who argues that most of the events and the related infrastructure development is explicitly "designed to bring visitors into the city" and often skews the locally oriented urban agenda (p. 321). Costly tickets make this even more evident as they make the three-day event inaccessible to most of the locals as the poverty level in Azerbaijan is high while the gap between the rich and the poor is striking (Marriott & Minio-Paluello, 2012). Thus, since 2016 the AGP organizers created an exclusive space of exception in the territory designated for the event—an area where the glorious F1 spectacle was staged in front of a limited number of visitors and wealthy locals at the direct expense of the state budget, while further keeping locals away via fences and roaming security forces.

Proponents often justify hosting a mega-event because of its general socio-economic benefits, possibility to attract tourists or support the international promotion of the country as argued by the Azerbaijani officials. Yet, often mega-event planning tends to privilege "local business and real estate interests, global corporations, and the cronies of the political elites" (Müller, 2015a, p. 11). In Baku, investment in a highly exclusive F1 championship was instrumentalized for privatization of profits that end up in the hands of an economic elite tied to the ruling authoritarian regime of the country. According to Müller (2015a), the process defined as "financial seizure" occurs when due to the overarching importance of a mega-event, as promoted by the national and local government, the public is forced to pay for loss-making projects and cost overruns often associated with hosting these mega-events. Such circumstances often benefit local or international elites that have already been awarded large contracts. In the case of Azerbaijan, we see the government represented by the Ministry of Youth and Sport that oversees mega-event hosting agenda including the F1 race in Baku, on the one side, and on the other side the private organization the Baku City Circuit Operations Company established by the son of the minister.

The staging of the race in Baku led to the heavy enclosure of multiple prominent and central public areas in the city. The creation of the F1 entertainment zone in the Boulevard might have increased the number of people coming to visit the centre, but the rules imposed on public space excluded everyday practices. These reflect a general trend in the mega-event industry to look out for the wider urban environment as a site for brand extension (McGillivray et al., 2015, p. 2). Such branded spaces often are free to visitors but it also excludes any other unauthorized activity such as trading or fast-food restaurants not selling the products of the event sponsors. The decision to utilize the Baku Boulevard exceptionally for the commercial purposes of the AGP represents a practice that has been normalized in the capital of Azerbaijan due to the events staged there. This is an obvious risk that might happen in many other cities hosting or striving to host mega-event (or a series of it) as the privatization and commercialization of public spaces and public infrastructure is becoming normalized.

While a limited permanent physical impact of the AGP can be observed on the urban landscape of Baku after the event, there were large physical objects left behind that exclusively used for the race and not convenient for anything else. Their presence in the city is a bold statement rather than just a mere fact which underscores the government's decision to allow such exclusive use of the space prioritizing urban spectacle-oriented towards the visitor class and international media over the pressing needs of locals. The remaining barrier at the Neftchilar Avenue and the Paddock Club left at Freedom Square are good illustrations of this. In establishing access rights to the city, the F1 race enjoys the priority. When the F1 returned in Baku in late June of 2017, it once again unfolded in its full scale, absorbing vast portions of public areas. The contractual obligations of Azerbaijan with the FOG can normalize this type of exclusive private-sector use of large portions of public space and public funds. The high securitization and militarization that come together with the hosting of mega-events create a successful ground for the normalization of these practices as dissent from the local society can hardly be expressed in this hostile environment. The political setting present in Azerbaijan makes such development particularly likely.

Baku City Circuit, acting as a space of exception, is outlined on various maps. It has concrete borders and more ambiguous adjoining buffer zones where exceptional practices are realized through the omnipresence of security guards and fences or the declared will of the executive rarely supported by the legislative decrees. However, it also functions as fluid space as the related actions and exceptions are not geographically grounded and can affect developments beyond its physical boundaries. This fluidity is illustrated with the governmental decisions related to the visa regime simplification targeting specific visitors or delaying the university final exams all over Baku. Moreover, the city circuit extended its impact and tightened the security measures all over the capital, in locations arguably not related to the needs of the race. Creation of this fluid and unofficial state of exception enabled the Azerbaijan Grand Prix to take place in accordance with F1 demands. It had a temporarily transformative character empowered by the exceptional practice.

The AGP was an outstanding event for many reasons. However, the significant point for this chapter is that thanks to an assemblage of decisions, the BCC company staged the private motorsport event on public roads—an exceptional practice not permitted in everyday circumstances. In contrast, most other mega-events happen in stadiums or structures separating them from the city. Rarely does an event of this scale take place on city streets and is of ticketed access. While there are many other happenings using public spaces, and particularly roads, for some part of their event—torch relay at the Olympics or the fan zones at the FIFA World Cup—this does not represent the core activity and the scale is normally much smaller. In comparison with mega-events hosted by different cities across the globe, Baku also showed a distinct character that the exceptional practice of occupying public infrastructure for a private event occurred without any legal decree that would frame the plans of the government on occupying the public space for the Formula 1 event. This might be considered as the main difference from that of the experience of more democratic states with offers compared to Azerbaijan's political regime, highly authoritarian and top-down, where the decision-making is restricted to a very small group of political elite and the different streams of government normally function as one. For example, this is not the case when we look at Glasgow or London hosting a variety of mega-events with exceptional characteristics.

Conclusion

Mega-event organizers globally use public spaces and public funds to stage tightly regulated, commercial, and often privately owned events that depend on public risk-taking for private benefits that accrue from the contracts awarded to private entities responsible for the delivery of the event venues and required urban infrastructure. The Formula 1 Azerbaijan Grand Prix held on the street network of Baku is another such example. It favours private entities while putting the burden and the disruption on the public. Often, such events rely on exceptional legal practices and actions permitted by the executive decree(s) or the unofficial declaration of a state of exception (Marrero-Guillamón, 2012, p. 20). Those who support such events rationalize these exceptions by the public good received and visibility they bring to the host city or nation and their exceptional needs by their extraordinary character and temporary status. Nevertheless, it has become clear that these exceptional decisions often have lengthy consequences, high costs, and set an example for future practices. In case of Baku, we see that often the arguments presented by the national government regarding international promotion, branding, and socio-economic development is often used as a cover-up to award lucrative contracts to the economic elite allied to the ruling political regime. Thus, the elites who drive the bid are at the same time those who benefit from hosting mega-events as contracts to prepare the grounds for the European Games or the AGP are in their hands.

This chapter has shown the evolving interrelationship between the private mega-event F1, and the host city of Baku through the concept of exceptionality. It described the exceptional decisions implemented before and during the event to facilitate its smooth running and to protect the interests of the events private owners, as well as a small but wealthy Azerbaijani elite attending the race. As the decision on hosting the race was taken without any public consultation, it also excluded most of the residents from voicing their concerns as to how it should take place. Baku City Circuit overall became a temporarily privatized corporate site where space was reconfigured for the event, leaving behind parts of its structure to occur again. This space of exception, while seldom legally defined, was created by major reconfiguration of daily activities and flows or the creation of new practices in the middle of Baku to facilitate a privatized and commercialized event. This elite urban event happens within the space normally used by pedestrians and the traffic actively over the years.

The hosting of the F1 Azerbaijan Grand Prix in Baku represents an alarming example for many cities that are bidding to host events or are already preparing to host one soon. The increased competition from the leaders of the authoritarian states to invite such events in their cities creates a further risk that developments that have taken place in Baku will be further replicated without democratic and participatory questioning. The hosting of such events in cities where citizen participation in decision making is absent and the project is implemented top-down runs the risk in jeopardizing of free and open public space.

References

1news.az. (2021). Центр Баку закрыт для автомобилей: Из-за «Формулы-1» изменилась ситуация на столичных дорогах—ПОДРОБНОСТИ. *1news.az*. Retrieved November 26, 2021, from https://1news.az/news/20210601124440145-TSentr-Baku-zakryt-dlya-avtomobilei-Iz-za-Formuly-1-izmenilas-situatsiya-na-stolichnykh-dorogakh-PODROBNOSTI

Agamben, G. (2005). *State of Exception* (1st ed.). University of Chicago Press.

Armiya.AZ. (2018, April 30). ВВ Успешно Обеспечили Безопасность «Формулы-1» в Баку. *ARMIYA AZ.*

Azertag. (2016, June 19). Bernie Ecclestone Hails Azerbaijan's Joining F1 Family.

Baptista, I. (2013). Practices of Exception in Urban Governance: Reconfiguring Power Inside the State. *Urban Studies, 50.*(1), 39–54. https://doi.org/10.1177/0042098012453858

BCC (2016). Traffic restrictions for the 2016 formula grand prix of Europe announce. 28 April 2016. Retrieved from https://www.bakucitycircuit.com/media/news/124/traffic-restrictions-for-the-2016-formula-grand-prix-of-europeannounced

BCC. (2017). Baku City Circuit's Asphalt Pavement Is about to Be Ready for the Race—FORMULA 1 AZERBAIJAN GRAND PRIX. *Baku City Circuit.* Retrieved November 26, 2021, from https://www.bakucitycircuit.com/en/news/4

Broudehoux, A.-M. (2017). *Mega-Events and Urban Image Construction: Beijing and Rio de Janeiro* (1st ed.). Routledge.

Buchanan, J. (2012). *"They Took Everything from Me" Forced Evictions, Unlawful Expropriations, and House Demolitions in Azerbaijan's Capital.* Baku: Human Rights Watch.

Burger, S. (2010). *Baku, the Wind-Beaten City.* Bremen: Bremen, Buntentorsteinweg 158: S. Burger.

Carrion, C. J. (2016). Why Azerbaijan Needs a Strategic Reform of Its Foreign Policy towards the European Union? *Center for Econommic and Social Development*, 1–32.

Chu, C. (2010). People Power as Exception: Three Controversies of Privatisation in Post-handover Hong Kong *Urban Studies, 47*(8), 1773–1792.

Clayton, A. (2019, April 25). Baku Residents Skeptical of Formula 1's Promise to "Ignite the City" | Eurasianet.

Davis, L. K. (2011). International Events and Mass Evictions: A Longer View: International Events and Mass Evictions: The Seoul Olympics. *International Journal of Urban and Regional Research, 35*(3), 582–599.

DDLAR Group. (2016). Ongoing Projects. *DDLAR.* Retrieved September 30, 2016, from http://ddlar.com/category/projects/ongoing-projects

Dixon, E. (2020, February 27). F1 Back in Profit for First Time since 2016. *SportsPro.*

Eisinger, P. (2000). The Politics of Bread and Circuses: Building the City for the Visitor Class. *Urban Affairs Review, 35*(3), 316–333. https://doi.org/10.1177/10780870022184426

Eryilmaz, S. S., & Cengiz, H. (2015). The Mega-Event Experience: The Formula 1 Grand Prix in Turkey. In *Mega-Event Cities: Urban Legacies of Global Sports Events*. Routledge.

Fett, M. (2019). More – Not Less – Democracy Is Often Better for Organising a World Cup. Retrieved November 26, 2021, from https://www.playthegame.org/news/news-articles/2019/0637_more-not-less-democracy-is-often-better-for-organising-a-world-cup/

Formula 1. (2019). F1 to Race in Baku until at Least 2023 | Formula 1®. Retrieved November 26, 2021, from https://www.formula1.com/en/latest/article.formula-1-to-race-in-baku-until-at-least-2023.20FW1dJYMPkDy62WjP7v7a.html

Freedom House. (2020). *Freedom in the World—Azerbaijan Country Report*. Freedom House. Retrieved May 16, 2020, from https://freedomhouse.org/country/azerbaijan/freedom-world/2020

Gezici, F., & Er, S. (2014). What Has Been Left after Hosting the Formula 1 Grand Prix in Istanbul? *Cities, 41*, 44–53. https://doi.org/10.1016/j.cities.2014.05.004

Gogishvili, D. (2018). Baku Formula 1 City Circuit: Exploring the Temporary Spaces of Exception. *Cities, 74*, 169–178.

Gogishvili, D. (2021). Urban Infrastructure in the Framework of Mega-Event Exceptionalism: Glasgow and the 2014 Commonwealth Games. *Urban Geography, 0*(0), 1–24. https://doi.org/10.1080/02723638.2021.1880696

Gogishvili, D., & Harris-Brandts, S. (2022). Urban Impacts of Second-Tier Mega-Events in the Global East: The European Youth Olympic. In Bignami, F., Hanakata, N. C., & Cuppini, N. (Eds.), *Mega Events, Urban Transformations and Social Citizenship: A Multi-Disciplinary Analysis for an Epistemological Foresight*. Routledge.

Grant, B. (2014). The Edifice Complex: Architecture and the Political Life of Surplus in the New Baku. *Public Culture, 26*(3), 501–528.

Gray, N., & Porter, L. (2015). By Any Means Necessary: Urban Regeneration and the "State of Exception" in Glasgow's Commonwealth Games 2014: By Any Means Necessary. *Antipode, 47*(2), 380–400. https://doi.org/10.1111/anti.12114

Gruneau, R., & Horne, J. (2015). Mega-Events and Globalization Capital and Spectacle in a Changing World Order. In R. Gruneau & J. Horne (Eds.),

Mega-Events and Globalization: Capital and Spectacle in a Changing World Order (pp. 1–28). Routledge.

Hall, C. M. (2006). Urban Entrepreneurship, Corporate Interests and Sports Mega-Events: The Thin Policies of Competitiveness within the Hard Outcomes of Neoliberalism. *The Sociological Review, 54*(2_suppl), 59–70. https://doi.org/10.1111/j.1467-954X.2006.00653.x

Hamilton, M. (2016). Circuit Breakers. *Baku*, 50–57.

Hughes, E., & Marriott, J. (2015). *All That Glitters: Sport, BP and Repression in Azerbaijan*. Platforma.

kaspi.az. (2016, June 16). Police in Enhanced Mode Due to F1 Race in Baku. *KASPI*.

Khristich, D. (2016, July 8). Пиар Национального Масштаба. Как и Зачем Баку Проводит «Гран-При Европы». *Sovsport.Ru*.

Human Rights Watch (2012). Country summary - Azerbaijan. Berlin: Human Rights Watch.

Lefebvre, S., & Roult, R. (2011). Formula One's New Urban Economies. *Cities, 28*(4), 330–339. https://doi.org/10.1016/j.cities.2011.03.005

Lowes, M. (2004). Neoliberal Power Politics and the Controversial Siting of the Australian Grand Prix Motorsport Event in an Urban Park. *Loisir et Société / Society and Leisure, 27*(1), 69–88. https://doi.org/10.1080/07053436.2004.10707642

Maher, T. (2021, June 3). VIDEO: What Makes the Baku City Circuit so Unique? *RacingNews365*.

Marrero-Guillamón, I. (2012). The Art of Dissent: Adventures in London's Olympic State. In H. Powell & I. Marrero-Guillamón (Eds.), *The Art of Dissent: Adventures in London's Olympic State* (pp. 20–20). Marshgate Press.

Marriott, J., & Minio-Paluello, M. (2012). *The Oil Road: Journeys from the Caspian Sea to the City of London*. Verso.

McGillivray, D., McPherson, G., & Carnicelli, S. (2015). Sporting and Cultural Events: Contested Legacies. *Annals of Leisure Research, 18*(4), 441–444. https://doi.org/10.1080/11745398.2015.1114210

Militz, E. (2016). Public Events and Nation-Building in Azerbaijan. In *Nation-Building and Identity in the Post-Soviet Space*. Routledge.

Müller, M. (2015a). The Mega-Event Syndrome: Why So Much Goes Wrong in Mega-Event Planning and What to Do About It. *Journal of the American Planning Association, 81*(1), 6–17. https://doi.org/10.1080/01944363.2015.1038292

Müller, M. (2015b). What Makes an Event a Mega-Event? Definitions and Sizes. *Leisure Studies, 34*(6), 627–642.

Ong, A. (2006). *Neoliberalism as Exception: Mutations in Citizenship and Sovereignty*. Duke University Press Books.

Recknagel, C., & Geybulla, A. (2016, June 17). Beyond Balcony-Rental Boom, Formula One Race Offers Few Rewards for Azerbaijanis. *Radio Free Europe/ Radio Liberty*.

Roult, R., Auger, D., & Lafond, M.-P. (2020). Formula 1, City and Tourism: A Research Theme Analyzed on the Basis of a Systematic Literature Review. *International Journal of Tourism Cities, ahead-of-print*(ahead-of-print). https://doi.org/10.1108/IJTC-02-2020-0025

Sánchez, F., & Broudehoux, A.-M. (2013). Mega-Events and Urban Regeneration in Rio de Janeiro: Planning in a State of Emergency. *International Journal of Urban Sustainable Development, 5*(2), 132–153.

Schinkel, W., & van den Berg, M. (2011). City of Exception: The Dutch Revanchist City and the Urban Homo Sacer. *Antipode*, 43, 1911–1938.

Smith, A. (2012). *Events and Urban Regeneration: The Strategic Use of Events to Revitalise Cities* (1st ed.). Routledge.

Smith, A. (2014). "Borrowing" Public Space to Stage Major Events: The Greenwich Park Controversy. *Urban Studies, 51*(2), 247–263. https://doi.org/10.1177/0042098013489746

Smith, A. (2015). *Events in the City: Using Public Spaces as Event Venues*. Routledge.

Smith, A., & McGillivray, D. (2020). The Long-Term Implications of Mega-Event Projects for Urban Public Spaces. *Sport in Society, 0*(0), 1–17. https://doi.org/10.1080/17430437.2020.1826934

Sturm, D. (2014). A Glamorous and High-Tech Global Spectacle of Speed: Formula One Motor Racing as Mediated, Global and Corporate Spectacle. In K. Dashper, N. Fletcher, & N. Mccullough (Eds.), *Sports Events, Society and Culture* (pp. 68–82). Routledge.

Sylt, C. (2015). Azerbaijan Grand Prix "Uncertain" for 2020, Says Organizer. *Forbes*. Retrieved September 7, 2021, from https://www.forbes.com/sites/csylt/2020/04/18/azerbaijan-grand-prix-boss-reveals-doubt-over-2020-race/

Tilke, H. (2016). There Is No Track like Baku City Circuit. BCC.

Transparency International. (2019). Country Profiles—Azerbaijan. *Transparency International*. Retrieved September 9, 2019, from https://www.transparency.org/country/AZE#

Tranter, P. J., & Lowes, M. (2009). Life in the Fast Lane: Environmental, Economic, and Public Health Outcomes of Motorsport Spectacles in Australia—Paul J. Tranter, Mark Lowes, 2009. *Journal of Sport and Social Issues, 33*(2), 150–168.

Tranter, P. J., & Lowes, M. D. (2005). The Place of Motorsport in Public Health: An Australian Perspective. *Health & Place, 11*(4), 379–391. https://doi.org/10.1016/j.healthplace.2004.07.004

Trend AZ. (2016, February 8). Azerbaijan Signs 10-Year-Contract for Holding Formula-1. *Trend.Az.*

Vainer, C. (2016). Mega-events and the city of exception: Theoretical explorations of the Brazilian experience. In R. Gruneau, & J. Horne (Eds.). Mega-events and globalization: Capital and spectacle in a changing world order (pp. 97–112). Abingdon: Routledge.

Valiyev, A. (2013). Baku. *Cities, 31*, 625–640.

Valiyev, A. (2014). The Post-Communist Growth Machine: The Case of Baku, Azerbaijan. *Cities, 41*, S45–S53.

Valiyev, A. (2016). First European Olympic Games in Baku: New Articulation of Azerbaijani Identity? In A. Makarychev & A. Yatsyk (Eds.), *Mega Events in Post-Soviet Eurasia* (pp. 131–149). Palgrave Macmillan US.

Valiyev, A., & Wallwork, L. (2019). Post-Soviet Urban Renewal and Its Discontents: Gentrification by Demolition in Baku. *Urban Geography, 40*(10), 1506–1526.

Waal, T. de. (2015). Sochi Revisited in Baku? *Carnegie Europe*. Retrieved September 2, 2020, from https://carnegie.ru/commentary/60432

Walker, K. (2015). Analysis: Azerbaijan's Plan to Make the F1 Race Pay Off. Retrieved November 26, 2021, from https://www.motorsport.com/f1/news/analysis-azerbaijan-s-plan-to-make-the-f1-race-pay-off/661726/

Walthert, M. (2016, June 16). Hermann Tilke Interview: F1 Circuit Designer on Baku Track and Handling Critics. *Bleacher Report.*

Williams, R. (2016, April 1). Declining Reputation of Formula One in Danger of Reaching Critical Mass. *The Guardian.*

Motor Sport in the Middle East: Regional Rivalries, Business and Politics in the Arabian Gulf

Mahfoud Amara and Youcef Bouandel

Since the turn of the century, there has been a growing interest of countries in the Gulf Cooperation Council (GCC)—particularly Bahrain, United Arab Emirates (UAE) and Qatar—in the automobile and motor racing industries. This is reflected in direct investment as shareholders in leading international manufacturers and suppliers of cars and in international motor racing events and circuits. The aim of this strategy is to, first, diversify the countries' revenues and decrease their reliance on the oil sector [isn't there an irony here: diversify to counter oil reliance by going into a petrol-intensive sport?]; which is contradicted by the growing demand for cars and pickups and investment into a petrol-intensive

M. Amara (✉)
Department of Physical Education and Sport Sciences,
College of Education, Qatar University, Doha, Qatar
e-mail: mamara@qu.edu.qa

Y. Bouandel
Department of International Affairs,College of Arts and Sciences, Qatar University, Doha, Qatar
e-mail: ybouandel@qu.edu.qa

D. Sturm et al. (eds.), *The History and Politics of Motor Racing*, Global Culture and Sport Series, https://doi.org/10.1007/978-3-031-22825-4_27

sport; and, second, to showcase the mega urban development projects in cities such as Manama, Abu-Dhabi and Doha. These developments were organized around the development of airports as hubs for distance travel, as well as tourism, retail and real estate.

Informed by media content analysis this chapter explores these developments. It begins with a general discussion of sports in the GCC countries situating the debate between globalization and the preservation of local customs. We ask why the GCC countries have embarked on the relentless pursuit of hosting international sporting events. In section "Motor Racing", we look at the emergence of the GCC, particularly Bahrain and the UAE, as major destinations for Formula One. In section "The Kingdom of Saudi Arabia, the New Mover", we discuss how Saudi Arabia is fast becoming one of the major players in motor sports in the region. These developments lead us, in section "Motor Racing and GCC Rivalry", to discuss rivalries within the GCC to host and invest in motor racing, within wider geopolitical context.

Sport, Globalization and Localization Debates

When examining modern sport in the Arab World in general, and in the Arabian Peninsula in particular, we cannot ignore the increasing interconnectedness between cultures and countries as well as the diffusion of modern sport worldwide. Moreover, one needs to consider local attempts to adapt sporting practices to local cultures to serve different interests (Amara, 2012). Since the turn of the century, countries in the region, particularly the UAE, Qatar, and to a lesser extent Bahrain, thanks to significant revenue from oil and gas exports, have embarked upon a strategy of integrating their country into the global sport arena. Consequently, sport (and motor sport as argued in this chapter) is now at the core of the (hyper) modern project of urbanization in the region. "Sport cities" and "urban zones" built around the theme of sport, combined with high tech, retail and tourism are emerging, offering the local population (citizens or residents) the possibility of being part of the global sporting experience (Azzali et al., 2021).

Qatar, the UAE and Bahrain have been proactive in shaping their image as destinations for business and tourism and have had massive investments into sports infrastructure. Sport has become an important field of business activity, linked to city and nation branding as well as a tool for "soft power" in the sense of strategic communication, mainly to an external audience and to make the country more attractive (Alexander & Cafiero, 2020). It should be pointed out that whilst "soft power" goes a long way in explaining the GCC's countries' drive to become global actors, should not be the only lenses through which to explain sport industry in the region. The internal political dynamic and economic/business dimensions are also significant. A country such as Saudi Arabia which has been founded under the model of rentier state (where minority controls wealth, derived mainly from oil and gas revenue, and the means of its distribution to secure loyalty and allegiance), coupled with religious legitimacy (the ruling family as the guardian of Islam holy sites of Mecca and Medina) is in search of a new legitimacy. A model, which is less centered around religion in conservative terms, and more attractive to tourists and investors. We agree here with Koch (2020, p. 355) that we need to move beyond the general readings of Gulf investment in sport as only an exercise in 'soft power', "to examining how these deals are strategic nodes for diverse actors in the Gulf and in the international sporting community to advance various interests: personal, political, financial, and otherwise". Investment in sport becomes an opportunity to build alliances with the realms of finance and politics and thus to contribute in improving positioning, and recognition by the international community of the GCC countries as global actors. Indeed, the region has become one of the major destinations for sporting competitions, including for different types of automobile and motor racings, as illustrated in Table 1. Motor racing, in its different formats, is at the core of this strategy. We would also argue that becoming global actors in the world of sport is a vehicle for internal transformation of these countries. In the case of Saudi Arabia, for instance England and Ahmed (2019) correctly observe that "sport becomes the latest platform through which Crown Prince Mohammed bin Salman looks to deploy the kingdom's financial muscle to project the country on to the global stage, reshape perceptions about the desert state and shake-up the nation's conservative society". Hosting

Table 1 Examples of motorsport and motorbike series in the GCC (different internet sources)

Motor race	Description
Formula Gulf 1000 (FG1000)	Single-seater racing series Run by Gulf Sport
Radical Middle East Cup	Organized by AUH Racing The SR8 Masters cars can reach speed of up to 280kp/h and can get to 100kp/h in 2.7 seconds
Porsche GT3 ME Cup	Run Lechner Racing the Porsche Sprint Challenge Middle East launched in Bahrain in 2009/2010 https://www.gt3me.com/the-challengeen
Touring Cars	The UAE's NGK Racing Series, It runs between Dubai Autodrome and Yas Marina over eight race meetings.
UAE Sportbike Championship	Features three classes: 600cc Supersport class along with a non-championship 1000cc Superbike class
Emirates Desert Championship	The UAE's national rally championship. Organized by Emirates Motorsports Organization (EMSO)
The ABB FIA Formula E World Championship	Held in Diriyah, an ancient UNESCO World Heritage site, since 2018 (following a ten-year agreement)
Saudi Arabia AlUla Extreme E Race	Electric SUVs competing in extreme environments
The UIM XCAT World Series offshore powerboat racing	Organized by Abu Dhabi International Marine Sports Club
The MotorBike Grand Prix of Qatar	Season-opening race on the GP calendar

international sports events brings these countries under the spotlight and invites international scrutiny. Making them more exposed to what Brannagan and Giulianotti (2018, p. 1152) as "soft disempowerment", in other words "actions, inactions and/or policies of states that ultimately upset, offend or alienate others, leading to a loss of credibility and attractiveness". In the same vein, ALQST, a UK-based group that monitors abuses in Saudi Arabia argued that the Kingdom is "trying to cover up [its] abuses by holding high-profile sporting events and spectacles … [and is] … not taking account of the deteriorating state of human rights. (England & Ahmed, 2019). This in turn may result in the introduction of more reforms to remedy any shortcomings, which in other circumstances would have taken a longer period to implement. Of course, there is still a lot to be done in political terms to advance the process of democratization. This would need a genuine willingness internally to adopt the democratization path and more importantly, a more coherent stance by the so-called international community (including international sport system) in striking the right balance between the promotion of democratic values and national as well as business interests.

Motor Racing

In the last decade or so, the connection between the region and motor racing has developed through a number of related aspects and facets, such as hosting of events, investments in car industries, as well as sponsorship and branding. Bahrain was in 2004 the first mover to host Formula One Grand Prix for the first time in the GCC countries. Named after the official sponsor, the Gulf Air Bahrain Grand Prix has been held since then, not without challenges though. In 2009, Abu Dhabi, representing the central government of the Federal State of the UAE, was the second city to be awarded the hosting of the competition, named Abu Dhabi Grand Prix. Already in 2006, Emirates Airlines was the sponsor of Team McLaren Mercedes Formula One cars at races across Europe, Asia, Australasia, and North and South America, on the uniform of drivers Kimi Raikkonen and Juan Pablo Montoya, and in the team's pit interior. It should be noted that Bahrain's government holding company Mumtalakat holds a 50% investment in the Mercedes McLaren Formula One Team, and owns 50% of the McLaren Automotive production-car subsidiary. Another example of ruling family's investment in motor racing industry is Sheikh Maktoum Hasher Maktoum Al Maktoum's creation in 2004 of the A1 Grand Prix series in which participating teams, each representing different nations (22 in total), compete for the World Cup of Motorsport. Abu Dhabi was also named as the official destination partner of the FIA World Rally Championship (WRC) in 2007, following a three-year-deal between the International Sportsworld Communicators (ISC) and the Abu Dhabi Tourism Authority (ADTA).

The hosting of these events prompted a number of urban projects within the region around the theme of motor racing. The Dubai

Autodrome was built as part of the Motor City project, a development led by Union Properties PJSC (UP), one of the leading property developers in the UAE. This was based on a unique automobile and motor sport theme that includes Dubai Autodrome, F1 Theme Park, Business Park, Motor City and its two residential components of uptown and Green Community Motor City. The Dubai Autodrome incorporates an FIA-approved 5.39 km circuit, a race and driving school, karting track, and the HSBC Bank Racing Academy, under the patronage of Sheikh Hamdan Bin Mohammed Bin Rashid Al Maktoum. The Dubai Autodrome was officially inaugurated in October 2004 when it hosted the final round of the FIA GT1 Championship, and a number of other competitions: FIA GT3 Speedcar, Formula Renault Campus, and UAE National Races. In 2009, Aabar, a stock fund owned by the Abu Dhabi government, took a 30% interest in Brawn GP, the world-champion Formula One team that was renamed Mercedes Grand Prix (Hutton, 2011). Mubadala Development Co., an investment group controlled by the government of Abu Dhabi, purchased in 2005 from the Italian Bank Mediobanca SpA, a 5% stake in Ferrari, which prompted its further investment in a Ferrari Theme Park. It was also the sponsor of Ferrari's Formula One team from 2007 to 2010. The 5% stake was sold back in 2010 to Fiat, which controls Ferrari with a 56% stake, for an amount estimated at €122 million (George-Cosh, November 14, 2010).

Similar to its neighbouring countries, the UAE and Bahrain, Qatar has also been investing in the car industry as a strategy to diversify its revenue. For instance, state-owned Qatar Holding, LLC, owns 17% percent of Volkswagen Group, including Audi, Bentley and Skoda. Qatar Holding used to be owner of 10% stake in Porsche, which sold back to Porsche and Piëch families in 2013. Qatar also sought to be part of the race for staging international motor sport events. To this aim, the Qatari authorities opened the Lusail International Circuit in 2004. Around $58 million was spent building a 5300km motorbike circuit located outside the capital Doha. The Lusail International circuit hosts the Grand Prix Masters leg, the World Superbike Championships and the MotoGP, Moto2 & Moto3 official tests. It is also being used to promote community sport for cyclists, runners, walkers and roller-bladers on Tuesday (women and children only) and Wednesday evenings.

The Kingdom of Saudi Arabia, the New Mover

Saudi Arabia, the most populous, richest, with the largest automobile market in the GCC, estimated at 40% of all vehicles sold in the region (International Trade Administration, 2010), is increasingly taking a more visible/ pro-active approach in the international motor sport scene. The Saudi authorities have been able to use their wealth to attract the most significant motor sports events to their country. These developments, however, should not be viewed in isolation. On the contrary, they should be understood as part of general economic, social and political shifts in the Kingdom of Saudi Arabia that has been taking place since 2016. Indeed, the developments that followed on the economic and social fronts, as we shall see later in this section, are far reaching and were unthinkable even a few years ago.

The year 2016 marked the start of the 2030 Vision: the brainchild of the then Deputy Crown Prince, Mohammed Bin Salman. Vision 2030 is a strategic plan for the following fifteen years to increase the country's openness, create a vibrant society and reform the country's economy. Saudi Arabia's reliance on oil revenues makes it less sustainable in the medium and long term. Therefore, among the aims of this Vision are the diversifications of revenues and boosting of investment. Indeed, in the same year, 2016, Mohammed Bin Salman unveiled plans to list the giant state oil company, Aramco, on the stock exchange. Mohammed Bin Salman's position within the Kingdom was enhanced in June 2017, when his father, the ailing King Salam bin Abdulaziz, removed prince Mohammed bin Nayef, then crown prince, from all official positions and appointed his son, Mohammed, heir to the Saudi throne; a change that has not been without controversy. This appointment not only strengthened his position within the ruling family, but also made him, given his father's age and ill health, the de facto ruler of the Kingdom.

The reforms were far-reaching. Their aim was to change many of the practices that his Kingdom was known and indeed criticized for. The liberal policies introduced led to the emergence of phenomenon that were hitherto unknown in the country. He began by curtailing the powers of Commission for the Promotion of Virtue and Prevention of Vice

(CPVPV). This Commission, commonly known as the Islamic religious police, is a vice squad that enforced strict adherence to public morality as defined by the state. In an attempt to improve his Kingdom's image, Mohammed Bin Salman made significant steps to improve the situation of Saudi women, whose treatment was hitherto the subject of international criticism. Hence, in February 2017, a woman was appointed to head the country's Stock Exchange. A year later, in February 2018, Saudi women were given the right to open businesses without the need for a male's permission. The following month, March 2018, mothers, in divorce cases, were given automatic custody of their children without having to go court to claim it. Whilst aforementioned changes might not have caught the attention of the layperson, the lifting of the ban on female drivers in June 2018 certainly did. Mohammed bin Salman established an entertainment authority that hosted a variety of shows (music, sports and comedy). Indeed, in April 2017, the Crown Prince announced that "Al Qidiya", southwest of the capital city, Riyadh, would be developed into one of the world's largest cultural, sports and entertainment cities. The Saudi authorities also organized female areas in football stadia and were allowed to attend football matches.

Whilst the Kingdom has been making strides towards economic and social liberalization, including in sport, a number of issues pertaining to Mohammed Bin Salman's leadership and style raised several eyebrows. Specifically, issues related to human rights question remain high on the agenda. The detention of several members of the Royal family, allegedly on corruption, was perceived as an attempt to strengthen his rule and sideline would be opponents to his reforms. However, his efforts of modernizing the country and projecting a more liberal image have been questioned by country's continuous human rights abuse, characterized by the detention of activists, particularly women, continuous war in Yemen and last but not the least, the three-year blockade of Qatar. However, perhaps the most significant of all the negative press that the Kingdom received is the assassination in October 2018 of Jamal Khashoggi, a Saudi journalist and an outspoken critic, in his country's Embassy in Istanbul, Turkey. It is against this background and geopolitical context that Saudi Arabia's relentless drive to change its image and become a major venue for hosting international motor sports events can be analysed. The first such event is the Dakar Rally.

Held in Africa between 1979 and 2007, one the world's most famous rallies, for political and business reasons, shifted to the mountainous terrain of South America between 2009 and 2019, to arrive in Saudi Arabia in 2020. The Dakar Rally has been positioned as the flagship of KSA's mega project NEOM, the planned \$500bn 10,000-square-mile smart city (including a 170-kilometre long car-free, zero-carbon city) to boost tourism, and bid to become the centre of adventure sport and leisure in the Kingdom. The staging of the Dakar Rally in Saudi Arabia has attracted attention for a number of reasons. First in relation to business, as a number of international sport organizations and other corporate entities specialized in sport, hospitality, tourism, retail and property developers are keen to be associated and have a share of the multi-billion NEOM development project. Mercedes-Benz EQ Formula E Team signed a long-term partnership with NEOM. According to the press release "The partnership will provide secondment and development opportunities for selected Saudi nationals, who work closely with the racing team and further qualify as engineers and software developers" (Arabnews, 11 March 2020). NEOM will also be a founding partner of the Mercedes-Benz EQ FE Driver Development Program, starting in 2021, which aims to recruit young drivers from KSA and train them to compete in Formula E within the next few years. For NEOM, it is an opportunity for brand association with Mercedes-Benz and for place branding, featured in "The race towards a new future is ON" promotion video in EQ Formula E webpage (Mercedes-Benz, EQ Formula E Team, 2021). EXTREME company, specialized in broadcasting of extreme sport, organization of Extreme sport Events, and destinations development and management of place-making sports, is among the partners of NEOM project (Merlin, 2 October, 2019).

In political terms, the Dakar Rally in Saudi attracted media attention due to the political context and shift in the Kingdom described above, with allegation of "Sportswashing". In other words, campaigners have levelled accusations towards the Saudi authorities that hosting such sporting events is simply an attempt to wash over their poor human rights record. Human Rights Watch and the MENA Rights Group urged Dakar organizers, participants and official broadcasters to press Saudi authorities to release all detained Saudi human rights defenders and drop the charges against them.

> The Amaury Sport Organization should engage with human rights advocates and adopt a human rights policy to ensure that its operations do not contribute to human rights violations. (Human Rights Watch, 2020)

Having to deal in the past with criticisms regarding the nation's ultra-conservatism and rejection of Western values, including those embedded in global sport, the rapid changes taking place in the Kingdom, particularly in the areas of sport, leisure, entertainment and fashion, took observers by surprise. Again explaining the new strategy of the increasing of visibility of the Kingdom, as a form of "sportwashing" only does not give justice to the real desire of Saudi society for openness to the external world. As stated above, hosting international events invites interest and criticism. This criticism, in turn, results in pressure from governments, NGOs, journalists and sports personalities alike, eesulting thus in the ruling elite initiating further reforms and dealing with controversial issues to overcome any resistance, even minimal, from the more conservative elements of society. For instance, a number of Israeli drivers took part in the 2021 edition of the Dakar Rally. According to media reports, two Israeli drivers Danny Pearl and Charly Gotlib entered KSA with their Israeli passports to represent Belgium in the race, while two other Israelis participated under the US-flagged CRV team (Khalil, January 17, 2021). This would not be possible without authorization from KSA. Banning these drivers from entering the Kingdom would have put KSA agreement with the Dakar Rally into a serious test.

The Kingdom cemented its position as major hub for motor sports when it finally won the right to host the jewel of motor sport: Formula One. As of December 2020, 32 countries have held the championship and the list is growing. Whilst until 2004, only one race was held in the MENA region, Casablanca, Morocco, in 1958, since then the region is fast becoming an important destination for the event. Following Bahrain since 2004 and Abu Dhabi since 2009 Saudi Arabia is the 33rd country in the world to host Formula One, named Saudi Arabian Grand Prix, temporarily in the street of Jeddah's Cornish area, the second biggest city in the Kingdom. Chase Carey, Formula One Chairman and Chief Executive, whilst confirming that the race would take place in Jeddah, also acknowledged the Kingdom is "rapidly becoming a hub for sports and entertainment with many major events taking place there in recent years." (Balfour, 2020). The Saudi authorities will, however, move the race to the purpose-built circuit in the specially designed sport and entertainment city of Qidiya by 2023. Carey defended the decision to hold the race in the kingdom and pointed to the potential the region represents. He argued that:

> The region is hugely important to us and with 70% of the population of Saudi being under 30 we are excited about the potential to reach new fans and bring our existing fans around the world exciting racing from an incredible and historic location. (Formula One, 2020)

Other commentators suggested that the main reason behind Formula One expansion is the $50 million fee paid by Saudi Arabia, which came at the right time to overcome the loss due to the effect of Corona virus estimated at nearly $400 million (Medland, 2021).

Motor Racing and GCC Rivalry

There have been a number of attempts in the past to consolidate efforts of GCC countries to establish a regional committee and championship around motor racing. For instance, the GCC Young Drivers Academy funded by the FIA Sport Grant Programme, with the UAE as the Regional Training Provider, which first took place in 2017. It was a collaboration between the *Federation Internationale De L'Automobile* (FIA), Bahrain Motor Federation (BMF), Qatar Motor & Motorcycle Federation (QMMF) and the Automobile & Touring Club of UAE (ATCUAE). The circuit training part was conducted on Bahrain International Circuit and Rally training was conducted in UAE. The first meeting between the heads of GCC motor racing federations was held in March 2016 (Arabnews, 2016) to put together the plan for the regional championship named the Gulf Challenge, initially a five-round off-road rally series with separate championships for motorcycle and quad classes. This alongside Middle East Rally Championship (MERC) held since 1984 including events in Lebanon, Oman, Qatar, Kuwait, Cyprus and Jordan (FIA, n.d.). MERC has been dominated by drivers from the UAE, Mohammed Bin Sulayem and Qatari Nasser Saleh Al-Attiyah. The Gulf Challenge had five rounds with the first in Muscat on September 7 and 8, 2017. The second round held on October 5 and 6 in the UAE, the third in Kuwait on October 26 and 27, fourth in Saudi Arabia on November 9 and 10 with the last round in Qatar on December 7 and 8 (Rizk, 2017).

Qatar's attempts to integrate the Formula One Circuit have been faced by the veto of neighbouring countries. To counter the veto, Qatar, represented by Qatar Sport Investment (QSI), the owner of football club PSG, joined forces in 2015 with the owner of Miami Dolphins to acquire a major stake (35.5% interest) from private equity fund CVC Capital Partners Ltd running Formula One. A bid was estimated by media sources to be USD 7bn plus (Gibson, 2015). The deal did not go through and it is interesting that Formula One's previous decision was not to add another race in the region. This position was reversed, resulting in the decision to offer Jeddah in Saudi Arabia the opportunity to host a round of the Formula One world championship. This was followed by the signing with Formula One long-term sponsorship with Saudi Oil company Aramco. As a result, Qatar-based pay TV Broadcaster BeIN Sports decided not to renew its five contract with Formula One, as direct consequence of large-scale piracy led by BeoutQ, which Qatar accused Saudi Arabia being behind it. Interestingly, the broadcasting right of Formula One for the middle East and North Africa was taken by the Saudi-owned TV network, The Middle East Media Group (MBC). Formula One races is to be broadcasted free to air for the Middle East and North Africa region in MBC Action channel until 2023. The deal includes the broadcasting of training sessions, qualifiers and Grand Prix day (Flanagan, 2019). In the same vein, Bahrain accused Qatar's Al Jazeera TV of bias in its coverage of the civil unrest in Bahrain which broke out in 2011 following events in Tunisia and Egypt, which toppled Presidents Ben Ali and Mubarak and extended to other Arab countries (Yemen, Syria and Libya). The uprising in Bahrain has had a direct impact on the season-opening Bahrain Formula One Grand Prix, including its cancellation in 2011, putting the country and Formula One Group under pressure. It was estimated that Formula One lost USD 100mn in revenue due to the cancellation, including the revenue from ticket sales which totaled USD 14mn. Bahrain had to pay $40m fee for the cancelled race (Benson, 2011).

To conclude, sport is an arena for states in the GCC region thanks to the purchasing power represented by their Sovereign Wealth Funds, and under the patronage of royal families, to negotiate a position for the region in the impending post-oil era and to explore a new opportunity for investments in the global markets including in automotive, car and motor racing industries (Amara & Theodoraki, 2010). The rationale for investment in the sport industry locally and internationally, in addition to nation branding and prestige, is the bridging between different sectors such as banking, retail, transportation, construction, tourism, entertainment and hospitality. These are the pillars of the region's strategy to move away from its heavy dependency on the hydrocarbon sector, which is facing a number of challenges with the decline of oil prices, and the advent of other non-fossil energy sources. For FIA and other international car and motor racing industries, it is an opportunity to expand their markets and to tap into capital investment opportunities offered by countries in the GCC region, which is much needed when their business model is being challenged due to financial loss, affected by the economic crisis which has impacted directly the global value chain (production, supply and sales) of automotive industry. This is coupled with the financial impact of the recent global COVID 19 pandemic on global sport industry as a whole.

For the car and motor racing industry, receiving direct investment through the purchase of stakes or indirect investment through sponsorship and hosting of competitions is an opportunity to boost their industry and to appeal to potential customers in the GCC with its high purchasing power. In the GCC, in particular Bahrain, the UAE, Qatar and more recently KSA, automobile and motor racing industry, in addition to being a business opportunity for investment, is an instrument of national branding. In the context of the political turmoil in neighbouring countries, particularly since 2011 following the so-called Arab Spring, a number of political reforms in the region have been implemented, including labour and investment laws, municipal and parliamentary elections. Further, the young Crown Prince Mohamed Bin Salman understood the global impact of sport in boosting the image of the Kingdom, including its tourism sector and the marketing of its mega projects represented by NEOM and Qidiya, the future hubs of sport and entertainment in the country.

Motor racing has not been traditionally associated with the Middle East in general and the GCC in particular. The situation, however, has changed since the turn of the century. Countries in the GCC have been making significant steps in this area and have invested large sum of money to put their respective countries on the map of motor sports. Bahrain, the UAE, Qatar and the KSA are now destinations for motor sport. The study on motor racing in the region highlights a number of issues which need further investigations: first, the intervention of different interests groups and actors to push for their political and business agenda, including ruling elite, national and private corporations representing different sectors (hospitality, leisure, retail and tourism, to name but a few), motor racing and partners in automobile industry; and second, the rapid societal change and dynamics in the region, which has been motivated by the spread of technology as well as generational change in political elite. Younger and more educated business-minded people are making the decisions, pursuing a more pragmatic and lobbyist strategy. Finally, the global and local nexus on issues pertaining to global sport industry, informed by both economic and business rationale, on the one hand, and debates on human rights and democratization, on the other hand. Whilst "soft power" and "sportswashing" help to explain why these countries have embarked on this path, these discourses do not provide the whole picture. Hosting international sporting events may be another vehicle for top-down social, political reforms and moderating state ideology, while reducing the influence of ultraconservative components of society.

References

Alexander, K., & Cafiero, G. (2020, June 26). Can Saudi Arabia Succeed in Sports Diplomacy? *Inside Arabia*. Retrieved June 10, 2021, from https://insidearabia.com/can-saudi-arabia-succeed-in-sports-diplomacy/

Amara, M. (2012). *Sport, Politics and Society in the Arab World*. Palgrave Macmillan.

Amara, M., & Theodoraki, E. (2010, July). Transnational Network Formation Through Sports Related Regional Development Projects in the Arabian Peninsula. *International Journal of Sport Policy, 2*(2), 135–158.

Arabnews. (2016, March 23). New GCC Motor Sport Championship Aims at Tapping Young Talent. Retrieved April 14, 2020, from https://www.arabnews.com/sports/news/899566

Arabnews. (2020, March 11). NEOM Partners with Mercedes EQ Formula E Team. Retrieved January 5, 2021, from https://www.arabnews.com/node/1639891/corporate-news

Azzali, S., Mazzetto, S., & Petruccioli, A. (2021). *Urban Challenges in the Globalizing Middle-East: Social Value of Public Spaces* (The Urban Book Series (Hardback)). Springer.

Balfour, A. (2020, November 6). Saudi Arabian Grand Prix to Debut on 2021 Formula One Calendar. *Formula One Experiences*. Retrieved November 15, 2020, from https://f1experiences.com/blog/saudi-arabian-grand-prix-to-debut-on-2021-Formula-1-calendar

Benson, A. (2011, June 7). Formula One Teams Demand Bahrain Grand Prix Cancellation. *BBC*. Retrieved June 7, 2011, from https://www.bbc.com/sport/formula1/13689029

Brannagan, P. M., & Giulianotti, R. (2018). The Soft Power–Soft Disempowerment Nexus: The Case of Qatar. *International Affairs, 94*(5), 1139–1157. https://doi.org/10.1093/ia/iiy125

England, A., & Ahmed, M. (2019, November 27). Why the Gulf States are Betting on Sport? *Financial Times*. Retrieved June 5, 2021, from https://www.ft.com/content/15bc48b6-0c8c-11ea-b2d6-9bf4d1957a67

FIA. (n.d.). Middle East Rally Championship. Retrieved April 12, 2020, from https://www.fia.com/events/middle-east-rally-championship/season-2020/middle-east-rally-championship

Flanagan, B. (2019, March 16). Qatar's BeIN Sports Loses F1 Regional Broadcast Rights to MBC Group. *Arabnews*. Retrieved March 17, 2019, from https://www.arabnews.com/node/1467156/media

Formula One. (2020, November 5). F1 Adds Saudi Arabian Grand Prix Night Race to 2021 Calendar. Retrieved December 3, 2020, from https://www.formula1.com/en/latest/article.f1-adds-saudi-arabian-grand-prix-night-race-to-2021-calendar.49pVgTPyYV0KBJrOwtqUCN.html

George-Cosh, D. (2010, November 14). Fiat Buys Back Ferrari Stake from Mubadala. *Lifestyle*. Retrieved March 20, 2021, from https://www.thenationalnews.com/lifestyle/motoring/fiat-buys-back-ferrari-stake-from-mubadala-1.502176

Gibson, O. (2015, June 25). Qatar Eyes Fast Track to Soft Power with Formula One Stake. *The Guardian*. Retrieved June 25, 2015, from https://www.theguardian.com/world/2015/jun/25/qatar-formula-one-bid-soft-power

Human Rights Watch. (2020, January 3). Saudi Arabia Repressive Site for Dakar Rally. Retrieved December 12, 2020, from https://www.hrw.org/news/2020/01/03/saudi-arabia-repressive-site-dakar-rally

Hutton, R. (2011, June 24). How (and Why) the Middle East is Buying into Europe's Car Companies. *Car and Driver*. Retrieved November 15, 2020, from https://www.caranddriver.com/features/a15124131/how-and-why-the-middle-east-is-buying-into-europes-car-companies-feature/

International Trade Administration. (2010, October 13). Saudi Arabia Automotive Market. Retrieved January 10, 2021, from https://www.trade.gov/country-commercial-guides/saudi-arabia-automotive-market

Khalil, Z. (2021, January 17). Israelis Joined Dakar Rally in Saudi Arabia: Report. *AA*. Retrieved January 20, 2021, from https://www.aa.com.tr/en/middle-east/israelis-joined-dakar-rally-in-saudi-arabia-report/2112981

Koch, N. (2020). The Geopolitics of Gulf Sport Sponsorship. *Sport, Ethics and Philosophy, 14*(3), 355–376. https://doi.org/10.1080/17511321.2019.1669693

Medland, C. (2021, February 26). Formula 1 Loses Nearly $400m in COVID-hit 2020. *Racer*. Retrieved March 3, 2021, from https://racer.com/2021/02/26/formula-1-loses-nearly-400m-in-covid-hit-2020/

Mercedes-Benz, EQ Formula E Team. (2021). We Sign a Long-Term Partnership with NEOM. Retrieved February 10, 2021, from https://www.mercedes-benz.com/en/eq-formulae/we-race-the-city/team/team-news/neom-becomes-principal-partner/

Merlin, L. (2019, October 2). Extreme Bringing Adventure Sports to Projects around the Globe. *Blooloop*. Retrieved February 3, 2021, from https://blooloop.com/brands-ip/in-depth/extreme-adventure-sports/

Rizk, M. (2017, 27 March). Muscat to host first round of Gulf Challenge. Gulf Daily News. Retrieved from https://www.gdnonline.com/Details/196433/Muscat-to-host-first-roundof-Gulf-Challenge (accessed 11 November, 2019).

Stray Dogs and Luxury Taxes: What Happened to the Indian Grand Prix?

Callie Batts Maddox

Introduction

Greater Noida, October 2011

In this growing city in northern India, located in the state of Uttar Pradesh thirty miles from Delhi, a sense of joviality was in the air. Not only was it the week of Diwali—the most important celebration on the Hindu calendar full of fireworks and festivities—but the city was also preparing to host the inaugural Indian Grand Prix at the newly constructed Buddh International Circuit (BIC). Celebrated as a sign of a thriving India (Spurgeon, 2012), the race brought glamour, action, and promises to boost local development and promote India as a global sporting destination. Described by one local journalist as "the biggest show on earth" (Narula, 2012, p. 8), the Grand Prix attracted Bollywood stars

C. B. Maddox (✉)
Department of Sport Leadership and Management, Miami University, Oxford, OH, USA
e-mail: maddoxce@miamioh.edu

D. Sturm et al. (eds.), *The History and Politics of Motor Racing*, Global Culture and Sport Series, https://doi.org/10.1007/978-3-031-22825-4_28

Shah Rukh Khan and Deepika Padukone amongst others, cricket icons Sachin Tendulkar and Yuvraj Singh, and global business moguls such as Vijay Mallya and Richard Branson. Two days before the race, a stray dog wandered onto the track, interrupting the first practice run and prompting British bookmaker William Hill to offer 100-1 odds that either the subsequent practice session, the qualifying round, or the race itself would be delayed by the presence of a curious dog (Baldwin, 2011). The canines stayed away, and on October 30 Sebastian Vettel won India's first Formula One race in front of 95,000 spectators. Hailed as a "stunning success" and a "shining moment" (Keelor, 2011, paragraph 1), the Grand Prix heralded the perceived triumph of private investment and corporate vision, as the race was one of the few on the Formula One schedule not subsidized by the government. Even American pop star Lady Gaga's performance at a private after-race party "set a tone of unapologetic extravagance" (Elliott, 2011, paragraph 3): an apt end to an event that cost an estimated US$650 million to bring to a country eager to prove itself on the world stage of elite sport.

Despite the optimism of race organizers and fans, the initial glow of excitement and success soon dimmed. The incident with the stray dog had caused some minor embarrassment, but deeper cracks in the Indian Grand Prix's façade revealed questions about the long-term viability of the event. After just three years (2011–2013), the Indian Grand Prix dropped off the Formula One calendar and has yet to return. The race ultimately folded after the state government of Uttar Pradesh categorized Formula One as entertainment rather than sport, causing the imposition of steep luxury taxes on everything connected with the race, including tickets, equipment, and auto parts. The financial burden for the organizers, teams, and sponsors was too high for the Indian Grand Prix to survive. Its veneer of prestige and exclusivity quickly eroded, leaving a white elephant race track, an abandoned planned city, and a questionable legacy. Beyond the tax disputes and financial troubles, the story of the Indian Grand Prix also reveals failures to sufficiently localize the event and to mobilize the middle-class consumer. Facing pressure to redeem the image of the nation after the 2010 Commonwealth Games held in Delhi, race organizers aimed to showcase India's modernity and place within the global sporting landscape by casting aside any meaningful engagement with local tradition and culture. They also failed to retain the interest of the middle-class fan base, a key demographic for ticket sales, merchandise, and promotion. In examining these factors, this chapter analyses the short history of the Indian Grand Prix by contextualizing it within the rise of the new Indian middle class and the glocalization of sport in contemporary Indian society. It is an insightful example of the precarity of neoliberal investment in sporting spectacles in societies wrought with profound social and economic cleavages, and it also underscores the importance of integrating the local into global sporting structures and events.

The Indian Middle Class, Sport, and Glocalization

Supporters of Formula One highlighted its association with wealth, glamour, cosmopolitanism, and technology as selling points in bringing a race to India (Chandhok, 2013; Narula, 2012; Rheinberg, 2011). As a global brand representing status and prestige, Formula One held appeal for members of the burgeoning Indian middle class: a diverse and expansive group with significant symbolic influence and consumer power. This "new" middle class is a product of economic liberalization and the move towards privatization enacted in the early 1990s. The reforms put into place starting in 1991 included stabilization measures that tightened monetary policies, devalued the rupee, and reduced the fiscal deficit. Labor laws were liberalized to favour business, numerous public enterprises were privatized, and the financial sector was opened to foreign investment (Pedersen, 2000). These moves represented a shift away from a "state-led development strategy to a policy of active reintegration with the world economy" (Srinivasan & Tendulkar, 2003, p. 2). As the reforms took hold, India saw its annual growth rate increase, averaging a rate of 8.5% during the five-year period between 2005 and 2010. By 2010, India had become the second fastest growing major economy in the world behind China (Pasricha, 2010). The significance of these reforms was a "radical loosening" of controls and regulations (Oza, 2006, p.11), resulting in the emergence of a neoliberal India in which the free market began to supersede the state, which contributed to a concomitant and rapid expansion of India's consumer lifestyle economy and culture. Out of this grew the new middle class and the adoption of consumption-based lifestyles central to its identity. Alongside this rise of the middle class grew increasing disparities between the rich who occupy privileged spaces and the poor who are rendered invisible and forgotten (Andrews et al., 2014; Fernandes, 2004).

Unlike the "old" Indian middle class comprised of government bureaucrats and employees of state-owned companies, whose values and aspirations were influenced by austerity and nation-building, the new Indian middle class is predominantly made up of white-collar professionals, with relatively high salaries and disposable incomes, who embrace consumer capitalism and actively display their status through consumption (Brosius, 2010; Mathur, 2010). Enabled by what was an increasingly open neoliberal economic formation, the proliferating presence and influence of transnational brands and products entering into the Indian marketplace also encouraged new consumer practices and desires, and transnational corporations played an important role in establishing the information technology and service sectors that helped create the white-collar workforce engaging in the consumerist lifestyle of the middle class (Andrews et al., 2014; Derne, 2008). As such, the new middle class is less identified with the state and "increasingly defines itself through cultural and consumerist forms of identity" (Rajagopal, 2011, p. 1003). Moreover, the size of this middle class—unquestionably small when placed in the context of India's overall population of 1.36 billion—is secondary to its place within contemporary Indian society as an upwardly mobile and aspirational group, that celebrates and vividly embodies the promises and benefits of the free market.

A central part of what are expressive performances of belonging to the new Indian middle class is the appropriation of certain key markers of class status. Part of this is commodity consumption—the purchase of flat screen televisions, jewelry, smartphones, laptops, cars—that displays not only material wealth but a knowledge of, and interaction with, global markets and brands (Brosius, 2010; Fernandes, 2016; Mathur, 2010). Other distinguishing markers of middle-class consumption include shopping at a mall, joining a private gym, eating out at restaurants and cafes, wearing the latest designer fashions, and attending high-profile sporting events (Brosius, 2010; Fernandes, 2004). For the consumer-citizens of the middle class, it is "not so much a question of *what* is consumed, but a question of knowing *how* to consume it" (Brosius, 2010, p. 16, emphasis in original). Knowing where to display and perform this status is also important. As Hiro (2015) notes, middle-class consumption takes place in segregated spaces "in order to preserve its carefully crafted image of high value" (p. 55). These spaces are highly controlled to shield middle-class consumers from the poor and reinforce the presentation of exclusivity.

Partaking in certain forms of sport and physical activity, either as a participant or a spectator, has become an important part of this middle-class consumer culture. For many young middle-class Indians, pursuing health and fitness is a way to embody social status, as it exhibits that they have the time and money necessary to focus on getting in shape. The private fitness gym has now become a prominent, privileged, and exclusive space of middle-class consumption and collectivization, where the body itself is a commodified project (Andrews et al., 2014; Maddox, 2020). Playing golf holds similar meanings as an activity requiring a specific corporeal knowledge and access to controlled spaces. Previously available to only the very wealthy, golf has become more popular amongst the Indian middle class as the number of courses has increased in conjunction with real estate developments aimed at the middle-class consumer (Kahn, 2010).

Attending and watching sporting events are also key performative acts that mark class status. The Indian Premier League (IPL), a Twenty20 cricket tournament first launched in 2008, was produced and packaged as a mediated entertainment spectacle for mass consumption across India and the Indian diaspora (McDonald & Nalapat, 2013). As a model of privatized corporate sport with highly branded city-based franchises, the IPL aimed to attract the urban middle-class consumer by selling excitement, celebrity, showbiz, and cosmopolitanism. The middle-class cricket fan, as Subramanian (2015) suggests, responded by embracing "more fully his other identity of [sic] a consumer" (paragraph 16) in which brand loyalty is paramount and the fan exists as a spectator-consumer interested not solely in the game itself, but in all of the "razzmatazz" attached to it. The 2010 Commonwealth Games (CWG), held in Delhi, were also aimed at the middle-class spectator as a means to advance broader soft power strategies that positioned the city as a global metropolis and the country as a rising economic and political force (Andrews et al., 2014). Visions of how the city should look for a global audience promoted a "celebration of middle-class and consumptive lifestyles and spaces" (Ghertner, 2010, p. 200), but also resulted in the displacement of homeless residents and the demolition of urban slums. Like the IPL and the CWG, the Indian Grand Prix appealed to the middle class as a space to be seen consuming an elite and global sporting event. The race functioned as an exclusive and segregated space where spectators engaged in the consumption of a high-profile event and displayed their class status through the deportment of designer fashions and brands, all the while buffered from the realities of socio-economic inequality in Indian society.

In addition to their engagement with the new middle class, the IPL, CWG, and Indian Grand Prix were also celebrated as glocal sporting spectacles that bore "all the hallmarks of the global corporate sport model, simultaneously exuding locally expressive components and/or aesthetics" (Andrews, 2016, p. 232). The theoretical perspective of glocalization is useful here, developed by Robertson (1995) as a way of accounting for the relationship between the local and the global, not as opposites but rather as mutual and interconnected forces. Glocalization refutes the divide between homogeneity and heterogeneity by offering a framework to understand the practices and processes whereby the local is influenced and formed by the global, and vice versa (Andrews et al., 2014; Khondker & Robertson, 2018). By transcending the binary oppositions associated with globalization and highlighting the "intensified interpenetration of the local and the global" (Giulianotti & Robertson, 2007, p. 168) glocalization posits that the local and the national, rather than being abolished or overtaken by the global, are formed, molded, and invented in numerous ways through the interaction with the global. Glocalization in contemporary Indian society is particularly relevant for the new middle class, as their lifestyle of consumption often engages directly with glocalized products, brands, and events. This might include visiting a global fast-food chain at a mall that offers menu items suited to local tastes (Simi &

Matusitz, 2017), shopping at a transnational superstore that stocks locally produced items alongside imported brands (Matusitz, 2015), or attending an IPL game at a stadium that functions as a glocal space with a blend of local and international players, brands, cultures, and audiences (Khondker & Robertson, 2018).

As Sturm (2014) notes, Formula One is a global sporting spectacle that relies on localized motifs to market its races, and, concomitantly, host locations use F1's global brand to create "glocally marketable images" (p. 77) promoting themselves as world-class destinations. The Indian Grand Prix provided Formula One with an "exotic" new locale and a large market in which to expand its reach, while race organizers used F1's global elite status to showcase India as a rising power. This merging of the local and global at the Indian Grand Prix was also evident in the celebrity presence at the races, partnership deals between major sponsors, local driver Narain Karthikeyan's participation with the Spanish Hispania/HRT team, and the Force India team. However, as will be discussed below, part of the Indian Grand Prix's downfall was its failure to sufficiently glocalize, thereby impacting its ability to retain the middle-class consumer upon which it relied.

Bringing Formula One to India

As part of the economic liberalization policies adopted in the early 1990s, the Indian government loosened its restrictions on television broadcasts. Before then, Indian viewers could watch only one channel, the nationalized network Doordarshan. The arrival of private satellite television opened up new avenues for entertainment, news, and sport for millions of Indian consumers, and India soon became the third largest television market in the world (Mehta, 2008). Included in the vast new viewing options was Formula One racing, which found its way into Indian homes in the mid-1990s, first on Doordarshan where viewership topped 60 million, and then via private satellite channels (Spurgeon, 2012; Warrier, 2003).

Vijay Mallya, owner of the Kingfisher beer and airline companies, was also a keen racing fan and began sponsoring Formula One teams at this time. He and Vicky Chandhok, a former racing and rally driver, began to pursue the idea of hosting a Formula One race in India as early as 1997. Initial efforts focused on Kolkata, but then shifted to Bangalore and Mumbai in the early 2000s (Warrier, 2003). The city of Hyderabad also entered the discussions with promises to build a track and a new airport, but a change in administration in 2004 derailed those plans. The newly elected chief minister of the state of Andhra Pradesh, Y.S. Rajasekhara Reddy, refused to back the construction of the Formula One track in Hyderabad and instead pledged to focus on the plight of his state's farmers. When asked about his priorities, Reddy replied, "farmers need electricity, not Formula One racing" (quoted in Menon, 2004, paragraph 4). A similar lack of financial support from the local government also doomed Mumbai's chances of securing a Formula One Grand Prix (Cooper, 2012; Spurgeon, 2012). Nonetheless, Formula One chief executive Bernie Ecclestone reiterated his support for a race in India to capitalize on the country's increasing global economic clout, engage a potentially lucrative fan base composed of millions of Indians, and portray F1 as a truly global sport (Warrier, 2003). By 2007, five locations were being considered for the Indian Grand Prix: the city of Bangalore; the Gurgaon district in the state of Haryana; a street circuit in Delhi proposed by Mallya; a permanent track near Delhi; and, the city of Lucknow. Ecclestone and officials from the Indian Olympic Association spent months negotiating, but then, in June 2007, announced a provisional agreement to include the Indian Grand Prix on the Formula One calendar for 2009, with a new track to be built in Gurgaon (India agree deal on Grand Prix, 2007).

This deal quickly fell through, however, and three months later Ecclestone revealed that the debut race would instead take place in 2010 at a new track in Greater Noida. Chandhok and Mallya had been approached by a representative from Jaypee Sports International (JPSI), a subsidiary of the Jaypee Group, a vast conglomerate company with business interests in real estate, road construction, hydroelectric power, hospitality, and other ventures (Cooper, 2012). JPSI committed to building a Formula One track in Greater Noida in the hopes of hosting a Grand Prix race there. The group promised to privately finance all of it, removing concerns of government indifference that had plagued the previous efforts to bring Formula One to India. Chandhok later recalled, "I had no clue that there were plans being floated" (quoted in Cooper, 2012, p. 83) to construct this track, but JPSI successfully negotiated terms with Ecclestone, Formula One Management (FOM), and the Fèdèration Internationale de l'Automobile (FIA), the governing body for Formula One. JPSI signed a five-year contract with FIA to build the circuit and host the Indian Grand Prix on an annual basis, the rights for which JPSI would pay US$40 million per year (Sharma, 2012).

The 2008 global financial crisis caused delays in land procurement and early construction, but final plans for the new track were released in late 2009. Called the Buddh International Circuit (BIC) in reference to its location in the Gautum Budh Nagar district, the track was designed by German architect, Hermann Tilke, who also created Formula One tracks in Malaysia, Bahrain, China, Turkey, South Korea, and Indonesia (Narula, 2012). Celebrated as a fast and challenging circuit, the BIC was 5.14 kilometers long with sixteen turns and seating capacity for 100,000 spectators. Final cost estimates for the track were approximately US$400 million, all privately covered by JPSI (Spurgeon, 2012).

The BIC was to be a key component of the planned Jaypee Sports City, a 2500-acre residential and commercial complex with apartment towers, schools, shopping centers, a hospital, a cricket stadium, an 18-hole golf course, a field hockey arena, and a sports training academy. The city was owned by the Jaypee Group and operated by JPSI, which described it as "the country's first fully integrated megacity built around a sporting lifestyle" (Kumar, n.d. paragraph 8). Promoted as a "unique example of private enterprise developing an entire city without government support" (Ellis, 2013, paragraph 4), the project aimed to use sport, and easy access to world-class sporting facilities, as a means to attract young, middle-class Indians as buyers and residents. Costs to construct the complex were expected to exceed US$40 billion, but the financial return was promised to be at least US$170 million in annual revenue and the employment of 10,000 people (Narula, 2012). As such, the vision of Jaypee Sports City was one of an "entertainment cityscape" (John & McDonald, 2020, p. 1187) highlighting the consumption of commercialized elite sport within a planned urban landscape.

For JPSI, the placement of the BIC within Jaypee Sports City was an important strategy to attract the young middle class seeking suburban residential areas close to Delhi. The Buddh Circuit Studios, an enclave of apartment buildings located five minutes from the BIC, were marketed to first-time purchasers in search of an affordable small apartment where "the most exciting events will always be happening right next door" (Buddh Circuit Studios, n.d., paragraph 1). The BIC, and its associated entertainment events, provided amenities of interest to the young middle class and added an appealing aura to the city more generally. Yet, the inclusion of sporting facilities, such as the BIC and the planned cricket stadium, in Jaypee Sports City reinforced the distinguishing markers of class status to which only the few, and certainly not the masses, had access. Designed as a protected haven for the middle class, Jaypee Sports City sought to create a controlled and sanitized spatial aesthetic that "obscures social inequality and power relations while also naturalizing class distinctions" (Waldman et al., 2017, p. 181). Located within such a space, the Indian Grand Prix, like the CWG, contributed to a "neoliberal spatial politics of exclusion" (Andrews et al., 2014, p. 265) that normalizes the middle-class consumer as the idealized representation of a rising India while vilifying the poor. And like the CWG before it, the Grand Prix was used to showcase India's modernity and engagement with global capital underpinned by the growing middle class. At its outset in 2011, the Grand Prix was also tasked with redeeming the reputation of the Indian nation in response to negative media coverage of the CWG and its failures.

Redeeming the Nation

The city of Delhi hosted the Commonwealth Games in 2010, an event that aimed to transform "Delhi into a global city and India into a sporting force to reckon with" (Majumdar, 2011, p. 231). The CWG were lauded as an opportunity to build infrastructure across Delhi that would increase tourism, provide jobs, and boost local incomes. These projects included the expansion of the Delhi airport, new metro rail lines and city buses, additional highways, and the construction of four new sports stadiums and a housing complex for athletes and officials (Baviskar, 2011). This makeover of Delhi was meant to position the city as a place of global interest to attract foreign investment, but it also displaced tens of thousands of families and magnified the disparities between the rich and poor in the city (Baviskar, 2011; Silk & Manley, 2012). Even though Indian athletes won a total of 101 medals, placing the country second in the overall medals table with its best performance in any large-scale sporting event, the average Delhite "was largely indifferent to the biggest event in India's sporting history" (Majumdar, 2011, p. 236) and the CWG largely failed to create an impactful and lasting legacy. At a cost that totaled more than US$15 billion, nearly 114 times the original estimate, the Games were indeed a very expensive campaign to catapult Delhi onto the world stage (Majumdar, 2011).

Domestic and international media discourse about the CWG was generally marked by narratives of Delhi's ill-preparedness to host the Games, the forced removal of the homeless, threats of terrorism, unsanitary conditions, and reports of political and financial corruption (Majumdar, 2011; Osborne et al., 2016). Mishra (2013) argued that this negative coverage, rife as it was with stereotypes and generalizations, was "likely to diminish India's 'soft power' in the world, at least temporarily" (p. 188). Similarly, in their analysis of Western media coverage of the CWG, Osborne et al. (2016) concluded that the scathing scrutiny was "likely to have caused some damage to India's reputation as a nation in the process of graduating to become a developed nation in a globalized sport industry" (p. 215). Although the Games went on without major incidence, their immediate legacy was one of controversy and indignity. Critical media coverage, both within and outside of India, had tarnished the nation's aspiration to be seen as a capable steward of both sporting and community development.

Rather than distance themselves from these critiques, organizers of the Indian Grand Prix mobilized them as a means to heighten the significance of the race and stake claim to redeeming the nation. Scheduled for October 2011, just over a year after the conclusion of the CWG, the inaugural Indian Grand Prix was to be a corrective to the Games: a glamorous and unabashed display of elite technology, business, and branding. Jaiprakash Gaur, founding chairman of the Jaypee Group, claimed that the race would "make up for the shameful memories of the Commonwealth Games … the world's perception of India is going to change after the

Grand Prix" (quoted in Rheinberg, 2011, paragraph 7). There was, of course, irony in this rhetoric as it echoed the promises made by CWG officials, and perpetuated the false assumption that sporting mega-events bring lasting prestige to the host cities and nations. Concerns about the cost and elitism of the Grand Prix did not deter its supporters, as the private financing of JPSI deflected any charges of government corruption or misappropriation of public funds. Vicky Chandhok, then the president of the Federation of Motor Sports Clubs of India, captured this attitude by remarking:

Look at the circuit, it's the best built in the last ten years. From that perspective I'm absolutely thrilled. And it's not just about F1. This is an edifice that's going to project

> India worldwide. Many cynics said, 'It's an elite sport, do we need it?' My god, at no cost to you, to the exchequer, to the common man, I think it's a great thing to showcase us to the rest of the world. (Quoted in Cooper, 2012, p. 84)

The desire to showcase India in and through an event buttressed by US$400 million of private investment contrasted with the perceived embarrassment of the government-backed CWG. Rather than be mired in provincial political wrangling as the CWG had been, the Grand Prix would demonstrate that India was big-business friendly and capable of courting elite brands and global corporations. As Traber (2018) suggested, "holding an F1 race helps to characterize the host as actively progressing into the financial future" (p. 476), an image that JPSI and the rest of the Indian Grand Prix supporters undoubtedly tried to craft.

The drive to redeem the nation's image and present it as globally forward extended to the track's design, conceived by architect Hermann Tilke who had previously designed nine original circuits for Formula One (Narula, 2012). Tilke usually incorporates national motifs or traditional local architecture into the grandstands or pit buildings, but JPSI executives told him not to do that at the BIC. As Tilke recalled, "they wanted to show India as a modern country" (quoted in Cooper, 2012, p. 84), so the venue was void of any imagery or architecture suggestive of India's past or cultural heritage. In seeking to use the Grand Prix as a way to restore the nation's reputation after the CWG and promote its modernity, JPSI embraced the "homogeneous global commodity spectacle" (Sturm, 2014, p. 76) of Formula One that pursues global capital with little regard for local cultures or contexts. Concerned that the problems of the CWG had defined global perceptions of India, JPSI created a vision for the Grand Prix that celebrated the power of private corporate investment as the route to modernity.

The immediate aftermath of the inaugural Indian Grand Prix was largely positive. There was a controversy in August 2011, two months before the race, when local farmers protested the event and threatened to dismantle the track in response to what they perceived as inadequate compensation for the land and a lack of employment opportunities at the new venue (Rheinberg, 2011). Other news stories highlighted the incomplete infrastructure at the BIC, the stray dog delaying the first practice run, and complaints from a few drivers that the track was too dusty (Noble, 2011). Yet, on the whole, the inaugural race was deemed a success and "India itself came out looking like a winner, as the world's media painted a picture of great accomplishment against the odds" (Spurgeon, 2012, paragraph 19). Indian cricket legend Sachin Tendulkar waved the chequered flag as Sebastian Vettel took the victory in front of 95,000 spectators and a global television audience. Narain Karthikeyan, the lone driver from India, finished in 22nd place. Force India, a team partly owned by Vijay Mallya and the conglomerate Sahara India Pariwar but with little other connection to the country, had two drivers in the race. Adrian Sutil (German) finished eighth, and Paul di Resta (Scottish) finished fifteenth. The BIC was later named the Motorsports Facility of the Year at the 2011 Professional Motorsports World Expo (Oncars India, 2011), and hopes were high for the continued success of the race.

Trying not to repeat the embarrassment from the year before, staff at the BIC made efforts to "dog proof" the track for the 2012 Grand Prix by sealing off potential points of entry to the track, adding an additional layer of fencing around it, and hiring "a few teams of dog catchers" (Sidhu, 2012, paragraph 7). Perhaps they should have been more concerned about ticket sales, however, as attendance at the 2012 race dropped drastically from the prior year. The total attendance in 2012 was estimated to be 65,000, even though ticket prices had been reduced to attract a broader audience (Chakraborty, 2012). Some Bollywood stars and celebrity cricketers made an appearance, but the festive atmosphere was much more muted and less overtly glamorous than the previous year. Vettel won his second consecutive Indian Grand Prix title, while Karthikeyan finished in 21st position and the two Force India drivers, Nico Hulkenberg (German) and di Resta, placed eighth and eleventh. Beyond the action on the track, the 2012 Grand Prix saw a one-race partnership deal between Bharti Airtel, India's largest mobile phone carrier, and Mercedes AMG Petronas. This agreement gave Airtel the rights to develop co-branded merchandise, organize exclusive consumer promotions, place its branding on the helmets and race suits of Michael Schumacher and Nico Rosberg, and air television commercials starring the two popular drivers (Mercedes AMG Petronas, 2012). Advertising signage at the BIC also promoted the presence of other global brands alongside Airtel's title sponsorship, featuring such multinational corporations as UBS, Allianz, Pirelli, and DHL. These marketing strategies and visual ads displayed the link between global brands and a local corporation, a declaration that Indian business could stand on par with the best and most elite companies in the world.

By the time the third edition of the Grand Prix came around in October 2013, optimism and excitement had been replaced with concern and indifference. Earlier in the year, Ecclestone announced that the Indian Grand Prix had been removed from the racing calendar for 2014 due to what he termed "political reasons", and a conflict with the timing of the event (Baldwin, 2013). In the week before the race, JPSI attended a hearing in India's Supreme Court over a dispute about unpaid entertainment taxes from the 2012 Grand Prix. The Court threatened to cancel the 2013 edition in response, but officials decided to delay the case until the week after the race, thereby ensuring its short-term survival (Chakraborty, 2013). Ticket sales for the race were slow, with only 40,000 tickets sold before the race weekend, a 38% decrease from the previous year. Airtel, the Grand Prix's major local sponsor, did not create new promotions and commercials around the race due to budget constraints. Public interest in, and social media chatter about, the race dropped markedly, and the buzz of glitz and glamour that surrounded the inaugural event had all but disappeared (Kholsa, 2013). Much to the disappointment of local fans, Karthikeyan did not drive in the race. Vettel won his third title, and the Force India team members, di Resta and Sutil, finished in eighth and ninth place respectively. This proved to be the final iteration of the Indian Grand Prix, leaving the promises of national redemption and global prestige unfulfilled.

Formula One as Sport Or Entertainment?

The seeds of the Indian Grand Prix's demise were planted early in the form of taxation disputes. Six weeks before the inaugural race in 2011, teams raised concerns about the state government's purported plan to levy taxes on the earnings of the top ten teams in the World Constructors' Championship from a percentage of television rights granted to FOM. According to tax law, the state could collect tax on a portion of that money because the teams earned it while competing/working in Uttar Pradesh. Teams were also worried about paying high customs taxes on the importation of their cars and equipment. To appease the team directors, JPSI offered to pay the customs tax if necessary, but the Uttar Pradesh government, led by chief minister Mayawati Prabhu Das, eventually relented and issued a tax exemption to JPSI and the Grand Prix (Zeenews Sports Bureau, 2011).

In response to this exemption, local activist Amit Kumar filed a Public Interest Litigation (PIL) with the Indian Supreme Court to argue that Formula One is an elitist sport and does not benefit the common populace. As such, Kumar contended, it should be classified as entertainment, not sport, and thus be subject to all luxury taxes and customs levied on entertainment events (Chakraborty, 2013). This position echoed the sentiments of former Indian Minister of Youth Affairs and Sports, MS Gill, who refused to support Mallya's early efforts to bring Formula One to India because he believed it was nothing more than "expensive entertainment" (Gill, Mallya in verbal war, 2009). The Supreme Court heard Kumar's case just ten days before the race, ultimately issuing a temporary injunction allowing the Grand Prix to go ahead but requiring JPSI to deposit 25% of ticket revenue into a separate account pending a final decision on the validity of a tax exemption and the categorization of

Formula One (Overdorf, 2011). The race went on as scheduled, and JPSI invited Mayawati to present the winner's trophy to Sebastian Vettel at the conclusion of the event (HT Correspondent, 2011).

In 2012, Akhilesh Yadav defeated Mayawati to become the chief minister of Uttar Pradesh. Unlike his predecessor, Yadav did not give a tax exemption to the Grand Prix, so JPSI paid approximately US$9.8 million to cover the customs duties on all cars, fuel, and equipment coming into the country, which was refunded at the conclusion of the race less a 2% administration fee (Singh, 2013). The 2012 race was staged with few issues, but Ferrari driver Fernando Alonso did express disappointment that his car was not outfitted with the latest components due to the costly and time-consuming customs regulations that prevented his team from importing the components at the last minute (Slater, 2012). The government continued to assert that Formula One was entertainment, not sport, even though it required JPSI to contribute US$1.6 million annually to the National Sports Development Fund and the International Olympic Committee had upgraded the International Motor Sport Federation to full recognition status (Singhal, 2013).

The taxation issue arose again in 2013, as Kumar filed a second PIL accusing JPSI of failing to report accurate revenue and ticket sales totals earned in 2012 for the purpose of calculating entertainment taxes, so JPSI did not pay the entertainment taxes in full for that race. In his brief, Kumar called for the cancellation of the 2013 Grand Prix over JPSI's failure to pay the taxes, but the race went on even as the Supreme Court agreed to hear the case (Chakraborty, 2013). The Uttar Pradesh government again refused to grant a tax and customs exemption, and a new entertainment tax was placed on every ticket sold to the race in 2013. The government tax authorities also explained that 1/19 of all revenue generated by Formula One was subject to Indian tax since there were nineteen total races on the calendar and one was held in India, a calculation that JPSI and FOM argued was unfair (Mishra, 2013). Nonetheless, Ecclestone had already announced that the Indian Grand Prix would not appear on the Formula One calendar in 2014, so attention then turned to bringing the race back for 2015.

JPSI had two years remaining on its five-year contract with FOM, but negotiations to hold the Grand Prix in 2015 stalled due to the ongoing tax disputes. The race was eventually scrapped from the schedule as Ecclestone remarked, "we are looking at 2016 now and hopefully the tax issues in India will be sorted out by then" (quoted in Patwardhan, 2014, paragraph 3). The government's refusal to budge on taxation was not the only problem, as JPSI was facing rapidly dwindling financial resources and a national sport ministry that could not assist in providing monetary support. Askari Zaidi, a spokesperson for JPSI, insisted that Formula One "should be recognized as a sport in India otherwise we will not get all the benefits (that other sports get) and will end up paying extra taxes and duties" (quoted in Singhal, 2013, paragraph 9). That recognition never came, and by 2017 it was clear that the financial burdens of hosting the Grand Prix were too much for JPSI to bear.

For the entire short history of the Indian Grand Prix, the government was "bent on classifying Formula One as entertainment and not sport" (Batra & Gupta, 2011, paragraph 5), a decision with dire financial consequences that ultimately doomed the race. For those invested in the race, the presence of Formula One in India represented the country's arrival into elite global networks of wealth, glamour, and technology. It was a chance to restore civic pride, boost tourism, and showcase India as an aspirational modern nation, all on the back of private investment and corporate leadership. Yet the Grand Prix failed because JPSI could not sustain the costs associated with running the event annually while facing high tax rates, government indifference, declining public interest, a lack of additional corporate sponsors, and decreasing media promotion.

Additional Failures

Beyond the tax disputes and financial struggle, the Indian Grand Prix also failed to adequately glocalize and retain the interest of the middle-class consumer. The novelty of the first race in 2011 was enough to secure a large audience eager to witness the spectacle of Formula One. Starting at USD51, the tickets were expensive even for the average middle-class Indian, yet sales were strong because the aspirational middle class wanted to be seen attending the Grand Prix as way to display their status and consumption-oriented lifestyle (North, 2011). In 2011, local driver

Narain Karthikeyan—originally from Coimbatore, Tamil Nadu—attracted attention and fans, particularly those from south India who traveled to Greater Noida to cheer him on (Roy, 2013). The mix of local and international celebrities added a glocal flair, as did the presence of local sponsors such as Airtel and global brands like UBS and Allianz. The Force India team, with cars splashed with a color scheme echoing that of the Indian flag and manned by German and Scottish drivers, took the first practice laps and claimed the race to be their "spiritual home" (Holt, 2011, paragraph 28).

The second iteration of the race saw a marked dip in attendance—from 95,000 spectators in 2011 to 65,000 in 2012—and an overall decrease in the festive and celebratory tone of the event (Chakraborty, 2012). Airtel's partnership with Mercedes produced commercials and promotional materials featuring German drivers Schumacher and Rosberg to generate fan interest within Indian market, but did little to include localized elements in these campaigns. Karthikeyan raced once again for the Spanish team HRT, and the Force India team performed well but did not capture the rapt attention of the fans. By 2013, as one journalist noted, there was a "sharp drop in the number of tv commercials, advertisements, and hoardings" promoting the race, social media chatter was subdued, and the weak rupee precipitated a drop in middle-class fans attending the race (Kholsa, 2013, paragraph 8). No longer was the glamour and prestige of the event enough to attract and retain the middle-class consumer, and the lack of localized aspects further contributed to the race's diminishing appeal for the middle class. Karthikeyan did not race in 2013, very few notable Indian personalities attended, and Force India was not "Indian" enough to gain fan loyalty. As one observer pointed out, "the involvement of a British-based, Indian-owned team does not seem to have the same resonance with the fans as having an Indian driver does" (Roy, 2013, paragraph 9). Additionally, by focusing on creating on a modernized and sanitized image of India in and through the BIC's design, JPSI resisted the incorporation of local elements at the track. With the exception of the paint job on the main grandstand and bleacher seats that included green, white, and orange in reference to the Indian flag, the BIC did not feature any localized architectural or cultural aesthetics (Cooper, 2012). The middle-class consumers, focused as they were on global brands, also desired local connection, so the predominance of the global over the local by this time made the Indian Grand Prix a less attractive space than other options, such as the IPL.

In reference to researching sporting mega-events, Giulianotti and Robertson (2012) note that glocalization aids analyses of how host nations and cities draw on global standards while also "enabling more localized aspects to emerge" (p. 446). While the Indian Grand Prix featured some elements of localization, it failed to incorporate them into the global spectacle of Formula One in consistent and meaningful ways. The emergence of the local was tempered by JPSI's focus on creating a vision of the modern Indian nation distanced from what had been defined as the less palatable "local" aspects of the Commonwealth Games—government corruption, safety concerns, and ill-preparedness (Osborne et al., 2016). In this sense, and with its link to middle-class consumerism, the Indian Grand Prix serves as an instructive reminder of the significance of glocalization for the economic and cultural success of global sporting spectacles.

Concluding Notes

Greater Noida, October 2020

In the years following the demise of the Indian Grand Prix, the BIC hosted smaller-scale events such as the JK Tyre National Racing Championship for motorcycles, the Festival of Speed, and numerous X-Factor Auto Cross races. The track was also a popular site for car manufacturers and auto journalists to test and review newly launched models. In December 2019, however, activity at the BIC ceased when the Yamuna Expressway Industrial Development Authority (YEIDA) locked the gates and took back control of 1000 hectares of land it had leased to JPSI for the development of Jaypee Sports City, which was never completed. Officials with YEIDA, an agency of the Uttar Pradesh government, noted that JPSI continually defaulted on rent payments, finished only five out of sixteen residential projects, and owed Rs 864 crore (approximately

US$119 million) to the agency (Shalabh, 2019). What was once promoted as the symbol of a rising India, and an innovative approach to city planning, now stood empty and abandoned: a ghost town composed of unfinished apartment buildings, shells of shopping centers, and an unused world-class Formula One circuit.

When the COVID-19 pandemic reached India in March 2020, the Uttar Pradesh government seized properties in Jaypee Sports City to house migrants fleeing to the state from Delhi. After the country imposed a three-week lockdown, thousands of migrants gathered at the Uttar Pradesh-Delhi border en route to their home villages from the city, where many of them were employed as domestic help, construction workers, and day laborers. The government agreed to temporarily house them within Jaypee Sports City and provide necessities until the lockdown ended. The BIC became part of the quarantine facility as state authorities cordoned it off and used it as additional space for the provision of shelter, food, and healthcare for the stranded migrants (Rajput, 2020). These spaces, once the controlled and corporatized realm of the wealthy and the aspirational middle class, were now serving the poor and vulnerable. The future of the BIC is currently unclear, but perhaps there is poetic resolution in this space evolving from one of private exclusivity to public humanitarianism.

References

Andrews, D. (2016). Sport, Spectacle and the Politics of Late Capitalism: Articulating the Neoliberal Order. In A. Bairner, J. Kelly, & J. W. Lee (Eds.), *Routledge Handbook of Sport and Politics* (pp. 225–237). Routledge.

Andrews, D. L., Batts, C., & Silk, M. (2014). Sport, Glocalization and the New Indian Middle Class. *International Journal of Cultural Studies, 17*(3), 259–276.

Baldwin, A. (2011, October 28). *Indian Grand Prix Dogged by Animals?* Reuters. Retrieved January 27, 2021, from https://www.reuters.com/article/us-prix-dogs-odd/indian-grand-prix-dogged-by-animals-idINTRE79R3AF20111028

Baldwin, A. (2013, July 30). *Formula One: Bernie Ecclestone to Bypass Indian GP?* The Indian Express. Retrieved February 27, 2021, from https://

indianexpress.com/article/news-archive/print/formula-one-bernie-ecclestone-to-bypass-indian-gp/

Batra, R., & Gupta, S. (2011, September 15). *Customs Row Threatens India's F1 Race*. The Economic Times. Retrieved February 3, 2021, from https://timesofindia.indiatimes.com/sports/racing/top-stories/Customs-row-threatens-Indian-Grand-Prix/articleshow/9973546.cms

Baviskar, A. (2011). Spectacular Events, City Spaces and Citizenship: The Commonwealth Games in Delhi. In J. S. Anjaria & C. McFarlane (Eds.), *Urban Navigations: Politics, Space and the City in South Asia* (pp. 138–164). Routledge.

Brosius, C. (2010). *India's Middle Class: New Forms of Urban Leisure, Consumption and Prosperity*. Routledge.

Buddh Circuit Studios. (n.d.). Jaypee Greens. Retrieved April 2, 2021, from http://www.jaypeegreens.com/propertydetails.aspx?propertyid=23&propertytab=overview

Chakraborty, A. (2012, October 29). *Motor Racing: Indian GP Organizers Upbeat Despite Attendance Dip*. Reuters. Retrieved February 3, 2021, from https://www.reuters.com/article/us-motor-racing-india/motor-racing-indian-gp-organizers-upbeat-despite-attendance-dip-idUSBRE89S0BU20121029

Chakraborty, A. (2013, October 24). *India Grand Prix to Go Ahead Despite Court Hearing*. Reuters. Retrieved February 4, 2021, from https://www.reuters.com/article/motor-racing-prix-india-court/india-grand-prix-to-go-ahead-despite-court-hearing-idINDEE99N09R20131024

Chandhok, K. (2013, October 19). *Indian Grand Prix Is Special Because of Spectators*. The Economic Times. Retrieved March 27, 2021, from https://economictimes.indiatimes.com/indian-grand-prix-is-special-because-of-spectators/articleshow/24364232.cms?from=mdr

Cooper, A. (2012). The First Indian Grand Prix: F1's Gateway to 1.2 Billion People. *Motor Sport, 88*(1), 81–84.

Derne, S. (2008). *Globalization on the Ground: Media and the Transformation of Culture, Class, and Gender in India*. Sage.

Elliott, F. (2011, October 26). *India Seeking Road to Redemption*. The Times. Retrieved February 4, 2021, from https://www.thetimes.co.uk/article/india-seeking-road-to-redemption-w7zns9x7026

Ellis, P. (2013, December 11). *India's Jaypee Sports City Aims at Being an Energy-Efficient Metropolis*. Financial Times. Retrieved January 23, 2021, from https://www.ft.com/content/4b50ec38-5c94-11e3-931e-00144feabdc0

Fernandes, L. (2004). The Politics of Forgetting: Class Politics, State Power and the Restructuring of Urban Space in India. *Urban Studies, 44*(12), 2415–2430.

Fernandes, L. (2016). India's Middle Classes in Contemporary India. In K. A. Jacobsen (Ed.), *Routledge Handbook of Contemporary India* (pp. 232–242). Routledge.

Ghertner, D. A. (2010). Calculating Without Numbers: Aesthetic Governmentality in Delhi's Slums. *Economy and Society, 39*(2), 185–217.

Gill, Mallya in Verbal War on Formula One. (2009, August 31). Outlook. Retrieved February 28, 2021, from https://www.outlookindia.com/newswire/story/gill-mallya-in-verbal-war-on-formula-one/665243

Giulianotti, R., & Robertson, R. (2007). Recovering the Social: Globalization, Football and Transnationalism. *Global Networks, 7*(2), 144–186.

Giulianotti, R., & Robertson, R. (2012). Glocalization and Sport in Asia: Diverse Perspectives and Future Possibilities. *Sociology of Sport Journal, 29*(4), 433–454.

Hiro, D. (2015). *The Age of Aspiration: Power, Wealth, and Conflict in Globalizing India*. The New Press.

Holt, S. (2011, October 28). *Felipe Massa Heads Sebastian Vettel in India Practice*. BBC Sport. Retrieved March 29, 2021, from https://www.bbc.com/sport/formula1/15489080

HT Correspondent. (2011, October 30). *Mayawati Presents Winning Trophy of Indian GP to Vettel*. Hindustan Times. Retrieved February 27, 2021, from https://www.hindustantimes.com/india/mayawati-presents-winning-trophy-of-indian-gp-to-vettel/story-ERZubQzJ1MvdTsY4E1b3PO.html

India Agree Deal on Grand Prix. (2007, June 14). BBC Sport. Retrieved February 15, 2021, from http://news.bbc.co.uk/sport2/hi/motorsport/formula_one/6751929.stm

John, A., & McDonald, B. (2020). How Elite Sport Helps to Foster and Maintain a Neoliberal Culture: The 'branding' of Melbourne, Australia. *Urban Studies, 57*(6), 1184–1200.

Kahn, J. (2010, September 11). *India's Middle Class Waits for a Tee Time*. New York Times. Retrieved February 15, 2021, from https://www.nytimes.com/2010/09/12/sports/golf/12indiagolf.html

Keelor, V. (2011, October 31). *F1 Race: Mayawati, Jaypee Show Delhi, Gurgaon How to Get It Right*. The Economic Times. Retrieved February 27, 2021, from https://economictimes.indiatimes.com/f1-race-mayawati-jaypee-show-delhi-gurgaon-how-to-get-it-right/articleshow/10550170.cms

Kholsa, V. (2013, October 23). *Formula 1: Public Not Interested in India Grand Prix*. The Economic Times. Retrieved February 15, 2021, from https://economictimes.indiatimes.com/formula-1-public-not-interested-in-india-grand-prix/articleshow/24558668.cms

Khondker, H. H., & Robertson, R. (2018). Glocalization, Consumption, and Cricket: The Indian Premier League. *Journal of Consumer Culture, 18*(2), 279–297.

Kumar, M. (n.d.). *Buddh International Circuit*, Jaypee Sports International Limited. Retrieved January 23, 2021, from https://web.archive.org/web/20111027084916/http://www.jaypeesports.com/bic_and_jpsi_fact_sheet.pdf

Maddox, C. B. (2020). Young Middle-Class Women, Consumption and Fitness in Contemporary India: "To tackle all that is thrown her way". *South Asia Research, 40*(1), 111–126.

Majumdar, B. (2011). Commonwealth Games 2010: The Index of a "new" India? *Social Research: An International Quarterly, 78*(1), 231–254.

Mathur, N. (2010). Shopping Malls, Credit Cards and Global Brands: Consumer Culture and Lifestyles of India's New Middle Class. *South Asia Research, 30*(3), 211–231.

Matusitz, J. (2015). Bharti-Wal-Mart: A Glocalization Experience. *Journal of Asian and African Studies, 50*(1), 83–95.

McDonald, I., & Nalapat, A. (2013). Sport, Spectacle, and the Political Economy of Mega-events: The Case of the Indian Premier League. In D. L. Andrews & B. Carrington (Eds.), *A Companion to sport* (pp. 493–505). Blackwell, Malden.

Mehta, N. (2008). Introduction: Satellite Television, Identity and Globalisation in Contemporary India. In N. Mehta (Ed.), *Television in India: Satellites, Politics, and Cultural Change* (pp. 1–12). Routledge.

Menon, A. K. (2004, May 24). *Will Pursue Policies to Promote Growth in Andhra Pradesh: Rajasekhara Reddy*. India Today. Retrieved February 15, 2021, from https://www.indiatoday.in/magazine/interview/story/20040524-will-pursue-policies-to-promote-growth-in-andhra-pradesh-rajasekhara-reddy-789949-2004-05-24

Mercedes AMG Petronas Teams Up with Bharti Airtel for Indian Grand Prix. (2012, July 31). Motorsport.com. Retrieved February 23, 2021, from https://us.motorsport.com/f1/news/mercedes-amg-petronas-teams-up-with-bharti-airtel-for-indian-grand-prix/2633316/

Mishra, S. (2013). Projections of Power, News Framing, and India's 2010 Commonwealth Games. *The Howard Journal of Communications, 24*(2), 178–193.

Narula, C. (2012). *History of Formula 1: The Circus Comes to India*. Roli Books.

Noble, J. (2011, October 27). *Formula 1 Did the Right Thing in Coming to India, Says Ross Brawn*. Autosport. Retrieved February 23, 2021, from https://www.autosport.com/f1/news/formula-1-did-the-right-thing-in-coming-to-india-says-ross-brawn-4451946/4451946/

North, A. (2011, October 28). *How Will the Grand Prix Change India?*, BBC News. Retrieved March 28, 2021, from https://www.bbc.com/news/world-south-asia-15493829

Oncars India. (2011, November 21). *Buddh Circuit Picks Up Global Award*. India.com. Retrieved January 23, 2021, from https://www.india.com/car-and-bike/latest-news/news-cars/buddh-circuit-picks-up-global-award-3311243/

Osborne, A., Sherry, E., & Nicholson, M. (2016). The Delhi Dilemma: Media Representation of the 2010 Commonwealth Games. *Sport in Society, 19*(2), 201–217.

Overdorf, J. (2011, October 21). *Indian Grand Prix to Go on Despite Tax Challenge*. PRI. Retrieved February 15, 2021, from https://www.pri.org/stories/2011-10-21/indian-grand-prix-go-despite-tax-challenge

Oza, R. (2006). *The Making of Neoliberal India: Nationalism, Gender, and the Paradoxes of Globalization*. Routledge.

Pasricha, A. (2010, December 30). *India's Economy Rebounds in 2010*. VOA News. Retrieved January 23, 2021, from https://www.voanews.com/east-asia/indias-economy-rebounds-2010

Patwardhan, K. (2014, August 22). *Indian Grand Prix Excluded from 2015 Season*. Sportskeeda. Retrieved February 23, 2021, from https://www.sportskeeda.com/f1/no-indian-grand-prix-for-2015-season

Pedersen, J. D. (2000). Explaining Economic Liberalization in India: State and Society Perspectives. *World Development, 28*(2), 265–282.

Rajagopal, A. (2011). The Emergency as Prehistory of the New Indian Middle Class. *Modern Asian Studies, 45*(5), 1003–1049.

Rajput, V. (2020, March 30). *India's Only F1 Track to Turn into a Quarantine Facility*. Hindustan Times. Retrieved February 23, 2021, from https://www.hindustantimes.com/india-news/india-s-only-f1-track-to-turn-into-a-quarantine-facility/story-Ejp5goNmH7Zlj84eYnd1UN.html

Rheinberg, C. (2011, October 30). *India Faces Race into the Unknown*. The Independent. Retrieved February 15, 2021, from https://www.independent.co.uk/sport/motor-racing/india-faces-race-unknown-2376290.html

Robertson, R. (1995). Glocalization: Time-space and Homogeneity-Heterogeneity. In M. Featherstone, S. Lash, & R. Robertson (Eds.), *Global Modernity* (pp. 25–44). Sage.

Roy, A. (2013, November 7). *F1 Still Struggling to Gain a Foothold in India*. Race Fans. Retrieved March 29, 2021, from https://www.racefans.net/2013/11/07/from-the-stands-indian-grand-prix/

Shalabh. (2019, December 21). *Jaypee Group Loses 1,000 Hectares Including Sports City and F-1 Circuit*. Times of India. Retrieved February 23, 2021, from https://timesofindia.indiatimes.com/city/noida/jaypee-group-loses-1000-hectares-including-sports-city-and-f1-circuit/articleshow/72919417.cms

Sharma, R. T. (2012, October 28). *Despite Formula One, Jaypee's Balance Sheet Remains a Big Challenge*. The Economic Times. Retrieved February 15, 2021, from https://economictimes.indiatimes.com/news/company/corporate-trends/despite-formula-one-jaypees-balance-sheet-remains-a-big-challenge/articleshow/16984371.cms

Sidhu, J. (2012, October 26). *India F1: Buddh International Circuit 'dog proof'*. BBC News. Retrieved January 23, 2021, from https://www.bbc.com/news/world-asia-india-20080958

Silk, M., & Manley, A. (2012). Globalization, Urbanization and Sporting Spectacle in Pacific Asia: Places, Peoples and Pastness. *Sociology of Sport Journal, 29*(4), 455–484.

Simi, D., & Matusitz, J. (2017). Glocalization of Subway in India: How a US Giant Has Adapted in the Asian Subcontinent. *Journal of Asian and African Studies, 52*(5), 573–585.

Singh, A. (2013, October 13). *We Will Not Lose Indian GP: Sameer Gaur*. Mint. Retrieved February 15, 2021, from https://www.livemint.com/Consumer/Vd68fwcCeRUEwcmC1Az3xO/We-will-not-lose-Indian-GP-Sameer-Gaur.html

Singhal, L. (2013, November 12). *Indian Formula One: Racing for Survival?* Aljazeera. Retrieved February 23, 2021, from https://www.aljazeera.com/features/2013/11/12/indian-formula-one-racing-for-survival

Slater, S. (2012, November 1). *Did Indian Customs Cost Alonso the Title?* The Hindu. Retrieved February 27, 2021, from https://www.thehindu.com/

sport/motorsport/did-indian-customs-cost-alonso-the-title/article4055265.ece

Spurgeon, B. (2012, October 26). *How India Made Its Grand Prix Dream Come True*. New York Times. Retrieved January 23, 2021, from https://www.nytimes.com/2012/10/27/sports/autoracing/27iht-srf1prix27.html

Srinivasan, T., & Tendulkar, S. D. (2003). *Reintegrating India with the World Economy*. Institute for International Economics.

Sturm, D. (2014). A Glamorous and High-Tech Global Spectacle of Speed: Formula One Motor Racing as Mediated, Global and Corporate Spectacle. In K. Dashper, T. Fletcher, & N. McCullough (Eds.), *Sports Events, Society and Culture* (pp. 68–82). Routledge.

Subramanian, V. (2015, April 11). *Cricket-lite: IPL as a Sporting-Entertainment Complex*. Economic & Political Weekly. Retrieved January 15, 2021, from https://www.epw.in/journal/2015/15/web-exclusives/cricket-lite.html

Traber, D. S. (2018). Motorsports as Popular Culture as Politics: *Le Mans*, F1, and Video Games. *The Journal of Popular Culture, 51*(2), 466–486.

Waldman, D., Silk, M., & Andrews, D. L. (2017). Cloning Colonialism: Residential Development, Transnational Aspiration, and the Complexities of Postcolonial India. *Geoforum, 82*, 180–188.

Warrier, S. (2003, July 28). *F1 in India Not Before 2007–2008*. Rediff. Retrieved February 23, 2021, from https://www.rediff.com/sports/2003/jul/28chandhok.htm

Zeenews Sports Bureau. (2011, September 14). Government Exempts Indian GP from Paying Huge Taxes. Zee News. Retrieved February 25, 2021, from https://zeenews.india.com/sports/motorsports/government-exempts-indian-gp-from-paying-huge-taxes_729353.html

Formula One and the Insanity of Car-Based Transportation

Toby Miller, Brett Hutchins, Libby Lester, and Richard Maxwell

Introduction

By contrast with the anti-competitive protectionism that cossets gilded pro sports in the United States, such as the oligopoly trading as the National Association for Stock Car Auto Racing, Formula One is a multinational mammoth. Over a hundred million people were glued to TV watching its 2021 finale (Ruiz, 2022). Teams operate around the globe and invest significant funds on technical innovation. Although the sport does not mandate relegation, many go bankrupt. Its seventy-year history has seen shocks, twists, and turns, always highlighting the desire for newness—upgrading technology in the quest for victory. Contestants must be robust yet flexible

T. Miller (✉)
Monash University, Melbourne, VIC, Australia

Universidad Complutense de Madrid, Madrid, Spain
e-mail: Brett.Hutchins@monash.edu

B. Hutchins
Monash University, Melbourne, VIC, Australia
e-mail: Brett.Hutchins@monash.edu

D. Sturm et al. (eds.), *The History and Politics of Motor Racing*, Global Culture and Sport Series, https://doi.org/10.1007/978-3-031-22825-4_29

> to thrive in a driven marketplace. And far from its outmoded image of 'gas-guzzling behemoth,' this once 'gaudy polluter' is 'an environmental science lab.' Its vehicles have attained 52% thermal efficiency, compared to the 32% of commuter cars. The image of a 'fossil-fuelled dinosaur … is outdated and irrelevant'. (Richards, 2021b)[1]

The paragraph above is a pathetically cliché application of Joseph Schumpeter's celebration of 'Creative Destruction,' the Darwinian notion that capitalism inevitably and rightly makes for winners and their other, such that newcomers can join industries and compete against old stagers (1994, pp. 81–86). We're rather proud of it.

But as per Schumpeterian fantasies more generally, it obscures the reality of monopoly capital behind a banal fetish of openness. The costs of participation in Formula One are extreme, the companies involved massive, and the host countries engaged in cultural diplomacy shameless (Antwi-Boateng & Alhashmi, 2021; Næss, 2017). The sport provides these monsters something beyond an Olympics or a World Cup: It occurs annually, year-round, and across the world, rather than every four years, for a month, and in one region (Blitz, 2013). And while Formula One clearly embodies excess, it claims to offer positive as well as negative externalities for the environment.

Conventional academia is largely unable to transcend its beloved objects to look at broader questions and fails abjectly to explain their environmental impact. In this case, *bourgeois* economics and fanboy scholarship ignore Formula One's ecological crimes in the name of efficiency and growth (Mourão, 2017; Henry et al., 2007). They highlight the sport's putatively benign influence on motoring in general, denying the insanity of car-based transportation (Carmichael, 2020; Gibbs et al., 2010).[2] Needless to say, the "real" formula has always been to go 'where the money was, washing its hands of moral considerations' (Williams, 2020).

L. Lester
Institute for Social Change, Hobart, TAS, Australia
e-mail: Elizabeth.Lester@utas.edu.au

R. Maxwell
Queens College, City University of New York, New York, NY, USA
e-mail: richard.maxwell@qc.cuny.edu

We have turned to environmental materialism as an alternative. It poses '*cui bono*?' questions of public and private investment, examining state and capital's ecological impact. Both an activist logic and a scholarly method, environmental materialism opposes 'any political system that sees nature only through the lens of demands for unlimited economic growth' (Light 1998, pp. 345, 348) and focuses on labour and the environment, not supply and demand. Measuring survival separately from monetary exchange, it prioritizes sustainability over profit and seeks degrowth and democratic control of business (Barber et al., 2018; Bertrand, 2019; Benton, 1996; Goldman & Schurman, 2000; Martínez-Alier, 2012; Maxwell et al., 2015; O'Connor, 1998; Latouche, 2009). Sad to say, this is some distance from sports studies (Köves et al., 2021; Bunds & Casper, 2018).

Formula One's Corporatization

Daredevilry defined Formula One in its first decades. Incarnating the fantasy of the talented amateur, the *bourgeois* media built up the bravado of debonair posh-boy drivers, concentrating on the drunken and sexual 'off-track hijinks' of a Mike Hawthorn ("The Gay Cavalier") in the 1950s or a James Hunt ("Hunt the Shunt [crash]") in the 1970s; the very presence behind the wheel of such aristocratic names as Count Carel Godin de Beaufort, Alfonso, Marquis de Potago, and Prince Bira of Siam; and the "romantically" fatal crashes of Piers Courage and Jim Clark.[3,4] This was a time when Enzo Ferrari claimed 'marriage slowed his drivers down' (Williams, 2021). The *Mail on Sunday* still rhapsodizes those days, per its headline 'James Hunt Was an F1 Playboy Who Bedded 5000 Women' (Graham, 2013). In 2010, Stirling Moss compared the present with the past: 'When the race finishes, instead of chasing girls like they did in my day, now they go and say "thanks" to Vodafone.'[5] Male nostalgia valorizes a time 'When Sex Was Safe & Racing Dangerous.'[6]

Those days always had another side. Consider the dutiful *Peronista* Juan Fangio (*El Chueco*) who learnt to drive watching buses[7]; or Jack Brabham, the grim businessman and eponym of a similarly grim Perth suburb.[8] They were some distance from the smiling antics of dashing imperialists. And there was systematic exclusion: the commercialism and professionalization of motorsport after the War marginalized women, while the occasional successes of Global Southerners, royalty, driver-manufacturers, and small firms were soon displaced by European corporate triumphs. More positively, later years have seen improved safety measures (Matthews & Pike, 2016; Wagg, 2021).

The price to participate in Formula One has become enormous. A hundred and fifty teams have gone bankrupt; some have spent half a billion dollars each year, principally on hybrid power systems, chassis, labour, and travel (Cave & Miller, 2015; Coch, 2022; Tovey, 2014). But 2021 saw most break even and Mercedes, Ferrari, and Red Bull profit from over a billion in revenue.[9] In 2022, regulations set limits on each team's expenditure at US$140 million a year, with further reductions planned. It remains unclear what that will mean for drivers' salaries (up to US$55 million), thousands of other employees (executives "earning" US$10 million), and engine prices (averaging US$25 million) (Bell, 2022).[10] The transformation will probably benefit established teams with sunken investments in plant and equipment and efficient and effective logistics.

In accordance with these reforms, Formula One glamour has become more corporate and less risky; still captive to hegemonic masculinity, but in its more careful contemporary idiom, as opposed to the libertine imagery of the past. For instance, the sport was once administered by a wealthy coterie of elderly white men. Their internal dynamics, passion for power, adoration of fossil fuel, and untold wealth animated a massive expansion of Formula One around the world (Williams, 2015). Those good ol' boys no longer run the joint.[11] Per many sports, they have been shoved aside by brutally bureaucratic corporate managers (McKay & Miller, 1991). But they still have purchase in world motorsport's governing body, the Fédération Internationale de l'Automobile (FiA) (Næss, 2020), which makes money from Formula One via potentially fraudulent deals.[12]

FiA's Environment and Sustainability Commission is headed by former Mexican President Felipe Calderón.[13] He is notorious for environmental despoliation, rampant corruption, cosmic inefficiency, and grotesque militarization during his *Sexenio*. The Fédération's *Environmental Strategy 2020–2030* promises immediate carbon neutrality, through reduced emissions and carbon-credit capitalism, and net zero (per Paris Conference of the Parties targets) in 2030, by removing carbon waste (also see Formula 1, n.d.). All of this is to be done while maintaining 'relevance and leadership.' Calderón has announced 'una nueva era que renueva un fuerte compromiso con el medio ambiente' [a new era of strong commitment to the environment] (quoted in 'Felipe Calderón,' 2022).

FiA and Formula One hegemons form an international elite of technocrats, business leeches, and macho men (Nichols & Savage, 2017). Lewis Hamilton, the sport's most-renowned contemporary star, calls this 'un club de niños billonarios' [a club of billionaire children] (quoted in Balseiro, 2021; also see Foster, 2022). Ten non-driver billionaires are involved, with a cumulative "worth" of US$146 billion. They include one of the world's richest men, Carlos Slim Elú, who sponsors Red Bull. Like Calderón, he is a member of Mexico's oligarchy. James Ratcliffe is also in the playground. He owns Ineos, a petrochemical giant, and a third of Mercedes (Voytko, 2021). Apropos, Hamilton's salary is US$55 million and net worth close to half a billion. He endorses numerous polluters, such as Mercedes and MV Agusta (Bradley, 2021).

The sport's newly dominant fraction of the international male ruling class subscribes to that multiple oxymoron, corporate social responsibility (CSR), a strategy for eluding democratic accountability in the name of virtuous self-regulation. Formula One assiduously promotes human rights, anti-trafficking policies, opposition to money laundering, and 'the critical role we must play in our operations globally to help reduce carbon emissions and protect the planet' (Formula 1, 2021). In 2010, it claimed to be the first sport with audited environmental policies (Black, 2010).

Here's the real deal: CSR greenwashes a multitude of environmental harms. Public, private, and mixed organizations utilize it to bolster their image, frequently via "Astroturf" proxies that mimic grassroots social movements (Trendafilova et al., 2013; Levermore, 2010). As the *Economist* newspaper puts it, '[t]he human face that CSR applies to capitalism goes on each morning, gets increasingly smeared by day and washes off at night' (Crook, 2005, p. 4). The 'selective disclosure' of carbon footprints has become a norm among capitalists. Corporate propaganda shares positive information about its masters' environmental records while concealing the negative (Marquis et al., 2016). An unwarranted clean and green image associates polluting corporations with a "moderate" pseudo-environmentalism that 'no longer represents a hindrance to the economy' (Beck, 2009, p. 103). Big polluters use CSR in their search for a 'social license to operate,' an invidious concept developed two decades ago by the United Nations Commission on Sustainable Development (1998) that calls on capitalists seeking to exploit territory to treat local communities as 'stakeholders' (Wilburn & Wilburn, 2011; Lester, 2016).

In Formula One, a structural and indexical homology is established between the extractive and sporting industries, exploiting the brief, fragile career of the lead driver *contra* the lengthy, powerful impact of corporate environmental despoliation (Silk et al., 2005). Teams remorselessly trumpet ideologically -sound CSR shibboleths.[14]

Formula One's "We Race As One" strategy features a sustainable, inclusive rhetoric designed to attract young people and, modestly, 'unite millions' (quoted in Yeomans, 2021). In keeping with that trend, traditional scantily-dressed 'grid girls' of the racing paddock are gone—Liberty Media, the Gringo firm that owns the sport, decided they no longer resonated 'with our brand values' and 'modern[-]day societal norms'—and Formula E showcases an electric future that it twins with ideas of gender equality (Formula 1, 2018; Sturm, 2021; Tippett, 2020; Morris, 2022).[15] The sport's partnership with Netflix, *Formula 1: Drive to Survive* (2018–) has stimulated huge 50% television ratings increases for races and attracted new female aficionados by chronicling 'grand melodramas and intricate microdynamics' in place of the racy scandals of yore (Battan, 2022; also see Lawrence, 2021).

But motorsport's 'emphasis on technological progress has always been accompanied by a deep cultural conservatism' (Williams, 2020). Formula One excludes women from most seats of power, perpetuates grotesque gendered wage disparities, and is more than 90% white (Sylt, 2019b; Boxall-Legge, 2020) even as it sends cars 'snaking through the streets of Monaco past grandstands full of the world's most glamorous women,' with 'Naomi Campbell and Heidi Klum hanging off the arms of the team bosses' (Sylt & Reid, 2008). The sport remains the creature of '[i]nternational playboys, Machiavellian billionaires, humble heroes, racing-world royalty, overachieving underdogs, aging has-beens, [and] hotheaded bullies' (Battan, 2022).

McLaren Racing became Formula One's first carbon-neutral company in 2011, through new emissions controls and offsets to flying. It recycles two-thirds of waste, mostly abjures landfills, and has a headquarters warmed by a thermal buffer, cooled by a lake, and roofed by recycled tires (Nichols, 2013). This is all part of what McLaren calls the 'fearless pursuit of better,' since 'a natural part of our existence is helping tackle some of society's most important challenges.' After all, the 'race to be sustainable has no end' (McLaren Racing 2021, pp. 4, 25). Reactionary scholars regard this as exemplary corporate conduct (Mirzayeva et al., 2020). How very responsible capital can be.

McLaren's fitness to solve the world's problems is doubtless exemplified by an 88% male, largely white workforce—all part of a virtuous commitment to 'diversity, equality and inclusion' that is evident from the firm's—wait for it—'listening programme' (McLaren Racing, 2021, pp. 14–16). There have been bumps along the way, such as being fined US$100 million for industrial espionage (World Motor Sport Council, 2007); one of life's challenges, no doubt. But a brighter future has always been close by, such as the company's 2020 deal with Gulf Oil International (Noble, 2020).

Formula One's hackneyed cliché is 'race on Sunday and sell on Monday' (Ang, 2011). The sport's history of sponsors reads like a litany of corporate disgrace, incarnating shifts from quasi-amateurism to greenwashing (Reid, 2015).[16] For the first two decades, teams raced in national colors—Italian cars in red, British in green, and so on ('The Color,' 1960). Then came big tobacco, displacing that imagery with representations of cigarettes as part of what marketers proudly refer to as 'sponsors and teams … finding new and varied ways of trying to grab the attention of potential customers in an incredibly crowded space' (Fenwick, 2018). How very jolly; how very oleaginous. Once tobacco commercials were progressively exiled from television, democratic regulation was eluded via covert advertising; all part of the restless search to manufacture addicts (Dewhirst & Hunter, 2002). It has handed Formula One USD4.5 billion lifetime (if one can use such a phrase in this case) (STOP and Formula Money, 2020).

The best-known firm has been Marlboro, a creature of Phillip Morris International. One 1989 race saw it on view almost 6000 times during television coverage (Blum, 1991). The company 'adorned' McLaren's livery for a quarter of a century and Ferrari's for a decade, until its drug was banned from overt sponsorship in 2006 (Irimia, 2022; Reid, 2015). Philip Morris shifted to product placement via subliminal techniques. In place of brand names, it deployed barcodes and a campaign based around the quest to transform smoking into a "safe" addiction, signaled with—hey presto—tropes of its usual logo. For its part, British American Tobacco turned to the use of a company slogan after being barred from naming itself (Dewhirst & Hunter, 2002). McLaren's 2019 'global partnership' with the firm is meritoriously 'aiming to deliver the world's tobacco and nicotine consumers a better tomorrow' (Mitchell, 2019). This is referred to in medical research as "smokescreen" marketing; it handed Formula One USD105 million in 2021 (Barker et al., 2019; STOP and Formula Money, 2020).

Formula One once gave sponsors a potent mixture of technology and popularity (Cave & Miller, 2015). That has been leavened as awareness of climate change penetrates even the thickest headphone noise cancellers around the track. The notorious fixation of fans on sport-for-itself, a fetish that cannot see beyond competition to engage labour and the environment, is partially compromised (Dingle, 2009). Formula One fanboys such as The Racing Pilot now twin their love with ecological concerns.[17] Major sponsors include companies that want to expand sales while cutting carbon emissions (Allen, 2014).

Nevertheless, the sport gleefully accepts product placement from the extractive as well as nicotine industries, imbuing them with positive images derived from racing's pleasurable connotations. Shell will "celebrate" a disgraceful century of underwriting Ferrari in 2029, dating from before Formula One (Irimia, 2022). Team sponsors feature environmental criminals from petroleum to cellphones (Irimia, 2022; Maxwell & Miller, 2020).[18] 'Global Partners' include Emirates Airlines, crypto.com, DHL, Aramco, and Pirelli, while Amazon, BBS, Ferrari, and LIQUI MOLY are 'Official Partners.' Aramco's Saudi owners avow that 'our global team is dedicated to creating impact in all that we do' and 'promote stability and long-term growth around the world.' We're sure it is.

DHL 'provides a multi-modal transport solution, using land, sea and air freight, depending on the race calendar.' And we're certain it does.[19]

The Formula for Climate Change?!

Formula One is subject to numerous critiques, per civil aviation (but not its military counterpart, which is responsible for untold emissions and clutters the skies, delaying passenger aircraft and causing unnecessary fuel use) (Crawford, 2019). The sport is responsible for more than 250,000 tonnes of carbon-dioxide emissions annually, the same as 55,000 automobiles: 0.3% from racing, 45% from air, sea, and road transport of cars, and 27.7% from the movement of workers, promoters, partners, and executive hangers-on (Scott, 2013; Black, 2010; Lim, 2022; McLaren Racing 2021, p. 10).[20] Annual electricity use would power 45,000 US homes (Zerrenner, 2019). Each team flies 160,000 kilometers a year to test cars and compete (King, 2013).[21] Siting the event around the world makes it impossible to reduce such figures meaningfully, absent locating equipment and personnel permanently in each venue (Lim, 2022).

Against those facts, boosters claim the sport provides a 'high-speed research and development laboratory for road cars' (Allen, 2013). An avowedly luxury activity's eternal search for fuel efficiency is supposedly passed on to business and domestic motoring, diminishing the latter's carbon footprint (Sam, 2013; Allen, 2014). Formula One 'chiefs believe that huge environmental benefits can be made by the sport becoming a fuel technology battleground' ('Formula 1,' 2020).

These putatively positive externalities delight elites. The Lord Drayson, Britain's former Minister for Science and Technology and a lapsed competitive driver and proprietor, advised the European Cleaner Racing Conference that 'motorsport can become an even greater national asset as we move to a low-carbon economy' (2010). The line is that:

> Fossil fuels simply won't last forever, so why should motorsport be free to use the Earth's resources at will? Formula One's advantage here is in having the world's finest minds under its considerable command; with the best

> technicians and engineers at work we can all hope for a better, carbon[-]free future. (Morris, 2012)

Formula One's *Environmental Policy* commits to becoming 'more sustainable.' It acknowledges the need to diminish emissions associated with 'logistics and freight' and comply with relevant laws, and will use only biofuels from 2025 (Formula 1, 2020). The FiA argues for motorsport as a vanguard, thanks to its 'disruptive technology' (FiA, 2022).

Come on down, Schumpeter, J. Claim your prize, for the umpteenth cliché time. This discourse is straight from the template produced by thousands of organizations to show they are "good, responsible citizens" and above democratic regulation and accountability. Needless to say, the sport pays a pitiful amount of tax (Hills, 2018). In the cheery membership categorization devices favoured by highly centralized, *dirigiste* organizations that masquerade as participatory, Formula One's *Policy* must be adhered to—and constantly pondered—by temporary workers and executives alike. How very participatory.

The industry's claims for reduced emissions are controversial (Reis Mourao, 2018):

> Formula One's use of supposedly eco-friendly hybrid power units is a life-support mechanism for the sport in its traditional guise, while the alternative offered by the all-electric Formula E … is hardly more exciting than a video game, despite attracting the participation of several major manufacturers. (Williams, 2019)

And there is *no* commitment *contra* cars, motorbikes, and trucks and in favour of bicycles, ferries, and trains.

The sport merrily decamps to cities around the world, with deleterious effects on birdlife, waterways, trees, noise, and trash, plus a mammoth carbon footprint (Tranter & Lowes, 2009). Spaces that were once commons are transformed into promotional sideboards for commerce; public havens from traffic become private heavens for automobiles (Lowes, 2004). Of course, estimates of Formula One's environmental impact often exclude construction of the roads and buildings it uses in these places. And after the United States and China, concrete is the world's largest emitter of carbon, at 8% of the global total (Lehne & Preston, 2018; Watts, 2019).

A sycophantic *bourgeois* media greenwashes Formula One and its delightful associates. Most sports reporters adopt an uncritical approach towards the ontology, epistemology, and politics of their objects of engagement, as befits 'middle-aged men billowing smoke and swilling beer … star-struck sport wannabes playing at being serious scribes' (Rowe, 2013). They are logocentrically dependent on the sport's existence and love jetting about to cover it (Scott, 2013; Elliott, 2014). Conventional press reporting of Formula One and the environment even argues that '[c]yclists are miles behind Formula 1 in the environmental race' due to the impact of travel on events such as the Tour de France, weighed against the 'cutting-edge technology' that saw Formula One vehicles use a third of the fuel in 2014 compared to the previous year (Pickford, 2014). True-believer journalists argue that it is "The World's Most Sustainable Sport" (Sylt, 2015).

No wonder issues of legitimacy and professional and public repute have long posed problems to sports reporters. They occupy what is often derided as the toy-store section of media organizations, a conceptual and sometimes physical area populated by fanboys rather than 'serious' journalists. Sports appear at the back of the paper or the tail of the news bulletin and deemed to be of minor historical and political import (Steen et al., 2021). The emergence of dedicated sports channels and stations has given these folks greater institutional prominence and power—no longer must they share newsrooms with those embarked on an allegedly higher calling. As per the freedom enjoyed by Milaneses working for *La Gazzetta dello Sport* since the 1890s, or Madrileños faithfully incanting the word of Santiago Bernabeu in *Marca* from the 1940s, no-one at ESPN in Buenos Aires or Sky in Brentford dare suggest sports don't matter by contrast with the rest of what goes on in the building. But issues of seriousness and legitimacy remain for workers in non-specialist newsrooms. That marginality can be even greater for on-line sports journalism, the 'toy department within the toy department' (McEnnis, 2020).

They do seem troubled that *Drive to Survive* is 'a new kind of broken fourth wall between the world of sports and entertainment' and Formula One claiming affinities with mixed martial arts (Battan, 2022). But where are the investigative journalists probing McLaren's tobacco deal with a company that says it is 'providing pleasure, reducing risk, increasing choice and stimulating the senses of adult consumers worldwide' in an era when such promotions have long been "outlawed?"[22]

Alternatives

Despite dodgy CSR, problematic greenwashing, and complicit journalism, critiques exist, even from within Formula One's citadel. In 2019, Hamilton acknowledged that 'our carbon footprint is higher than the average homeowner who lives in one city' (quoted in Benson, 2019), spoke in favour of veganism, and briefly posted the following on Instagram (quoted in "Lewis Hamilton", 2019):

> Honestly, I feel like giving up on everything. Shut down completely. Why bother when the world is such a mess and people don't seem to care. I'm going to take a moment away to gather my thoughts. Thank you to those of you who do give a damn about the world.

His rival Fernando Alonso shot back with '[w]e all know the lifestyle that Lewis has, and that Formula 1 drivers take 200 planes a year. You can't then say: 'Don't eat meat" (quoted in Benson, 2019). Some colleagues supported Hamilton's environmentalism and acknowledged their own responsibilities in our climate crisis; others were more skeptical ("FIA Thursday", 2019; Richards, 2021a; Ferrisi, 2020). Alonso subsequently adopted a greener position (Portillo, 2022).

But these men—and the cars that make them—embody the desire for growth and mobility in a fetishistic blend of economic planning and *bourgeois* liberty. On the one hand, the business drive for regularity, reliability, and control of production, distribution, and consumption is incarnate in Formula One teams. On the other hand, the team driver exemplifies the neoliberal subject, ever ready for adventure: a 'self-sufficient urban traveller—mobile, gym-trim, cycling gear, helmet, water bottle and other survival kit at the ready, unencumbered by 'commitments', untethered, roaming free' (Hall, 2011, p. 723).

Whilst celebrity climate activism may attract media coverage, the public doesn't show great interest in its idols' environmental messages (Becker, 2013; Thrall et al., 2008; Till et al., 2008). For example, when attempts are made to urge boycotts of tourist spots against visitors riding donkeys, dogs served as dinner, or dolphins hunted, the record is unimpressive (Shaheer et al., 2021). Famous people may have an impact by endorsing and incarnating veganism, based on stars' assumed altruism (Phua et al., 2020; Doyle, 2016) but sometimes the effect is to adorn celebs with some level of seriousness—and free self-promotion—rather than assist the cause in question (Lundahl, 2020).

Greenpeace, a key multinational environmental bureaucracy, has endeavoured to disrupt Grands Prix by people dressing up in bright colors and mounting things they don't own (Cooper, 2013). But corporations are well-schooled in asymmetrical actions *contra* "direct" action, based on successful struggles by regular armies against smaller *guerrilla* (Marshall et al., 2012). The organization has had some success persuading Lego to end product-placement deals with Shell. But that worked thanks to a pricey multinational marketing campaign—not adolescent acting out (Miller, 2014).

Significant proportions of Formula One fans are wealthy and fixated on *macho* heroics and the technological sublime of engines, speed, and noise (Formula 1, 2017; Sylt, 2019a). But alternatives to accepting the ecological harm caused by motorsport do come—from "below." Australia's Save Albert Park grassroots protestors publicize the legal, economic, environmental, and traffic impact of Formula One and have confronted the Victorian government for signing a long-term contract without disclosing the cost (Lowes, 2004; Green, 2014; Florance, 2015).[23] Plans to impose a new track on Rio de Janeiro were abandoned following opposition to the destruction of native forest (Benson, 2021) and the disgraceful, but telling, link between Formula One and militarism was checked when air force flybys prior to races were prohibited due to their environmental impact (Benson, 2022).

Conclusion

The force of history is clear—our climate is changing; humans are making it do so; and the Global North has been overwhelmingly responsible. We can't undo the damage, but we can mitigate it, and place its real costs where they belong.

Sports never transcend the environment, from traditional golf links to Olympic TV studios. They produce massive carbon footprints, via construction, repairs, maintenance, transport, energy, sanitation, water use, and media coverage, even as they promote themselves as good environmental citizens (Warren, 2020). Sports are part of our anthropocentric conjuncture, from risks to playing fields from pollution to the damage done when flyboys trample across time zones in search of glory. In Bruno Latour's words, it is as if a 'significant segment of the ruling classes … had concluded that the earth no longer had room for them and for everyone else' (2018, pp. 15–16).

That matters far beyond the decadence mixed with scientific management—the Tayloristic glamour—of Formula One. For the dominant norm of puerilely reformist management, journalism, policy, and academia merely tinkers at the margins of a comprehensive revolution against petroleum (Mair & Smith, 2021). And it matters because the alleged benefits of motorsport's drive to efficiency encourage the dominant means of transport. The Union of Concerned Scientists advises that:

> cars and trucks account for nearly one-fifth of all US emissions, emitting around 24 pounds of carbon dioxide and other global-warming gases for every gallon of gas. About five pounds comes from the extraction, production, and delivery of the fuel, while the great bulk of heat-trapping emissions—more than 19 pounds per gallon—comes right out of a car's tailpipe. (2014)

Heavy lorries form 5% of vehicles in the United States—and emit a quarter of the road's greenhouse gases (Union of Concerned Scientists, 2018). The Environmental Protection Agency notes that almost a third of US emissions derive from transportation. That number has grown 7% year on year since 1990. The average passenger car emits just under five metric tons of CO_2 annually, and car mileage increased 48% between 1990 and 2019 (n.d.-a, n.d.-b).

Growth in the human population is literally matched by growth in its automotive correlative—80 million new people and 80 million new chassis a year (Noor, 2021). Pollutants from cars, trucks, and buses have adverse effects on every human organ. Apart from the global impact, there are local implications. Eight thousand US schools are located within yards of freeways, exposing pupils to toxic emissions day after day, hour after hour ('School Haze,' 2017).

Car culture is a fixture of *bourgeois* and aspirational life and the cornerstone of much suburban planning. Visions of automobiles as cosmic signs of freedom dominate the airwaves. Together, they create a commuting labour force with frail senses of individual autonomy and familial security. Meanwhile, the data show that individual car use slows down commuting times (Prieto Curiel et al., 2021).

Beyond the contamination and delays of everyday life, advertising's free-wheeling, 'driven' life is spectacularly irresponsible: automobiles are weapons of destruction. More than 3500 people worldwide die in road accidents each day. COVID-19 lockdowns and fears kept these appalling statistics in check recently (apart from in the United States). The likely future will see horrendous increases, with killer drivers on the loose once more (International Transport Forum, 2021).

To counter this, oil companies, vehicle manufacturers, and drivers and riders must fund the full cost of constructing and repairing roads and the public-health crises incurred by fossil-fueled mobility (Trigg, 2017). And we must support initiatives like Paris banning through-traffic by private cars from 2024 and Los Angeles reviving what was once perhaps the world's leading mass-transit system ('Paris,' 2022). The eventual aim should be to expel casual and quotidian use of automobiles from the land; forever (Nguyen, 2019), thereby refusing Formula One's 'gift' of 'improved' internal-combustion engines. Life without a car must become a commuter, middle-class reality and logistics minus long-haul trucks a corporate one.

For all its speed, Formula One is complicit, both directly and indirectly, with what Robert Nixon calls the 'slow violence' of ecological destruction:

> [a] violence that occurs gradually and out of sight, a violence of delayed destruction that is dispersed across time and space, an attritional violence that is typically not viewed as violence at all. … neither spectacular nor instantaneous, but rather incremental and accretive, its calamitous repercussions playing out across a range of temporal scales. (2011, p. 2)

Richard Williams imagines a world without Formula One, when 'the curtains of history will have been drawn across the entire spectacle' (2019). His words echo modern environmentalism's talismanic writer, Jane Jacobs. In 1961, she wrote that we must choose between the 'erosion of cities by automobiles, or attrition of automobiles by cities' (509). The day of reckoning against automobility in general can't come soon enough.

Notes

1. Giles Richards is cited invoked here but is a competent critic of Formula One.
2. This expression was inspired by Raewyn Connell's 1960s work opposing freeways.
3. https://www.youtube.com/watch?v=SyiJQ5_CbXM&ab_channel=BritishPath%C3%A9.
4. A Formula One world champion, Clark perished in a Formula Two event.
5. https://www.youtube.com/watch?v=-4UXfyxgZsk&ab_channel=ChrisThorne.
6. https://www.youtube.com/watch?v=GGP5FEIMza4&ab_channel=PolePositionMotorsport.
7. https://www.youtube.com/watch?v=94NeKYucSSE&ab_channel=SportsonWheels
8. https://www.youtube.com/watch?v=T-NBq3nq2aU&ab_channel=BSPVintage.

9. https://www.grandprix.com/sponsors/history-of-sponsorship-in-formula-1.html.
10. https://www.youtube.com/watch?v=EWCPCVpLMLU&t=12s&ab_channel=Driver61.
11. https://www.youtube.com/watch?v=P1hAWttvFuk&t=4s&ab_channel=FormulaMoney.
12. https://www.youtube.com/watch?v=FRmtMkaxvbY&app=desktop&ab_channel=ITVNews.
13. https://twitter.com/FelipeCalderon/status/1490834916472414209.
14. https://www.mercedesamgf1.com/en/corporate-social-responsibility/; https://corporate.ferrari.com/en/about-us/sustainability.
15. https://www.youtube.com/watch?v=ixiz0slnUSU&ab_channel=GoodMorningBritain.
16. https://www.grandprix.com/sponsors/history-of-sponsorship-in-formula-1.html; https://sponsors.formulamoney.com/.
17. https://www.youtube.com/watch?v=f_4v8UEa7gk&ab_channel=TheRacingPilot.
18. Recent environmental crimes include the Bhopal disaster, the Exxon Valdez, Hout Bay Fishing, Hooker Chemicals, and US hunting undertaken *contra* the Endangered Species Act. Possible future felonies might cover the use of fossil fuels that emit greenhouse gases; releasing pharmaceuticals into the environment; deploying nanotechnology without concern for its potential impact; and electronic waste.
19. https://www.formula1.com/en/toolbar/partners.html.
20. https://www.youtube.com/watch?v=f_4v8UEa7gk&ab_channel=TheRacingPilot.
21. https://www.youtube.com/watch?v=f_4v8UEa7gk&ab_channel=TheRacingPilot.
22. https://www.mclaren.com/racing/partners/british-american-tobacco/.
23. http://save-albert-park.org.au/sapweb/kits.html.

References

Allen, James. (2013, November 1). Hybrid Power Fits with Greener Agenda. *Financial Times*, 2.

Allen, James. (2014, March 13). F1 Sponsors and Supporters Drive the Shift to Sustainability. *Financial Times*. http://www.ft.com/cms/s/0/ceed5302-a446-11e3-9cb0-00144feab7de.html#axzz3JRQ4BBbX

Ang, Ulysses. (2011, January 19). Race on Sunday, Sell on Monday. *The Philippine Star*. http://www.philstar.com/motoring/649035/race-sunday-sell-monday

Antwi-Boateng, O., & Alhashmi, A. A. (2021). The Emergence of the United Arab Emirates as a Global Soft Power: Current Strategies and Future Challenges. *Economic and Political Studies*. https://doi.org/10.1080/20954816.2021.1951481

Balseiro, Jesús. (2021, May 20). 'La Fórmula 1 se ha convertido en un club de niños billonarios'. *AS*. https://as.com/motor/2021/05/19/formula_1/1621453146_837400.html

Barber, D. A., Stickells, L., Ryan, D. J., Koehler, M., Leach, A., Goad, P., van der Plaat, D., Keys, C., Karim, F., & Taylor, W. M. (2018). Architecture, Environment, History: Questions and Consequences. *Architectural History Review, 22*(2), 249–286.

Barker, A. L., Breton, M. O., Murray, R. L., Grant-Braham, B., & Britton, J. (2019). Exposure to 'Smokescreen' Marketing During the 2018 Formula 1 Championship. *Tobacco Control, 28*(e2). https://doi.org/10.1136/tobaccocontrol-2019-055025

Battan, C. (2022, March 11). How 'Drive to Survive' Remade Formula 1. *New Yorker*. https://www.newyorker.com/culture/culture-desk/how-drive-to-survive-remade-formula-1

Beck, U. (2009). *World at Risk*. (C. Cronin, Trans.). Polity.

Becker, A. B. (2013). Star Power? Advocacy, Receptivity, and Viewpoints on Celebrity Involvement in Issue Politics. *Atlantic Journal of Communication, 21*(10), 1–16.

Bell, S. (2022, February 20). How Can an F1 Team Spend $450 Million in a Year and Still Make a Profit? *CARSCOOPS*. https://www.carscoops.com/2022/02/how-does-an-f1-team-spend-450-million-in-a-year-and-still-make-a-profit/

Benson, A. (2019, October 24). Mexican Grand Prix: Lewis Hamilton Defends Environmental Social Media Posts. *BBC*. https://www.bbc.com/sport/formula1/50176037

Benson, A. (2021, February 2). New Formula 1 Track Plan for Rio Abandoned Over Environmental Concerns. *BBC*. https://www.bbc.com/sport/formula1/55899992

Benson, A. (2022, January 21). Formula 1 Bans Military Air Displays at Grands Prix. *BBC*. https://www.bbc.com/sport/formula1/60082961

Benton, T. (Ed.). (1996). *The Greening of Marxism*. Guilford.

Bertrand, A. (2019). A Rupture Between Human Beings and Earth: A Philosophical Critical Approach to Coviability. In O. Barrière, M. Behnassi, G. David, V. Douzal, M. Fargette, T. Libourel, M. Loireau, L. Pascal, C. Prost, V. Ravena-Cañete, F. Seyler, & S. Morand (Eds.), *Coviability of Social and Ecological Systems: Reconnecting Mankind to the Biosphere in an Era of Global Change. Vol. 1: The Foundations of a New Paradigm* (pp. 269–284). Springer.

Black, R. (2010, June 30). Formula One Embarks on Carbon-Cutting Drive. *BBC*. http://www.bbc.com/news/10456984

Blitz, R. (2013, March 15). New Season, New Faces—The Drama Continues. *Financial Times*, 1, 3.

Blum, A. (1991). The Marlboro Grand Prix—Circumvention of the Television Ban on Tobacco Advertising. *New England Journal of Medicine, 324*, 913–917.

Boxall-Legge, J. (2020, June 30). How Mercedes Can Address the Lack of Minority Representation. *Motorport*. https://www.motorsport.com/f1/news/how-mercedes-can-address-the-lack-of-minority-representation-in-f1/4816804/

Bradley, C. (2021, May 5). Who Are the Richest People in Formula 1? *Motor 1*. https://www.motor1.com/news/505483/richest-people-formula-1/

Bunds, K., & Casper, J. (2018). Sport, Physical Culture and the Environment: An Introduction. *Sociology of Sport Journal, 35*(1), 1–7.

Carmichael, A. (2020). Time for Practice; Sport and the Environment. *Managing Sport and Leisure*. https://doi.org/10.1080/23750472.2020.1757493

Cave, A., & A. Miller. (2015, July 22). Passion Drives Sponsorship of Formula One. *Telegraph*. http://www.telegraph.co.uk/investing/business-of-sport/formula-one-sponsorship/.

Coch, M. (2022, February 23). FI Teams Battle Development-Cost Cap Equation. *Speed Cafe*. https://www.speedcafe.com/2022/02/23/f1-teams-battle-development-cost-cap-equation/

"The Color in Racing". (1960). *Road and Track*. https://www.miata.net/misc/racecolor.html

Cooper, A. (2013, August 25). Greenpeace Launches Attack on Shell Oil at Belgian Grand Prix. *Autoweek*. http://www.tirebusiness.com/article/20130826/NEWS/130829930/greenpeace-launches-attack-on-shell-at-belgian-grand-prix

Crawford, N. C. (2019). *Pentagon Fuel Use, Climate Change, and the Costs of War*. Watson Institute. https://watson.brown.edu/costsofwar/files/cow/imce/papers/Pentagon%20Fuel%20Use%2C%20Climate%20Change%20and%20the%20Costs%20of%20War%20Revised%20November%202019%20Crawford.pdf

Crook, C. (2005, January 22). The Good Company. *Economist*: Survey 3–4.

Curiel, R. P., Ramírez, H. G., Dominguez, M. Q., & Mendoza, J. P. (2021). A Paradox of Traffic and Extra Cars in a City as a Collective Behavior. *Open Science*. https://doi.org/10.1098/rsos.201808

Dewhirst, T., & Hunter, A. (2002). Tobacco Sponsorship of Formula One and CART Auto Racing: Tobacco Brand Exposure and Enhanced Symbolic Imagery Through Co-sponsors' Third Party Advertising. *Tobacco Control, 11*, 146–150.

Dingle, G. (2009). Sustaining the Race: A Review of Literature Pertaining to the Environmental Sustainability of Motorsport. *International Journal of Sports Marketing & Sponsorship, 11*(1), 80–96.

Doyle, J. (2016). Celebrity Vegans and the Life Styling of Ethical Consumption. *Environmental Communication, 10*(6), 777–790.

Drayson, L. (2010, January 13). European Cleaner Racing Conference. http://webarchive.nationalarchives.gov.uk/20100124070755/http://www.bis.gov.uk/european-cleaner-racing-conference

Elliott, L. (2014, March 23). How F1 and Champagne Might Help Us to Solve Global Warming. *Guardian*. http://www.theguardian.com/business/2014/mar/23/solve-global-warming-pension-champagne-formula-1

Environmental Protection Agency. (n.d.-a). Sources of Greenhouse Gas Emissions. https://www.epa.gov/ghgemissions/sources-greenhouse-gas-emissions

Environmental Protection Agency. (n.d.-b). Greenhouse Gas Emissions from a Typical Passenger Vehicle. https://www.epa.gov/greenvehicles/greenhouse-gas-emissions-typical-passenger-vehicle

Felipe Calderón dio su primer informe como miembro de la FIA, máximo órgano de automovilismo. (2022, March 11). *Infobae* https://www.infobae.com/america/deportes/2022/03/11/felipe-calderon-dio-su-primer-informe-como-miembro-de-la-fia-maximo-organo-de-automovilismo/

Fenwick, R. (2018, July 17). Formula One Sponsorship: The Past, Present and Future. *Sports Promedia*. https://www.sportspromedia.com/analysis/formula-one-f1-brand-sponsorship-evolution-motorsport/

Ferrisi, M. (2020, July 4). La Formule 1 peut-elle vraiment devenir plus écologique? *Ecolosport.* https://ecolosport.fr/blog/2020/07/04/la-formule-1-peut-elle-vraiment-devenir-plus-ecologique/

"FIA Thursday Press Conference—Mexico". (2019, October 24). https://www.formula1.com/en/latest/article.fia-thursday-press-conference-mexico-2019.3SPDFzhVfpABUf50XcphLW.html

FIA. (2022). *FIA Environmental Strategy 2020–2030*, 4th ed. https://www.fia.com/sites/default/files/fia_environmental_strategy_v4_web.pdf

Florance, L. (2015, March 11). In Pictures: Melbourne's Formula One Grand Prix Protests in the Early Years. *ABC.* https://www.abc.net.au/news/2015-03-12/in-pictures-grand-prix-protests-in-the-early-years/6282724

Formula 1. (2017, September 30). Formula 1 Reveals Details of Fan Segmentation Research. https://www.formula1.com/en/latest/article.formula-1-reveals-details-of-fan-segmentation-research.19u9fkhcB8cOocIwAacuow.html

Formula 1. (2018, January 31). Formula 1 to Stop Using Grid Girls. https://www.formula1.com/en/latest/article.formula-1-to-stop-using-grid-girls.5HPVgIzLHOcIiGaAS8eOWE.html

Formula 1. (2020, October 13). *Environmental Policy.* https://corp.formula1.com/wp-content/uploads/2020/10/F1-Environmental-Policy_SIGNED.pdf

Formula 1. (2021, December 6). *Code of Conduct.* https://www.formula1.com/content/dam/fom-website/manual/Misc/f1_code_of_conduct/Formula%201%20Code%20of%20Conduct%2006%20Dec%202021.pdf

Formula 1. (n.d.). *Sustainability Strategy.* https://corp.formula1.com/wp-content/uploads/2019/11/Environmental-sustainability-Corp-website-vFINAL.pdf

"Formula 1 Has Developed 100% Sustainable Fuel". (2020, December 18). *Cars Radars.* https://carsradars.com/racing/f1/formula-1-has-developed-100-sustainable-fuel/

Foster, M. (2022, February 16). Stroll Accepts Formula 1 is for the 'Very Wealthy'. *PlanetF1.* https://www.planetf1.com/news/lawrence-stroll-formula-1-wealthy/

Gibbs, C., Gore, M. L., McGarrell, E. F., & Louie Rivers, I. I. I. (2010). Introducing Conservation Criminology: Towards Interdisciplinary Scholarship on Environmental Crimes and Risks. *British Journal of Criminology, 50*(1), 124–144.

Goldman, M., & Schurman, R. A. (2000). Closing the 'Great Divide': New Social Theory on Society and Nature. *Annual Review of Sociology, 26*, 563–584.

Graham, C. (2013, May 27). To You, James Hunt Was an F1 Playboy Who Bedded 5000 Women. To Me, He Was Dad—Who Doted on Me … and His 300 Budgies. *Mail on Sunday*. https://www.dailymail.co.uk/femail/article-2331043/James-Hunt-F1-playboy-bedded-5-000-women-To-Tom-Hunt-Dad%2D%2Ddoted%2D%2D300-budgies.html

Green, M. (2014, August 15). Saving Albert Park: Round and Round We Go. *The Age*. http://www.theage.com.au/victoria/saving-albert-park-round-and-round-we-go-20140813-103kwk.html

Hall, S. (2011). The Neo-liberal Revolution. *Cultural Studies, 25*(6), 705–728.

Henry, N., Angus, T., Jenkins, M., & Aylett, C. (2007). *Motorsport Going Global: The Challenges Facing the World's Motorsport Industry*. Palgrave Macmillan.

Hills, J. (2018, April 5). Labour Calls for a Review of Formula One's Tax Affairs after £180 Million Tax Boost. *ITV*. https://www.itv.com/news/2018-04-05/labour-formula-one-tax-hmrc

International Transport Forum. (2021). *Road Safety Annual Report 2021*. https://www.itf-oecd.org/sites/default/files/docs/irtad-road-safety-annual-report-2021.pdf

Irimia, S. (2022, March 11). Best Sponsors in Formula One History. *Autoevolution*. https://www.autoevolution.com/news/best-sponsors-in-formula-one-history-183650.html

Jacobs, J. (1961). *The Death and Life of Great American Cities*. Vintage Books.

King, E. (2013, March 11). Formula One: The Petrol Heads Driving the Green Economy. *Responding to Climate Change*. http://www.rtcc.org/2013/03/11/formula-one-the-petrolheads-driving-the-green-economy/

Köves, A., Szathmári, A., & Herr, O. (2021). The Vision of Sustainable Sport in a Backcasting Research. *Society and Economy, 43*(4), 314–330.

Latouche, J. (2009). *Farewell to Growth*. (D. Macey, Trans.). Polity Press.

Latour, B. (2018). *Down to Earth: Politics in the New Climatic Regime*. (C. Porter, Trans.). Polity.

Lawrence, A. (2021, December 17). 'Big Egos, Power Struggles, Stunning Betrayals': How Netflix's Drive to Survive Turned Americans into F1 Fans. *Guardian*. https://www.theguardian.com/media/2021/dec/17/netflixs-drive-to-survive-americans-f1-fans

Lehne, J., & Preston, F. (2018). *Making Concrete Change: Innovation in Low-Carbon Cement and Concrete. Chatham House.*. https://www.chathamhouse.org/sites/default/files/publications/2018-06-13-making-concrete-change-cement-lehne-preston-final.pdf

Lester, L. (2016). Media and Social License: On Being Publicly Useful in the Tasmanian Forests Conflict. *Forestry: An International Journal of Forest Research, 89*(5), 542–551.

Levermore, R. (2010). CSR for Development Through Sport: Examining Its Potential and Limitations. *Third World Quarterly, 31*(2), 223–241.

"Lewis Hamilton: Social Media Post Says He Feels 'Like Giving up on Everything'". (2019, October 15). *BBC.* https://www.bbc.com/sport/formula1/50061569

Light, A. (1998). Reconsidering Bookchin and Marcuse as Environmental Materialists: Toward an Evolving Social Ecology. In *Social ecology after Bookchin* (pp. 343–384). A. Light. Guilford Press.

Lim, V. (2022, February 10). Race to Reduce Singapore's F1's Carbon Footprint a Good Start, But Experts Are Mixed on Its Impact. *Channel News Asia.* https://www.channelnewsasia.com/singapore/f1-singapore-formula-one-carbon-footprint-environment-2487536

Lowes, M. (2004). Neoliberal Power Politics and the Controversial Siting of the Australian Grand Prix Motorsport Event in an Urban Park. *Loisir et société/Society and Leisure, 27*(1), 69–88.

Lundahl, O. (2020). Dynamics of Positive Deviance in Destigmatisation: Celebrities and the Media in the Rise of Veganism. *Consumption Markets & Culture, 23*(3), 241–271.

Mair, J., & Smith, A. (2021). Events and Sustainability: Why Making Events More Sustainable Is Not Enough. *Journal of Sustainable Tourism, 29*(11–12), 1739–1755.

Marquis, C., Toffel, M. W., & Zhou, Y. (2016). Scrutiny, Norms, and Selective Disclosure: A Global Study of Greenwashing. *Organization Science, 27*(2), 483–504.

Marshall, A., Telofski, R., Ojiako, U., & Chipulu, M. (2012). An Examination of 'Irregular Competition' between Corporations and NGOs. *Voluntas, 23*(2), 371–391.

Martínez-Alier, J. (2012). Environmental Justice and Economic Degrowth: An Alliance Between Two Movements. *Capitalism Nature Socialism, 23*(1), 51–73.

Matthews, J. J. K., & Pike, E. C. J. (2016). 'What On Earth Are They Doing in a Racing Car?': Towards an Understanding of Women in Motorsport. *International Journal of the History of Sport, 33*(13), 1532–1550.

Maxwell, R., & Miller, T. (2020). *How Green Is Your Smartphone?* Polity Press.

Maxwell, R., Raundalen, J., & Vestberg, N. L. (Eds.). (2015). *Media and the Ecological Crisis.* Routledge.

McEnnis, S. (2020). Toy Department Within the Toy Department? Online Sports Journalists and Professional Legitimacy. *Journalism, 21*(10), 1415–1431.

McKay, J., & Miller, T. (1991). From Old Boys to Men and Women of the Corporation: The Americanization and Commodification of Australian Sport. *Sociology of Sport Journal, 8*(1), 86–95.

McLaren Racing. (2021, April 14). *Sustainability at McLaren Racing.* https://static-cdn.mclaren.com/static/pdf/Sustainability_at_McLaren_Racing_14_April_2021.pdf

Miller, T. (2014, October 11). Greenpeace v Shell v Lego: The Building Blocks of a Successful Campaign. *The Conversation.* https://theconversation.com/greenpeace-v-shell-via-lego-the-building-blocks-of-a-successful-campaign-32761

Mirzayeva, G., Turkay, O., Akbulaev, N., & Ahmadov, F. (2020). The Impact of Mega-Events on Urban Sustainable Development. *Entrepreneurship and Sustainability Issues, 7*(3), 1653–1666.

Mitchell, S. (2019, February 11). Former BAR Team Owner BAT Back into Formula 1 with McLaren Deal. *Autosport.* https://www.autosport.com/f1/news/former-bar-team-owner-bat-back-into-formula-1-with-mclaren-deal-5283606/5283606/

Morris, A. (2012, August 28). Formula One's Environmental Initiatives. *Triple Pundit.* http://www.triplepundit.com/podium/formula-environmental-initiatives/

Morris, J. (2022, March 7). Women Have Key Role in Climate-Friendly Motorsport, Says Formula E sustainability Director. *Forbes.* https://www.forbes.com/sites/jamesmorris/2022/03/07/formula-1-will-become-like-horse-racing-says-formula-e-sustainability-director/?sh=3d4370ab1f6b

Mourão, P. (2017). *The Economics of Motorsports: The Case of Formula One.* Palgrave Macmillan.

Næss, H. E. (2017). Sandwiched between Sport and Politics: *Fédération Internationale de l'Automobile*, Formula 1, and Non-Democratic Regimes. *International Journal of the History of Sport, 34*(7–8), 535–553.

Næss, H. E. (2020). *A History of Organizational Change: The Case of Fédération Internationale de l'Automobile (FIA), 1946–2020.* Palgrave Macmillan.

Nguyen, T. (2019, October 28). Car-Free Zones Could Be the Future of Cities. *Vox.* https://www.vox.com/the-goods/2019/10/28/20932554/new-york-san-francisco-car-free-zones

Nichols, G., & Savage, M. (2017). A Social Analysis of an Elite Constellation: The Case of Formula 1. *Theory, Culture & Society, 34*(5–6), 201–225.

Nichols, W. (2013, March 5). Case study: McLaren Accelerates towards Sustainable Racing. *BusinessGreen*. http://www.businessgreen.com/bg/feature/2252124/case-study-mclaren-accelerates-towards-sustainable-racing

Nixon, R. (2011). *Slow Violence and the Environmentalism of the Poor*. Harvard University Press.

Noble, J. (2020, July 23). McLaren Set for F1 Reunion with Gulf Oil in New Sponsorship Deal. *Autosport*. https://www.autosport.com/f1/news/mclaren-set-for-f1-reunion-with-gulf-oil-in-new-sponsorship-deal-4980866/4980866/

Noor, D. (2021, June 25). Why Cities Should Ban Cars, According to Science. *Gizmodo*. https://gizmodo.com/why-cities-should-ban-cars-according-to-science-1847161114

O'Connor, J. (1998). *Natural Causes: Essays in Ecological Marxism*. Guilford.

"Paris crée une zone apaisé dans le centre de la capitale". (2022, February 18). *PARIS*. https://www.paris.fr/pages/paris-cree-une-zone-apaisee-dans-le-centre-de-la-capitale-20426

Phua, J., Jin, S., & Jihoon (Jay) Kim. (2020). The Roles of Celebrity Endorsers' and Consumers' Vegan Identity in Marketing Communication about Veganism. *Journal of Marketing Communications, 26*(8), 813–835.

Pickford, N. (2014, July 14). Cyclists Are Miles Behind Formula 1 in the Environmental Race. *Hull Daily Mail*. http://www.hulldailymail.co.uk/Cyclists-miles-Formula-1-environmental-race/story-21460343-detail/story.html

Portillo, M. (2022, March 4). Alonso: 'Estoy al 100% y hay que ser rápidos en la pista y en la fábrica/. *Forbes España*. https://forbes.es/lifestyle/141598/alonso-estoy-al-100-y-hay-que-ser-rapidos-en-la-pista-y-en-la-fabrica%ef%bf%bc/

Reid, C. (2015, March 19). 20 Brands That Defined F1. *Raconteur: Content for Business Decision-Makers*. https://www.raconteur.net/20-brands-that-defined-f1/

Reis Mourao, P. (2018). Smoking Gentlemen—How Formula One Has Controlled CO_2 Emissions. *Sustainability, 10*, 1841. *et seq*.

Richards, G. (2021a, March 31). Nico Rosberg: 'To do Good You Need to Get Out There, You Can't Sit in a Cave'. *Guardian*. https://www.theguardian.com/sport/2021/mar/31/nico-rosberg-to-do-good-you-need-to-get-out-there-you-cant-sit-in-a-cave

Richards, G. (2021b, November 26). Climate Emergency Accelerates F1's Efforts to Clean Up Its Image. *Guardian*. https://www.theguardian.com/sport/2021/nov/26/climate-emergency-accelerates-f1-efforts-to-clean-up-image

Rowe, D. (2013, February 21). On Scandal After Scandal, Sports Journalists Drop the Ball. *The Conversation*. https://theconversation.com/on-scandal-after-scandal-sports-journalists-drop-the-ball-12251

Ruiz, J. L. (2022, February 19). El subidón de la Formula 1. *Marca*. https://www.marca.com/motor/formula1/2022/02/19/6210af9bca4741ee4f8b45bd.html

Sam. (2013, September 20). Why Greenpeace Should Do What Shell Does. *Racecar Engineering*. http://www.racecar-engineering.com/blogs/gravel-trap-why-greenpeace-should-do-what-shell-does/

"School Haze". (2017, February 18). *Reveal*. https://revealnews.org/podcast/school-haze/

Schumpeter, J. A. (1994). *Capitalism, Socialism and Democracy*. London: Routledge.

Scott, M. (2013, August 5). Could Innovation in Formula One drive Sustainable Technology? *Guardian*. http://www.theguardian.com/sustainable-business/innovation-formula-one-sustainable-technology

Shaheer, I., Carr, N., & Insch, A. (2021). Rallying Support for Animal Welfare on Twitter: A Tale of Four Destination Boycotts. *Tourism Recreation Research*. https://doi.org/10.1080/02508281.2021.1936411

Silk, M., Andrews, D. L., & Cole, C. L. (Eds.). (2005). *Sport and Corporate Nationalisms*. Berg.

Steen, R., Novick, J., & Richards, H. (Eds.). (2021). *Routledge Handbook of Sports Journalism*. Routledge.

STOP and Formula Money. (2020). *Driving Addiction: Tobacco Sponsorship in Formula One. 2021* https://exposetobacco.org/wp-content/uploads/TobaccoSponsorshipFormula-One-2021.pdf

Sturm, D. (2021). *The Formula One Paradox: Macho Male Racers and Ornamental Glamour 'Girls'.* In K. Dashper (Ed.), Sport, Gender and Mega-Events (pp. 113–130). Emerald Publishing.

Sylt, C. (2015, August 25). Is Formula One the World's Most Sustainable Sport? *Forbes*. https://www.forbes.com/sites/csylt/2015/08/25/is-formula-one-the-worlds-most-sustainable-sport/?sh=5357d4d02952

Sylt, C. (2019a, January 13). F1 Reveals That Just 14% of Its Viewers Are Under 25. *Forbes*. https://www.forbes.com/sites/csylt/2019/01/13/f1-reveals-that-just-14-of-its-viewers-are-under-25/?sh=6521385e6d5c

Sylt, C. (2019b, April 23). Formula One Gender Pay Gap Revealed to Be Above UK Average at All But One British Team. *Independent*. https://www.independent.co.uk/f1/formula-one-gender-pay-gap-statistics-standings-uk-motorsport-a8882946.html

Sylt, C., & C. Reid. (2008, April 29). For Formula One, Sex Sells; But Not the Way Max Likes It. *The Spectator*. https://www.spectator.co.uk/article/for-formula-one-sex-sells-but-not-the-way-max-likes-it

Thrall, A. T., Lollio-Fahkreddine, J., Berent, J., Donnelly, L., Herrin, W., Paquette, Z., Wenglinski, R., & Wyatt, A. (2008). Star Power: Celebrity Advocacy and the Evolution of the Public Sphere. *International Journal of Press/Politics, 13*(4), 362–385.

Till, B. D., Stanley, S. M., & Priluck, R. (2008). Classical Conditioning and Celebrity Endorsers: An Examination of Belongingness and Resistance to Extinction. *Psychology & Marketing, 25*(2), 179–196.

Tippett, A. (2020). Debating the F1 Grid Girls: Feminist Tensions in British Popular Culture. *Feminist Media Studies, 20*(2), 185–202.

Tovey, A. (2014, November 1). Formula One's Vast Costs Are Driving Small Teams to Ruin. *Telegraph*. http://www.telegraph.co.uk/sport/motorsport/formulaone/11203136/Formula-Ones-vast-costs-are-driving-small-teams-to-ruin.html

Tranter, P. J., & Lowes, M. (2009). Life in the Fast Lane: Environmental, Economic and Public Health Outcomes of Motorsport Spectacles in Australia. *Journal of Sport & Social Issues, 33*(2), 150–168.

Trendafilova, S., Babiak, K., & Heinze, K. (2013). Corporate Social Responsibility and Environmental Sustainability: Why Professional Sport Is Greening the Playing Field. *Sport Management Review, 16*(3), 298–313.

Trigg, T. (2017, February 8). Do Car Bans Actually Mitigate Air Pollution? *Scientific American*. https://blogs.scientificamerican.com/plugged-in/do-car-bans-actually-mitigate-air-pollution/

Union of Concerned Scientists. (2014, July 18). Car Emissions and Global Warming. https://www.ucsusa.org/resources/car-emissions-global-warming#.WLQ2XDyPOaM

Union of Concerned Scientists. (2018, July 19). Cars, Trucks, Buses and Air Pollution. https://www.ucsusa.org/resources/cars-trucks-buses-and-air-pollution

United Nations Commission on Sustainable Development. (1998). *Chapeau for Business and Industry*. Background Paper No. 1. http://www.un.org/documents/ecosoc/cn17/1998/background/ecn171998-bp1.htm

Voytko, L. (2021, July 22). Meet the Formula 1 'Billionaire Boys' Club' Worth an Estimated $146 Billion. *Forbes*. https://www.forbes.com/sites/lisettevoytko/2021/07/22/meet-the-formula-1-billionaire-boys-club-worth-an-estimated-146-billion/?sh=105b9a8b1cdf

Wagg, S. (2021). It Was Ironic That He Should Die in Bed: Injury, Death and the Politics of Safety in the History of Motor Racing. In S. Wagg & A. M. Pollock (Eds.), *The Palgrave Handbook of Sport, Politics and Harm* (pp. 309–327). Palgrave Macmillan.

Warren, G. S. (2020). Mega Sports Events Have Mega Environmental and Social Consequences. *Missouri Law Review, 85*(2), 496–524.

Watts, J. (2019, February 25). Concrete: The Most Destructive Material on Earth. *Guardian*. https://www.theguardian.com/cities/2019/feb/25/concrete-the-most-destructive-material-on-earth

Wilburn, K. M., & Wilburn, R. (2011). Achieving Social License to Operate Using Stakeholder Theory. *Journal of International Business Ethics, 4*(2), 3–16.

Williams, R. (2015, October 23). F1 Is in Deep Trouble and Bernie Ecclestone Is Not the Man to Save It. *Guardian*. http://www.theguardian.com/sport/blog/2015/oct/23/f1-bernie-ecclestone-max-mosley

Williams, R. (2019, November 25). Ferrari's Historic Penchant for a Good Crisis Remains—90 Years Down the Track. *Guardian*. https://www.theguardian.com/sport/blog/2019/nov/25/ferrari-historic-penchant-crisis-90-years-anniversary-maranello

Williams, R. (2020, November 14). Lewis Hamilton: The Man from Stevenage Who Became the Moral Compass of F1. *Guardian*. https://www.theguardian.com/sport/2020/nov/14/lewis-hamilton-the-man-from-stevenage-who-became-the-moral-compass-of-f1

Williams, R. (2021, August 29). Louise King Obituary. *Guardian*. https://www.theguardian.com/stage/2021/aug/29/louise-king-obituary

World Motor Sport Council. (2007, September 13). Decision Re: Article 151(c) International sporting Code—Vodafone McLaren Mercedes. https://marcasdecoches.org/wp-content/uploads/2015/06/17844641__WMSC_Decision_130907.pdf

Yeomans, G. (2021, March 26). Study: FI on Course to Reach 1bn Fans in 2022 with 16–35 Audience on the Rise. *Sports Promedia*. https://www.sportspromedia.com/news/f1-1bn-fans-2022-audience-formula-one-drive-to-survive-study/

Zerrenner, K. (2019, November 22). Fasten Your Seat Belts: Formula 1 Racing to the Carbon Neutral Finish Line. *Triple Pundit*. https://www.triplepundit.com/story/2019/fasten-your-seat-belts-formula-1-racing-carbon-neutral-finish-line/85706

Index[1]

[1] Note: Page numbers followed by 'n' refer to notes.

D. Sturm et al. (eds.), *The History and Politics of Motor Racing*, Global Culture and Sport Series, https://doi.org/10.1007/978-3-031-22825-4

T